Introduction to Public Health

Second Edition

Mary-Jane Schneider, PhD
Director of Interdisciplinary Programs
and Clinical Associate Professor of Health Policy,
Management, and Behavior
School of Public Health
University at Albany
State University of New York
Rensselaer, New York

Drawings by Henry Schneider

JONES AND BARTLETT PUBLISHERS
Sudbury, Massachusetts
BOSTON   TORONTO   LONDON   SINGAPORE

World Headquarters
Jones and Bartlett Publishers
40 Tall Pine Drive
Sudbury, MA 01776
978-443-5000
info@jbpub.com
www.jbpub.com

Jones and Bartlett Publishers Canada
6339 Ormindale Way
Mississauga, Ontario L5V 1J2
CANADA

Jones and Bartlett Publishers International
Barb House, Barb Mews
London W6 7PA
UK

Jones and Bartlett's books and products are available through most bookstores and online booksellers. To contact Jones and Bartlett Publishers directly, call 800-832-0034, fax 978-443-8000, or visit our website www.jbpub.com.

Substantial discounts on bulk quantities of Jones and Bartlett's publications are available to corporations, professional associations, and other qualified organizations. For details and specific discount information, contact the special sales department at Jones and Bartlett via the above contact information or send an email to specialsales@jbpub.com.

Production Credits
Publisher: Michael Brown
Production Director: Amy Rose
Associate Production Editor: Tracey Chapman
Editorial Assistant: Kylah Goodfellow McNeill
Associate Marketing Manager: Marissa Hederson
Manufacturing and Inventory Coordinator: Amy Bacus
Composition: GGS Book Services
Cover Design: Anne Spencer
Printing and Binding: Malloy, Inc.
Cover Printing: Malloy, Inc.

Library of Congress Cataloging-in-Publication Data
Schneider, Mary-Jane, 1939-
    Introduction to public health / Mary-Jane Schneider.— 2nd ed.
        p. ; cm.
    Includes bibliographical references and index.
    ISBN 0-7637-3000-9 (pbk.)
    1. Public health.
    [DNLM: 1. Public Health. 2. Public Health Practice. WA 100 S359i 2006] I. Title.
    RA425.S28 2006
    362.1—dc22

                                                                                            2005008642

Printed in the United States of America
09 08 07 06   10 9 8 7 6 5 4 3 2

*To Edie, beloved Mom
and Grandma,
and to the memory of my parents,
Al and Mildred Tunis*

TABLE OF CONTENTS

PREFACE TO THE FIRST EDITION

As a laboratory scientist, a science writer, and a citizen, I always had a vague sense of uncertainty when I heard or read the term *public health*. When in 1986 I accepted a position as an administrator to help build the new School of Public Health in Albany, New York, a collaboration between the University at Albany and the New York State Department of Health, that sense of uncertainty became more acute. What is public health? If we don't understand what it is, how can we create a school to teach it? I found that I was not alone in my confusion. When I asked the question of those around me, some struggled to explain, while others admitted that their understanding was as vague as mine.

Fortunately, two events rescued me from my confusion. One was the publication in 1988 of the Institute of Medicine's report, *The Future of Public Health*.[1] The report set out, first of all, to clearly define public health, went on to state that the general public and policymakers do not understand public health and its importance, and urged that we who work in public health reach out to educate the public about what it is. Reading the report reassured me that at least I had not been alone in my ignorance.

What helped most to clarify my understanding of the concept was the assignment to work with the public health professionals of the New York State Department of Health to create the School's Master of Public Health (MPH) program. The MPH is the quintessential degree for public health professionals, and it is designed to provide students with a broad understanding of the whole interdisciplinary field of public health, together with a set of skills that will equip them to work at protecting and promoting the health of the public. In designing the University at Albany's public health program, I worked with committees of Health Department epidemiologists, biomedical scientists, environmental health specialists, social and behavioral scientists, biostatisticians, and health policy makers – people who were actually doing public health – searching, questioning, and debating over what should be part of a public health education. For me, it was an inspiration to observe the idealism and commitment of these busy professionals, clearly dedicated to the health of the people of New York State, who were willing to volunteer their time and effort toward the goal of preparing the public health professionals of the future. The process gave me a better sense not only of what public health is, but also of the ethic and ideal of public health as a basic principle of social justice.

Once the School was firmly established and the MPH program was functioning, some of us began to think about the Institute of Medicine report's mandate to inform the public about public health and, specifically, to "expose undergraduates to concepts, history, current context, and techniques of public health."[1(p.17)] Because schools of public health are primarily graduate schools, most college students don't have the opportunity to take a course in public health or even know enough about the field to be curious about it. Public health does not fall neatly into any traditional academic category and I would be surprised if it earned more than passing mention in courses in history, government, or political science – fields that might be expected to include public health as a topic of study – or microbiology, sociology, or anthropology, disciplines that contribute to the field of public health. To help remedy the deficiency, the faculty of the School developed a course called "Introduction to Public Health," which has been taught annually to undergraduates at the University at Albany since 1994.

This book was written as a textbook for "Introduction to Public Health," for which I am the course coordinator. The audience I have in mind for the book includes people such as I was before I came to work at the School of Public Health, people who feel vaguely uncertain about what is being referred to when they hear or read about public health. The material on which I base most of the book arises out of the course, which is taught by faculty from all departments of the School. Because many of the faculty of the School of Public Health at Albany are first of all public health practitioners at the New York State Department of Health, many of the lectures consist of these wonderful people talking about what they do every day to promote and protect the health of the population of New York State. I have continued to learn by attending these lectures and have found it a fascinating and inspiring way to learn about public health. I believe the students who have taken the course have likewise been fascinated and inspired.

I hope that the existence of this textbook will inspire faculty at other colleges and universities to teach public health to undergraduate students. Americans are still largely uninformed about what public health is and what it does for us. A poll conducted by Louis Harris and Associates in 1996 found that "few Americans have any real idea what the words 'public health' mean," although when it was explained to them, "almost everyone" believed it to be very important.[2] I believe that every citizen of the United States should know something about public health, just as they should know something about democracy, law, and other functions of government. One step toward achieving this goal would be to include public health as a general education course in college. Ideally the concept of public health should also be introduced in high school courses, an objective that could be achieved if future teachers were introduced to the subject in college.

I have tried to make this book easily comprehensible to the general reader. Public health issues are featured almost every day on the front pages of our newspapers and in the headlines of our television news programs. Often, they are not labeled as public health, and this is why so many of us are confused as to what those two words mean. This book is my effort to spread the word about the crucial role that public health plays in maintaining and improving the health of us all.

REFERENCES

1. Institute of Medicine (U.S.), Committee for the Study of the Future of Public Health, *The Future of Public Health* (Washington, DC: National Academy Press, 1988).
2. H. Taylor, "Public health: Two Words Few People Understand Even Though Almost Everyone Thinks Public Health Functions Are Very Important," Louis Harris and Associates, Inc., January 6, 1997.

PREFACE TO THE SECOND EDITION

In the Preface to the first edition, I wrote of the public's general ignorance of the field of public health. That situation seems to have improved somewhat since the book was published, in part because of the attention paid to public health as a result of the anthrax attacks in fall 2001 and the recognition that defense against bioterrorism requires a strong public health system. Each time I begin a new semester of teaching this course at SUNY-Albany, I ask the class what they think public health is. Clearly, recent students have displayed more understanding of the field than did the students of the 1990s.

Teaching public health to undergraduate students has become more widespread in recent years, and some universities have begun to offer undergraduate minors and majors in public health. I am happy for whatever contribution this textbook has made toward expanding general knowledge of the field and inspiring students to choose public health as a career.

The second edition of this textbook follows the plan of the first edition, bringing it up to date and including new developments in infectious diseases, women's health, environmental health controversies, the FDA, and many other issues encompassed by the always newsworthy field of public health. A new chapter has been added, prompted by the events of fall 2001 together with the timely publication by the American Public Health Association of *Public Health Management of Disasters: The Practice Guide*, written by Linda Landesman. Disaster preparedness has always been an important but under-appreciated component of public health, and Landesman's book is the result of an effort, supported by the Association of Schools of Public Health and the Centers for Disease Control and Prevention, to develop a disaster curriculum for schools of public health.

Public health is a fascinating field. The fact that it depends on political decisions is frustrating to many practitioners, but it is often the politics that put public health in the headlines. I hope that this book will help give you all a better idea of the sciences and politics of public health.

ACKNOWLEDGMENTS

This book is in a sense a joint effort by all the faculty of the School of Public Health who have cooperated in teaching the undergraduate course, Introduction to Public Health, at SUNY-Albany. Much of what I have written is taken from their lectures. Any errors, however, are my own.

Dan Beauchamp was an important influence in the early days of Albany's School of Public Health. His idealism about public health as a force for social cohesion inspired us all. Dan's lessons on the philosophy, ethics, and politics of public health opened my eyes to the rich variety of the subject, which I hope this book will help to communicate to others.

David Strogatz was one of the small group of faculty who originally planned the course and he anchored the course in the early years with his discussion of the basic science of public health. I have based much of my epidemiology section on his lectures.

Jack Conway was another member of the original planning team and was a regular lecturer in the course. My section on environmental health follows his lead to a great extent.

In the area of social and behavioral aspects, Michelle van Ryn and Barry Sherman were always thought-provoking on why these factors have such a major influence on health, and why certain social groups are at special risk for poor health. I have learned most of what I know of this complex and important field from them. In recent years, Mary Gallant and Ben Shaw have taken over the task of explaining for the class the role of social and behavioral sciences in public health.

Gene Therriault has been the principal statistics lecturer for the course, explaining statistical concepts and methods with remarkable lucidity. I am grateful to him for bringing to life a difficult subject. Peter Millock explains the legal basis of public health each year with great panache.

I am indebted to two people who no longer participate in the School of Public Health, but who taught me most of what I know about their areas of expertise: Susan Standfast in injury control and Jack Guzewich in food safety.

Thanks also to the following people who have been taking a regular and important role in the course, with lessons I have incorporated into the book: in the area of biomedical sciences, Chuck Trimarchi on rabies, Ken Pass on newborn screening, Michele Caggana on human genetics, Kathleen McDonough on tuberculosis, and Lou Smith on the biomedical basis of HIV/AIDS; in epidemiology, Barbara Wallace on epidemiologic surveillance, Nancy Wade on the epidemiology of HIV/AIDS, and Betsy Lewis-Michl on the difficulties of cancer epidemiology; in the collection and uses of data, Sid Prasad on the U.S. census, Mike Medvesky on community health assessment, and Mike Zdeb, who delights in pointing out the errors and uncertainties in the statistical data on which public health depends so heavily; in the area of environmental health, Roger Sokol on water quality, Tom Gentile on air quality, Lloyd Wilson on solid and hazardous wastes, and Ron DePersis on occupational health; in the area of social and behavioral factors in health, Russell Sciandra on tobacco control programs, Mary Applegate on unintended pregnancy and infant mortality, Wendy Shotsky on AIDS/HIV prevention programs, and Judy Levin on the obesity epidemic; in the area of the U.S. medical care system, Diane Dewar on the rising costs of medical care, Barbara Frankel on managed care, Tim Hoff on medical errors, and Nancy Persily on the aging population.

Bob Westfall, Director of the School of Public Health's Center for Public Health Preparedness, introduced me to the field of emergency planning and preparedness through his lectures in the course, and he kindly reviewed my new chapter on that subject.

David Carpenter, founding dean of the school who supported the original proposal to teach an undergraduate course, has stimulated many discussions on controversial public health risks, some of which I have referred to in these chapters. He gave me my start in public health.

I have depended heavily for published materials on the Dickerman Library of the New York State Department of Health, and I thank the library staff, especially Rae Clark, who is always there late when I most need help. Thanks also to Carol Whittaker for encouragement and moral support.

Finally, I could not have reached the end of this project without the loving support of my husband, Allan, who has always encouraged me to explore my professional interests. I wish also to express pride in my son Henry, the economist, who did the wonderful drawings that lighten the tone of a rather serious book, and my son Joseph, also multi-talented, who is beginning a new career in health care.

Public Health in the News

What is public health? It is an abstract concept, hard to pin down. Reports about public health appear in the news every day, but they are not labeled as public health stories and most people do not recognize them as such. Here in the prologue are four major public health stories of the past two decades that bring the abstraction to life. The ongoing AIDS epidemic, arguably the greatest challenge that public health has faced in the past half century, illustrates the multidisciplinary nature of the field and the complex ethical and political issues that are often an inherent component of public health. The outbreak of water-borne disease that sickened more than 400,000 people in Milwaukee, Wisconsin in 1993, was the consequence of a breakdown in a routine public health measure that has protected the populations of developed countries for most of the century. Lest Americans forget that maintaining the health of the population requires constant vigilance, the dramatic decline in all measures of health in Russia presents a cautionary lesson of what can happen to a society that loses the will to protect its people. Finally, the terrorist attacks of fall 2001 made it clear that the national security of the United States depends not only on the Defense Department but also on the American public health system.

AIDS EPIDEMIC

On July 3, 1981, the *New York Times* ran a story with the headline: "Rare Cancer Seen in 41 Homosexuals."[1] The cancer was Kaposi's sarcoma, a form of skin cancer, rarely fatal, which usually occurred in elderly men of Mediterranean descent. Now the victims were young, gay men living in New York City or San Francisco, and eight of the forty-one had died within twenty-four months of being diagnosed. The report noted that several of the victims had been found to have severe defects in their immune systems, but it was not known whether the immune defects were the underlying problem or had developed later. Most of the victims had had multiple and frequent sexual encounters with different partners, the article said, but there was no evidence that the disease was contagious, since none of the patients knew each other.

On August 29, there was another story: "2 Fatal Diseases Focus of Inquiry."[2] A rare kind of pneumonia called pneumocystis had been striking gay men and killing 60 percent of them. According to the *New York Times*, fifty-three cases of pneumocystis had been diagnosed. Also, the number of cases of Kaposi's had grown to forty-seven, and seven patients had both diseases. No one knew why gay men were affected, but there was speculation that there might be a link to their sexual lifestyle, drug use, or some other environmental cause. The article noted without comment that one woman had also been reported with pneumocystis pneumonia. A scientific task force had been formed at the Centers for Disease Control and Prevention (CDC) to investigate what was going on. There was no further news in the *New York Times* about what was to be known as AIDS until May 1982.[3] In that article, the underlying commonality of the immune defect was recognized and the condition was called gay-related immune deficiency syndrome (GRID). While immune deficiencies had been known and studied previously, most were genetic conditions that afflicted children from birth or were caused by immunosuppressive drugs used to prevent rejection of transplanted organs. The total suppression of the immune system by whatever means leads to many infections, one of which eventually kills the victim. Speculation as to the cause of GRID generally focused on a sexually transmitted infectious agent, although there was a suspicion that multiple factors might be involved, perhaps including drugs or an immune response to the introduction of sperm into the blood through sexual contact.

As the number of reported cases grew, CDC scientists interviewed people with GRID, questioning them about their sexual behavior and partners. The scientists learned about, and the news media began to report on, sexual activities of gay men—promiscuous and anonymous sex in public baths, use of drugs to enhance sexual pleasure—which tended to worsen many people's already negative view of gay men. Linkages were found that began to confirm that a sexually transmitted infectious agent was responsible. But the investigations were hampered by lack of funding. President Ronald Reagan had been inaugurated in January 1981 on a conservative platform. His administration was not interested in a disease that affected people who behaved in ways so unappealing to the general population. Nor was there much concern on the part of the general public. Most people felt no threat to themselves, although people who lived New York, San Franciso, Los Angeles, and Miami, where most of the cases had been reported, might have gone out of their way to avoid gay men.

Since early in the epidemic, however, there had been occasional reports of the immune deficiency in women and heterosexual men, many of them intravenous drug users. By summer of 1982, cases of the syndrome had also been reported in people with hemophilia, who were exposed to blood products used to make a clotting factor, and patients who had received blood transfusions. A study of female sexual partners of men with the syndrome suggested that the disease may be transmitted by heterosexual relations. A number of babies turned up with a syndrome that resembled GRID, possibly transmitted from their mothers before or at birth. It was clear that the condition was not limited to gay men, and its name was changed to Acquired Immune Deficiency Syndrome (AIDS). The public began to take notice.

By mid-1983, the public began to panic. A report by a pediatrician in New Jersey suggested that AIDS had spread within a family by routine household contact. That scared a lot of people: AIDS was a fatal disease, and people did not want to take any chances of catching it. Inmates in a New York State prison refused to eat meals in a mess hall used by a fellow inmate who had died of AIDS. A New York City sanitation worker with no known risk factors contracted AIDS, perhaps from a syringe protruding from a trash bag. In San Francisco, with its large gay population, the police officers demanded special masks and gloves for handling people suspected of being infected with AIDS. Blood banks reported that blood supplies were critically low because people wrongly feared that they could contract AIDS through donating blood. In New York City, tenants of a cooperative apartment building tried to evict a doctor known for treating people with AIDS. In a few well-publicized incidents, schools refused to allow children with AIDS—usually hemophiliacs—into the classroom. A special telephone information number on AIDS, set up by the federal government, was swamped with 8,000 to 10,000 calls a day. Fundamentalist preachers and conservative legislators fulminated that AIDS was God's punishment for abominable behavior and that people with AIDS deserved their fate.

Meanwhile, although controversy still restricted federal funding for AIDS research, biomedical scientists were competing to identify the infectious agent, which most scientists believed would turn out to be a virus. Despite the ill repute of many AIDS patients, the disease was of great scientific interest, and the growing public concern promised to reward with acclaim and financial benefits the scientist who isolated the virus. On April 23, 1984, the Secretary of Health and Human Services convened a press conference to announce that Dr. Robert Gallo of the National Cancer Institute had discovered the virus—now known as the human immunodeficiency virus (HIV)—and that a vaccine would be available within five years.[4] While both those statements proved to be less than accurate—Gallo's priority was disputed and eventually disproved, and after twenty years an effective vaccine has still not been developed—the discovery did promise to allow testing of blood for exposure to the virus. Just a year later, blood banks in the United States began screening donated blood, greatly reducing the risk to transfusion recipients and people with hemophilia.

Now, more than two decades after the first reports on AIDS were publicized, most of the hysteria has faded, while many of the most dire predictions have been realized. By the end of 2002, 859,000 people in the United States had been diagnosed with AIDS and over 500,000 had died.[5] An estimated 384,900 Americans are living with HIV infection. The proportion of women diagnosed with AIDS is steadily increasing, amounting to 26 percent in 2002. A great deal more is known about the disease. New drugs have "miraculously" restored health to some dying patients and offer hope that HIV is becoming a chronic, manageable condition rather than a progressively fatal disease. However, there is still no cure, and long-term prospects for HIV-infected individuals are at best uncertain. The only prevention is the avoidance of risky behaviors.

The question of how the government should respond to the AIDS epidemic has raised some of the most difficult ethical and political issues imaginable in public health. Every new scientific discovery stimulated new dilemmas. Most of the controversies pitted two opposing principles against each other: the protection of the privacy and freedom of the individual suspected of being ill, on the one hand, and the protection of the health of potential "innocent" victims at risk of being exposed, on the other. This conflict is common to many public health problems. Historically, the protection of the public has taken precedence over the rights of the individual. Thus, the principle of quarantining patients with dangerous infectious diseases such as typhus, cholera, or yellow fever has been generally accepted and upheld by the courts. However, in the case of AIDS, the issues have been more complicated.

Because people with AIDS belonged to stigmatized groups who may have been exposed to the virus because of illegal behavior (intravenous drug use or homosexual acts that were still illegal in many states), they bitterly opposed being publicly identified. Gay men, who had only recently achieved a degree of liberation from public oppression, were very well organized politically; they effectively opposed some measures that would have normally been considered standard public health practice, such as reporting the names of diagnosed patients to the health department. They had well-founded fears of being discriminated against in jobs, housing, access to health insurance, and so on. Major political battles erupted over issues such as whether gay bathhouses should be closed and whether the names of people who have tested positive for HIV should be reported to the local health department. As HIV infection has become more controllable, some of the controversy has subsided.

AIDS is particularly difficult for government to deal with because the only effective way to prevent its spread is to change people's behavior. There are precedents for governmental efforts at promoting behavior change—campaigns to promote smoking cessation, use of bicycle helmets, and healthy diet and exercise—but their success has been modest. Generally, the weight of a law adds significantly to the government's success in promoting healthy behavior, as in the case of seat belt laws and laws against drunk driving. However, behavior that spreads HIV is very difficult to control by law: intravenous drug use is already illegal everywhere in the United States, and homosexual acts were also illegal in many states until the U.S. Supreme Court declared these laws unconstitutional in 2003. From the beginning, public health officials recognized that AIDS could be prevented only by persuading people to reduce their risk by limiting their exposure, which requires convincing them to control powerful biological and social urges.

Beginning with the earliest attempts at AIDS education, conflict arose between the attempt to communicate effectively with people most likely to be at risk and the likelihood of offending the general public by seeming to condone obscene or illegal acts. Conservatives argued—and still argue—that the only appropriate AIDS education message is abstinence from sex and drugs. C. Everett Koop, President Reagan's surgeon general, was originally known for his right-to-life views. Later he became an unexpected hero to public health advocates by taking a strong stand in favor of frank AIDS education. While stressing the importance of mutually faithful monogamous sexual relationships and avoidance of injected drugs, he nevertheless advocated education about the advantages of condoms and clean needles, and he urged schools to teach children about safe sex. In response, Senator Jesse Helms, a powerful conservative from North Carolina, denounced safe sex materials aimed at gay men as "promotion of sodomy" by the government and sponsored an amendment banning the use of federal funds "to provide AIDS education, information, or prevention materials and activities that promote or encourage, directly or indirectly, homosexual activities."[6(p.218)] Today, television advertising of condoms, the most effective barrier to HIV transmission, while not as restricted as it was two decades ago, is still usually limited to late-night time slots.[7] Despite the abundance of sexually explicit programming and widespread advertising of Viagra and similar drugs, condom manufacturers still fear the ire of political conservatives and moralists.

Drug regimens introduced in the mid-1990s that are capable of controlling the damage the virus wreaks on the immune system stimulated new medical, ethical, and economic challenges. The drugs have side effects that may prove fatal for some patients and have long-term adverse effects in others. Complicated regimens for taking many pills a day have been simplified, but new problems of viral strains resistant to the drugs have arisen. These strains may be transmitted to others. Moreover, the drugs are expensive, costing an average of $13,000 for a year's supply,[8] well beyond the budget of most patients, although government programs pay for the treatment of many patients. Estimated medical costs of caring for HIV-infected adults in the United States are $6.7 billion per year.[9]

The history of the AIDS epidemic vividly illustrates that public health involves both science and politics. It took the science of epidemiology, the study of disease in human populations, to determine the basic nature of the disease and how it is transmitted. The biomedical sciences, especially virology and immunology, were crucial in identifying the infectious agent, determining how it causes its dire effects on the human organism, developing methods to identify virus-infected blood, and devising drugs that can hold the virus at bay. Biostatisticians help to design the trials that test the effectiveness of new drugs and, eventually, vaccines—believed to be the greatest hope for controlling the virus. In the meantime, behavioral scientists must find ways to convince people to avoid actions that spread the virus.

The politics of the AIDS epidemic shows the tension between individual freedom and the health of the community. There is a strong tradition of the use of police powers to protect the health of the public in all civilized societies. In the United States, there is also a strong tradition of individual liberty and civil rights. Politics determines the path the government will take in balancing these traditions. Public health is not based on scientific facts alone. It depends on politics to choose the values and ethics that determine how science will be applied to preserve people's health while protecting their fundamental rights.

CRYPTOSPORIDIUM IN MILWAUKEE WATER

In early April 1993, an outbreak of "intestinal flu" struck Milwaukee, causing widespread absenteeism among hospital employees, students, and school teachers. The symptoms included watery diarrhea that lasted for several days. The Milwaukee Department of Health, concerned, contacted the Wisconsin state health department and an investigation was begun.[10]

Stool samples from the most severely ill patients had been sent to clinical laboratories for testing, and these tests yielded the first clues to the cause of the illness. Two laboratories reported to the city health department that they had identified cryptosporidium in samples from seven adults. This organism was not one that most laboratories routinely tested for, but starting April 7, all fourteen clinical laboratories began looking for it in all stool samples submitted to them—and they began finding it. Ultimately, 739 stool samples tested between March 1 and May 30 were found positive for cryptosporidium.

Cryptosporidium is an intestinal parasite that is most commonly spread through contaminated water. In people who are basically healthy, the severe symptoms last a week or so. In addition to the watery diarrhea, the symptoms include varying degrees of cramps, nausea, vomiting, and fever. The infection can be fatal in people with a compromised immune system, such as AIDS patients or people taking immunosuppressive drugs for organ transplants or cancer treatment.

In Milwaukee, public health officials immediately suspected the municipal water supply, which comes from Lake Michigan. They inspected records from the two water treatment plants that supplied the city, and suspicion immediately fell on the southern plant. The inspectors noted that the water's turbidity, or cloudiness, which was monitored once every eight hours, had increased enormously beginning on March 21, an ominous sign. On April 7, city officials issued a warning advising customers of the Milwaukee Water Works to boil their water before drinking it. On April 9, they temporarily closed the plant. Looking for evidence that the water was indeed contaminated with cryptosporidum, they discovered that a southern Milwaukee company had produced and stored blocks of ice on March 25 and April 9. Testing confirmed that the organism was present in the ice.

Meanwhile public health investigators were trying to determine how many people had been made sick by the contaminated water. Reasoning that only the most severely affected patients would go to a doctor and have their stool tested, they began a telephone survey of Milwaukee residents. On April 9, 10, and 12, they called randomly selected phone numbers and asked the first adult who answered whether anyone in the household had been sick since March 1. Of 482 respondents, 42 percent reported having had watery diarrhea, which was considered to be the defining symptom of the illness. In a more extensive telephone survey conducted on 1,663 people in the greater Milwaukee area between April 28 and May 2, 30 percent of the respondents reported having had diarrhea. Half of the respondents whose water came from the southern plant reported the symptoms, while only 15 percent of those whose homes did not get water from the Milwaukee Water Works had been ill. These individuals had probably been exposed at work or from visiting in the affected region.[10]

The investigators, who reported the results of their study in the *New England Journal of Medicine*, estimated that at least 403,000 people were made ill by the cryptosporidium contamination of the Milwaukee water supply.[10] The number of deaths has been estimated to be fifty-four; 85 percent of them were AIDS patients.[11] In discussing how the contamination had occurred, the investigators speculated that unusually large amounts of the organism may have come from cattle farms, slaughterhouses, or human sewage swept into Lake Michigan by heavy spring rains and snow runoff. Flaws in the water treatment process of the southern plant led to inadequate removal of the parasites. After the problem was diagnosed, the southern water treatment plant was thoroughly cleaned and a continuous turbidity monitor was installed that automatically sounds an alarm and shuts down the system if the turbidity rises above a certain level.

Cryptosporidum contamination is probably much more common than is recognized. A 1993 report by the Natural Resources Defense Council stated that the organisms had been found in water supplied by 100 utility systems to at least forty-five million Americans.[12] In a workshop held at the CDC in 1994, experts agreed that low levels of cryptosporidium contamination are common in treated water and that little is known on the associated health risks. They suggested that immunocompromised people can reduce their risk by boiling all their drinking water.[13]

The United States has always been proud of its safe drinking water. Times are changing, however. While many communities are still using water treatment technology dating to World War I, population growth, modern agricultural technology, and toxic industrial wastes are challenging cleanup efforts, which are expensive. However, waterborne disease outbreaks are also expensive. An analysis of the cost of the Milwaukee outbreak in medical costs and productivity costs, done by scientists from the CDC, the City of Milwaukee Department of Health, the Wisconsin State Division of Public Health, and Emory University, yielded an estimate of $96.2 million.[14] These authors estimated that, based on the approximately 7.7 million cases of waterborne disease annually, waterborne disease outbreaks cost $21.9 billion each year in the United States. They recommended that the cost of the outbreaks should be considered when costs of maintaining safe water supplies are calculated. Safe drinking water, one of the most fundamental public health measures, is by no means assured in the United States.

WORST CASE SCENARIO: PUBLIC HEALTH IN RUSSIA

The Soviet Union set a high priority on public health soon after the Russian Revolution, when the population was suffering from the effects of war, including famine, plague, and a general lack of sanitation. The communist government ran educational campaigns to teach people to practice basic hygiene and prevent disease. It promised free medical care to all; it trained physicians and built hospitals and tuberculosis sanitariums. The incidence of typhus, typhoid fever, and dysentery were dramatically cut. By the 1930s, Western visitors were impressed with the nation's progress in raising the health of the population to near European levels. However, the promise was soon eroded by the abuses of the Soviet system. Progress was choked off by Stalin's suppression of science, the policy of secrecy that concealed bad news, and the Soviet industrial planning process that pushed for continuously increased production at all costs.[15]

The extent of the public health disaster was not known until the late 1980s when Gorbachev began the policy of "glasnost," or openness. Westerners—and Russians themselves—learned that infant mortality rates had been rising since the 1970s but were not published because they were embarrassing to the government. The extent of environmental degradation throughout the former Soviet Union, together with increasing rates of cancer, respiratory disease, and birth defects, had become obvious. The corruption and incompetence in the Soviet medical system were also clear: shortages of vaccines, drugs, and medical supplies; unhygienic practices including the re-use of needles for injections and immunizations; poor training of physicians and shortages of nurses. Alcoholism was rampant.[15]

After the Soviet Union disintegrated in 1991, public health in Russia and other former Soviet states grew dramatically worse. In Russia, death rates increased and birth rates declined so that, by the mid-1990s, deaths were almost twice as common as births. This has led to a rapid decline in the size of the population, which is predicted to fall by a third to a half of its present size by the year 2050.[16] The life expectancy at birth for Russian men, which was sixty-four years in 1989, fell to 58.9 in 2001.[16,17] (Life expectancy for American men was 74.3.)[18] The infant mortality rate fell during the 1990s, but still it was 15.9 per 1,000 live births in 2001, double that of the United States.[17,18] Abortions, the most common method of birth control, were twice as common as childbirth; recent government efforts to restrict abortions, together with the increased availability of birth control, reduced their number; still, there were thirteen abortions for every ten live births in 2002.[19]

Infectious diseases, which had been well controlled during the Soviet era, have reappeared, with outbreaks of cholera, diphtheria, plague, typhoid fever, and typhus.[16] Tuberculosis has been surging, fed by overcrowded conditions in prisons; when prisoners are released, they spread the disease to their community. Improper use of antibiotics has led to drug resistance in many of these cases.[20] Infection with HIV, the virus that causes AIDS, has been spreading out of control. A recent report by the Russian government estimated that one and a half million Russians now carry the virus, roughly twice the number in the United States, which has double the population. The report predicts that the total number of Russians infected could reach as many as one in twenty-five over the next five years.[21]

Although many factors contribute to the alarming statistics, much of the blame appears to fall on the economic stress and social breakdown that accompanied the breakup of the former Soviet Union. Middle-aged men have been the group most severely impacted by the changes in the system. They are dying in large numbers from motor vehicle accidents, suicide, homicide, drowning, alcohol poisoning, and cardiovascular disease. Alcohol contributes to many of these deaths; the per capita consumption of alcohol averages 4.4 gallons per year, the highest in the world.[22] One Russian official has been quoted as saying that every third death in Russia is alcohol related.[23] Among men, half of all deaths occur on Monday after a weekend drinking binge. Although smoking is widespread and the Russian diet is poor, the effects of alcohol are said to outstrip all other health risks.

Attention has also focused on environmental pollution. The Soviet emphasis on industrialization and competitiveness in waging the cold war led to a neglect of environmental protection and civilian public works. Soviet factories of 1930s vintage still spew black smoke and toxic chemicals into the air, causing asthma and chronic bronchitis in cities across the nation. Raw sewage and industrial wastes pour into rivers used for drinking water: almost three-quarters of the nation's surface water is polluted. Rivers used for irrigation have run dry, leaving contaminated dust to blow in the wind. Soil and water are heavily contaminated by the excessive use of pesticides, many of them banned in the United States because of their toxicity. The accident at the Chernobyl nuclear power station in 1986 poured quantities of radioactive material into the atmosphere that contaminated water and soil over 50,000 square miles of the Ukraine, Belorus, and western Russia. Other, less publicized nuclear accidents, as well as atomic tests and deliberate dumping of nuclear materials, have exposed thousands of citizens to dangerous levels of radiation. Genetic damage, caused by exposure to radiation and toxic chemicals, is one hypothesis put forward to explain the dramatic increases in birth defects and other health problems that are taking their toll on the Russian people.[15]

The medical system is vastly underfunded: sterile equipment is rare; drugs are in short supply; physicians and other medical workers are poorly paid.[24] According to World Health Organization figures, the Russian government spends $405 per person annually on health, compared to annual expenditures of $4,490 in the United States.[17,18] With 38 percent of the population living below subsistence level, people who most need medical care cannot afford to pay for private care, and health insurance is almost non-existent.[25] The Russian diet, high in cholesterol-rich animal fats and eggs and low in fruit and vegetables, contributes to abnormally high rates of cardiovascular disease and some cancers.[26] High rates of alcoholism and tobacco addiction and the apparent reluctance of women to bear children (as demonstrated by low birth rates and high abortion rates) are symptoms of social breakdown, in which people have so little faith in their future that they feel it is not worth worrying about their health. Considering also the high crime rates and economic chaos, the conditions in Russia are not conducive to good public health.

The public health disaster in Russia serves to remind Americans how lucky they are and how wise they have been to—through local, state, and federal governments—take measures to protect the environment and their health. Americans take most public health protections for granted—safe water, clean air, freedom from exposure to dangerous radiation, sterile medical instruments, the availability of effective antibiotics to treat infections, and access to immunizations against formerly common diseases. Most Americans expect to live a long and healthy life. However, the benefits of effective public health measures require continued vigilance. The Russian experience illustrates the worst that can happen if these protections are not maintained.

PUBLIC HEALTH AND TERRORISM

On September 11, 2001, the United States was struck by foreign terrorists, and Americans entered a new phase of civic life. Four passenger airliners were simultaneously hijacked: three were crashed into buildings filled with people going about their work routines, and one crashed in an empty field in Pennsylvania, apparently headed for another target but wrestled from the hijackers by resistant passengers.

The immediate public reaction to these disasters was the activation of emergency response plans in the regions where the crashes occurred. Police, firefighters, and ambulances rushed to the scenes; hospital emergency rooms were alerted; extra doctors and nurses were called in. In the New York City area, health care facilities in the whole region readied themselves to receive the expected large numbers of people wounded at the World Trade Center. Unfortunately, much of this preparation was not utilized because there were so few survivors.

Although the disaster of September 11 was unprecedented in its magnitude, it was similar in kind to other emergencies and disasters that communities plan for: plane and train crashes, factory explosions, earthquakes, hurricanes, and so on. In New York, public health agencies were concerned not only with coordinating emergency medical care, but also with ensuring the safety of cleanup workers and area residents. Problems with polluted water, contaminated air, spoiled food, infestation of vermin, and so on, had to be dealt with in lower Manhattan just as they must be dealt with after any natural disaster.

The longer term response to September 11 has focused on law enforcement and national defense, with the goal of preventing future hostile acts by terrorists. The federal government has tightened security at airports and borders; it has attacked or warned foreign countries thought to harbor terrorists; and national intelligence agencies have increased their surveillance of persons and groups suspected of being a threat to the United States, to the extent that there are concerns that civil liberties are being eroded.

In contrast to the dramatic events of September 11, the second terrorist attack of fall 2001 became apparent only gradually. On October 2, Robert Stevens, an editor for a supermarket tabloid, was admitted to a Florida hospital emergency room suffering from a high fever and disorientation. An infectious disease specialist made a diagnosis of anthrax, in part because of heightened suspicions of bioterrorism provoked by the September 11 attacks. The doctor notified the county health department, which notified the state and the CDC. After further tests, the health agencies announced on October 4 that a case of inhalational anthrax had been confirmed. An intensive investigation into the source of exposure began at once. Mr. Stevens died on October 5.[27,28]

On that same day, another case was diagnosed in a co-worker at the tabloid offices. Tests done throughout the building detected a few anthrax spores on Mr. Stevens's computer keyboard and more in the mailroom.

The building was closed, and all employees were offered antibiotics to protect them against the development of disease.

On October 9, the New York City Department of Health announced that a newsroom worker at NBC in New York City had developed cutaneous anthrax. She had handled a suspicious letter containing a powder, later identified as anthrax spores. Shortly after, a seven-month-old infant, who had visited his mother's workplace at ABC-TV two weeks earlier, was diagnosed with cutaneous anthrax. The child had developed a severe, intractable skin lesion that progressed to severe anemia and kidney failure, but anthrax had not been suspected as a cause of these symptoms.[29] By this time, it was clear that the outbreak was intentionally caused and that a bioterror attack was under way.

On October 15, a staff member working in Senator Tom Daschle's office in Washington, DC opened a letter and noticed a small burst of powder from it. Alert to the threat of anthrax, the aide notified the police and the FBI, and the area was vacated. The letter tested positive for anthrax. Staff and visitors who were potentially exposed were offered antibiotics, as were workers in the Capitol mail rooms.[30]

The bad news continued. At about the same time that workers in the media and in Congress were being exposed, the disease was breaking out in postal workers in New Jersey, Maryland, and Virginia, although it took days or weeks to recognize what was happening. While it was known by mid-October that anthrax spores were being sent through the mail, they were not believed to escape from sealed envelopes. As it turned out, postal workers were among the most affected by the outbreak. The Brentwood Mail Processing and Distribution Center in the District of Columbia was closed on October 21 after four postal workers were hospitalized with inhalational anthrax; two of these workers died.[31]

All told, a total of twenty-two cases of anthrax were diagnosed over a two-month period, of which eleven were the inhalational form. Five of the latter group died, one of whom was a ninety-four-year-old woman in Connecticut whose source of exposure was never verified. It was surmised that a piece of mail received at her home had been cross-contaminated by another piece of mail at a postal facility.[32] The CDC estimated that 32,000 potentially exposed people received prophylactic antibiotic therapy, which may have prevented many more cases.[33] Contaminated buildings, including five U.S. Postal Service facilities, had to be closed and laboriously decontaminated; some of these building could not be reopened for more than a year.[34,35]

Investigation of postal service records determined that letters to the media were mailed in Trenton, New Jersey in mid-September. The letter to Senator Daschle and one to Senator Patrick Lahey, which was not opened until it was irradiated to kill the bacteria, were mailed in Trenton on October 9. A number of hoax letters, similar to the anthrax letters, some containing innocuous white powder, were also mailed to media and government offices from St. Petersburg, Florida. Since they were sent before the news broke about the anthrax letters, they were presumably sent by the same person. The perpetrator of the anthrax mailings has still not been identified.[36]

The anthrax attacks terrorized the population far beyond the actual damage done. They also disrupted the public health and emergency response systems out of proportion to the actual threat. Any encounter with white powder evoked panic, causing people to send samples to public health laboratories for testing. At New York State's Wadsworth Center in Albany, scientists worked around the clock throughout the fall, testing more than 900 samples. Some of the unlikely specimens sent for testing were a pair of jeans, a box of grape tomatoes, a box of Tic Tacs breath freshener, and several packets of cash from automatic teller machines. The largest amount of cash submitted at one time was $8,000, carefully guarded and picked up by police immediately after the anthrax tests proved to be negative.[37]

The events of fall 2001 disturbed Americans' sense of security within their borders. The terrorists' hijacking of four airplanes prompted major efforts to strengthen homeland security through more rigorous screening of airline passengers and of international travelers at the borders, precautions that are now routine and are expected to be maintained. The anthrax attacks called attention to the fact that the public health system is America's best protection from bioterrorism. Increased funding for disease surveillance, public health laboratories, and emergency response systems has strengthened the ability of the public health system to respond to bioterrorist attacks as well as to natural disasters and epidemics. These precautions are just as important as other homeland security measures for Americans to be safe in their homeland.

REFERENCES

1. L. Altman, "Rare Cancer Seen in 41 Homosexuals," *New York Times* (July 3, 1981): A20.
2. Associated Press, "2 Fatal Diseases Focus of Inquiry," *New York Times* (August 29, 1981): 9.
3. L. Altman, "New Homosexual Disorder Worries Health Officials," *New York Times* (May 11, 1982): C1.

4. L. Garrett, *The Coming Plague: Newly Emerging Diseases in a World Out of Balance* (New York: Farrar, Straus, and Giroux, 1994).
5. U.S. Centers for Disease Control and Prevention, *HIV/AIDS Surveillance Report 2002*, 14.
6. R. Bayer, *Private Acts, Social Consequences: AIDS and the Politics of Public Health* (New York: The Free Press, 1989), 218.
7. "A Brief History of Condoms and Condom Advertising," American Foundation for AIDS Research Web site, *www.amfar.org/cgi_bin/iowa/newsrecord.html?record=28*, February 8, 2002. Accessed May 24, 2004.
8. J. Bhattacharya et al., "The Link between Public and Private Insurance and HIV-Related Mortality," *Journal of Health Economics* 22 (2003): 1105–1122.
9. S. Bozette et al., "Expenditures for the Care of HIV-Infected Patients in the Era of Highly Active Antiretroviral Therapy," *New England Journal of Medicine* 324 (2001): 1897–1904.
10. W. R. MacKenzie et al., "A Massive Outbreak in Milwaukee of Cryptosporidium Infection Transmitted Through the Public Water Supply," *New England Journal of Medicine* 331 (1994): 161–167.
11. N. J. Hoxie et al., "Cryptosporidiosis-Associated Mortality Following a Massive Waterborne Outbreak in Milwaukee, Wisconsin," *American Journal of Public Health* 87 (1997): 2032–2035.
12. S. Terry, "Drinking Water Comes to a Boil," *New York Times Magazine* (September 26, 1993): 42–65.
13. U.S. Centers for Disease Control and Prevention, "Assessing the Public Health Threat Associated with Waterborne Cryptosporidiosis: Report of a Workshop," *Morbidity and Mortality Weekly Report Recommendations and Reports*, 44, No. RR-6 (1995).
14. P. S. Corso et al., "Cost of Illness in the 1993 Waterborne Cryptosporidium Outbreak, Milwaukee, Wisconsin," *Emerging Infectious Diseases* 9 (2003): 426–431.
15. M. Feshbach and A. Friendly Jr., *Ecocide in the USSR: Health and Nature Under Siege* (New York: Basic Books, 1992).
16. M. G. Field, "The Health and Demographic Crisis in Post-Soviet Russia: A Two-Phase Development," in M. G. Field and J. L. Twigg, *Russia's Torn Safety Nets: Health and Social Welfare during the Transition* (New York: St. Martin's Press, 2000), 11–42.
17. World Health Organization Web site, *www.who.int/country/rus/en*. Accessed January 5, 2004.
18. World Health Organization Web site, *www.who.int/country/usa/en*. Accessed January 5, 2004.
19. S. L. Myers, "New Russian Limits on Abortion Reflect a Wider Concern," *New York Times* (August 24, 2003): 3.
20. A. Zuger, "Russia Has Few Weapons as Infectious Diseases Surge," *New York Times* (December 5, 2000): F1.
21. M. Wines, "Rise of H.I.V. in Russia Is Quickening, Official Says," *New York Times* (May 22, 2003): A9.
22. M. Wines, "An Ailing Russia Lives a Tough Life That's Getting Shorter," *New York Times* (December 3, 2000): A1.
23. B. Aris, "Russia's Health Crisis Fuels 20-Year Cut in Lifespan Estimates," *The Lancet* 362 (2003): 4785.

24. M. Wines and A. Zuger, "In Russia, the Ill and Infirm Include Health Care Itself," *New York Times* (December 4, 2000): A1.
25. J. W. LeSar et al., "Russian Federation," in C. E. Koop et al., *Critical Issues in Global Health* (San Francisco: Jossey-Bass, 2001).
26. P. R. Magrab and P. C. Van Dyck, "Childhood Survival: Policies in Perspective," *Central European Health & Environment Monitor* 5, no. 1 (1997): 8.
27. U.S. Centers for Disease Control and Prevention, "Update: Investigation of Anthrax Associated with Intentional Exposure and Interim Public Health Guidelines, October 2001," *Morbidity and Mortality Weekly Report* 50 (2001): 889–891.
28. S. G. Stolberg, "Anthrax Threat Points to Limits in Health System," *New York Times* (October 14, 2001): A1.
29. D. Grady, "Report Notes Swift Course of Inhalational Anthrax," *New York Times* (February 20, 2002): A11.
30. U.S. Centers for Disease Control and Prevention, "Update: Investigation of Bioterrorism-Related Anthrax and Interim Guidelines for Exposure Management and Antimicrobial Therapy, October 2001," *Morbidity and Mortality Weekly Report* 50 (2001): 909–919.
31. U.S. Centers for Disease Control and Prevention, "Evaluation of Bacillus anthracis Contamination Inside the Brentwood Mail Processing and Distribution Center— District of Columbia, October 2001," *Morbidity and Mortality Weekly Report* 50 (2001): 1129–1133.
32. U.S. Centers for Disease Control and Prevention, "Update: Investigation of Bioterrorism-Related Anthrax—Connecticut, 2001," *Morbidity and Mortality Weekly Report* 50 (2001): 1077–1079.
33. U.S. Centers for Disease Control and Prevention, "Update: Investigation of Bioterrorism-Related Anthrax and Adverse Events from Antimicrobial Prophylaxis, 2001," *Morbidity and Mortality Weekly Report* 50 (2001): 973–976.
34. U.S. Centers for Disease Control and Prevention, "Follow-Up of Deaths Among U.S. Postal Service Workers Potentially Exposed to Bacillus anthracis—District of Columbia, 2001–2002," *Morbidity and Mortality Weekly Report* 52 (2003): 937–938.
35. I. Peterson, "Postal Center Hit by Anthrax Is Now Clean, Officials Say," *New York Times* (February 10, 2004): B7.
36. B. H. Rosenberg, Federation of American Scientists. Analysis of the Anthrax Attacks, *www.fas.org/bwc/news/anthraxreport.htm*, September 22, 2002. Accessed January 2004.
37. L. Sturman, personal communication.

PART I

What is Public Health?

CHAPTER 1

Public Health: Science, Politics, and Prevention

Medical Care versus Public Health

One expectation about living in a civilized society is that the living conditions will be basically healthy. Unless something unusual happens, like the outbreak of cryptosporidium in the Milwaukee water supply (discussed in the Prologue), people assume that they are basically safe: their water is safe to drink; the hamburger they buy at the fast food restaurant is safe to eat; the aspirin they take for a headache is what the label says it is; and they are not likely to be hit by a car—or a bullet—if they use reasonable caution in walking down the street. Even after the attacks of fall 2001, which severely disrupted their sense of security, most Americans regained a sense of trust in the safety of their environment.

In historical terms, this expectation is a relatively recent development. In the mid-nineteenth century, when record-keeping began in England and

Wales, death rates were very high, especially among children. Of every ten newborn infants, two or three never reached their first birthday. Five or six died before they were six, and only about three of the ten lived beyond the age of 25.[1] Tuberculosis was the single largest cause of death in the mid-nineteenth century. Epidemics of cholera, typhoid, and small-pox swept through communities, killing people of all ages, and making them afraid to leave their homes. Injuries—often fatal—to workers in mines and factories were common due to unsafe equipment, long working hours, poor lighting and ventilation, and child labor.

There are a number of reasons why people's lives are basically healthier today than they were a century and a half ago: cleaner water, air, and food; safe disposal of sewage; better nutrition; education concerning healthy and unhealthy behaviors; and many others. Most of these factors fall in the domain of public health. In fact, the term "public health" refers to two different but related concepts. We can say that the public health has improved since the nineteenth century, meaning that the general state of people's health is now much better than it was. But the measures that people take as a society to bring about and maintain that improvement are also known as public health.

Although many sectors of the community may be involved in promoting public health, people most often look to government—at the local, state, or national level—to take the primary responsibility. Governments provide pure water and efficient sewage disposal. Governmental regulations ensure the safety of the food supply. They also ensure the quality of medical services provided through hospitals, nursing homes, and other institutions. Laws regulating people's behavior prevent them from injuring each other. Laws requiring immunization of school-aged children prevent the spread of infectious diseases. Governments also sponsor research and education programs on causes and prevention of disease.

WHAT IS PUBLIC HEALTH?

Public health is not easy to define or to comprehend. A telephone survey of registered voters conducted in 1999 by a charitable foundation found that over half of the 1,234 respondents misunderstood the term.[2] Leaders in the field have themselves struggled to understand the mission of public health, to explain what it is, why it is important, and what it should do. Charles-Edward A. Winslow, a theoretician and leader of

American public health during the first half of the twentieth century, defined ~~public health~~ in 1920 as:

𝑝 The science and the art of preventing disease, prolonging life, and promoting physical health and efficiency through organized community efforts for the sanitation of the environment, the control of community infections, the education of the individual in principles of personal hygiene, the organization of medical and nursing services for the early diagnosis and preventive treatment of disease, and the development of the social machinery which will ensure to every individual in the community a standard of living adequate for the maintenance of health.[3(p.1)]

Winslow's definition is still considered valid today.

Over the following decades, public health had many successes, carrying out many of the tasks described in Winslow's definition. It was highly effective in reducing the threat of infectious diseases, thereby increasing the average lifespan of Americans by several decades. By the 1980s, public health was taken for granted, and most people were unaware of its activities. But there were signs that the system was not functioning well. Government expenditures on health were alarmingly high, but most of the spending was directed towards medical care. No one was talking about public health. At the same time, new health problems were appearing: the AIDS epidemic broke out, concern about environmental pollution was growing, the aging population was demanding increased health services, and social problems such as teenage pregnancy, violence, and substance abuse were becoming more common. There was a sense that public health was not prepared to deal with these problems, in part because people were not thinking of them as public health problems.

A study conducted by the Institute of Medicine and published in 1988, called *The Future of Public Health*, refocused attention on the importance of public health and has done a great deal to revitalize the field. One of the first tasks the study committee set for itself was to re-examine the definition of public health, reasoning that for it to be effective, public health had to be broadly defined.[4] The committee's report gives a four-part definition describing public health's mission, substance, organizational framework, and core functions.

The Future of Public Health defines the *mission* of public health as "the fulfillment of society's interest in assuring the conditions in which people can be healthy."[4(p.40)] The *substance* of public health is "organized community efforts aimed at the prevention of disease and the promotion of health."[4(p.41)] The *organizational framework* of public health encompasses "both activities undertaken within the formal structure of government and the associated efforts of private and voluntary organizations and individuals."[4(p.42)] The core functions of public health are defined as:

1. assessment
2. policy development
3. assurance.[4(p.43)]

PUBLIC HEALTH VERSUS MEDICAL CARE

One way to better understand public health and its functions is to compare and contrast it with medical practice. While medicine is concerned with individual patients, public health regards the community as its patient, trying to improve the health of that population. Medicine focuses on healing patients who are ill. Public health focuses on preventing illness.

In carrying out its core functions, public health—like a doctor with his/her patient—assesses the health of a population, diagnoses its problems, seeks the causes of those problems, and devises strategies to cure them. Assessment constitutes the diagnostic function, in which a public health agency collects, assembles, analyzes, and makes available information on the health of the population. Policy development, like a doctor's development of a treatment plan for a sick patient, involves the use of scientific knowledge to develop a strategic approach to improving the community's health. Assurance is equivalent to the doctor's actual treatment of the patient. Public health has the responsibility of assuring that the services needed for the protection of public health in the community are available and accessible to everyone. These include environmental, educational, and basic medical services. If public health agencies do not provide these services themselves, they must encourage others to do so or require such actions through regulation.

Public health's focus on prevention makes it more abstract than medicine, and its achievements are therefore more difficult to recognize. The doctor who cures a sick person has achieved a real, recognizable benefit, and the patient is grateful. Public health cannot point to the people who have been spared illness by its efforts. As Winslow wrote in 1923,

"If we had but the gift of second sight to transmute abstract figures into flesh and blood, so that as we walk along the street we could say 'That man would be dead of typhoid fever,' 'That woman would have succumbed to tuberculosis,' 'That rosy infant would be in its coffin,'—then only should we have a faint conception of the meaning of the silent victories of public health."[3(p.65)]

This "silence" accounts in large part for the relative lack of attention paid to public health by politicians and the general public in comparison with medical care. It is estimated that only about one percent of the nation's total health spending is spent on public health. In 1992, when the average cost of medical care for each American was $3,007, the amount spent per person on public health was only about $34 per person.[5] During the health care reform debate of 1993 and 1994, virtually all the discussion focused on paying for medical care, while very little attention was paid to funding for public health. Although federal resources devoted to some public health activities increased dramatically after September 11, 2001, as discussed in Chapter 29, budget deficits are again putting downward pressure on public health allocations.

Effective public health programs clearly save money on medical costs in addition to saving lives. Moreover, public health contributes a great deal more to the health of a population than medicine does. According to one analysis, the life expectancy of Americans has increased from forty-five to seventy-five years over the past century.[6] Only five of those thirty additional years can be attributed to the work of the medical care system. The majority of the gain has come from improvements in public health, broadly defined as including better nutrition, housing, sanitation, and occupational safety. One responsibility of public health, therefore, as noted in an Institute of Medicine report, is to educate the public and politicians about "the crucial role that a strong public health capacity must play in maintaining and improving the health of the public . . . By its very nature, public health requires support by members of the public—its beneficiaries."[4(p.32)]

Public health, like medical practice, is based on science. However, even when public health scientists are certain they know all about the causes of a problem and what should be done about it, a political decision is generally necessary before action can be taken to solve it. When a doctor diagnoses a patient's illness and recommends a treatment, it is up to the patient to accept or reject the doctor's recommendation. When the "patient" is a community or a whole country, it is usually a government—federal, state, or local—that must make the decision to accept or reject the recommendations of public health experts. Sometimes the process starts within the community when, like a patient going to a doctor with a complaint, the people recognize a problem and demand that the government take action. This has occurred in many communities when victims of drunk drivers form organizations such as Mothers Against Drunk Driving (MADD) to lobby for stricter laws, or when neighbors of pollution-generating factories demand that the government force the industry to clean up their environment.

Politics enters the public health process as part of the policy development function and especially the assurance function. Since the community will have to pay for the "treatments," usually through taxes, they must decide how much "health" they are willing to fund. They also must decide whether they are willing to accept the possible limitations of their freedom that may be required to improve the community's health. Among the assurance functions of public health is the provision of basic medical services: how this should be done is a matter of great political controversy, as was apparent during the national debate over health care reform in 1993 and 1994. Public health professionals are often impatient with politics, as an Institute of Medicine report notes, seeming to "regard politics as a contaminant of an ideally rational decision-making process rather than as an essential element of democratic governance."[4(p.5)]

THE SCIENCES OF PUBLIC HEALTH

The scientific knowledge on which public health is based spans a broad range of professional disciplines. An Institute of Medicine report notes that "public health is a coalition of professions united by their shared mission" as well as by "their focus on disease prevention and health promotion; their prospective approach in contrast to the reactive focus of therapeutic medicine, and their common science, epidemiology."[4(p.40)] The disciplines of public health can be divided somewhat arbitrarily into six areas. *Epidemiology* and *statistics* are the basis for the assessment functions of public health, including the collection and analysis of information. Both assessment and policy development need an understanding of the causes of health problems in the community, an understanding that depends on *biomedical sciences*, *social and behavioral sciences*, and *environmental sciences*. As part of the assurance function, public health seeks to understand the medical care system in an area of study generally referred to as *health policy and management* or *health administration*.

Epidemiology has been called the basic science of public health. As its name suggests, epidemiology is the study of epidemics. It focuses on human populations, usually starting with an outbreak of disease in a community. Epidemiologists look for common exposures or other shared characteristics in the people who are sick, seeking the causative factor.

Epidemiology often provides the first indications of the nature of a new disease. When AIDS was first recognized in the early 1980s, the cause was unknown. Doctors reported cases of this unusual disease to the U.S. Centers for Disease Control and Prevention, and epidemiologists began looking for common characteristics of the patients. Epidemiologic research indicated that it was an infectious disease spread through blood and body fluids and suggested a virus as the cause. This prompted the biomedical scientists to step in and look for the virus.

Epidemiology is important not only for deciphering the causes of exotic new diseases, but for preventing the spread of old, well-understood diseases. Epidemiologists are mainstays of local health departments. In what is commonly known as "shoe-leather epidemiology," they track down, for example, the source of a food-poisoning outbreak and force a restaurant to clean up its kitchen. Or they trace everyone who has been in contact with a college student diagnosed with meningitis in order to administer high doses of antibiotic to prevent further spread of that dangerous disease. Epidemiologic studies have also been important in identifying the causes of chronic diseases such as heart disease and cancer.

Because public health deals with the health of populations, it depends very heavily on statistics. Governments collect data on births and deaths, causes of death, outbreaks of communicable diseases, cases of cancer, occupational injuries, and many other health-related issues. These numbers are diagnostic tools, informing experts how healthy or sick a society is, and where its weaknesses are. For example, the fact that the United States ranks twenty-eighth in infant mortality among the nations of the world is one indication that the public health in this country is not as good as that in many others.[7]

To understand what the numbers mean, it is necessary to understand certain statistical concepts and calculations. The science of statistics is used to calculate risks from exposure to environmental chemicals, for example. Statistical analysis is an integral part of any epidemiologic study seeking the cause of a disease or a clinical study testing the effectiveness of a new drug.

Both public health and medicine depend on the biomedical sciences. A major proportion of human disease is caused by microorganisms. Prevention and control of these diseases in a population requires an understanding of how these infectious agents are spread and how they affect the human body. Control of infectious diseases was a major focus of public health in the nineteenth and early twentieth centuries. Biomedical research was very successful in gaining an understanding of the major killers of that period, providing the information and techniques from which successful public health measures could bring these diseases under control.

Biomedical research is still important to the understanding and control of new diseases such as AIDS, which has become the major epidemic of the late twentieth century worldwide. It has also contributed increasingly to an understanding of non-infectious diseases such as cancer and heart disease, which have become increasingly important as infectious diseases have been controlled. Recent progress in understanding human genetics is providing new insights into people's inherent susceptibility to various diseases, raising new hopes of a cure as well as concerns about discrimination.

Environmental health science, a classic component of public health, is concerned with preventing the spread of disease through water, air, and food. While it is not strictly a separate science, because it shares concerns about the spread of infectious organisms with biomedical sciences and depends on epidemiology to track environmental causes of disease outbreaks, it is usually considered a separate area of public health. Much of the great improvement in public health in the United States over the past century is due to improved environmental health, especially the fact that most Americans have safe drinking water. In its concern with safe water and waste disposal, environmental health depends on engineering to design, build, and maintain these systems.

Despite the fact that the importance of safe air, water, and food have been recognized for so many decades, there are many new challenges to environmental health. Not only do old systems fail, as occurred in Milwaukee (see the Prologue), but new problems arise, brought about by modern lifestyles. Thousands of new chemicals enter the environment every year, while little is known about their effects on human health. Chemicals known to be toxic have accumulated in the environment, and methods must be devised to dispose of them safely. Other environmental threats to health include ultraviolet rays in sunlight, an increasing problem as the ozone layer of the earth's atmosphere is depleted, and exposure to other kinds of radiation.

Increasingly, public health is concerned with social and behavioral sciences. As biomedical and environmental sciences have conquered many of the diseases that killed people of previous generations, people in modern societies are dying of diseases caused by their behavior and social environment. Heart disease is related to nutrition and exercise patterns; many forms of cancer are caused by smoking; abuse of drugs and alcohol is a notorious killer. Violence is a significant cause of death in our society and attracts ongoing concern.

Some subgroups of the population have poorer health overall than others, for reasons that, while not completely understood, relate to social and behavioral factors. People with low income are less healthy than those with higher socioeconomic status. Black Americans have lower life expectancy overall than white Americans, even when their incomes are similar. Other ethnic minority groups, including Hispanics, Asians, and American Indians are at increased risk for a variety of health problems.

Social and behavioral sciences involve more unanswered questions than biomedical and environmental sciences do. Very little is known about why racial and ethnic groups differ in their health-related behavior, why many people of all races behave in unhealthy ways, and how to prevent self-destructive behaviors. In the social and behavioral sciences, of all areas, research and application of its findings are most likely to make a difference in the future.

Until the beginning of the twentieth century, public health and medicine overlapped substantially in their spheres of interest and activity. Both fields were concerned primarily with understanding the causes and prevention of infectious disease, because medicine was relatively powerless to cure them. With the discovery of antibiotics, however, medicine gained the power to work miracles of healing, leading to a period of rapidly growing influence. Meanwhile, because of its less glamorous task of preventing disease, public health faded into obscurity.

Over the past few decades, it has become apparent that our society's emphasis on curing disease rather than preventing it has gone out of control. Medical care has become so expensive that an increasing proportion of the population cannot afford it, and spending for medical care has eaten up resources that could more profitably be used for education, housing, and the environment. Concern about runaway costs, lack of access, and questionable quality has led to an increasing interest in studying the medical care system, its effectiveness, efficiency, and equity, a science called health services research. Traditional categorization of public health fields puts this study into the area of health policy and management or health administration.

PREVENTION AND INTERVENTION

Public health's approach to health problems in a community has been described as a five-step process:

1. Define the health problem
2. Identify the risk factors associated with the problem
3. Develop and test community-level interventions to control or prevent the cause of the problem
4. Implement interventions to improve the health of the population
5. Monitor those interventions to assess their effectiveness[5]

Thus, a main task of prevention is to develop *interventions* designed to prevent specific problems that have been identified either through an assessment process initiated by a public health agency or through community concern raised by an unusual course of events. For example, statistical data may show that a community has a high rate of cancer in comparison with other similar communities. Or a series of fatal crashes caused by drunk driving may mobilize a community to demand action to prevent further tragedies.

Public health has developed systematic ways of thinking of such problems that facilitate the process of designing interventions to prevent the undesirable health outcomes. One approach is to think of prevention on three levels: primary prevention, secondary prevention, and tertiary prevention. Primary prevention prevents an illness or injury from occurring at all, by preventing exposure to risk factors. Secondary prevention seeks to minimize the severity of the illness or the damage due to an injury-causing event once the event has occurred. Tertiary prevention seeks to minimize disability by providing medical care and rehabilitation services.

Thus interventions for primary prevention of cancer include efforts to discourage teenagers from smoking and encourage smokers to quit. In secondary prevention, screening programs are established to detect cancer early when it is still treatable. Tertiary prevention involves the medical treatment and rehabilitation of cancer patients.

This way of thinking was very effective in developing traffic safety programs that, over the past four decades, have significantly reduced the rates of injury from motor vehicle crashes (as discussed in Chapter 17). Primary prevention focused on preventing crashes from occurring, for example, by building divided highways and installing traffic lights. Secondary prevention included the design of safer automobiles with stronger bumpers, padded dashboards, seat belts, and airbags. It also included laws requiring drivers and passengers to wear the seat belts. And tertiary prevention required the development of emergency medical services including ambulances, 911 networks, and trauma centers.

Another approach to designing interventions is to think of an illness or injury as the result of a chain of causation involving an agent, a host, and the environment. This approach is traditional when thinking of infectious diseases: the agent may be a disease-causing bacterium or virus; the host is a susceptible human being; and the environment includes the means of transmission by which the agent reaches the host, which may be contaminated air, water, or food, or it may be another human being who is infected. Prevention is accomplished by interrupting the chain of causation at any step. The chain can be interrupted by rendering a potential host unsusceptible through immunization, for example. Or the bacterium infecting a host can be killed through the use of antibiotics. Or the environment can be sanitized through the purification of water and food.

The chain of causation model can also be used for other kinds of illnesses or injuries. For example suicide is the third leading cause of death in the age group fifteen to twenty-four.[7] In applying the model to prevention of youth suicide, the host is the susceptible young person; the agent is most often a gun or an overdose of pills; the environment includes the young person's whole social environment, including family, school, and the media. A public health intervention could focus on how to make young people less susceptible to self-destructive thinking; it could try to change the messages presented by television and schoolmates that may lead a young person to think he or she is unattractive or otherwise inferior. However, the public health perspective tends to be, as discussed in Chapter 17, that the most effective target of intervention for youth suicide prevention is the agent, especially guns. Many adolescents are susceptible to depressed moods and think of killing themselves, but the best predictor of whether they will succeed is whether they have access to a gun.

PUBLIC HEALTH AND TERRORISM

The events of fall 2001 disturbed the sense of complacency many people felt about the health and safety of their living conditions. Evidence that there were groups or individuals who not only wanted to cause harm to Americans at home but who had the resources and the will to succeed in that goal forced us to think about how to prevent similar events in the future. While prevention of violent acts such as hijacking airplanes is primarily a responsibility of law enforcement, public health has an important role to play in controlling the damage caused by such events. In other words, primary prevention of terrorist acts may be out of the domain of public health, but secondary and tertiary prevention are very much a part of public health's mission.

The crashing of two planes into the World Trade Center triggered the activation of emergency response plans in place for New York City and New York state. Hospital emergency rooms were alerted, doctors and nurses were called in. The health care system in the whole region readied itself to receive the expected large numbers of people wounded in the disaster. Unfortunately, much of this preparation was not utilized because there were so few survivors.

The public health response to the terrorism of September 11, 2001 was essentially the same as the response needed for other emergencies and disasters: factory explosions, plane and train crashes, earthquakes, hurricanes, and so on. Public health was concerned not only with coordinating emergency medical care, but also with ensuring the safety of cleanup workers and area residents. Problems with polluted water, contaminated air, spoiled food, infestation of vermin, and so on, had to be dealt with in downtown Manhattan just as they must be dealt with after a natural disaster.

The importance of public health became even more obvious in the aftermath of the anthrax mailings. These bioterrorism attacks did not announce themselves in the dramatic fashion of the airplane hijackings. The first signs that a terrorist event had occurred were not recognized as such. No alarm bells rang when a few patients showed up in hospital emergency rooms with hard-to-diagnose illnesses. Anthrax announced itself in the same way that AIDS appeared, as an outbreak of something new that was reported to public health authorities, who then investigated.

The damage done by the anthrax mailings was relatively minor. However, the potential disaster that would result if a more infectious microorganism were used in a bioterror attack forced many sectors of society to pay attention to public health. In speculating about what would happen if a terrorist clandestinely released smallpox virus into a crowd, public health authorities realized that only epidemiologic methods for controlling natural epidemics could even begin to deal with the crisis. Suddenly the media and politicians began talking about public health. Ironically, the threat of bioterrorism did more to teach the public about public health than any educational program. As Robert F. Meenan, dean of the Boston University School of Public Health, is quoted as saying, the anthrax attacks provided "a marketing campaign we could never have bought."[8]

CONCLUSION

This chapter has shown that *public health* is a broad term that is difficult to define. It includes a goal—maximum health for all—as well as the means of attempting to achieve that goal. Public health is concerned with the prevention of disease and disability. It is aimed at benefiting the entire population in contrast with medicine, which focuses on the individual.

The functions of public health in a community can be compared with the functions of a physician in caring for a patient. Public health diagnoses and treats the community's ills by way of assessment, policy development, and assurance. It relies on the tools of science and politics. The public health sciences of epidemiology and statistics are applied in assessing a population's health. Policy is developed based on biomedical sciences, social and behavioral sciences, environmental health sciences, and the study of the medical care system. Public health depends on politics for decision making. Decisions on public health interventions to be taken by the community, insofar as they require government action, are reached through politics.

Public health focuses on prevention of disease and disability. Preventive measures can be applied at three levels: primary prevention aims to prevent a disease or injury from occurring at all; secondary prevention aims to minimize the damage caused by the illness or injury-causing event when it occurs; and tertiary prevention seeks to minimize any ensuing disability by providing medical care and rehabilitation.

Public health prevention programs function through interventions designed to interrupt the chain of causation that leads to an illness or an injury. Interventions can be directed toward eliminating or suppressing the agent that causes an illness or injury, strengthening the resistance of the host to the agent, or changing the environment in such a way that the host is less likely to encounter the agent.

Public health is an abstract concept that is not well understood and is often neglected. The dramatic events of fall 2001 forced the government and the media to pay attention to the importance of public health, both in mitigating the effects of obvious disasters, and in recognizing and controlling the more insidious effects of bioterrorism.

REFERENCES

1. T. McKeown, *The Role of Medicine: Dream, Mirage or Nemesis?* (Oxford: Basil Blackwell, 1979).
2. U.S. Centers for Disease Control and Prevention, "Public Opinion About Public Health—United States, 1999," *Morbidity and Mortality Weekly Report* 49 (2000): 258–260.
3. C.-E. A. Winslow, *The Evolution and Significance of the Modern Public Health Campaign* (New Haven: Yale University Press, 1923); reprinted by the *Journal of Public Health Policy*, 1 (1984).
4. U.S. Institute of Medicine, Committee for the Study of the Future of Public Health, *The Future of Public Health* (Washington, DC: National Academy Press, 1988).
5. U.S. Public Health Service, *For a Healthy Nation: Returns on Investment in Public Health* (Washington, DC: U.S. Government Printing Office, 1994).
6. J. P. Bunker et al., "Improving Health: Measuring Effects of Medical Care," *The Milbank Quarterly* 72 (1994): 225–258.
7. U.S. National Center for Health Statistics. *Health, United States, 2003* (Hyattsville, Maryland: Public Health Service, 2003), 130.
8. Smith, J. S. "Personal Predicament of Public Health." *Chronicle of Higher Education* (June 27, 2003).

CHAPTER 2

Why Is Public Health Controversial?

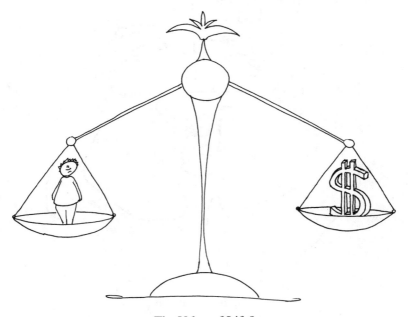

The Value of Life?

The mission of public health as defined by the Institute of Medicine report on *The Future of Public Health*—"fulfilling society's interest in assuring conditions in which people can be healthy"[1(p.40)]—is very broad. The conditions include many factors that might not normally be thought of as relevant to public health. For example, as Chapter 14 discusses, the factor most significant in determining the health of a community is its economic status: people with higher incomes tend to be healthier for a variety of reasons. This expansive view of public health is not new. Winslow's eighty-year-old definition specifically includes as part of public health's role, "the development of the social machinery which will ensure to every individual in the community a standard of living adequate for the maintenance of health."[2(p.1)]

Restricting Individual Freedom

Indeed, the early history of U.S. public health was closely tied to social reform movements. In addition to sanitary science and public hygiene, nineteenth-century reformers campaigned for improved housing, trade unions, the abolition of child labor, maternal and child health, and temperance. Winslow thought of public health as a military-style campaign and wrote of "whole populations mobilized for the great war against preventable disease."[3(p.27)]

Public health can be viewed as a broad social movement. Dan E. Beauchamp, a noted public health philosopher, has written that "public health should be a way of doing justice, a way of asserting the value and priority of all human life."[4(p.8)] In an influential 1974 paper entitled, "Public Health as Social Justice," Beauchamp calls on public health to challenge the ideology that prevails in the United States, an ideology that he calls "market justice." Market justice, he writes, emphasizes individual responsibility, minimal obligation to the common good, and the "fundamental freedom to all individuals to be left alone."[4(p.4)] Under market justice, powerful forces of environment, heredity, and social structure prevent a fair distribution of the burdens and benefits of society. Social justice, on the other hand, suggests that minimal levels of income, basic housing, employment, education, and health care should be seen as fundamental rights. According to Beauchamp, "The historic dream of public health that preventable death and disability ought to be minimized is a dream of social justice."[4(p.6)]

Political conservatives have tended to resist this broad vision of public health. They would prefer to limit public health to a technical enterprise focused on controlling communicable disease or as a safety net that provides medical care to the indigent. This restricted view of public health was encouraged by physicians, concerned about government encroachment on their economic and professional independence; their political power helped to limit federal health funding in the 1930s and 1940s to programs, run by local health departments, which were narrowly focused on providing services for child health, venereal disease control, tuberculosis, and dental health.

Concerns about health threats from environmental pollution that arose in the 1960s were addressed independently of the traditional public health system, and separate agencies were set up to deal with them. Similarly, social problems such as homelessness, drug abuse, and violence were not thought of as public health problems, although they had adverse health consequences. It was this fragmentation of public health that led the Institute of Medicine committee to conclude in 1988 that public health was "in disarray"[1(p.19)] and to affirm the comprehensive view of public health expressed by Winslow and Beauchamp.

The broad view of public health's scope generates considerable controversy in America's individualistic, market-oriented society. The notion that government has an obligation to provide healthy conditions for citizens who are unwilling or unable to provide such conditions for themselves—and indeed to provide medical care for those who need it, as most other industrialized countries do—has often been attacked as socialist. Conservative politicians have won office by campaigning against taxes, starving governments of funds that could provide health services for all. Many Americans reflexively oppose being told what to do and resist the idea of governmental restrictions on their behavior even when the intent is to protect their own health and that of others. Moreover, many health problems have their roots in unhealthy behaviors that are so personal and intimate that moralists oppose even discussing them. Three issues—economic, libertarian, and moral—tend to come up repeatedly in any debate over public health actions or activities.

ECONOMIC IMPACT

Most public health measures have a negative economic impact of some kind on some segment of the population or on some industry. Consequently, any new proposal for a public health regulation is likely to inspire opposition from some quarter, on the grounds that it might cost jobs, add to the price of a product, or require a tax increase. It might also cut into a company's profits. Consequently, industries resist change: milk producers resisted pasteurization, landlords resisted building codes, automobile manufacturers resist design changes to improve safety. There are several reasons why these conflicts are particularly difficult to resolve.

The difficulty in dealing with the economic impact of public health measures has been illustrated by conflicts with the tobacco industry. Tobacco is clearly harmful to health, causing thousands of deaths and millions of dollars in medical costs annually. Yet, until recently, only mild restrictions and regulations were instituted to discourage use of the product. Tobacco is a major industry in the South, supporting jobs and providing profits for tobacco companies. Cigarette sales also are a significant source of income for many small businesses. Owners of bars and restaurants have fought laws restricting smoking on their premises, fearing that they would lose the patronage of smokers. Politicians are not eager to institute strong public health measures that would have such a major economic impact. Only in the past two decades, with the shift of public opinion against the tobacco industry, together with the industry's need to protect itself against a potentially bankrupting flood of lawsuits by injured smokers, have federal, state, and local governments begun to take serious measures to control smoking.

In many circumstances, controversy arises because those who pay for a public health measure are not the ones who benefit. Environmental regulations such as restrictions on timber harvesting in the Pacific Northwest are currently under attack because they may cost jobs in the lumber industry, although they may preserve jobs in the fishing and tourist industries as well as contribute in the long term to a more stable climate. Regulations that protect the health and safety of workers may require expensive protective equipment, thus driving up the costs to consumers.

In times of economic difficulty, people are often unwilling to pay short-term costs in order to obtain a benefit in the long term. In both the fishing and lumber industries, stocks have been dangerously depleted, and there is a risk of killing off all the fish and cutting down all the timber, thereby destroying the industries altogether. Yet few workers in the fishing or lumber industries are willing to voluntarily cut back on their own harvests. Companies resist tough pollution control laws even though less polluting technology may lead to a long-term benefit not only for the environment but also for a company's competitiveness in international markets.

A recent example of how economics affects public health regulation is the alarm raised by a case of "mad cow" disease in an American cow. The diagnosis was made weeks after the cow was slaughtered and its meat sent to consumers around the country. News reports taught the American people a great deal about how beef is produced and distributed in this country, and the news was not reassuring. Many safeguards instituted in Europe and Japan after mad cow outbreaks there, such as testing all cattle at slaughter and using methods of tracing each animal through the production system, were not required in the United States. These methods are expensive and were resisted by the industry on the argument that they were unnecessary because the disease had not been detected here. The result of this inaction, however, was that import of American beef was banned in many countries around the world, dealing a major blow to the profitability of the industry. Now, some beef producers are supporting stricter regulations in an attempt to reassure international buyers that American beef is safe.

The costs of public health measures are usually much easier to calculate than the benefits. For example, experts may know the cost of reducing smog in Los Angeles to a level that reduces deaths from lung disease by ten percent. But how do they calculate whether this benefit is worth the cost? It is very difficult to put a dollar value on life and health. Furthermore, it is often difficult to quantify what the risk really is and how to balance it against other risks. People are concerned, for example, about farmers' use of pesticides, which may leave toxic residues on fruits and vegetables. Scientists can estimate the health risks the average person faces by consuming that residue. But fruits and vegetables are an important part of a healthy diet. If the use of pesticides were forbidden, the crops might be less abundant, and the price of the produce might rise, perhaps discouraging some people from eating these nutritious foods. Thus, an effort to protect health might have a negative impact on health overall.

INDIVIDUAL LIBERTY

One of the primary purposes of government is to "promote the general welfare," as called for in the U.S. Constitution. Health and safety, together with economic well-being, are the major factors that contribute to the general welfare. While the government cannot guarantee health and safety for each individual, its role is to provide for maximum health and safety for the community as a whole. One of the central controversies in public health is the extent to which government can and should restrict individual freedom for the purpose of improving the community's health.

There has long been general agreement that it is acceptable to restrict an individual's freedom to behave in such a way as to cause direct harm to others. Laws against assault and murder are found in the Bible and even the Babylonian Code of Hammurabi, which dates to the eighteenth century B.C. When the harm is less direct, however, the issues become more controversial. Most controversial are governmental restrictions on people's freedom to harm themselves.

Government restrictions on behavior that causes indirect harm to others is the way to prevent what Garrett Hardin, in 1968, called the "tragedy of the commons."[5] Hardin describes a pasture open to all herdsmen in a community. The land can support a limited number of grazing cattle. If each herdsman tries to maximize his gain by keeping as many cattle as possible on the pasture—the commons—the pasture will be overgrazed. The cattle will starve, and the herdsmen will be ruined. The only way for the community to save the pasture is to agree to restrict the freedom of the herdsmen, placing fair and equitable limits on the number of cattle each can keep there.

In the industrialized world of today, the "commons" is the air, water, and other elements of the environment that all people share. Because no individual has the power to control the quality of his or her own personal environment independent of the behavior of his or her neighbors, government action is required to protect these common resources. While the general principle of protecting the "commons" is accepted by most citizens, there is plenty of room for controversy in defining what to include among the protected resources, as well as how extensive the protective measures should be.

The United States has made great progress over the past thirty-five years in cleaning up air and water through federal legislation. Now questions are being raised as to whether the laws have gone too far in restricting the "freedom" to pollute. Companies have been required to limit emissions from their smokestacks; automobile makers have been required to install emission control devices on every car they manufacture. These regulations may have driven up the costs of automobiles and other products, but they have not limited anybody's freedom. However, California still has a serious air pollution problem. Proposed regulations for the state to meet the federal mandates for clean air have included a ban on gas-driven lawn mowers, elimination of drive-through windows in banks and fast food restaurants (to cut the pollution that results from idling car engines), and a ban on charcoal lighting fluid. None of these activities on an individual basis—mowing a lawn, sitting in an idling car waiting for a hamburger, or lighting a few chunks of charcoal—contributes in any major way to the pollution of California's air, but when done by thousands of residents each day, they add up to a significant problem. Are Americans willing to accept such significant limitations on their behavior in order to achieve the desirable goal of clean air to breathe?

Most controversial of public health measures are requirements that restrict people's freedom for the purpose of protecting their own health and safety. Examples of such measures include requirements to wear seat belts when traveling in a car and helmets when riding a motorcycle. Such laws inspire allusions to "the tyranny of health"[6] and "the health police," although restrictions on many drugs, such as heroin, cocaine, marijuana, LSD, and—during Prohibition in the early twentieth century—alcohol have been generally accepted.

Such restrictions on individual behavior are often criticized as "paternalism." Libertarians, in the words of John Stuart Mill, argue that "the only purpose for which power can be rightfully exercised over any member of a civilized community, against his will, is to prevent harm to others . . . In the part [of his conduct] which merely concerns himself, his independence is . . . absolute."[7(p.90)] The one form of paternalism generally accepted is that children and young people can be restricted in their behavior, on the basis that they are not yet mature enough to make considered judgments as to their own best interests. Thus, there are laws that prevent juveniles from buying tobacco and alcohol, that require them to wear bicycle helmets and seat belts (even where adults are not required to wear them), and that require parental permission to obtain birth control information or an abortion, or to go sky-diving.

According to the libertarian view, which has a strong tradition in the United States, it is acceptable to outlaw drunk driving but not drunkenness itself. Similarly, smoking in indoor public places can be outlawed because the smoke bothers others (although there is still strong resistance in many places), while smoking itself cannot be regulated in adults.

Restrictions on individual liberty are sometimes justified on the basis that their purpose is really to protect others, even when the argument is a bit strained. For example, unhelmeted motorcyclists could be a threat to others because of the possibility of their losing control if hit by flying debris. Unhelmeted cyclists and unbelted motorists, severely injured in road accidents, drive up insurance rates for others and in extreme cases may become expensive wards of the state. Alcoholics and drug users bring harm to their families and are a nuisance to their neighbors.

Most public health advocates believe that there are more fundamental justifications for restrictions on individual behavior for the sake of the public health. Beauchamp, the philosopher, explores the reasons in his book, *The Health of the Republic*,[4] arguing that such laws are needed most for behaviors that are common and carry small risks. Consistent use of seat belts, for example, prevents thousands of deaths and injuries in the population as a whole, although the risk people face on any one trip, when they must decide whether to buckle up, is quite small. While each individual's choice to take the risk of driving unbuckled may be rational, society's interest in preventing the thousands of deaths and injuries outweighs the minor inconvenience of obeying the seatbelt law.

Beauchamp's argument in favor of limiting individual liberty for the common good is consistent with his view of public health as social justice. Death and disability are collective problems, he says, and collective action is needed to promote the common welfare. The U.S. tradition of supporting private liberty above all is wrong, as noted by that early critic of the American character, Alexis de Tocqueville, in that it "disposes [citizens] not to think of their fellows and turns indifference into a sort of public virtue."[8(p.16)]

MORAL AND RELIGIOUS OPPOSITION

Public health often arouses controversy on moral grounds, most often when it confronts sexual and reproductive issues. AIDS, other sexually transmitted diseases, teenage pregnancy, and low birthweight babies are major public health problems in the United States. The public health approach to these problems includes sex education and the provision of contraceptive services, especially condoms. These measures are often vigorously opposed by members of certain religious groups who believe that they promote immoral behavior. Safe and legal abortion to terminate unwanted pregnancy is even more controversial. While there is no question that the safest and healthiest lifestyle is to abstain from sexual activity before marriage and then to be faithful to one's spouse, experience has long shown that preaching morality has limited efficacy in preventing sexually transmitted diseases and unwanted pregnancy. Chapter 13 discusses these issues further.

AIDS has been an especially divisive issue because so many people with AIDS contract the disease through behavior that is widely regarded as immoral—homosexual acts and intravenous drug use. Consequently, AIDS-related policy has often been confounded by moral revulsion against the disease and its victims. While not supported by the evidence, it is commonly believed that education on how to protect oneself against contracting the virus that causes AIDS may encourage homosexuality and promiscuous sexual behavior in general. Similarly, moralists frown on the practice of providing clean needles to drug addicts because, while it is effective in reducing the spread of the virus, they believe it condones the use of intravenous drugs.

Moralism also enters into discussions of alcohol and drug policy. Libertarians could argue against regulation of alcohol and bans on addictive drugs on the basis that consumption of drugs is private behavior that does not directly hurt others. In fact, however, most citizens accept the validity of such regulation. The power of government to limit drug and alcohol consumption is well established in the United States and corresponds with the tradition of limiting individual behavior for the common good.

While regulation for the common good is valid, trying to legislate morality has often proven to be ineffective, self defeating, and a threat to liberty, in part because people differ in what they view as moral. When morality is the justification for banning certain behaviors, rational discussion is often impossible. Free speech is repressed, victims are demonized, practitioners of the behavior are driven underground, and the "epidemic"—whether AIDS, drug abuse, or teenage pregnancy—spreads more easily.[4]

Moral and religious concerns may interfere with scientists' studying how to prevent the spread of the human immunodeficiency virus (HIV) and other diseases and conditions caused by unhealthy behavior. As Chapter 13 discusses, up to half of the deaths in the United States are preventable, many of them caused by unhealthy behavior. Yet a small fraction of the research funded by the federal government is devoted to understanding why people behave in unhealthy ways and how to encourage them to change these behaviors. Such research tends to be highly controversial and is vulnerable to attacks by conservative groups. For example, in fall 2003, a group called the Traditional Values Coalition drew up a list of projects funded by the National Institutes of Health and requested that a congressional committee investigate why taxpayer money was being "wasted" on these studies, which involved HIV transmission and sexual behavior.[9] Although the investigation did not lead to withdrawal of funding from any of these projects, such episodes do have the effect of discouraging scientists and funding agencies from conducting research on many important public health problems.

POLITICAL INTERFERENCE WITH SCIENCE

While there are legitimate differences of opinion on how to weigh the competing interests in making policy that affects public health, these decisions should be informed by science to the extent possible. In today's polarized political climate, concerns have been raised that the Bush administration has gone beyond previous political practices in manipulating and distorting scientific evidence to fit its political agenda. In February 2004 the Union of Concerned Scientists (UCS), a nonprofit advocacy group, released a report called "Scientific Integrity in Policymaking," which was signed by more than sixty leading scientists, including twenty Nobel-Prize winners.[10] The report documented many instances of the administration's misrepresentation or suppression of scientific information and stacking of scientific advisory committees to obscure the fact that policy decisions are based on its political agenda, which usually favors right-wing constituencies and large corporations.

One example cited by the UCS report was pressure on the Centers for Disease Control and Prevention (CDC) to promote abstinence-only programs for preventing teen pregnancy. The CDC was required to remove from its Web site information on "Programs that Work," five sex education programs for teenagers that had been found effective in scientific studies. Similarly, the CDC replaced information on the effectiveness of condoms in preventing the spread of HIV/AIDS with a document that emphasizes condom failure rates and the effectiveness of abstinence. While there is no dispute that abstinence is the most effective way to prevent pregnancy and HIV transmission, scientific studies have found abstinence-only programs to be ineffective. In 2003, the *New York Times* reported that the National Cancer Institute's Web site contained information suggesting that having an abortion increased a woman's risk of breast cancer. This issue had long been discredited by a number of epidemiologic studies, and the publicity forced the Institute to remove the inaccurate information.[11]

Other examples cited by the UCS included suppression of the release of scientific information by the Environmental Protection Agency (EPA) and other government agencies. A comparison by EPA scientists of a Bush administration proposal to change air pollution rules with an alternative proposal from several senators had found that the senators' proposal would cut pollution sooner and more effectively than the administration proposal at "negligible" cost to industry (see Chapter 20). However, the EPA report was not released until it was leaked to the *Washington Post*.[12] Similarly, a scientist at the Department of Agriculture was prohibited from publicizing his research on health hazards caused by antibiotic-resistant bacteria in the air near hog confinement operations in Iowa and Missouri (see Chapter 19). Global warming is an issue on which the Bush administration has especially sought to suppress information and discredit scientific evidence. According to the UCS, the political environment over this issue was so hostile, the EPA decided to omit an entire climate change section from a major report on the environment rather than compromise its credibility by misrepresenting the scientific consensus[13] (see Chapter 24).

Another way the administration has sought to distort scientific information, according to the UCS report, is by packing scientific advisory committees with ideologues and industry representatives. For example, the President's Council on Bioethics was created to consider research on embryonic stem cells, which offers the hope of curing many degenerative diseases, but has been strongly opposed by abortion opponents. In early 2004, President Bush dismissed two of the members, scientists who were supporters of such research. "It seems like an act of desperation to keep the bioethics commission from coming up with advice [the president] doesn't want to hear," said a Nobel-prize winning geneticist.[14] An advisory committee on Childhood Lead Poisoning Prevention was about to recommend that the CDC issue a stricter federal standard for exposure to lead, which damages children's brains and nervous systems, when the

Secretary of Health and Human Services replaced highly qualified scientists on the committee with members who had financial ties to the industry (see Chapter 19). "The Bush administration has the right to implement the policies it chooses," said one of the signers of the UCS statement. "We object to the administration pretending the science supports these policies, when in fact it doesn't."[14]

CONCLUSION

Public health is controversial because, depending on how it is defined, it may challenge people's values and demand sacrifices. The battle between an expansive and a restrictive view of public health is ongoing. The expansive view asks people to give up a degree of personal liberty for the common good.

At its most idealistic, public health is a broad social movement, a campaign to maximize health for everyone in the population through distributing benefits and responsibilities in an equitable way. Health is therefore "a political endeavor as much as, or at times even more than, a medical one."[15(p.15)]

Public health measures are often controversial because they have an economic impact. The people or industries that must pay the price may not be the ones that will benefit from the new protections. Costs are usually more concrete than benefits. Moreover, the price may need to be paid sooner while the benefit may not be achieved until later.

Public health may be affected by personal and intimate behaviors, which are often embarrassing and even offensive to discuss. Thus some public health measures are controversial because they arouse moral or religious objections.

Although there are legitimate differences of opinion on how to weigh competing interests in making public health policy, concerns have been raised recently that the Bush administration is misusing and distorting scientific evidence to pretend that its policies are based on science when they really are not.

REFERENCES

1. U.S. Institute of Medicine, Committee for the Study of the Future of Public Health, *The Future of Public Health* (Washington, DC: National Academy Press, 1988).

2. C.-E. A. Winslow, *The Evolution and Significance of the Modern Public Health Campaign* (New Haven: Yale University Press, 1923); reprint, *Journal of Public Health Policy*, 1984: 1.

3. C.-E. A. Winslow, "The Contribution of Hermann Biggs to Public Health: The 1928 Biggs Memorial Lecture," *The American Review of Tuberculosis* 20 (1929): 1–28.

4. D. E. Beauchamp, "Public Health as Social Justice," *Inquiry* 13 (1976): 1–14.

5. G. Hardin, "The Tragedy of the Commons," *Science* 162 (1968): 1243–1248.

6. F. T. Fitzgerald, "The Tyranny of Health," *New England Journal of Medicine* 331 (1994): 196–898.

7. J. S. Mill, On Liberty, quoted in D. E. Beauchamp, *The Health of the Republic: Epidemics, Medicine, and Moralism as Challenges to Democracy* (Philadelphia: Temple University Press, 1988), 90.

8. A. de Toqueville, Democracy in America, quoted in Beauchamp, *The Health of the Republic* 16.

9. J. Kaiser, "NIH Roiled by Inquiries Over Grants Hit List," *Science* 302 (2003): 758.

10. Union of Concerned Scientists, *Scientific Integrity in Policymaking: An Investigation into the Bush Administration's Misuse of Science* (Cambridge, Massachusetts: 2004).

11. Union of Concerned Scientists, Scientific Knowledge on Breast Cancer Distorted, *www.ucsusa.org/global_environment/rsi/page.cfm?pageID=1357*. Accessed June 8, 2004.

12. Union of Concerned Scientists, Multiple Air Pollutants Information Censored, *www.ucsusa.org/global_environment/rsi/page.cfm?pageID=1365*. Accessed June 8, 2004.

13. Union of Concerned Scientists, Climate Change Research Distorted and Suppressed, *www.ucsusa.org/global_environment/rsi/page.cfm?pageID=1363*. Accessed June 8, 2004.

14. American Public Health Association, "Politics Outweighing Science in Policy Decisions, Report Says," *Nation's Health* (April 2004): 1.

15. L. Wallack et al., *Media Advocacy and Public Health: Power for Prevention* (Newbury Park, California: Sage Publications, 1993), 15.

CHAPTER 3

Powers and Responsibilities of Government

Federal, State, Local . . .

Governments ultimately have the responsibility of making the organized community efforts necessary to protect the health of the population, although many other organizations and community groups are also important participants. Government's role is determined by law; that is, government's public health activities must be authorized by legislation at the federal, state, or local levels. The public health law is further defined by decisions of the courts at the various levels of government. The broad decisions of the legislative and judicial branches of government are worked out in detail by the executive branch, usually the agencies which issue regulations and carry out public health programs. The ultimate authority that allows the laws to be written is the constitution or charter, whether federal, state, or local. Thus the body of public health law is massive, consisting of all the written statements relating to health by any of the three branches of government at the federal, state, and local level.

Many nongovernmental organizations play an important role in public health, especially through educational programs and lobbying. In recent years, stimulated in part by the Institute of Medicine's *The Future of Public Health*,[1] there has been increasing emphasis on community involvement in public health planning and in generating support for and participation in public health activities. This process expands the concept of the public health system to include, for example, hospitals, businesses, and charitable and religious organizations.

FEDERAL VERSUS STATE AUTHORITY

The U.S. Constitution does not mention health. Because the Tenth Amendment states that "the powers not delegated to the United States by the Constitution . . . are reserved to the States respectively," public health has been a responsibility primarily of the states. Most state constitutions provide for the protection of public health, and the original states already had laws concerning health before the Constitution took effect.[2]

All states have laws such as mandates to collect data about the population, immunize children before they enter school, regulate the environment for purposes of sanitation, and regulate safety. To a varying extent, responsibility for some public health activities may be delegated by the state to local governments. Figure 3–1, an organization chart of a small state health department, shows public health activities typically provided for in state law.

The Constitution, in the Preamble, includes among the fundamental purposes of government, "to promote the general welfare." It gives the federal government authority to regulate interstate commerce and to "collect taxes . . . to pay the debts and provide for the common defense and the general welfare." These powers are the basis for the federal role in public health.

The interstate commerce provision, for example, justifies the activities of the Food and Drug Administration (FDA), which oversees extensive federal regulation of foods, drugs, medical devices, and cosmetics, most of which are distributed across state lines. It is obviously more efficient and economical for the industries that produce these products to be bound by uniform national rules rather than having to comply with fifty different sets of state regulations.

The power to tax and spend is a way for the federal government to achieve goals that it may lack the authority to achieve directly. It can provide funds to the states subject to certain requirements. For example, in 1967 the federal government mandated that, as a precondition for receiving highway construction funds, states must pass laws requiring motorcyclists to wear helmets. The effectiveness of the mandate was demonstrated

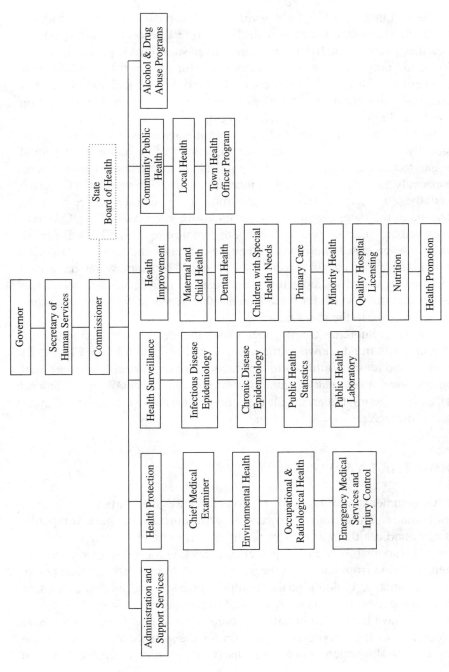

Figure 3–1 Organization Chart of a State Health Department
Source: Anon.

by the fact that, by 1975, forty-seven states had passed such laws, with the result that motorcyclist deaths declined by 30 percent in these states.[3] Another example of federal influence over state health programs is the Medicaid program of providing health care for the poor. The federal government provides 50 to 80 percent of the funding for Medicaid. States and counties administer the Medicaid program, providing the remaining funds, and must follow the guidelines established by Congress.[2]

Since World War II, the federal government has used these powers to steadily widen its role in public health, among other matters. That trend began to reverse in the 1980s. In a political climate hostile to government, especially the federal government, there was a strong movement in Congress and the Supreme Court to cut government regulation and return more powers to the states. In an early example of the reversal, in 1976 Congress removed the financial penalty for lack of motorcycle helmet laws. By 1980, twenty-seven states had repealed their helmet laws and motorcycle deaths rose in those states by 38 percent.[3] The Medicaid program, which has grown enormously expensive since it was established in 1965, has also been a target of Congress, which for some time has threatened, so far without success, to hand it over to the states entirely.

The U.S. Supreme Court under Chief Justice William Rehnquist has begun a new trend known as the new federalism, which limits Congress's powers and returns authority to the states. For example, in 1995, the Court struck down a law making gun possession within a school zone a federal offense, rejecting the argument that gun possession was a matter of interstate commerce.[4]

HOW THE LAW WORKS

Governments have broad power to act in ways that curtail the rights of individuals. These police powers of governments are basic to public health, and are the reason why public health must ultimately be government's responsibility.[5] Police powers are invoked for three reasons: to prevent a person from harming others; to defend the interests of incompetent persons such as children or the mentally retarded; and, in some cases, to protect a person from harming himself or herself.[6]

Laws have been used to enforce compliance in health matters for over a century. In 1905, a precedent was set for the state's police power in the area of health when the Massachusetts legislature passed a law that required all adults to be vaccinated against smallpox. A man named Jacobson refused to comply and went to court, arguing that the law infringed on his personal liberty. The trial court found that the state was within its power to enforce the law. Jacobson appealed his case all the way to the U.S. Supreme Court. He lost: the Supreme Court upheld the right of the state to restrict an individual's freedom "for the common good."[4]

The public health law has become more complex over the years, but it follows the same pattern. At any level of government, a legislature, perceiving a need, passes a statute. The statute may be challenged in court and the decision of the court may be appealed to higher courts. Generally, on issues of constitutionality, a state court may overturn a local law or court decision, and a Federal court may overturn a state law or court decision.

Since public health increasingly involves complex technical issues, legislatures at the levels of government generally set up administrative agencies to perform public health functions. The legislature, recognizing that it lacks the necessary expertise, authorizes these agencies to set rules that define in detail how to accomplish the purpose of the legislation. The courts may then be called on to interpret the authority of the agencies under the laws and to determine whether certain rules or decisions of an agency are within its legal authority.

As an example of the interplay of legislation, agency rule making, and the role of the courts, consider the Occupational Safety and Health Act, passed by Congress in 1970. The legislation stated that "personal injuries and illnesses arising out of work situations impose a substantial burden upon . . . interstate commerce," and thus used the federal government's authority over interstate commerce to pass a public health statute.[7(p.180)] The law established the Occupational Safety and Health Administration (OSHA) within the Department of Labor. OSHA was authorized, among other things, to set standards regulating employees' exposure to hazardous substances. Representatives of industry challenged the constitutional authority of Congress to pass the law but were unsuccessful.

Industries that feel economically harmed by OSHA standard setting have used other routes to weaken the agency's power. One of the substances that OSHA decided to regulate was benzene, which caused a variety of toxic effects among workers in the rubber and petrochemical industries. In 1971, OSHA set a standard limiting benzene exposure to 10 parts per million (ppm) in air, averaged over an eight-hour period. Epidemiologic evidence indicated, however, that exposure to lower concentrations of benzene over time might increase the risk of leukemia, and there was laboratory evidence to support those studies. Therefore, in 1978, OSHA lowered the standard to 1 ppm over an eight-hour period. Representatives of the affected industries appealed the new regulations in court, claiming that evidence that benzene causes leukemia was not sufficiently strong, and that complying with the new standard would be too expensive. The court, in a ruling upheld later by the Supreme Court, agreed that OSHA did not have sufficient evidence to support the need for the new standard and thus had exceeded its authority in issuing the regulation.[7] The standard remained at 10 ppm until 1987, when evidence for the carcinogenicity of benzene was deemed convincing enough to justify the lower value.[8]

The courts did not rule on whether the cost of complying with a standard should be considered in the process of setting it. The act had specified that standards should ensure the health of workers "to the extent feasible."[7(p.180)] Industry argued that OSHA should have done a cost-benefit analysis before issuing the regulation. This issue was decided in another case, in which the courts determined that a formal cost-benefit analysis was not required in the law.[7] Usually, the expected cost of implementing regulations is considered together with the potential benefits when decisions are made. However, there is plenty of room for controversy over the relative magnitudes of the costs and benefits, as discussed in Chapter 2.

Since regulatory activities of federal and state governments are so fundamental to public health, they will often be discussed throughout this book.

HOW PUBLIC HEALTH IS ORGANIZED AND PAID FOR IN THE UNITED STATES

Local Public Health Agencies

The organization of public health at the local level varies from state to state and even within states. The most common local agency is the county health department. A large city may have its own municipal health department, and rural areas may be served by multicounty health departments. Some local areas have no public health department, leaving their residents to do without some services and to depend on state government for others.

Local health departments have the day-to-day responsibility for public health matters in their jurisdiction. These include collecting health statistics; conducting communicable disease control programs; providing screening and immunizations; providing health education services and chronic disease control programs; conducting sanitation, sanitary engineering, and inspection programs; running school health programs; and delivering maternal and child health services and public health nursing services. Mental health may or may not be the responsibility of a separate agency.

In many states, laws assign local public health agencies the responsibility for providing medical care to the poor. While this task may be considered part of the assurance function defined in *The Future of Public Health*,[1] the Institute of Medicine found that this role tends to consume excessive resources and distract local health departments from performing their assessment and policy development functions. The provision of medical services by public health clinics has often been a source of friction with the medical establishment, as discussed in Chapter 25. Functions of a typical county health department are shown in the organization chart, Figure 3–1.

The source of funds for local health department activities varies widely among states. Some states provide the bulk of funding for local health departments while others provide very little. The federal government may fund some local health department activities directly, or federal funds may be passed on from the states. A portion of the local health budget usually comes from local property and sales taxes, and from fees that the department charges for some services. The extent to which local health departments are responsive to mandates from the state and federal government is likely to depend on how much of the local agency's budget is provided by these sources. When the bulk of a local health department's budget is determined by a city council or county legislature, the local agency's capacity to perform core functions may depend on its ability to educate the legislative body about public health and its importance.

State Health Departments

The states have the primary constitutional responsibility and authority for the protection of the health, safety, and general welfare of the population, and much of this responsibility falls on state health departments. The scope of this responsibility varies: some states have separate agencies for social services, aging, mental health, the environment, and so on. This may cause problems, for example, when the environmental agency makes decisions that impact the population's health without consulting the health agency, or—in one example described by the Institute of Medicine—when the Indian Health Service, the state health agency, and the state mental health agency argued about which was responsible for adult and aging services.[1] Some state health departments are strongly centralized, while others delegate much of their authority to the local health departments. State health departments depend heavily on federal money for many programs, and their authority is thus limited by the strings attached to the federal funds.

State health departments define to varying degrees the activities of the local health departments. The state health department may set policies to be followed by the local agencies, and they generally provide significant funding, both from state sources and as channels for federal funds. The state health department coordinates activities of the local agencies and collects and analyzes the data provided by the local agencies. Laboratory services are often provided by state health departments.

State health departments are usually charged with licensing and certification of medical personnel, facilities, and services, with the purpose of maintaining standards of competence and quality of care. An organization chart of a typical state health department is shown in Figure 3–2.

People who lack private health insurance are generally the concern of state health departments, although many states pass this responsibility on to localities. Some of these people are covered by Medicaid, the joint federal-state program for the poor. States have significant—though not total—flexibility in how to administer the Medicaid program, determining eligibility rules for coverage as well as setting payment amounts for the doctors, hospitals, and other providers of medical care. Most states also provide some kind of funding to hospitals to reimburse them for treating uninsured patients who arrive in the emergency room and must be treated.

Funding for state health department activities comes mostly from state taxes and federal grants.

Federal Agencies Involved with Public Health

Most traditional public health activities at the federal level, other than environmental health, fall under the jurisdiction of the Department of Health and Human Services (HHS). A list of HHS agencies is shown in Figure 3–3. The predominant agencies are the Centers for Disease Control and Prevention (CDC), the National Institutes of Health (NIH), and the FDA. The Surgeon General is the nation's leading spokesperson on

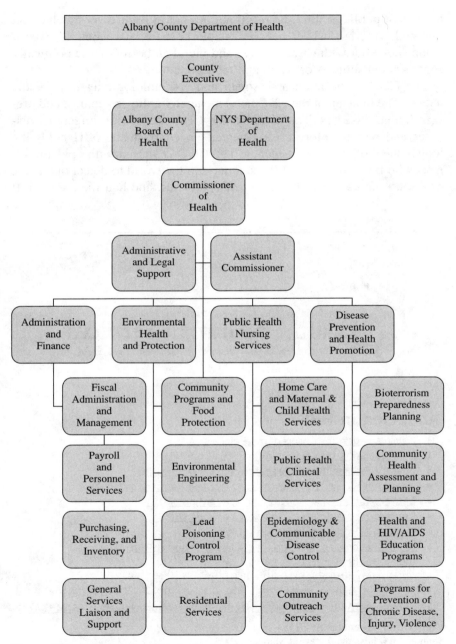

Figure 3–2 Organization Chart of a County Health Department
Source: Albany County DOH.

matters of public health. The position does not in itself carry much direct line authority, but it became very visible in the 1980s when C. Everett Koop spoke out with great courage and moral authority on the politically controversial subjects of AIDS and tobacco.

The CDC is the main assessment and epidemiologic agency for the nation. The mission of the CDC is, as its name implies, to control and prevent human diseases. Traditionally, the CDC focused on infectious diseases and was therefore crisis-oriented. In contrast, the NIH holds the longer view of a research agency. The CDC is staffed with epidemiologists who travel throughout the country and the world to detect outbreaks of disease, track down the causes of epidemics, and halt their spread. It

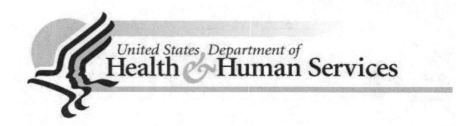

Agencies in HHS

- Administration for Children and Families (ACF)
- Administration on Aging (AoA)
- Agency for Healthcare Research and Quality (AHRQ)
- Agency for Toxic Substances and Disease Registry (ATSDR)
- Centers for Disease Control and Prevention (CDC)
- Centers for Medicare & Medicaid Services (CMS)
- Food and Drug Administration (FDA)
- Health Resources and Services Administration (HRSA)
- Indian Health Service (IHS)
- National Institutes of Health (NIH)
- Program Support Center (PSC)
- Substance Abuse and Mental Health Services Administration (SAMHSA)

Figure 3–3 Agencies in HHS
Source: www.hhs.gov. Accessed March 6, 2005.

also has laboratories at its headquarters in Atlanta, where biomedical scientists study the viruses and bacteria linked with the epidemics. One of the twelve centers, institute, and offices in the CDC is the National Center for Health Statistics, which is the national authority for collecting, analyzing, and disseminating health data for the United States.

The CDC has expanded its mission over recent decades to include chronic diseases, genetics, injury and violence, and environmental health. The CDC's change in focus is justified by the argument that infectious diseases no longer are the leading causes of death and disability in the United States and that these other problems must be addressed in order to make further progress in preventing and controlling disease. However, the CDC's involvement in programs to prevent cancer and heart disease, injury, and violence is more controversial politically, in that it embroils the agency in discussions of the hazards of smoking and firearms, which may offend members of Congress who are supporters of those industries.

A list of CDC Centers, Institute, and Offices is shown in Figure 3–4. CDC issues a weekly publication called *Morbidity and Mortality Weekly*

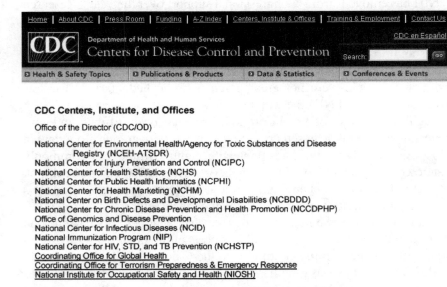

Figure 3–4 CDC Centers, Institute, and Offices
Source: www.cdc.gov. Accessed June 27, 2005.

Report (*MMWR*), which is widely distributed in print and electronically via the Internet. *MMWR* reports on timely public health topics that the CDC deals with, such as outbreaks of infectious diseases and new environmental and behavioral health hazards. The first published report that heralded the onset of the AIDS epidemic appeared in *MMWR* on June 4, 1981.[9] The CDC's journal *Emerging Infectious Diseases*, published in print and online, discusses new infectious disease threats that occur naturally as well as potential bioterrorist threats.

The NIH is the greatest biomedical research complex in the world, with its own research laboratories, most of which are located in Bethesda, Maryland, as well as a program that provides grants to biomedical scientists at universities and research centers throughout the United States. NIH supports research ranging from basic cellular processes to the physiological errors that underly human diseases. NIH's Clinical Center in Bethesda is a research hospital where medical researchers test experimental therapies. NIH also includes the National Library of Medicine, which serves as a reference library for medical centers around the world. Its computerized bibliographic service can be accessed on the Internet. Figure 3–5 shows a list of the NIH institutes and centers.

NIH has enjoyed strong Congressional support over the years. Research aimed at curing human diseases is a popular cause and, for the most part, is generally agreed to be a proper activity for the federal government. States and private companies could not afford to do biomedical research, except to a limited extent, and until recently the prospects for corporate profit in this field were not great. Even periodic budgetary constraints have usually spared NIH the worst of the ax.

Regulation of the food and drug industries has been difficult and controversial since Massachusetts passed the first American pure-food law in 1784. As recently as the late nineteenth century, milk was commonly watered down, then doctored with chalk or plaster of Paris to make it look normal.[10] The Pure Food and Drugs Act of 1906 was opposed by the food canning industry, drug and patent medicine manufacturers, whiskey interests, and, of course, the meat packing industry. That law was passed soon after the publication of Upton Sinclair's best selling novel, *The Jungle*, an exposé of brutal and filthy conditions in the Chicago stockyards.

The modern FDA was established in 1931, and the current law provides for the agency, in addition to ensuring that the food supply is safe and nutritious, to evaluate all new drugs, food additives and colorings, and certain medical devices, approving them only if they are proven safe and, in

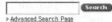

U.S. DEPARTMENT OF HEALTH AND HUMAN SERVICES

National Institutes of Health

Home   Health   Grants   News   Research   Institutes   About NIH

Search

▸ Advanced Search Page

 Institutes, Centers & Offices

National Cancer Institute (NCI)

National Eye Institute (NEI)

National Heart, Lung, and Blood Institute (NHLBI)

National Human Genome Research Institute (NHGRI)

National Institute on Aging (NIA)

National Institute on Alcohol Abuse and Alcoholism (NIAAA)

National Institute of Allergy and Infectious Diseases (NIAID)

National Institute of Arthritis and Musculoskeletal and Skin Diseases (NIAMS)

National Institute of Biomedical Imaging and Bioengineering (NIBIB)

National Institute of Child Health and Human Development (NICHD)

National Institute on Deafness and Other Communication Disorders (NIDCD)

National Institute of Dental and Craniofacial Research (NIDCR)

National Institute of Diabetes and Digestive and Kidney Diseases (NIDDK)

National Institute on Drug Abuse (NIDA)

National Institute of Environmental Health Sciences (NIEHS)

National Institute of General Medical Sciences (NIGMS)

National Institute of Mental Health (NIMH)

National Institute of Neurological Disorders and Stroke (NINDS)

National Institute of Nurshing Research (NINR)

National Library of Medicine (NLM)

Center for Information Technology (CIT formerly DCRT, OIRM, TCB)

Center for Scientific Review (CSR)

John E. Fogarty International Center (FIC)

National Center for Complementary and Alternative Medicine (NCCAM)

National Center on Minority Health and Health Disparities (NCMHD)

National Center for Research Resources (NCRR)

NIH Clinical Center (CC)

Figure 3–5 NIH Institutes, Centers, and Offices
Source: www.nih.gov. Accessed March 6, 2005.

the case of drugs, effective. The agency also regulates vaccines and diagnostic tests, animal drugs, and cosmetics. The FDA is frequently under attack in the current anti-regulatory climate in Congress.

Other components of HHS include the Centers for Medicare and Medicaid Services and the Agency for Health Care Research and Quality, which supports research on health care quality and cost such as that discussed in Chapter 27. The Indian Health Service operates hospitals and health clinics for Native Americans.

Responsibility for environmental health is scattered throughout the federal government, including the CDC's Center for Environmental Health and the NIH's National Institute of Environmental Health Sciences. The prime agency for the environment is the Environmental Protection Agency (EPA), established in 1970 to carry out programs dealing with water pollution, air pollution, toxic substances control, and other issues of environmental contamination. The EPA is one of the most controversial federal public health agencies. It has often been attacked by Congress and, in recent years, its policies have been watered down by the White House.

Many other federal agencies have public health responsibilities. For example, although meat safety concerns were a major factor in the establishment of the FDA, standards of meat safety are the province of the Department of Agriculture. The Department of Agriculture also oversees food and nutrition programs, including food stamps and school lunches. The Department of Education oversees health education and school health and safety programs. The Department of Labor has OSHA, which is concerned with occupational health and prevention of occupational injury. The Department of Veterans Affairs administers its own health and medical services. The Department of Defense, which provides medical care for the armed forces, has long had to deal with public health concerns relating to threats from infectious diseases in foreign climates as well as health effects from toxic chemicals and radiation.

NONGOVERNMENTAL ROLE IN PUBLIC HEALTH

While government bears the major responsibility for public health, many nongovernmental organizations play important roles, especially in education, lobbying, and research. Organizations that focus on specific diseases, such as the American Heart Association, the American Cancer Society, the Alzheimer's Disease and Related Disorders Association, and the American Diabetes Association, lobby Congress for resources and policies to benefit their causes. They also conduct campaigns to educate the public and may sponsor research concerned with their disease. Professional membership organizations, such as the American Public Health Association, the American Medical Association, and the American Nurses Association also are active in lobbying Congress in support of public health issues such as research related to the health effects of smoking. However, the American Medical Association is also known for its opposition to some public health-related programs such as President Clinton's universal health care proposal of 1994. Other organizations that will play an important role in defining the future of public health include the National Association of City and County Health Officers, the Association of State and Territorial Health Officers, and the Association of Schools of Public Health.

Several major philanthropic foundations provide funding to support research or special projects related to public health. For example, the Rockefeller Foundation focuses on world population issues; the Robert Wood Johnson Foundation on providing health care to the poor as well as on AIDS, alcoholism, and drug abuse; the Pew Charitable Trusts on health, AIDS, and drug abuse; the Kaiser Family Foundation on health and public policy; and the Commonwealth Fund also on health and public policy, especially concerning minorities, children, and elderly people. Bill Gates of Microsoft has endowed a new Bill and Melinda Gates Foundation, the mission of which is to improve global health.

Consumers groups organized around specific issues have sometimes had a major impact on national or regional policy related to public health. For example, Ralph Nader's traffic safety campaign in the 1960s forced Congress to pass legislation requiring the automobile industry to build safer cars. The Gay Men's Health Crisis played a critical role in the 1980s in starting up community health services for AIDS victims in New York City.

One of the lessons of the Institute of Medicine report was that governments alone cannot achieve the objectives of public health. Organized community efforts to prevent disease and prolong life must involve all sectors of the community, including providers of health care services, local business, community organizations, the media, and the general public. In the words of one public health leader, "Public health, unlike virtually all other important social efforts, is dependent on its ability to obtain the participation of other agencies to solve its problems."[11(p.399)] Thus, public health leaders must be adept at negotiation and coalition building. Chapter 30 discusses some efforts—led by the federal government with the participation of other governmental and nongovernmental organizations—of the past decades to develop a framework for public health planning and action that involves all sectors of the community at the local, state, and national levels.

CONCLUSION

As an organized community effort, public health is primarily the responsibility of government, although a successful public health enterprise must involve all sectors of the community. Because the U.S. Constitution does not mention health, the states have the primary legal responsibility for public health. In turn, local governments, as the level of government closest to the people, provide the bulk of public health services. Despite the lack of explicit constitutional authority, the federal government has established a significant presence in public health. Federal agencies establish and enforce laws and regulations on issues that need a national scope. Through its authority to tax and spend, the federal government leads and assists state and local governments in providing public health services.

REFERENCES

1. U.S. Institute of Medicine, Committee for the Study of the Future of Public Health, *Future of Public Health* (Washington, DC: National Academy Press, 1988).
2. T. Christoffel, *Health and the Law: A Handbook for Health Professionals* (New York: The Free Press, 1982), 51–52.
3. G. S. Watson et al., "The Repeal of Helmet Use Laws and Increased Motorcyclist Mortality in the United States, 1975–1978," *American Journal of Public Health* 70 (1980): 579–585.
4. L. O. Gostin, "Public Health Law in a New Century, Part II: Public Health Powers and Limits," *Journal of the American Medical Association* 283 (2000): 2979–2984.
5. L. O. Gostin, "Public Health Law in a New Century, Part I: Law as a Tool to Advance the Community's Health," *Journal of the American Medical Association* 283 (2000): 2837–2841.
6. L. O. Gostin, "Public Health in a New Century, Part III: Public Health Regulation: A Systematic Evaluation," *Journal of the American Medical Association* 283 (2000): 3118–3122.
7. K. R. Wing, *The Law and the Public's Health* (Ann Arbor, Michigan: Health Administration Press, 1990), 180.
8. I. L. Feitshans, "Law and Regulation of Benzene," *Environmental Health Perspectives* 82 (1989): 299–307.

9. U.S. Centers for Disease Control and Prevention, "Pneumocystis Pneumonia—Los Angeles," *Morbidity and Mortality Weekly Report* (June 4, 1981).
10. R. M. Deutsch, *The New Nuts Among the Berries: How Nutritional Nonsense Captured America* (Palo Alto, California: Bull Publishing Company, 1977).
11. G. Pickett, "Book Review: The Future of Public Health," *Journal of Public Health Policy*, Autumn 1989: 397–401.

PART II

Analytical Methods of Public Health

CHAPTER 4

Epidemiology: The Basic Science of Public Health

Epidemiologic Surveillance

C.-E. A. Winslow, the great public health leader of the early twentieth century, called epidemiology "the diagnostic discipline of public health."[1(p.vii)] Epidemiologic methods are used to investigate causes of diseases, to identify trends in disease occurrence that may influence the need for medical and public health services, and to evaluate the effectiveness of medical and public health interventions. Epidemiology is used to perform

51

public health's assessment function called for in the Institute of Medicine's *The Future of Public Health.*[2]

Epidemiology studies the patterns of disease occurrence in human populations and the factors that influence these patterns. The term is obviously related to *epidemic* (derived from the Greek word meaning "upon the people"). An epidemic is an increase in the frequency of a disease above the usual and expected rate, which is called the *endemic* rate. Thus, epidemiologists count cases of a disease and when they detect signs of an epidemic, they ask *who*, *when*, and *where* questions: Who is getting the disease? Where and when is the disease occurring? From this information, they can often make informed guesses as to *why* it is occurring. Their ultimate goal is to use this knowledge to control and prevent the spread of disease.

HOW EPIDEMIOLOGY WORKS

The first example of the use of epidemiology to study and control a disease occurred in London between 1853 and 1854, and it stands as an illustration of what epidemiology is and how it works. It was conducted by a British physician, John Snow, who is known as the father of modern epidemiology.

Snow was concerned about a cholera epidemic that had struck London in 1848. He noticed that death rates were especially high in parts of the city with water supplied by two private companies, both of which drew water from the Thames River at a point heavily polluted with sewage. Between 1849 and 1854, the Lambeth Company changed its source to an area of the Thames that was free of pollution from London's sewers. Snow noticed that the number of cholera deaths declined in the section of London supplied by the Lambeth Company, while there was no change in the sections supplied by the Southwark and Vauxhall Company. He formulated the hypothesis that cholera was spread by polluted drinking water.[3]

In 1853 there was a severe outbreak of cholera concentrated in the Broad Street area of London, in which some houses were supplied by one water company and some by the other. This provided an opportunity for Snow to test his hypothesis in a kind of "natural experiment," in which "people of both sexes, of every age and occupation, and of every rank and station . . . were divided into two groups without their choice, and, in most cases, without their knowledge . . ."[4(p.6–7)] Snow went to each house in which someone had died of cholera between August 1853 and January 1854 to determine which company supplied the water. When he tabulated the results, he found that in 40,046 houses supplied by the Southwark and Vauxhall Company, there were 1,263 deaths from cholera. By comparison, in 26,107 houses supplied by the Lambeth Company, only ninety-eight deaths occurred. The rate of cholera deaths was thus eight and one-half times higher in houses supplied by the Southwark and Vauxhall Company than those supplied by the Lambeth Company. This was convincing evidence that deaths from cholera were linked with the source of water. See Table 4–1.

Snow would not have been able to formulate his hypothesis without the data on cholera deaths, which had been collected by the British government as part of a system for routine compilation of births and deaths, including cause of death, since 1839. Now, the governments of all developed countries collect data on births, deaths, and other vital statistics, as will be discussed in Chapter 8. These data are often used for epidemiologic studies.

Because it is preferable to recognize that an epidemic is occurring before many people start dying, governments also use a system called *epidemiologic surveillance*, requiring that certain "notifiable" diseases be reported as soon as they are diagnosed. These are usually infectious diseases whose spread can be prevented if the appropriate actions are taken. In the United States, approximately fifty diseases have been identified by law as notifiable at the federal level, including, for example, tuberculosis, hepatitis, measles, and syphilis. Some states require reporting of addi-

Table 4–1   Deaths from Cholera by Company Supplying Water to the Household

Water Company	Number of Houses	Deaths from Cholera	Deaths in Each 10,000 Houses
Southwark and Vauxhall Company	40,046	1263	315
Lambeth Company	26,107	98	37
Rest of London	256,423	1422	59

Source: Reprinted from *Epidemiology: An Introductory Text*, 2e, Mausner JS, p. 202, copyright (1985), with permission from Elsevier.

tional infectious diseases. There may also be requirements for reporting birth defects, cancer, and other non-infectious conditions. All physicians, hospitals, and clinical laboratories must report any case of a notifiable disease or condition to their local health department, which in turn reports to the state health department and the Centers for Disease Control and Prevention (CDC). The timely reporting of cases of notifiable diseases allows public health authorities to detect an emerging epidemic at an early stage. Measures can then be taken to control the spread of infectious diseases, as discussed later and in Chapter 9. Reporting of chronic diseases is less widespread, but some public health agencies have urged a system to monitor conditions such as birth defects, Alzheimer's disease, asthma, and a variety of cancers.[5] Such a system would help to identify causes of these diseases, including environmental causes that could be controlled or eliminated, preventing further harmful effects.

While the surveillance system was created to control the spread of known diseases, the established network of reporting can facilitate the recognition that a new disease may be emerging. The first step in recognizing that a community is facing a new problem is usually a report to the local or state health department or the CDC by a perceptive physician who notices something unusual that he or she thinks should be investigated further. This is how AIDS came to be recognized early in the epidemic.

A TYPICAL EPIDEMIOLOGIC INVESTIGATION: OUTBREAK OF HEPATITIS

Hepatitis A is a notifiable disease in all fifty states. Because it is caused by a virus that contaminates food or water, it is important to identify the source of any outbreak so that wider exposure to the virus can be prevented. Although hepatitis is not usually fatal to basically healthy people, it can make people quite sick for several weeks and sometimes require hospitalization.

Because hepatitis is a notifiable disease, the local public health department is able to recognize when an outbreak occurs. A county may normally record only a few cases of hepatitis each year. This is the endemic level, the background level in a population. A sudden increase in the number of cases signifies an epidemic and calls for an epidemiologic investigation to determine why it is occurring.

The investigation requires asking the who, where, and when questions. This kind of medical detective work is nicknamed "shoeleather epidemiology." The investigator starts with the reported cases—the *who*—although other, unreported cases may turn up once the investigator starts asking questions. Each victim must be interviewed and asked the *when* question: on what date did the first symptoms appear? Knowing that hepatitis has an incubation period of about thirty days, it is possible to work back to an estimated date of exposure. The *where* question is the hardest: where did the victims obtain their food and water during the period of likely exposure and what sources did they have in common?

It may be that they all had eaten at the same restaurant. The epidemiologist would visit the restaurant and might find that the chef had developed hepatitis about a month earlier and been hospitalized; so the contamination of the food had stopped, and the epidemic would also stop. Alternatively, the chef may have had only a mild, perhaps unrecognized case and continued to work, thereby continuing to spread the infection. The health department might have to close the restaurant down, if necessary, until the chef is declared healthy.

Such investigations are a frequent task of epidemiologists at local health departments. A large number of these investigations deal with food poisoning outbreaks caused by contamination with salmonella or shigella, bacteria that commonly infect carelessly prepared or preserved food, both of which cause notifiable diseases. The Milwaukee cryptosporidiosis outbreak described in the Prologue was solved by such an epidemiologic investigation. Although cryptosporidiosis was not a notifiable disease, the epidemic was recognized because it was so severe and widespread. If the disease had been notifiable, it might have been recognized and halted earlier. Cryptosporidiosis was added to the national list of notifiable diseases in 1995. Table 4–2 gives a list of diseases that are reportable at the national level in 2002.

With some diseases, even a single case amounts to an epidemic. Measles, which is highly contagious, is preventable by vaccination. Although measles immunization for children was required by all states beginning in the 1970s, a number of measles epidemics occurred between 1989 and 1991 on college campuses. A reported case triggered a need for mass immunizations on campus. When epidemiologists found that many of the affected students had been immunized as infants, they concluded that a second vaccination was necessary for teenagers. The new policy put a halt to measles epidemics on campuses.

Table 4–2   Infectious Diseases Designated as Notifiable at the National Level and Number of Cases Reported During 2002

AIDS	42,745
Anthrax	2
Botulism, total	118
Foodborne	28
Infant	69
Brucellosis	125
Chancroid	67
Chlamydia trachomatis, genital inf.	834,555
Cholera	2
Coccidioidomycosis	4,968
Cryptosporidiosis	3,016
Cyclosporiasis	156
Diphtheria	1
Ehrlichiosis, human granulocytic	511
Human monocytic	216
Encephalitis/meningitis, Calif. serogroup	164
Eastern equine	10
Powassan	1
St. Louis	28
West Nile	2,848
Western equine	—
Enterohem. *E. coli* (EHEC), O157:H7	3,840
EHEC serogroup non-O157	194
EHEC, not serogrouped	60
Giardiasis	21,206
Gonorrhea	351,852
H. influenzae, invasive disease	1,743
Hansen disease	96
Hantavirus pulmonary syndrome	19
Hemolytic uremic syndrome, postdiarrheal	216
Hepatitis A, acute	8,795
Hepatitis B, acute	7,996
Hepatitis C/non-A, non-B, acute	1,835
HIV infection*	31,805
Adult (> 13 yrs.)	31,595
Pediatric (< 13 yrs.)	210
Legionellosis	1,321
Listeriosis	665
Lyme disease	23,763
Malaria	1,430
Measles	44
Meningococcal disease	1,814
Mumps	270

Pertussis	9,771
Plague	2
Poliomyelitis, paralytic	—
Psitticosis	18
Q fever	61
Rabies, animal	7,609
Rabies, human	3
Rocky Mountain spotted fever	1,104
Rubella	18
Rubella, congenital syndrome	1
Salmonellosis	44,264
Shigellosis	23,541
Streptococcal disease, invasive, group A	4,720
Strep. pneumoniae, drug-resistant, invasive	2,546
Strep. pneumoniae, invasive, <5 yrs	513
Streptococcal toxic-shock syndrome	118
Syphilis, primary and secondary	6,862
Total, all stages	32,871
Tetanus	25
Toxic-shock syndrome	109
Trichinosis	14
Tuberculosis	15,075
Tularemia	90
Typhoid fever	321
Varicella (chicken pox)	22,841
Varicella deaths	9
Yellow fever	1

*33 areas with confidential name-based HIV infection reporting
Source: U.S. Centers for Disease Control and Prevention, "Summaries of Notifiable Diseases in the United States, 2002," *Morbidity and Mortality Weekly Report* 51 (2004): 17–18.

Since the bioterror attacks of fall 2001, the CDC has added to the list of notifiable diseases several infectious diseases that are potential agents of bioterrorism. As discussed in Chapter 29, the first sign of a bioterror attack could be the report of a single case identified in a hospital emergency room.

LEGIONNAIRES' DISEASE

In July 1976, the American Legion held a four-day convention in Philadelphia. Before the event was over, conventioneers began falling ill with symptoms of fever, muscle aches, and pneumonia. By early August, 150 cases of the disease and twenty deaths had been reported to the

Pennsylvania Department of Health, and the CDC was called in to help determine what was causing the epidemic. The investigation determined that the site of exposure was most likely the Hotel Bellevue-Stratford, one of four Philadelphia hotels where convention activities were held.[6,7] Delegates who stayed at the Bellevue-Stratford had a higher rate of illness than those who stayed at other hotels, and many of those who fell ill had attended receptions in the hotel's hospitality suites. However, cases also occurred in people who had only been near, not in, the hotel, suggesting that exposure could have occurred on the streets or sidewalks nearby. The evidence suggested that the causative agent was airborne, but it did not appear to spread person-to-person to the patients' families.

While the epidemiologists were conducting their investigation, they enlisted the help of the CDC's biomedical scientists to look for evidence of viruses or bacteria in the body tissues of the victims. They also considered the possibility of a toxic chemical, but no evidence of a cause could be found. It was not until the following January that the biomedical scientists found the bacteria that were responsible for the epidemic, which by then was called Legionnaires' disease. The hotel was searched for the source of the bacteria. It was eventually found in the water of a cooling tower used for air conditioning. Legionella bacteria had been pumped into the cooled air and inhaled by the victims.

Once the Legionella bacteria were identified, they were found responsible for a number of other outbreaks of pneumonia around the country. The bacteria were also identified in preserved blood and tissue samples collected in 1965 from victims of a previously unsolved outbreak of pneumonia which affected some eighty patients at St. Elizabeth's psychiatric hospital in Washington, D.C., killing fourteen of them.[7] Thus Legionnaire's disease had probably been around but unrecognized as a specific disease at least since the invention of air conditioning. Federal air conditioning standards were changed after the Philadelphia epidemic; stringent requirements for cleaning of cooling towers and large-scale air-conditioning systems were introduced. Legionnellosis is now a notifiable disease.

EOSINOPHILIA-MYALGIA SYNDROME

Although infectious agents are usually suspected first in any outbreak of a new disease, epidemiologists must also consider exposure to a toxic substance as an alternative cause. Physicians and epidemiologists found this to be the case in a puzzling outbreak first reported in New Mexico. In October 1989, several Santa Fe doctors were comparing notes on three patients suffering from a novel condition involving fatigue, debilitating muscle pain, rashes, and shortness of breath. Blood tests on all three had revealed very high counts of white blood cells called eosinophils. The doctors knew of no known condition that could explain these findings. However, they were struck by the fact that all three patients, when questioned about drugs or medications they were taking, had mentioned a health food supplement called L-tryptophan. L-tryptophan is a "natural" substance, a component of proteins, that had been publicized as a treatment for insomnia, depression, and premenstrual symptoms. Believing that more than coincidence was involved in these three cases, the doctors reported them to the New Mexico State Health Department.[8]

The Health Department reported the cases to the CDC and began an investigation to determine if additional cases existed and whether there was a consistent link with L-tryptophan. By searching the records of clinical laboratories in Santa Fe, Albuquerque, and Los Alamos, they discovered twelve additional patients whose blood had exhibited high white cell counts since May 1. A team of health department investigators interviewed these twelve people and found that they all had used L-tryptophan. They also interviewed twenty-four people of the same age and sex as the patients who lived in the same neighborhoods—a control group—and found that only two had taken the supplement. This strongly suggested that there was a link between L-tryptophan exposure and the illness. The CDC notified other state health departments, which conducted their own investigations, and by November 16 the CDC has received reports from thirty-five states of 243 possible cases of the new disease, called eosinophilia-myalgia syndrome (EMS). On November 17, the Food and Drug Administration announced a nationwide recall of products containing L-tryptophan. The publicity brought forth a flood of new reports of the syndrome, but then new cases began to drop off. By August 1, 1992, 1,511 cases had been reported by all fifty states. Many patients were left with permanent disabilities and thirty-eight people had died, but the epidemic was over.[9]

Why had this natural substance caused such severe consequences? L-tryptophan is an amino acid, present in many foods including meat, fish, poultry, and cheese. It is also added to infant formulas, special dietary foods, and intravenous and oral solutions administered to patients with special medical needs. No cases of EMS had been reported from these products. Tests on the recalled tablets indicated that a toxic contaminant, formed as a result of a recent change in one factory's method of production, may have been responsible for the epidemic of 1989. However, there is evidence that earlier, unrecognized cases had occurred since the product was introduced in 1974.[10] The fact that many people took the supplements with no apparent harm suggests that individual variations in susceptibility may exist.

Serious outbreaks of illness caused by toxic contamination of food, through production errors, or outright fraud, have occurred a number of times over the past few decades. It is usually epidemiologists who identify the source of the problem. To many public health experts, the EMS epidemic of 1989 resembled an illness with similar symptoms that affected some 20,000 people in Spain in 1981, killing more than 300 of them. An infectious agent had first been suspected, but epidemiologists noted an odd geographical distribution of the outbreak. Patients lived either in a localized area south of Madrid or in a corridor along a road north of the city. The epidemiologists found that the affected households had bought oil for cooking from itinerant salespeople, who were illegally selling oil that had been manufactured for industrial use.[11] Laboratory scientists investigating the nature of the contaminants and how they might have caused the symptoms have not specifically identified a single chemical as being responsible. They now suspect that a range of chemicals, even at very low concentrations, may induce autoimmune responses in susceptible people, causing the body's immune system to attack its own tissues. Such outbreaks caused by toxic contamination of foods and drugs may be much more common than is generally recognized.[12] In cases of toxic oil syndrome and EMS, government action to remove the contaminated product put an end to the epidemic.

Epidemiologic surveillance is a major line of defense in protecting the public against disease. It is the warning system that alerts the community that something is wrong, that a gap has opened in the protective bulwark against preventable disease or that a new disease has appeared on the horizon. The sooner the surveillance system kicks in, the sooner action can be taken to stop the epidemic. Before the health department is notified, individual doctors are trying to cure individual patients, often unaware that the problem is more widespread. After the epidemic is recognized, all the resources of the community—local, state, or national—can be mobilized to prevent the disease's spread. Whether through vaccination campaigns against measles, isolation of hepatitis-infected food workers, new regulations on air conditioning systems, or recall of contaminated food or drugs, the government must act to protect the health of the public. Epidemiologic surveillance has become even more important as concerns about bioterrorism have increased, as Chapter 29 discusses.

EPIDEMIOLOGY AND THE CAUSES OF CHRONIC DISEASE

Epidemiology has had a different role to play in investigating the causes of the diseases common in older age, such as cancer and heart disease, which are quite different from infectious diseases or acute poisoning. Until the twentieth century, these conditions were thought of as a natural part of aging, and no one thought to look for causes or try to prevent them.

Cancer, heart disease, and other diseases of aging do not have single causes. They tend to develop over a period of time, are often chronic and disabling rather than rapidly fatal, and cannot be prevented or cured by any vaccine or "magic bullet." The best hope for protecting the public against these diseases is to learn how to prevent them, or at least to delay their onset. Prevention, however, requires an understanding of the cause, or causes, of a disease and the factors that influence how they progress. Epidemiology has made major contributions to the current understanding of the causes of heart disease and some cancers and what can be done to prevent them. Epidemiologic studies will continue to yield information on how people can protect themselves against cancer, Alzheimer's disease, and other afflictions of aging.

Epidemiologic studies of these chronic diseases are much more complicated and difficult than investigations of acute outbreaks of infectious diseases or toxic contamination. Except for the clear link between smoking and lung cancer (discussed later in this chapter), most chronic diseases cannot be attributed to a single cause. There may be many different factors that play a part in causing a disease, factors that epidemiologists call "risk factors." The long period over which these diseases develop also contributes to the difficulty of determining the causative factors. Epidemiologists must determine which of a person's many experiences over the previous decades are relevant, and what significant exposures might have occurred ten or twenty years ago that may have increased the person's risk of developing the disease today.

Epidemiology has developed a number of methods to study chronic diseases and try to answer the difficult questions. This chapter describes a few of the best-known studies that have had a major impact in understanding the causes of heart disease and cancer. Chapter 5 discusses in a more systematic way the major types of epidemiologic studies.

HEART DISEASE

Since the 1920s, when infectious disease mortality had dropped to approximately its current low levels, heart disease has been the leading cause of death in the United States for both men and women. Deaths from heart disease increased dramatically during the first half of the twentieth century. After World War II, one in every five men was affected with heart disease before the age of sixty, and little was known about why. In 1948, an epidemiologic study was launched in Framingham, Massachusetts, to investigate what factors might be causing the problem. It was the first major epidemiologic study of a chronic disease. More than half the middle-aged population of the town, more than 5,000 healthy people, were examined and data were recorded on their weight, blood pressure, smoking habits, the results of various blood tests, and other characteristics. Two years later, the same people were examined again, and these tests have been and will continue to be repeated every two years for the rest of their lives.[13]

As early as ten years later, the Framingham Heart Study had revealed a great deal about how to predict which of their subjects were likely to develop heart disease. The study identified three major risk factors: high blood pressure, high blood cholesterol, and smoking. As a result of the findings, concepts of "normal" blood pressure and cholesterol levels changed significantly. Doctors had previously believed that blood pressure naturally increased as people aged and that the increase was normal and healthy. The Framingham Study found that some people maintained their youthful blood pressure and cholesterol values as they got older and that these people remained healthier. Weight gain and lack of exercise were found to be associated with increased blood pressure and cholesterol values and with an increased risk of heart disease.[14]

Remarkably, the Framingham findings had a major impact on the course of the heart disease epidemic. Publicity on the information gained by the study, confirmed and supported by other studies, persuaded some people to change their behavior and formed the basis of public health programs to encourage others to do the same. By the 1970s, it was clear that death rates from heart disease were falling in the United States. The Framingham Study itself found in 1970 that the death rate over the previous ten years had declined by 60 percent from that in 1950.[14] This improvement was associated with a decline in risk factors in 1970: blood cholesterol levels were lower, blood pressure was lower, and smoking was less common. These beneficial trends have continued. In 2002, the age adjusted death rate from heart disease was 61% lower than it was in 1950, as shown in Figure 4–1.

Meanwhile, the Framingham Study has continued and expanded, and much more has been learned. For example, a smoker's risk of heart disease rapidly drops back to that of nonsmokers soon after the smoker quits; but low-tar, low-nicotine cigarettes are no better than the old-fashioned kind

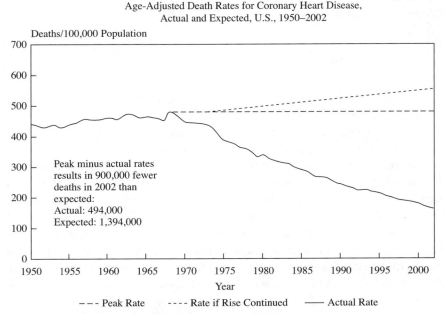

Figure 4–1 Crude Death Rates for Morbidity & Mortality
Source: www.nhlbi.nihgov/resources/docs/04_chtbk.pdf.

in their effects on risk of heart disease.[14] Various forms of cholesterol have been identified, including high-density lipoprotein (HDL) cholesterol—the "good" kind that is protective and low-density lipoprotein (LDL) cholesterol—the "bad" kind. Drinking alcohol in moderation has been found to increase HDL cholesterol and protect against heart disease. Exercise also raises HDL levels.[13] The scope of the Framingham Study has expanded: in 1978, the subjects began to be given neurological examinations in addition to tests for cardiac risk factors. The investigators are watching for the development of Alzheimer's disease in the aging study population, hoping that they will be able to detect risk factors for this increasingly common and tragic condition.[15]

An offshoot of the original study, the Framingham Offspring Study, was created in 1971; it included about 5,000 children of the original participants. Investigators use comparisons of risk factors within families and across generations, hoping to sort out the roles of genetics and environment in heart disease. The younger study population is being tested with more advanced cardiology equipment and more sophisticated blood tests. In 2001, the National Institutes of Health announced another expansion to form the Third Generation Study, which will enroll grandchildren of the study's original participants.[16]

LUNG CANCER

Epidemiologic studies seeking causes of cancer began soon after the Framingham Study. However, studies of most kinds of cancer had much less success than the studies of heart disease; epidemiologists had few strong clues about possible causes or risk factors.

An exception was the link between smoking and lung cancer. Mortality from lung cancer had been increasing dramatically since the 1930s, as shown in Figure 4–2. Because it was logical to suppose that the cause might be something that was inhaled, the two main hypotheses proposed to explain this increase were tobacco smoking and air pollution, both having increased during the same period that lung cancer was rising. Several early studies conducted in England and the United States beginning in the late 1940s questioned lung cancer patients about their smoking habits. All these studies found that a high proportion of these patients were heavy smokers.

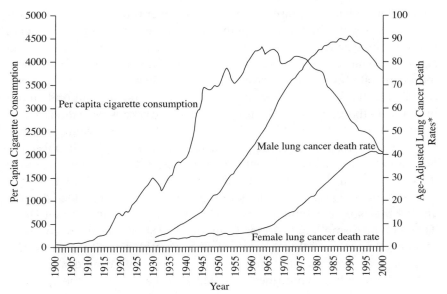

*Age-adjusted to 2000 US standard population.

Figure 4–2 Cigarette Consumption and Lung Cancer Deaths in the U.S., 1900–2000
Source: Copyright 2005 American Cancer Society, Inc. www.cancer.org. Reprinted with permission.

In late 1950 and early 1952, two major epidemiologic studies were started that convincingly established a link between lung cancer and tobacco smoking. The British epidemiologists Richard Doll and A. Bradford Hill sent out a questionnaire to all physicians in the United Kingdom, asking whether they were smokers, past smokers, or nonsmokers. Smokers and ex-smokers were asked to provide additional information on their age at starting to smoke and the amount of tobacco smoked, and ex-smokers were asked when they had quit smoking. Over 40,000 doctors responded to the survey.[17]

During the following years, Doll and his collaborators, by arrangement with the British Medical Association and the Registrar General of the United Kingdom, gathered information on which doctors had died each year and what was the cause of death. A little over four years after the survey began, several important conclusions were apparent: First, the death rate from lung cancer was about twenty times higher among smokers than among nonsmokers, increasing as the amount smoked increased. Second, the death rate among ex-smokers was lower than that of smokers and declined as the length of time increased since the doctor had quit smoking. Third, the contrast in lung cancer mortality between smokers and nonsmokers was the same whether the doctors lived in rural or urban areas. Therefore, the difference could not be attributed to air pollution. Fourth, deaths from heart attacks were also significantly higher among heavy smokers aged thirty-five to fifty-four than among nonsmokers.[18]

A similar study on a much larger group of people was conducted in the United States by epidemiologists E. Cuyler Hammond and Daniel Horn. They obtained smoking histories from almost 188,000 men and followed them over a period of three years and eight months. For all the study participants who died, they determined the cause of death from death certificates. Their findings confirmed and extended the results of the Doll and Hill study of British doctors. First, cigarette smokers were more than ten times more likely to die of lung cancer than nonsmokers. Second, cigarette smokers were about five times more likely to die of cancer of the lip, tongue, mouth, pharynx, larynx, and esophagus as nonsmokers. Several other types of cancer were also more common among smokers. Third, heavy smokers (two or more packs a day) were 2.4 times more likely to die of heart disease than nonsmokers.[19]

The British study continued until 1971, tracking all the doctors for twenty years, by which time about one-third of them had died. The longer period of observation confirmed the results obtained earlier. An interesting finding was that many physicians reacted to the earlier reports by quitting smoking. By 1971, the average number of cigarettes smoked per day by the physicians in the study was less than half what it had been in 1951, and as a result, lung cancer became relatively less common as a cause of death in this group.[18]

The Framingham Study and the two lung cancer studies are examples of prospective cohort studies, following large numbers of people over extended periods of time. These are considered among the most reliable kinds of epidemiologic studies for investigating causes of chronic diseases. Other such studies have been done and continue at present, many of them seeking causes of various kinds of cancer. Chapter 5 discusses the major types of epidemiologic studies. More on what is known about cancer and heart disease will be discussed in Chapters 11, 15, and 16.

CONCLUSION

Epidemiology is an important component of the assessment function of public health. Epidemiologists investigate epidemics of known and unknown diseases by counting the number of cases and how they are distributed by person, place, and time. Using this information, they can often determine a probable cause of a new disease or a reason for an outbreak of a previously controlled disease. This knowledge allows public health workers to institute methods to prevent and control the spread of the disease.

An early achievement of epidemiology was the recognition in the nineteenth century that cholera was spread by polluted water. In 1993, similar epidemiologic methods determined that polluted water had caused an outbreak of crytosporidiosis in Milwaukee. The same approach has been successful in halting outbreaks of illness caused by toxic contaminations. "Shoeleather epidemiology" by local health departments provides the front line of defense against acute diseases. Epidemiologic surveillance, including mandatory reporting of notifiable disease, alerts a local health department that an epidemic is beginning in time for an agency to investigate the reasons and take preventive action.

Epidemiology also provides information on the causes of chronic disease. Formal long-term studies of heart disease and lung cancer provided the earliest information on the risk factors that contributed to these diseases. The Framingham Study, which has tracked citizens of Framingham, Massachusetts for five decades, identified high blood pressure, high blood cholesterol, and smoking as risk factors for heart disease. Two epidemiologic studies conducted in the 1950s—one on the smoking habits of British doctors and a similar study on a group of 188,000 American men—indicated a clear link between smoking and lung cancer.

Epidemiology's role in identifying causes of disease leads directly and indirectly to prevention and control. In some cases, regulatory action by a local government is necessary to eliminate the conditions that are causing disease. Sometimes simply publicizing the results of a study allows people to modify their behavior to avoid risk factors for a disease. For example, information released in the 1950s on results from the Framingham Study and the studies regarding smoking and lung cancer contributed to a significant decline in smoking in the United States, accompanied by a drop in mortality from both heart disease and lung cancer since the 1950s. To achieve additional improvements in public health, health agencies build on epidemiologic information to develop policy and plan programs aimed at reducing risk and promoting health in the population.

REFERENCES

1. C.-E. A. Winslow et al., quoted in R. C. Brownson and D. B. Petitti, eds., *Applied Epidemiology: Theory to Practice* (New York: Oxford University Press, 1998), vii.
2. Institute of Medicine, *The Future of Public Health* (Washington, DC: National Academy Press, 1988).
3. C. J. Hennekens and J. F. Buring, *Epidemiology in Medicine* (Boston: Little, Brown, 1987).
4. J. Snow, *On the Mode of Communication of Cholera* (London: Churchill, 1955). Quoted in Hennekens and Buring, *Epidemiology in Medicine* (Boston: Little, Brown, 1987).
5. P. J. Hilts, "Panel Urges Monitoring of Chronic Diseases," *New York Times* (September 12, 2000): F12.
6. D. W. Fraser et al., "Legionnaire's Disease," *New England Journal of Medicine* 297 (1977): 1189–1203.
7. L. Garrett, *The Coming Plague: Newly Emerging Diseases in a World Out of Balance* (New York: Farrar, Straus, and Giroux, 1994).
8. U.S. Centers for Disease Control, "Eosinophilia-Myalgia Syndrome—New Mexico," *Morbidity and Mortality Weekly Report* 38 (1989): 765–767.
9. S. L. Nightingale, "Update on EMS and L-Tryptophan," *Journal of the American Medical Association* 268 (1992): 1828.
10. T. A. Medsger Jr., "Tryptophan-Induced Eosinophilia-Myalgia Syndrome," *New England Journal of Medicine* 322 (1990): 926–928.
11. E. M. Kilbourne et al., "Clinical Epidemiology of Toxic-Oil Syndrome: Manifestations of New Disease," *New England Journal of Medicine* 309 (1983): 1408–1414.
12. M. Posada de la Paz et al., "Toxic Oil Syndrome: The Perspective After 20 Years," *Epidemiology Reviews* 23 (2001): 231–247.
13. J. Brody, "Heart Disease: Big Study Produces New Data," *New York Times* (January 8, 1985), III, I.
14. W. B. Kannel, "The Framingham Experience," in M. Marmot and P. Elliott (eds.), *Coronary Heart Disease Epidemiology: From Aetiology to Public Health* (New York: Oxford University Press, 1992).
15. D. L. Backman et al., "Incidence of Dementia and Probable Alzheimer's Disease in a General Population: The Framingham Study," *Neurology* 43 (1993): 515–519.
16. National Institutes of Health, News Release: "Framingham Heart Study Enters New Phase," Washington, DC: November 8, 2001.
17. R. Doll and A. B. Hill, "Smoking and Carcinoma of the Lung: Preliminary Report," *British Medical Journal* (September 30, 1950): 739–748.
18. R. Doll and R. Peto, "Mortality in Relation to Smoking: 20 Years' Observations on Male British Doctors," *British Medical Journal* 2 (1976): 1525–1536.
19. E. C. Hammond and D. Horn, "Smoking and Death Rates—Report on Forty-Four Months of Follow-up of 187,783 Men," *Journal of the American Medical Association* 166 (1958): 1294–1308.

CHAPTER 5

Epidemiologic Principles and Methods

Risk Factors

This chapter examines epidemiology more closely, defining some of its basic terms and describing how epidemiologists use the terms to describe the patterns of disease occurrence. The chapter also explains the different kinds of epidemiologic studies, with examples of the types of information each form of epidemiologic study can provide.

Epidemiology is defined as "the study of the *distribution* and *determinants* of *disease frequency* in *human populations*." (emphasis added)[1(p.1)] Each of these terms must be clearly understood.

First, the epidemiologist must define the *disease* in a clear way so that there is no doubt about whether an individual case should or should not be counted. Some diseases are easier to identify than others. In a hepatitis outbreak, the symptoms are fairly nonspecific and not every patient who comes to an emergency room with vomiting and diarrhea has hepatitis. Therefore, the epidemiologist must include the results of blood tests for liver function in his/her case definition. In a study of deaths from gunshot wounds, on the other hand, the cases are fairly easy to count since virtually 100 percent of deaths are reported, and the cause of death is usually identified easily and listed on the death certificate. With a new disease like eosinophilia myalgia syndrome (described in Chapter 4), working out the case definition might be the most important part of the investigation.

In defining a disease to be studied, epidemiologists use the term *disease* broadly: "health outcome" is a more accurate but cumbersome description of what is to be studied. For example, epidemiologists might study the frequency and distribution of high blood cholesterol, which is not a disease but is related to the risk of heart attack, or they might study injuries due to traffic accidents, which are not diseases but are certainly significant to health. In both cases, an epidemiologic study may point to ways of preventing the negative health outcome.

In measuring disease *frequency*, it is necessary not only to count the number of cases but to relate that number to the size of the population being studied, yielding a *rate*. Six cases of Legionnaires' disease among a thousand vacationers on a cruise ship, as happened in June 1994, is of much greater concern than if the same number of cases were diagnosed in the whole country. In calculating a rate, the denominator is generally the *population at risk*. The rate of ovarian cancer in a city of one million, for example, would be calculated by dividing the number of cases by the female population, not the total population of the city.

Two kinds of frequency measures are commonly used in epidemiology: incidence rates and prevalence rates. *Incidence* is the rate of new cases of a disease in a defined population over a defined period of time. For notifiable diseases, it is ascertained by counting cases reported to the local or state health departments and dividing by the population at risk. Incidence measures the probability that a healthy person in that population developed the disease during that time. Incidence rates are useful in identifying causes of a disease. For example, the incidence of birth defects in Europe rose dramatically in 1960 after the introduction of thalidomide, a drug used as a sleeping pill. This sudden increase and its timing aroused suspicions that thalidomide use by pregnant women was the cause of limb deformities in their infants, a suspicion that was soon confirmed by epidemiologic studies.[2]

Prevalence is the total number of cases existing in a defined population at a specific time. It would generally be measured by doing a survey. Incidence and prevalence are related to each other, but the relationship depends on how long people live with the disease. If the disease tends to kill people in a short period of time, or if people recover from it rapidly, incidence could be high and prevalence low. However, for chronic diseases that are not lethal—arthritis, for example—the prevalence will be much higher than the incidence. For most diseases, prevalence rates change slowly and are less useful for epidemiologic studies. They are most useful in assessing the societal impact of a disease and planning for health care services.

Death rates, or mortality rates (the incidence of death), are often used as a measure of frequency for diseases that are usually fatal. Death rates are close to incidence rates for the most lethal diseases, such as pancreatic cancer. For diseases such as breast cancer, which many women survive, the mortality rate will be much smaller than the incidence rate. Death rates are not at all useful as a measure of frequency for diseases that are rarely fatal, such as arthritis.

The *distribution* of disease is the answer to the *who, when,* and *where* questions described in Chapter 4. The *who* question characterizes the disease victims by such factors as age, sex, race, and economic status. For example, the incidences of cancer and heart disease are greater in older people; measles and chicken pox occur more often in the young. Old women and young men are more likely to suffer broken bones than old men and young women. During the early months of the AIDS epidemic, the answer to the *who* question was gay men and intravenous drug abusers. This information led to some obvious hypotheses as to how the disease was transmitted.

The *when* question looks for trends in disease frequency over time: is the incidence increasing, decreasing, or remaining stable? The incidence of lung cancer in American men, for example, increased steadily from the 1930s to about 1990, when it peaked and began to decrease (see Figure 4–2). Meanwhile the incidence of stomach cancer has been declining. Posing another kind of *when* question, epidemiologists look for seasonal variations in incidence. The incidence of respiratory infections is always higher in the winter.

The *when* question is crucial in tracking an outbreak of infectious diseases such as hepatitis and legionellosis. Epidemiologists construct *epidemic curves,* like those shown in Figures 5–1 and 5–2, plotting the number of cases identified over a period of time. Figure 5–1 shows the epidemic curve for the 1976 outbreak of Legionnaires' disease in Philadelphia. It is clear from the epidemic curve that most of the victims were exposed to the virus at about the same time, and therefore, probably from the same source. Comparing the dates of onset with the dates of possible exposure, epidemiologists calculated an incubation period of two to ten days. An epidemic curve such as that shown in Figure 5–2 is typical of a disease that has been passed from one person to another.

The *where* question looks at comparisons of disease frequency in different countries, states, counties, or other geographical divisions. It may

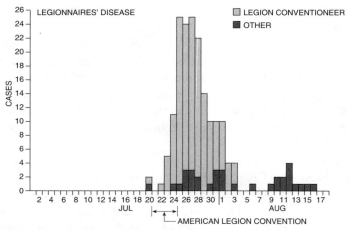

Dates of Onset of Illness in Cases of Legionnaires' Disease in Philadelphia, July 1–August 18, 1976
(Dates of onset of two cases are unknown)

Figure 5–1 Epidemic Curve for Legionnaires' Disease Outbreak
Source: Reprinted with permission from *The New England Journal of Medicine* 297 (22)
(1997): 1193. Copyright © 1977, Massachusetts Medical Association.

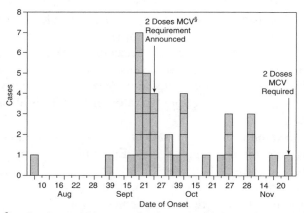

#A confirmed case was laboratory confirmed or met the clinical case definition and was
epidemiologically linked to a confirmed case. A clinical case was defined as an illness
characterized by generalized rash lasting ≥ 3 days; temperature ≥ 101°F (≥38.3°C); and
either cough, coryza, or conjunctivitis, n = 33.
†n = 33.
§Measles-containing vaccine.

Figure 5–2 Number of Confirmed# Measles Cases, by Date of Rash Onset,
by 3-Day Interval—Anchorage, Alaska, August 10–November 23, 1998†
Source: U.S. Centers for Disease Control and Prevention, "Transmission of Measles
Among Highly Vaccinated School Population—Anchorage, Alaska, 1998, "*Morbidity
and Mortality Weekly Report* 47 (1999): 1109–1110.

also look at comparisons between urban and rural populations. The hypothesis that fluoride protects against tooth decay arose from the observation that dental cavities were less common in children who lived in parts of the country that had high concentrations of fluoride in the water. Statistics on causes of death in different countries can be very suggestive in generating hypotheses as to causes of disease. The wide international variation in death rates from heart disease has been interpreted in a variety of ways, including that diet is a factor and that the pressures of urban life have a negative effect on health.

Thus, information on the *distribution* of disease leads to clues as to the *determinants* of disease. International comparisons of cancer mortality have led to hypotheses on causes of various kinds of cancer. For example, cancer of the colon and rectum is much more common in industrialized countries than in developing countries, which has led to the hypothesis that the difference is due to differences in diet: Americans eat meals rich in fat, meat, and dairy products, while diets in China are traditionally high in fiber, cereals, and vegetables. Evidence that environmental factors rather than genetics are to blame comes from studies of people who move from a low-rate country to a high-rate country. They tend to develop higher rates of the disease as they acquire the habits of the host country. In Japan, the rates of colorectal cancer have more than doubled since the 1950s, as Japanese have adopted more Western-style diets.[3] International patterns of breast cancer are somewhat similar to those of colorectal cancer, suggesting that similar dietary factors may play a role.[4,5] Rates of stomach cancer, on the other hand, are much higher in China and Japan than in the United States, evidence that different dietary factors may be involved. Stomach cancer rates in Japan have not fallen as much as colorectal cancer rates have risen, however, and breast cancer rates have not increased. Thus the diet, cancer relationship is not clear. Figure 5–3 illustrates these differences in cancer rates for the United States, Great Britain (which has a diet similar to Americans'), China, and Japan.

The relevance of the *who* and *when* questions are clearly illustrated in the evidence that smoking is a determinant of lung cancer. As seen in Figure 4–2, men began smoking cigarettes early in the twentieth century, and lung cancer rates began rising twenty years later. Women did not begin smoking in large numbers until the 1940s and 1950s. Lung cancer rates for women did not begin to rise sharply until the 1960s.[6]

Why are broken bones in young people more common in males, while among the elderly, they are more common in females? This question leads

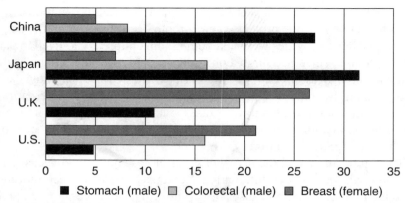

Figure 5–3 Cancer Rates in Four Countries, 2002
Source: Data from American Cancer Society, *Cancer Facts and Figures 2005*.

to an investigation of the determinants of broken bones. It turns out that these injuries in boys and young men are usually the result of accidents stemming from reckless behavior, which males are more likely to engage in than females. In the elderly, however, broken bones are usually the result of osteoporosis, or weakening of the bones, which is more common in females.

Epidemiology studies *human populations*, usually using observational rather than experimental methods. The alternative approach to investigating causes of disease is the biomedical approach, often using animal models of the disease, discussed in Part III. There are advantages and disadvantages to each approach. Experiments done on animals can yield clear answers as to cause and effect, while for ethical reasons experiments cannot usually be done on humans. However, there are always uncertainties about the relevance of animal studies to humans and whether the findings on animals can be extrapolated to people. The uncertainties and sources of error in the epidemiologic approach are examined in Chapter 6, and the problems in interpreting the results of animal experiments are discussed in Chapter 11.

KINDS OF EPIDEMIOLOGIC STUDIES

Answers to the *who*, *when*, and *where* questions provide clues as to the causes of a disease or the source of an outbreak. This type of analysis is called descriptive epidemiology. The hypotheses generated by descriptive epidemiology are tested by formal epidemiologic studies, designed to confirm or disprove the hypothesis. For example, in investigating the eosinophilia-myalgia syndrome (EMS) outbreak in New Mexico, described in Chapter 4, epidemiologists found an apparent link with the use of L-tryptophan. To test the hypothesis, they conducted a study comparing twelve cases of EMS with twenty-four controls, a case-control study (see the following section) that confirmed the link.[7]

Epidemiologic studies are sometimes referred to as prospective or retrospective. *Prospective* studies start in the present and monitor groups of people into the future, or they may start at a point in time in the past and look forward from there. *Retrospective* studies look into the past for causes of diseases that people currently suffer from. In both cases, investigators are looking for associations between *exposure* to the suspected causative factor and *disease* (or other health outcome).

INTERVENTION STUDIES

Intervention studies are the exception to the rule that epidemiologists do not do experiments. These studies are conducted in very much the same way as are laboratory experiments on animals. They are usually done to test a new treatment for a disease, such as a chemotherapy drug for cancer, or a preventive measure, such as a vaccine. In a clinical trial, one group is exposed to the intervention while a control group is not exposed. The investigators then watch and wait to see whether the response of the treatment group is different from the control group. Of course, only a limited number of interventions lend themselves to being tested in clinical trials for ethical reasons or because a trial is too difficult to conduct. In testing treatments for serious diseases, there must be enough doubt about the effectiveness of the intervention to justify withholding it from people who could be helped and enough evidence that it will not harm the people on whom it is tested.

The control group may be given a *placebo*—an inactive substance similar in appearance to the drug or vaccine being tested. When a treatment for a disease is already known to exist, trials may compare the new treatment with the existing treatment. The purpose of the placebo is to prevent subjects from knowing whether they are receiving the intervention. Many trials over the years have found that up to a third of patients respond to a placebo as if it were the intervention, reporting that they feel better or that they suffered side effects. This is the *placebo effect*. The drug being tested must show a higher response rate than the placebo if it is to be considered effective.

The most convincing clinical trials are conducted in a *randomized, double-blind* manner. *Randomized* means that each subject is assigned to the treatment group or the control group at random. This helps to equalize the groups with respect to unknown and known factors that might affect the results. *Double-blind* means that both the patient and the doctor are blind as to whether the patient is receiving the drug or a placebo. One reason that the doctor should also be blinded is that studies have shown patients to respond more favorably to a treatment that the doctor believes in. Another reason is to prevent the possibility that doctors might interpret the patient's condition differently if they know how the patient was being treated.

In a therapeutic clinical trial, both the experimental group and the control group are patients who have the disease for which a therapy is being tested. Therapeutic trials are being conducted at all times by pharmaceutical companies testing new drugs. The Food and Drug Administration (FDA) requires that the safety and effectiveness of a new drug must be demonstrated in a properly conducted clinical trial before it can be approved for marketing.

A classic example of a randomized, double-blind clinical trial of a preventive intervention is the field trial of the polio vaccine in 1954. Polio, then a greatly dreaded disease in the United States, killed and paralyzed children and adults. President Franklin Roosevelt, for example, had paralysis of the legs from polio, which he had contracted at the age of thirty-nine when he was already active in politics and public service.[8] In 1952, 21,269 cases of paralytic polio were reported in the United States.[9] The development of a vaccine by Jonas Salk offered great hope for prevention of this scourge. Preliminary tests had shown the vaccine to be safe and to stimulate disease-fighting antibodies in the blood of people who had been vaccinated. Before the vaccine could be approved for widespread use, however, it had to be tested in a clinical trial to determine if it really could protect a large number of people against the disease. In 1954, some 400,000 school children in eleven states were given the Salk vaccine or a "dummy" vaccine (the placebo), and were then tracked through the end of the year to determine if they became ill with polio. The incidence of polio among the children who had received the vaccine was less than half that of those given the placebo vaccine.[10] This result demonstrated that polio immunization could reduce the incidence of disease; in fact, the use of the vaccine (or an oral vaccine developed by Albert Sabin in the 1960s) has virtually eliminated polio in the United States.

Another randomized controlled trial of a preventive intervention is the Physicians' Health Study, in which 22,000 American physicians participated. Two hypotheses were being tested: whether aspirin reduced mortality from heart disease and whether beta carotene decreased the incidence of cancer. The physicians were randomly divided into four groups: those who took aspirin and beta carotene, those who were given one or the other and a placebo, and those who were given placebos only. The trial began in 1983 and was scheduled to run until 1995. The aspirin part of the trial was halted in 1988, however, because it was clear by that time that the physicians taking aspirin had a much reduced risk of suffering a heart attack.[11] They were only 56 percent as likely to have a heart attack as the group taking the placebo. The beta carotene part of the trial, which continued until 1995, found no significant difference in the incidence of cancer between the group receiving the beta carotene and the placebo group.[12]

The Kingston-Newburgh study of fluoride for the prevention of tooth decay was another form of intervention study, a community trial. Before the study began, the schoolchildren of these two small cities on the Hudson River in New York State were similar in general health and the prevalence of tooth decay. For the study, fluoride was added to the water supply of Newburgh, beginning in 1945, while Kingston's water was not fluoridated. Ten years later, dental examinations were conducted on the schoolchildren in both cities. The children of Newburgh were found to have approximately half as many decayed, missing, or filled teeth as the children of Kingston had. No adverse health effects were found in the Newburgh children. This evidence was strongly supportive of the value of fluoridation in preventing tooth decay.[13]

COHORT STUDIES

Since such experiments are not possible for most hypotheses that epidemiologists want to test, methods have been devised by which investigators can link exposures to results by observation alone, without actively intervening in the lives of the study subjects. Probably the most accurate of these methods is the *cohort study*. In a typical cohort study, large numbers of people—all healthy at the time the study begins—are questioned concerning their exposure. They are then observed over a period of time, watching to see whether those who were exposed are more likely to develop the disease than those who were not. This approach is similar to performing an experiment, except that the people themselves have chosen whether they belong to the "exposed" group or the control group.

The Framingham Heart Study is a cohort study, as were the Doll-Hill and Hammond-Horn studies of smoking and lung cancer described in Chapter 4. Another well-known cohort study, still under way, is the Nurses' Health Study, which since 1976 has been following some 120,000 married female nurses, looking for factors that may be related to the development of breast cancer and other diseases. The participating nurses have been sent questionnaires every two years, asking about their diet, drinking and smoking habits, and use of drugs, including oral contraceptives. The study found that nurses had a 50 percent higher risk of breast cancer while they were taking oral contraceptives, but the risk fell back to normal after they stopped taking them. Another finding was that regular consumption of alcohol increases the risk of breast cancer by 10 to 40 percent.[14,15]

Epidemiologic studies are designed to determine not only the existence of an association between an exposure and a disease, but also the strength of that association. The measure of the strength of association obtained by cohort studies and intervention studies is the *relative risk*, which is the ratio of the incidence rate for persons exposed to the factor to the incidence rate for persons in the unexposed group. A relative risk of 1.0 means that there is no association between the exposure and the disease. A value greater than 1.0 indicates an increased risk from exposure, while a value less than 1.0 indicates a decreased risk.

Doll and Hill, in their study of British physicians, found that the relative risk of lung cancer in heavy smokers compared to nonsmokers was 23.7, a major effect.[16] The calculation that led to this conclusion is shown in Table 5–1. In the Nurses' Health Study, the relative risk of breast cancer for current contraceptive use is 1.5, while that for past use is 1.0, findings that are not very dramatic but suggest further studies are called for.[15] In the Physicians' Health Study, the relative risk of a heart attack for men taking aspirin was 0.56.[11] The decrease was significant enough to recommend that most older men might benefit from this preventive measure, but the recommendation would carry much less weight than a recommendation to stop smoking.

Table 5–1 Relative Risk for Lung Cancer in Heavy Smokers Compared to Nonsmokers

Exposure Category	Lung Cancer Death Rates Per 100,000 Persons
Heavy smokers	166
Nonsmokers	7
Relative risk	166/7 = 23.7

Source: Data from R. Doll and A. B. Hill, Lung Cancer and Other Causes of Death in Relation to Smoking: A Second Report on the Mortality of British Doctors, *British Medical Journal* (1956): 1071–1081.

CASE-CONTROL STUDIES

In contrast with cohort studies, which start out by measuring exposure and watching for the development of disease, *case-control studies* start with people who are already ill and look back to determine their exposure. Case-control studies are much more efficient than cohort studies in that they focus on a smaller number of people and can be completed relatively quickly. In a case-control study, cases—people who have the disease—are compared with controls, healthy individuals chosen to match the cases as much as possible in age, sex, and other factors that might be relevant to the disease. The investigator asks all participants the same questions concerning the extent of their exposure to factors hypothesized to have caused the disease. Small case-control studies are commonly done to follow up a hypothesis generated by "shoeleather epidemiology," as was done in the investigation of eosinophilia-myalgia syndrome and L-tryptophan described in Chapter 4 and previously in this chapter.

An important case-control study conducted in the mid-1980s sought the cause of Reye's syndrome, a deadly disease of children that occurred a few weeks after a child had recovered from a viral infection such as chicken pox. The study tested the hypothesis that the development of Reye's syndrome was linked to medications the child was given during the viral illness.[17] The cases were children who had been diagnosed with Reye's syndrome and reported a previous respiratory or gastrointestinal illness or chicken pox. Controls were children who did not have Reye's syndrome but who had recently been diagnosed with chicken pox or a

Table 5–2   Use of Salicylates and Reye's Syndrome

	Cases of Reye's Syndrome	Controls
Used salicylates	26	53
Did not use salicylates	1	87
Total	27	140

Odds Ratio: $\dfrac{26/1}{53/87} = \dfrac{26 \times 87}{53 \times 1} = \dfrac{2262}{53} = 42.7$

Source: From D. E. Lilienfeld and P. D. Stolley, *Foundations of Epidemiology*, 3rd ed. 1994. Oxford University Press, Inc. Data from E. S. Hurwitz et al., *Journal of the American Medical Association* 257 (1987): 1905–1911.

respiratory or gastrointestinal illness. Parents of the children in both groups were asked about what medications their children had received during the viral illness. Results of the study are shown in Table 5–2.

Case-control studies estimate the strength of the association between exposure and disease by calculating an *odds ratio*, which is an estimate of what the relative risk would be if a cohort study had been done. The odds ratio is calculated by dividing the ratio of exposed to nonexposed in the case group by the ratio of exposed to nonexposed in the control group. In the Reye's syndrome study, a link was found with the use of aspirin during the initial viral infection. From Table 5–2, the odds ratio is 26:1 divided by 53:87 = 42.7. The study indicates that children who are given aspirin to treat a viral infection are 42.7 times more likely to develop Reye's syndrome than children who did not take aspirin, a very strong association. As a result of this study, the FDA required drug producers to put warning labels on aspirin containers and pediatricians to advise parents to give their children acetominophen (Tylenol) rather than aspirin to treat infections.

A number of case-control studies have been done seeking causes of breast cancer, a particularly intractable problem as Chapter 11 discusses. The results of a British study exploring a possible link between breast cancer and the use of oral contraceptives are shown in Table 5–3. The cases consisted of 351 female breast cancer patients ages forty-five years and younger interviewed in eight hospitals between 1980 and 1984. The controls were 351 women of similar age who were hospitalized for other conditions during the same period. All the women were asked whether they had ever taken oral contraceptives and, if so, for how many years. Odds ratios were calculated for various exposures to oral contraceptives. The

Table 5–3 Relative Risk of Breast Cancer by Duration of Oral Contraceptive Use

Contraceptive Use	Breast Cancer Cases	Hospital Controls	Odds Ratio (Estimated Relative Risk)
No Use	235	273	1.0
<1 year	27	26	1.2
1–4 years	43	29	1.7
>4 years	46	23	2.3

Source: From D. E. Lilienfeld and P. D. Stolley. *Foundations of Epidemiology*, 3rd ed. 1994. Oxford University Press, Inc. Data from McPherson et al., *Brit J Cancer* 56 (1987): 653–660.

results indicate that use of oral contraceptives did increase the risk of developing breast cancer for women aged forty-five and under and that the risk increases with longer exposure. Women who took oral contraceptives for more than four years had more than double the risk of breast cancer compared to those who had never taken oral contraceptives.[17]

The results of the British breast cancer study are fairly consistent with those of the Nurses' Health Study, indicating that oral contraceptives increase the risk of breast cancer. However, the certainty of this conclusion is much smaller than the certainty that aspirin is a risk for Reye's syndrome. A smaller odds ratio (or relative risk) leads to a much less certain conclusion, as Chapter 6 further explains. In fact, a more recent case-control study that included large numbers of women, found no increased risk of breast cancer among women who had used oral contraceptives.[18] The study compared 4,575 women with breast cancer and 4,682 controls and found that the relative risk of breast cancer among current users of oral contraceptives was 1.0; among former users the relative risk was 0.9.

CONCLUSION

Epidemiologists study the distribution and determinants of frequency of disease in humans. Disease frequency is usually expressed as *incidence* rate: the number of new cases in a defined population at risk over a defined period of time, or *prevalence* rate: the number of existing cases in a defined population at a single point in time. Incidence rate is most useful in identifying causes of disease.

Descriptive epidemiology looks at distribution of disease by characteristics of the person (age, sex, ethnicity, personal habits, etc.), the place (variations by geographical areas), and the time (changes in incidence over the long term, seasonal variations, or time since an epidemic began). This information on the distribution of disease may lead to hypotheses about the determinants, or causes, of disease.

Hypotheses generated through descriptive epidemiology can be tested through systematic epidemiologic studies. There are several types of epidemiologic studies. Intervention studies are true experiments, in which subjects are assigned to either a test group (people who receive the intervention) or a control group (people who do not receive the intervention). The most common and rigorous type of intervention study is the randomized, double-blind clinical trial, used to test new drug treatments or preventive measures.

For most situations in which epidemiologists wish to investigate whether a certain exposure causes a certain disease, it would be unethical to conduct an intervention study. The next best thing is a cohort study, in which subjects are questioned about their exposures and then tracked over time, comparing the exposed group with the unexposed group to see whether the exposed group is more likely to develop the disease. The third major type of study is the case-control study, which begins with cases of the disease and questions each case about what they had been exposed to, comparing their answers with those of a healthy control group.

Epidemiologists study human populations, which limits the types of studies that can be done. However, epidemiology has provided some of the most useful information about factors that affect human health.

REFERENCES

1. B. MacMahon and D. Trichopoulos, *Epidemiology: Principles and Methods* (Boston: Little, Brown, 1996).
2. C. G. Hennekens and J. F. Buring, *Epidemiology in Medicine* (Boston: Little, Brown, 1987).
3. R. Doyle, "Colorectal Cancer Mortality among Men," *Scientific American* (January 1996), 27.
4. J. Kelsey and P. L. Horn-Ross, "Breast Cancer: Magnitude of the Problem and Descriptive Epidemiology," *Epidemiology Reviews* 15 (1993): 7–16.
5. American Cancer Society, *Cancer Facts and Figures—2004* (New York: 2004).
6. C. E. Bartecchi et al., "The Human Costs of Tobacco Use," *New England Journal of Medicine* 330 (1994): 907–912.

7. U.S. Centers for Disease Control and Prevention, "Eosinophilia-Myalgia Syndrome—New Mexico," *Morbidity and Mortality Weekly Report 38* (1989): 765–767.

8. J. P. Lash, *Eleanor and Franklin: The Story of Their Relationship* (New York: W.W. Norton, 1971).

9. M. B. Gregg and B. M. Nkowane, "Poliomyelitis," in ed. J. Last, Maxcy-Rosenau *Public Health and Preventive Medicine* (Norwalk, Connecticut: Appleton-Century-Croft, 1986), 173–176.

10. G. D. Friedman, *Primer of Epidemiology* (New York: McGraw Hill, 1994).

11. Steering Committee of the Physicians' Health Study Research Group, "Final Report on the Aspirin Component of the Ongoing Physicians' Health Study," *New England Journal of Medicine* 321 (1989): 129–135.

12. C. H. Hennekens et al., "Lack of Effect of Long-Term Supplementation with Beta Carotene on the Incidence of Malignant Neoplasms and Cardiovascular Disease," *New England Journal of Medicine* 334 (1996): 1145–1149.

13. E. R. Schlesinger et al., "Newburgh-Kingston Caries-Fluorine Study XIII. Pediatric Findings after Ten years," *Journal of the American Dental Association* 52 (1956): 296–306.

14. R. J. Lipnick et al., "Oral Contraceptives and Breast Cancer: A Prospective Cohort Study," *Journal of the American Medical Association* 255 (1986): 58–61.

15. M. P. Longnecker, "Alcoholic Beverage Consumption in Relation to Breast Cancer: Metaanalysis and Review," *Cancer Causes and Control* 5 (1994): 73–82.

16. R. Doll and A. B. Hill, "Lung Cancer and Other Causes of Death in Relation to Smoking: A Second Report on the Mortality of British Doctors," *British Medical Journal* 2 (1956): 1071–1081.

17. D. E. Lilienfeld and P. D. Stolley, *Foundations of Epidemiology* (New York: Oxford University Press, 1994), 227–228.

18. P. A. Marchbanks et al., "Oral Contraceptives and the Risk of Breast Cancer," *New England Journal of Medicine* 346 (2002): 2025–2032.

CHAPTER 6

Problems and Limits of Epidemiology

The Study of Humans

The ultimate goal of many epidemiologic studies is to determine the causes of disease. This is generally done by, first, observing a possible association between an exposure and an illness; second, by developing a hypothesis about a cause and effect relationship; and, third, by testing the hypothesis through a formal epidemiologic study. While the formal study can strongly support the conclusion that a certain exposure causes a certain disease, there are many potential sources of error in drawing such a conclusion. Studies of chronic diseases, which often have multiple determinants and develop over long periods of time, are especially prone to error.

PROBLEMS WITH STUDYING HUMANS

All epidemiologic studies have the advantage of studying humans rather than experimental animals; but also all are limited by that fact. Each type of epidemiologic study has its own strengths and weaknesses.

Consider the design of an epidemiologic study to test the hypothesis that a low-fat diet reduces the risk of heart disease. The average American already eats a high-fat diet and has a high risk of heart disease compared to residents of many other countries, so there is no ethical problem in asking people to participate in such an experiment, which should not harm their health more than their current practice.

The randomized controlled trial, the most rigorous form of intervention study described in Chapter 5, is the most similar in concept to a biomedical scientist's experiment with rats. Suppose researchers choose a group of subjects who have been eating an average American diet and divide them randomly into an experimental group, who will be instructed to eat a strict low-fat diet over the next five years, and a control group, who will be told to continue eating normally. Researchers will monitor both groups, watching for signs of heart disease and expect that, if their hypothesis is correct, fewer people in the low-fat group will become ill.

In fact, researchers are likely to be disappointed with the results. The problem is that it is impossible to control the behavior of human beings under such circumstances. If the experiment was being conducted using rats, researchers would feed them the assigned diets and could thus be certain of the relative exposures of the two groups. With people, however, even if researchers could find enough of them who would agree to participate in the experiment, it is unlikely that they would remain on the appropriate diet over the necessary length of time. People in the experimental group might succumb to temptation and drop out of the study or lie about what they have eaten. People in the control group might become concerned about their health and voluntarily cut back on the amount of fat they eat. It is unrealistic to expect to succeed at a randomized controlled trial that requires people to alter their behavior over a significant period of time, unless the subjects have a special motivation to participate—if they are suffering from a serious disease, for example—and participation in a trial is their only chance to have access to a new, potentially more effective treatment.

To test the dietary hypothesis, researchers might try, instead of a randomized controlled trial, a cohort study. They would choose a large group of people, ask them detailed questions about their diets, and then, over the next five years, compare the health of those who already eat a low-fat diet with those who eat an average American diet. This would not require people to change their behavior. The problem with this scenario is that people who have voluntarily chosen to eat a low-fat diet may differ in other respects from the group who eat the average diet. The low-fat group members are likely be more health conscious in general. They may be less likely to smoke and more likely to exercise, for example. These people, therefore, would have a reduced risk of heart disease even if a low-fat diet did not have a protective effect.

The third type of study, the case-control study, has its own difficulties. In this study, researchers would choose a group of people who already have heart disease; perhaps they would go to a hospital and interview patients recovering from a heart attack. A comparable group of people who do not have heart disease would serve as the control group. Researchers would question people in both groups about their diets over the past five years and decide whether the diets should be classified as high-fat or low-fat. If the researchers' hypothesis is correct, the patients who have had a heart attack will report a diet higher in fat than the control group. This approach also has obvious problems. People are not likely to remember what they ate in the past, or they might be embarrassed to admit how self-indulgent they have been. The information researchers obtain concerning exposure in the case-control trial may not be reliable.

These difficulties do not mean that no valid conclusion can be drawn from any kind of epidemiologic study. However, they demonstrate the types of errors that different kinds of studies may be prone to and alert researchers about what to watch out for in choosing a study design and interpreting the results.

SOURCES OF ERROR

News reports of new health studies can often be confusing. Sometimes there are conflicting reports on the health effects of various substances. Coffee is reported to cause heart disease; then it is reported that there is no such effect. Oat bran is reported to prevent cancer; then it is reported to make no difference. Fish is good for your heart; fish is full of toxic chemicals that may cause harm. All these contradictions tend to make people distrustful of the news and uncertain about how to protect their health. Since most of these news reports are based on epidemiologic studies, it is useful to understand possible sources of error in such studies and how to look for the truth in the reports.

One of the most common reasons for a study to lead to a wrong conclusion is that the reported result is merely a random variation and that the association is merely due to chance. Chapter 7 discusses some of the factors involved in determining whether a result is statistically significant. As a general rule, epidemiologic studies of chronic diseases require large numbers of subjects to draw valid conclusions. Causes of these diseases are usually complex, and there are usually long periods between exposures to possible causes and the development of illness, making it difficult to draw conclusions about associations between exposure and disease. The cause-and-effect relationship is not obvious—as it is, for example, when a bullet in the heart causes death, or exposure of an unvaccinated child to the measles virus causes the child to develop measles in ten to twelve days. The weaker the relationship between exposure and disease, the larger the group of people that must be studied for the relationship to be evident. If the group being studied is too small, a cause-and-effect relationship is likely to be missed or a spurious relationship will show up by chance alone. One of the reasons that the Doll-Hill and Hammond-Horn results concerning smoking and lung cancer are so convincing is that they involved such large numbers of subjects (see Chapter 4).

There are a number of other possible sources of error that well-designed studies may be able to avoid. For example, the cohort study of a low-fat diet proposed previously may be invalidated by the presence of *confounding variables*, smoking and exercise. Confounding variables are factors that are associated with the exposure and that may independently affect the risk of developing the disease. Such an error may have occurred in a 1980s study that suggested coffee drinking could cause pancreatic cancer, a finding that has not been replicated in other studies. Since many heavy coffee drinkers were also smokers, there are suspicions that the cancer was caused by the smoking rather than the coffee.[1] To eliminate the errors caused by smoking as a confounding variable, researchers might conduct the study only on nonsmokers. Alternatively, there are statistical techniques for adjusting the results to compensate for confounding variables as long as the investigator is clever enough to think of possible factors that may affect the result and to take them into consideration when collecting the data and calculating the results. While the investigators in the study of coffee corrected for smoking over the five-year period before the cancer was diagnosed, the correction may have been inadequate.

Bias, or systematic error, may be introduced into a study in a number of ways. *Selection bias* is a particular problem in choosing subjects for a case-control study. For example, if the cases of heart disease are chosen from hospitalized patients recovering from heart attacks, and the controls are hospitalized patients being treated for a digestive disorder that causes extreme discomfort from eating fatty foods, the study may suggest an exaggerated effect of dietary fat on heart disease. The results would probably be different if the controls were patients recovering from the effects of motor vehicle crashes, whose diet might be more like the average American's. Selection bias may also occur when there is a systematic difference between people who choose—or are chosen—to participate in a study and those who do not. For example, in a case-control study that found exposure to high electromagnetic fields (EMF) from power lines increased the risk of childhood cancer, the controls were chosen by a process of telephone random digit dialing until a child was located who matched a case by age and sex. Cases and controls were compared, and cases were found to have higher exposure to EMF. However, the cases also were also found to be of lower socioeconomic status; they were more likely to live in areas of high traffic density, and their mothers were more likely to smoke. The random digit dialing had created a bias: the control group was more affluent and consequently less exposed to confounding poverty-associated factors.[1]

An extreme example of selection bias—one that no well-trained epidemiologist would make—was seen in the report of the author Shere Hite on male and female relationships. Out of 100,000 questionnaires on women's attitudes about men and sex that Hite distributed, only 4,500 replies were received. Hite reported that 84 percent of the women in the study were dissatisfied with their intimate relationships, results that were widely publicized. The low response rate suggests that selection bias was operating and that the most dissatisfied women were responding preferentially to the survey.[2]

Cohort studies, which tend to extend over many years, are likely to suffer from a form of selection bias caused by people dropping out or being untraceable when results are being sought. If people who get sick drop out at a different rate from those who remain healthy, the results will be compromised. Subjects who are lost to follow-up may be more likely than those who are traceable to have entered an institution or moved in with family, indicating a serious health problem. A high dropout rate casts doubt on the results of any epidemiologic study.

Reporting bias or *recall bias* is a common problem in case-control studies. It occurs if the study group and the control group systematically report differently even if the exposure was the same. Subjects' reports of their dietary intake are notoriously unreliable. For example, underweight individuals consistently overreport their fat intake, while obese individuals underreport it.[1] Similarly, studies attempting to relate certain diseases to alcohol consumption may suffer from reporting bias because people who drink heavily tend to underreport their consumption. Case control studies that attempt to determine causes of birth defects are especially subject to recall bias, since the mother of a child born with a malformation is likely to have thought a great deal about what might have caused the problem, while mothers of healthy children would be less likely to notice an unusual exposure.

PROVING CAUSE AND EFFECT

For the most part, epidemiologic studies, no matter how well designed to avoid error, cannot prove cause and effect. However, there are several factors that can be combined to make the cause-and-effect relationship almost certain.

As discussed previously, a study with a large number of subjects is more likely to yield a valid result than a small study. The stronger the association measured between exposure and disease—the higher the relative risk or odds ratio—the more likely that there is a true cause-and-effect relationship. For example, the Reye's syndrome case-control study described in Chapter 5 found a 42.7 odds ratio from exposure to aspirin during a viral infection. The British case-control study linking birth control pills to breast cancer found only a 2.3 odds ratio, while the Nurses' Health Study—a cohort study—found at most a 1.5 relative risk of breast cancer from oral contraceptives. The much stronger association found in the Reye's syndrome study makes it highly probable that aspirin causes the syndrome in children, while the breast cancer results could possibly be due to some error or alternative explanation.

A dose-response relationship between the exposure and the risk of disease is evidence supporting the exposure as the cause of the disease. Some of the earliest evidence that long-term exposure to low levels of x-rays had adverse health consequences came from a study comparing the mortality rates of physicians exposed to different amounts of radiation. Radiologists had the lowest life expectancy of the three groups of specialists studied. Ophthalmologists-otolaryngologists, who have little exposure to radiation, had the highest life expectancy. Internists, whose exposure was intermediate, had intermediate life expectancy, confirming a dose-response effect—the higher the dose of radiation, the greater the effect on lifespan.[3]

Epidemiologic evidence is more convincing if there is a known biological explanation for an association between an exposure and a disease. Studies suggesting that EMFs cause leukemia and other forms of cancer have been looked on with skepticism because of the lack of a known mechanism by which such low energy fields could have a biological effect. The question is unresolved. However, a number of other exposures have been identified by epidemiologic studies as causes of disease before a biological explanation was found. For example, strong epidemiologic evidence that cigarette smoking was a major cause of heart disease existed long before there was any biological explanation, and the mechanism is still not well understood.

The most important indication that an epidemiologic result is valid is that it is consistent with other investigations. If several independently designed and conducted studies lead to the same conclusion, it is unlikely that the conclusion resulted from bias or other error. If the reports are conflicting, however, people must be wary of accepting any of the results.

EPIDEMIOLOGIC STUDIES OF HORMONE REPLACEMENT THERAPY—CONFUSING RESULTS

When women reach menopause at age fifty or so, their natural production of the hormone estrogen drops significantly. Many women at this stage of life begin to have menopausal symptoms that can be troubling: hot flashes that disturb their well-being during the day and their sleep at night and vaginal dryness that causes discomfort and interferes with sexual activity. Prescription of estrogen supplements relieves these symptoms, and this treatment became popular in the 1960s. Estrogen was promoted to help keep women "feminine forever" as promised in a best-selling book of that title by Robert Wilson, published in 1966.[4] Large numbers of post-menopausal women took the hormone in the hope that it would keep them looking and feeling younger, improve their memory, and stave off other effects of aging. When evidence appeared in the 1970s that women taking estrogen had an increased risk of uterine cancer, the problem was averted by adding another hormone, progesterone, to the prescription. Progesterone countered the effect of the estrogen on the uterus without appearing to diminish its positive effects on other organs. There was good reason to believe that these female hormones protect women. Rates of cardiovascular disease are well-known to be much lower among women than men until middle age, increasing after menopause to match the rates among men. And older women are much more likely to suffer from osteoporosis, thinning of the bones that leads to fractures. It was reasonable to think that hormone supplements might also protect women against these problems.

Numerous epidemiologic studies over the years supported the protective role of estrogen for bones and hearts. Most notably, the Nurses' Health Study, the large cohort study, ongoing since 1976, found that women taking hormone therapy had a 61 percent lower risk of heart disease and a 75 percent lower risk of hip fractures.[5] These studies found small increases in breast cancer risk, but the trade-off seemed worthwhile for many women. In 1999, approximately 38 percent of postmenopausal women in the United States were using hormone-replacement therapy (HRT).[6]

Then in July 2002 the news broke that HRT was not as beneficial as it had seemed. The previous positive evidence had all come from observational studies. Meanwhile, a huge clinical trial, called the Women's Health Initiative (WHI), had been under way since 1991. The researchers announced in 2002 that the WHI had been stopped early on the basis that the risks had been found to outweigh the benefits.[7] Women randomly assigned to take a combination pill of estrogen plus progesterone were found to have a higher risk of breast cancer than women taking a placebo, which was not surprising. The surprise was that women taking the pill were also found to have a higher risk of heart attack, stroke, and blood clots. The women in the experimental group had fewer hip fractures and fewer cases of colorectal cancer than the control group, but this protective effect was not enough to outweigh the risks.

The news from the WHI study seemed to contradict the overwhelming evidence from cohort studies that HRT protected women against heart disease. However, the WHI was a clinical trial, the gold standard of epidemiologic studies, and thus was much less likely to be subject to bias.

Since reports of the study were published, epidemiologists have been struggling to understand why the two kinds of studies produced such conflicting results. There are still many unanswered questions, but one important factor seems to be selection bias. Women in the observational studies who chose to take hormones were healthier to begin with and had healthier habits than the women who did not take the hormones. Many other factors appear to be involved, including biologic differences between the women in the two types of studies (women in the Nurses' Health Study were younger and thinner than the women in the WHI) and a bias stemming from the fact that cohort studies tend to miss adverse events that occur very soon after a therapy is begun.[8] Now that the WHI has been halted, it is unlikely that all the questions will be answered. For ethical reasons, no future study could randomly assign healthy women to take HRT.

ETHICS IN EPIDEMIOLOGY

Most epidemiologic studies are observational and have little potential for harm. There are exceptions, however, especially in the conduct of intervention studies. Nowadays, strict ethical limitations apply in any study involving humans. These rules were developed in reaction to abuses such as those by Dr. Joseph Mengele, who conducted medical experiments on concentration camp prisoners during World War II. Ethical abuses have not been limited to Nazi war criminals, however. At one time, medical researchers in the United States were not overly concerned with the rights of the experimental subjects, who were often poor patients or captive populations such as prisoners or inmates of mental institutions. That changed in 1972, when news of the Tuskegee syphilis study shocked the nation.

Syphilis was a dreaded disease for hundreds of years, inspiring some of the same moral revulsion as AIDS sometimes does today. Spread by sexual contact, syphilis had an unpredictable course that, over a variable number of years, could lead to a range of grim symptoms, including blindness, heart disease, dementia, and paralysis. It was sometimes treated with an arsenic-containing drug called salvarsan, which had been shown to cure syphilis in rabbits but which was not always effective in human patients and sometimes killed them. Some scientists suspected that the disease was not as uniformly dire as its reputation suggested and that the treatment might be worse than the disease. This conclusion was supported by the results of a Norwegian study of untreated syphilis done during the early part of the twentieth century, which found that up to 75 percent of the patients were symptom-free after more than twenty years of the disease.[9]

In 1932, the U.S. Public Health Service and scientists from Tuskegee Institute began a similar study of about 400 black men in Macon County, Alabama, where syphilis was rampant: 40 percent of the population suffered from the disease. The purpose was to observe the course of the disease in these men, who were not to receive treatment. In part because it was not common practice at the time, and in part because the subjects were poor, black, and uneducated, the investigators did not try to explain what they intended to do or ask the subjects' permission. The men were told they had "bad blood" and were enticed to participate with free "treatments" and physical examinations, free hot lunches, and free burials. In the 1940s, penicillin was discovered and became standard treatment for syphilis, but the Tuskegee subjects did not receive the antibiotic until after the story broke in 1972.[9]

There is some question about whether the men were physically harmed by the withholding of antibiotic treatment. The course of the disease is complicated and the surviving subjects were in a late, noninfectious stage by the time penicillin was discovered, perhaps too late to help most of them. However this study raised a number of ethical issues, the major one being that the men were deceived. They were not told what syphilis was or that they were part of a study, and they were led to believe that they were receiving treatment. Furthermore, one of the tests that was done on the subjects was a spinal tap, a painful procedure that uses a needle to withdraw spinal fluid, which has the potential of causing harmful side effects, including—rarely—paralysis. This treatment would not likely have been tolerated by white, middle class Americans, and many critics have concluded that the study was racist.

The outcry that followed the publicity about the Tuskegee study in 1972 led directly to the establishment of rules for the conduct of human experimentation. All institutions that receive federal funds must follow these rules. The rules require that every research subject must be informed of the purpose of a study and its risks and benefits. The subjects must freely consent to participate. In addition, any such study must be approved in advance by an institutional review board, a committee that includes representatives of the community as well as other scientists, who must agree that the study is well designed, that its benefits outweigh its risks, and that the subjects are truly given the opportunity for informed consent. Clinical trials are halted if the treatment group is clearly showing better or worse results than the control group. This was done, for example, in the portion of the Physicians' Health Study that looked at aspirin's effectiveness in preventing heart attacks when it became clear that subjects taking aspirin were suffering fewer heart attacks than those in the placebo group.[10] It was also done in the WHI study of HRT, described previously.

Even with the current strict ethical guidelines, there are a number of controversial issues surrounding clinical trials, including whether such trials should be conducted at all, who should participate, whether informed consent is truly possible, and whether unproven treatments should be available outside of clinical trials.

All these controversies came to the foreground several years ago in connection with the AIDS epidemic. People with AIDS knew they had a fatal disease that had no known cure, and they were desperate. Many of them were very politically active. People with AIDS argued that they did not have time to wait for clinical trials to test the efficacy of every promising new drug. They wanted immediate access to any new drug that showed promise in the laboratory, because they would prefer to try something— anything that had the slightest chance of working—rather than face certain death. On the other side of the argument is the history of useless therapies that have been employed for years or decades because no one had ever done a scientific test of whether they worked. This is a true ethical dilemma pitting the individual against society. Can we deny today's AIDS patient a treatment that "can't hurt" and might help so that future patients will have access to treatment whose effectiveness is proven? The pressure for untested therapies has now been eased somewhat by the development of new drugs that have been found effective in clinical trials.

The use of bleeding by eighteenth century physicians as a treatment for almost any illness is well known. The argument for this therapy appears foolish to us today, but the absence of curative power was not obvious to the people of the time. Similarly, tonsillectomies were performed on more than half of all children in the 1930s through the 1950s in the belief that the operation prevented rheumatic fever and other complications of strep throat. In fact, there was no evidence for this benefit. It is now believed that a tonsillectomy may make strep infection more difficult to diagnose and treat.[11] Unfortunately, it is difficult to do a randomized controlled study on a treatment that is already in wide use, because people do not want to risk being randomized to a placebo treatment if they suspect the active therapy is effective.

Such was the case in the 1990s with bone marrow transplant as a treatment for advanced breast cancer. With conventional chemotherapy, a patient had a 40 to 45 percent chance of living for five more years. A procedure that removed a woman's bone marrow, administered a much higher dose of chemotherapy, and then replaced the bone marrow, in theory gave her a better chance of surviving the cancer. However, the procedure was itself arduous and risky, subjecting the woman to a 5 percent chance of dying of complications of the treatment. It was also expensive, costing up to $200,000. The National Cancer Institute sponsored three large national trials of bone marrow transplants for breast cancer. The trials required women to be randomly assigned to the transplant group or to conventional therapy. Many were reluctant to participate in a trial because they wanted the most aggressive treatment, perceiving that this offered them the best chance of survival. There were questions whether it was ethical to deny women the chance to choose the procedure, forcing them into a trial. On the other hand, might the practice of offering the transplant outside of a trial be unethical because surgeons and hospitals have a conflict of interest, perhaps influencing patients to choose a treatment from which they, the surgeons and hospitals, stand to profit financially? Insurance companies were forced through lawsuits and political pressure to pay for these expensive and arduous procedures without evidence that they saved lives.[12]

Fortunately, enough women ultimately enrolled in the clinical trials to test the hypothesis. The women are still being followed, so the answer is not yet final, but an analysis published in 2004 of five randomized controlled trials strongly suggested that the intensive procedure did not lead to better survival for women who underwent it and, in fact, led to more treatment-related deaths and adverse side effects than suffered by the controls.[13] Meanwhile, the authors pointed out, over 40,000 American women with breast cancer had the procedure done outside of clinical trials, while only 1,000 were recruited to participate in the clinical trials. If the clinical trials had not been completed, bone marrow transplant might have become the standard treatment, although, like bleeding and tonsillectomies, they appear to do more harm than good.

CONCLUSION

Epidemiologic studies are susceptible to many sources of error. Confounding factors may influence the results, suggesting an association where none exists. Bias may be introduced in the selection of cases or controls, in the reporting of exposures or outcomes, or in the disproportionate loss to follow-up of exposed and unexposed groups. Nevertheless, epidemiology is the basic science of public health. It is the only science of disease that focuses on human experience.

Epidemiology cannot prove cause and effect. However, certain characteristics of well-designed studies can make them very convincing. Studies with large numbers of subjects are more likely to be valid than smaller studies. A strong measure of association between exposure and disease, in the form of a high relative risk or odds ratio, is likely to indicate a true cause-and-effect relationship. A dose-response relationship that shows increasing risks from higher exposures adds to the validity of a study. A known biological explanation for an association between an exposure and a disease makes epidemiologic evidence more convincing than if there is no known mechanism.

While observational studies have little potential for harming people, many ethical questions have been raised about clinical trials. In response to well-publicized abuses of the past, clinical trials and many other epidemiologic studies are required to be approved by committees, called institutional review boards, that ensure that the subjects' rights are protected. Other ethical concerns have been raised about the availability of treatments that have not been tested in clinical trials.

Despite its flaws, epidemiology is still of necessity the basic science of public health. Epidemiologic data, when confirmed by repeated, well-designed studies and supported by the results of biomedical experiments in the laboratory, provide the best certainty as to the causes and cures of human disease.

REFERENCES

1. G. Taubes, "Epidemiology Faces Its Limits," *Science* 269 (1995): 164–169.
2. S. Hite, *Women and Love: A Cultural Revolution in Progress* (New York: Alfred A. Knopf, 1987), described in V. Cohn and L. Cope, *News and Numbers: A Guide to Reporting Statistical Claims and Controversies in Health and Other Fields, 2nd ed,* (Ames: Iowa State University Press, 2001), 154–156.
3. R. Seltser and P. E. Sartwell, "The Influence of Occupational Exposure to Radiation on the Mortality of American Radiologists and Other Medical Specialists," *American Journal of Epidemiology* 81 (1965): 2–22.
4. R. A. Wilson, *Feminine Forever* (New York: M. Evans and Company, 1966).
5. G. Kolata, "Hormone Studies: What Went Wrong?" *New York Times* (April 22, 2003): F1.
6. J. E. Manson and K. A. Martin, "Postmenopausal Hormone-Replacement Therapy," *New England Journal of Medicine*, 345 (2001): 34–40.

7. G. Kolata, "Citing Risks, U.S. Will Halt Study of Drugs for Hormones," *New York Times* (July 9, 2002): A1.
8. F. Grodstein et al., "Understanding the Divergent Data on Postmenopausal Hormone Therapy," *New England Journal of Medicine* 348 (2003): 645–650.
9. G. E. Pence, *Classic Cases in Medical Ethics: Accounts of the Cases That Have Shaped Medical Ethics, with Philosophical, Legal, and Historical Backgrounds* (New York: McGraw-Hill, 1990).
10. Steering Committee of the Physicians' Health Study Research Group, Final Report on the Aspirin Component of the Ongoing Physicians' Health Study, *New England Journal of Medicine* 321 (1989): 129–135.
11. E. Braunwald et al., eds., *Harrison's Principles of Internal Medicine* (New York: McGraw-Hill, 1987).
12. G. Kolata, "Women Resist Trials to Test Marrow Transplants," *New York Times* (February 15, 1995): E8.
13. C. Farquhar et al., "High Dose Chemotherapy and Autologous Bone Marrow or Stem Cell Transplantation versus Conventional Chemotherapy for Women with Metastatic Breast Cancer," *Cochrane Database of Systematic Reviews* 2 (2004).

CHAPTER 7

Statistics: Making Sense of Uncertainty

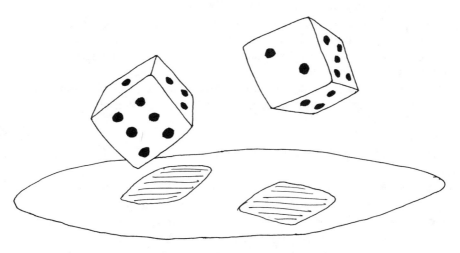

Understanding Uncertainty

The science of epidemiology rests on statistics. In fact, all public health, because it is concerned with populations, relies on statistics to provide and interpret data. Chapter 8 discusses the kinds of data government collects to assess the need for public health programs and evaluate public health progress. The term *statistics* refers to both the numbers that describe the health of populations and the science that helps to interpret those numbers.

The science of statistics is a set of concepts and methods used to analyze data in order to extract information. The public health sciences discussed in this book depend on the collection of data and the use of statistics to interpret the data. Statistics makes possible the translation of data into information about causes and effects, health risks, and disease cures.

Because health is determined by many factors—genes, behavior, exposure to infectious organisms or environmental chemicals—that interact in complex ways in each individual, it is often not obvious when or whether specific factors are causing specific health effects. As Chapter 6 discussed, there are ethical limits to the kinds of studies that can be conducted on human populations, and as Chapter 9 explains, there are limits to the conclusions that can be drawn from biomedical studies. Only by systematically applying statistical concepts and methods can scientists sometimes tease out the one influence among many that may be causing a change in some people's health. Often however, statistics indicates that an apparent health effect may be simply a random occurrence.

The problems and limits of epidemiology discussed in Chapter 6 are defined in large part by the uncertainties that are the subject of the science of statistics. This chapter discusses the science of statistics in more detail, describing how it is used to clarify conclusions from a study or a test, to put numbers into perspective so that researchers can make comparisons and discern trends, and to show the limits of human knowledge.

THE UNCERTAINTY OF SCIENCE

People expect science to provide answers to the health questions that concern them. In many cases, science has satisfied these expectations. But the answers are not as definitive as people want them to be. Science has shown that the human immunodeficiency virus (HIV) causes AIDS. But that does not mean that a woman will definitely contract AIDS from having sex with an HIV-positive man. Her chance of becoming infected with the virus from one act of unprotected intercourse is about one in 1,000.[1] Similarly, scientific studies show that as a treatment for early breast cancer, a lumpectomy followed by radiation is as effective as a mastectomy. However, a woman who chooses the lumpectomy still has a 10 percent chance of cancer recurrence.[2] Both the woman who had unprotected intercourse and the woman who chose the lumpectomy would dearly like to believe that they will be one of those in the majority of cases who will have a positive outcome, but science cannot promise them that. It can only say, statistically, that if 1,000 women like her have unprotected sex with an HIV positive man, 999 probably will fare well while one will not, and if 100 women with early breast cancer have a lumpectomy with radiation, ninety probably will be cancer-free after twelve years while ten will have a recurrence.

In many cases, there are not enough data even to give us that degree of certainty, or the data that exists are too ambiguous to allow a valid conclusion. In 1995, the *New England Journal of Medicine* published a report that the Nurses' Health Study (a cohort study), which had monitored 122,000 nurses for fourteen years, found a 30 to 70 percent increased risk of breast cancer in women who had taken hormone replacement therapy after menopause.[3] One month later, the *Journal of the American Medical Association* published the results of a case-control study that found no increased risk from the hormones. Five hundred women who had newly diagnosed breast cancer were no more likely to have taken postmenopausal hormones than a control group of 500 healthy women.[4] In the *New York Times* article reporting on the studies, each researcher is quoted suggesting possible flaws in the other study.[5] There is little comfort in these results for women seeking certainty on whether the therapy will improve their health. According to one view, postmenopausal estrogen was clearly worth the possible risk of cancer because it appeared to decrease a woman's risk of heart disease and osteoporosis. In the opposing argument, women could achieve similar benefits without the possible risk through exercise, avoiding smoking, eating a low fat diet, maintaining a normal weight, and taking aspirin. Now, as discussed in Chapter 6, a clinical trial has contradicted some of the findings of each of these studies; hormone replacement therapy has been found to increase cancer risk and not to benefit the heart.

Contradictory results from epidemiologic studies are common. As discussed in Chapter 6, there are many possible sources of error in this kind of research, including bias and confounding, which are factors irrelevant to the hypothesis being tested that may affect a result or conclusion. Later in this chapter, additional factors to be considered in assessing whether to believe a study's conclusions are examined.

People sometimes demand certainty even when science cannot provide it, as occurred in 1997 over the issue of whether women ages forty through forty-nine should be screened for breast cancer using mammography. Studies have shown that routinely testing women aged fifty and over with the breast x rays could reduce breast cancer mortality in the population. However, studies done on younger women had not demonstrated a life-saving benefit overall for this group. Routine screening of these women increases their radiation exposure, perhaps raising the risk of causing cancer. It also yields many false alarms, leading to unnecessary medical testing, and major expense. The follow-up testing itself may cause complications, and many of the women remain anxious even after cancer is ruled out.[6]

When Dr. Richard Klausner, the director of the National Cancer Institute (NCI), called together a panel of experts in early 1997 to advise him on the issue, the panel concluded that the benefit did not justify the risks and costs and recommended that each woman make the decision in consultation with her doctor, considering her own particular medical and family history. The public and political response was heated: after a barrage of media publicity, the Senate voted ninety-eight to zero to endorse a non-binding resolution that the NCI should recommend mammography for women in their forties. A letter signed by thirty-nine congresswomen stated that, "without definitive guidelines, the lives of too many women are at risk to permit further delay," assuming that screening could save lives despite the lack of evidence.[7(p.1104)] In the end, director Klausner, with the support of President Clinton and Secretary of Health and Human Services Donna Shalala, recommended that women in their forties should be screened. It seems clear that pressure from politicians eager to get credit for supporting women's health led to a pretense of scientific certainty where none existed.

On this question, further analysis supported the politicians. While the "melee that followed the meeting will not qualify for a place in the history of public health's most distinguishing scientific or policy moments," in the words of one analyst, there is now a far better understanding of the issue, and mammography has been shown to be life-saving for women forty to forty-nine.[8] In part this is due to improved technology that is more sensitive at detecting tumors in the denser breast tissue of younger women. In part it is due to the recognition that tumors occurring in younger women tend to grow more rapidly, meaning that screening must be done more often to be effective at recognizing cancer early enough to save lives. The evidence now shows that mammography screening should be done annually in women under fifty, while every two years may be sufficient for older women.

There are few instances when politicians pressure scientists to change their opinion as they did in the breast cancer screening case. However, many people concerned about how to protect their health find it frustrating when today's news seems to contradict yesterday's. As this example shows, science is a work in progress. In the words of Dr. Arnold Relman, former editor of the *New England Journal of Medicine*, "Most scientific information is of a probable nature, and we are only talking about probabilities, not certainty. What we are concluding is the best opinion at the moment, and things may be updated in the future."[9(p.11)]

PROBABILITY

Scientists quantify uncertainty by measuring *probabilities*. Since all events, including all experimental results, can be influenced by chance, probabilities are used to describe the variety and frequency of past outcomes under similar conditions as a way of predicting what should happen in the future. Aristotle said that, "the probable is what usually happens." Statisticians know that the improbable happens more often than most people think.[9(p.19)]

One concept scientists use to express the degree of probability or improbability of a certain result in an experiment is the p value. The p value expresses the probability that the observed result could have occurred by chance alone. A p value of 0.05 means that if an experiment were repeated 100 times, the same answer would result ninety-five of those times, while five times would yield a different answer. If a person tosses a coin five times in a row, it is improbable that it will come up the same—heads or tails—every time. However, if each student in a class of sixteen conducts the experiment, it is probable that one student will get the identical result in all five tosses. The probability of that occurrence is one chance in 16, or 0.0625 ($p = 0.0625$). Thus a p value of 0.05 says that the probability that an experimental result occurred by chance alone is less than the probability of tossing five heads or five tails in a row. A p value of 0.05 or less has been arbitrarily taken as the criterion for a result to be considered statistically significant.

Another way to express the degree of certainty of an experimental result is by calculating a confidence interval. This is a range of values within which the true result probably falls. The narrower the confidence interval, the lower the likelihood of random error. Confidence intervals are often expressed as margins of error, as in political polling, when a politician's support might be estimated at 50 percent plus or minus 3 percent. The confidence interval would be 47 percent to 53 percent.[9]

While p values and confidence intervals are useful concepts in deciding how seriously to take an experimental result, it is wrong to place too much confidence in an experiment just because it yields a low p value or a narrow confidence interval. There may be up to 10,000 clinical trials of cancer treatment under way at any time. If a p value of 0.05 is taken to imply statistical significance, five out of every 100 ineffective treatments would appear to be beneficial, errors caused purely by chance.[9] Thus, large numbers of cancer treatments could be in clinical use that are actually not effective. Other reasons that a low-p-value study could lead to an erroneous conclusion could be bias or confounding, which are systematic errors. The results of the study discussed in Chapter 6 that linked coffee-drinking with pancreatic cancer were statistically significant with a p value of 0.001.[10] The conclusion is thought to be wrong not because of random error but because the cancer was caused by smoking rather than coffee drinking.[11]

The fact that the probable is not always what happens leads to the Law of Small Probabilities.[9] The most improbable things are bound to happen occasionally, like throwing heads five times in a row, or even—very rarely—ninety-nine times. This means, for example, that a few people with apparently fatal illnesses will inexplicably recover. They may be convinced that their recovery was caused by something they did, giving rise— if their story is publicized—to a new vogue in quack therapies. But because their recovery was merely a random deviation from the probable, other patients will not get the same benefit.

Another consequence of the Law of Small Probabilities is the phenomenon of cancer clusters. Every now and then a community will discover that it is the site of an unusual concentration of some kind of cancer, such as childhood leukemia, and everyone will be highly alarmed. Is there a carcinogen in the air or the drinking water that is causing the problem? Could the cause be electromagnetic fields, which residents blamed for the cluster of six cases of childhood cancer between 1981 and 1988 among the pupils of an elementary school in Montecito, California?[12] Under great political pressure, the local and state government will investigate, but no acceptable explanation will be found. In the case of the electromagnetic fields, it could not be proven that they were *not* responsible for the cluster, but as more studies are done the evidence is still ambiguous. Most such clusters are due to statistical variation, like an unusual run of tails in a coin toss. Such an explanation tends to be unsatisfactory to community residents, who may accuse the government of a cover-up; but after the investigation the number of new cases usually returns to more or less normal levels, and the sense of alarm subsides.

If a cluster is very large, it is likely not to be a random variation—just as in coin tossing, fifty heads in a row is a much less likely outcome than five heads unless there is something wrong with the coin. A large number of cases is said to confer *power* on a study. Power is the probability of finding an effect if there is, in fact, an effect. Thus, an epidemiologic study that includes large numbers of subjects is more powerful than a small study, and the results are more likely to be valid, although systematic errors due to bias or confounding can be present in even the largest studies.

In designing studies of any kind, statisticians can calculate the size of the study population necessary to find an effect of a certain size if it exists. Studies with low power are likely to produce *false negative* results (i.e., to find no effect when there actually is one). *False positives* occur when the study finds an effect that is not real (i.e., when a random variation appears to be a true effect). In a study of epidemiologic studies, a statistician examined the power of each of seventy-one clinical trials that reported no effect. He concluded that 70 percent of the studies did not have enough patients to detect a 25 percent difference in outcome between the experimental group and the control group. Even a 50 percent difference in outcome would have been undetectable in half the studies.[9] This common weakness in epidemiologic studies is probably one reason for the contradictory results so often reported in the news.

In the review of high dose chemotherapy and bone marrow transplant for advanced breast cancer, described in Chapter 6, the authors addressed the question of whether the studies had enough power to detect a 15 percent improvement in survival for the treated women. They concluded that the individual studies did not have sufficient power, but that the systematic review of all studies combined did have the power to detect a 15 percent difference if it existed. No difference was detected at a 95 percent confidence level.[13] They noted, however, that a smaller difference in outcomes might still be possible and raised the question of how much difference would be clinically relevant. Would it be acceptable for a woman to undergo the arduous treatment if her chance of survival was only 10 percent better? That is a question that cannot be answered by statisticians.

THE STATISTICS OF SCREENING TESTS

In public health's mission to prevent disease and disability, secondary prevention—early detection and treatment—plays an important role. When the causes of a disease are not well understood, as in breast cancer, little is known about primary prevention. The best public health measure is to screen the population at risk so as to detect the disease early, when it is most treatable. Screening is also an important component of programs to control HIV/AIDS by identifying HIV-infected individuals so that they can be treated and counseled about how to avoid spreading the virus to others. As discussed in Chapter 12, newborn babies are routinely screened for certain congenital diseases that can be treated before permanent damage is done to the infants' developing brains and bodies.

While laboratory tests to be used in screening programs should ideally be highly accurate, most are likely to yield either false positives or false negatives. Tests may be highly *sensitive*, meaning that they yield few false negatives, or they may be highly *specific*, meaning that they yield few false positives. Many highly sensitive tests are not very specific and vice versa. For most public health screening programs, sensitive tests are desirable in order to avoid missing any individual with a serious disease who could be helped by some intervention. However, inexpensive, sensitive tests chosen to encourage testing of as many at-risk individuals as possible are often not very specific. When a positive result is found, more specific tests are then conducted to determine if the first finding was accurate. For example, if a sensitive mammogram finds a suspicious spot in a woman's breast, the test is usually followed up with a biopsy to determine whether the spot is indeed cancerous.

When screening is done for rare conditions, the rate of false positives may be as high as or higher than the number of true positives, leading to a lot of follow-up testing on perfectly normal people, a problem with screening women in their forties with mammography for breast cancer. Such a situation occurred in 1987 when the states of Illinois and Louisiana mandated premarital screening for HIV.[14] With the rate of HIV infection in the general, heterosexual population quite low, a great many healthy people were unnecessarily alarmed and subjected to further tests, while very few HIV-positive people were identified. Some couples went to neighboring states to marry to avoid the nuisance. The programs were discontinued within a year.

RATES AND OTHER CALCULATED STATISTICS

As seen in Chapter 5, epidemiology makes extensive use of *rates* in studies of disease distribution and determinants. Rates put the raw numbers into perspective by relating them to the size of the population being considered. As Chapter 8 discusses, vast quantities of health-related data are collected on the American population, data that are used to assess the people's health and to evaluate the effectiveness of public health programs. For these purposes too, the raw numbers are subjected to statistical adjustments that yield various rates useful in making comparisons and identifying trends.

For example, knowing that a city has 500 deaths per year is not very informative unless the population of the city is known. Death rates are generally expressed as the number of deaths per 1,000 people. Five hundred deaths per year is a low number for a city of 100,000, while it is high for a city of 50,000. The overall death rate in the United States was 8.3 per 1,000 people in 2003.[15] The same data may yield different rates depending on the population referred to. For example, the birth rate, like the death rate, is defined as the number of live births per 1,000 people. The fertility rate, by contrast, gives the number of live births per 1,000 women ages fifteen to forty-four. Two communities with the same fertility rate may have quite different birth rates if one contains many young women and the other is older with a higher proportion of men. Both rates start with the same raw number—the number of live births—but use a different population for reference. In 2002, the birth of 4,021,726 babies in the United States led to a birth rate of 13.9 per thousand people overall. The fertility rate ranged from 57.4 per 1,000 non-Hispanic white women to 102.8 per 1,000 women of Mexican origin.[16]

Other rates commonly used as indicators of a community's health are the infant mortality rate and the maternal mortality rate, as discussed in

Florida's Population is Older than Average

Chapter 18. The infant mortality rate is the number of infants that die before their first birthday in a year, divided by the number of live births in that year. The maternal mortality rate is the number of deaths among women associated with pregnancy and delivery in a year, divided by the number of live births in that year.

For some purposes, the numbers can be made still more useful by converting *crude rates* into *adjusted rates*. Death rates are often adjusted for the age of the population. The adjustment uses a statistical calculation to make the populations being examined equivalent to one another. For example, the crude mortality rate in Florida is much higher than the crude mortality rate in Alaska. There is no cause for alarm in Florida, however. Since the average age of the Floridians is significantly higher than the average age of Alaskans—in fact many residents of other states retire to Florida and die there, while people who move to Alaska are likely to be young—it is to be expected that a higher percentage of Floridians die each year. After adjusting the mortality rate to what it would be if the average ages of the two populations were the same, the differences fade away. The age-adjusted mortality rates are almost the same, as seen in Table 7–1. Rates may also be adjusted for other factors relevant to health, such as gender, race, ethnicity, and so forth. For example, because males have higher mortality rates at all ages than females, it may sometimes be useful to calculate a gender-adjusted mortality rate for a population that has a higher proportion than average of one gender.

Rates are also calculated on a *group-specific* basis. Researchers may calculate rates for males alone or females alone, blacks, whites, Hispanics, members of other racial or ethnic groups, and people in defined age groups. This kind of data informs us, for example, that males have higher

Table 7–1   Age-Adjusted Mortality Rates for Florida and Alaska, 2002

	Florida	Alaska
Crude death rate per 100,000	1,004.1	471.1
Age-adjusted death rate per 100,000	786.4	790.5

Source: Data from *National Vital Statistics Reports. Deaths: Preliminary Data for 2002.* National Center for Health Statistics (2004).

mortality rates than females in the same age group, and that blacks have higher mortality rates than whites of the same sex and age. It is common to break down death rates from various causes by age group, revealing that different age groups are more likely to die of different causes. For example, death rates from cancer, stroke, and heart disease increase steadily with age. Death rates from AIDS, however, are highest for the thirty-five to forty-four year age group and fall to almost zero for those older than seventy-five years.[17(Table 42)] Death rates from firearms injuries and motor vehicle injuries are highest in the twenty to twenty-four age group, although death rates from motor vehicle injuries are almost as high for people over seventy-five.[17(Table 47)]

Further calculations can be done using age-specific death rates to yield *life expectancies*, data that is intuitively meaningful in describing the health of a population. Life expectancy is the average number of years of life remaining to people at a particular age, and it reflects the mortality conditions of the period when the calculation is made. Life expectancies may be determined by race, sex, or other characteristics using age-specific death rates for the population with that characteristic. The most common figure used in comparing the health of various populations is the life expectancy at birth. As seen in Table 7–2, life expectancies at birth in the United States have been increasing since 1900. In Russia, however, as the Prologue discusses, life expectancies have been declining since the fall of the Soviet Union, reflecting many societal ills that have led to poorer health of the population there. Table 7–3 shows the life expectancy at birth for males and females of selected countries.

Another calculated concept that is sometimes used as a measure of premature mortality is *years of potential life lost (YPLL)*. It gives greater weight to deaths of young people, appropriate to the priorities of public health, which has the goal not of eliminating death entirely but of enabling people to live out their natural lifespan with a minimum of illness and disability. Calculation of YPLL arbitrarily chooses seventy-five as the age before which a death is considered premature (age sixty-five was used before 1996). As an example, the death of a person fifteen to twenty-four years of age counts as 55.5 YPLL before age seventy-five. Unintentional injuries rank relatively high in YPLL because they are likely to kill young people, who have more years to lose. Table 7–4 shows a comparison of the leading causes of death in the United States with the leading causes of YPLL.

Table 7-2 Life Expectancy at Birth According to Race and Sex, United States, Selected Years 1900–2002

Specified Age and Year	All Races			White			Black or African American[1]		
	Both Sexes	Male	Female	Both Sexes	Male	Female	Both Sexes	Male	Female
At Birth				Remaining Life Expectancy in Years					
1900[2,3]	47.3	46.3	48.3	47.6	46.6	48.7	33.0	32.5	33.5
1950[3]	68.2	65.6	71.1	69.1	66.5	72.2	60.8	59.1	62.9
1960[3]	69.7	66.6	73.1	70.6	67.4	74.1	63.6	61.1	66.3
1970	70.8	67.1	74.7	71.7	68.0	75.6	64.1	60.0	68.3
1980	73.7	70.0	77.4	74.4	70.7	78.1	68.1	63.8	72.5
1985	74.7	71.1	78.2	75.3	71.8	78.7	69.3	65.0	73.4
1990	75.4	71.8	78.8	76.1	72.7	79.4	69.1	64.5	73.6
1991	75.5	72.0	78.9	76.3	72.9	79.6	69.3	64.6	73.8
1992	75.8	72.3	79.1	76.5	73.2	79.8	69.6	65.0	73.9
1993	75.5	72.2	78.8	76.3	73.1	79.5	69.2	64.6	73.7
1994	75.7	72.4	79.0	76.5	73.3	79.6	69.5	64.9	73.9
1995	75.8	72.5	78.9	76.5	73.4	79.6	69.6	65.2	73.9
1996	76.1	73.1	79.1	76.8	73.9	79.7	70.2	66.1	74.2
1997	76.5	73.6	79.4	77.1	74.3	79.9	71.1	67.2	74.7
1998	76.7	73.8	79.5	77.3	74.5	80.0	71.3	67.6	74.8
1999	76.7	73.9	79.4	77.3	74.6	79.9	71.4	67.8	74.7
2000[4]	77.0	74.3	79.7	77.6	74.9	80.1	71.9	68.3	75.2
2001	77.2	74.4	79.8	77.7	75.0	80.2	72.2	68.6	75.5
2002	77.3	74.5	79.9	77.7	75.1	80.3	72.3	68.8	75.6

Source: National Center for Health Statistics. *Health, United States, 2004,* Table 27. www.cdc.gov/nchs/data/hus/hus04.pdf

[1]Data shown for 1900–60 are for the nonwhite population.

[2]Death registration area only. The death registration area increased from 10 States and the District of Columbia in 1900 to the coterminous United States in 1933. See Appendix II, Registration area.

[3]Includes deaths of persons who were not residents of the 50 States and the District of Columbia.

[4]Life expectancies (LEs) for 2000 were revised and may differ from those shown previously.

Table 7–3 Life Expectancy at Birth, According to Sex, Selected Countries, 1980 and 1999

Country	Male		Female	
	1980	*1999*	*1980*	*1999*
Hong Kong	71.6	77.7	77.9	83.2
Japan	73.4	77.1	78.8	84.0
Sweden	72.8	77.1	78.8	81.9
Switzerland	72.8	76.8	79.6	82.5
Israel	72.2	76.6	75.8	80.6
Canada	71.7	76.3	78.9	81.7
Australia	71.0	76.2	78.1	81.8
New Zealand	70.0	75.7	76.3	80.8
Norway	72.3	75.6	79.2	81.1
Italy	70.6	75.6	77.4	82.3
Singapore	69.8	75.6	74.7	79.7
Greece	72.2	75.5	76.8	80.6
Netherlands	72.5	75.3	79.2	80.5
England and Wales	70.8	75.3	78.8	80.1
Spain	72.5	75.1	78.6	82.1
Austria	69.0	75.1	76.1	81.0
France	70.2	75.0	78.4	82.5
Costa Rica	71.8	74.9	77.0	79.8
Germany	69.6	74.7	76.1	80.7
Belgium	79.0	74.4	76.8	80.6
Northern Ireland	68.3	74.3	75.0	79.2
Denmark	71.2	74.2	77.7	79.0
United States	70.0	73.9	77.4	79.4
Ireland	70.1	73.9	75.6	79.1
Finland	69.2	73.8	77.6	81.0
Cuba	72.2	73.3	—	77.5
Scotland	69.0	72.7	75.2	78.1
Chile	—	72.4	—	78.1
Portugal	67.7	72.2	75.2	79.2
Czech Republic	66.8	71.4	73.9	78.2
Puerto Rico	70.8	70.7	76.9	79.8
Slovakia	66.8	69.0	74.3	77.2
Poland	66.0	68.2	74.4	77.2
Bulgaria	68.5	67.4	73.9	74.9
Romania	66.6	67.1	71.9	74.2
Hungary	65.5	66.4	72.7	75.2
Russian Federation	61.4	59.4	73.0	72.0

Source: Health United States, 2004, Table 26. National Center for Health Statistics.

Table 7–4   YPLL before Age 75 by Cause of Death and Rank, 2002

Cause of Death	YPLL	Rank by YPLL	Rank by No. of Deaths
Cancer	1,622.7	1	2
Heart Disease	1,212.7	2	1
Unintentional injuries	1,079.2	3	5
Suicide	346.7	4	11*
Homicide	274.4	5	13*
Cerebrovascular disease	208.1	6	3
Chronic lower respiratory disease	184.5	7	4
Diabetes	184.3	8	6
HIV disease	161.8	9	**
Chronic liver disease and cirrhosis	160.5	10	12*
Influenza and pneumonia	82.7	11	7

*in 2001.
**not one of the 15 leading causes of death in 2001.
Source: Data from *Health, United States, 2004*, Table 30. National Center for Health Statistics 2001 data from National Vital Statistics System, National Center for Health Statistics.

RISK ASSESSMENT AND RISK PERCEPTION

While some statistical concepts may seem difficult and confusing, people have an intuitive understanding of statistics affecting their everyday lives. They understand that the future is full of uncertainties, and they intuitively try to minimize risks or at least weigh risks against expected benefits. Their intuitive judgment of risks, however, often does not coincide with the more scientific estimates of statisticians. It turns out that while judgments of risk by the average person include statistical estimates that are often fairly accurate, they are also influenced by psychological factors that should perhaps be taken into consideration by the public health professionals.

Public health's mission to protect the population from disease and injury requires governments to minimize risks or at least weigh risks against expected benefits, just as individuals do in their own lives. The formal process of *risk assessment* identifies events and exposures that may be harmful to humans and estimates the probabilities of their occurrence as well as the extent of harm they may cause.

Risk assessment is often done on the basis of historical data: for example, one may predict that the number of motor vehicle crashes next year will be similar to the number this year, increasing or decreasing according to the trend established over the past several years. Risks that certain chemicals cause cancer in humans are usually estimated by analogy with data obtained from animal studies. For many situations, however, there is little basis on which to make comparisons. In such cases, assessing risks involves making many assumptions, some of which may be little better than guesses. To estimate the probability of a mishap in a new technology, various possible chains of events are considered, and a risk for something going wrong is estimated for each step, perhaps by analogy with conventional technology. Risks of the individual steps are then added or multiplied to obtain a risk for the whole. This approach was used, for example, when nuclear power plants were first introduced, and it helped engineers to identify what kind of safety devices should be incorporated to reduce the probability of failure.[18] Still, the assessment appears to have underestimated the risk at Three Mile Island, as discussed later in this section.

Using such methods, scientists calculate probabilities that various injurious events will occur and rank them in order, as shown in Table 7–5. According to an analysis published in 1987, experts said that the most risky activities and technologies were motor vehicles, smoking, alcoholic beverages, handguns, and undergoing surgery. When the representatives of the general public were asked for their perceptions of risks, however, they headed their list with nuclear power, which was ranked twentieth by the experts. Other risks that people tend to rank higher than the experts do are electromagnetic fields, genetic engineering, and radioactive waste.[19]

As a result of the apparent irrationality of the public in response to risks that the experts estimated to be small, a field of study has developed concerning *risk perception*. While experts assess risk on the basis of expected mortality as predicted from historical data, the general public includes other considerations in its assessments. When these additional criteria are analyzed, it appears that the public's perception may not be so irrational after all.

Risk perception researchers have found that people's concern about a risk is affected by certain associated factors. For example, familiar risks are more acceptable than unfamiliar ones. Risks that people perceive they have control over are more acceptable than those that are uncontrollable. A risk with potentially catastrophic consequences is unacceptable, even if it is highly unlikely to occur. People are more likely to accept a risk from

Table 7–5   Ordering of perceived risk for 30 activities and technologies. The ordering is based on the geometric mean risk ratings within each group. Rank 1 represents the most risky activity or technology.

Activity or Technology	League of Women Voters	College Students	Experts
Nuclear power	1	1	20
Motor vehicles	2	5	1
Handguns	3	2	4
Smoking	4	3	2
Motorcycles	5	6	6
Alcoholic beverages	6	7	3
General (private) aviation	7	15	12
Police work	8	8	17
Pesticides	9	4	8
Surgery	10	11	5
Fire fighting	11	10	18
Large construction	12	14	13
Hunting	13	18	23
Spray cans	14	13	26
Mountain climbing	15	22	29
Bicycles	16	24	15
Commercial aviation	17	16	16
Electric power (non-nuclear)	18	19	9
Swimming	19	30	10
Contraceptives	20	9	11
Skiing	21	25	30
X-rays	22	17	7
High school and college football	23	26	27
Railroads	24	23	19
Food preservatives	25	12	14
Food coloring	26	20	21
Power mowers	27	28	28
Prescription antibiotics	28	21	24
Home appliances	29	27	22
Vaccinations	30	29	25

Source: Reprinted with permission from P. Slovic *Science* 236: 281. Copyright 1987, AAAS.

an activity that is perceived as beneficial, but they want the risks and benefits to be distributed equitably.

Risk perception researchers classify risks on two scales: dreadness and knowability. The more dread the risk, the less acceptable it is; similarly,

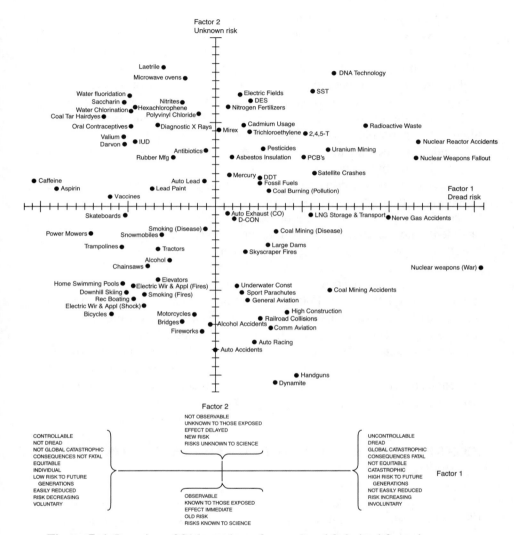

Figure 7–1 Location of 81 hazards on factors 1 and 2 derived from the relationships among 18 risk characteristics. Each factor is made up of a combination of characteristics as indicated by the lower diagram
Source: Reprinted from P. Slovic et al., in *Perilous Progress: Managing the Hazards of Technology*, (p. 108) by R. W. Kates et al., ed., with permission of P. Slovic.

unknown risks are less acceptable than known risks. Figure 7–1 maps various risks according to the concern they evoke on the two scales. Thus although driving an automobile is, statistically, one of the most risky activities, it does not arouse great anxiety because it is neither dread nor unknown. Moreover, people perceive that they have control when they are driving, and the benefit is obvious to them. Conversely, a nuclear reactor accident is highly dread, and thus is perceived by the public as more risky than the experts believe it to be. People perceive that they lack control over nuclear reactors, and the benefits of nuclear power may not be clear to people who live in their vicinity.

The public's perception about nuclear power gained credibility after the 1979 accident at the Three Mile Island nuclear reactor in Pennsylvania. According to the experts, numerous safeguards were in place to prevent an accident, and the chance of a serious breakdown was remote. In fact, the safety systems worked to the extent that there was no disaster; no one was killed, and there was no significant radiation leak. Nevertheless, the fact that the breakdown occurred at all sent a signal that the experts may have underestimated the risks. Public opposition to nuclear power increased dramatically, and stricter requirements for reactor safety were imposed, raising construction and operating costs. The coup de grace for nuclear power came with the 1986 reactor meltdown at Chernobyl, in the Ukraine, which did cause lost lives and widespread radioactive contamination of the environment. Since then, no new nuclear reactors have opened in the United States.[19]

COST-BENEFIT ANALYSIS AND OTHER EVALUATION METHODS

Other types of statistical calculations are frequently carried out as part of public health decision-making. One of these is *cost benefit analysis*, discussed in Chapter 3 in relation to the controversy over setting occupational exposure limits to benzene.

Cost benefit analysis weighs the estimated cost of implementing a policy against the estimated benefit, usually in monetary terms. In the benzene example, the industry argued that setting a low exposure limit would be very expensive and that the benefit in lives saved would be small. Part of the difficulty in conducting such an analysis is the determination of what monetary value to place on a life saved. In other situations, the analysis provides a clearer justification for a program. For example, an analysis of the costs and benefits of immunizing children against measles, mumps, and rubella—comparing the costs of the immunization program with the costs of caring for the thousands of patients whose disease would not have been prevented if no immunizations had been done—yielded a 13 to 1 ratio of benefits to costs.[20]

Another evaluation technique is *cost-effectiveness analysis*, which compares the efficiency of different methods of attaining the same objective. For example, it may be so expensive to prevent heart attacks in healthy men by prescribing cholesterol-lowering drugs that a cost-effectiveness analysis would conclude that it is cheaper to skip the drugs and provide cardiac care for the men who do suffer an attack. Cost benefit analysis and cost-effectiveness analysis "cannot serve as the sole or primary determinant of a health care decision," according to a congressional report, but the process of identifying and considering all the relevant costs and benefits can improve decision-making.[21(p.211)]

CONCLUSION

The world is full of uncertainty. Science may not always be able to provide answers to people's questions. Statistics is a way to learn, at least, how certain people can be about what they think they know.

Statistics is a tool widely used in public health. Most epidemiologic studies and most studies in the other public health sciences depend on statistics to analyze data and interpret findings. Statistical analyses can establish the probability that what was observed occurred by chance alone. A measure commonly used to indicate the probability that a study finding is the result of chance is the p value. Even when a low p value indicates that a result is statistically significant, there is still a chance that the result is not valid, even if all sources of bias are ruled out. Studies with large numbers of subjects are more likely to be valid than small studies, although sources of error other than random variation are still possible in large studies.

Knowledge of statistics is also important in evaluating screening tests, used as a secondary prevention approach to detect diseases so that they can be treated at an early stage. Tests that are highly sensitive tend to yield false positives, while tests that are highly specific tend to yield false negatives. Most screening programs use sensitive tests and follow up positive results with more expensive tests that are both highly sensitive and highly specific. For conditions that are rare in the population being screened, the rate of false positives may be higher than the rate of true positives.

To put numbers into perspective, they are often converted into rates. Rates are useful in epidemiology and as a way of understanding the importance of the vast quantities of data used for assessment of the public's health and evaluation of public health programs. Rates commonly used as public health indicators are mortality (death) rates, birth rates, fertility rates, infant mortality rates, and maternal mortality rates. Rates may be statistically adjusted to make them comparable from one population to another. Age-specific rates can also be calculated. Other statistical concepts useful as public health indicators are life expectancy and years of potential life lost.

Public health's efforts to protect the population may require calculations of risk. Risk assessment is a formal process of calculating probabilities of various injurious events. The scientific assessment of risk sometimes conflicts with people's perception of risk.

Public health is based on science, including the science of statistics, which is the science of uncertainty. To paraphrase statistician and author Robert Hooke, scientific studies are often the only way to answer people's questions, but the studies do not produce "unassailable, universal truths that should be carved on stone tablets." Instead, they produce statistics, which must be interpreted.[9(p.64)]

REFERENCES

1. R. Royce et al., "Sexual Transmission of HIV," *New England Journal of Medicine* 336 (1997): 1072–1078.
2. B. Fisher et al., "Reanalysis and Results After 12 Years of Follow-Up in a Randomized Clinical Trial Comparing Total Mastectomy With Lumpectomy With or Without Irradiation in the Treatment of Breast Cancer," *New England Journal of Medicine* 333 (1995): 1456–1467.
3. G. A. Colditz et al., "The Use of Estrogens and Progestins and the Risk of Breast Cancer in Postmenopausal Women," *New England Journal of Medicine* 332 (1995): 1589–1593.
4. J. L. Stanford et al., "Combined Estrogen and Progestin Hormone Replacement Therapy in Relation to Risk of Breast Cancer in Middle Aged Women," *Journal of the American Medical Association* 274 (1995): 137–142.
5. G. Kolata, "Cancer Link Contradicted by New Hormone Study," *New York Times* (July 12, 1995): A1.
6. H. C. Sox, "Benefit and Harm Associated with Screening for Breast Cancer," *New England Journal of Medicine* 338 (1998): 1145–1146.

7. V. L. Ernster, "Mammography Screening for Women Aged 40 through 49—A Guidelines Saga and a Clarion Call for Informed Decision Making," *American Journal of Public Health* 87 (1997): 1103–1106.

8. R. A. Smith, "Breast Cancer Screening among Women Younger than 50: A Current Assessment of the Issues," *CA-A Cancer Journal for Clinicians* 50 (2000): 312–336.

9. V. Cohn and L. Cope, *News and Numbers: A Guide to Reporting Statistical Claims and Controversies in Health and Other Fields*, 2nd ed. (Ames: Iowa State University Press, 2001), 11.

10. B. MacMahon et al., "Coffee and Cancer of the Pancreas," *New England Journal of Medicine*, 304 (1981): 630–633.

11. G. Taubes, "Epidemiology Faces Its Limits," *Science* 269 (1995): 164–169.

12. P. Brodeur, *The Great Power-Line Cover-Up: How the Utilities and the Government Are Trying to Hide the Cancer Hazards Posed by Electromagnetic Fields* (Boston: Little, Brown, 1993).

13. C. Farquhar et al., "High Dose Chemotherapy and Autologous Bone Marrow or Stem Cell Transplantation versus Conventional Chemotherapy for Women with Metastatic Breast Cancer," *Cochrane Database of Systematic Reviews* 1 (2005) http://gateway.ut.ovid.com/gw1/ovidweb.egi. Accessed April 25, 2005.

14. R. Bayer, *Private Acts, Social Consequences: AIDS and the Politics of Public Health* (New York: The Free Press, 1989).

15. U.S. Centers for Disease Control and Prevention, "Births, Marriages, Divorces, and Deaths: Provisional Data for 2003," *National Vital Statistics Report* 52, No. 22 (June 10, 2004).

16. J. A. Martin et al., "Births: Final Data for 2002," *National Vital Statistics Report* 52, No. 10 (December 17, 2003).

17. U.S. Centers for Disease Control and Prevention, *Health, United States, 2003*.

18. R. Wilson and E. A. C. Crouch, "Risk Assessment and Comparisons: An Introduction," *Science* 236 (1987): 267–270.

19. P. Slovic, "Perception of Risk," *Science* 236 (1987): 280–285.

20. C. C. White et al., "Benefits, Risks and Costs of Immunization for Measles, Mumps and Rubella," *American Journal of Public Health* 75 (1995): 739.

21. G. Pickett and J. J. Hanlon, *Public Health: Administration and Practice* (St. Louis, Missouri: Times Mirror/Mosby, 1990), 211.

CHAPTER 8

The Role of Data in Public Health

Collecting Data

Just as a doctor monitors the health of a patient by taking vital signs—blood pressure, heart rate, and so forth—public health workers monitor the health of a community by collecting and analyzing health data. These data are called health statistics. Statistics are a vital part of public health's assessment function, used to identify special risk groups, detect new health threats, plan public health programs and evaluate their success, and prepare government budgets. The statistics collected by federal, state, and local government are the raw material for research on epidemiology, environmental health, social and behavioral factors in health, and the medical care system.

At the federal level, the primary agency that collects, analyzes, and reports data on the health of Americans is the National Center for Health Statistics (NCHS), part of the Centers for Disease Control and Prevention (CDC). NCHS collects its data in two main ways: First, states periodically transmit data they have compiled from local records; vital statistics, including virtually all births and deaths, are routinely collected this way. Second, NCHS conducts periodic surveys of representative samples of the population, seeking information on certain characteristics such as health status, lifestyle and health-related behavior, onset and diagnosis of illness and disability, and the use of medical care. Some of these surveys are conducted on a state-by-state basis and the data is thus useful to states and local communities. In addition, other federal agencies that collect data for their own purposes share it with NCHS.

VITAL STATISTICS

Births and deaths are the most basic, reliable, and complete data collected. Virtually every birth and death in the United States is recorded on a birth certificate or death certificate. Certificates are filed with the local registrar by the attending physician, midwife, undertaker, or other attendant. The state health department is generally responsible for collecting these reports and transmitting them periodically to the NCHS.

Birth certificates contain information supplied by the mother about the child's family, including names, addresses, ages, race and ethnicity, and education levels. Medical and health information is supplied by the hospital, doctor, or other birth attendant concerning prenatal care, birth weight, medical risk factors, complications of labor and delivery, obstetrical procedures, and abnormalities in the newborn. In the past decade many states have added a question on the mother's use of tobacco to the birth certificate. Much of the information on the certificate is confidential, withheld even from the person represented by the certificate. Its main use is for public health research, providing the data that can be used to relate features of the mother and her pregnancy to the health of the child.

The information on death certificates is subject to a number of uncertainties, depending on how well the informant knew the deceased and the circumstances of the death. For example, information on parents, education, and occupation may not be known if the decedent is an elderly person with no surviving relatives. There is often difficulty in the accuracy and consistency with which causes of death are specified. Incorrect diagnoses are common; in the absence of an autopsy, the exact cause of death may not be known. If a number of conditions contribute to the fatal process, underlying causes and immediate causes may be confused. For some conditions such as AIDS or suicide, the cause of death may be misstated deliberately by the local official because of social stigma.

In addition to births and deaths, vital statistics include marriages and divorces, spontaneous fetal deaths, and abortions. Data on marriages and divorces are legal events that require universal reporting, but they are not very interesting from a public health point of view. Reporting of spontaneous fetal deaths is incomplete, especially for those that occur relatively early in a pregnancy; many may be unrecognized. Induced abortions are also probably somewhat under-reported. In some states, the name of the woman who had the abortion is not included in the report for reasons of confidentiality.

Because infant mortality is an important public health issue, the NCHS has set up a special computer system which links vital records of infants born during a given year who died before their first birthday. The linkage allows researchers to compare information on the death certificates with that on the birth certificates, providing insight into factors that contribute to infant deaths.

THE CENSUS

As discussed in Chapter 7, the data collected through the vital statistics system and other methods must be converted into rates if they are to be useful for many public health purposes. The calculation requires information on the number of people in the population being referred to, the number that serves as the denominator when a vital statistic is used as the numerator. To calculate age-adjusted or age-specific rates it is necessary to know how many people are in each age group. To determine sex-specific or race-specific rates, one needs to know how many males and females there are and how many blacks, whites, Hispanics, and people of other races in each sex and each age group. This information is collected by the U.S. Census Bureau, part of the Department of Commerce. Without an accurate count of the American population and all its characteristics, the government's health statistics would not be accurate.

As every schoolchild knows, the Constitution requires that the population of the United States be counted every ten years to determine each state's representation in the House of Representatives. Based on that simple mandate, the Census Bureau has developed a national survey that provides data not only on the geographical distribution of the population and its sex, age, and ethnic characteristics, but also on a wide variety of social and economic characteristics, including education, housing, and health insurance status. Furthermore, because the population is always in flux and its circumstances tend to change fairly quickly, the Census Bureau tracks trends in the population between the ten-year censuses, using polls and surveys and other sources of data such as birth and death records, immigration and emigration records, and school statistics. Census Bureau data are vital for the operation of the nation's social, political, economic, and industrial systems and essential for the practice of public health.

Because census data can determine the political composition of the U.S. Congress and the distribution of federal funds to states and communities, various interest groups carefully monitor how the data is collected. Two issues were particularly controversial in preparing for the year 2000 census, both of which have impact on the statistics used to evaluate the public's health. One question concerned how a person's race is determined. The broad categories previously used in the census were white, black, Hispanic, Asian and Pacific Islander, and American Indian and Alaska native. Individuals identify their own race and ethnic category. The issue has been further complicated by the fact that interracial marriage and parenthood has become increasingly common in the United States, and many of mixed racial parentage wanted an "interracial" category to be included on the year 2000 census. After considerable debate, the Census Bureau decided against such a category, but it allowed individuals to check more than one racial category for themselves.[1] This new policy affects race-specific health statistics, but the effect is still small. Only 2.4 percent of the population chose to check more than one race in 2000.[2]

An even more politically controversial issue for the year 2000 census was whether the Census Bureau would be allowed to use statistical sampling to correct for the inability to count every individual person in the United States. Every individual in the nation is supposed to be accounted for, with the head of every household completing a short questionnaire sent by mail. Census workers follow up in person to count the people in households that did not return questionnaires. Already, sampling methods are used to estimate answers to some of the questions, those included only in the long form sent to one in six households. In all previous censuses, the Bureau tried very hard to count everyone, but inevitably some people were missed or counted twice. The missing ones were likely to be the poorest and most marginal members of the population—the homeless, illegal immigrants, fugitives from the law. Wealthy people who own more than one home might be counted twice. It is estimated that in the 1990 census, eight to ten million people were missed and more than four million were double counted.[3] Such errors can lead to systematic inaccuracies in health statistics. For example, blacks tend to be undercounted in the census, while black births and deaths are more accurately recorded, meaning that birth and death rates calculated for blacks tend to be higher than their true value would be if correct population numbers were used for the denominator.

In planning for the year 2000, the Census Bureau declared its intent to use statistical sampling methods to obtain a more accurate count than it has been able to achieve in previous censuses and to do so at lower cost, since tracking down nonresponders is very expensive. The plan to use sampling aroused intense political opposition among Republicans. Since many federal funding programs distribute the funds according to population, a more accurate count might lead to financial gains to some traditionally Democratic geographical areas. More accurate population figures might also increase Congressional representation of Democratic urban areas at the expense of Republican suburbs. In February 1998, Republican Newt Gingrich, then the speaker of the House of Representatives, filed suit in U.S. District Court to prevent the use of sampling, and in August 1998, the court ruled that sampling would violate federal law.[4] The ruling was appealed to the Supreme Court, which in early 1999 issued a mixed decision that resulted in the Census Bureau's producing two counts, one including sampling and one not.[5] In the end, the Census Bureau announced that the 2000 census missed at least 6.4 million people and counted at least 3.1 million people twice.[6] From a public health perspective, of course, sampling is desirable because it will provide more accurate statistics.

The decision against sampling applied only to the actual enumeration of the population for the purpose of determining representation in Congress, information obtained on the short form of the census. The long form, which provided more details on people's education, economic status, housing and so forth, has generally been sent to only a sample of the population and its results were generalized using statistical techniques to draw conclusions about the whole population. Because there is a need for more timely information, the Census Bureau has been conducting an ongoing survey, called the American Community Survey, that collects much of the data normally on the long form.[7] It is possible that in future censuses there will no longer be a need for the long form.

NCHS SURVEYS AND OTHER SOURCES OF HEALTH DATA

As noted previously, the NCHS, in addition to collecting data from the states, actively conducts a number of surveys to gather additional information on the health of the American population. Follow-back surveys are a way to expand on the vital statistics data the NCHS has received. In these periodic studies, the NCHS chooses a sample of birth certificates to investigate further, sending questionnaires to the mothers, doctors, and hospitals to learn more about family characteristics as well as the circumstances of the pregnancy and birth. Such a survey was conducted in 1988. Called the National Maternal and Infant Health Survey, the survey followed back a sample of fetal deaths and infant deaths, allowing researchers to study factors related to poor pregnancy outcomes.[8] Similar surveys are periodically conducted on a sampling of deaths; the person who filled out the death certificate is asked to provide more information on the lifestyle of the deceased as well as what medical care he or she received.

Two NCHS surveys aim to assess the health of the population as a whole, estimate the prevalence of selected diseases and risk factors, and look for trends. Each year, interviewers for the National Health Interview Survey (NHIS) contact about 50,000 households and ask questions about illnesses, injuries, impairments, chronic conditions, utilization of medical resources, and other health topics.[9] The National Health and Nutrition Examination Survey (NHANES) is designed to obtain even more detailed and accurate information; doctors and nurses are sent in vans to conduct physical and dental examinations and laboratory tests on a carefully selected sample of the population. Each year, fifteen counties are visited, and about 5,000 individuals of all ages are selected to undergo the tests. Data is collected on the prevalence of chronic conditions and risk factors for those conditions, such as smoking, alcohol consumption, sexual practices, physical fitness and activity, weight, and dietary intake.[10]

NCHS is also collaborating with the National Institute on Aging on several follow-up studies of the population surveyed in previous NHIS surveys. In one follow-up study, over 7,000 individuals who were seventy years of age or older in the 1984 NHIS were re-interviewed in 1986, 1988, and 1990. A similar follow-up study on over 9,000 individuals who were seventy years or older in 1994 were re-interviewed in 1997–98 and 1999–2000. The interview data is linked to Medicare records and death certificates. The purpose of these studies is to describe the process by which older people function in the community, become dependent, are institutionalized, and die. Information is also collected on use of medical care and services. The second study looks for trends in healthy aging. The information provided by these followup studies is expected to be very valuable in relating the clinical, nutritional, and behavioral factors identified more than two decades ago to subsequent health status as people age, including their need for hospitalization or institutionalization in a nursing home.[11]

The Behavioral Risk Factor Survey (BRFSS) conducted by the states, which report their findings to the CDC, is another way of obtaining information on health-related behavior. It asks questions about health, including high blood pressure, high blood cholesterol, diabetes, and weight, as well as about high-risk behaviors such as cigarette smoking, excessive alcohol consumption, drinking and driving, and physical inactivity. It also asks whether people get preventive medical care such as mammograms, Pap smears, colon cancer screening, and immunizations.[12] The BRFSS gathers some of the same information as NHANES, but it has the advantage of surveying many more people, and it allows analysis of how the factors vary from one state to another. However, the information is self-reported and may be less reliable than that obtained in NHANES. For example, the BRFSS finds that, according to people's own reports, about 21 percent of adults are obese,[13] while the NHANES survey, using direct measurements, found a rate of about 31 percent.[14] This finding accords with previous observations that overweight people generally report that they weigh less than they do.

Other governmental agencies collect health-related data according to the focus of their responsibilities. For example, the Environmental Protection Agency carries out surveillance for health hazards in the environment, including air pollutants and releases of toxic chemicals, as discussed in Chapter 20. The National Cancer Institute coordinates a program called Surveillance, Epidemiology, and End-Results (SEER), used to monitor long-term trends of cancer incidence and mortality. The Center for Medicare and Medicaid Services has billing records for the Medicare program, which are useful for research on utilization and outcomes of medical care, as discussed in Chapter 27. The Food and Drug Administration collects reports of adverse reactions to drugs after they have been approved and are on the market, sometimes ordering recalls if a serious problem appears that was not noted during preapproval testing. Surveillance for product-related injuries is conducted by the Consumer Product Safety Commission.

IS SO MUCH DATA REALLY NECESSARY?

While it seems that the government collects enormous amounts of information on its citizens, there is never too much. These data are critically important in making up the surveillance systems that form the basis of effective public health practice as well as the planning and evaluation efforts that are increasingly being used in public health programming.

The statistics collected by federal, state, and local agencies are used in all areas of public health. Early notification of communicable disease cases is a classic use of public health information to protect the public's health. The need for public health intervention to control other problems may not be obvious without an analysis of data. This explains the Institute of Medicine committee's insistence on the importance of assessment as a core function of public health (see Chapter 1). As discussed in Chapter 30, public health leaders are increasingly stressing the importance of planning, setting goals, and managing public health programs to meet these goals, a process that requires data at the local, state, and federal levels. For example, a community may not recognize that it has a problem with unintended pregnancy and low birth weight unless it analyzes the data from birth certificates. Recognition of the problem might persuade local public health leaders to consider school-based birth control education and services.

Throughout this book, during discussions of public health issues (including biomedical, social and behavioral, environmental, and medical care issues), problems are defined according to the data that is available. In any area of public health, problems are identified in terms of statistics. The success of intervention programs to confront a problem is evaluated based on if it improves the statistics.

In an era when people tend to frown on "big government" and yearn for lower taxes, there is always pressure to cut back fiscal support for data collection and analysis, activities that seem less urgent than fighting a known epidemic, for instance. Yet without data, experts cannot recognize that an epidemic is beginning. Inspired by the recommendations of *The Future of Pubic Health*[15], the CDC has taken a lead in coordinating and encouraging the use of data in public health assessment. Recent events, including the emergence and resurgence of infectious diseases and the fear of bioterrorism, have stimulated the development of new surveillance systems within the United States and around the world.

With or without adequate data, decisions affecting public health policy and the allocation of scarce resources from government budgets must be made. It is increasingly important that these policy and fiscal decisions be made on the basis of timely and accurate information.

ACCURACY AND AVAILABILITY OF DATA

British economist Sir Josiah Stamp (1880–1941) wrote in 1929, "The Government [is] very keen on amassing statistics. They collect them, add them, raise them to the nth power, take the cube root and prepare wonderful diagrams. But you must never forget that every one of those figures comes in the first instance from the village watchman, who just puts down what he damn well pleases."[16]

The process of data collection is always imperfect. Data for even births and deaths, the most accurately reported health events, may be flawed. The census produces errors, and there are political difficulties in trying to rectify them. Most other sources of health information, relying as they do on surveys or voluntary reports, are even more incomplete or subject to bias. For example, the Youth Behavioral Factor Risk Survey of high school students, conducted by states and reported to the CDC, misses adolescents who have the highest risks—those who have dropped out of school.

Errors in reporting cause of death on death certificates, a prime example of what Stamp warns about, are especially worrisome for public health in that mortality data have such a strong influence on planning and priority setting for public health programs. Autopsies are being done with declining frequency, in part because of cost concerns, but also because doctors may believe that sophisticated diagnostic technology has rendered autopsies obsolete. In 1961, autopsies were performed in 41 percent of hospital deaths; in the mid-1990s, that number had fallen to 5 to 10 percent.[17] Cause of death information is still subject to uncertainty in many cases, however, and several studies have found that evidence obtained from an autopsy contradicted the clinical judgment of doctors in 15 to 32 percent of cases. Information gained from an autopsy answers the question, did the patient receive the correct treatment for the correct disease?

This information can improve the quality of medical care for future patients as well as improve the accuracy of vital statistics.

Because some of the inaccuracies on birth and death certificates may result from carelessness on the part of the busy health professionals who file them, new electronic methods of filing that are being introduced in some states are expected to improve the quality of the data. For example, maternal deaths are suspected of being underreported because doctors often fail to check off on a women's death certificate whether she was pregnant or gave birth in the time period prior to her death. If an electronic death certificate is used, the computer will refuse to accept the form— "send" to it—until that question is answered.[18]

Computers are extensively used in the analysis of public health data, of course, and new applications are continually improving the timeliness and accessibility of the data. Weekly reports of notifiable diseases from state and local health agencies are transmitted electronically to the CDC, allowing prompt response to new outbreaks. Laboratory results are also reported electronically, facilitating the rapid identification of bacterial and viral strains that may be causing illness in scattered locations around the country. Databases that are kept up-to-date by electronic filings can provide rapid feedback on the effectiveness of new public health interventions as well as help detect emerging problems.

The new information technology—or public health informatics as it is sometimes called—has vastly improved the accessibility of public health information to public health workers and the general public. The CDC and most other federal and state public health agencies make information available over the Internet. For example, *Morbidity and Mortality Weekly Reports* is searchable online, and articles can be downloaded from the CDC's Web page. The National Cancer Institute provides the latest information on cancer therapies and prognoses tailored for doctors and for patients. Some data sets require users to have special passwords before they are allowed access; others are available to authorized users only on diskettes or CDs.

CONFIDENTIALITY OF DATA

When anyone collects information on other people, questions always arise about how the information is going to be used and who is going to be allowed access to it. In general, all information collected from individuals by governments for whatever purpose is considered confidential and cannot be divulged without the consent of the individual. In most cases, the information is entered into a massive database from which individual names and addresses are removed. For research purposes, an identifying number may remain attached to the data to enable researchers to match information in one database with that in another. This technique is used, for example, in matching birth and death records as described above in order to learn more about the factors that contribute to infant mortality.

There is always concern that a determined snoop who works in an agency or knows an employee could obtain confidential information on an individual and use it to that individual's detriment. Agencies that handle confidential data impose stringent rules on access. Researchers must explain and justify their need for the data and promise to safeguard its confidentiality. Most agencies have an institutional review board or data protection committee, often including members from the community, which weighs the researchers' claims and decides whether to grant permission for access. Other than its use for research, the only exception made to the promise of confidentiality is when people must be notified that they have been exposed to a communicable disease.

The conflict between the need for confidentiality and the need for open access to information has been played out over various aspects of the AIDS epidemic, as discussed in the Prologue. Because HIV-positive individuals feared, with good reason, that they might be discriminated against if employers, landlords, and others learned of their infection, public health practitioners were concerned that patients would refuse to be tested unless confidentiality was ensured. Hence, the rules for reporting HIV were handled differently from other communicable diseases: anonymous testing was allowed, and the system for reporting cases to many state health departments and the CDC was modified to maintain anonymity. Recently, however, with the advent of new drugs that can clearly help AIDS patients and slow the onset of AIDS in HIV-infected individuals, HIV's exempt status has, for the most part, been discontinued, and it is treated like other communicable diseases.

CONCLUSION

Statistics are the vital signs of public health. Local, state, and federal governments collect data on their citizens, starting with birth certificates and ending with death certificates. The U.S. census, conducted every ten years, provides information on the age, sex, and ethnic composition of communities, information that allows the calculation of birth rates, death rates, infant mortality rates, life expectancies, and other data that form the basis for public health's assessment function.

The NCHS is the repository for the vital statistics data received from the states. The NCHS also conducts a number of periodic and ongoing surveys to collect additional information on Americans, including information on family structure, specific health conditions, behavioral risk factors, and other data useful in planning public health intervention programs.

Health statistics are used for all aspects of public health policy development and evaluation. Uses of the data include health needs identification, analysis of problems and trends, epidemiologic research, program evaluation, program planning, budget preparation and justification, administrative decision making, and health education.[19]

Increasingly, electronic means are being used to collect, transmit, store, and analyze data and to make the data available to public health workers and the general public. Strict precautions are taken to ensure confidentiality of information about individuals.

REFERENCES

1. S. A. Holmes, "People Can Claim One or More Races On Federal Forms," *New York Times* (October 30, 1997): A1.
2. U.S. Census Bureau, "Census 2000 Shows America's Diversity," Press Release (March 12, 2001).
3. S. A. Holmes, "The Path to the Next Census Has Been Far from Routine," *New York Times* (February 1, 1999): A18.
4. S. A. Holmes, "Court Voids Plan to Use Sampling for 2000 Census," *New York Times* (August 25, 1998): A1.
5. L. Greenhouse, "In Blow to Democrats, Court Says Census Must Be by Actual Count," *New York Times* (January 26, 1999): A1.
6. E. Schmitt, "Count of the 2000 Census Is Said to Err by Millions," *New York Times* (March 16, 2001): A12.
7. C. Holden, "New Annual Survey Brings Census Into 21st Century," *Science* 295 (2002): 2202–2203.
8. National Center for Health Statistics, *www.cdc.gov/nchs/about/major/nmihs/abnmihs.htm*, reviewed April 9, 2004. Accessed August 15, 2004.
9. National Center for Health Statistics, *www.cdc.gov/nchs/nhis.htm*, reviewed August 13, 2004. Accessed August 15, 2003.
10. National Center for Health Statistics, "National Health and Nutrition Examination Survey: Overview," May 2003.

11. National Center for Health Statistics, "Aging Activities," *www.cdc.gov/nchs/agingact. htm*, reviewed April 2, 2004. Accessed August 15, 2004.
12. U.S. Centers for Disease Control and Prevention, "Health Risks in the United States: Behavioral Risk Factor Surveillance System," *www.cdc.gov/nccdphp/aag/aag_brfss. htm*, reviewed April 6, 2004. Accessed July 20, 2004.
13. A. H. Mokdad et al., "Prevalence of Obesity, Diabetes, and Obesity-Related Health Risk Factors, 2001," *Journal of the American Medical Association* 289 (2003): 76–79.
14. K. Flegal et al., "Prevalence and Trends in Obesity Among U.S. Adults 1999–2000," *Journal of the American Medical Association* 288 (2002): 1723–1727.
15. U.S. Institute of Medicine, Committee for the Study of the Future of Public Health, *The Future of Public Health* (Washington, DC: National Academy Press, 1988).
16. J. Stamp, *Some Economic Factors in Modern Life* (London: P.S. King, 1929), 258–259, quoted in R. Goodman and R. Berkelman, "Physicians, Vital Statistics, and Disease Reporting," *New England Journal of Medicine* 258 (1987): 379.
17. National Center for Health Statistics, "The Autopsy, Medicine, and Mortality Statistics," *Vital and Health Statistics*, Series 3, Number 32 (2001).
18. Michael Zdeb and Mary Applegate, personal communication.
19. G. Pickett and J. J. Hanlon, *Public Health: Administration and Practice* (St. Louis, Missouri: Times Mirror/Mosby, 1990), 151–153.

PART III

Biomedical Basis of Public Health

CHAPTER 9

The "Conquest" of Infectious Diseases

Rabid Kitten

Throughout history, until the beginning of the twentieth century, infectious diseases were the major killers of humans. Bubonic plague, the "Black Death," is said to have wiped out as much as three-quarters of the population of Europe and Asia in the fourteenth century. Tuberculosis was the number one killer in England in the mid-nineteenth century. An example of the toll of infectious diseases is demonstrated in Figure 9–1, which provides death rates of the population of New York City over the period 1804 to 2000. Epidemics of smallpox and cholera swept through the city

137

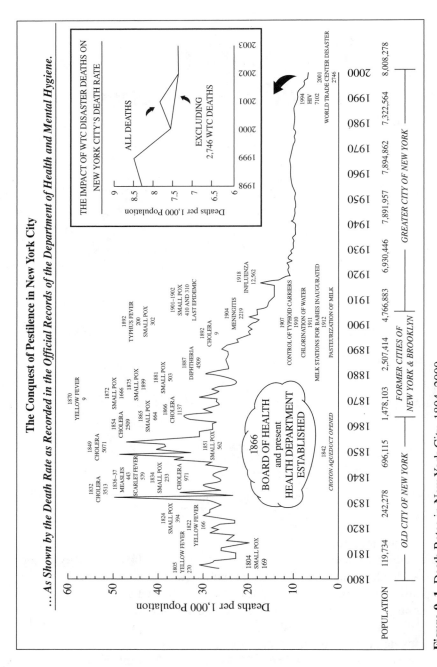

Figure 9–1 Death Rates in New York City, 1804–2000
Source: www.nyc.gov/html/doh/downloads/pdf/v5/2001sum.pdf. Accessed June 30, 2005.

every few years, killing many people in each wave. In the mid-nineteenth century, background mortality rates—largely from tuberculosis, typhoid, and miscellaneous respiratory and gastrointestinal diseases—were double what they became by 1930.

These infectious diseases were largely conquered through public health measures, including purification of water, proper disposal of sewage, pasteurization of milk, and immunization, as well as improved nutrition and personal hygiene. The discovery of antibiotics also played a role. In fact, by the 1960s, the threat of infectious diseases seemed to have been reduced to a minor nuisance.

In contrast to the fear, drama, and excitement that accompanied efforts to understand and control infectious diseases in the late nineteenth and early twentieth centuries, public health in the 1960s and 1970s seemed to have become routine and boring. This period in the history of public health corresponds to the time when, according to the Institute of Medicine, public health was falling into disarray because of complacency.[1] Chapter 10 discusses why the declaration of victory in the war against infectious diseases was premature. This chapter will focus on the battles public health practitioners have won. It will discuss the causes of infectious diseases, how they are transmitted, and how classic public health measures have brought them under control.

INFECTIOUS AGENTS

The major epidemic diseases are caused by bacteria, viruses, or parasites. The fact that each of these diseases is caused by a specific microbe was established in the 1880s and 1890s, at a time of great scientific excitement, when almost every year marked a discovery of a new disease-causing bacterium.

Robert Koch, a German physician, developed techniques to classify bacteria by their shape and their propensity to be stained by various dyes. Since billions of bacteria—most of them harmless to humans—inhabit the skin, throat, mouth, nose, large intestine, and vagina, it was necessary to develop a set of rules that could be used to prove that a specific organism caused a specific disease. These rules, called "Koch's postulates," are (1) the organism must be present in every case of the disease; (2) the organism must be isolated and grown in the laboratory; (3) when injected with the laboratory-grown culture, susceptible test animals must develop the disease; and (4) the organism must be isolated from the newly infected animals and the process repeated.[2]

Koch applied these rules in his proof that tubercle bacilli were the cause of tuberculosis, the leading cause of death in Europe at that time. Bacilli are bacteria that appear rod shaped when observed under the microscope. Koch identified another bacillus, vibrio cholera, as the cause of cholera. Other disease-causing bacilli identified during that period were those that cause plague, typhoid, tetanus, diphtheria, and dysentery.

Round-shaped bacteria, called cocci, include streptococci, which cause strep throat and scarlet fever; staphylococci, which cause wound infections; and pneumococci, which cause pneumonia. Syphilis is caused by a corkscrew-shaped bacterium called a spirochete. All these bacteria were identified by the beginning of the twentieth century.

For some infectious diseases, however, no bacterial agent could be found. Smallpox, for example, was known to be transmitted from a sick person to a healthy one by something in the pus of the patient's lesions. Yet attempts

BACILLI   COCCI   SPIROCHETE

to isolate a microorganism were unsuccessful. The agent that caused the disease could pass through the finest available filters and could not be observed in any existing microscope. Smallpox was recognized to be one of a number of diseases caused by such "filterable agents" or viruses. It was not until 1935, when the American scientist W. M. Stanley crystallized tobacco mosaic virus, that the nature of viruses was demonstrated.

While bacteria are living, single-celled organisms that can grow and reproduce outside the body if given the appropriate nutrients, viruses are not complete cells. They are simply complexes of nucleic acid and protein that lack the machinery to reproduce themselves. Various kinds of viruses infect not only animal cells but also plant cells—as tobacco mosaic virus infects tobacco—and even bacteria. They can survive extreme conditions such as treatment with alcohol and drying in a vacuum and become active again when they are injected into a living cell. They reproduce themselves by taking control of the cell's machinery, often killing the cell in the process. The human diseases caused by viruses include smallpox, yellow fever, polio, hepatitis, influenza, measles, rabies, and AIDS, as well as the common cold.

Human diseases can also be caused by protozoa, or single-celled animals that can live as parasites in the human body. Malaria, spread by mosquitoes; cryptospiridiosis, which caused the Milwaukee diarrhea epidemic; and giardiasis, also known as "beaver fever" are examples of protozoal diseases. Other parasites, such as roundworms, tapeworms, hookworms, and pinworms, are the most common source of human infection in the world. Except for pinworms, they are not common in the United States today.

MEANS OF TRANSMISSION

Infectious diseases are spread by a variety of routes, directly from one person to another or indirectly by way of water, food, or vectors such as insects and animals. Bacteria and viruses that cause respiratory infections, including colds, influenza, and tuberculosis, are transmitted through the air on *aerosols*, water droplets produced when an infected person coughs or sneezes. They can also be transmitted from an infected person to objects he or she touches, such as doorknobs, utensils, or towels, to be picked up by the next person to touch the contaminated object and transferred by hand to the nose. The early European settlers made use of this route of transmission to inflict a primitive form of germ warfare on the

ROUNDWORM

HOOKWORM

PINWORM

TAPEWORM

Native American people, giving them blankets that had been used by patients suffering from smallpox. The disease decimated Native American populations because they had no immunity to the virus.

Gastrointestinal infections such as cholera, cryptospiridiosis, and diphtheria, are generally spread by the *fecal-oral* route, by which fecal matter from an infected person reaches the mouth of an uninfected person. This may occur as a result of poor personal hygiene or by contamination of drinking water because of inadequate sanitary systems. Vector-born diseases, including malaria, yellow fever, and West Nile encephalitis, generally use a more complex route from one person to another most often through an insect.

Each disease has its own pattern of development after a person is infected, and the time during which the patient is capable of transmitting the infection to others varies from one disease to another. Some diseases are most likely to be transmitted during the most symptomatic phase, for example, when a patient suffering from tuberculosis or the common cold is most actively coughing and sneezing. Others, such as measles and mumps, are most communicable during the day or two before noticeable symptoms develop. A few diseases can exist in a carrier state, in which the infected person can transmit the disease without having symptoms, as demonstrated by the infamous case of Typhoid Mary.[3]

Mary Mallon worked as a cook in a series of wealthy New York homes at the beginning of the twentieth century. After an increasing number of family members in these homes became sick with typhoid fever, some of them fatally, suspicion fell on the cook. Because she was healthy, and because cooking was the only way she knew to support herself, Mary resisted medical tests and, when finally proven to be a carrier of the bacteria, refused to accept the results. Eventually she had to be incarcerated to prevent her from taking jobs where she spread the disease by the fecal-oral route. She remained in the custody of the New York City Health Department for the rest of her life. It was Mary's occupation, of course, that made her such a threat to the public health. The discovery of antibiotics, too late to help Mary, made it possible to eliminate the bacteria in typhoid carriers. However some viruses, such as herpes and hepatitis B, can persist in carrier states, and no treatment is known to eliminate them.

CHAIN OF INFECTION

Control of infectious diseases is still an important component of public health. The public health approach to controlling infectious diseases is to interrupt the chain of infection. Many methods used to accomplish this interruption have now become routine, but vigilance is always required.

The chain of infection, a term used to describe the pattern by which an infectious disease is transmitted from person to person, is composed of several links, as illustrated in Figure 9–2. These are:

1. Pathogen. The pathogen is a virus, bacterium, or parasite that causes the disease in humans.

2. Reservoir. The reservoir is a place where the pathogen lives and multiplies. Some pathogens spread directly from one human to another and have no other reservoir. Others, however, may infect nonhuman species, spreading from them to humans only occasionally. Plague, for example, is a disease of rodents that is transmitted to humans by the bite of a flea. Rats are the reservoir of plague. Raccoons and bats are reservoirs for rabies, which spreads to humans only through the bite of a rabid animal. Contaminated water or food may also serve as reservoirs for human disease.

3. Method of transmission. The pathogen must have a way to travel from one host to another, or from a reservoir to a new host. The flea is a vector for plague, transferring the plague bacillus from rat to human by sucking it up when it bites the rat and then injecting it into a human host with a second bite. Food-borne diseases are transmitted when a person eats contaminated food; water-borne diseases are transmitted when someone drinks contaminated water. Many respiratory diseases are transmitted by aerosol. AIDS, syphilis, gonorrhea, and a number of other diseases are transmitted by sexual contact.

4. Susceptible host. Even if the pathogen gains entry, a new potential host may not be susceptible because the host has immunity to the pathogen. Immunity may develop as a result of previous exposure to the pathogen, or the host may naturally lack susceptibility for a variety of reasons. Most microorganisms are specifically adapted to infect certain species. Canine distemper virus, for example, does not infect humans. Even within species, susceptibility to specific viruses varies among individuals. Scientists have been puzzled why a very few people who have been repeatedly exposed to the human immunodeficiency virus (HIV) do not become infected; recent studies have found a genetic mutation that makes them resistant to the virus.

Public health measures to control the spread of disease are aimed at interrupting the chain of infection at whichever links are most vulnerable. At link 1, the pathogen could be killed, for example, by using an antibiotic

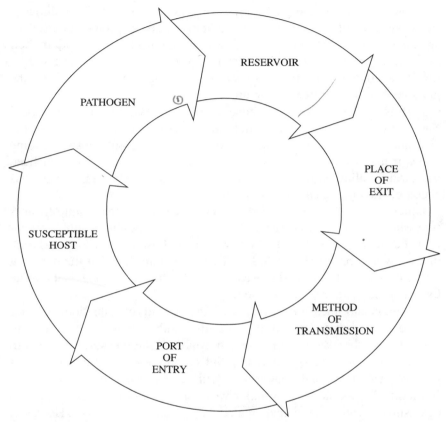

Figure 9–2 Chain of Infection
Henry Schneider

---

to destroy the disease-causing bacteria. At link 2, one could eliminate a reservoir that harbors the pathogen. For example, controlling rat populations in cities by picking up garbage is a way of preventing the spread of plague to humans. Adequate water and sewage treatment prevents the spread of water-borne diseases, and proper food handling methods eliminate reservoirs of food-borne pathogens.

At link 3, transmission from one host to another could be prevented by quarantining infected individuals, for example, or by warning people to boil their water if the water supply becomes contaminated. Hand washing is an important way to prevent the spread of disease for restaurant workers to avoid contaminating food, hospital workers to avoid carrying pathogens from one patient to another, and all individuals to protect themselves against pathogens they may pick up from the environment and put in their mouth. The spread of sexually transmitted diseases can be prevented by use of a condom, a simple matter of blocking the movement of the pathogens to the uninfected person.

At link 4, the resistance of hosts can be increased by immunization. Vaccination not only keeps the individual from contracting a disease but also makes it harder for the pathogen to find susceptible hosts. In some cases, it may even be possible to completely eliminate a pathogen from the earth by eliminating the susceptibility of its potential hosts. This was accomplished in the case of smallpox, as discussed below.

Other links are often included separately as part of the chain of infection when it is useful to consider them as sites for public health intervention. For example, the *port of entry* into the host for a mosquito-borne disease would be the skin, a link that could be interrupted if the potential host wears long sleeves and gloves. Similarly, the *place of exit* is the route by which the pathogen leaves the host.

Public health measures to control the spread of infectious disease include both routine prevention measures and emergency measures to control an outbreak once it has begun. Many of the measures referred to above—especially those concerning links 2 and 3—come under the category of "environmental health" and will be discussed further in Part V. Immunization—link 4—is a major weapon which has had great success against the dread diseases that created the epidemics of the past. However, vaccines do not exist for all diseases—notably, a vaccine has not yet been developed against AIDS. Even when vaccines do exist, some diseases are too rare to justify the trouble and expense of vaccinating everyone. This is where surveillance is especially important.

Epidemiologic surveillance—discussed in Chapter 4—is the system by which public health practitioners watch for disease threats so that they may step in and break the chain of infection, halting the spread of disease. In the early history of public health, the solution was often quarantine—isolation of the patient to prevent him or her from infecting others. Quarantine is still used occasionally, when the disease is serious and there is no effective vaccine. For example, a patient diagnosed with tuberculosis—which is slow to respond to medication—might be ordered to stay home for two to four weeks after treatment is started until the disease is no longer infectious.

More often, the public health response when an outbreak is detected by surveillance is to locate people who have had contact with the infected individual and immunize them or give them medical treatment, as appropriate. For tuberculosis, contact tracing is used in addition to quarantine: people who have been exposed to the patient are given prophylactic doses of antibiotics. Tuberculosis has presented new and more difficult problems to the public health system in recent years because of the development of drug resistant strains of the bacteria. Chapter 10 discusses this issue further.

Contact tracing is also routinely used for controlling sexually transmitted diseases, such as syphilis and gonorrhea. Syphilis, which tends to affect the poor, the homeless, drug users, and prostitutes, can be diagnosed by a blood test. Because it has few symptoms in the early stages, it may go untreated and is easily spread. The challenge for public health is to identify those with the disease through screening programs carried out, for example, in a city jail. Once a case is identified, public health workers try to discreetly alert those who have been exposed. The public health worker asks the person who has been diagnosed to identify sexual contacts; the worker then notifies the contacts that they have been exposed without identifying the source of the exposure. Syphilis is readily cured by penicillin. If untreated, it may cause long-term damage to the heart and brain; congenital syphilis in infants born to infected mothers can be lethal.

The classic public health measures of surveillance and quarantine were key components in combating severe acute respiratory syndrome (SARS), a highly infectious new disease that first broke out in southern China in November 2002. Because China did not at first report the disease, it was not recognized as a major threat until March 2003, when the World Health Organization (WHO) issued a global alert and a travel advisory. WHO had been alerted by Dr. Carlo Urbani, an infectious disease specialist working in Vietnam, who noticed that a patient who had recently arrived in Saigon from Hong Kong was suffering from an atypical form of pneumonia. Dr. Urbani himself soon contracted the disease and died. Epidemiologic detective work found that the patient in Saigon, as well as patients soon identified in Toronto and Singapore, had all stayed in the same hotel in Hong Kong where a traveler from southern China had spent one night before falling ill with the syndrome. More than a dozen guests at the hotel had been infected by that one traveler, and they carried the disease to several other countries.[4]

By July 5, 2003, when WHO declared that SARS had been contained, the disease had infected 8,439 people in thirty countries and killed 812 people.[5]

Although a virus was identified, lab tests could not diagnose the disease until weeks after a patient had developed symptoms. No drug has been found effective against the virus, and treatment requires intensive respiratory therapy during extended hospital stays. SARS was contained by old-fashioned measures: quickly isolating patients who were suspected to have the disease—because of fever, cough, and previous contact with a known SARS patient—and quarantining anyone who had come in contact with them. The epidemic had severe economic impact wherever it broke out, keeping business and vacation travelers from affected areas and even scaring away visitors from Chinatowns in American cities.

There was concern that the disease would be seasonal and break out again in 2004, but this did not occur. A few small outbreaks in 2004 stemmed from inadequate safety measures in research laboratories, but alert health workers kept the disease from spreading. Scientists are attempting to develop a vaccine against SARS, which could be used to break the chain of infection when and where the virus might appear again.

RABIES

Rabies, a fatal disease of the nervous system, is caused by a virus. Transmission of the disease to humans is very effectively prevented by routine public health measures, including epidemiologic surveillance. Although there is an effective vaccine against rabies, routine immunization of everyone is not recommended. Human exposure to the rabies virus is relatively rare and the vaccine is expensive and inconvenient to deliver, requiring several injections over a period of approximately a month.

The rabies virus infects only mammals, and it is almost always transmitted when a rabid animal bites another animal or a human. Since the animal most likely to bite a human is the dog, mandatory immunization of dogs against rabies is the first line of defense in the protection of people. Wild animals serve as the reservoir of rabies, and dogs are most likely to be exposed by being bitten by a rabid wild animal. Domestic cats are also at risk for exposure to rabies from wildlife, and immunization is recommended for them as well.

The public health system has defined clear guidelines for responding to a report of a person's being bitten by a domestic or wild animal, depending on the likelihood that the animal is rabid. Because immunization of dogs is widespread in the United States, only about 200 cases of rabies occur annually in the fifty million dogs in this country, and a dog bite is considered unlikely to transmit the disease.[6] If the biting dog (or cat) appears to be healthy, it need only be observed for ten days to ensure that it remains healthy. Rabies virus affects the brain and from there travels to the salivary glands and is secreted in saliva. An animal capable of transmitting the virus in its saliva will already have brain involvement, exhibit symptoms, and be dead within a few days. That is sufficient time for the bitten person to be given the series of vaccinations that will protect him or her from the disease.

If the biting animal is wild, or if there is other reason to suspect that it is rabid, it must be killed and its brain tested for signs of rabies virus infection. There is no way to determine definitively whether a living animal is rabid. If the test shows the animal to be rabid, the bite victim receives the vaccinations. If no sign of rabies is found, no vaccinations are given. There is no room for error in these tests, because once symptoms of rabies appear, it is too late to save the victim. Public health laboratories take this responsibility very seriously. Generally, immunizations are given to anyone who is bitten by a wild animal that cannot be captured and tested.

To control rabies, public health practitioners conduct surveillance for rabies in wildlife. When raccoons, skunks, and foxes in a geographic area are infected with the virus, they are likely to be a threat to humans and domestic animals. In Europe and in some parts of the United States, public health officials are attempting to control rabies in wildlife by distributing a bait containing an oral rabies vaccine.

Bats are the most dangerous rabies threat to humans. Even in parts of the country where the disease is not endemic among most wildlife, rabid bats are likely to be found. Because the animals are nocturnal and elusive, contact with bats may go unnoticed. During the period between 1990 and 2000, twenty-four of the thirty-two cases of human rabies in the United States were caused by a strain of the virus that is associated with bats. Only two of these victims were aware of having been bitten by a bat.[7]

The rabies surveillance system has been remarkably successful. The cost of rabies control is significant, however. Testing the brain of an animal for rabies costs about $100, and the price of a series of vaccinations for a person suspected of being exposed may amount to $1,500. In 1994, after a kitten in a New Hampshire pet store tested positive for rabies, 665 people received post-exposure treatment, the most expensive single episode on record in the United States.[8]

SMALLPOX, MEASLES, AND POLIO

While constant vigilance is required to protect people from rabies because wild animals serve as a reservoir of the disease, some pathogenic viruses, including measles and polio, have no nonhuman reservoir. It is possible, therefore, that universal immunization against these diseases could eliminate the measles and polio viruses from the earth. This has been achieved with smallpox, one of public health's greatest victories.

Smallpox was a particularly feared disease that is believed to have first emerged in Asia about the time of Christ and tended to spread in major epidemics that claimed millions of lives in China, Japan, the Roman Empire, Europe, and the Americas.[2] It was highly contagious, spread by aerosol or by touch. The concept of vaccination originated with smallpox: the observation that survivors of the disease were immune to future infection inspired the idea that people could be protected against serious illness by inoculating them with small amounts of infected matter from a person suffering a mild case. While the procedure was not entirely safe, the practice became widespread in the American colonies, and George Washington ordered his entire army to be inoculated. In 1796, the practice of immunization became less risky when the British physician Edward Jenner—inspired by the observation that milkmaids appeared to be immune to smallpox—proved that inoculation with cowpox matter, which was harmless to humans, provided immunity against smallpox.[9]

By 1958, routine immunization had eliminated smallpox in the United States and other industrialized countries. However, it was still widespread in thirty-three underdeveloped countries, killing two million people a year. With support from both the United States and the Soviet Union, WHO developed plans for a program to eliminate smallpox. Between 1967 and 1977, medical teams traveled all over the world, in search of outbreaks of the disease. Local governments were mobilized to vaccinate residents of areas where an outbreak was occurring. Because the lesions of smallpox were so conspicuous, it was possible for the investigators to track outbreaks by showing pictures of victims and asking people if they knew of anyone with this disease. Once a patient was located, he or she could be quarantined and everyone in the vicinity vaccinated, sometimes by force. The last case was found in Somalia in October 1977.[2]

Now smallpox virus officially remains in only two places, stored in laboratories at the Centers for Disease Control and Prevention and in a Russian laboratory in Siberia. By international agreement, genetic studies were being conducted, after which both stocks of the virus were scheduled to be destroyed in 1999.[10] The decision to destroy the virus was controversial, with some scientists believing that valuable information might be gained in future studies using techniques that are not yet known. In 1999, WHO decided to defer the destruction for a few more years.[11]

Meanwhile, word was leaking out of the former Soviet Union that the Soviets had been working on smallpox as a bioweapon. There were fears that they had shared their stocks of the virus with rogue states such as Iraq and North Korea. The anthrax attacks of 2001 have further raised fears about bioterrorism. Plans for destruction of the virus have been put on hold, and research priorities have focused on developing an improved vaccine and finding drugs that would be effective against the virus. Chapters 10 and 29 discuss bioterrorism further.

Poliovirus, like smallpox virus, infects human beings only and similarly has the potential to be eradicated. In 1988, WHO set a goal of eradicating polio by the year 2000. This goal was not met, but substantial progress has been made against this crippling disease: polio has been essentially eliminated from the Western Hemisphere and has been reduced by more than 90 percent worldwide. Many countries hold National Immunization Days each year, distributing doses of oral polio vaccine to millions of children. At the end of 2003, polio was endemic in only six countries, and fewer than 700 cases were recorded.[12]

Only Southern Asia and Sub-Saharan Africa still have a significant incidence of polio. An important reason that eradication did not succeed in these countries is that some Muslim politicians and religious leaders, especially in Nigeria, have claimed that the polio vaccine had been deliberately contaminated to cause AIDS or infertility.[13] WHO warned in mid-2004 that sub-Saharan Africa was on the verge of the largest polio epidemic in recent history.[14] The number of cases in Nigeria was five times that of the previous year, and the virus had spread to several other African countries that had previously been polio free. Under pressure from WHO, Nigeria resumed polio immunizations at the end of July 2004. The United States spends about $200 million a year on polio immunizations[15] and eight to ten Americans each year contract the disease from the vaccine itself.[16] Eradication of the virus would eliminate the need for immunization.

Measles, another viral disease that could be eradicated, offers an example what happens when public health relaxes its vigilance. Before a vaccine was available, almost all children contracted measles. While not usually fatal, measles can have complications that leave permanent brain and nerve damage. A vaccine became available in 1963, and the number of cases dropped precipitously reaching a low of 1,497 in 1983, compared with over 400,000 reported cases in 1962. In 1978, the U.S. Department of Health and Human Services set a goal to eradicate measles from the United States by 1982. That ambition proved overly optimistic. Two problems interfered.[17]

First, outbreaks of measles began to occur among high school and college students who had been vaccinated as babies. It became clear that the immunity conferred by vaccination in infancy wears off and a booster vaccination is necessary in older children, a practice that is now recommended at the age of four to six. The booster should be given to adolescents if they did not receive it earlier.

The greater problem was that too many children were not being immunized until it was required for entry into school. This was particularly true in large cities among poor African-American and Hispanic children. Immunization rates in the United States were worse than those of some third-world countries. More than 27,000 American children contracted measles in 1990, and eighty-nine died.[18] Even the surveillance system was doing poorly: a study in New York City during 1991 found that up to 50 percent of cases were not reported.[19] The public health system was shaken by this evidence of failure, and a better job is now being done on measles immunization. In fact, measles is no longer endemic in the United States, meaning that all cases can be traced to individuals who contracted the disease outside the country and brought it here. In 2003, forty-two cases were reported.[20] But the prospects for eradication are not clear. Public health leaders hope that when and if polio is eradicated, the organizational and medical resources that had been mobilized in that campaign can then be used in a vaccination campaign against measles.

An attempt to eradicate an eradicable disease can backfire if it is not conducted with sufficient political will, knowledge, and resources. This was the case with malaria, which was the target of an international eradication campaign in the 1950s and 1960s. The primary weapon was the pesticide DDT, used to kill mosquitoes, the vectors that carry the disease-causing parasites. While the campaign produced dramatic results, funding ran out before the objective was achieved, and there was a resurgence of the disease with greater impact than ever. A combination of factors contributed to the calamity: DDT-resistant mosquitoes emerged; the pathogen developed resistance to the main antimalarial drug, chloroquine; and populations in former malarial areas lost their immunity to the disease because of lack of exposure.[2] Now, malaria is one of the most widespread potentially fatal infectious diseases in the world, striking an estimated 300 million to 500 million people annually.[21] The disease occurs mainly in tropical and subtropical areas and has been largely eliminated in the United States, but global climate change and international travel could contribute to the reemergence of malaria as a public health problem in the South.

FEAR OF VACCINES

The benefits of vaccination are obvious to public health and medical professionals. However, just as Muslim leaders in Nigeria have resisted polio vaccination with the rumor of infertility, so suspicion has spread in the United States that measles immunization causes autism. Autism often becomes apparent at about the age when the vaccine is given. Consequently, some parents refused to allow their children to be vaccinated against measles. Similarly, unfounded stories about side effects of the pertussis (whooping cough) vaccine—that it might cause sudden infant death syndrome (SIDS)—led many parents to resist the vaccine.[22]

The rumors that measles vaccine caused autism were disproved by a major study done in Denmark, where records of a half million children were analyzed. About one in five children had not received the vaccine, and the researchers found that these children developed autism at the same rate as children who had received the vaccine.[23] Some vaccines do have real risks, including fever and seizures that occur in a small number of infants after they are vaccinated for pertussis and rare cases of polio caused by the oral polio vaccine. These risks are much smaller than the risks of the diseases in an unvaccinated population. However, many American parents are too young to remember the fears aroused by polio in the past, and they may be unaware that formerly common childhood diseases such as measles and chicken pox sometimes had serious complications. Whooping cough can be fatal in infants exposed to unvaccinated older siblings who contract the disease. Because of the success of vaccinations, people have never seen these diseases and thus no longer fear them.

It is often in wealthy communities that parents refuse to subject their children to the small risk of immunization. They count on the fact that most other children are vaccinated to protect their own children from being exposed. However, much of the protection afforded by a high rate of immunization in a population comes from "herd immunity," the phenomenon by which even infants too young to be vaccinated, old people with weakened immune systems, and those who refuse to be immunized are unlikely to be exposed to a disease because the majority of the population is immune. If the percentage of immunity in the population falls too low, however, outbreaks are likely. Then even vaccinated people are at risk, because no vaccine is perfect.[24]

Another drawback of people's fear of vaccines is that pharmaceutical companies have become reluctant to invest in developing them. Parents' tendency to blame a recent immunization for any serious health problem suffered by their children leads them to sue the company that made the vaccine. This experience, together with the fact that prices that can be charged for vaccines tend to be low, has caused many companies to drop vaccine production altogether. While immunization is considered the most effective intervention for preventing disease and promoting health, it is not clear that even the current vaccines will continue to be available.[25]

The development of resistance to the chemical arsenal for combating disease will be discussed in Chapter 10, together with other new and emerging problems in infectious diseases. While public health has had some successes and could have more with sufficient vigilance and will, infectious diseases are now more threatening than they seemed a few decades ago. New variations of pathogenic bacteria and viruses constantly arise to challenge the public health system. It has become clear that infectious diseases are far from being conquered.

CONCLUSION

Public health has had great success in controlling infectious diseases. Classic public health measures prevent transmission of disease-causing bacteria, viruses, and parasites by interrupting the chain of infection. Measures employed at various links in the chain include killing the pathogen, eliminating the reservoir that harbors the pathogen, preventing transmission from one host to another or from reservoir to host, and increasing the resistance of hosts by immunization.

Rabies is an example of a disease that has been successfully controlled by public health measures. Immunization of dogs is the primary barrier protecting humans from the reservoir of the virus, which is wild animals. By maintaining surveillance and intervening with vaccination when a person has been exposed to a possibly rabid animal, public health has kept the number of human deaths from rabies very low. SARS, a new, highly communicable disease first recognized in Asia in 2003, was successfully controlled by the classic public health measures of surveillance, isolation, and quarantine.

Smallpox, measles, and polio are viral diseases against which effective vaccines have been developed and which have no nonhuman reservoir. In theory, therefore, they could be eliminated from the earth. This has been accomplished with smallpox, with only two known stocks of the virus remaining. Polio has been eliminated from the United States and many other parts of the world, and a campaign is underway to eradicate it. The prospects for measles eradication are unclear. The United States has had epidemics of measles as recently as the early 1990s, and cases of measles still occur when infected people enter this country from endemic areas. Reluctance by some parents to vaccinate their children weakens herd immunity and threatens to cause outbreaks of infectious diseases that could have been controlled.

Success in controlling infectious diseases requires adequate resources and political will to maintain effective immunization programs and ongoing epidemiologic surveillance.

REFERENCES

1. U.S. Institute of Medicine, Committee for the Study of the Future of Public Health, *The Future of Public Health* (Washington, DC: National Academy Press, 1988), 19.
2. L. Garrett, *The Coming Plague: Newly Emerging Diseases in a World out of Balance* (New York: Farrar, Straus & Giroux, 1994), 403.
3. G. Pickett and J. J. Hanlon, *Public Health: Administration and Practice* (St. Louis, Missouri: Times Mirror/Mosby, 1990).
4. J. M. Hughes, "The SARS Response—Building and Assessing an Evidence-Based Approach to Future Global Microbial Threats," *Journal of the American Medical Association* 290 (2003): 3251–3253.
5. K. Bradsher, "SARS Declared Contained, with No Cases in Past 20 Days," *New York Times* (July 6, 2003): 4.
6. D. B. Fishbein and L. E. Robinson, "Rabies," *New England Journal of Medicine* 329 (1993): 1633–1638.
7. U.S. Centers for Disease Control and Prevention, "Human Death Associated with Bat Rabies—California, 2003," *Morbidity and Mortality Weekly Report* 53 (2004): 33–35.
8. D. L. Noah et al., "Mass Human Exposure to Rabies in New Hampshire: Exposures, Treatment, and Cost," *American Journal of Public Health* 86 (1996): 1149–1151.
9. G. Rosen, *A History of Public Health* (Baltimore, Maryland: Johns Hopkins University Press, 1993).
10. E. Marshall, "Bioterror Defense Initiative Injects Shot of Cash," *Science* 283 (1999): 1234–1235.
11. L. Altman, "Killer Smallpox Gets a New Lease on Life," *New York Times* (May 25, 1999): F3.

12. U.S. Centers for Disease Control and Prevention, "Brief Report: Global Polio Eradication Initiative Strategic Plan, 2004," *Morbidity and Mortality Weekly Report* 53 (2004): 107–108.
13. L. Roberts, "Health Workers Scramble to Contain African Epidemic," *Science* 305 (2004): 24–25.
14. World Health Organization, "Global Polio Eradication Initiative Welcomes Immunization Campaign in Kano, Nigeria," Press Release, August 3, 2004.
15. L. Schlein, "Hunting Down the Last of the Poliovirus," *Science* 279 (1998): 168.
16. U.S. Centers for Disease Control and Prevention, "Paralytic Poliomyelitis—United States, 1980–1994," *Morbidity and Mortality Weekly Report* 48 (1997): 79–83.
17. U.S. Centers for Disease Control and Prevention, "Measles Prevention: Recommendations of the Immunization Practices Advisory Committee," *Morbidity and Mortality Weekly Report* 38, No. S-9 (1989): 1–11.
18. U.S. Centers for Disease Control and Prevention, "Measles—United States, 1990," *Morbidity and Mortality Weekly Report* 40 (1991): 369–372.
19. S. F. Davis et al., "Reporting Efficiency During a Measles Outbreak in New York City, 1991," *American Journal of Public Health* 83 (1993): 1011–1015.
20. U.S. Centers for Disease Control and Prevention, "Measles Outbreak in a Boarding School—Pennsylvania, 2003," *Morbidity and Mortality Weekly Report* 53 (2004): 305–309.
21. P. Kachur and P. B. Bloland, "Malaria," in ed. R. B. Wallace, *Maxcy-Rosenau-Last, Public Health and Preventive Medicine* (Stamford, Connecticut: Appleton and Lange, 1998), 313–326.
22. E. W. Campion, "Suspicions about the Safety of Vaccines," *New England Journal of Medicine* 347 (2002): 1474–1475.
23. K. M. Madsen et al., "A Population-Based Study of Measles, Mumps, and Rubella Vaccination and Autism," *New England Journal of Medicine* 347 (2002): 1477–1482.
24. D. G. McNeil, "When Parents Say No to Child Vaccinations," *New York Times* (November 30, 2002): A1.
25. R. Rappuoli et al., "The Intangible Value of Vaccination," *Science* 297 (2002): 937–939.

CHAPTER 10

The Resurgence
of Infectious Diseases

Bacterial Resistance

The appearance of AIDS in the early 1980s challenged the widely held belief that infectious diseases were under control. However, there had been intimations during the previous two or three decades that the microbes were not as tamed as generally believed. The influenza virus was proving stubbornly unpredictable, deadly new variants of known bacteria were beginning to crop up, and the familiar old bacteria were becoming strangely resistant to antibiotics. That trend has continued, and the importance of public health in combating these growing problems has become increasingly apparent.

THE BIOMEDICAL BASIS OF AIDS

In just over twenty years, the exotic disease that seemed to strike only gay men has turned into a world-wide scourge: the human immunodeficiency virus (HIV) infects over forty-two million individuals and has killed over twenty million.[1] In the United States as of 2002, some 500,000 people had died of AIDS.[2] Since the outbreak was first recognized, a great deal has been learned about HIV, how it causes AIDS, and how it is spread.

HIV is a *retrovirus*, a virus that uses RNA as its genetic material instead of the more usual DNA. Retroviruses have long been known to cause cancer in animals and have been extensively studied for clues to the causes of human cancer. Two human retroviruses—causing two types of leukemia—were known before HIV was discovered. Retroviruses infect cells by copying their RNA into the DNA of the cell, penetrating the genetic material like a "mole" in a spy agency. This DNA may sit silently in the cell, being copied normally along with the cell's genetic material for an indefinite number of generations. Or it may take over control of the cell's machinery, causing the uncontrolled reproduction typical of cancer.

The target of HIV is a specific type of immune cell called the CD4-T lymphocyte, or T4 cell. T4 cells are just one of many components of the complicated immune machinery that is activated when the body recognizes a foreign invader such as a bacterium or virus. The T4 cell's role is to divide and reproduce itself in response to such an invasion and attack the invader. In a T4 cell that is infected with HIV, activation of the cell activates the virus also, which then produces thousands of copies of itself in a process that kills the T4 cell. The T4 cells are a key component of the immune system because, in addition to attacking foreign substances, they also regulate other components of the immune system, including the cells that produce antibodies. Thus destruction of the T4 cells disrupts the entire immune system.[3]

The course of infection with HIV takes place over a number of years. After being exposed to HIV, a person may or may not experience mild, flu-like symptoms for a few weeks, during which time the virus is present in the blood and body fluids and may be easily transmitted to others by sex or other risky behaviors. The body's immune system, including specific antibodies—the component detected by diagnostic screening tests— then eliminates most of the circulating viruses. The infection then enters a latent period, with the viruses mostly hidden in the DNA of the T4 cells, although a constant battle is taking place between the virus and the immune system. Billions of viruses are made, and millions of T4 cells are destroyed daily.[4] During this time, the person is quite healthy and is less likely to transmit the virus than during the early stage of infection. Eventually, after several years, the immune system begins to lose the struggle, and so many of the T4 cells begin to die that they cannot be replaced rapidly enough. When the number of T4 cells drops below 200 per cubic millimeter of blood, about 20 percent of normal, symptoms are likely to begin appearing, and the person is vulnerable to opportunistic infections. At the same time, the number of circulating viruses increases, and the person again becomes more capable of transmitting the infection to others.[5]

The development and licensing of a screening test in 1985 was a major step forward in the fight against HIV. The test measures antibodies to the virus, which begin to appear two to six months after the original infection. This test is relatively fast and inexpensive and is a sensitive screening test, giving the first indication that the individual may be HIV positive. The test is used for three purposes: diagnosing individuals at risk to determine whether they are infected so that they may be appropriately counseled and, if necessary, treated; monitoring the spread of HIV in various populations via epidemiologic studies; and screening of donated blood or organs to ensure that they do not transmit HIV to a recipient of a transfusion or transplant. A major drawback of the antibody screening test is the absence of antibodies in the blood during the initial two-month period after infection. This "window" of nondetectability may give newly infected people a false sense of security. More accurate tests that look for the virus itself in the blood are now available. These tests are used to confirm infection in people who have tested positive in the screening test. In the United States, they are also done on all donated blood to ensure that no virus-infected blood is used for transfusions.

Tests that directly measure virus in the blood have contributed a great deal to understanding the biomedical basis of HIV infection. Measurements of "viral load"—the concentration of viruses in the blood—are a valuable tool in evaluating the effectiveness of therapeutic drugs. Viral load has also been found to influence the individual's chances of transmitting the virus by sexual and other means. Thus a therapy that is effective in reducing viral load can help to control the spread of HIV.

The major pathways of HIV transmission vary in different populations. Homosexual relations between men are still the leading route of exposure for men in the United States. Injection drug use accounts for about 15 percent of HIV infections.[2] Transmission by heterosexual relations, especially male to female, is becoming increasingly common in this country and is the leading route of infection for females. In the developing countries of Asia and Africa, where HIV infection is spreading rapidly, heterosexual relations are the most common means of transmission.

Sharing of needles is a common route of transmission in developing countries because of insufficient supplies of sterile equipment for medical use. In poor countries, including Russia and some nations in Eastern Europe, medical personnel often use one syringe repeatedly for giving immunizations or injections of therapeutic drugs. If one of the patients is HIV-positive, this practice may transmit the infection to everyone who later receives an injection with the same needle. According to the World Health Organization (WHO), 40 percent of injections worldwide are given with unsterile needles.[6] Transfusion with HIV-contaminated blood is no longer a significant source of HIV infection in the United States, but it still occurs in countries too poor to screen donated blood.

A special case of HIV transmission is that from mother to infant. In the absence of treatment, one-fourth to one-third of infants of HIV-infected women are themselves infected with the virus. However, all such infants will test positive during the first few months after birth. This is because fetuses in the womb receive a selection of their mothers' antibodies, providing natural protection against disease (though not HIV) during their first months of life. Testing a baby's blood for HIV antibodies provides evidence of the mother's HIV status. Many states in the United States routinely perform HIV screening tests on newborns' blood as part of their newborn screening programs, discussed in Chapter 12. The special issues raised by maternal-fetal transmission of the virus have been the subject of ethical, legal, and political controversy at the national and state level. New therapies are now capable of preventing transmission of the virus from mother to infant in 99 percent of cases.[7]

Progress in treating HIV/AIDS over the past two decades has been dramatic. Early therapy focused on treating opportunistic infections, which were often the immediate cause of death in AIDS patients. The first antiretroviral therapy, zidovudine (AZT), was approved by the Food and Drug Administration in 1987.[8] The drug interfered with the replication of HIV by inhibiting the enzyme that copies the viral RNA into the cell's DNA. However the virus's tendency to mutate rapidly leads to the development of resistance to the drug, meaning that its effectiveness in treating patients wears off rapidly.

As scientists gained a better understanding of the virus, they developed drugs that target different stages of viral replication. Protease inhibitors, which interfere with the ability of newly formed viruses to mature and become infectious, were introduced in 1995.[8] At the same time, scientists recognized that treating patients with a combination of drugs that attack the virus in different ways reduces the opportunity for HIV to mutate and develop resistance. The introduction of these drug combinations, called highly active anti-retroviral therapy (HAART), led to dramatic improvements in the survival of HIV-infected patients. As a result, the number of AIDS deaths fell by more than half between 1995 and 2002.[2]

The development of effective treatments for HIV/AIDS has had many beneficial consequences. HAART can reduce viral load to undetectable levels in the blood and body fluids of many patients, which greatly reduces the likelihood that the virus will be transmitted to others through sexual contact and other means. The availability of effective therapy also encourages at-risk people to be tested and counseled on ways to protect themselves and prevent transmission of the virus to others. Scientists hoped that HAART would be able to completely eradicate HIV from the body, but this hope has not been realized. The virus manages to survive in protected reservoirs of the body, rebounding into active replication when the drugs are withdrawn.[8] For some patients, side effects of the drugs can be severe and even fatal; about 40 percent of patients treated with protease inhibitors develop lipodystrophy, characterized by abnormal distributions of fat in the body, sometimes accompanied by other metabolic abnormalities.[9]

New drugs continue to be developed, including a new class called fusion inhibitors, introduced in 2003, which interfere with HIV's ability to enter a host cell. Thus for many patients, HIV infection has become a chronic disease, necessitating life-long therapy but enabling them to live a relatively normal life. The drugs are expensive however, costing an average of $13,000 per year per patient.[10] Many HIV-infected individuals who could benefit from therapy do not have access to it.

The greatest hope for controlling AIDS, especially in the developing world where the new drugs are unaffordable, is to develop an effective vaccine. Prevention through immunization has been the most effective approach for the viral scourges of the past, including smallpox, measles, and polio. Early hopes for the rapid availability of a vaccine against AIDS have faded, however. It should perhaps not be surprising that a virus that is so well adapted to disabling the immune system should be so effective at eluding attempts to employ that same immune system against it. Part of the difficulty in developing an effective vaccine is that the virus itself is constantly changing its appearance, making it unrecognizable to the immune mechanisms that have been mobilized against it. This quality is common to RNA viruses.

At present, the most effective way to fight AIDS is to prevent transmission (step 3 in the chain of transmission; see Chapter 9). This requires education and efforts at motivating people to change their high risk behavior, an exceedingly difficult task, as Chapter 14 explains.

HIV seems to have appeared from nowhere and spread over the entire world within a decade. Where did the virus come from? Genetic studies of HIV show that it is related to viruses that commonly infect African monkeys and apes, and it seems likely that a mutation allowed one of these viruses to infect humans. There is evidence that this type of event—cross-species transmission of viruses—may occur fairly frequently. Monkeys and chimpanzees are killed for food in parts of Africa, which could explain how humans were exposed.[8] However, HIV is remarkable for the speed with which it has spread into the human population worldwide.

Scientists conjecture that the human form of the virus may have existed in isolated pockets of Africa for some time, but that its rapid spread was the result of social conditions in Africa and the United States in the late 1970s. Because symptomatic AIDS does not appear until several years after the original infection, the first victims of the 1980s were probably infected in the early and mid 1970s. Investigators trying to track the early spread of the epidemic have gone back to screen stored blood samples drawn in earlier times and found HIV-infected samples from as early as 1966, in the blood of a widely traveled Norwegian sailor who died of immune deficiency. The sailor's wife and one of his three children later died of the same illness, and their stored blood, when tested, was also found to be infected with HIV.[11] An even older blood sample drawn from an African man in 1959 has been found to contain fragments of the virus, but it is not known whether the man developed AIDS.[12] Sporadic early outbreaks of the disease in isolated African villages would have gone undetected, perhaps for decades.

The reasons for the recent emergence of HIV disease as a significant problem include the disruption of traditional lifestyles by the movement of rural Africans to urban areas, trends magnified by population growth, waves of civil war, and revolution. The apparent worldwide explosion of AIDS then occurred because of changing patterns of sexual behavior and the use of addictive drugs in developed and developing countries, together with the ease of international air travel.

OTHER EMERGING VIRUSES

In 1976, before the AIDS epidemic was recognized but while, as scientists now believe, the virus was spreading silently into African cities, another viral illness broke out with much more dramatic effect in Zaire and Sudan. Symptoms caused by the previously unidentified Ebola virus included fever and severe bleeding from various bodily orifices. Several hundred people became ill from the disease and up to 90 percent of its victims died. The disease spread rapidly from person to person, affecting especially family members and hospital workers who had cared for patients. Investigators from the Centers for Disease Control and Prevention (CDC) and WHO identified the virus and helped to devise measures, including quarantine, to limit the spread of the disease, which eventually disappeared. The Ebola virus broke out again in Zaire in the summer of 1995, killing 244 people before it again seemed to vanish.[13] Since then, at least eight Ebola outbreaks occurred among people in Central Africa by 2004.[14] The Ebola virus infects monkeys as well as humans, and on a number of occasions, infected monkeys have been imported into the United States. In 1989, a large number of monkeys imported from the Philippines died of the viral infection at a primate quarantine facility in Reston, Virginia. In that episode, which served as the basis for Richard Preston's book, *The Hot Zone*, several laboratory workers were exposed to the virus, which fortunately turned out to be a strain that did not cause illness in humans.[15] Scientists have been searching for an animal species that serves as a reservoir for the virus between outbreaks in the human population. There are indications that, like HIV, Ebola may spread to humans when they handle the carcasses of apes used for food. Unlike HIV, the Ebola virus kills the apes it infects, leading to significant declines in populations of gorillas and chimpanzees; outbreaks in humans have been preceded by the discovery of dead animals near villages where the outbreaks occur.[14]

Other new or resurgent viruses have appeared in various parts of the world, including the United States, over the past several years. In May and June 2003, for example, public health authorities in Illinois and Wisconsin received reports of a disease similar to smallpox among people who had had direct contact with prairie dogs. Prompt investigation by state officials and the CDC identified the cause as monkeypox virus, which was known from outbreaks in Africa. Although known to infect monkeys, the primary hosts for monkeypox are rodents.[16]

The outbreak in the United States spread to seventy-two people in six midwestern states. Fortunately, monkeypox is not highly contagious in humans, and it is a less severe disease than smallpox. No one died in the outbreak. However, the incident raised alarms about exotic pets. The illness in the prairie dogs was traced back through pet stores and animal distributors to an Illinois distributor, who in April had imported several African rodents, including a Gambian giant rat that had died of an unidentified illness. In June 2003, the U.S. government banned the import of all rodents from Africa. Careful surveillance and isolation of exposed people and animals halted the outbreak by the end of July. However, there is still concern about the possibility that infected prairie dogs might have been released into the wild and spread the virus, turning monkeypox into an endemic disease in the United States.[16]

In 1993, the CDC was called in when two healthy young New Mexico residents living in the same household died suddenly within a few days of each other of acute respiratory distress, their lungs filled with fluid. Within three weeks, biomedical scientists had recognized that the illness, which had claimed several other victims in the Four Corners area of the Southwest, was caused by hantavirus. Named after the Hantaan River in Korea, the hantavirus had been responsible for kidney disease among thousands of American soldiers in Korea during the 1950s. In New Mexico, the virus was found to be carried by deer mice, which had been unusually plentiful in the Four Corners area because of an unusually wet winter. All the human victims of hantavirus had had significant exposure to mouse droppings, either in their homes or their places of work.[17]

The CDC declared hantavirus pulmonary syndrome (HPS) a notifiable disease in 1995, and as of June 2002, 318 cases had been reported in 29 states.[18] Over one-third of the victims have died, often in a matter of hours. It is hoped that adding HPS to the list of notifiable diseases will help medical workers to recognize it more readily. In the case of a Rhode Island college student who may have contracted the disease from exposure to mouse droppings while making a film at his father's warehouse, the hospital did not recognize that he was seriously ill and sent him home from the emergency room the first time he appeared there; two days later he returned much sicker and died five hours after being hospitalized.[19]

Rodents are suspected as carriers of several hemorrhagic fevers with symptoms similar to those caused by hantavirus or the Ebola virus: Bolivian hemorrhagic fever (caused by the Machupo virus), Argentine hemorrhagic fever (caused by the Junin virus), and Lassa fever in Sierra

Leone are all carried by rats. Well-known, insect-borne viruses, such as yellow fever and equine encephalitis, are resurgent in areas of South and Central America where they had been thought to be vanquished. Dengue fever, also spread by mosquitoes, has taken on the new, deadly form of a hemorrhagic fever and is spreading north through Central America, threatening people along the southern border of the United States.[13]

In the summer of 1999, the United States first experienced the effects of West Nile virus, which spread rapidly across the country over the next few years. The first sign of the new disease was a report to the New York City Health Department by an infectious disease specialist in Queens, New York that an unusual number of patients had been hospitalized with encephalitis, an inflammation of the brain. The disease was suspected to be St. Louis encephalitis, a mosquito-borne disease that is endemic in the southern United States, and the diagnosis was supported by the patients' reports that they had been outdoors in the evenings during peak mosquito hours. Soon, however, it became obvious that a great number of dead crows were being found in the New York area, and a veterinarian at the Bronx Zoo reported that there had been unprecedented deaths among the zoo's exotic birds. Lab tests confirmed that the virus causing the human disease was the same as the one that was killing the birds, but St. Louis encephalitis virus was known not to infect birds. West Nile virus was well known in Africa, West Asia, and the Middle East. It is known to be fatal to crows and several other species of birds. It also infects horses. Fifty-six patients were hospitalized in the New York epidemic, seven of whom died.[20, 21]

How the West Nile virus came to New York is not known. The most likely explanation is that it came in an infected bird, perhaps a tropical bird that was smuggled into the country. The virus is easily spread among birds by several species of mosquitoes, some of which also bite humans. Although the threat disappeared with the mosquitoes after the first frost in the fall, the next summer saw a spread of the disease to upstate New York and surrounding states. Carried by migratory birds, the virus has now arrived in forty-six states. It appears that West Nile virus is here to stay. In 2003 it caused illness in more than 9,800 people, 4,146 horses, and countless birds.[22,23] Public health professionals fight the virus by educating the public about eliminating standing water where mosquitoes breed, wearing long sleeves, and using repellant. A vaccine is available for horses, and scientists are working on developing a vaccine that will be effective for humans.

A variety of environmental factors are responsible for the recent emergence of so many new pathogens. Human activities that cause ecological changes, such as deforestation and dam building, bring people into closer contact with disease-carrying animals. Modern agricultural practices, such as extreme crowding of livestock, intensify the risk that previously unknown viruses will incubate in crowded herds and be widely dispersed to human consumers. International distribution of meat and poultry may help to spread new pathogens. The popularity of exotic pets in the United States also can lead to the spread of pathogens, like monkeypox and perhaps West Nile virus, from animals or birds to people. A breakdown of public health efforts such as mosquito control programs because of complacency or insufficient funding has resulted in the reappearance of insect-borne diseases. Spread of the viruses is facilitated by urbanization, crowding, war, and the breakdown of social restraints on sexual behavior and intravenous drug use. U.S. residents will not be able to escape the effects of these new pathogens. The ease and speed of international travel means that a new infection first appearing anywhere in the world could traverse entire continents within days or weeks. This was dramatically illustrated by the emergence and rapid spread of SARS, as described in Chapter 9. The SARS virus is believed to have been transmitted to humans from an animal species used for food in China, possibly the civet cat.

INFLUENZA

Influenza—the "flu"—may seem like an old familiar infectious disease. However, it can be a different disease from one year to the next and has the capacity to turn into a major killer. This happened in the winter of 1918–1919, when the flu killed twenty million to forty million people worldwide, including 196,000 people who died in the United States in October.[24] Even in the average year, influenza kills 500,000 to one million people worldwide.[25] Although normally most deaths from flu occur in people over sixty-five, the 1918 epidemic preferentially struck young people.

Influenza virus has been studied extensively, and vaccination can be effective, but constant vigilance is necessary to protect people from the disease. Like HIV, influenza is an RNA virus, constantly changing its appearance and adept at eluding recognition by the human immune system. Because of the year-to-year variability of the flu virus, flu vaccines must be changed annually to be effective against the newest strain. Each winter, viral samples are collected from around the world and sent to WHO, where biomedical scientists conduct experiments designed to predict how the virus will mutate into next year's strain. These educated guesses form the basis for next year's vaccine.

At unpredictable intervals, however, a lethal new strain of the flu virus can come along, as it did in 1918. A strain that caused the Asian flu emerged in 1957, and a third, called Hong Kong flu, arrived in 1968. Neither of the latter outbreaks was as deadly as the 1918 epidemic, although a not insignificant 70,000 Americans died from the Asian flu. In 1976, CDC scientists thought they had evidence that another deadly strain—swine flu—was emerging, and the country mobilized for a massive immunization campaign. That time, the scientists had made a mistake, and the anticipated epidemic never occurred. Most infectious disease experts believe that, by now, the world is overdue for a lethal new epidemic.

New strains of influenza virus, especially those that have undergone major changes, tend to arise in Asia, particularly China, and then spread around the world from there. One of the reasons China is an especially fertile source of new flu strains is that animal reservoirs for influenza—pigs and birds—are common there, living in close proximity to humans. Human and animal influenza viruses incubate in a pig's digestive system, forming new genetic combinations, and are then spread by ducks as they migrate. While such hybrid viruses, containing human and animal genes, are only rarely capable of infecting humans, those that are able to do so are the most likely to be deadly.

Until recently, little was known about what made the 1918 strain of influenza so deadly, or how to predict the lethality of new strains that come along. Recently, however, genetic studies have been possible using samples of the 1918 virus. Tissue taken from soldiers who died in 1918 had been stored at the Armed Forces Institute of Pathology in Washington, D.C., and from victims in an Alaskan village who were buried in permanently frozen ground. Scientists have found that the 1918 virus has features in common with avian flu viruses which make it especially dangerous to humans, and it also resembles the human virus enough so that it can spread easily among people.[26] Similar avian features were found in the viruses that caused epidemics in 1957 and 1968.

Thus influenza experts were alarmed in 1997, when a three-year old Hong Kong boy died from a strain of influenza virus that normally infected chickens. There had been an epidemic of the disease in the birds a few months earlier. Antibodies to the virus were found in the blood of the boy's doctor, although he did not become ill, and public health authorities watched for more cases with great concern. Two dozen other people became sick by December, and six died. To prevent further transmission from chickens to humans, the Hong Kong government ordered that all one and one-half million chickens in the territory be killed. That action seems to have been effective in halting the epidemic in humans.[27]

Bird flu emerged again in 2003. It appears to have become widespread in poultry in several Asian countries despite efforts to eliminate it by killing millions of birds.[28] Human deaths from bird flu were recorded in 2003 and 2004 in Thailand and Vietnam. Thus far it appears that all the human victims of the bird flu had caught the virus from chickens, not from other humans. There is great concern that mixing of the viral genes could occur in a person infected with both the bird virus and a human flu virus, resulting in a much more virulent strain capable of spreading among humans. The new virus could start a global pandemic of a lethal form of the disease, as in 1918. Scientists are trying to develop a vaccine against the bird flu virus, but this is proving more difficult than making existing flu vaccines. One new drug has been found effective against the disease, but it is expensive and not yet available in the large quantities that would be necessary if there is a pandemic.

The public health approach to influenza control can serve as a model for how to predict and possibly prevent the spread of other new viral threats. As the AIDS epidemic has shown, a new virus can come from "nowhere" and wreak havoc all over the world within a few years. Complacency over the "conquest" of infectious diseases led governments to cut budgets and reduce efforts at monitoring disease. That should not happen again. The public health information gathering network is more important than ever.

NEW BACTERIAL THREATS

Bacteria, which two decades ago seemed easily controllable because of the power of antibiotics to wipe them out, have, like viruses, emerged in more deadly forms. Previously unknown bacterial diseases such as Legionnaires' and Lyme disease have appeared. More baffling is the fact that some ordinary bacterial infections have turned unexpectedly lethal. A great cause for concern is the development of resistance to drugs. Resistance can spread among pathogens of the same species and even from one bacterial species to another.

Legionnaires' and Lyme diseases are not new, but it is only recently that they became common enough to be recognized as distinct entities and for their bacterial causes to be identified. As described in Chapter 4, legionnella bacteria were able to flourish in water towers used for air conditioning. Regulations requiring antimicrobial agents in the water have been effective in limiting the spread of Legionnaires' disease. The conditions that promote the spread of Lyme disease, however, are more difficult to change. The pathogen that causes Lyme disease was identified in 1982 as a spirochete that is spread by the bite of an infected deer tick.[29] The reservoir for Lyme disease is the white-footed mouse, on which the deer tick feeds and becomes infected. Deer, on which the ticks grow and reproduce, are an important step in the chain of infection, and it is because of the recent explosion in the deer population in suburban areas that Lyme disease has now become such a problem for humans.

Infection with streptococci, the bacteria that cause strep throat, had normally been easily cured with penicillin. However, for reasons that are not well understood, a more lethal strain of the bacteria, called Group A streptococci, has become increasingly common. The sudden death of Muppets puppeteer Jim Henson in 1990 from fulminating pneumonia and toxic shock was caused by this new, virulent strain. The headline-grabbing "flesh-eating bacteria" that infect wounds to the extent of necessitating amputations and even causing death are also Group A streptococci. The Group A strain, which produces a potent toxin, was prevalent in the early part of the twentieth century, when it caused scarlet fever, frequently fatal in children. For decades, the Group A strain was superseded by strains B and C, which were much milder in their pathogenic effects, but now, for reasons that are not clear, the trend seems to be reversing.[30]

Another bacterium that has recently become more deadly is E. coli, which is normally present without ill effect in the human digestive tract. In 1993, the new threat gained national attention when a number of people became severely ill after eating hamburgers at a Jack in the Box restaurant in Seattle, and four children died of kidney failure. The culprit was found to be a new strain of E. coli, which had acquired a gene for shiga toxin from a dysentery-causing bacterium. The toxin, against which there is no treatment, causes kidney failure, especially in children and the elderly. The shiga toxin gene had "jumped" from one species of bacteria to another while they were both present in human intestines. The resulting strain, called E. coli O157:H7, is now quite common in ground beef, leading public health authorities to recommend or require thorough cooking of hamburgers.[11] The "jumping gene" phenomenon has also been found in cholera and diphtheria bacteria, bacterial strains that can be benign or virulent depending on the presence or absence of genes that produce toxins.

Since the finding that E. coli O157:H7 is common in hamburger, it has been discovered to cause illness by a number of other exposures, including unpasteurized apple cider and alfalfa sprouts.[31] In 1999, there was an outbreak in upstate New York among people who had attended a county fair. The bacteria were found in the water supplied to food and drink vendors. It turns out that E. coli O157:H7 is widespread in the intestines of cattle, especially calves, which excrete large quantities of the bacteria in manure. The manure may contaminate apples fallen from trees or other produce, which if not thoroughly washed before being consumed, may spread the disease to people. At the New York State county fair, the water was contaminated because heavy rain washed manure from the nearby cattle barn into a well.[32]

Perhaps the most disturbing development in infectious diseases is the antibiotic resistance among many species of bacteria, a development that leaves physicians powerless against many diseases they thought were conquered. The process by which bacteria become resistant to an antibiotic is a splendid example of evolution in action. In the presence of an antibiotic drug, any mutation that allows a single bacterium to survive confers on it a tremendous selective advantage. That bacterium can then reproduce without competition from other microbes, transmitting the mutation to its offspring. The result is a strain of the bacteria that is resistant to that particular antibiotic. The mutated gene can also "jump" to other bacteria of the same or different species by the exchange of plasmids, small pieces of DNA that can move from one bacterial organism to another. Different mutations may be necessary to confer resistance to different antibiotics. Some bacteria become resistant to many different antibiotics, making it very difficult to treat patients infected with those bacteria.

Improper use of antibiotics favors the development of resistance, and the current widespread existence of resistant bacteria testifies to the carelessness with which these lifesaving drugs have been used. For example, since antibiotics are powerless against viruses, the common practice of prescribing these drugs for a viral infection merely affords stray bacteria the opportunity to develop resistance. Another example of improper use is the common tendency of patients to stop taking an antibiotic when they feel better instead of continuing for the full prescribed course. The first few days' dose may have killed off all but a few bacteria, the most resistant, which may then survive and multiply, becoming much more difficult to control. In some countries, antibiotics are available without a prescription, increasing the likelihood that they will be used improperly.

A practice that significantly contributes to antibiotic resistance is the widespread use in animal feeds of low doses of antibiotics, which makes livestock grow bigger and healthier. More antibiotics are used in this manner than in medical applications, and the practice has clearly led to the survival of resistant strains of bacteria that may not only contaminate the meat but also spread the antibiotic resistance genes to other bacteria.[33] Because the agricultural industry benefits from the practice, government has been reluctant to impose regulations on it. Routine use of antibiotics in animal feed has been banned in Europe.

The bacteria salmonella and campylobacter are estimated to cause 3.8 million cases of food-borne illness in the United States each year. In a 1999 study, 26 percent of the salmonella cases and 54 percent of the campylobacter cases were found to be resistant to at least one antibiotic, probably because of antibiotic use in animal feed.[34] Resistance to erythromycin and other common antibiotics is increasingly found in Group A streptococci, discussed above.[35] One study done in Atlanta in 1994 found that pneumococci isolated from 25 percent of patients were resistant to multiple drugs, and over 40 percent of white children under six years of age harbored strains that were resistant to penicillin.[36] Infection with multidrug-resistant staphylococci is a major problem in hospitals, burn centers, and nursing homes, where hospital staff may carry the bacteria from one vulnerable patient to another. Hospital-acquired infections, many of them caused by drug resistant bacteria, are estimated to cost $4.5 to $5.7 billion and contribute to some 90,000 deaths annually in the United States.[37]

MULTIDRUG-RESISTANT TUBERCULOSIS

Tuberculosis used to be a major killer in the United States. Between 1800 and 1870, it accounted for one out of every five deaths in this country. Worldwide, it is still the leading cause of death among infectious diseases. It is a disease associated with poverty, thought to be conquered in the affluent United States, where the incidence of tuberculosis steadily declined between 1882 and 1985. Much of the success came from the early public health movement, which emphasized improvement of slum housing, sanitation, and pasteurization of cows' milk, which harbored a bovine form of the bacillus that was pathogenic to humans. Patients were isolated in sanatoriums, where they were required to rest and breathe fresh air and, incidentally, were prevented from infecting others. With the introduction of antibiotics in 1947, mortality from tuberculosis was dramatically reduced, sanatoriums were closed, and tuberculosis seemed vanquished.

In 1985, however, the trend reversed. There were several reasons for the increase in the incidence of tuberculosis, which was particularly concentrated in cities. The HIV epidemic was certainly a major factor. People with defective immune systems are more susceptible to any infection, but HIV-positive people are especially vulnerable to tuberculosis. An increasing homeless population and the rise in intravenous drug use, both of which are associated with HIV infection, were also factors in increasing tuberculosis rates. Homeless shelters, prisons, and urban hospitals are prime sites for the transmission of tuberculosis.

But tuberculosis is not limited to the "down and out" or those who participate in high risk behavior. "The principal risk behavior for acquiring TB infection is breathing," as one expert says.[38(p.1058)] People have been infected with tuberculosis bacilli in the course of a variety of everyday activities: a long airplane trip sitting within a few rows of a person with active tuberculosis,[39] hanging out in a Minneapolis bar frequented by a homeless man with active tuberculosis,[40] and, most frightening, attending a suburban school with a girl whose tuberculosis went undiagnosed for thirteen months.[41]

When tuberculosis bacilli are inhaled by a healthy person, they do not usually cause illness in the short term. Most often, the immune system responds by killing off most of the bacilli and walling off the rest into small calcified lesions in the lungs called tubercles, which remain dormant indefinitely. Evidence that a person has been exposed shows up in tuberculin skin tests, which cause a conspicuous immune response when a small extract from the bacillus is injected under the exposed person's skin. For reasons that are not well understood, probably having to do with individual immune system variations, a small percentage of people develop active disease soon after exposure; others may harbor the latent infection for years before it becomes active. Infected people have a 10 percent lifetime risk of developing an active case. The risk for people who are HIV positive is much higher: 60 to 80 percent.[31] Most cases of active tuberculosis are characterized by growth of the bacilli in the lungs, causing breakdown of the tissue and the major symptom—coughing—which releases the infectious agents into the air.

Before the introduction of antibiotics, about one-half the patients with active tuberculosis died. Antibiotics dramatically reduced not only the mortality rate, but the incidence rate as well, since the medication relieved coughing and therefore inhibited the spread of disease. However, the development of multidrug resistance in some strains of the bacilli has meant that people with disease caused by these strains have a 50 percent risk of dying, equal to the risk patients had before the drugs were available.

The increased prevalence of the antibiotic resistant strains in all parts of this country during the 1980s is thought to be due to the fact that many patients did not take their medications regularly. The tuberculosis bacillus is a particularly difficult pathogen to deal with because it grows slowly and diagnostic testing can take several weeks. Once the disease is diagnosed, even the most potent antibiotic must be taken for several months to wipe out the pathogens. Patients commonly begin to feel better after two to four weeks of taking an effective prescribed drug and, if they stop taking the medication at that point, they may relapse with a drug-resistant strain.

That multidrug-resistant tuberculosis can be a threat to all strata of society was made clear by an epidemic that was finally recognized in a suburban California school in 1993. The source of the outbreak was a sixteen-year-old immigrant student who had contracted the disease in her native Vietnam.[41] She had developed a persistent cough in January 1991, but her doctors had failed to diagnose the cause as tuberculosis until thirteen months later. Even then, they did not report the case to the county health department, as required by law, and when the case was reported by the laboratory that had analyzed her sputum, the doctors refused to cooperate with the health department. By the time the county authorities took over her case in 1993, the girl had developed a drug-resistant strain. In accordance with standard public health practice, the health department then began screening all the girl's contacts for tuberculosis infection. Twenty-three percent of the 1,263 students given the tuberculin skin test were found to be positive for exposure to the infection. Thirteen students had active cases of the drug-resistant strain of the disease. Fortunately no one died.[42]

It is clearly in the community interest to ensure that all tuberculosis patients be properly diagnosed and provided a full course of medications, whether or not they can afford to pay, to prevent them from spreading the disease. New York City has proven that, by applying public health measures, it is possible to reverse the trend of increasing multidrug-resistant tuberculosis, a trend that had been worse in that city than anywhere else in the nation. In 1992, the number of tuberculosis cases diagnosed in the

city had nearly tripled over the previous fifteen years, and 23 percent of
new cases were resistant to drugs. The city and state began intensive public health measures, which included screening high-risk populations and
providing therapy to everyone diagnosed with active tuberculosis. A program of directly observed therapy was instituted for patients who were
judged unlikely to take their medications regularly. Outreach workers
traveled to patients' homes, workplaces, street corners, park benches, or
wherever necessary to observe that each patient took each dose of his or
her medicine. As a result of these measures, the number of new cases of
tuberculosis fell in 1993, 1994, and 1995, and the percentage of cases that
were multidrug-resistant also fell by 30 percent in a two year period.[43]
New York's success has been echoed by national trends, as shown in
Figure 10–1, giving hope that concerted public health efforts can eliminate tuberculosis as a serious public health threat in the United States.

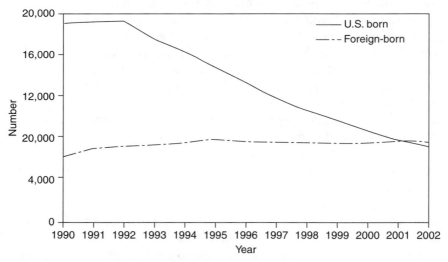

Figure 10–1 TUBERCULOSIS. Reported Cases Among U.S.-Born
and Foreign-Born Persons,* by Year—United States, 1990–2002
*For 120 cases, origin of patients was unknown.
The number of tuberculosis cases among foreign-born persons in the United States
increased from 6,262 (25% of the total number) in 1990 to 7,659 (51% of the total)
in 2002.
Source: www.cdc.gov/MMWR/PDF/WK/MM5153.pdf. Accessed 6/30/05.

Throughout the world, more than one-third of the population is infected with the tuberculosis bacillus.[44] The prevalence of antibiotic-resistant strains is still relatively low, but they have been found in every country and are especially common in parts of China, Russia, and other eastern European countries.[45] The spread of HIV around the world has made tuberculosis more deadly than ever. Because of immigration and international travel, the United States will need to continue tuberculosis control programs at home and to actively participate in global efforts to control the disease around the world to avoid future outbreaks in this country.

It is clear that in the struggle between microbes' ability to evolve new variations and human ingenuity in devising new defenses against them, the microbes are gaining. In a special issue of *Science* magazine devoted to emerging infections, a CDC scientist says that a "post-antimicrobial era may be rapidly approaching," when effective antibiotics will no longer be available to treat bacterial infections.[46(p.1055)] That era will force public health professionals back to more emphasis on prevention of disease transmission with classical public health measures such as surveillance, immunization, sanitation, and infection control procedures.

PRIONS

As if new viruses and drug-resistant bacteria were not worrisome enough, a novel form of infectious disease grabbed headlines in the 1990s. Creutzfeldt-Jacob disease (CJD) is a rare and devastating disorder in which the patient becomes demented and ultimately dies, and the brain appears spongy on autopsy because many brain cells have died. Similar diseases in animals can be transmitted by injecting brain tissue from an infected animal into the brain of a previously healthy one. However, no virus or bacteria has been found responsible for causing the condition. In 1997, Stanley Prusiner, a scientist at the University of California Medical School in San Francisco, won the Nobel Prize for his controversial theory that this type of disease is caused by particles called prions, which contain protein but no nucleic acid and thus no traditional genetic material.

In 1996, a paper appeared in a British medical journal reporting that ten persons in the United Kingdom under the age of forty-five had been diagnosed with a CJD-like condition, an unusually high incidence in a group much younger than those usual struck by the disease.[47] The authors suggested a link with an epidemic of bovine spongiform encephalopathy (BSE), known as "mad cow disease," which had killed over 160,000 cattle in Britain over the previous decade. The disease was spread by the practice, now discontinued, of grinding up discarded animal parts and adding them to feed for other cattle. A flurry of alarm and a European ban on British beef led the British government in 1996 to order the mass slaughter of all at-risk cattle to prevent the possibility of human exposure to infected beef.[48]

The evidence is strong that consumption of contaminated beef is the cause of new variant CJD (vCJD). As of December 1, 2003, 153 cases had been reported worldwide, of which 143 were in the United Kingdom. Most of the others had lived there during the years of the BSE outbreak among cattle.[49] There is great controversy about whether enough is being done to protect American cattle from BSE. Regulations on cattle feed have been tightened and restrictions have been introduced that prohibit certain cattle parts from entering the food supply. However, many critics believe more should be done. In Japan, all cattle to be used for food are tested for mad cow disease at the time of slaughter. In France, about half of the slaughtered cattle are tested. In the United States, tests are done on only a small fraction of the slaughtered cattle. One case of BSE was identified in late 2003 in a cow imported from Canada. Critics say that the American policy on testing is based more on economic factors than health concerns and that the Agriculture Department does not want to find diseased cows for fear of damaging the market for exports of American beef.[50]

PUBLIC HEALTH RESPONSE TO EMERGING INFECTIONS

The American public health system, criticized in 1988 for being in disarray, has taken many steps toward responding to the emerging threats of infectious diseases. While still underfunded and challenged from all sides, American public health agencies have devoted significant resources to developing plans and priorities for confronting the threats.

In 1992, the Institute of Medicine (IOM) released a report called *Emerging Infections: Microbial Threats to Health in the United States*, which focused attention on the seriousness of microbial threats. In response, the CDC in 1994 developed a strategic plan for how the U.S. public health system should respond to emerging infectious diseases. In 2001, the IOM was again asked to review the nation's knowledge and preparedness for confronting infectious disease. A second report, *Microbial Threats to Health: Emergence, Detection, and Response*, was published in 2003.[51]

Recommendations from both IOM reports and the CDC agree on the importance of efforts in several areas. Some of these efforts are underway, as described in Chapter 29. Priorities specifically identified by the 2003 IOM report include:

1. Global surveillance for infectious diseases.
2. Rebuild domestic public health capacity at federal, state, and local levels.
3. Improve domestic surveillance through better disease reporting, not only by medical health care providers but also by veterinary health care providers.
4. Explore innovative systems of surveillance and data collection, especially electronic systems.
5. Develop and use diagnostic tests to direct appropriate treatment and reduce inappropriate use of antibiotics.
6. Education and training of the workforce that deals with microbial threats.
7. Need for the development and production of new vaccines.
8. Need for new antimicrobial drug.
9. Reduce inappropriate use of antimicrobial drugs, including use for growth promotion in animals.
10. Vector-borne and zoonotic (animal-borne) disease control.

PUBLIC HEALTH AND THE THREAT OF BIOTERRORISM

The late 1990s saw a burst of concern in the United States about the possibility that biological organisms could be used as agents of warfare and terrorism. The anthrax attacks of 2001, described in the Prologue, demonstrated that the concern was well founded. Earlier incidents had raised awareness of the possible threat, including revelations by a Russian defector that the Soviets had developed systems for loading smallpox virus on ballistic missiles.[52] Concern was heightened by evidence that Iraq had produced missile warheads and bombs containing anthrax spores and botulinum toxin.[52] The Aum Shinrikyo cult that released sarin gas in a Tokyo subway was found later to have experimented with releases of aerosolized anthrax and botulinum toxin throughout the city.[53] Closer to home, a 1984 outbreak of salmonellosis that sickened 751 people in The Dalles, Oregon was eventually traced to intentional contamination of salad bars in several restaurants, details of which were revealed much later in a criminal prosecution of the Baghwan religious cult that was responsible for the incident.[54]

Even before the anthrax attacks of 2001, the CDC had developed plans for dealing with biological terrorism. It was clear that, in contrast with bombings or chemical attacks, dissemination of biological agents is likely to be done in a covert way. Thus, the first signs of an attack are likely to be seen by physicians and hospital emergency rooms. Local health departments will carry out the initial investigations of unusual disease outbreaks, and good surveillance is vital for recognizing outbreaks as early as possible. In sum, the approach to bioterrorism preparedness is much the same as the response to an epidemic of any other origin. In fact, the IOM report, *Microbial Threats to Health*, discussed previously, includes intentionally introduced biological agents as one of many emerging threats, to be defended against according to the same recommendations.[51] Preparedness for bioterrorism is discussed further in Chapter 29.

CONCLUSION

Infectious diseases have increasingly threatened the health of Americans over the past two decades, in a challenge to the earlier view that infectious diseases were under control. The appearance of AIDS in the early 1980s was an early sign that a new disease could appear out of "nowhere" and rapidly become a lethal, world-wide epidemic. Other viruses such as Ebola and other hemorrhagic fevers have emerged in tropical areas and could be brought to the United States if conditions were right. A deadly hantavirus appeared in the United States in 1993 and has been reported in twenty-nine states. West Nile virus was first recognized in New York City in 1999 and has spread across the country to almost all states. Monkeypox, a virus similar to smallpox that primarily infects rodents, was brought to the United States in exotic pets imported from Africa and sickened a number of people in 2003. Influenza is a highly infectious disease that can spread rapidly all over the world. While the public health system has worked internationally, adapting vaccines to keep up with the rapidly mutating viruses, everyone is frightened by the prospect of another worldwide flu epidemic like the one in 1918 that killed twenty to forty million people.

New bacterial diseases have also been appearing in the United States as ecological and cultural conditions change. Lyme disease and Legionnaires' disease have been significant problems in the past two decades. Streptococci and E. coli have become much more deadly in recent years. Many bacteria, including M. tuberculosis have developed resistance to antibiotics, making them much less vulnerable to treatment.

To combat today's emerging infectious threats, public health professionals must update measures successful in the early part of the twentieth century. Plans are in place to fortify the public health system to improve surveillance and response to the new threats. As with many other aspects of public health, however, political controversy and economic concerns tend to impede the implementation of effective measures, such as those needed to deal with antibiotic resistance stimulated by agricultural practices. New concerns about the threat of biological terrorism have added urgency to the call for strengthening the public health system in the United States.

REFERENCES

1. "20 Years of HIV Science (editorial)," *Nature Medicine* 9 (2003): 801.
2. U.S. Centers for Disease Control and Prevention, *HIV/AIDS Surveillance Report, 2002* 14: 16.
3. W. C. Greene, "AIDS and the Immune System," *Scientific American* (September 1993): 99–103.
4. M. Pope and A. T. Haase, "Transmission, Acute HIV-1 Infection and the Quest for Strategies to Prevent Infection," *Nature Medicine* 9 (2003): 847–852.
5. M. A. Nowak and A. J. McMichael, "How HIV Defeats the Immune System," *Scientific American* (August 1995): 58–65.
6. R. O. Valdiserri et al., "Accomplishments in HIV Prevention Science: Implications for Stemming the Epidemic," *Nature Medicine* 9 (2003): 881–886.
7. R. J. Pomerantz and D. L. Horn, "Twenty Years of Therapy for HIV-1 Infection," *Nature Medicine* 9 (2003): 867–873.
8. A. S. Fauci, "HIV and AIDS: 20 Years of Science," *Nature Medicine* 9 (2003): 839–843.
9. A. Garg, "Acquired and Inherited Lipodystrophies," *New England Journal of Medicine* 350 (2004): 1220.
10. J. Bhattacharya, "The Link between Public and Private Insurance and HIV-Related Mortality," *Journal of Health Economics* 22 (2003): 1105–1122.
11. L. Garrett, *The Coming Plague: Newly Emerging Diseases in a World Out of Balance* (New York: Farrar, Straus and Giroux, 1994).
12. T. Zhu et al., "An African HIV-1 Sequence from 1959 and Implications for the Origin of the Epidemic," *Nature* 391 (1998): 594–597.
13. B. Le Guenno, "Emerging Viruses," *Scientific American* (October 1995): 56–64.
14. E. M. Leroy et al., "Multiple Ebola Virus Transmission Events and Rapid Decline of Central African Wildlife," *Science* 303 (2004): 387–390.
15. R. Preston, *The Hot Zone* (New York: Random House, 1994).

16. K. D. Reed et al., "The Detection of Monkeypox in Humans in the Western Hemisphere," *New England Journal of Medicine* 350 (2004): 342–350.

17. U.S. Centers for Disease Control and Prevention, "Outbreak of Acute Illness—Southwestern United States, 1993," *Morbidity and Mortality Weekly Report* 42 (1993): 421–424.

18. U.S. Centers for Disease Control and Prevention, "Hantavirus Pulmonary Syndrome—United States: Updated Recommendations for Risk Reduction," *Recommendations and Reports* 51 (RR09) (2002): 1–12.

19. U.S. Centers for Disease Control and Prevention, "Hantavirus Pulmonary Syndrome—Northeastern United States, 1994," *Morbidity and Mortality Weekly Report* 43 (1994): 548–549, 555–556.

20. U.S. Centers for Disease Control and Prevention, "Outbreak of West Nile-Like Viral Encephalitis—New York, 1999," *Morbidity and Mortality Weekly Report* 48 (1999): 845–849.

21. U.S. Centers for Disease Control and Prevention, "Update: West Nile Virus Encephalitis—New York, 1999," *Morbidity and Mortality Weekly Report* 48 (1999): 944–946.

22. U.S. Centers for Disease Control and Prevention, "West Nile Virus Activity—United States, November 20–25, 2003," *Morbidity and Mortality Weekly Report* 52 (2003): 1160.

23. U.S. Centers for Disease Control and Prevention, *http://westnilemaps.usgs.gov/background.html*, July 6, 2004. Accessed July 29, 2004.

24. R. M. Henig, "Flu Pandemic," *New York Times Magazine* (November 20, 1992): 28–67.

25. S. P. Layne et al., "A Global Lab Against Influenza," *Science* 293 (2001): 1729.

26. E. C. Holmes, "1918 and All That," *Science* 303 (2004): 1787–1788.

27. E. C. J. Claas et al., "Human Influenza A H5N1 Virus Related to a Highly Pathogenic Avian Influenza Virus," *The Lancet* 351 (1998): 472–477.

28. U.S. Centers for Disease Control and Prevention, "Update: Influenza Activity—United States and Worldwide, 2003–04 Season, and Composition of the 2004–05 Influenza Vaccine," *Morbidity and Mortality Weekly Report* 53 (2004): 547–552.

29. F. S. Kantor, "Disarming Lyme Disease," *Scientific American* (September 1994): 34–39.

30. R. M. Krause, "The Origin of Plagues: Old and New," *Science* 257 (1992): 1073–1078.

31. J. Chin, *Control of Communicable Diseases Manual* (Washington, DC: American Public Health Association, 2000), 155–158.

32. U.S. Centers for Disease Control and Prevention, "Public Health Dispatch: Outbreak of *Escherichia coli* O157:H7 and *Campylobacter* Among Attendees of the Washington County Fair—New York 1999," *Morbidity and Mortality Weekly Report* 48 (1999): 803.

33. W. Witte, "Medical Consequences of Antibiotic Use in Agriculture," *Science* 279 (1998): 996–997.

34. S. L. Gorbach, "Antimicrobial Use in Animal Feed—Time to Stop," *New England Journal of Medicine* 345 (2001): 1202–1203.

35. P. Hudvinen, "Macrolide-Resistant Group A Streptococcus—Now in the United States," *New England Journal of Medicine* 346 (2002): 1243–1245.

36. J. Hofmann et al., "The Prevalence of Drug-Resistant Streptococcus Pneumoniae in Atlanta," *New England Journal of Medicine* 333 (1995): 481–486.

37. J. P. Burke, "Infection Control—A Problem for Patient Safety," *New England Journal of Medicine* 348 (2003): 651–656.

38. B. R. Bloom and C. J. L. Murray, "Tuberculosis: Commentary on a Reemergent Killer," *Science* 257 (1992): 1055–1064.

39. T. A. Kenyon, "Transmission of Multidrug-resistant Mycobacterium Tuberculosis During a Long Airplane Flight," *New England Journal of Medicine* 334 (1996): 935–938.

40. S. Kline et al., "Outbreak of Tuberculosis Among Regular Patrons of a Neighborhood Bar," *New England Journal of Medicine* 333 (1995): 222–227.

41. "California School Becomes Notorious for Epidemic of TB," *New York Times* (July 18, 1994): A1.

42. R. Ridzon et al., "Outbreak of Drug-Resistant Tuberculosis with Second-Generation Transmission in a High School in California," *Journal of Pediatrics* 131 (1997): 863–868.

43. T. R. Frieden et al., "Tuberculosis in New York City—Turning the Tide," *New England Journal of Medicine* 333 (1995): 229–233.

44. P. M. Small, "Management of Tuberculosis in the United States," *New England Journal of Medicine* 345 (2001): 189–200.

45. M. A. Espinal et al., "Global Trends in Resistance to Antituberculosis Drugs," *New England Journal of Medicine* 345 (2001): 1294–1303.

46. M. I. Cohen, "Epidemiology of Drug Resistance: Implications for a Post-Antimicrobial Era," *Science* 257 (1992): 1050–1055.

47. R. G. Will et al., "A New Variant of Creutzfeldt-Jacob Disease in the U.K.," *The Lancet* 347 (1996): 921–925.

48. P. G. Smith and S. N. Cousens, "Is the New Variant of Creutzfeldt-Jacob Disease from Mad Cows?" *Science* 273 (1996): 748.

49. U.S. Centers for Disease Control and Prevention, "Fact Sheet: New Variant Creutzfeldt-Jakob Disease," *www.cdc.gov/ncidod/diseases/cjd/cjd_fact_sheet.htm*, January 20, 2004. Accessed August 1, 2004.

50. D. G. McNeil Jr., "Doubling Tests for Mad Cow Doesn't Quiet Program Critics," *New York Times* 9 (February 9, 2004): A8.

51. U.S. Institute of Medicine, *Microbial Threats to Health: Emergence, Detection, and Response* (Washington, DC: National Academy Press, 2003).

52. C. J. Davis, "Nuclear Blindness: An Overview of the Biological Weapons Programs of the Former Soviet Union and Iraq," *Emerging Infectious Diseases* 5 (2000): 509–512.

53. K. B. Olson, "Aum Shinrikyo: Once and Future Threat?" *Emerging Infectious Diseases* 5 (2000): 513–516.

54. T. J. Torok, "A Large Community Outbreak of Salmonellosis Caused by Intentional Contamination of Restaurant Salad Bars," *Journal of the American Medical Association* 278 (1997): 389–395.

CHAPTER 11

The Biomedical Basis
of Chronic Diseases

Evolution of the Research Study

The early successes of public health against infectious diseases led to a change in the major causes of illness and death beginning in the 1920s. Chronic degenerative diseases, especially heart disease and cancer, are now the leading causes of death in the United States. While they are primarily diseases of old age—when everyone must die of something—they also strike people in their prime, robbing them of productive years of life. Cancer is the leading cause of death among Americans aged forty-five to sixty-five, and cardiovascular disease runs a close second. Other significant diseases of current public health concern include diabetes, arthritis, and Alzheimer's disease, which may not be as deadly in the short run but have severe impact on the quality of life. It is the mission of public health to prevent such premature death and disability.

Prevention of disease usually requires some understanding of the cause, a requirement that is generally much more difficult to fulfill for chronic diseases than for infectious ones. There is no single pathogen that causes cancer or heart disease, nor is there one for arthritis, diabetes, or Alzheimer's disease. In most cases, chronic diseases have multiple causes, making it more difficult for scientists to recognize significant factors and establish preventive measures. Moreover, these diseases tend to develop over long periods of time, further complicating the task of pinning down causes. In some cases, however, the gradual onset provides the advantage of early detection, permitting secondary prevention—interventions early in the disease process that can mitigate its impact.

As chronic degenerative diseases became a growing problem during the twentieth century, scientists began to focus on efforts to understand their causes. The growth of the National Institutes of Health (NIH), which sponsors most biomedical research in the United States, has reflected the growth of concern about these diseases. In its early days as a one-room Laboratory of Hygiene that opened in 1887, the NIH conducted research primarily on infectious diseases. Congress created the National Cancer Institute in 1937 and the Heart Institute—now called the National Heart, Lung, and Blood Institute (NHLBI)—in 1948. Now there are nineteen different institutes, each of them focused on a different organ or problem, mostly chronic diseases. One institute, for example, is concerned with arthritis, one with diabetes, and one with neurological disorders and stroke. (See list of institutes and centers in Chapter 3, Figure 3–5.)

Research into the causes of chronic disease, like research into the causes of infectious disease, relies on the epidemiologic methods discussed in Chapters 4, 5, and 6 and on laboratory research, which usually includes studies of animals as models, or stand-ins for human patients. The importance of research on animal models to the understanding of human disease cannot be overemphasized. Epidemiology is generally limited to observation and analysis of events that occur spontaneously. Ethical concerns severely limit the experiments that can be done on humans. In experiments on laboratory animals, scientists can carefully control the conditions so that cause and effect relationships can be clearly proven. Mice and rats are the most commonly used laboratory animals; as mammals, they share the majority of biochemical and physiological processes with humans. Because of their short life spans, the effects of various exposures and interventions can be studied over the lifetime of the animals. However, mammals can differ in unpredictable ways in their susceptibility to infectious or toxic agents. Different experimental animals have proven useful for studying different diseases, and extrapolation of results from other mammals to humans is not always valid.

The identification of an animal model can significantly improve progress toward understanding a disease. It is not always easy to find an experimental animal that is susceptible to the disease one wishes to study. For instance, there is no good animal model for AIDS, a fact that has hampered progress in developing drug therapies or vaccines. Asian macaque monkeys, which can be made sick by simian immunodeficiency virus, a relative of human immunodeficiency virus (HIV), are the closest substitute. Only chimpanzees can be infected with HIV, and chimps are no longer used for research for ethical and cost reasons.[1] Animals also differ in how they metabolize some chemicals; a dose of dioxin that would kill a guinea pig has no effect on a mouse or rat, and it is difficult from this evidence to predict the chemical's toxicity to humans.

Scientists have been increasingly successful in devising methods of growing cells and tissues in laboratory glassware for studying biomedical processes. Such laboratory cultures are commonly used to investigate the cancer-causing potential of various chemicals. Much of the research on HIV has been done using cultured cells, and a great deal has been learned. However, such experiments provide oversimplified conditions that may lead to invalid conclusions about the complex interactions that occur in intact animals. In the case of HIV, for example, a number of drugs that appeared to inactivate the virus in test tube experiments have proved to be ineffective in human patients.

CARDIOVASCULAR DISEASE

Cardiovascular disease encompasses two of the three leading causes of death in the United States: heart disease and stroke. The causes of cardiovascular disease have been relatively well established through epidemiologic studies, including the Framingham Study described in Chapter 4, as well as through animal experiments and examination of the bodies of people who have died of the disease. Understanding of cardiovascular disease has been facilitated by its prevalence in the United States and the fact that it follows a similar progression in many of its victims. The important role of blood components in determining individual risk was readily established because blood is easy to study; it can be drawn from patients and experimental subjects without major discomfort or ethical objections.

It has been known for decades that atherosclerosis—hardening of the arteries—is part of the development of cardiovascular disease. Pathologists performing autopsies on people who died of heart attacks found, within the inner wall lining of the deceased's arteries, a buildup of plaque composed of fat and cholesterol, blood cells, and clotting materials. The formation of plaque begins at an early age in the United States. Fatty streaks, the first stage in the development of plaque, have been found on autopsy in half the children aged ten to fourteen who died of accidental causes.[2] A classic study, published in 1955, examined the arteries of American soldiers killed in the Korean War and found that 77 percent of the men, whose average age was twenty-two, showed some signs of atherosclerosis.[3] More recent studies have confirmed these findings and showed that plaque was more likely to be found in adolescents and young adults with risk factors such as smoking, hypertension, obesity, and high levels of low-density lipoprotein cholesterol.[4]

Animal studies showed that diet plays a role in the formation of plaque. Rabbits fed milk, meat, and eggs instead of their normal vegetarian diet were found to develop atherosclerotic plaque very similar to that found in humans.[5] It was easy to deduce that the American diet was responsible for the high rate of cardiovascular disease in the United States.

Experiments on rats, rabbits, and monkeys have clarified the process by which high cholesterol and fat in the blood interact with other risk factors such as smoking, high blood pressure, and diabetes to form plaque in the arteries.[5] These factors cause chronic injury of the artery's inner wall, which the body attempts to repair, leading to a "healing" process that runs wild, becoming a disease in itself. The higher the levels of cholesterol and other fats in the blood, the more they are incorporated into the scab-like buildup and the faster the plaque forms. A heart attack or stroke results when the plaque ruptures, releasing clots that may block an artery in the heart or brain, cutting off the blood supply.

Recently, scientists have begun considering evidence that atherosclerosis may have an infectious component caused by bacteria that are often found in plaque.[6] The blood cells in plaque are characteristic of an immune response, and some scientists have reasoned that atherosclerosis is therefore an inflammatory condition like arthritis. This possibility is still controversial, and the implications for prevention, diagnosis, and treatment of atherosclerosis are not clear.

With the risk factors for cardiovascular disease well established, much of the recent epidemiologic and biomedical research has focused on trying to understand what determines the relative presence or absence of risk factors. A great deal has been learned about the various lipids (fats) in the blood, each of which plays a role in the individual's risk of cardiovascular disease, and how their concentrations may be increased or decreased. Factors that affect blood pressure have also been extensively studied.

Diabetes, which has its own research institute at NIH, greatly increases the risk of cardiovascular disease (see the following section for a discussion of the biomedical basis of diabetes). All these risk factors are determined in part by genetics, but they can be significantly modified by individual behavior and are thus susceptible to public health intervention.

High blood cholesterol is a well-known risk factor for atherosclerosis and heart disease. Cholesterol levels of 175 mg/dl (milligrams per deciliter of blood) or below are considered desirable: persons with that level of cholesterol have less than one-half the heart attack risk of those with levels between 250 and 275 mg/dl. Most of the cholesterol in the blood is bound up with protein in various forms, and some forms are more harmful than others. For example, if a high percentage of a person's cholesterol is in the form of high-density lipoprotein (HDL), sometimes called "good cholesterol," the person's risk of heart disease is much lower than that of someone with a high percentage of cholesterol in the form of low-density lipoprotein (LDL), "bad cholesterol." Many current studies try to identify factors that affect not only total cholesterol, but also the relative concentrations of HDL and LDL.

The main sources of cholesterol in the American diet are eggs, meat, and milk. In humans, as in rabbits, vegetarians have lower cholesterol levels than meat eaters. Vigorous exercise lowers total cholesterol and increases HDL. Moderate consumption of alcoholic beverages has a similar effect, although heavy drinking damages the heart. Other dietary substances such as fish, olive oil, and oat bran also appear to have favorable effects on blood lipids. Smoking lowers HDL levels. Genes play a role in the HDL-LDL balance also. Some people can eat lots of fat with very little effect on their blood cholesterol, while others must work much harder to maintain favorable levels.

In the last decade, the use of cholesterol-lowering drugs called statins has increased dramatically. The number of people who took the drugs grew from about two million in 1998 to more than ten million in 2004, when the NHLBI published new cholesterol guidelines that more than doubled the number of people who should take the drugs. Epidemiologic studies have clearly shown that statins can prevent heart attacks, even in people with cholesterol levels previously considered normal, and they appear to be safe for long-term use.[7] However, from a public health perspective, the trend toward prescribing drugs for healthy people to take for the rest of their lives is troubling. Moreover, statins are expensive. As a spokesman for the American Heart Association is quoted as saying,

"If you're going to increase my health insurance because my next door neighbor has borderline high cholesterol, and if he's sitting around and watching TV and eating and getting fat, do you want me to pay for that?"[8]

While the availability of statins appears to be good news for secondary prevention in people who already have atherosclerosis or who have risk factors that put them at high risk, the preferable public health approach to preventing heart disease is primary prevention. This means promoting healthy behavior, including exercise, not smoking, and eating a healthy diet. Eating a healthy diet is not easy in American society. Chapters 16 and 23 discuss the role of public health in promoting good nutrition. Other aspects of social and behavioral factors in health are also discussed in Part IV.

High blood pressure—hypertension—is a major risk factor for cardiovascular disease, contributing to the injury in the artery walls that is part of atherosclerosis. While some medical conditions are known to cause high blood pressure, most cases occur without known cause, and these people are said to have "essential hypertension." Factors that have been linked with essential hypertension are obesity, smoking, and stress. Dietary salt is believed to be a factor in causing some cases of essential hypertension, but sensitivity to salt is variable and is probably determined by genetics. Some strains of rats get high blood pressure when fed large amounts of salt, while rats of other strains do not seem to react to salt. Rats of one sensitive strain tend to have strokes when subjected to salt and stress, while rats of some other strains are unaffected.[9] The NHLBI recommends that everyone limit their salt intake to about a teaspoon a day, but researchers are divided whether the evidence supports the view that this measure would reduce blood pressure. Some studies suggest that deficiencies in calcium and other nutrients found in dairy products, fruits, and vegetables may be more significant in causing high blood pressure than excess amounts of dietary salt.[10]

Many people can keep their blood pressure under control by eating a healthy diet, exercise, and abstention from smoking, the same behavior that promotes healthy cholesterol levels. Secondary prevention is important: people should know their own blood pressure and take appropriate measures if it is too high. In the United States, 140/90 is generally considered the borderline above which blood pressure is considered too high. In this reading, 140 is the systolic pressure, that pressure exerted by the blood on the artery walls during the heart's contraction when the pressure is greatest. The diastolic pressure—90 in this case—occurs between contractions, when the heart is relaxed. New evidence prompded the NHLBI to issue guidelines in 2003 that classified blood pressure as "normal" only if it is below 120/80.

Since the risk of stroke rises continuously as blood pressure rises, people are advised to take medication if necessary to maintain a healthy blood pressure. The U.S. government launched a major blood pressure awareness program in 1972; since then, the annual rate of fatal strokes has been cut by more than half.[9,11]

Smoking is believed to increase the risk of cardiovascular disease through the actions of two components of tobacco smoke: nicotine and carbon monoxide. Nicotine, the addictive component of tobacco (as discussed in Chapter 15), is a stimulant that raises blood pressure, increases the pulse rate, stimulates release of stress hormones, and increases irritability of the heart and blood vessels. Carbon monoxide, a poisonous gas, binds to hemoglobin in the blood, blocking the hemoglobin's ability to carry oxygen throughout the body. Both nicotine and carbon monoxide place stress on the heart and blood vessels, with the long-term effect of contributing to atherosclerosis. In the short term, the effects of nicotine and carbon monoxide can provoke irregularities in heartbeat, which may result in sudden death.

Tobacco is especially significant as a cause of heart attack in younger adults. While heart attacks are relatively rare among people in their thirties and forties, those that do occur are likely to be caused by smoking. One epidemiologic study found that smokers in this age group have a five times greater rate of heart attacks than nonsmokers.[12]

CANCER

Cancer has proven much more difficult to understand than cardiovascular disease, in part because it has so many different manifestations. It is sometimes said that cancer is not one disease, but one hundred diseases. In many ways, breast cancer is different from lung cancer, which is different from leukemia. They typically differ as to risk factors, appearance under a microscope, response to various forms of treatment, and so forth. For the biomedical scientist and the public health professional trying to understand cancer cause and prevention, each kind of cancer must be studied separately. Despite the features specific to the particular organ in which the tumor forms, all cancer develops in basically the same way.

Cancer arises when the activities of a cell are transformed and the cell begins to grow out of control. Understanding cancer, therefore, requires understanding normal cell function—knowledge that has begun to be available only in the last decade or two. Increasingly sophisticated laboratory research has shown that, in general, a normal cell turns cancerous through a mutation in the genetic material, DNA—in particular, a mutation in one of the genes that regulate cell growth and differentiation. When that cell divides, the mutation is transmitted to the daughter cells, which, because of the disruption in control caused by the mutation, tend to divide more rapidly than normal. As the cells continue to divide abnormally, errors tend to occur as the DNA is copied, leading to additional mutations and more abnormalities in the cells that are becoming a tumor.[13]

To achieve the public health goal of preventing disease, it is important to know what causes the mutations that initiate the cancer. It turns out that mutations in DNA can be caused by many different types of agents, including chemicals, viruses, and radiation. Other factors, such as hormones and diet, play a role in determining whether a mutation progresses to the development of a tumor. Hormones, which function in the body to stimulate or inhibit cell growth, may have an enhanced effect on a mutated cell. The mechanisms by which dietary factors influence the development of cancer—in addition to the fact that some foods may contain carcinogens, or cancer-causing chemicals—are less well understood. There is some evidence that dietary fiber protects against cancer, perhaps because it speeds the passage of possible carcinogens through the digestive tract, lessening the likelihood that they will be absorbed. High fat in the diet increases the risk of many forms of cancer, but it is not clear why. Diets high in fruits and vegetables seem to be protective.

Exposure to certain kinds of radiation have long been known to cause cancer in humans. Many of the early scientists who unsuspectingly worked with radioactive materials died of the disease, including Marie Curie, the Nobel prize winner who discovered radium. Curie died of leukemia at age sixty-six.[14] Laboratory studies demonstrated clearly that ionizing radiation was capable of damaging DNA and causing mutations in all forms of life, from bacteria to plants to mammals. Later, exposure to certain chemicals was observed to cause some of the same kinds of genetic damage as did radiation, and many of these same chemicals could be demonstrated to cause cancer in laboratory animals.

Viruses have long been known to cause some cancers in plants and animals, but only recently have some human cancers, including liver cancer and cervical cancer, been shown to be of viral origin. Cancer viruses transform cells by integrating themselves into the DNA of the host cell; the viral genes may override the host's genes, for example, by turning on inappropriate cell division. In fact, viruses that cause cancer in humans have been found to carry altered forms of human genes.

The knowledge gained by studying cancer viruses has helped scientists to understand more generally how mutation of the cell's own genes can turn a normal cell into a cancer cell by inappropriately turning on cell division. Some of the genes that, when mutated, lead to cancer—known as oncogenes—stimulate cell division; others, known as tumor suppressor genes, normally function to keep cell division turned off. The new genetic understanding of cancer causation also helps to explain why some families are more susceptible to some kinds of cancer. Since in most cases more than a single mutation is required before a cell is fully malignant, a member of a family that carries one mutation in a gene might need only one additional event to develop a tumor.

The public health approach to primary prevention of cancer is to prevent human exposure to the agents that cause mutation. In the case of ionizing radiation, the danger of which was recognized early, government standards have been developed to protect the population against exposure from various sources such as nuclear power plants, medical and dental x rays, and radon gas. Sunlight, another proven cause of cancer, cannot be regulated: education in the importance of sunscreen and hats is the favored approach. Because viruses have only recently been recognized to cause cancer in humans, the public health response to these agents is evolving. Immunization is one approach: Hepatitis B vaccination is now recommended for all children, not only to prevent acute hepatitis infection but because chronic infection with hepatitis B virus has been shown to lead to liver cancer.

The extent to which chemicals in the environment cause cancer is one of the most difficult and controversial questions in public health. The tars in tobacco smoke are clearly a major cause, and the American Cancer Society estimates that almost one-third of cancer deaths in the United States are due to tobacco use.[15] Although Americans are greatly concerned about the possibility of cancer-causing chemicals in their food, water, or air, little is known about whether these sources contribute significantly to the number of cases diagnosed each year. Most industrial chemicals have not been tested for carcinogenicity. Chemicals added to food, however, must be tested. Regulations on food additives are discussed in Chapter 23.

The testing of chemicals for carcinogenicity in humans is fraught with difficulties. The standard, most definitive approach is a controlled experiment in which a large group of rats, mice, or guinea pigs is fed a diet containing the suspect chemical over their whole lifetime—about two years for these animals—and the incidence of tumors in this group is compared with that in an equivalent group of animals that did not receive the chemical. If the exposed animals have more tumors than the unexposed, the chemical is labeled a carcinogen. Aside from the potential frustration of the experiment by some unpredictable factor—for example, an epidemic of mouse flu that kills off all the animals after the first year, necessitating a new start—there are many reasons why this approach may not accurately predict carcinogenicity in humans. Differences in metabolism between mouse and human sometimes mean differences in carcinogenicity of a chemical in the two species; or the dose of the chemical necessary to produce a detectable increase in tumors may be so high that it disrupts the animals' metabolism, making the results meaningless.

Another approach to determining carcinogenicity—one that is much faster, simpler and cheaper—is to test whether the chemical can cause mutations in a colony of cells growing in a laboratory dish. This test has its own drawbacks. While mutation is necessary for the development of cancer, all chemicals that cause mutations are not carcinogens. These test tube experiments ignore the role of hormones and other secondary influences that determine whether a mutated cell will actually grow into a tumor.

Part V discusses further the importance of environmental factors in causing cancer.

DIABETES

The number of Americans diagnosed with diabetes is rising rapidly, having more than doubled in the past twenty years.[16] Diabetes ranks seventh as a cause of death in the United States, but it is a major cause of disability. Although it is usually treatable and can be controlled over long periods of time, there seems to be little that public health can do to prevent the disease except to make unpopular recommendations for changes in lifestyle. The Centers for Disease Control and Prevention refers to twin epidemics of diabetes and obesity,[17] because obesity greatly increases the risk of diabetes, and the number of Americans who are obese has been increasing rapidly, as discussed in Chapter 16.

Diabetes is a deficiency in the body's ability to metabolize sugar, a function that is normally controlled by the hormone insulin. There are two major forms of diabetes: Type I diabetes, which usually has its onset in childhood, is caused by a failure of the insulin-producing cells of the pancreas; type II diabetes, more common with increasing age, is a more complex mix of impaired insulin production and resistance to the hormone's action. Both forms of diabetes are significantly affected by genetics. Research on the causes of diabetes has thus far yielded very little information on how type I diabetes could be prevented. Type II is closely correlated with obesity, and is largely preventable with proper diet and exercise. However, public health has not been very successful in persuading most people to adopt such healthy behaviors, which could prevent a number of other chronic diseases as well, as discussed in Chapter 16.

While public health may not be able to prevent diabetes, it is concerned with preventing the disability that is inevitable when the disease is not well controlled. The American Diabetes Association estimates that one-third of people with diabetes are unaware that they have it.[18] This is a major public health problem because the high blood sugar that is typical of uncontrolled diabetes causes damage to blood vessels throughout the body, especially the eyes and kidneys. Complications of diabetes include blindness, kidney failure, poor wound healing, and amputations of the extremities. Secondary prevention requires early diagnosis of the disease so that treatment can begin at an early stage. Lack of access to routine medical care—a common problem in the United States—contributes to the seriousness of diabetes as a public health problem. The necessary long-term monitoring and treatment required to manage a case of diabetes can be complicated and expensive, and those who need it the most may have the greatest difficulty in receiving care, as discussed in Chapters 25 and 26.

OTHER CHRONIC DISEASES

There is much more to learn about other diseases that have a major impact on the health of the population. Mental illness is a major cause of disability in this country, and yet very little is known about its causes and prevention. Alzheimer's disease and other forms of dementia in older people cause anguish to their families and force affected people into nursing homes at a tremendous cost to society. The NIH and other funding sources are supporting a great deal of research on understanding genetic and other factors that affect people's risk of developing dementia as they age, but not much is known yet on how people can protect themselves. Arthritis, while not a major killer, can severely impact the quality of life for many older people, causing great pain and suffering in their last years.

CONCLUSION

Chronic diseases are the leading causes of death and disability in the United States, with cardiovascular diseases and cancer leading the list. Preventing these diseases—an important public health priority—is based on understanding their causes. The success of biomedical science and epidemiology in understanding causes of cardiovascular disease and how to prevent or delay its onset serves as a model for what society would hope to achieve for all the diseases that cause premature death or disability. Progress in understanding the functioning of normal cells and what goes wrong when they turn malignant gives researchers hope that they will eventually learn to prevent many kinds of cancer.

Despite the tremendous progress made by biomedical science in the understanding of the basis of chronic disease, a great deal is left to learn about what can go wrong with the human body and how to prevent it. People cannot expect, and maybe would not wish, to live forever, but biomedical research holds the key to preventing many premature deaths, as well as much of the pain and anguish that many people suffer toward the end of their lives. Because it offers such hope, NIH's work is generally well supported by Congress and the American people.

REFERENCES

1. J. Cohen, "Monkey Puzzles," *Science* 296 (2002): 2325–2326.
2. R. Ross, "The Pathogenesis if Atherosclerosis: A Perpective for the 1990s," *Nature* 362 (1993): 801–809.
3. W. F. Enos Jr. et al., "Pathogenesis of Coronary Disease in American Soldiers Killed in Korea," *Journal of the American Medical Association* 158 (1955): 912–914.
4. H. C. McGill and C. A. McMahan, "Starting Earlier to Prevent Heart Disease," *Journal of the American Medical Association* 290 (2003): 2320–2322.
5. S. J. Dudrick et al., "Experimental and Clinical Atherosclerosis: Their Experimental Reversal," in *Unnatural Causes: The Three Leading Killer Diseases in America*, ed. R. C. Maulitz (New Brunswick, New Jersey: Rutgers University Press, 1989), 35–61.
6. S. O'Connor et al., "Potential Infectious Etiologies of Atherosclerosis: A Multifactorial Perspective," *Emerging Infectious Diseases* 7 (2001): 780–788.
7. E. J. Topol, "Intensive Statin Therapy—A Sea Change in Cardiovascular Prevention," *New England Journal of Medicine* 350 (2004): 1562–1564.

8. G. Kolata, "A Broader Benefit Is Found in a Drug Against Cholesterol," *New York Times* (May 27, 1998): A1.
9. J. J. Nora et al., *Cardiovascular Diseases: Genetics, Epidemiology, and Prevention* (New York: Oxford University Press, 1991).
10. D. A. McCarron, "Diet and Blood Pressure—The Paradigm Shift," *Science* 281 (1998): 933–934.
11. National Center for Health Statistics, *Health, United States, 2003*. (Hyattsville, Maryland: 2003), 162.
12. R. Collins et al., "Cigarette Smoking, Tar Yields, and Non-Fatal Myocardial Infarction," *British Medical Journal* 311 (1995): 471–477.
13. W. K. Cavenee and R. L. White, "The Genetic Basis of Cancer," *Scientific American* (March 1995): 50–57.
14. *The New Encyclopedia Britannica*, Vol. 3 (Chicago: Encyclopaedia Britannica, 1995), 799.
15. American Cancer Society, *Cancer Facts and Figures—2004* (Atlanta: 2004).
16. U.S. Centers for Disease Control and Prevention, *www.cdc.gov/diabetes/statistics/prev/national/figpersons.htm*, reviewed May 14, 2004. Accessed August 13, 2004.
17. U.S. Centers for Disease Control and Prevention, "Twin Epidemics of Diabetes and Obesity Continue to Threaten the Health of Americans CDC Says," press release, September 11, 2001.
18. American Diabetes Association, *www.diabetes.org/diabetes-statistics.jsp*. Accessed August 13, 2004.

CHAPTER 12

Genetic Diseases and Other Inborn Errors

Bad Genes

Congenital defects are a major cause of death and disability in infants and children. Three to four percent of newborns have a major abnormality apparent at birth. Other problems show up later; up to 7.5 percent of children are diagnosed with a congenital defect in their first five years.[1] Such abnormalities may be inherited in the child's genes, or they may be caused by birth injury or by the mother's exposure to an infectious agent or toxic substance during pregnancy. Genes also play a role in many diseases of later life.

Because the birth of healthy children has been a high priority traditionally for public health, education and prenatal care for pregnant women have been encouraged, as discussed in Chapter 18. As more has been learned about how certain infectious agents, drugs, and chemicals can cause birth defects, greater public health efforts have been directed toward preventing women's exposure to these substances. Until the past few decades, little could be done to prevent genetic abnormalities. Now, however, technological developments have opened up vast possibilities in the detection of defective genes. These discoveries have had many clear benefits, but they have also raised many difficult ethical questions.

ENVIRONMENTAL TERATOGENS

Birth defects may be caused by a variety of environmental agents, called teratogens, which include some bacteria and viruses, various drugs and chemicals, and radiation. Many teratogens are also carcinogens, capable of causing cancer. In some cases, the teratogenic effect, like the carcinogenic effect, is known to be the result of mutation in the DNA. However, much less is known about the disruptions of fetal development that lead to birth defects than is known about carcinogenesis.

Infectious diseases known to damage the fetus include syphilis, rubella (German measles), and toxoplasmosis. Congenital syphilis, caused by bacteria passed from a mother to her fetus through the placenta, was a devastating disease of newborns before penicillin was discovered. The disease damaged the infants' nerves, bones, and skin and often resulted in blindness and mental retardation. Beginning in the 1930s, many states required blood tests for syphilis—the Wasserman test—for all couples about to be married in an effort to identify and treat infected people before they could transmit the disease to a child.[2] Most states have discontinued that requirement.

Rubella, ordinarily a mild disease of childhood, causes profound deafness in children whose mothers were infected by the virus while pregnant. Routine vaccination of children against rubella accomplishes the longer term purpose of immunizing childbearing women, and the incidence of congenital deafness has been dramatically reduced. Toxoplasmosis, a parasitic disease that may go unnoticed in adults, can cause major neurological damage in the fetus. Since cats are a reservoir for the parasite and the route of transmission is most commonly through cat feces, toxoplasmosis is best prevented by education—warning pregnant women about the risks of contracting the disease through gardening and contact with litter boxes.

A pregnant woman's exposure to teratogenic drugs and environmental chemicals can have very obvious results because the effects become apparent within nine months, dramatically altering a young life. One memorable tragedy occurred in the 1950s at Minamata, Japan, where a plastics factory contaminated the bay with high levels of mercury. A highly toxic form of the mercury accumulated in the fish, the staple of the community's diet. While adults were relatively unaffected, many children were born with severe neurological deformities including profound brain damage.[3] The tragedy of Minamata, captured by the famous photographs of W. Eugene Smith and Eileen M. Smith, alerted the world to the dangers of environmental pollution. Laws controlling air and water pollution and disposal of toxic wastes have been effective in preventing such disasters in the United States, but they continue to occur in other parts of the world, including the former Soviet Union, as described in the Prologue.

Another famous teratogenic event was the epidemic of limb deformities that occurred in Europe and Australia in the early 1960s and was caused by the sedative thalidomide. Women who took the drug to relieve morning sickness gave birth to babies whose arms and legs were drastically shortened into flipper-like appendages.[3] The United States escaped the epidemic because one skeptical Food and Drug Administration (FDA) official, Dr. Frances Kelsey, was suspicious of the drug and resisted great pressure from the manufacturer before and then the dangers became apparent. Recently, in a controversial decision, thalidomide has been approved by the FDA as an effective treatment for leprosy, AIDS, and some autoimmune diseases. However, it will be used only under very strict regulations that require women taking it to undergo monthly pregnancy tests and use two forms of birth control.[4]

It is one of the FDA's most important missions to protect American citizens against such tragic side effects of drugs by prohibiting them entirely if their value is not judged to be worth the risk or by mandating clear communications about risks when there are also clear benefits. The antibiotic tetracycline, the anti-epilepsy drug Dilantin, the hormone diethylstilbestrol, and the acne medication Accutane are among the common prescription drugs that have been found by painful experience to cause birth defects. Pregnant women are now advised to refrain from taking any medication that is not absolutely necessary.

Alcohol was recognized to be a teratogen only in the 1970s. Although most cases of fetal alcohol syndrome have been identified in children of heavy drinkers, no level of alcohol has been judged safe for the fetus, and pregnant women are advised not to drink at all. Tobacco smoke, while not a teratogen, can have harmful effects on the fetus because it cuts off oxygen in the uterine blood flow and may inhibit fetal growth. Cocaine and heroin use by pregnant women causes addiction in the fetus, bringing about painful withdrawal symptoms in the newborn and sometimes leaving permanent neurological damage.

Genetic Diseases

Essentially all the information required for the development of a new human being is contained in the genetic material located in the forty-six chromosomes, half of which come from the mother's egg and half from the father's sperm. Mistakes are common in the reproductive process.

The most visible are chromosomal abnormalities, which can be seen under a microscope. Such defects cause a variety of malformations in the developing fetus, many of which are incompatible with survival. More than half of pregnancies in healthy women end in spontaneous abortion, and chromosomal abnormalities are obvious in many of these aborted fetuses.[1] When the affected fetus does survive, the disability is usually profound, almost always including mental retardation and often leading to early death. Down syndrome, caused by an extra copy of chromosome 21, is the best-known disorder of this type, largely because its effects are less lethal than those of other chromosomal defects, and most affected infants survive.

The majority of genetic diseases are caused by defects that are not visible under a microscope. Those that are best known and understood are caused by a defect in a single gene inherited more or less according to classical Mendelian genetics. (See Figure 12–1.) In the first part of the figure, the pattern of inheritance of a dominant gene is shown. The father carries the gene for Huntington's disease on one of a pair of chromosomes. The mother carries two normal genes. Half of the children will inherit the disease from the father. In the second part of the figure, the pattern of inheritance of a recessive gene is shown. Both parents carry one recessive gene, but neither parent has symptoms and the parents may be unaware that they are carriers. One-quarter of the children will inherit two recessive genes and have the disease. One-half the children will be carriers.

In other words, of the two copies of each gene that the individual inherits, one from each parent, the gene for the disease may be dominant or recessive. When the presence of a single copy is sufficient to cause the disease—an autosomal dominant disorder—the affected person will transmit that gene on average to half of his or her children. (Autosomal genes are on a non-sex chromosome.) Examples of autosomal dominant disorders are Huntington's disease, a mid-life deterioration of the brain whose best-known victim was the folk singer Woody Guthrie; achondroplasia, a type of dwarfism made famous by the French painter Toulouse-Lautrec; and Marfan's syndrome, characterized by extreme height and cardiovascular abnormalities, which occasionally makes the news after the sudden death of an unsuspecting basketball player.[1]

Autosomal recessive disorders do not become obvious unless the individual inherits two copies of the gene. The disease may appear unexpectedly in a child of two parents who were unaware that they each carried one copy of the gene. The best-known autosomal recessive disorders tend to predominate in certain ethnic groups: Tay-Sachs disease in Jews of

Pattern of Inheritance of a Dominant Gene: Huntington's Disease

Father

	H	h
h	Hh	hh
h	Hh	hh

(Mother labels the rows)

H = dominant gene for Huntington's disease
h = normal gene

The father carries the gene for Huntington's on one of a pair of chromosomes.
The mother carries two normal genes. Half of the children will inherit the disease from the father.

Pattern of Inheritance of a Recessive Gene: Sickle Cell Disease

Father

	S	**S**
S	*SS*	*S*S
S	S*S*	SS

(Mother labels the rows)

S = recessive gene for Sickle cell disease
S = normal gene

Father and mother both carry one recessive gene. Neither parent has symptoms and they may be unaware they are carriers. One-quarter of the children will inherit two recessive genes and have the disease. One half the children will be carriers.

Figure 12–1 Mendelian Genetics

Eastern European descent, szickle cell anemia in Africans and African-Americans, cystic fibrosis in people of northern European ancestry, and thalassemia in populations of Mediterranean or Asian descent.[1]

X-linked disorders, such as hemophilia and Duchenne's muscular dystrophy, are caused by a defective gene on the female sex chromosome, called the X chromosome. These diseases occur predominantly in males. Since females have two X chromosomes, inheritance of the defective gene has minimal impact because of the second, normal gene's presence. Males, who inherit an X chromosome from the mother and a Y chromosome from the father, can inherit the disease only from the mother.

While the patterns of inheritance are well established for many genetic diseases, new mutations may sometimes occur, affecting a child whose family has no history of the disease. Many autosomal dominant conditions cause such severe handicaps that the affected individuals are unable or unlikely to reproduce; for these conditions, the majority of cases arise from mutations. With recessive and X-linked genetic defects, birth of an affected infant into a family that lacks a history of the condition may or may not indicate that a new mutation has occurred. A recessive gene would not be apparent unless someone who carried it married another carrier. X-linked genes might not appear for several generations in small families or those in which most of the children happened to be girls.

Some genetic conditions vary in their impact depending on environmental factors. For example, anencephaly—the absence of a brain—and the related spinal cord defect, spina bifida, appear to be the result of a combination of genetic and environmental factors. The incidence of these disorders has been found to vary by geographical area, a hint that further research will provide evidence that environmental factors are involved. One important finding is that if a woman takes dietary supplements of folic acid before conception and during early pregnancy, the risk of these devastating conditions is substantially reduced.

Genetic makeup also influences people's susceptibility to most of the common diseases of adulthood. As discussed in Chapter 11, genes for cholesterol and other blood lipids affect an individual's risk of cardiovascular disease. High blood pressure has a genetic component. A variety of genes affect people's risk for various forms of cancer. Susceptibility to diabetes is strongly influenced by genes. Mental disorders including schizophrenia, manic depression, and Alzheimer's disease are also believed to be affected by genetics. Environmental factors also seem to play a role in all these conditions, although for some the evidence is fragmentary. It is well known that if people have high cholesterol they can lower their risk of heart disease by exercising, eating a healthier diet and, if necessary, taking appropriate medications. On the other hand, with current knowledge, there is little that can be done to counteract a family history of Alzheimer's disease. One can only hope that, with advances in biomedical research, prevention will someday be possible.

GENETIC AND NEWBORN SCREENING PROGRAMS

Short of performing surgery on the genetic material, the public health mandate of preventing death and disability from many genetic diseases can be fulfilled only by predicting and preventing the birth of affected children. The process involves various methods of prenatal diagnosis and, when an affected fetus is identified, termination of the pregnancy. One of the most common genetic abnormalities, Down syndrome, is caused by an extra copy of chromosome 21. The risk is well known to increase with the mother's age, and women over thirty-five are advised to undergo prenatal testing. With the option of abortion available, this practice has reduced the incidence of Down syndrome births by 25 percent.[1]

There is a more significant role for public health in the prevention of disorders that are caused by recessive genes. When the gene is known, members of populations that have a high incidence of the disease can be screened for carrier status, allowing young people to make informed decisions about marriage and child bearing. In the 1970s, after the gene for Tay-Sachs disease was identified, a major voluntary program offered screening to Jewish people. The response was enthusiastic because the horror of the disease was well known: apparently healthy infants began to deteriorate soon after birth, developing paralysis, dementia, and blindness, and died by age three or four. In ultra-orthodox communities that practice arranged marriage, a confidential registry was established that allowed matchmakers to avoid arranging marriages between Tay-Sachs carriers. As a result of the availability of screening, Tay-Sachs disease has been reduced by more than 90 percent in the at-risk population.[5]

It is also possible to prevent the death and disability caused by genetic diseases by screening newborns for the more common metabolic disorders that can be treated if diagnosed soon after birth. The first such condition to be recognized was phenylketonuria (PKU), which was identified as the cause of mental retardation in a significant number of institutionalized adults. Biomedical scientists found that the problem was a genetic inability to metabolize the amino acid phenylalanine, which therefore accumulates in the blood with toxic effects on the brain. They recognized that if affected infants could be identified early they could be put on a special diet low in phenylalanine, and the damage would be prevented.

Dr. Robert Guthrie, a pediatrician from Buffalo, New York, who is considered the "father of newborn screening," developed a simple, inexpensive test that could diagnose PKU from a drop of a baby's blood placed on a piece of filter paper. Routine newborn screening for PKU began in the 1960s and is now mandated in all states and most developed countries. Before each baby is discharged from the hospital, the blood sample is obtained by a prick of the baby's heel. Filter paper specimens bearing the dried blood spots are sent to state public health laboratories for testing.[6] A sample specimen form is shown in Figure 12–2.

A number of other inborn errors can be identified from testing the same dried drop of blood, and tests for these conditions are mandated by various states depending on the characteristics of their populations. In addition to PKU, all states screen for congenital hypothyroidism, a deficiency of thyroid hormone leading to mental retardation and dwarfism that can be easily treated with regular doses of the hormone. The newborn blood samples are used in some states to identify infants who may have been exposed to the human immunodeficiency virus (HIV) prenatally.

Laboratory tests used for newborn screening have become increasingly sophisticated. A method called tandem mass spectrometry searches for more than twenty metabolic disorders in one process, using the dried blood-spot specimen.[7] However, the technical ability to detect these disorders has confronted states with dilemmas of how extensively to implement screening for them. Resources are needed to follow up on an abnormal test result, including further testing to confirm the presence of a disease and counseling of parents and pediatricians about a condition that may be extremely rare. There are concerns about who is responsible for treating a disease that has been identified through screening. For example, the special diet required for infants with PKU may be considered a food rather than a drug and thus not be covered by a family's health insurance. In some cases, no treatment exists. States differ not only on which conditions they screen for, but also on whether parental consent is required before screening, whether a fee is charged, and the extent of services provided for followup.[8]

The information gained from a genetic test or the screening of a newborn is not always so unambiguous as a fatal diagnosis of Tay-Sachs

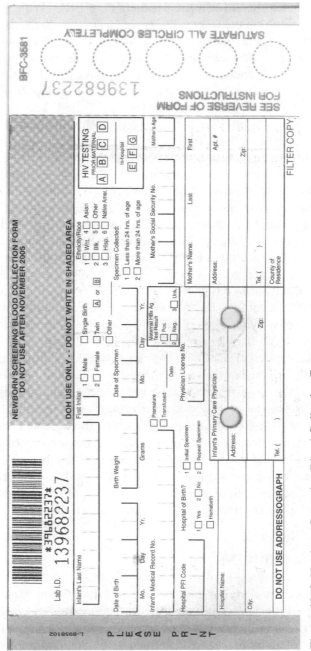

Figure 12–2 Newborn Screening Blood Collection Form
Source: Wadsworth Center, New York State Department of Health.

disease or a clear need for a special diet, as in PKU. With many conditions, uncertainties in the test results as well as in the prognosis complicate decision making. For example, cystic fibrosis, which causes abnormal secretions of the lungs, pancreas, and sweat glands, is the most common potentially lethal genetic diseases in the United States.[9] About one in twenty-five Caucasians of European descent, the group at highest risk, carries the recessive gene, which has been identified. The screening test, which measures an enzyme in the blood, yields many false positives. Scientists learned that the accuracy of the diagnosis could be improved by following up the enzyme test with a test on the DNA. As scientists studied the gene, however, they found hundreds of different mutations that could cause cystic fibrosis, and there seemed to be little correlation between the mutation and the symptoms. While many patients with cystic fibrosis die young of breathing problems associated with thick mucus in the lungs, some individuals identified by genetic tests have much milder symptoms. Although only a few states now include cystic fibrosis in their newborn screening programs, a major epidemiologic study done by the state of Wisconsin found that early identification of affected infants helped to prevent some of the nutritional deficits and deterioration of lung function suffered by children who were identified only when they developed symptoms at an older age.[10]

The identification of the cystic fibrosis gene allows prospective parents to be tested for carrier status, as in Tay-Sachs disease. However, in the case of cystic fibrosis, test results are not as clear. Each of the many possible mutations must be tested for individually, and it is not feasible for laboratories to test for all of them. Currently, the accepted approach for white Americans is to test for the twenty-five most common mutations. About 78 percent of carrier couples can be identified this way, but one in five couples with a normal test result is still at risk to bear a child with cystic fibrosis. The frequencies of mutations are different in other ethnic groups, and identification of carriers is even less reliable.[11]

GENOMIC MEDICINE

The science underlying human genetics has made great advances over the past decade, facilitated by the federally sponsored Human Genome Project, which aims to analyze the whole of human DNA and make a map of all human genes. The successful identification of key genes has enabled many couples cursed with a family heritage of crippling disease to bear a healthy child. Most diseases of later life are more complex, not single gene defects, and thus the presence or absence of a specific gene does not provide any definite predictions. Nevertheless, an individual's risk of developing some cancers, heart disease, diabetes, Alzheimer's disease, and other major afflictions of adulthood are closely tied to his or her genetic makeup. Knowledge of the genes can potentially provide benefits in preventing the diseases as well as better treatments when the individual becomes sick with one of these diseases later in life. The study of how genes act in the body, and how they interact with environmental influences to cause disease is called genomics, a science that is transforming the prospects of medical practice and has major implications for public health.

There are many potential benefits of identifying genetic risks early in life. For example, scientists are investigating ways to prevent the onset of type 1 diabetes in children whose genes put them at high risk. Antibodies detectable in the blood of these children attack and ultimately destroy the insulin-producing cells of the pancreas, but there is hope of disrupting this process with appropriate drugs or immune modifiers. If these experiments are successful, diabetes risk could be included in newborn screening programs, and treatment could avert the need for lifelong insulin therapy and lifestyle modifications.[12]

Genes have been identified that increase a woman's risk of breast cancer. The BRCA1 and BRCA2 genes can be screened for, but they account for a relatively small percentage of breast cancer; these genes also increase the risk of ovarian cancer. Screening may benefit women who have a family history of breast cancer, especially when the cancer occurs at an early age, as tends to happen with inherited BRCA mutations. The most effective intervention currently available for BRCA carriers is the surgical removal a woman's breasts and ovaries. Scientists hope that, in the future, a better understanding of the genes' actions may lead to less drastic therapy.[13]

Genetic mutations are now known that affect an individual's risk of developing a variety of diseases. Because the risk may also be affected by environmental and behavioral factors, it is possible that a person could be counseled to alter his or her lifestyle based on knowledge of his or her genetic risk. For example, some genetic mutations raise blood cholesterol levels, so that an individual would be advised early in life to adjust his or her diet and exercise levels to reduce the risk. Different forms of a gene that controls metabolism of certain toxins affect a smoker's risk of developing lung cancer. Susceptibility to some infectious diseases is also known to be affected by genes; for example, some individuals are almost completely resistant to HIV infection because of a genetic mutation.[14]

Findings from the Human Genome Project are expected to have major implications for the use of drugs in the treatment of diseases. A great deal is being learned about how genes affect the metabolism of various drugs. It has been known for some time that different individuals may respond to a drug in different ways. Medicines that are dramatically effective in some patients may be ineffective in others with the same disease and may cause major side effects in still others. It is becoming possible to predict which patients will respond to a drug and even to determine that some patients may require higher or lower doses of the drug than others. Scientists are also able to design drugs for specific patients depending on their genetic makeup. Cancer therapy is especially suitable for targeted drug therapy: already there have been successes in blocking tumor growth using specially designed drugs that attack cellular mechanisms specific to certain mutations. Lives of patients with leukemia, gastric cancer, melanoma, and colon cancer have been extended with such drugs.[15]

ETHICAL ISSUES AND GENETIC DISEASES

There has been great excitement about the potential uses of genetics and genomics in preventing and treating disease. However, the discoveries have opened a Pandora's box of ethical, legal, social, and scientific questions.[16]

There are lessons to be learned from the mistakes made in early attempts to screen for sickle cell disease, a disorder of hemoglobin, the oxygen-carrying protein in the blood. In sickle cell disease, painful crises of impaired blood circulation occur in individuals who have inherited two copies of the recessive gene, which was identified in the 1970s. However, well-meaning attempts to initiate screening programs for sickle cell disease, inspired by the success of Tay-Sachs screening in Jews, caused widespread confusion and ill feeling among African-Americans, the group at highest risk for carrying the sickle cell gene. The meaning of the tests was not understood, and many people who were healthy carriers of one gene were discriminated against in school and in employment and were denied health insurance. Many African-Americans became suspicious that the intent of the program was genocidal.[16] Considerable time, effort and money were required to overcome the early mistakes. Now, most states include sickle cell disease in their newborn screening programs. While there is no cure for sickle cell disease, infant and childhood mortality is reduced by prophylactic treatment with penicillin, which prevents infections associated with the crises.[17]

Difficult questions always arise when a serious disorder is diagnosed in a fetus or the genetic potential for such a problem is recognized in the parents. Aborting a fetus with a genetic or teratogenic abnormality is often the only alternative to the birth of a child with a handicap. Many Americans are uncomfortable with, if not morally opposed to, abortion. However, attitudes vary with the severity of the abnormality: most people would support the parents' decision to abort a fetus with anencephaly, the absence of a brain, a condition that is rapidly and inevitably lethal. The acceptability of a Down syndrome child varies significantly among prospective parents, however: some couples choose abortion, while others are happy to have the child.

Matters become even more complicated when the genes being identified are those that are known to cause diseases of later life. One of the cruelest of these is Huntington's disease, a single gene defect in which symptoms first appear between the ages of thirty and fifty. During the next ten to twenty years, the disease progresses toward death, with symptoms that include extreme involuntary movements, intellectual deterioration, and psychiatric disturbances. Because Huntington's disease is inherited in an autosomal dominant fashion, each child of an affected individual has a 50 percent chance of developing the disease. Although a test is now available that allows individuals to learn whether they carry the gene and are thus destined to develop the symptoms, many people who are at risk have decided they would prefer not to know. The psychological impact of such knowledge can be devastating, and the potential for being denied insurance or employment is significant. On the other hand, individuals with a family history of Huntington's disease may wish to know whether they carry the gene before deciding to beget children.[5]

With the increasing availability of genetic tests, there is great concern about how the information will be used. The knowledge can help individuals to make informed decisions about their lifestyle. However, it can be harmful when, for example, insurance companies use the information to deny coverage to affected individuals. Already, there is evidence that employers are using such knowledge to discriminate against prospective employees who may be more vulnerable to factors in the work environment or who may be potentially more expensive to insure.[18]

There is a fine line between the worthy goal of preventing disease and disability and the use of genetic screening and abortion to select desirable traits and eliminate undesirable ones from the gene pool. The former is part of the mission of public health, but the latter comes dangerously close to the kind of eugenics practiced by Nazi Germany. The Human Genome Project has set aside three to five percent of its funding to study the many social, ethical, and legal dilemmas that result from better understanding of human heredity. Since genetic screening first became possible in the 1960s, various groups have proposed guidelines for how screening should be done and who should be screened. Most of the principles are consistent with the recommendations proposed by an Institute of Medicine committee, which include the following:

- Newborn screening should be done only when there is a clear indication of benefit to the newborn, when a system is in place to confirm the diagnosis, and when treatment and followup are available for affected infants.
- Carrier identification programs should be voluntary and confidential, and they should include counseling about all choices available to the identified carriers.
- Prenatal diagnosis should include education and counseling before and after the test, informing the parents about risks and benefits of the testing procedure and the alternatives available to them.
- All tests should be of high quality, because life and death decisions are based on the results. New tests should be evaluated by the FDA and there should be more government oversight of laboratory proficiency.
- There should be more education for the general public about genetics.[5]

The information coming from the Human Genome Project is so new that governments have not yet developed ways of dealing with it. Laws against genetic discrimination exist in several states, but as of mid-2004, there has been no federal legislation. Genetic tests are being patented and commercialized. Companies will promote the use of their tests, perhaps promising that the tests provide an unrealistic level of certainty. There is a great need for safeguards on how this new technology is used. According to some estimates, every individual carries at least five to ten genes that could make him or her sick under the wrong circumstances or could adversely affect his/her children.[6] All people have an interest in ensuring that any knowledge about their genetic makeup will be used to do them good and not harm.

From a public health perspective, there is danger that the enthusiasm for genomics may deflect attention and resources from the important mission of preventing disease in the population. Although individuals differ in their genetic susceptibility to the most common diseases, these diseases are associated with well-known environmental and behavioral risks that are traditional targets of public health intervention. Smoking, for example, increases risk for heart disease, several kinds of cancer, and a number of other diseases. To reduce smoking in the whole population is a far more efficient and effective approach to improving the population's health than attempts to identify risk genes in individual smokers. There is a place for genomics in understanding diseases that cannot be prevented with existing knowledge, such as breast cancer, type 1 diabetes, and Alzheimer's disease. However, many public health advocates believe that resources would be better spent on research and interventions aimed at modifying health-related behaviors, including smoking, diet and physical activity patterns, and sexual behavior.[19]

According to one skeptical epidemiologist, the benefits of genomics are likely to be greatest for treatment rather than prevention, and "our resources allocated to treatment already massively outweigh those spent for disease prevention."[20]

CONCLUSION

People's health is determined significantly by their genes, and sometimes by prenatal exposure to infectious agents and toxic substances. Pubic health measures can sometimes prevent unfortunate health outcomes caused by genes or by exposures before birth.

A number of bacteria, viruses, and parasites are known to damage a developing fetus. Immunization of children against some of these infectious agents prevents infections from affecting future generations. Some chemical substances, including several well-known prescription drugs as well as alcohol and illegal drugs, can also cause birth defects. Public health efforts to prevent these exposures include environmental protection and regulation by the FDA.

With increasing knowledge about the genetic basis of some diseases, public health is able to take some actions to minimize their impact. Some conditions, such as Down syndrome, can be easily detected during pregnancy, permitting parents to choose whether to bear an affected child. For a few notorious diseases in children who receive a defective gene from each parent, such as Tay-Sachs and sickle cell disease, prevention involves screening at-risk populations, allowing potential parents to choose whether to conceive an affected child. A major public health effort is focused on diagnosing severe metabolic disorders that can be treated if detected soon after birth. All states have newborn screening programs that test dried spots of blood taken from each infant soon after birth.

The increasing knowledge about the role of genetics in health and the growing capacity to test for individuals' genetic makeup raise many ethical issues concerning how the information should be used and whether application of this knowledge will divert resources from public health's mission of preventing disease in the whole population.

REFERENCES

1. P. A. Baird and C. R. Scriver, "Genetics and the Public Health," in *Maxcy-Rosenau Public Health and Preventive Medicine*, eds. J. M. Last and R. B. Wallace (Norwalk, Connecticut: Appleton and Lange, 1992), 983–994.
2. W. B. Long and J. A. Goldberg, *Handbook of Social Hygiene* (Philadelphia: Lea and Febiger, 1938), 414–418.
3. A. Nadakavukaren, *Our Global Environment: A Health Perspective* (Prospect Heights, Illinois: Waveland Press, 1995).
4. S. G. Stolberg, "Thalidomide, Once Banned, Is in Demand," *New York Times* (November 28, 1997): A1.
5. U.S. Institute of Medicine, Committee on Assessing Genetic Risks, *Assessing Genetic Risks: Implications for Health and Social Policy* (Washington, DC: National Academy Press, 1994), 42–44.
6. R. Guthrie, "Newborn Screening: Past, Present, and Future," in *Genetic Disease Screening and Management*, eds. T. Carter and A. M. Willey (New York: Alan R. Liss, 1986), 318–339.
7. U.S. Centers for Disease Control and Prevention, "Using Tandem Mass Spectrometry for Metabolic Disease Screening Among Newborns," *Morbidity and Mortality Weekly Reports* 50 (RR03) (2001): 1–22.
8. American Academy of Pediatrics Newborn Screening Task Force, "Serving the Family from Birth to the Medical Home," *Pediatrics* 106 (2000): 389–422.
9. U.S. Centers for Disease Control, "Newborn Screening for Cystic Fibrosis: A Paradigm for Public Health Genetics Policy Development," *Morbidity and Mortality Weekly Report* 46 (RR 16) (1997): 1–22.

10. P. M. Farrell et al., "Nutritional Benefits of Neonatal Screening for Cystic Fibrosis," *New England Journal of Medicine* 337 (1997): 963–969.

11. L. A. Bradley and I. Lubin, "Carrier Testing for Cystic Fibrosis: Transition from Research to Clinical Practice," in Centers for Disease Control and Prevention, Office of Genomics and Disease Prevention, *Genomics and Population Health: United States 2003* (Atlanta, Georgia: 2004).

12. E. A. M. Gale, "Can We Change the Course of Beta-Cell Destruction in Type 1 Diabetes?" *New England Journal of Medicine* 346 (2002): 1740–1741.

13. J. Couzin, "Choices—and Uncertainties—for Women with BRCA Mutations," *Science* 302 (2003): 592.

14. A. Guttmacher and F. S. Collins, "Genomic Medicine—A Primer," *New England Journal of Medicine* 347 (2002): 1512–1520.

15. A. Pollack, "Drugs May Turn Cancer Into Manageable Disease," *New York Times* (June 6, 2004): 1.

16. J. Rennie, "Grading the Gene Tests," *Scientific American* (June 1994): 89–97.

17. U.S. Centers for Disease Control and Prevention, "Mortality Among Children with Sickle Cell Disease Identified by Newborn Screening During 1990–1994—California, Illinois, and New York," *Morbidity and Mortality Weekly Report* 47 (1998): 169–172.

18. K. L. Hudson et al., Genetic Discrimination and Health Insurance: An Urgent Need for Reform, *Science* 270 (1995): 391–393.

19. K. R. Merikangas and N. Rich, "Genomic Priorities and Public Health," *Science* 302 (2003): 599–601.

20. W. C. Willett, "Balancing Life-Style and Genomics Research for Disease Prevention," *Science* 296 (2002): 695–598.

PART IV

Social and Behavioral Factors in Health

CHAPTER 13

Do People Choose
Their Own Health?

The Leading Causes of Death

Early successes of public health, in its mission to prevent death and disability, often came from focusing on specific diseases or groups of diseases, seeking particular causes, and finding ways to interrupt the cause and effect relationships. This approach was validated in the early twentieth century by victories over infectious diseases. Public health professionals learned to break the chains of infection, most often by removing etiologic agents (bacteria, viruses, parasites) from the environment (water, food) or by developing vaccines to immunize potential hosts.

As infectious diseases were brought under control and chronic diseases became more significant as causes of death and disability, it became increasingly apparent that the challenges faced by public health regarding chronic diseases would be more complex. Compare the leading causes of death in the United States in 1900 with those in 2000, as shown in Tables 13–1 and 13–2. The top three killers of 1900, which were of infectious origin, have moved down or disappeared from the 2000 list, while heart disease has moved from fourth to first and cancer from eighth to second. The diseases at the top of the 2000 list have complex causes and most have no clear etiologic agent. Despite decades of biomedical research, there are no vaccines or environmental solutions to the problems of cancer and heart disease.

Table 13–1   Leading Causes of Death in the United States, 1900

Cause	% of All Deaths
Pneumonia and influenza	11.8
Tuberculosis (all forms)	11.3
Diarrhea, enteritis, ulceration of intestines	8.3
Diseases of the heart	8.0
Intracranial lesions of vascular origin	6.2
Nephritis	5.2
All accidents	4.2
Cancer and other malignant tumors	3.7
Senility	2.9
Diphtheria	2.3

Source: National Center for Health Statistics. 1900–1940 tables ranked in National Office of Vital Statistics, December 1947. www.cdc.gov/nchs/data/dvs/lead1900_98.pdf

Table 13–2   Leading Causes of Death in the United States, 2000

Cause	Number of Deaths	% of All Deaths
Diseases of heart	710,760	29.6
Malignant neoplasms (cancer)	553,091	23.0
Cerebrovascular diseases	167,661	7.0
Chronic lower respiratory diseases	122,009	5.1
Accidents (unintentional injuries)	97,900	4.1
Diabetes	73,249	3.0
Influenza and pneumonia	65,313	2.7
Alzheimer's disease	49,558	2.1
Kidney diseases	37,251	1.5
Septicemia	31,224	1.3

Source: National Center for Health Statistics. National Vital Statistics System, 2002. www.cdc.gov/nchs/data/dvs/LCWK1_2000.pdf

In 1990 a group of public health experts from the Centers for Disease Control and Prevention (CDC) decided that they should look at the data in a different way. They observed that the leading causes were not, in fact, root causes but merely the diagnoses identified at the time of death. These diseases result from a combination of inborn (largely genetic) and external factors. The panel of experts undertook to identify, where possible, the underlying causes of death from each of the leading diseases. They came up with a list of nongenetic factors that they called the leading actual causes of death.[1] While the mortality figures are only estimates, they are based on the best data available. These factors are highly significant for public health because they are preventable causes of death and disability and they provide targets for public health intervention. In 2000, CDC scientists repeated the analysis with new data and found some changes, although the order of importance is almost the same.[2] Table 13–3 shows the leading actual causes of death in 2000.

Tobacco was found to be the leading actual cause of death in the United States. According to the study, tobacco accounts for 30 percent of all cancer deaths and 21 percent of cardiovascular disease deaths. In addition, it causes chronic obstructive lung disease, infant deaths due to low birth weight, and burns. Of the 435,000 deaths attributed to tobacco smoking, 35,000 were caused by second-hand smoke.

Table 13–3   Actual Causes of Death in the United States, 2000

Cause	Number of Deaths	% of All Deaths
Tobacco	435,000	18.1
Poor diet and physical inactivity	365,000	15.2
Alcohol consumption*	85,000	3.5
Microbial agents	75,000	3.1
Toxic agents	55,000	2.3
Motor vehicle	43,000	1.8
Firearms	29,000	1.2
Sexual behavior	20,000	0.8
Illicit drug use	17,000	0.7

*16,653 deaths from alcohol-related crashes are included in both alcohol consumption and motor vehicle death categories.
Source: A. H. Mokdad, J. S. Marks, D. F. Stroup, and J. L. Gerberding, "Actual Causes of Death in the United States, 2000." *Journal of the American Medical Association* 291 (2004): 1238–1245; 293 (2005): 298.

Poor diet and physical inactivity are listed as the second most important actual cause of death. These two factors are closely related to each other, with overeating and inactivity combining to lead to obesity. Dietary fat, sedentary behavior, and obesity have all been associated with heart disease, stroke, several forms of cancer, and diabetes. The number of deaths attributed to this factor increased by 22 percent from the 1990 estimates, the largest change among all actual causes of death. The prevalence of overweight and obesity among Americans increased dramatically during the 1990s.

In 2005, an analysis by scientists from the CDC and other respected institutions found fault with the calculations of obesity as a leading cause of death.[3] The new calculations led to the conclusion that being moderately overweight was actually protective, especially in older people, although obesity still caused premature deaths. The publication of this study prompted great glee among critics of the "health police" and libertarians who object to being told what to do by the government. It is not clear why this analysis produced such different conclusions from the previous ones. The evidence is still strong that excess weight increases risks for heart disease, diabetes, high blood pressure, and some kinds of cancer. One possible explanation for the new findings is that medical care has become increasingly effective in preventing deaths from these diseases. Despite the controversy, public health professionals will continue to regard excess weight and obesity as a major threat to people's health. Chapter 16 discusses evidence for the impact of the "obesity epidemic" and public health approaches to combat it.

Misuse of alcohol was listed as the third actual cause of death, causing 35 to 40 percent of motor vehicle fatalities, as well as chronic liver disease and cirrhosis, home injuries, drownings, fire fatalities, job injuries, and 3 to 5 percent of cancer deaths.

Number four on the list—microbial agents—encompasses the top three killers of 1900. The fact that mortality from infectious diseases has become so much less significant is testimony to public health's successes, described in Parts II and III. As discussed previously, however, infectious diseases have by no means been conquered, and they could move to a higher position on the list in the future.

The fact that toxic agents—the environmental threats discussed in Part V—are listed fifth as an actual cause of death is evidence of successes in environmental health. The list's authors call this figure the most uncertain; environmental threats may actually belong farther up the list. Certainly, environmental pollution is much more significant as a cause of death in the former Soviet Union, where environmental health has not been given the priority it has in the United States. (See the Prologue.)

Firearms, sexual behavior, motor vehicles, and the illicit use of drugs round out the list. The authors, recognizing that some deaths may have multiple causes, choose what they believe to be the most significant. For example, they attribute most AIDS deaths to sexual behavior or drug use, although they recognize of course that a microbial agent is involved. The number of deaths attributed to these actual causes has declined since 1990 because of improved treatments for human immunodeficiency virus (HIV). Deaths from alcohol-related motor vehicle crashes have also declined since 1990, largely due to better enforcement of drunk driving laws.[2]

These nine actual causes of death identified by the experts account for approximately half of all deaths in the United States. The other half includes genetic factors, which were specifically excluded from the analysis, and other less clearly identifiable causes. Lack of access to health care was cited as a significant factor. Presumably, many deaths could legitimately be attributed to old age. The nine identified factors are of particular public health significance because they cause premature deaths; they are often preceded by impaired quality of life; and many could be prevented by public health measures.

In trying to prevent premature death and disability, public health must focus on these nine factors. Two of them—microbial agents and toxic agents—have traditionally been public health issues. The other seven are rooted in the behavioral choices of individuals. This is the biggest challenge now faced by public health. How can people be persuaded to behave in healthier ways in a democratic society, where every step is fraught with political, economic, and moral controversy?

There are two obvious approaches that the government has traditionally taken to promote healthy behavior: *education* and *regulation*. Both of these approaches have had successes and both have had failures. Both continue to be important components of public health's struggle to accomplish its mission.

EDUCATION

Most simply, education informs the public about healthy and unhealthy behavior. Many people who are concerned about their health and that of their families do in fact adjust their behavior in accordance with new information. For example, the 1964 surgeon general's report called *Smoking and Health*,[3] the first authoritative statement from the federal government that smoking caused cancer and other life-threatening diseases, had a significant impact on the prevalence of smoking in the United States, as discussed in Chapter 15. Many people quit the habit after learning the information, and the prevalence of smoking began to decline for the first time after 1964.

Information on healthful eating habits has traditionally been provided by the federal government. In the early twentieth century, concern focused on nutritional deficiencies, and the government conducted research on requirements for various vitamins and minerals, leading to listings of recommended dietary allowances or daily values. The educational process was furthered by Food and Drug Administration (FDA) requirements for labeling of prepared foods, which must accurately identify the percentage of the daily value provided by each serving.

While the prevention of nutritional deficiencies is still a valid concern, especially among the poor, the focus of government educational programs on nutrition has shifted to the prevention of the major killers—cancer, cardiovascular disease, and diabetes. Research over the past several decades has led to a greater understanding of the importance of overall dietary pattern in the onset of these diseases. The government's educational efforts have stressed the importance of eating less fat (especially saturated fat), less salt, and more fruits, vegetables, and grains. The FDA has revised its labeling requirements to provide consumers with the information that will allow them to follow its guidelines. There is evidence that Americans have responded to the message that they should cut down on fat in their diet and that this behavior may have helped bring down the high rates of heart disease over the past thirty years (see Chapter 4).

Results of efforts to modify dietary and smoking behaviors, while showing some success, also illustrate the limitations of the educational approach. The impact of both messages has been limited. While the percentage of Americans who smoke has declined, one in four adults maintains the habit despite widespread knowledge about the dangers of tobacco. Evidence of dietary improvement is difficult to verify, since surveys of people's eating habits are notoriously unreliable. While the decline in heart disease is encouraging, the prevalence of obesity has increased, casting doubt on the extent to which Americans have really improved their eating habits.

Educational efforts to modify health-related behavior can be controversial, even when the messages seem benign and obvious. For decades the tobacco industry used all its political and economic power to dispute the evidence that smoking was harmful, as discussed in Chapter 15. Even the government's policy on diet has generated opposition, for example, from the meat industry, which has fought to delay the release of proposed recommendations that people eat less meat and more fruits, vegetables and grains—recommendations that, if widely followed, would financially harm the industry.[4] Similarly, the sugar industry has fought government recommendations that people should reduce sugar in the diet.[5]

The educational messages most guaranteed to generate controversy, however, are those concerning sexual behavior. American attitudes about sex are notoriously ambivalent. Though movies and television shows frankly depict sexual activity, many people are puritanically reluctant to talk about how people can protect themselves against the natural consequences of that activity: unintended pregnancy and sexually transmitted diseases. For example, the tenure of Joycelyn Elders as President Clinton's surgeon general was extremely controversial because she spoke out openly on these issues, recommending condom use and masturbation, until she was forced by political pressures to resign her office.

Schools are naturally a prime site for health education programs. The goal is to teach children from an early age how to live healthy lives, providing information, for example, on diet, exercise, and the dangers of smoking, alcohol use, and drug abuse. Studies have shown that school education programs are effective in teaching children the facts about health and safety. It is less clear, however, that they actually influence young people to behave in healthier ways.

Sex education in the schools is highly controversial. Opponents have argued for years that teaching young people about sex encourages them to indulge in immoral behavior. When AIDS came along, the controversy became more intense because it meant that sexual behavior could be a matter of life and death. Many proponents of explicit education about safe sex argue that young people have sex no matter what they are taught and that they should be informed about how to protect themselves. Opponents argue that condoms are only partially effective in preventing HIV transmission and that young people should be taught that they can protect themselves only by abstinence. This has been the policy of the Bush administration.

In fact, a number of studies have shown that students who have received comprehensive sex education in school are less likely to be sexually active and more likely to use contraception when they do have sex.[6] And while the use of condoms cannot guarantee protection against HIV transmission, condoms do decrease risk. Nevertheless, the controversy continues in many communities. The decision on what students should be taught about sex is made by local school boards and depends on "community standards."

An extension of the educational approach to changing behavior is the use of advertising to reinforce the public health message. Most people are subjected to large doses of media messages promoting unhealthy behavior, including cigarette ads in magazines, beer commercials on television, and movie portrayals of unsafe sex. The occasional public service announcements meant to convey countervailing messages are feeble weapons in the battle for public health, although there is evidence that counter advertising about the dangers of smoking helped to reduce smoking rates in the 1960s, as discussed in Chapter 15. The "just say no" antidrug campaign during the Reagan Administration was strong enough to make an impression; whether it persuaded people to change their behavior is uncertain. Recently there have been efforts to develop more effective approaches to conveying public health messages in the media. One of these is the successful Harvard School of Public Health campaign to persuade several television producers to write "designated drivers" into their sitcom scripts as a way of advocating an alternative to drinking and driving.[7]

Health education messages may also be delivered by a medical professional during an office visit. Doctors who care for people with chronic diseases such as diabetes and asthma know that they can keep their patients healthier if they include a health education component in their treatment plans. Studies have shown that, while patients do not always follow the doctor's orders, a physician's recommendation can increase the likelihood that people will change their behavior.[8]

As discussed in Chapter 1, public health's mission is to prevent disease, while medicine traditionally focuses more on treatment and cure. However, the fact that the medical profession can—and often does—play an important role in communicating public health messages about healthy behavior means that public health has a role to play in educating medical providers about health risks and health-related behaviors.

REGULATION

As discussed in Chapter 3, governments have always regulated people's behavior by passing and enforcing laws. The regulatory approach is clearly warranted when its intent is to restrain people from harming others.

Laws against murder and assault are in effect public health laws, and there is no question about their legitimacy. Traffic laws—also aimed at protecting public health—are clearly accepted as necessary. Though not scrupulously obedient, everyone recognizes the importance of stopping at red lights, keeping to the right side of the road (in the United States), and driving at speeds appropriate to the conditions.

Most states have laws concerning alcohol and tobacco use aimed at protecting the public's health. Laws against drunk driving are clearly justified as a means of protecting others. Laws that regulate smoking in indoor public places are also justified on the basis that smokers create a health hazard by polluting the air that others must breathe. Most adults agree with laws aimed at preventing children and teenagers from behaving in ways that may harm their health, such as restrictions on access to alcohol and tobacco. The greatest controversy about governmental attempts to regulate behavior arises when these efforts are perceived as interfering with an individual's freedom to take risks with his or her own health. Laws requiring seat belt use or motorcycle helmets, accordingly, are less well accepted than speed limits.

Controversy over public health laws is not new, as discussed in Chapter 2. In the nineteenth century, major controversies raged in Britain and the United States over laws requiring immunization against smallpox. In the United States the matter was decided in the 1905 Supreme Court decision *Jacobson v. Commonwealth of Massachusetts*, which upheld that state's right to require vaccination "for the common good."[9]

Another hot issue in the nineteenth century, both in Britain and the United States, was the control of venereal diseases, a campaign fraught with moral and social implications that presaged recent controversies over AIDS. In Britain, a series of Contagious Diseases Acts were passed in the 1860s and 1870s, providing for compulsory medical examinations of known and suspected prostitutes and detention of those found to carry disease. Such laws were justified by arguing that venereal diseases were a national defense issue: military recruits affected by syphilis and gonorrhea would be unfit for service. Proponents also argued that irresponsible men, infected by prostitutes, carried diseases home to their innocent wives. It was especially urgent to prevent the spread of syphilis, which can be transmitted from an infected woman to her fetus during pregnancy, causing severe damage to the child. In the United States, most states adopted laws that required couples to be certified free of disease before they could obtain a marriage license.[10]

Many of the themes that occurred in the debates over venereal disease control have recurred today in debates about AIDS prevention, as described in the Prologue and Chapter 2. In fact, two states passed laws in the 1980s requiring premarital screening for HIV infection—similar to the old requirement for syphilis testing. However, these laws were soon repealed, as the syphilis laws have been. Changes in social norms mean that premarital screening occurs too late to protect women—or men—against sexually transmitted diseases. The conflict between, on the one hand, the protection of the privacy and freedom of the infected individual and, on the other hand, the protection of the health of potential "innocent" victims is the same with AIDS as it was with syphilis. However, the political power of gay men, the group most affected by AIDS in the early days of the epidemic, was much stronger than was the power of prostitutes in the nineteenth century. The gay community fought against many proposals designed to prevent the spread of the virus. For example, legal battles were fought in San Francisco and New York over the closing of gay bathhouses, which were the site of many unsafe sexual practices. New York State's 1985 decision to close the bathhouses in New York City was upheld by the courts. In San Francisco, legal action by the gay community forced an overturn of the city's order to close the bathhouses. However, the court ordered bathhouse owners to hire monitors to prevent high-risk sexual activity.[11]

DOES PROHIBITION WORK?

The most ambitious attempt by the U.S. government to regulate the behavior of its citizens was Prohibition, passed by a constitutional amendment in 1919 that was repealed fourteen years later. Common wisdom holds that Prohibition was a failure, but today's society treats "recreational" drugs—marijuana, heroin, cocaine—in much the same way that the Eighteenth Amendment treated alcohol, and few public health leaders are willing to call for an end to the "war on drugs." In fact, the Prohibition approach to regulating behavior appears to have mixed results, combining success and failure in a complex way.

The movement to legally ban alcohol became a moral crusade in the late nineteenth century, with prohibitionists blaming alcohol for all the ills of society. According to the rhetoric, drinking drove men to violence, especially against their wives and children; drunkards were a threat to public safety; and drunkenness itself was looked on as a sin and a crime.

In fact, public disapproval had convinced many people to cut down on or quit their use of alcohol, and consumption had declined even before the Eighteenth Amendment was approved.[12] During Prohibition, the rate of cirrhosis of the liver declined to half that of 1910. Despite the image of the Roaring Twenties—with speakeasies, flappers, and bathtub gin—consumption of alcohol fell by two-thirds.[13] However, it was also true that flouting of the law became socially acceptable, and organized crime flourished.

The debate about Prohibition resurfaces occasionally in the context of illegal drugs. In an exchange of letters published in the *Wall Street Journal* in 1989, two prominent conservatives debated whether the war on drugs was doing more harm than good.[14,15] The economist Milton Friedman argued that while drugs are "tearing asunder our social fabric, ruining the lives of many young people, and imposing heavy costs on some of the most disadvantaged among us," much of the harm results from the fact that the drugs are illegal.[14(p.A14)] The illegality drives up the price of the drugs, providing a financial incentive to drug dealers, causing desperate addicts to commit crimes to pay for their addiction, and corrupting law enforcement officials tempted by bribery. Removing the "obscene profits" from the drug market, Friedman wrote, would reduce the motivation of drug pushers to recruit future addicts among vulnerable young people.

Opposing this view was William Bennett, who was the leader of the first President Bush's drug control efforts. Bennett admitted that the war on drugs is costly, but argued that the cost of not enforcing laws against drugs would be higher. He claimed that after repeal of Prohibition, the consumption of alcohol soared by 350 percent and asked if the country could afford such a dramatic increase in drug use. He blamed current levels of drug use for lost productivity, rising health insurance costs, flooding of hospitals with drug overdose emergencies, and drug-caused accidents. He disputed the argument that addicts turn to crime to support their habit, claiming that many addicts were criminals before they turned to drugs.[15]

There is no clear answer to the question of whether or not a Prohibition-like approach works. As has been seen from the experience with alcohol and drugs, laws cannot eliminate the use of illegal substances. On the other hand, they can discourage the use of drugs and reduce the number of people who use them. Laws are more effective when they are supported by public opinion. The United States is not likely to abandon the war on drugs in the near future. However, in advocating for wider availability of treatment programs, the public health view differs from the dominant punitive approach. In addition, it is clear that, even when banning a substance is not feasible, there are legal approaches to controlling its use in ways that minimize the harm it can cause while maintaining public support for the law. These approaches, which have been used with alcohol, include limits on advertising, age restrictions on who may obtain the substance, and bans on driving while under the influence of the substance.

Chapter 14 undertakes a more theoretical discussion of what influences people to behave in the ways that they do. It is clear that, to be effective, public health must expand beyond the traditional approaches of education and regulation in its attempt to change people's unhealthy behaviors. Chapter 15 discusses ways in which a combination of education and regulation is being used to change people's behavior in relation to the substance that tops the list of hazards to health: tobacco smoking.

CONCLUSION

As infectious diseases have become less predominant causes of death in the United States, a major focus of public health programs has shifted to people's behavior. An analysis conducted by a group of public health leaders has concluded that the top three actual causes of death are smoking, poor diet and physical inactivity, and alcohol consumption. Other behavioral factors that are among the top nine causes of death are firearms, sexual behavior, motor vehicles, and the illicit use of drugs. For public health to significantly reduce the death rates beyond what it can achieve in controlling infectious diseases, it must find ways to promote behavioral change.

Two approaches that government has traditionally taken to persuade people to change their behavior are education and regulation. Education about health includes simply informing people about risks, which can be an effective strategy when new knowledge becomes available, as occurred with the 1964 surgeon general's report called *Smoking and Health*. Food labeling is also part of an educational effort to encourage Americans to eat a healthier diet. Regulation is another effective approach to promoting behavioral change, although it is often unpopular. Historically, the most ambitious attempt to regulate Americans' behavior was Prohibition, which did in fact improve their health by reducing the rate of cirrhosis of the liver.

Research in the social and behavioral sciences has led to the development of theories of why people behave as they do and how they can be influenced to change their behavior. The evidence indicates that health promotion programs are most effective when they target individuals at many different levels of influence. Chapter 14 discusses some of the theories of health behavior. In the chapters that follow, as several specific problematic health behaviors are addressed, there will be examples of programs aimed at changing those behaviors.

REFERENCES

1. J. M. McGinnis, and W. H. Foege, "Actual Causes of Death in the United States," *Journal of the American Medical Association* 270 (1993): 2207–2212.
2. A. H. Mokdad, J. S. Marks, D. F. Stroup, and S. L. Gerberding, "Actual Causes of Death in the United States, 2000," *Journal of the American Medical Association* 291 (2004): 1238–1245.
3. *Smoking and Health: Report of the Advisory Committee to the Surgeon General of the Public Health Service* (Washington, DC: U.S. Department of Health, Education and Welfare, 1964).
4. M. Nestle, *Food Politics* (Berkeley, California: University of California Press, 2002).
5. Editorial. The Food Pyramid Scheme. *New York Times* (September 1, 2004).
6. R. Gardner, "Female Adolescent Health Care: International Perspective," in *Reproductive Health Care for Women and Babies*, eds. B. P. Sachs et al. (New York: Oxford University Press, 1995), 40–56.
7. K. C. Montgomery, "Promoting Health Through Entertainment Television," in *Mass Communication and Public Health: Complexities and Conflicts*, ed. C. Atkin and L. Wallack (Newbury Park, California: Sage Publications, 1990), 114–128.
8. U.S. Public Health Service. *Healthy People 2000: National Health Promotion and Disease Prevention Objectives,* Publication No. (PHS) 91-50212 (Washington, DC: Department of Health and Human Services, 1990), 153–154.
9. T. Christoffel, *Health and the Law: A Handbook for Health Professionals*, (New York: The Free Press, 1982).
10. H. M. Leichter, *Free to Be Foolish: Politics and Health Promotion in the United States and Great Britain* (Princeton, New Jersey: Princeton University Press, 1991).
11. R. Bayer, *Private Acts, Social Consequences: AIDS and the Politics of Public Health,* (New York: The Free Press, 1989).
12. G. Pickett, and J. J. Hanlon, *Public Health: Administration and Practice* (St. Louis, Missouri: Times Mirror/Mosby, 1990).
13. D. Beauchamp, *The Health of the Republic: Epidemics, Medicine, and Moralism as Challenges to Democracy* (Philadelphia: Temple University Press, 1988).
14. M. Friedman, "An Open Letter to Bill Bennett," *Wall Street Journal* (September 7, 1989): A14.
15. A. Bennett, "A Response to Milton Friedman," *Wall Street Journal* (September 19, 1989): A30.

CHAPTER 14

How Psychosocial Factors Affect Health Behavior

Healthy, Wealthy, and Wise

While individual behavior plays a major role in determining a person's health, as Chapter 13 discussed, many factors influence individual behavior. Humans are social creatures, and their behavior is strongly affected by their social environment. This accounts, at least in part, for the fact that diseases tend to be distributed in the population according to certain patterns: certain groups have characteristic disease patterns that remain constant over time even when individuals in the group change. From a public health perspective, it may be more efficient to try to change the social environment that influences people to behave in unhealthy ways than to try to change people's behavior one individual at a time.

Another reason to consider the social environment in studying health behavior is that when the focus is on the individual, the conclusion is likely to be that the person is to blame for his or her illness. Unhealthy behaviors may be maintained and reinforced by aspects of the social environment that are beyond the individual's control. It may be more appropriate for public health intervention programs to focus on these social aspects or at least consider them in designing programs aimed at promoting healthy behavior.

Demographic factors—including race, gender, and marital status—are consistently found to influence health. Statistics show that ethnic minorities in the United States have significantly higher mortality rates from most diseases than whites. Males have higher mortality rates than females at all ages, although females tend to suffer more from chronic illness. Married people are in general healthier than people who are not married, whether single, separated, widowed, or divorced. The reasons for these differences are believed to be primarily social.

The most important predictor of health is *socioeconomic status* (SES), a concept that includes income, education, and occupational status, factors that tend to be strongly associated with each other. SES accounts in part, though not entirely, for the health differences by race, sex, and marital status. For example, blacks tend to be less healthy than whites, and they generally have lower SES than whites. However, even wealthy, educated blacks have higher mortality rates than whites of comparable SES.[1]

Groups with the lowest SES have the highest mortality rates, a fact that is true in many different countries and has been true for centuries, for reasons known and unknown.[2] In London in 1665, the poor were more likely to die in the plague epidemic because of poor nutrition and sanitation and because they could not flee the city to escape infection as the wealthy did. In the United States today, the health of the poor is threatened by the adverse environmental conditions of the inner cities, such as lead paint and air pollution, crime, and violence. Poor people also have poorer nutrition, less access to medical care, and more psychological stress.

It is not only the effects of poverty that account for socioeconomic variations in health, however. The association is seen at all levels of the socioeconomic scale, the very rich being healthier than the rich, who are healthier than the middle class, and so on. In a study of British civil servants called the Whitehall Study, mortality rates over a ten-year period were compared across four levels of employment grade. Top administrators were compared with executives and professionals, the clerical staff, and unskilled laborers.[3] As seen in Figure 14–1, higher employment status was associated with lower risk of dying.

Part of the reason that people with higher SES are healthier seems to be that people with more education behave in healthier ways. A study of 2,138 middle-aged American women found that of those with a high school education or less, 43 percent smoked, while only 22 percent of college graduates and 19 percent of those with advanced degrees smoked.[4]

Wealth = health

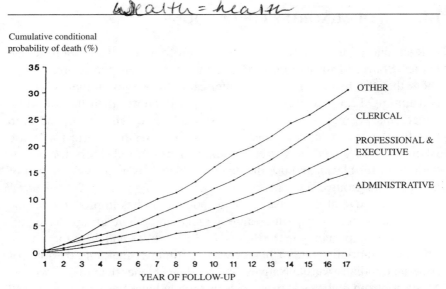

Figure 14–1 Mortality from All Causes by Year of Follow-Up and Grade of Employment, in Whitehall (U.K.) Male Civil Servants, Initially Aged 40–64. *Source:* M. G. Marmot, M. J. Shipley, and G. Rose, Inequalities in Death-Specific Explanations of a General Pattern? *The Lancet*, 1:1003 © By The Lancet Ltd. 1984a.

Those with more education also had lower cholesterol, lower blood pressure, and less body fat, all indicators that women with more education were more likely to practice healthy behaviors. Similarly, the Whitehall Study questioned subjects about their habits and found that those in higher employment grades were less likely to smoke, more likely to exercise, and more likely to eat a healthful diet that included skim milk, whole grains, and fresh fruits and vegetables.[3]

Variations in access to medical care is another factor that has been blamed for some of the socioeconomic differences in health. In the United States, where 15 to 20 percent of the population—mostly those in low socioeconomic groups—lacks health insurance, it is often argued that universal health insurance could reduce health inequalities. However, the SES differences in mortality are also seen in Britain, Scandinavian nations, and other countries that have national health programs. The British civil servants in the Whitehall Study all had the same medical coverage by the National Health Service; yet the mortality risks were still higher at lower employment grades even when behavioral factors were taken into consideration.

HEALTH OF MINORITY POPULATIONS

Race and ethnicity have been seen to profoundly affect health in the United States. Most data on health status of different population groups show that the health of African Americans, the largest minority group, constituting 12.3 percent of the population, is poorer than that of white Americans. A smaller amount of data is available on Hispanics, and even less for American Indians/Alaska Natives and Asian Americans/Pacific Islanders. Many studies, therefore, contrast health indicators for whites with those for blacks and use the health of blacks as a "proxy" for that of all nonwhite groups.

While the overall health of the U.S. population has improved over the past decades, health disparities among racial and ethnic groups have persisted.[5] Life expectancy in 2001 was 77.7 for whites and 72.2 for blacks. The infant mortality rate of blacks was 2.3 times higher, and the rate for American Indians/Alaska Natives was 1.7 times higher than that of whites. Mortality from diabetes is over twice as high in blacks as in whites. Black men die of prostate cancer at 2.5 times the rate of white men. Of Americans living with AIDS, about half are black, way out of proportion to their percentage of the population.

The health disparities may be accounted for in part by the lower SES of blacks, who lived in households with median incomes $13,000 less than the average for the nation.[6] Over one-third of black children were living in poverty in 2003, as compared with one out of ten white non-Hispanics. Blacks have less education on average than whites, and they have higher unemployment rates. The reasons for the socioeconomic disparities are complex and somewhat inaccessible to public health interventions. Moreover, the relationship between socioeconomic status and health is not entirely understood. Nevertheless, public health must find ways to improve the health of groups that have historically been disadvantaged economically, educationally, and politically. The federal government predicts that by 2050, nearly half of Americans will belong to racial and ethnic minorities. If the health disparities are not remedied, the overall health of the U.S. population is likely to decline.[7]

Public health interventions aimed at improving the health of minority groups include efforts to influence their health behaviors. These efforts begin with attempts to understand what factors influence health and health behavior, how these factors may affect people of various ethnic and racial groups differently, and what kind of interventions can be effective in modifying these factors. This chapter and later chapters that consider specific health behaviors will examine how minority groups differ from the majority white population and how those differences may be related to the observed disparities in health.

STRESS AND SOCIAL SUPPORT

A number of psychological factors have been found to influence health, some of which may have a role in the health effects of SES. One of these factors is stress, which is due to the adverse physical and social conditions associated with lower SES, which may act both directly, by affecting physiological processes, and indirectly, by influencing individual behavior. Early evidence of the health effects of stress came from observations that widows and widowers seemed to have an unusually high risk of dying soon after the death of their spouses. Several studies in the 1960s and 1970s found that mortality rates of survivors are 40 to 50 percent higher during the six months after the death of a spouse compared to the mortality of married people of the same age. These studies were expanded to include the effects of other stressful life events such as death of other family members, divorce, and loss of a job, all of which were found to increase the risk of illness or death.[8]

Stress is well established as a contributor to heart disease, a relationship that has been demonstrated in a variety of epidemiologic studies. A particularly convincing example is a study of the male employees of two banks. At first, the two groups were similar, but one bank changed its management policies to become commercial. The employees of the commercial bank had to deal with considerable competition, risk, and responsibility for investing funds; employees of the other bank, a semipublic savings bank, had less competition and fewer responsibilities. Over a ten-year period, the employees of the commercial bank were found to have 50 percent higher rates of heart attacks and sudden death.[9]

Experiments on animals ranging from rats to baboons have found that various psychosocial stresses induce physiological changes such as decreased immune response and increased atherosclerosis. A 1991 experiment on humans demonstrated that stress suppresses the immune response in humans also. In that experiment, investigators measured levels of psychological stress in 420 healthy volunteers, then administered nasal drops containing cold viruses to all but a small control group. They found that the subjects whose stress levels were higher were more likely to be infected with cold viruses and more likely to develop colds, with symptoms including sneezing, coughing, eye watering, nasal discharge, sore throat, and increased use of tissues.[10] A whole new field of research called psychoneuroimmunology has arisen to study the impact of stress on health.

There are many reasons why lower SES exposes people to greater life stress. Daily hassles are greater at lower levels on the SES hierarchy: cars break down, landlords complain about late rent checks, child care is unreliable, officials are rude. Members of racial and ethnic minorities may be exposed to incidents of racial prejudice. These minor but constant stresses may be as debilitating as such major life events as deaths in the family. Higher income and education provide resources that help to buffer the impact of life's hassles, thereby protecting health.

There are a number of factors that help people cope with life's stresses. Money, of course, can solve a multitude of problems. Education is important because it provides the information and skills to solve problems. Family and friends can also help by providing both emotional and instrumental assistance. In fact, *social support* has proven to be surprisingly significant in determining an individual's health.

Early evidence for the influence of social support on health came from an epidemiologic cohort study conducted on residents of Alameda County in California. Persons aged thirty to sixty-nine were surveyed in 1965 on their physical, mental, and social well-being as well as their health-related habits such as exercise and the use of cigarettes and alcohol. They were also asked about their social networks, such as marital status, number of close friends and relatives, church membership, and affiliation with other organizations. Death certificates were then monitored over the next nine years to assess mortality rates and, in 1974, a follow-up survey was conducted on survivors to assess their health status.[11]

The study, as expected, found a strong association between certain unhealthy behaviors and higher mortality rates. More surprising, the study also found that an individual's health status and risk of dying were strongly associated with the extent and nature of his or her social network. This was true for both men and women and for individuals of high SES and low SES. The association remained true even after unhealthy behaviors were taken into consideration. Throughout the socioeconomic spectrum, men and women with few social contacts had mortality rates two to three times higher than those with many social connections.

Many more recent studies have supported the conclusions of the Alameda County study. Absence of social support has been related to an increase in coronary heart disease, complications in pregnancy and delivery, suicide, and other unhealthy outcomes.[12] Why social support should have such a broad and consistent effect on health is very poorly understood. It probably acts in part through its ability to buffer stress. A better understanding of the relationship between social support and health may come from research in the field of psychoneuroimmunology.

PSYCHOLOGICAL MODELS OF HEALTH BEHAVIOR

While public health does not have much power to change people's SES, stressful life events, or social networks, it is hoped that understanding how these factors affect health may permit more effective interventions to promote healthier behavior. With this goal, social and behavioral scientists have proposed various theories and models attempting to explain how psychosocial factors affect health-related behavior. Some of these theories focus on individual psychology, while others attempt to explain the effect of the social environment on individual behavior. The goal of these analyses is to understand the most effective ways to promote healthier behavior.

The classic frame of reference for understanding health behavior, and especially behavior change, is the *health belief model*. Assuming that people act in rational ways, the health belief model specifies three factors that determine whether a person is likely to change behavior when faced with a health threat. These factors are (1) the extent to which the individual feels vulnerable to the threat, (2) the perceived severity of the threat, and (3) the perceived effectiveness of taking an action to prevent or minimize the problem as compared to barriers to and costs of taking such an action.

Based on the health belief model, the public health approach to changing behavior would be to convince people that they are vulnerable, that the threat is severe, and that certain actions are effective preventive measures. For example, applying the model to encourage the practice of breast self examination (BSE) for early detection of breast cancer, a disease that terrifies many women, several studies focused on factor 3, the perceived effectiveness of the practice. Women who already felt vulnerable to the disease were taught how to perform BSE as well as the benefits of early detection and treatment. Follow up found that women who were convinced of BSE's effectiveness were more likely to practice it.[13]

A second major psychological approach to understanding health behavior involves the concept of *locus of control*. People who are confident that they can control their lives are said to have an internal locus of control. They are also said to have high *self-efficacy*. People who believe their lives are subject to chance or external forces are said to have an external locus of control, or low self-efficacy.

A sense of control is beneficial for health in a number of ways. Clearly, it reduces stress. A number of studies in both humans and animals have shown that an individual's perception of the stressfulness of an event can be reduced by two factors: knowledge of when the stressful event will occur and the ability to regulate the timing and intensity of the event. This knowledge and ability give the individual a sense of control, or self-efficacy. The lowest self-efficacy is seen in people (or animals) who have experience of being unable to avoid noxious events, especially if they have repeatedly tried and failed. They may develop a pattern of "learned helplessness," a pattern described as a "numbed acceptance of a negative situation, so that an individual no longer tries to change that situation for the better because he or she does not expect those efforts to make any difference."[14(p.44)]

According to locus of control theory, people with an internal locus of control, or high self-efficacy, are more likely to engage in health-promoting behavior than those with an external locus, or low self-efficacy. An attitude of learned helplessness is common in people who have repeatedly tried and failed to quit smoking or lose weight.

The extent to which women practice BSE has been used to test the locus of control theory; as in testing the health belief model, BSE is a useful measure of health behavior because women practice it only for health reasons, while other behaviors such as eating healthful food and exercising may involve other motivations—appearance, for example. A study of female college students that asked them to complete questionnaires concerning their beliefs and health behaviors found that women who valued health highly and had a high internal locus of control were more likely to improve their practice of BSE over their college career than those who rated lower on these two qualities.[14]

A great deal of research has been focused on how to increase people's self efficacy, thereby helping to motivate them to practice healthy behaviors. An individual's self-efficacy is increased by previous successful performance of the behavior in question. It may also be increased by seeing others successfully perform the behavior, especially if the model is similar to the individual. For example, the most successful school drug prevention programs include role-modeling, small group exercises, and skills practice to teach students how to identify and resist internal and external pressures to use drugs. These programs have been found to be much more effective in enhancing students' self-efficacy to resist drugs if they are led by older teens, with whom they can identify, rather than by adult health educators.[15]

The health belief model and locus of control theory are not contradictory; they are merely alternative ways of looking at what may be the same psychological factors. Research on psychosocial aspects of health behavior is still at a fairly primitive stage, and there is no way to measure the comparative value of different models. Both models can be useful in designing public health messages aimed at changing behavior.

ECOLOGICAL MODEL OF HEALTH BEHAVIOR

In accordance with the recognition that individual beliefs and behaviors occur in a social context and that health promotion may be more effectively achieved through changing the social environment, so-called ecological models have been proposed for understanding health behavior.[16] An ecological model looks at how the social environment, including interpersonal, organizational, community, and public policy factors, supports and maintains unhealthy behaviors. The model proposes that changes in these factors will produce changes in individual behavior.

The ecological model, illustrated in Figure 14–2, describes five levels of influence that determine health related behaviors, each level a potential target for health promotion intervention. The first level—intrapersonal factors—encompasses the knowledge, attitudes and skills of the individual. This is the level that has been explored by the psychological theories discussed earlier in this chapter. The second through fifth levels—interpersonal relations, institutional factors, community factors, and public policy— each have an impact on individual behavior both directly and indirectly, by interaction with the factors at other levels of influence.

The second level of influence, interpersonal relations—including family, friends, and coworkers—has very important effects on health-related behavior. Families, of course, are the origin of many health behaviors, especially habits learned early in life such as tooth brushing, exercising, and eating patterns. In the teen years, pressure from peers becomes more significant in influencing individual behaviors, such as smoking, using alcohol and drugs, and engaging in other risk-taking behavior. On the

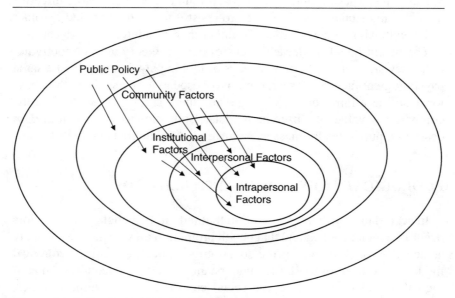

Figure 14–2 Ecological Model of Health Behavior

positive side, family and peer relationships provide the social support discussed earlier in this chapter.

Application of the ecological model at the interpersonal level would lead to different strategies in a teen drug prevention program depending on the nature of the teens' social relationships. A teen who belongs to a dense, homogeneous network will be more influenced by the norms and values of that group than a teen who relates individually to a number of separate individuals. In the close-knit group, drug prevention programs would have to focus on changing the norms about drug use within the existing network. When social networks are more loosely organized, the program might focus on creating drug-free networks, encouraging teens to associate with those networks, and reducing the desirability of membership in drug-using networks.

The third level of influence is significant because people spend one-third to one-half of their lives in institutional settings, especially schools and workplaces, which may have profound effects on their health and health-related behavior. In the workplace, employees may encounter hazardous chemicals or risks from injuries and accidents. Stress may be a problem. Alternatively, organizations may provide a corporate culture that supports positive behavior change. Workplace or school cafeterias may provide health-conscious menus; exercise facilities may be available and their use encouraged; smoking restrictions may prevail. Schools and workplaces provide ideal settings for public health intervention.

The larger community—the fourth level—can be a significant influence on behavior. Organizations can work together in a community to jointly promote healthy goals. An understanding of community organization and networks can offer insight into promising avenues for health promotion. For example, churches are the social centers for many black and rural communities and may provide a focal point for health-related interventions. Conversely, community factors may sabotage public health efforts to promote healthy behavior. In the South, where tobacco is a pillar of local economies, public health advocates may find it difficult to even raise the issue of the health consequences of smoking.

At the fifth level, public policy encompasses the regulations and limitations on behavior that have been discussed in previous chapters, including Chapters 2 and 13. These are the most explicit and controversial measures that local, state, and national governments take to promote healthy behaviors. Such measures include smoking restrictions, age limits on alcohol sales, seat-belt laws, and so forth.

HEALTH PROMOTION PROGRAMS

As social and behavioral scientists gain a better understanding of how people's behavior is affected by their own beliefs and by the various levels of influence in their social environment, theories such as the health belief model and the ecological model are being used to design more effective public health and disease prevention programs. A good example is provided by an AIDS prevention program targeted at gay men in San Francisco in the mid-1980s.[17] Prevention of infection through behavior change is the most effective approach to AIDS control because there is as yet no biomedical solution to the problem—no vaccine and no proven cure.

In the 1980s, San Francisco was the city with the second highest number of AIDS cases in the United States. Most of the cases occurred in gay men, and the primary means by which the virus was transmitted was by sexual intercourse between men. Almost as soon as this was understood, a prevention campaign was launched by the city health department in collaboration with community-based AIDS organizations and a research group from the University of California. They mounted an intensive media effort to inform at-risk individuals about the practice of safer sex. However, researchers understood that merely providing knowledge was not sufficient to change people's behavior. By interviewing small groups of gay men, they identified key beliefs that must be addressed if the messages were to be acted on by the target population.

This approach combines elements of the three theories discussed above: the health belief model, locus of control theory, and the ecological model. The campaign's goals were to promote the following beliefs among high-risk individuals:

1. Belief in personal threat. ("I am susceptible to infection")
2. Belief in response efficacy. ("There is something I can do that will lessen the threat of infection")
3. Belief in personal efficacy. ("I am capable of making these changes")
4. Belief that new behaviors are consistent with group norms. ("My peers support new behaviors")[17]

The first belief was relatively easy to achieve because of the extensive publicity about AIDS in the general media. News and entertainment media aimed at gay men, including gay newspapers, comic books and leaflets, and telephone hot lines could be used to focus more on the second and third beliefs. Gay organizations held small group training sessions to teach skills in the use of condoms as well as interpersonal communication skills such as the ability to negotiate safer sex practices with prospective sex partners; this helped to enhance perceptions of self-efficacy among those at risk. To achieve the fourth belief, messages sought to encourage the perception that low-risk behaviors could be pleasurable and satisfying.

The first three elements of the campaign targeted individual health beliefs and self efficacy. The fourth belief addressed interpersonal and community influences. The campaign also targeted community influences by providing educational programs for bartenders in establishments frequented by gay men. Condoms were made widely available in bars and small group meetings and were distributed by volunteers on street corners. The public policy, government level of influence was brought in through provision by the city of free, confidential testing for the human immunodeficiency virus (HIV) antibody. Because public bathhouses were a frequent site of high-risk behavior, there was pressure on the city government to close them, as was done in New York City. However, the campaign as a whole was so successful in changing the behavior of gay men that business at the bathhouses fell off and public health officers were satisfied with merely posting warnings to the clientele about safe sex.[18]

The San Francisco AIDS prevention program was highly successful. Surveys done between 1984 and 1988 found that gay men dramatically reduced their high-risk sexual behaviors during that period. For example, the percentage of men who reported engaging in unprotected receptive anal intercourse—the behavior most likely to transmit HIV—fell from 44 percent to 3 percent over the four years of the study.[19] When rates of seroconversion among gay men from HIV-negative to HIV-positive were analyzed, the researchers found that the behavior changes had paid off: between 1982 and 1986, seroconversion rates fell from 13 percent to only 1 percent.

The early success of AIDS prevention programs among gay men, in the rest of the country as well as in San Francisco, was attributable largely to the fact that the gay community is in general well educated and politically astute. In other words, the epidemic's potential victims tended to be of high SES, motivated to preserve their health and able to mobilize resources to cope with the impending threat. Thus, they were more receptive to the health promotion campaign than other groups at risk for HIV. Even so, more recent surveys have found that occasional lapses into unsafe behavior are not uncommon. More troubling, younger gay men who became sexually active after awareness of AIDS had become widespread have been found by a follow-up study in San Francisco to be practicing risky behavior and converting to HIV-positive status at rates almost as high as those in the early days of the epidemic.[20] A recent national survey in seven U.S. cities of men aged fifteen to twenty-two years old who have sex with men found a high incidence of HIV, especially in African American men.[21] Unfortunately, health promotion and disease prevention programs cannot be done once and for all. They must be repeated for every generation and every new at-risk group.

CHANGING THE ENVIRONMENT

As more is being learned about what influences people to behave the way they do, many advocates believe that public health programs, to be effective, must concentrate less on individual behavior and more on changing the environment—both the social environment and the physical environment—to make it easier for people to behave in healthy ways. For example, there are many fewer deaths from motor vehicle crashes now than there were two decades ago, as discussed in Chapter 17. This public health success comes less from educational programs about safe driving than it does from safer design of highways and automobiles.

Environmental factors also influence people's diet and activity patterns, which are the second most important factor in Americans' poor health. As discussed in Chapter 16, the government recommends that people eat five servings daily of fresh fruit and vegetables, but educating people who live in poor areas of the inner city will not help improve their diets if they do not have access to supermarkets or produce stands. Similarly, federal policies that since World War II have favored a suburban lifestyle must bear much of the blame for Americans' lack of exercise: people live in their cars because most places are not within walking distance.

The environmental perspective forces people to think of public health problems as social and political issues that require collective action. Instead of blaming smokers for lack of will power, public opinion has shifted its focus to the tobacco industry and the enormous resources the industry has put into making their product attractive to young people, a way of thinking that has led to a remarkable change in public attitudes toward smoking. People take action, as black activists did against the alcoholic beverage industry when it began aggressively marketing high-powered malt liquors to young black males.[22] This approach may lead to confrontations with very powerful economic interests, and it will not always be successful. However, when whole communities become involved, it has the potential of being the most effective way to bring about major changes in health and behavior.

CONCLUSION

Because health is so strongly affected by behavior, it is important for public health advocates to understand what influences people to behave in healthy or unhealthy ways. The social and behavioral sciences offer insights into why people behave as they do and provide a basis for developing interventions aimed at persuading people to change their behavior.

There is evidence that factors such as race, gender, marital status, and especially SES influence health, and the reasons for these differences are likely to be social. Life expectancy, infant mortality, and mortality rates from a variety of diseases vary profoundly among different racial and ethnic groups. Stress, which may be brought on by social factors, has an adverse effect on health for a number of reasons. Social support has been found to have a positive effect on health, probably in part by providing a buffer against stress. The health of black Americans tends to be poorer than that of the white majority. Health data on the population is usually analyzed by race and ethnicity, and public health efforts focus on understanding the disparities and trying to eliminate them.

Theories of health behavior include the health belief model and the theory of self efficacy or locus of control. Both theories focus on the individuals' attitudes and beliefs as determinants of their behavior. A broader perspective is provided by the ecological model of health behavior. This model considers all the levels of influence that may affect the individual's attitudes and beliefs, including interpersonal relationships such as family and friends, institutional influence such as school and work, the larger community and its values and beliefs, and public policy including laws and regulations.

The most effective public health intervention programs influence people's beliefs at several levels with the goal of creating a social environment favorable to healthy behavior. The San Francisco AIDS prevention program is an example of an effective program that succeeded in significantly reducing the transmission of HIV. Evidence shows, however, that to maintain the success of such a program, intensive public health efforts must be maintained, both to prevent relapses into unhealthy behavior and to educate new generations of at-risk people.

Increasingly, public health advocates realize that the most effective ways of improving health-related behavior of individuals is to focus on involving whole communities in improving the social and physical environment to be more conducive to healthy behavior.

REFERENCES

1. P. D. Sorlie, E. Backlund, and J. B. Keller, "U.S. Mortality by Economic, Demographic, and Social Characteristics: The National Longitudinal Mortality Study," *American Journal of Public Health* 269 (1995): 949–956.
2. N. Adler, T. Boyce, M. A. Chesney, S. Folkman, and S. L. Syme, "Socioeconomic Inequalities in Health: No Easy Solution," *Journal of the American Medical Association* 269 (1993): 3140–3145.
3. M. G. Marmot et al., "Health Inequalities Among British Civil Servants: the Whitehall II Study," *Lancet* 337 (1991): 1387–1393.
4. K. A. Matthews et al., "Educational Attainment and Behavioral and Biological Risk Factors for Coronary Heart Disease in Middle Aged Women," *American Journal of Epidemiology* 129 (1989): 1132–1144.
5. National Center for Health Statistics, *Health, United States, 2003 with Chartbook on Trends in the Health of Americans* (Hyattsville, Maryland: Public Health Service, 2003).
6. C. DeNavas-Walt, B. D. Proctor, and R. J. Mills, U.S. *Census Bureau, Income, Poverty, and Health Insurance Coverage in the United States: 2003* (Washington, DC: U.S. Government Printing Office, 2004).
7. U.S. Centers for Disease Control and Prevention, "Health Disparities Experienced by Racial/Ethnic Minority Populations," *Morbidity and Mortality Weekly Report* 53 (2004): 755.
8. K. J. Helsing, and M. Szklo, "Mortality after Bereavement," *American Journal of Epidemiology* 114 (1981): 41–52.
9. F. Kittel, M. Kornitzer, and M. Dramaik, "Coronary Heart Disease and Job Stress in Two Cohorts of Bank Clerks," *Psychotherapy and Psychosomatics*, 34 (1980): 110–123.
10. S. Cohen, D. A. J. Tyrrell, and A. P. Smith, "Psychological Stress and Susceptibility to the Common Cold," *New England Journal of Medicine* 325 (1991): 606–612.
11. L. F. Berkman, and L. Breslow, *Health and Ways of Living: the Alameda County Study* (New York: Oxford University Press, 1983), 31–54.
12. J. S. House, K. R. Landis, and D. Umberson, "Social Relationships and Health," *Science* 241 (1988): 540–545.
13. J. P. Kirscht, "The Health Belief Model and Predictions of Health Actions," in *Health Behavior: Emerging Research Perspectives*, ed. D. S. Gochman (New York: Plenum Press, 1983), 27–41.

14. R. R. Lau, "Beliefs about Control and Health Behavior," in *Health Behavior: Emerging Research Perspectives*, ed. D. S. Gochman (New York: Plenum Press, 1983), 43–63.

15. C. A. Marlatt, J. S. Baer, and L. A. Quigley, "Self-Efficacy and Addictive Behavior," in *Self Efficacy in Changing Societies*, ed. A. Bandura (Cambridge: Cambridge University Press, 1995), 289–315.

16. K. R. McLeroy, D. Bibeau, A. Steckler, and K. Glanz, "An Ecological Perspective on Health Promotion Programs," *Health Education Q.* 15 (1988): 351–377.

17. A. L. McAlister, P. Puska, M. Orlandi, L. L. Bye, and P. L. Zbylot, "Behaviour Modification: Principles and Illustrations," in eds. W. Holland, R. Detels, and G. Knox, *Oxford Textbook of Public Health*, 2nd ed. Vol. 3. (Oxford: Oxford University Press, 1991), 3–16.

18. R. Bayer, *Private Acts, Social Consequences: AIDS and the Politics of Public Health* (New York: The Free Press, 1989).

19. L. McKusick, T. J. Coates, S. F. Morin, L. Pollack, and C. Hoff, "Longitudinal Predictors of Reductions in Unprotected Anal Intercourse among Gay Men in San Francisco: The AIDS Behavioral Research Project," *American Journal of Public Health* 80 (1990): 978–983.

20. D. H. Osmond et al., "HIV Infection in Homosexual and Bisexual Men 18–29 Years of Age: The San Francisco Young Men's Health Study," *American Journal of Public Health* 84 (1994): 1933–1937.

21. U.S. Centers for Disease Control and Prevention, "HIV Incidence Among Young Men Who Have Sex With Men—Seven U.S. Cities, 1994–2000," *Morbidity and Mortality Weekly Report* 50 (2001): 440–444.

22. L. Wallack, L. Dorfman, D. Jernigan, and M. Themba, *Media Advocacy and Public Health: Power for Prevention* (Newbury Park, California: Sage Publications, 1993).

CHAPTER 15

Tobacco—Public Health Enemy Number One

Deadly Habit

Cigarette smoking—the leading actual cause of death in the United States according to the analysis described in Chapter 13—is clearly the nation's most significant public health issue. The problem of tobacco-caused disease embodies the complex interactions by which psychological, social, cultural, economic, and political factors influence individual behavior to cause over 400,000 deaths each year. Table 15–1 lists the

Table 15–1 Major Diseases Caused by Smoking and Estimated Annual Number of Deaths, 1995–1999

Disease	Annual Number of Deaths
Cardiovascular disease	148,605
Lung cancer	124,813
Respiratory disease, including pneumonia, influenza, bronchitis, emphysema, and chronic airway obstruction	98,007
Other cancers, including laryngeal, oral, esophageal, pancreatic, urinary	30,948
Diseases among infants	1,007
Burns	966

Source: *Morbidity and Mortality Weekly Report* 51 (14) (2002): 300–303.

major diseases caused by smoking and estimates the annual number of deaths from each disease.

The struggle to understand and deal with tobacco-caused illness involves all areas of public health. Epidemiology provided the first solid evidence that smoking caused cancer and heart disease and has continued to yield information on the health effects of this very human habit (see Chapter 4). Biomedical studies were slow to provide evidence because laboratory animals could not be persuaded or forced to smoke cigarettes, but eventually they yielded valuable information on the role of tobacco in the causation of cancer and heart disease. In recent years, smoking has increasingly been seen as an environmental health threat, producing indoor air pollution that has been shown to cause adverse health effects in non-smokers. Ultimately, however, smoking is a behavior, and it is the social and behavioral sciences that must provide insights into why people smoke and how they can be persuaded to quit.

Public health faces a fundamental dilemma in confronting the current epidemic of tobacco-caused disease: What should be the role of a democratic government in confronting a behavior that is practiced by one out of four adults and will kill up to half of them? Political and economic forces that favored tobacco have opposed strong government measures against cigarettes. Public health efforts involving education and health promotion campaigns have persuaded many people to stop smoking but seem to have reached the limit of their effectiveness in bringing smoking prevalence down to about 23 percent among adults.

However, the 1990s saw a major shift in federal and state governments' attitudes toward smoking. Recognition that the nicotine in tobacco is addictive, together with evidence that cigarette companies have purposely manipulated nicotine levels in cigarettes to keep people hooked, have forced politicians to look with suspicion on what was previously considered a freely chosen behavior. Moreover, evidence of the high economic costs paid by government-financed programs, including Medicare and Medicaid, for the treatment of tobacco-caused disease has forced governments to question their previous assumptions about the economic advantages of supporting the tobacco industry.

BIOMEDICAL BASIS OF SMOKING'S HARMFUL EFFECTS

The basic fact underlying the popular success of cigarettes is that they deliver nicotine, an addictive drug. Nicotine is absorbed by the linings of the mouth and the respiratory tract and travels rapidly to the heart and then to the brain. The drug produces a sense of enhanced energy and alertness, while also having a calming effect on addicted smokers. When people try to quit smoking, they experience withdrawal reactions with unpleasant physical and psychological symptoms. In the 2002 Health Interview Survey, over 40 percent of smokers reported that during the past year they had tried to quit and failed.[1]

In addition to nicotine, an important component of tobacco smoke is tar, the residue from burning tobacco that condenses in the lungs of smokers. Tars provide the flavor in cigarette smoke; they are also a major source of its carcinogenicity. As early as the 1930s, experiments were done in which these tars were painted on the ear linings of rabbits or the shaved backs of mice and found to cause tumors. Decades of studies by biomedical researchers—and clandestinely by tobacco companies, which did not wish to publicize their results—have confirmed the carcinogenicity of the tars as well as other ingredients of the smoke, including arsenic and benzene. When filters were added to cigarettes with the ostensible purpose of removing tars and other harmful ingredients, it turned out that they tended also to remove the taste and "satisfaction" from smoking. Thus filter cigarettes, to be acceptable to smokers, had to deliver significant levels of tar and nicotine, meaning that there were limits to how "safe" a cigarette could be.

Tars not only cause cancer but also contribute to other lung diseases through their tendency to damage cilia, the tiny hairs on the linings of the respiratory tract that sweep the lungs and bronchi clear of microbes, irritants, and toxic substances. Damage to cilia and irritation of respiratory tract linings by components of smoke increase susceptibility to infectious diseases like bronchitis, influenza, and pneumonia as well as to diseases brought on by chronic irritation such as emphysema and asthma.

In contrast to the long-term processes leading to cancer and emphysema, the effect of smoking on the cardiovascular system can be very rapid. The nicotine in cigarette smoke raises blood pressure and heart rate. It may also cause spasms in the blood vessels of the heart, especially if damage already exists, increasing the risk of sudden cardiac death. Carbon monoxide in cigarette smoke interferes with the oxygen-carrying capacity of red blood cells, leading to oxygen shortages in the hearts of patients suffering from coronary artery disease. Smoking increases the risk of stroke and heart attacks by altering the clotting properties of blood. Components of cigarette smoke also have been shown to raise total blood cholesterol levels and reduce levels of HDL, the "good" cholesterol (see Chapter 11).

HISTORICAL TRENDS IN SMOKING AND HEALTH

Although it has been smoked and chewed for hundreds of years, tobacco was not used intensively enough to cause widespread illness until the twentieth century. Before then, almost all tobacco was smoked in pipes and cigars or used as chewing tobacco and snuff. Cigarette-rolling machines and safety matches were invented in the 1880s, but cigarette smoking began to increase dramatically only after 1913, when Camel, followed by other brands, began mass marketing campaigns.[2] The distribution of free cigarettes to soldiers during the two world wars further stimulated smoking among men. Smoking among women was frowned on early in the century, but women began to take up the habit during and after World War II, and by 1960 about 34 percent of American women smoked.[2] While estimates of the percentage of men and women who smoked during the early part of the century are imprecise [they were done before the Centers for Disease Control and Prevention (CDC) began systematic surveys of the population in 1965], a general idea of the trends since the middle of the century can be seen in Figure 15–1. A better sense of the extent of smoking in this country, and the circumstances influencing it comes from U.S. Department of Agriculture data on total manufactured cigarette consumption, as shown in Figure 15–2.

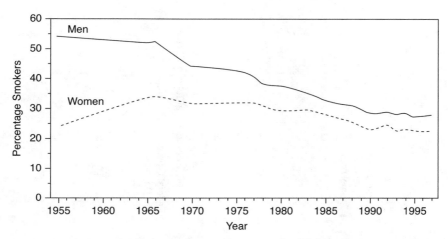

Figure 15–1 Trends in Cigarette Smoking* among Persons Aged ≥18 Years, by Sex—United States, 1955–1997
*Before 1992, current smokers were defined as persons who reported having smoked ≥100 cigarettes and who currently smoked. Since 1992, current smokers were defined as persons who reported having smoked ≥100 cigarettes during their lifetime and who reported now smoking every day or some days.
Sources: 1955 Current Population Survey: 1965–1997 National Health Interview Survey. U.S. Centers for Disease Control and Prevention. Morbidity and Mortality Weekly Report 48 (1999)988

The first disease clearly linked to smoking was lung cancer, which is caused almost exclusively by smoking and is rare in nonsmokers. Lung cancer was virtually nonexistent in the United States and Britain in 1900. In the 1930s, the increase in deaths from lung cancer began to attract attention, and a link to cigarette smoking began to be suspected. This link was confirmed in the epidemiologic studies published in the 1950s (see Chapter 4). Cigarette consumption dropped as a result of these reports (as shown in Figure 15–2) but began to climb again when tobacco companies promoted filter cigarettes as a safer alternative.

In 1964, the U.S. surgeon general released a report, *Smoking and Health*, a summary of the evidence to date, the result of an exhaustive deliberation by a panel of ten renowned scientists.[3] The panel unanimously agreed and wrote that cigarette smoking caused lung cancer and chronic bronchitis and was strongly associated with cancer of the mouth and larynx. It also reported that smoking increased the risk of heart disease. The surgeon general's report was

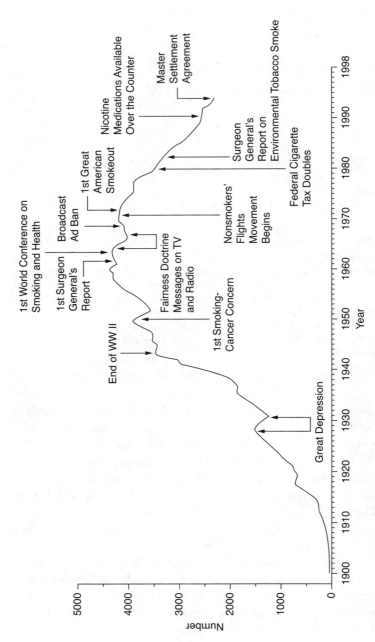

Figure 15–2 Annual Adult per Capita Cigarette Consumption and Major Smoking and Health Events—United States, 1900–1998

Sources: U.S. Department of Agriculture; 1985 Surgeon General's Report. U.S. Centers for Disease Control and Prevention. Morbidity and Mortality Weekly Report 48 (1999)986 very influential, convincing many smokers to quit and providing ammunition for advocates wishing to impose controls on the tobacco industry.

Women were hardly mentioned in the 1964 surgeon general's report. Lung cancer was rare in women, and all the studies had been done on men. However, women soon began to catch up. In 1980 the surgeon general issued another report which focused entirely on women. *Health Consequences of Smoking for Women* addressed "the fallacy of women's immunity."[4] The report points out that the first signs of an epidemic of smoking-related diseases among women were just beginning to appear, because women had only begun smoking intensively twenty-five years after men had (Figure 15–1 and Figure 4–2). Indeed, lung cancer was about to surpass breast cancer and become the leading cause of cancer death in women.[5] The report noted that, in addition to suffering the same ill health effects as men, female smokers are at increased risk for complications of pregnancy and that infants of female smokers are more likely to be premature or lagging in physical growth.

Historically, the prevalence of smoking among black men was higher than that for white men; accordingly, lung cancer mortality rates have been higher among black men. Rates of smoking among blacks have declined and are now similar to those among whites at about 23 percent of adults. American Indians and Alaskan Natives smoke at much higher rates than other ethnic groups, averaging 40.8 percent overall. Very large differences in smoking rates are seen among groups of different socioeconomic status, and there is a particularly strong association with lack of education. Prevalence of smoking is only about 12 percent among male and female college graduates, while 38.1 percent of men with only nine to eleven years of education are smokers.[1]

REGULATORY RESTRICTIONS ON SMOKING— NEW FOCUS ON ENVIRONMENTAL TOBACCO SMOKE

Public health efforts at discouraging smoking have had to contend with the enormous economic and political power of the tobacco industry. Congress, which still provides subsidies to tobacco growers, has been very reluctant to pass legislation opposed by the industry. However, the 1964 surgeon general's report carried great credibility, and its publication led to a number of government actions aimed at restricting cigarette marketing. These included Federal Trade Commission requirements that cigarette packages contain warning labels and a Federal Communications Commission mandate that radio and television advertisements for cigarettes be balanced by public service announcements about their harmful effects. The latter requirement, called the Fairness Doctrine, was so effective in countering the tobacco companies' ads, as seen in the drop in cigarette consumption shown in Figure 15–2, that in 1971 the industry submitted to a total ban on cigarette advertising on radio and television. In return, the public service announcements ceased. The tobacco companies shifted their advertising efforts to magazines, newspapers, billboards, product give-aways, and sponsorship of sporting and cultural events.[2]

Over the past three decades, new awareness of the harm caused by "second-hand smoke" has led to some of the most effective actions against smoking. Studies began to show that exposure to environmental tobacco smoke caused some of the same health problems as active smoking. For example, the nonsmoking spouses of smokers have an increased risk of lung cancer and heart disease, and children of parents who smoke are more likely to suffer from asthma, respiratory infections, and sudden infant death syndrome. In 1992, the Environmental Protection Agency issued a report that declared environmental tobacco smoke to be a carcinogen, causing 3,000 lung cancer deaths a year.[6] Evidence of the harm caused by passive smoking inspired the nonsmokers rights movement, which largely bypassed the Congress and focused political pressure on state and local governments.

In 1974 Connecticut was the first state to enact restrictions on smoking in restaurants. Minnesota passed a comprehensive statewide clean indoor air law in 1975. In 1983, San Francisco passed a restrictive law against smoking in the workplace, including private workplaces. The clean indoor air movement blossomed. At the state level, laws were passed that restricted smoking on public transit and in elevators, cultural and recreational facilities, schools, and libraries. Over the objections of the tobacco industry, a ban on smoking on all domestic airline flights was passed by Congress in 1989.[2] Restrictions on indoor smoking became more widespread in the 1990s. By the end of 2003, five states had banned smoking in all public places, including work sites, restaurants, and bars. More than 1,600 counties and municipalities have passed legislation to promote clean indoor air.[7]

The effectiveness of the nonsmokers' rights movement stems from its success in transforming smoking into a socially unacceptable activity. Bans in so many public places force smokers to refrain for extended periods and to segregate themselves when they wish to smoke, often by going outdoors. By making smoking inconvenient, bans encourage people to quit. As Figure 15–2 shows, cigarette consumption has declined steadily since the nonsmokers rights movement began.

EMPHASIS ON YOUTH—ADVERTISING

While smoking rates among adults have fallen, public health advocates have become increasingly concerned about smoking among youth. Teenagers tend to be less worried about their health in the distant future than they are with their image and social status among their peers. Tobacco companies exploit those concerns in their attempts to win over young people to smoking.

In order to maintain a constant number of customers over time, the tobacco industry must persuade two million people to take up the habit each year to balance the number of smokers who die or quit.[8] Cigarette advertising and promotional expenditures have continuously increased, amounting to $11.2 billion in 2001, almost double the amount spent in 1998.[9] Because the teen years are the critical period for smoking initiation— 90 percent of adult smokers started when they were teenagers, and the average age at which they took up the habit is fourteen and a half— tobacco companies target their advertising toward children and young people.[2] For example, Joe Camel ads were strongly appealing to children. A 1991 study found that 91 percent of six-year-olds recognized the cartoon character, the same percentage that recognized the Mickey Mouse logo of the Disney channel. Ninety-eight percent of high school students recognized Joe Camel, compared with only 72 percent of adults.[10] Between 1988, when the Joe Camel ad campaign was introduced, and 1990, it is estimated that Camel cigarette sales to minors went from $6 million to $476 million.[2] In response to an outburst of negative publicity and public anger at the tobacco companies, Joe Camel was retired in 1997.

Tobacco companies also target youth with promotional items, such as T-shirts, caps, and sporting goods bearing a brand's logo. They have managed to evade the ban on broadcast advertising by sponsoring sporting events, at which brand names are displayed in the background, ensuring that they will be visible on television throughout the event.

Advertising is also targeted at women and minorities, groups identified as promising sources of new smokers. Young women have been attracted by suggestions that smoking will help them lose weight, beginning with the Lucky Strike ads of the 1920s which advised, "Reach for a Lucky instead of a sweet." Today's Virginia Slims ads take a similar approach. Shortly after the Virginia Slims advertising campaign began in the 1960s, the proportion of fourteen- to seventeen-year-old girls who started smoking nearly doubled.[2] Also targeted are African Americans, who have historically had higher rates of smoking—and of lung cancer—than whites.

Tobacco companies win over black leaders by donating to black causes, such as the National Association for the Advancement of Colored People and the United Negro College Fund, and by sponsoring black cultural events such as jazz festivals. They advertise heavily in African American publications and, before the Tobacco Master Settlement Agreement (MSA, discussed below), blanketed neighborhoods with billboards

As part of the 1998 MSA, discussed later, major tobacco companies agreed to stop advertisements targeted at children. Although the most blatant appeals to youth are gone, there is evidence that today the companies' ads, while ostensibly anti-tobacco, are actually more sophisticated messages designed to encourage youth smoking.[11] Nevertheless, a combination of public health efforts have contributed to a decline in the number of teens who smoke. The CDC's biannual survey of high school students found in 2001 that 28.5 percent had smoked in the previous month, down from 36.4 percent in 1997, the year when the highest number of students reported having smoked.[12]

All states have laws prohibiting the sale of tobacco to minors, but most high school students find it easy to obtain cigarettes. In 1999, according to the CDC survey, 23.5 percent of students who smoked reported that they usually purchased their cigarettes in a store. Most of these students said they had not been asked to show proof of age. Enforcement of the laws has increased since 1995, when purchase in a store was the source for 38.7 percent of students. However, almost 30 percent of the student smokers reported that they usually gave money to someone else to buy cigarettes for them. Other students reported that they usually obtained cigarettes by stealing or borrowing them.[13] There is evidence that increasingly, youths are buying cigarettes via the Internet, and there is no federal law that bans the practice.[14] These studies have shown that, while strict enforcement can reduce young people's commercial access to cigarettes, reducing overall access is more difficult.

TAXES AS A PUBLIC HEALTH MEASURE

Antismoking activists, supported by economics research, have concluded that one of the most effective measures to discourage young people from smoking is to raise the tax on cigarettes. One reason is that a pack of cigarettes represents a more significant proportion of a teenager's disposable income than it does for adults, and the higher price is likely to have more impact on someone who is not yet addicted.

Recent research on teenage smoking suggests that teenagers are indeed sensitive to price. For example, after Philip Morris cut the price of Marlboro cigarettes, a brand favored by young people, by 40 percent in April 1993, the proportion of teenagers in eighth, tenth, and twelfth grades who smoked rose from 23.5 percent to 28 percent in 1996. Other studies have shown that a 10 percent increase in price reduces the number of teenagers who smoke by approximately 7 to 12 percent.[15] "Raising tobacco taxes is our number one strategy to damage the tobacco industry," an American Cancer Society executive was quoted as saying. "The industry has found ways around everything else we have done, but they can't repeal the laws of economics."[15(p.293)]

Raising taxes on cigarettes is effective in reducing smoking among adults as well. In 1989, California increased cigarette taxes from 10 cents to 35 cents per pack. The law specified that 20 percent of the proceeds were to be designated for programs designed to prevent and reduce tobacco use, especially among children. Surveys conducted before and after implementation of the tax increase found that the prevalence of cigarette smoking among adults in California was reduced from 26.7 percent in 1988 to 22.2 percent in 1992 to 16.7 percent in 1995.[16,20] It is difficult to determine the share of the decline that can be attributed to the price increase as compared with other anti-smoking measures, including indoor smoking bans and the antismoking campaign funded by the tax.

In recent years, state and local governments have found that raising taxes on cigarettes is a painless way of closing budget shortfalls, and many states have followed this policy. In 2004, for example, New Jersey had the highest rate, with a tax of $2.05 per pack. In New York, the state tax was $1.50 per pack, and New York City had imposed an additional tax of $1.50. In contrast, tobacco-producing states have low cigarette taxes: Virginia's rate was 2.5 cents per pack and Kentucky's was 3 cents.[17] California, a leader in raising cigarette taxes for public health goals, had fallen to a rank of nineteenth among states, with a tax of 87 cents per pack.

Opponents of high cigarette taxes have argued that such measures unfairly penalize low-income and minority smokers. However, a CDC study found that tax increases are especially effective in persuading these groups to quit or reduce their smoking. Based on an analysis from the National Health Interview Survey, the CDC estimates that a 50 percent increase in the price of a pack of cigarettes would cut consumption by 7 percent among whites, 16 percent among African Americans, and up to 95 percent among Hispanics. Moreover, young people were most affected by the price hikes.[18] Because members of low-income and minority groups tend to smoke at higher rates than others, public health advocates believe that the taxes are justified, but that the states have a moral obligation to pay for cessation programs to help these smokers quit.[9]

CALIFORNIA'S TOBACCO CONTROL PROGRAM

California's voter-initiated tobacco control program, funded by a 25-cent tax increase on cigarettes beginning in 1989, launched an experiment in the community, multipronged efforts to reduce smoking statewide. The initiative mandated mass media anti-tobacco advertising as well as school and community education and intervention activities. It also mandated that the effectiveness of the program be evaluated after a decade. Thus, the California experience has provided evidence on what methods are effective in reducing smoking.

The tax increase itself contributed to the success of the program, as discussed in the previous section. Immediately after the increase was implemented, the rate of decline in cigarette consumption increased significantly in California compared with the rest of the nation. The rate of decline then leveled off until the media campaign was launched in 1990 and 1991, when there was a further 12 percent decline.[19] In 1994, the California legislature passed a law prohibiting smoking statewide in all workplaces except bars, taverns, and casinos. The law has since been strengthened to include all workplaces.

Overall, per capita cigarette consumption in California fell by 60 percent between 1988 and 2001.[20] This reduction is achieved by a combination of a reduction in the number of smokers and reduction of the number of cigarettes each smoker consumes per day. In California, according to the CDC's Behavioral Risk Factor Survey, the prevalence of smoking was 16.6 percent in 2002, compared to 23 percent in the nation as a whole.[20,1] Even in years when the number of smokers remained steady or increased, the average number of cigarettes smoked per day continued to fall.[21] California's anti-tobacco campaign suffered budget cuts after the first few years, and tobacco companies stepped up their political efforts to oppose the state's control measures, as well as their advertising and promotion of cigarettes; but the permanent changes in policy, as well as additional tax increases, have helped California to maintain its lead over other states in keeping smoking levels relatively low.

California's campaign included an aggressive advertising component, which contributed significantly to the campaign's overall success. Studies of the effectiveness of anti-smoking messages have shown that some messages are much more effective than others. In fact, some programs sponsored by the tobacco industry, which are presented as smoking prevention efforts, have been shown to make smoking more attractive to youths. For example, these advertisements often present the messages that smoking is an "adult" choice, that parents have a responsibility to help their kids fight peer pressure for smoking, and that "it's the law" that retailers not sell cigarettes to youth. Examination of industry documents, discussed in the next section, has found that the industry has purposely used these "forbidden fruit" messages to generate good public relations and fight restrictive legislation without actually discouraging youth smoking.[22]

The evaluation component of California's media campaign identified which anti-smoking messages were most effective in reaching youth. Researchers found that the message most effective in reaching both youths and adults is that "Tobacco industry executives use deceitful, manipulative, dishonest practices to hook new users, sell more cigarettes and make more money."[23(p.774)] One such successful ad, called "Nicotine Soundbites," showed the actual footage of tobacco executives testifying before Congress in 1994, raising their right hands and swearing that nicotine is not addictive. Ads with this message made both adults and teenagers angry, because no one likes to learn that they are being manipulated.

Another message that was found to be effective among both adults and teens was that secondhand smoke harms others. One ad portrayed a boy smoking, sitting with his little sister watching television. The little girl begins coughing and smoke comes out of her mouth. In the early 1990s, California also ran ads that encouraged quitting and provided information on smoking cessation programs, including toll-free quit lines, and calls to the quit lines dramatically increased. Ads with some other messages, including those that focused on health effects, were found to be ineffective.[23]

Researchers concluded that, to be effective, anti-tobacco advertisements need to be "ambitious, hard-hitting, explicit, and in-your-face."[23(p.776)] The industry recognized the effectiveness of the ads and worked hard to limit them. R. J. Reynolds threatened to sue the California Department of Health and the television stations that ran the Nicotine Soundbites ad; the lawsuit was not filed, but the ad was later dropped. During the state campaign, the tobacco industry tried to counter the anti-tobacco efforts by increasing its spending in California on advertising, incentives to merchants, and promotional items. One study calculated that after 1993, the industry spent nearly $10 for every $1 spent by the state.[19]

THE MASTER SETTLEMENT AGREEMENT

The 1990s saw dramatic developments in the battle against smoking, and suddenly it seemed possible that effective tobacco control measures would be enacted at the federal level. The changes resulted from several separate political and legal events, as well as public revelations that have discredited the tobacco industry.

In February 1994, David Kessler, then Commissioner of the Food and Drug Administration (FDA), launched an offensive against the tobacco industry by asserting that his agency has the authority to regulate tobacco. Kessler, who was appointed by the first President Bush but now had the support of an anti-smoking president, Bill Clinton, based his claim on thoroughly documented evidence that nicotine is an addictive drug and cigarettes are drug delivery systems. He proposed a series of measures aimed to protect children and teenagers against tobacco company efforts to get them hooked.

Coincidentally, in March 1994, a class-action lawsuit was filed against American tobacco companies in federal district court in Louisiana on behalf of "all nicotine-dependent persons in the U.S." and their families and heirs, seeking compensatory and punitive damages, attorneys fees, an admission of wrongdoing, and other remedies. Although this suit was dismissed, it was followed by other major lawsuits, including one in May 1994 by Michael Moore, the attorney general of Mississippi, who sought to recover the medical costs that the state had incurred treating smoking-related illnesses. Attorneys general from most of the other states followed suit over the next three years.[24]

Also in 1994, an anonymous informant from the Brown & Williamson tobacco company, who called himself "Mr. Butts" after the Doonesbury comic strip character, sent a box of top-secret tobacco industry internal documents to Stanton Glantz, a professor of medicine at the University of California at San Francisco and a well-known critic of the tobacco industry. The papers provided a wealth of information on discrepancies between what the industry knew about the ill effects of tobacco and what they were telling the public. For example, a lawyer for Brown & Williamson had written in a 1963 internal memo, "Nicotine is addictive. We are, then, in the business of selling nicotine, an addictive drug effective in the release of stress mechanisms."[25(p.58)] Glantz, with the support of University of California lawyers and librarians, published the papers on the Internet.

The tobacco companies, of course, challenged the FDA's authority to regulate tobacco, and they also vigorously defended against the lawsuits by attorneys general and injured smokers. However, the documents released by Glantz, together with other internal industry documents that have been leaked, have seriously undermined the industry's ability to defend itself in court. In April 1997, a North Carolina court affirmed the FDA's authority over tobacco as a drug, although it struck down some of the advertising restrictions proposed by the agency. However, in August 1998, an appeals court ruled the other way, stating that only Congress has authority to regulate the tobacco industry. The Supreme Court agreed to take up the issue and in 2000 supported the appeals court decision that the FDA did not have the authority to regulate tobacco.[26]

In early 1997, when the tobacco industry was on the defensive, it began negotiations with the attorneys general, hoping to reach a settlement that would protect them against unlimited lawsuits and possible financial ruin. A historic settlement was announced in June, in which the companies agreed to pay $368.5 billion over a twenty-five year period to compensate states for treating smoking-related illnesses and to set up a fund to pay damage claims for ill smokers, as well as for other purposes including financing of nationwide anti-smoking programs. The industry also agreed to a number of restrictions on advertising and promotion and to allow the FDA to regulate the nicotine in cigarettes. However, the settlement required Congressional approval, which did not materialize. In 1998, the tobacco industry reached a more limited settlement with the attorneys general, agreeing to pay forty-six states $206 billion over twenty-five years and accepting some restrictions on advertising, including a ban on billboard ads. The settlement also provided $1.7 billion over a five-year period to create the American Legacy Foundation, which used the funds for public education and other tobacco control activities.[27]

The MSA has been something of a disappointment for public health advocates. It was hoped that the states would use some of the settlement dollars for tobacco control programs. Smoking-cessation programs that include counseling and nicotine-replacement therapy, such as nicotine gum or patches, can double or even triple a smoker's chance of quitting.[27] Telephone quit lines, sponsored by some states and sometimes by voluntary organizations, can be effective at motivating people to quit. However, most states have used little of the MSA funds for such programs, using the windfall to close state budget gaps. On the other hand, tobacco companies have had to increase the price of cigarettes by 45 cents a pack to pay for the settlement. As discussed previously, higher prices discourage people from smoking, especially young people.

The American Legacy Foundation has used its part of the settlement to run aggressive ad campaigns against smoking targeted at youth, called the "truth" campaign. Drawing on findings from evaluations of the California and other tobacco control programs, the ads convey the message that tobacco companies manipulate the truth, deny health effects and the addictive nature of tobacco, and try to make smoking appear attractive. The "truth" ads feature statements such as: "In 1984, one tobacco company referred to new customers as 'replacement smokers'" and "In 1990 tobacco companies put together a plan to stop coroners from listing tobacco as a cause of death on a death certificate."[28] One commercial features youths piling body bags outside of a tobacco company's headquarters and using megaphones to announce that these represent the 1,200 people killed daily by tobacco. The "truth" ads were placed in youth-oriented magazines and television programs. Two national youth surveys, used to evaluate the effect of the "truth" campaign, found that young people who had seen the ads were significantly more likely than those who had not seen them to hold negative attitudes toward tobacco.[29] The "truth" campaign, together with the increased tobacco taxes, has contributed to reducing youth smoking to a twenty-seven-year low.[27] The American Legacy Foundation's funding from the MSA expired in 2003, and it is not clear how much it will have to spend in the future. Ads for the truth campaign can be seen on the Foundation's website at www.thetruth.com.

The original agreement negotiated by the state attorneys general and the tobacco companies contained a provision allowing the FDA to regulate tobacco. Because that agreement was not approved by Congress, the MSA did not contain such a provision. There are many advantages to giving regulatory authority over tobacco to the FDA. At present, there are no legal restrictions concerning ingredients in tobacco smoke or on labeling or advertising concerning health claims by the companies. There is evidence, for example, that companies manipulate nicotine levels in tobacco to promote addiction, and they add ammonia to increase the effect of the nicotine. Tobacco smoke contains toxic chemicals such as nitrosamines and arsenic in addition to the tars known to be carcinogenic. The FDA could require companies to list ingredients on cigarette labels, as is required of food. It could regulate health-related claims made by the companies and insist that such claims be proven. It is possible that cigarettes could be made safer, so that smokers who cannot or will not quit would suffer less harm. However, unless the government has the authority to verify claims, tobacco companies could continue to label their products "light" or "safer" without needing to actually reduce the hazards of smoking.[26]

"The key to public health action on the tobacco front seems to lie in combining strategies to discourage children from smoking and in producing a safer and less addictive cigarette for those who cannot, or will not, resist the temptation to smoke," wrote the ethicist George Annas in January 1997,[30(p.307)] when the possibility of a negotiated settlement was first being considered. Whether Congress or the courts or both will finally make possible the demotion of tobacco as public health enemy number one remains to be seen.

CONCLUSION

Cigarette smoking is the leading actual cause of death in the United States. It has been known since the 1950s that smoking causes lung cancer, and the behavior has been responsible for an epidemic of lung cancer, the leading cause of cancer death among both men and women. Smoking also causes cardiovascular disease, chronic lung disease, low birth weight in infants, and a number of other unhealthy conditions.

Since the surgeon general's *Smoking and Health* report was published in 1964, summarizing the evidence about the harm caused by smoking, public health advocates have been attacking the habit in as many ways as possible. Cigarette consumption in the United States peaked in the early 1960s and has declined since then, demonstrating significant success from the public health efforts. In the 1990s, however, there was a leveling off of the percentage of adults who smoke. Currently about 23 percent of the adult population smoke cigarettes, down from over 42 percent in 1965.

Public health has fought the tobacco industry on many fronts. In the 1960s, Congress passed legislation that required that cigarette ads on radio and television be balanced by counter-advertising about the harmful effects of smoking. This publicity, together with warning labels on cigarette packages, helped to persuade many people to quit. Tobacco companies have become increasingly sophisticated about marketing their products, especially to children, and public health has had to work hard to oppose them. Since nicotine in tobacco is addictive, it has become clear that the most effective approach to reducing smoking is to prevent young people from taking up the habit.

Public health interventions that have demonstrated some success in preventing the onset of smoking and in reducing its prevalence include the enactment and enforcement of laws prohibiting the sale of tobacco to minors, restrictions on indoor smoking, and—most effectively—increases in cigarette prices through imposition of taxes.

California has been a leader among states in imposing a tax on cigarettes to be used for tobacco control programs. Evaluation of its mass media advertising campaign has helped anti-smoking activists to understand what messages are most effective in persuading youths not to smoke. California was also a leader in legislation to ban smoking in public places.

In the mid- and late-1990s, legal and regulatory attacks on the tobacco industry were launched by the Clinton administration and a number of states. The MSA between the attorneys general of forty-six states and the tobacco industry contained restrictions on tobacco advertising aimed at young people and provided billions of dollars to the states to compensate them for medical costs they incurred for treating smoking related illnesses. It also provided funds to establish the American Legacy Foundation, which has run an effective media campaign to discourage young people from smoking. The battle continues. It seems that progress is being made, but prospects for victory in public health's battle against the powerful tobacco industry are uncertain.

REFERENCES

1. U.S. Centers for Disease Control and Prevention, "Cigarette Smoking Among Adults—U.S. 2002," *Morbidity and Mortality Weekly Report* 53 (2004): 427–431.
2. C. E. Bartecchi, T. D. MacKenzie, and R. W. Schrier, "The Global Tobacco Epidemic," *Scientific American* (May 1995): 44–51.
3. U.S. Public Health Service, *Smoking and Health: Report of the Advisory Committee to the Surgeon General* (Washington, DC: 1964).
4. U.S. Public Health Service, *Health Consequences of Smoking for Women, Report of the Surgeon General* (Rockville, MD: 1980).
5. American Cancer Society, *Cancer Facts & Figures—1998*.
6. Environmental Protection Agency, *Health Effects of Passive Smoking: Lung Cancer and other Disorders* (Washington, DC: U.S. Dept. of Health and Human Services, 1992).
7. R. Bayer, and J. Colgrove, "Science, Politics, and Ideology in the Campaign Against Environmental Tobacco Smoke," *American Journal of Public Health* 91 (2002): 949–954.

8. R. Kluger, "A Peace Plan for the Cigarette Wars," *New York Times Magazine* (April 7, 1996): 28–30, 35, 50, 54.

9. C. Healton, and K. Nelson, "Reversal of Misfortune: Viewing Tobacco as a Social Justice Issue," *American Journal of Public Health* 94 (2004): 186–191.

10. P. M. Fischer, M. P. Schwartz, J. W. Richares Jr., A. O. Goldstein, and T. H. Rojas, "Brand Logo Recognition by Children Aged 3 to 6 Years: Mickey Mouse and Old Joe the Camel," *Journal of the American Medical Association* 266 (1991): 3145–3148.

11. J. Ellis, and M. E. Northridge, "Tobacco and the Media, editorial," *American Journal of Public Health* 92 (2002): 895.

12. U.S. Centers for Disease Control and Prevention, "Trends in Cigarette Smoking Among High School Students—United States, 1991–2001," *Morbidity and Mortality Weekly Report* 51 (2002): 409–412.

13. S. E. Jones, D. J. Sharp, C. G. Husten, and L. S. Crossett, "Cigarette Acquisition and Proof of Age Among U.S. High School Students Who Smoke," *Tobacco Control* 11 (2002): 20–25.

14. K. M. Ribisi, A. E. Kim, and R. S. Williams, "Are the Sales Practices of Internet Cigarette Vendors Good Enough to Prevent Sales to Minors?" *American Journal of Public Health* 92 (2002): 940–941.

15. M. Grossman, and F. J. Chaloupka, "Cigarette Taxes: The Straw to Break the Camel's Back," *Public Health Reports* 112 (1997): 291–297.

16. T. W. Hu, "The Impact of California Proposition 99, A Major Anti-Smoking Law, on Cigarette Consumption," *Journal of Public Health Policy* (Spring 1994): 26–36.

17. "State Excise Tax Rates on Cigarettes (January 1, 2004)," *www.taxadmin.org/fta/rate/cigarett.html*. Accessed September 16, 2004.

18. U.S. Centers for Disease Control and Prevention, "Response to Increases in Cigarette Prices by Race/Ethnicity, Income, and Age Groups—United States, 1976–1993," *Morbidity and Mortality Weekly Report* 47 (1998): 605–609.

19. J. P. Pierce et al., "Has the California Tobacco Control Program Reduced Smoking?" *Journal of the American Medical Association* 280 (1998): 893–899.

20. California Department of Health Services, "California's Adult Smoking Declines to Historic Lows." News Release. May 26, 2004.

21. California Department of Health Services, "Cigarette Consumption," *www.dhs.ca.gov/tobacco*. Accessed September 15, 2004.

22. A. Landman, P. M. Ling, and S. A. Glantz, "Tobacco Industry Youth Smoking Prevention Programs: Protecting the Industry and Hurting Tobacco Control," *American Journal of Public Health* 92 (2002): 917–930.

23. L. K. Goldman, and S. A. Glantz, "Evaluation of Antismoking Advertising Campaigns," *Journal of the American Medical Association* 279 (1998): 772–777.

24. J. M. Broder, "Cigarette Makers in a $368 Billion Accord to Curb Lawsuits and Curtail Marketing," *New York Times* (June 21, 1997): A1.

25. S. A. Glantz et al., *The Cigarette Papers* (Berkeley: University of California Press, 1996).

26. M. L. Myers, "Protecting the Public Health by Strengthening the Food and Drug Aministration's Authority over Tobaco Products," *New England Journal of Medicine* 343 (2003): 1806–1809.

27. S. A. Schroeder, "Tobacco Control in the Wake of the 1998 Master Settlement Agreement," *New England Journal of Medicine* 350 (2004): 203–301.

28. American Legacy Foundation web site. *www.thetruth.com/index.cfm?crazyworld=truth.* Accessed September 17, 2004.
29. M. C. Farrelly et al., "Getting to the Truth: Evaluating National Tobacco Countermarketing Campaigns," *American Journal of Public Health* 92 (2002): 901–907.
30. G. Annas, "Tobacco Litigation as Cancer Prevention: Dealing with the Devil," *New England Journal of Medicine* 336 (1997): 304–308.

CHAPTER 16

Public Health Threat Number Two and Growing: Poor Diet and Physical Inactivity

Pear-Shaped is Healthier

Throughout evolutionary history, humans had to exert a great deal of physical activity to obtain their food. Only over the past century has a substantial and increasing percentage of the population had access to an excess of food with no need to exercise. The consequence of this imbalance has been that Americans are becoming fatter, an exceedingly unhealthy trend. Today, poor diet and physical inactivity have been ranked second among the factors identified as leading actual causes of death in the United States, although the analysis is controversial as discussed in Chapter 13. (See Table 13–3.)

Many studies have shown that weighing too much increases people's risk of cardiovascular disease, diabetes, most kinds of cancer, and a variety of other diseases. Thus, it is in the interest of public health to reduce the prevalence of overweight and obesity, which in 2000 affected about 64 percent of the adult population.[1] Getting people to lose weight, however, seems to be even more difficult than getting them to quit smoking, although many of them want to be thinner. According to the 1998–2000 National Health Interview Survey, 44 percent of women and 29 percent of men are trying to lose weight, most of them unsuccessfully.[2] An Institute of Medicine report on the problem states, "It is paradoxical that obesity is increasing in the United States while more people are dieting than ever before, spending, by one estimate, more than $33 billion per year on weight-reduction products (including diet foods and soft drinks, artificial sweeteners, and diet books) and services (e.g., fitness clubs and weight-loss programs)."[3(p.27)]

The association of obesity with certain health risks is easy to measure, but the relationship may not be a simple one of cause and effect. Obesity is a complex condition, influenced by genes as well as by many individual and social factors that include eating and exercise patterns. While being overweight has a health impact in itself, a person's disease risk may be also be affected independently by dietary patterns and the amount of physical activity, whether or not he or she is overweight. Public health advocates, therefore, seek to promote healthier eating patterns among Americans, to encourage them to exercise more, and to reduce the percentage of people who are overweight.

EPIDEMIOLOGY OF OBESITY

Obesity is, to an extent, in the eyes of the beholder—often the beholder who is looking in the mirror. In the public health perspective, obesity is usually defined more precisely in terms of body-mass index (BMI). BMI is calculated by dividing a person's height in meters by the square of his

Table 16–1   Body Mass Index Table

To use the table, find the appropriate height in the left-hand column labeled Height. Move across to a given weight (in pounds). The number at the top of the column is the BMI at that height and weight. Pounds have been rounded off.

BMI	19	20	21	22	23	24	25	26	27	28	29	30	31	32	33	34	35
Height (inches)							Body Weight (pounds)										
58	91	96	100	105	110	115	119	124	129	134	138	143	148	153	158	162	167
59	94	99	104	109	114	119	124	128	133	138	143	148	153	158	163	168	173
60	97	102	107	112	118	123	128	133	138	143	148	153	158	163	168	174	179
61	100	106	111	116	122	127	132	137	143	148	153	158	164	169	174	180	185
62	104	109	115	120	126	131	136	142	147	153	158	164	169	175	180	186	191
63	107	113	118	124	130	135	141	146	152	158	163	169	174	180	186	191	197
64	110	116	122	128	134	140	145	151	157	163	169	174	180	186	192	197	204
65	114	120	126	132	138	144	150	156	162	168	174	180	186	192	198	204	210
66	118	124	130	136	142	148	155	161	167	173	179	186	192	198	204	210	216
67	121	127	134	140	146	153	159	166	172	178	185	191	198	204	211	217	223
68	125	131	138	144	151	158	164	171	177	184	190	197	203	210	216	223	230
69	128	135	142	149	155	162	169	176	182	189	196	203	209	216	223	230	236
70	132	139	146	153	160	167	174	181	188	195	202	209	216	222	229	236	243
71	136	143	150	157	165	172	179	186	193	200	208	215	222	229	236	243	250
72	140	147	154	162	169	177	184	191	199	206	213	221	228	235	242	250	258
73	144	151	159	166	174	182	189	197	204	212	219	227	235	242	250	257	265
74	148	155	163	171	179	186	194	202	210	218	225	233	241	249	256	264	272
75	152	160	168	176	184	192	200	208	216	224	232	240	248	256	264	272	279
76	156	164	172	180	189	197	205	213	221	230	238	246	254	263	271	279	287

Source: National Institutes of Health, "Body Mass Index Table," *www.nhlbi.nih.gov/guidelines/obesity/bmi_tbl.htm.* Accessed February 27, 2005.

or her weight in kilograms. Table 16–1 presents BMIs in terms of inches and pounds for a range that includes most Americans.

Most studies show that weight-associated health risks begin to appear at a BMI of about 25, and rise more significantly above 30, with the risks increasing in proportion to the severity of an individual's obesity. The National Institutes of Health and the Centers for Disease Control and Prevention (CDC) have agreed on a definition of overweight as a BMI between 25 and 29.9 and obesity as a BMI of 30 or greater.[4] Using this definition, 67 percent of men and 62 percent of women twenty years of age and older were found to be overweight or obese in the National Health and Nutrition Examination Survey (NHANES) conducted between 1999 and 2000.[5] Obesity had a prevalence of 27.7 percent in men and 34.0 percent in women.

The prevalence of obesity has increased dramatically over the past three decades, as shown in Figures 16–1 and 16–2. There are significant racial differences in the prevalence of obesity among women: 76 percent of nonpregnant black women are overweight, compared with 58 percent of white women. Black men are less likely than white men to be overweight:

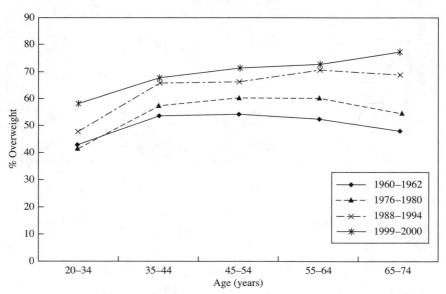

Figure 16–1 Percentage of Overweight Males
Source: Data from U.S. Centers for Disease Control and Prevention, *Health, United States,* 2003.

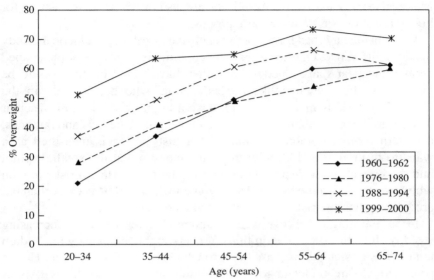

Figure 16–2 Percentage of Overweight Females
Source: Data from U.S. Centers for Disease Control and Prevention, *Health, United States,* 2003.

59 percent of black men compared with 67 percent of white men.[5] The health effects of overweight and obesity are less marked among blacks. The optimal BMI has been calculated to be 23 to 25 for whites, while it is 23 to 30 for blacks.[6] Obesity increases with age, as seen in Figures 16–1 and 16–2, but declines in the age group 75 years and older as discussed in Chapter 28.

Socioeconomic status has a significant influence on the prevalence of obesity. College graduates of both sexes are thinner than men and women with fewer years of education. The difference is especially significant among females: those with less than twelve years of education are nearly two and one-half times more likely to be obese than female college graduates. Similarly, poorer women are much more likely to be overweight than wealthier women, although the prevalence of obesity in men does not vary much with income.[7]

The greater prevalence of obesity in black women compared to white women doubtless contributes to poorer health among blacks. As discussed in Chapter 14, rates of cardiovascular disease and diabetes are higher in blacks than in whites, and an unhealthy diet is likely to be part of the problem.

Many Hispanics and Native Americans are also overweight, accounting for high rates of diabetes among these groups.

While being fat is bad for people's health, the distribution of fat on the body makes a difference. Obesity researchers distinguish between apple-shaped people and pear-shaped people, and they have found health risks to be greater for those shaped like apples. People who gain weight in the abdominal area, as men usually do, have a higher risk of cardiovascular disease and diabetes than people who gain weight in the hips and buttocks, a pattern more common in females. Fat distribution is measured as a waist-to-hip ratio (WHR), with the waist measured at the smallest point and the hips at the widest point around the buttocks. Health risks in men who have a WHR more than 1.0 and women whose WHR is more than 0.8 are greater than the risks due to obesity alone.[3]

In an alarming trend, overweight among children has been increasing steadily since the 1960s. Definitions of overweight and obesity in children are complex calculations, based on growth curves of BMI for age. Health professionals are reluctant to label children as obese; so the NHANES survey identifies children at or above the 95th percentile on the growth curves as overweight and children between the 85th and the 95th percentile as at risk for overweight.[8] (Some surveys use the term obese for children at or above the 95th percentile.) The prevalence of overweight among children and adolescents six to nineteen years old increased from about 5 percent in the earliest surveys to more than 15 percent in the 1999–2000 NHANES. The prevalence of overweight is higher in some ethnic groups: among Mexican American teenage boys, more than 27.5 percent are overweight, while the prevalence is 25.7 percent among black teenage girls.[5]

Children who are fat are likely to become fat adults and suffer the concomitant risks of chronic disease. For example, a study that tracked 679 school children for sixteen years found that weight during childhood was a good predictor of whether an adult would exhibit risk factors for cardiovascular disease and diabetes.[9] Overweight children are for the first time being diagnosed with type 2 diabetes, which is sometimes called "adult-onset diabetes" because until recently it was believed to occur almost exclusively in adults.[10] Obesity in children also tends to cause psychological problems such as depression and low self esteem. Children who are worried about their weight may undertake diets that affect their physical as well as their psychological health. While the issues are not well understood, children preoccupied with weight and dieting appear to be at increased risk for eating disorders such as anorexia and bulimia.

DIET AND NUTRITION

Obesity is caused by unhealthy eating patterns combined with inadequate physical activity, each a factor that influences people's health whether or not they weigh too much. The public health aspects of physical activity will be discussed later in this chapter. This section and the next explore the role of diet in the prevention of chronic diseases, including obesity, and describe public health efforts to encourage people to eat a healthier diet.

Most analyses find that Americans eat too much protein and fat and too few fruits and vegetables. This pattern contributes to high levels of cholesterol and other blood lipids and to high blood pressure—risk factors for cardiovascular disease, as discussed in Chapter 11. The evidence is less clear how the American diet increases cancer risk, but epidemiologic studies show that breast and colon cancer risks are greater in populations that eat diets high in meat and low in fruits and vegetables. Diet is a major factor in type 2 diabetes, which is often brought on by obesity and which can be controlled by careful eating. Osteoporosis, a debilitating disease of the elderly, especially white women (see Chapter 28), is likely to become increasingly common because young women are not getting enough calcium, best obtained in low-fat dairy products.

The federal government, in a number of reports over the years by various advisory committees, has developed recommendations on how Americans should eat to maintain health and prevent chronic disease. Since 1980, the U.S. Department of Agriculture and the Department of Health and Human Services have reviewed the recommendations every five years and released reports called *Dietary Guidelines for Americans*.[11] Agreeing on recommendations has often proved controversial, because the food industry opposes any recommendation that calls for eating less of any food substance.[12] However, evidence clearly supports the recommendations included in the 2000 guidelines that people should eat more dark green vegetables, orange vegetables, legumes, fruits, whole grains, and low-fat milk and milk products and less refined grains, total fats (especially cholesterol, and saturated and trans fats), added sugar, and calories. The guidelines contain special recommendations for specific population groups. The eating pattern now recommended is "the traditional eating pattern of poor people throughout the world."[13(p.739)]

While the 2005 food guidelines did not change significantly from those issued in 2000, the food guide pyramid, shown in Figure 16–3, was significantly revised in an attempt to make its recommendations more

Figure 16–3 Food Guide Pyramid
Source: www.mypyramid.gov/downloads/MiniPoster.pdf

understandable. The new pyramid comes in twelve versions for people of different ages, sexes, and activity levels, with specific recommendations that are more individualized than the pyramid of the past. People can visit the web site MyPyramid.gov and find guidelines appropriate for them. Another change is the addition of a recommendation for physical activity, illustrated by the stick figure climbing steps on the side of the pyramid.

Dietary surveys conducted by the Department of Agriculture have shown that while the diet of Americans has improved over the past several decades, people fall far short of the federal recommendations. One-third of the population eats at least some food from all food groups, but only 1 to 3 percent eat the recommended number of servings from all food groups on a given day. Fruits are the most commonly omitted item. Intake of fat and added sugars continues to be too high. While people appear to eat close to the recommended number of vegetable servings, half of these servings are iceberg lettuce, potatoes (including chips and fries), and canned tomatoes.[12] One unfortunate trend is that African Americans of low socioeconomic status, who used to eat a more healthful diet than wealthy whites, have now adopted eating patterns that have traditionally been associated with higher incomes. It is as if, as one commentator suggests, they feel they are now "able to afford steak instead of having to 'fill up' on bread or peas or beans."[13(p.739)]

Federal surveys suggest that, among the causes of increasing obesity, especially in children, is the increased intake of sweetened beverages. The proportion of calories that the average American obtained from soft drinks and fruit drinks more than doubled between 1977 and 2001.[14] The trend was similar for all age groups, but the numbers were highest in the younger age groups, rising from 4.8 to 10.3 percent of calories in the two- to eighteen-year-old group and from 5.1 to 12.3 percent among those between nineteen and thirty-nine. Meanwhile, consumption of milk decreased by 38 percent overall, including among children age two to eighteen, the group for whom milk consumption is most important for future health. Consumption of other beverages has not changed significantly over the period studied. These trends are unhealthy, not only because soft drinks and sweetened juice drinks contain "empty calories" that contribute to weight gain, but also because consuming milk products appears to help people control their weight. According to the researchers, reducing soft drink and fruit drink intake "would seem to be one of the simpler ways to reduce obesity in the United States."[14(p.209)]

PROMOTING HEALTHY EATING

It might seem that what each individual eats is under his or her individual control. But many social, cultural, and economic factors contribute to dietary patterns. Eating habits and dietary preferences develop over a lifetime, influenced by family, ethnicity, the media, and other factors in the social environment. The high prevalence of overweight in the United States combined with the large numbers of people who are trying unsuccessfully to lose weight makes it clear that changing eating patterns is very difficult, even for highly motivated people. Studies of patients with a variety of medical conditions requiring special diets have found that even they have difficulty sticking to the prescribed diet. The rate of adherence to a diet by people with diabetes ranged from 20 to 53 to 73 percent in three different studies. People with kidney failure who were on dialysis were found to have a rate of adherence to the recommended diet of 39 percent and 42 percent in two separate studies. Another study found that the ability of people with high cholesterol to adhere to a low-cholesterol diet was only 30 percent.[15]

Public health efforts concerning diet have attempted to apply the ecological model of health behavior as discussed in Chapter 14, to create a social environment that favors healthier eating. For example, making nutritious foods more readily available—intervention at the community and institutional levels—should encourage people to choose their foods more wisely. There is evidence that the food industry is responding to many consumers' concerns about weight and health by providing a greater choice of low-fat and low-calorie foods. Many restaurants offer "heart healthy" selections on the menu and label them thus. Worksite and school cafeterias provide healthy food choices including salad bars. While such measures do not guarantee that people will eat a healthier diet, they remove barriers that make it hard for people to do so.

Enhancing self-efficacy and providing social support are ways of promoting healthy eating at the level of the individual and his or her family and friends.[15] Social support is provided when a whole family is willing to adopt a diet together, or by group programs such as Weight Watchers. Self efficacy can be improved by "point of choice" postings of nutritional information, which can help shoppers who are concerned about the nutritional content of food but do not know how to make wise choices. Several major campaigns using point of choice postings have been conducted by supermarket chains in collaboration with health advocacy organizations such as the American Heart Association, but the results have been mixed. Other approaches to enhancing self-efficacy and adherence to diets include demonstrations of healthy cooking methods and practice in calculating portion sizes.

Despite such efforts, the continuing rise in the proportion of Americans who are overweight attests to public health's failure thus far to make significant changes in dietary patterns. In fact, several major public health campaigns conducted in entire communities and aimed at reducing cardiovascular risks found that obesity was the most difficult risk factor to control. The Stanford Three-Community Study, the Stanford Five-City Study, the Minnesota Heart Health Program, and the North Karelia (Finland) Project all had reasonable success in reducing risk factors such as smoking, hypertension, and blood cholesterol, but none of them interrupted the increase in the prevalence of obesity in the communities studied.[3]

The Institute of Medicine, after a thorough study aimed at developing criteria for evaluating the outcomes of programs to prevent and treat obesity, concluded in a report called *Weighing the Options* that prospects were dim for people seeking to lose weight. "The fact is that despite the billions of dollars spent, few people reduce their body weight to a desirable or healthy level and even fewer maintain the weight lost beyond two or three years."[3(p.158)] The report notes that for most people, weight is not lost once and for all but that its control demands continuing effort. Accordingly, the Institute of Medicine recommends thinking in terms of lifelong weight management, encouraging overweight people to try at least to avoid gaining additional weight. According to the report, even small weight losses can raise self-esteem and improve the health of people suffering from obesity-related chronic conditions.

Public health advocates look at evidence from antismoking campaigns for ideas on how to improve the social environment to affect the American diet. The success of the public service announcements of the 1960s, together with later bans on cigarette advertising in the broadcast media, in reducing smoking prevalence (see Chapter 15) has inspired a number of media campaigns to promote more healthful eating. One such campaign was California's "5-a-Day" Campaign for Better Health, which attempted to increase fruit and vegetable consumption among state residents to five servings per day.[12] The program proved to be successful in increasing consumption of fruits and vegetables in the state. Later, the National Cancer Institute launched the program nationwide, although funding was never adequate to maintain the early successes of the California program. As in the case of antismoking campaigns, public health advocates must compete with well-financed advertising campaigns by food manufacturers promoting highly attractive but nonnutritious foods.

The food and beverage industries use some of the same approaches for increasing their sales as the tobacco companies have used. As documented in Marion Nestle's book, *Food Politics: How the Food Industry Influences Nutrition and Health*,[12] companies do everything they can to encourage Americans to eat more. They do this by processing foods to make them taste good, which often means sweet, fat, or salty. They push larger portions, often by promoting them as good buys; for example, a large serving of fries might cost only pennies more than a small serving while it might have twice as many calories. The companies also advertise extensively, especially to children. They take advantage of the fact that, with most women working outside the home, convenience and efficiency are major factors in food choice and fewer family meals than in the past are home cooked. As Nestle describes, food companies "conduct systematic, pervasive, and unrelenting . . . campaigns to convince government officials, health organizations, and nutrition professionals that their products are healthful or harmless, to undermine any suggestion to the contrary, and to ensure that federal dietary guidelines and food guides will help promote sales."[12(p.26)] Like tobacco companies, food companies argue that diet is a matter of individual choice, and they use science to sow confusion about the harm their products can do.

A number of proposals have been made to tackle the obesity epidemic with tools similar to those that proved successful in the "tobacco wars." They include educational campaigns such as the one for "5-a-Day" fruits and vegetables. They also include regulations to improve the social environment for healthy eating and the imposition of taxes to discourage unhealthy eating. Food labeling and advertising should be required to carry information on calorie, fat, and sugar content, and should be prohibited from making misleading health claims. Fast food restaurants should be required to provide nutritional information on packages and wrappers. The nutritionist Nestle proposes taxes on soft drinks and other junk foods to fund "eat less, move more" campaigns and perhaps to subsidize the costs of fruits and vegetables.[12(p.367)]

Because the impact of lawsuits against tobacco companies was so successful in forcing the companies to raise prices, limiting their advertising and marketing, and publicizing their fraudulent claims, public health advocates are beginning to think about similar lawsuits against fast food companies. Although a lawsuit against McDonald's by obese teenagers was laughed out of court, some lawyers see potential for challenging the fast food companies on deceptive advertising and marketing practices, using consumer protection laws. One lawyer who was involved in tobacco cases and is now reportedly preparing suits against food companies is quoted as saying, "The issue is what goes on with the kids, the advertising, what's in schools. That's an issue that has some oomph to it."[16]

Many public health advocates believe that the best hope of preventing obesity in adulthood is to influence children's habits. Thus a great deal of attention is being paid to preventing overweight in children. One proven approach is to encourage breastfeeding, which has many other health advantages as well, for both mother and infant. A number of studies have shown that breastfeeding has a long-term protective effect against obesity in children. It also helps the mother to lose weight she gained during pregnancy.[17]

It is also important to increase parents' awareness that their children are at risk. In a follow-up to the 1988–1994 NHANES survey, after children were weighed and measured, mothers were asked whether their child was overweight, underweight, or about the right weight. Nearly one third of mothers of overweight children reported that their child was about the right weight.[18] The state of Arkansas has addressed this problem by mandating that schools send home a weight report card.[19] There is evidence that treatment of obesity in children with interventions that involve their parents has a much greater chance of success than treatment of adults. In one study, health educators gave instructions on a low-fat prudent diet to parents of infants, an intervention that significantly reduced the prevalence of obesity in children up to three years old.[3] However, such programs must overcome the influence of television advertising designed to promote foods that are not necessarily nutritious. One cereal manufacturer, for example, claimed that its television spot was seen by 95 percent of all children ages two through eleven an average of 107 times within the first year of its new cereal's introduction.[20]

In 2005, the Institute of Medicine published a report called *Preventing Childhood Obesity: Health in the Balance*.[21] Calling childhood obesity a "critical public health threat,"[21(p.2)] the report recommends steps that federal, state, and local governments should take to make prevention of obesity in children and youth a national priority. Recommendations include developing guidelines for advertising and marketing of foods and beverages to children and giving the Federal Trade Commission authority and resources to monitor compliance. Governments should also develop and implement nutritional standards for all foods and beverages sold or served in schools. Food and beverage companies have invaded schools with vending machines selling unhealthy drinks and snacks, fast food in school cafeterias, and special educational programs and materials accompanied by advertisements for fast food and junk food.

As discussed below, obesity and chronic disease are as much a result of lack of physical activity as they are of unhealthy diets. Weight loss programs are most successful, in adults as well as in children, when they combine diet and exercise. "Exercise is today's best buy in public health," one commentator notes. "It is positive and acceptable, has insignificant side effects, and can be inexpensive."[22(p.252)]

PHYSICAL ACTIVITY AND HEALTH

Most studies on how to lose weight have found that the most effective approach combines dieting and physical activity. Dieters who are physically active are more likely to lose fat while preserving lean mass. This combination not only promotes a healthier distribution of body weight (a lower WHR), but it also helps people avoid the weight loss plateaus that can result from dieting. Since lean mass burns more calories than fat burns, a dieter who loses muscle mass will end up with a higher proportion of his or her weight consisting of fat, and thus fewer calories will be needed to maintain the new weight, making it more difficult to lose additional pounds. Exercising when dieting helps to ensure that the weight lost will be fat. Raising the amount of physical activity without reducing calorie intake, while a relatively inefficient way to lose pounds, is likely to reduce the waist-to-hip ratio and thus improve health.[23]

A number of epidemiologic studies have demonstrated that people who are more physically active live longer. For example, a study of almost 17,000 male Harvard alumni found that those who engaged in vigorous activities for three or more hours per week were less than half as likely to die within the twelve- to sixteen-year follow-up period than those who had the lowest activity levels.[24] Among Harvard graduates who were sedentary at the beginning of the study, those who took up moderate sports activity at some time during the follow-up period had a 23 percent lower death rate than those who remained sedentary.[25]

Exercise clearly protects against cardiovascular disease, as demonstrated by epidemiologic studies and through biomedical evidence. The Framingham Study found, as early as the 1970s, that the risk for both men and women of dying from cardiovascular disease was highest among those who were the least physically active and that more activity was associated with lower risk.[26] Exercise offers the greatest protective effect against heart disease; the evidence for protection against stroke is equivocal. Several studies have indicated that inactive men and women are more likely to develop high blood pressure than those who are active and that moderate intensity exercise may help reduce blood pressure in people whose pressure is elevated.

There is some biomedical evidence for how physical activity protects against cardiovascular disease. One major factor is the effect on blood cholesterol, especially the tendency for exercise training to increase levels of high density lipoprotein, "the good cholesterol." Even a single episode of physical activity has been found to improve the balance of blood lipids, an effect persisting for several days.[27] By lowering cholesterol levels in the blood, exercise protects against atherosclerosis. Studies on monkeys have demonstrated that exercise has a protective effect even when the animals are fed a diet high in cholesterol and fats.[28] Other favorable effects of physical activity on the cardiovascular system include a lowering of blood pressure, an increase in circulation to the heart muscle, and a reduced tendency of blood to form clots. Moreover, physical activity reduces the risk of diabetes, which is an important risk factor for cardiovascular disease.

Type 2, or adult-onset diabetes is related to weight gain in adults, especially weight gain distributed in an "apple" shape, a consequence of insufficient physical activity. The high prevalence of obesity among Americans contributes to the ranking of diabetes as the sixth leading cause of death, probably an underestimate because many cardiovascular deaths have diabetes as an underlying cause.

Early suspicions that physical inactivity contributed to diabetes were raised by observations that prevalence of the disease was higher in societies or groups that moved from a traditional lifestyle to a more technologically advanced environment. This transition has been extensively studied in certain Native American and Pacific Islander communities. While the increased risk stems in part from changes in diet and increased prevalence of obesity, physical activity may be an independent risk factor.[29] The Nurses' Health Study and the Physicians' Health Study have both found that regular physical exercise reduces the incidence of type 2 diabetes.[30,31] The protective effect of exercise against the development of diabetes seems to work largely by increasing the sensitivity of muscle and other tissues to insulin.

There are indications that physical activity may also protect against cancer, although the relationship is clear only in the case of colon cancer. A number of epidemiologic studies have found that men and women who are physically active have lower risks of colon cancer than those who are inactive.[23] Studies examining the association of breast and prostate cancer with lack of exercise have been inconclusive, although there is a suggestion that physical activity during adolescence and young adulthood may protect women against later development of breast cancer.

HOW MUCH EXERCISE IS ENOUGH, AND HOW MUCH DO PEOPLE GET?

There is some controversy over how much exercise is enough to provide a health benefit. Part of the problem is that it is difficult to obtain reliable measures of study subjects' degree of activity. Most studies use self-reported information given on questionnaires, and many measure activity at a single point in time. Since the studies suffer from weaknesses in measurements of exposure (to exercise), most do not yield a clear dose-response effect. However most researchers agree that the amount of benefit increases with the intensity, frequency, and duration of the physical activity, and that the activity must be regular and ongoing to provide an ongoing benefit.[23]

To send a clear message to Americans about the importance of increasing their physical activity, a panel of researchers convened by the CDC and the American College of Sports Medicine (ACSM) developed recommendations for how much and what kind of exercise people should aim for.[23] They arrived at a minimum standard of about 150 kilocalories of energy per day of light to moderate activity, which could be broken up over the course of the day. People can achieve the expenditure of 150 kilocalories each day by walking briskly for about thirty minutes or by running at ten minutes per mile for about fifteen minutes, or by performing other activities shown in Table 16–2. This recommendation, endorsed in a surgeon general's report, is supported, for example, by a study of almost 74,000 women ages fifty to seventy-nine, which found that those who did the recommended amount of exercise for thirty minutes a day five days a

Table 16–2 Duration of Various Activities to Expend 150 Kilocalories for an Average 70 kg Adult

Intensity	Activity	Metabolic Equivalents METs	Approximate Duration in Minutes
Moderate	Volleyball, noncompetitive	3.0	43
Moderate	Walking, moderate pace (3 mph, 20 min/mile)	3.5	37
Moderate	Walking, brisk pace (4 mph, 15 min/mile)	4.0	32
Moderate	Table tennis	4.0	32
Moderate	Raking leaves	4.5	32
Moderate	Social dancing	4.5	29
Moderate	Lawn mowing (powered push mower)	4.5	29
Hard	Jogging (5 mph, 12 min/mile)	7.0	18
Hard	Field hockey	8.0	16

Source: U.S. Department of Health and Human Services. *Physical Activity and Health: A Report of the Surgeon General*, 1996.

week had 30 percent less heart disease than those who were less active.[23] More exercise was better, but the greatest benefit was gained in going from being sedentary to thirty minutes of walking.[32]

Some scientists have disputed the validity of the CDC/ACSM recommendation, arguing that more vigorous, sustained exercise is necessary to achieve a significant benefit.[33] This view is supported by an Institute of Medicine report issued in 2002 that calls for sixty minutes a day of moderate exercise. The report concluded that thirty minutes a day is not adequate to maintain normal weight.[34] The new *Dietary Guidelines for Americans* follow the Institute of Medicine recommendations for exercise. Others argue, however, that it is preferable to set realistic goals for modest improvement, given that a very small percentage of the population gets even the minimal amount of exercise recommended by the CDC/ACSM panel.

In fact, about one out of four Americans report that they engage in no physical activity at all during their leisure time, according to 2002 Behavioral Risk Factor Surveillance System data. Lack of activity is more common in females than males and more common in African Americans and Hispanics than whites. People with less education and lower incomes are more likely to be inactive than those of higher socioeconomic status, and older adults tend to be more inactive than younger ones. The good news is that the percentage of adults who report no physical activity declined since 1996 by an average of 1 percent a year for all age groups.[35] Reasons for the decline in inactivity are not known; it has apparently not been sufficient to halt the continued increase in overweight and obesity.

Lack of physical activity is a major factor in the trend toward increasing prevalence of obesity in children. While most younger children report having engaged in exercise that makes them "sweat and breathe hard," surveys show that activity falls off dramatically during the high school years. Among ninth grade students, in 2003, 8.4 percent of boys and 9.7 percent of girls reported no participation in vigorous or moderate physical activity during the preceding seven days. By the time they reached twelfth grade, 10.9 percent of boys and 17.0 percent of girls were physically inactive. Only 44.5 percent of boys and 34.6 percent of girls were enrolled in physical education classes when they were in twelfth grade, and fewer than half of them had physical education class every day.[36]

There is evidence that television may be an important factor in children's physical inactivity. American children spend more time watching television and videotapes and playing video games than doing anything else except sleeping.[37] A national study of children and adolescents from diverse socioeconomic backgrounds found that obesity was directly associated with the amount of time spent watching television.[38] A trial conducted among third and fourth grade students in a California school found that reducing the hours they spent watching television by half to a third over a period of six months reduced their BMI significantly compared with a control group.[37] Television encourages not only physical inactivity, but also snack consumption; children are bombarded with television commercials for nonnutritious food products.

PROMOTING PHYSICAL ACTIVITY

As with most attempts to change people's behavior, the most effective approach to promoting physical activity is likely to employ the ecological model, intervening at a number of levels of influence. Efforts to motivate individuals to be more active must be combined with interventions that make the physical and social environment more conducive to physical activity. In part because research on the effectiveness of these interventions is difficult to do, most studies have focused on short-term changes in exercise behavior. There is very little evidence that any program has had long-term success in increasing physical activity among significant numbers of people.

A physician's recommendation has been found to significantly influence some sedentary people to become more physically active. However, a 1996 survey of primary care physicians found that only 49 percent of them believed that regular daily physical activity was very important for the average patient.[39] Accordingly, some organizations, such as the American Heart Association and the American Medical Association, have recommended that physicians include physical activity counseling in routine patient visits. Some programs have focused on educating physicians on the importance of physical activity and providing training on how to counsel patients.

Even when individuals are motivated to be active, there are environmental barriers that prevent people from carrying out their good intentions. The suburban lifestyle, which requires people to drive to wherever they want to go, is a major barrier that is very hard to overcome. Other barriers include inconvenience and inaccessibility of exercise facilities and unsafe conditions for exercise. As part of health promotion programs, some communities build walking trails or persuade shopping malls to open early for "mall walkers." Schools are a greatly underused resource for community recreation.[23] Residents of some high-crime neighborhoods have persuaded police departments to increase their surveillance; in others, residents have formed neighborhood watch groups. Surveys of bicycle riders suggest that many more people would commute to work by bicycle if safe bike paths or bike lanes were available, and some communities have responded to this evidence by building such routes.

Community trials designed to increase physical activity—usually as part of a "healthy heart" program—have incorporated such environmental modifications while also employing communications strategies, from public service announcements about physical activity to signs that provide cues to action. In one study, signs that said, "Stay Healthy, Save Time, Use the Stairs," were placed next to an escalator. This measure increased the percentage of people who used the stairs from 8 percent to 15 to 17 percent. For the most part, however, community trials aimed at increasing physical activity among adults have had disappointing results.[23]

Many public health advocates believe that the best hope for increasing population-wide physical activity is to focus on developing the habit of exercise in children and adolescents. Most young children engage in physical activity because they enjoy it. The CDC recommends that physical education classes teach school-age children about the health benefits of physical activity and help them to develop skills that can be applied in lifelong physical fitness activities, such as jogging, tennis, and aerobic dance. Such classes might be the most widely available resource for promoting physical activity among young people. However, only 26 percent of states require high schools to offer a course on physical activity that can be practiced throughout one's lifetime.[23] Among most young people, especially girls, physical activity declines significantly during late childhood and adolescence.

Americans' lack of exercise is one of the most intractable problems facing public health today. Very little is known about psychosocial, cultural, environmental, and public policy factors that may influence physical activity. The surgeon general's *Physical Activity and Health* report called for more research on various interventions and their long-term effects.[23] There is much to learn about how to motivate Americans to exercise adequately. In the words of one researcher, "The return of physical activity as the norm in everyone's everyday life—the 'restoration of biological normality'—will require cultural change on a scale similar to that which has occurred with smoking."[22(p.253)]

CONFRONTING THE OBESITY EPIDEMIC

The prevalence of overweight and obesity has increased so rapidly over recent decades (see Figures 16–1 and 16–2) that public health professionals have taken to calling it an epidemic. The health risks caused by overweight and obesity threaten to reverse many of the improvements in public health that were achieved in the twentieth century. Costs of treating the diseases caused by overweight and obesity are estimated to account for 9.1 percent of total U.S. medical expenditures and, when nursing home expenditures are included, the costs may have reached as high as $92.6 billion in 2002.[40] About half of the costs are paid by Medicare and Medicaid, the government health insurance plans, and the other half by private health insurance and by individuals.

In 2000, then surgeon general David Satcher organized a public "listening session" on the problem, which led to the publication of *The Surgeon General's Call to Action to Prevent and Decrease Overweight and Obesity.*[41] The purpose was to develop a national plan and to forge coalitions of governments, organizations, and individuals to "promote healthy eating habits and adequate physical activity, beginning in childhood and continuing across the lifespan." As Dr. Satcher states in the report's forward, "Many people believe that dealing with overweight and obesity is a personal responsibility. To some degree they are right, but it is also a community responsibility. When there are no safe, accessible places for children to play or adults to walk, jog, or ride a bike, that is a community responsibility. When school lunchrooms or office cafeterias do not provide healthy and appealing food choices, that is a community responsibility. When new or expectant mothers are not educated about the benefits of breastfeeding, that is a community responsibility. When we do not require daily physical education in our schools, that is also a community responsibility. There is much that we can and should do together."[41(p.xiii)]

CONCLUSION

Poor diet and physical inactivity have been ranked second among the behavioral factors identified as the leading actual causes of death in the United States. The combination of eating too much and exercising too little causes a very high prevalence of obesity among Americans. Obesity contributes to many health problems, including cardiovascular disease, diabetes, and most kinds of cancer. It is not only the extra pounds, but how the weight is distributed that adversely affects health. Extra weight in the hips and buttocks is less harmful to health than extra weight in the midsection.

Americans eat too much protein and fat and too few fruits and vegetables. This pattern of eating is itself unhealthy even if it did not lead to obesity. Increases in the consumption of sweetened beverages and decreases in the consumption of milk over the past two-and-a-half decades, especially among children, have contributed to the obesity epidemic.

Recommendations for a healthy diet call for people to eat more vegetables, fruits, whole grains, and low-fat milk products. However, people have great difficulty in changing their eating patterns, as seen from the large numbers who are trying to lose weight, most of them without success. Public health programs to promote healthy eating employ the ecological model, trying to create a favorable social environment by conducting media campaigns, encouraging the ready availability of nutritious foods, and providing nutritional information so that people will choose their foods wisely.

Exercise helps to protect against cardiovascular disease, diabetes, and some forms of cancer, in addition to helping to control weight. People who are physically active live longer than those who are inactive. Americans get far too little exercise, a factor that contributes to the high prevalence of obesity. Most public health interventions to promote physical activity apply the ecological model of behavior, using interpersonal and media messages to motivate people to exercise and removing environmental barriers that hinder them.

Because of the difficulty in changing diet and physical activity patterns of adults, the best hope of improving the population's behavior may be to focus on children. The prevalence of obesity in children is increasing in the United States. Breastfeeding can help protect children against being overweight. Some studies have shown that interventions that involve the whole family can be effective in reducing children's obesity. In school, physical education classes that help children develop skills they can use later in life may encourage them to develop the habit of being physically active. One of the most important obstacles to the development of healthful diet and activity patterns in children is television watching, which not only promotes inactivity but also tempts children with advertisements for non-nutritious snacks.

REFERENCES

1. National Center for Health Statistics, "Prevalence of Overweight and Obesity among Adults: United States, 1999-2000." *www.cdc.gov/nchs/products/pubbs/oybd/hestats/obese/obse99.htm*. Accessed September 23, 2004.
2. M. K. Serdula et al., "Prevalence of Attempting Weight Loss and Strategies for Controlling Weight," *Journal of the American Medical Association* 282 (1999): 1353–1358.
3. U.S. Institute of Medicine, *Weighing the Options: Criteria for Evaluating Weight-Management Programs* (Washington, DC: National Academy Press, 1995).
4. National Center for Chronic Disease Prevention and Health Promotion, "Defining Overweight and Obesity," *www.cdc.gov/nccdphp/dnpa/obesity/defining.htm*. Accessed September 23, 2004.
5. National Center for Health Statistics, *Health, United States, 2003 with Chartbook on Trends in the Health of Americans* (Hyattsville, Maryland: Public Health Service, 2003).
6. K. R. Fontaine et al., "Years of Life Lost Due to Obesity," *Journal of the American Medical Association* 289 (2003): 187–193.
7. National Center for Health Statistics, *Health, United States, 1998 with Socioeconomic Status and Health Chartbook* (Hyattsville, Maryland: Public Health Service, 1998).
8. National Center for Chronic Disease Prevention and Health Promotion, "BMI for Children and Teens." *www.cdc.gov/nccdphp/dnpa/bmi-for-age.htm*. Accessed September 23, 2004.
9. A. Sinaiko et al., "Relation of Weight and Rate of Increase in Weight During Childhood and Adolescence to Body Size, Blood Pressure, Fasting Insulin, and Lipids in Young Adults: The Minneapolis Children's Blood Pressure Study," *Circulation* 99 (1999): 1471–1476.
10. A. Fagot-Camapagna et al., "Type 2 Diabetes Among North American Children and Adolescents: An Epidemiologic Review and a Public Health Perspective," *Journal of Pediatrics* 135 (2000): 664–672.
11. Dietary Guidelines for Americans 2005. *www.healthierus.gov/dietaryguidelines/index.html*. Accessed May 12, 2005.
12. M. Nestle, *Food Politics: How the Food Industry Influences Nutrition and Health* (Berkeley, California: University of California Press, 2002).
13. S. Kumanyika, "Improving Our Diet—Still a Long Way To Go," *New England Journal of Medicine* 335 (1996): 738–739.
14. S. J. Nielsen, and B. M. Popkin, "Changes in Beverage Intake Between 1977 and 2001," *American Journal of Preventative Medicine* 27 (2004): 205–210.
15. J. M. Chrisler, "Adherence to Weight Loss and Nutritional Regimens," in *Handbook of Health Behavior Research II: Provider Determinants*, D. S. Gochman, ed. (New York: Plenum Press, 1997), 323–333.
16. K. Zernike, "Lawyers Shift Focus From Big Tobacco to Big Food," *New York Times* (April 9, 2004).
17. L. M. Grummer-Strawn, and Z. Mei, "Does Breastfeeding Protect Against Pediatric Overweight? Analysis of Longitudinal Data From the Centers for Disease Control and Prevention Pediatric Nutrition Surveillance System," *Pediatrics* 113 (2004): 81–86.

18. L. M. Maynard, D. A. Galuska, H. M. Blanck, and M. K. Serdula, "Maternal Perceptions of Weight Status of Children," *Pediatrics* 111 (2003): 1226–1231.

19. K. Zernike, "Is Obesity the Responsibility of the Body Politic?" *New York Times* (November 9, 2003), Section 4, p. 3.

20. U.S. Institute of Medicine, *Improving America's Diet and Health: From Recommendations to Action* (Washington, DC: National Academy Press, 1991): 204–205.

21. Institute of Medicine (U.S.), *Preventing Childhood Obesity: Health in the Balance* (Washington, DC: National Academy Press, 2005).

22. J. N. Morris, "Exercise Versus Heart Attack: History of a Hypothesis," in M. Marmot and P. Elliott, eds. *Coronary Heart Disease Epidemiology: From Aetiology to Public Health* (Oxford, England: Oxford Medical Publications, 1992), 242–255.

23. U.S. Department of Health and Human Services, *Physical Activity and Health: A Report of the Surgeon General* (Atlanta, Georgia: Centers for Disease Control and Prevention, National Center for Chronic Disease Prevention and Health Promotion, 1996).

24. R. S. Paffenbarger Jr. et al., "Physical Activity, All-Cause Mortality, and Longevity of College Alumni," *New England Journal of Medicine* 314 (1986): 605–613.

25. R. S. Paffenberger Jr. et al., "The Association of Changes in Physical Activity Level and Other Lifestyle Characteristics with Mortality Among Men," *New England Journal of Medicine* 328 (1993): 538–545.

26. W. B. Kannel and P. Sorlie, "Some Health Benefits of Physical Activity: The Framingham Study," *Archives of Internal Medicine* 139 (1979): 857–861.

27. A. D. Tsopanakis et al., "Lipids and Lipoprotein Profies in a 4-Hour Endurance Test on a Recumbent Cycloergometer," *American Journal of Clinical Nutrition* 49 (1989): 980–984.

28. D. M. Kramsch et al., "Reduction of Coronary Atherosclerosis by Moderate Conditioning Exercise in Monkeys on an Atherogenic Diet," *New England Journal of Medicine* 305 (1981): 1483–1489.

29. T. J. Orchard et al., "Diabetes," in *Maxcy-Rosenau-Last Public Health and Preventive Medicine*, R. B. Wallace, ed. (Stamford, Connecticut: Appleton and Lange, 1998), 973.

30. J. E. Manson et al., "Physical Activity and Incidence of Non-Insulin-Dependent Diabetes Mellitus in Women," *Lancet* 338 (1991): 774–778.

31. J. E. Manson et al., "A Prospective Study of Exercise and Incidence of Diabetes Among U.S. Male Physicians," *Journal of the American Medical Association* 268 (1992): 63–67.

32. J. E. Manson et al., "Walking Compared with Vigorous Exercise for the Prevention of Cardiovascular Events in Women," *New England Journal of Medicine* 347 (2002): 716–725.

33. M. Baringa, "How Much Pain for Cardiac Gain?" *Science* 276 (1997): 1324–1327.

34. U.S. Institute of Medicine, *Dietary Reference Intakes for Energy, Carbohydrate, Fiber, Fat, Fatty Acids, Cholesterol, Protein, and Amino Acids* (Washington, DC: National Academies Press, 2002).

35. U.S. Centers for Disease Control and Prevention, "Prevalence of No Leisure-Time Physical Activity—35 States and the District of Columbia, 1988–2002," *Morbidity and Mortality Weekly Report* 53 (2004): 82–86.

36. U.S. Centers for Disease Control and Prevention. "Youth Risk Behavior Surveillance—United States, 2003." *Morbidity and Mortality Weekly Report* SS-2; 23–24.
37. T. N. Robinson, "Reducing Children's Television Viewing to Prevent Obesity." *Journal of the American Medical Association* 282 (1999): 1561–1567.
38. W. H. Dietz and S. L. Gortmaker, "Do We Fatten Our Children at the Television Set? Obesity and Television Viewing in Children and Adolescents," *Pediatrics* 75 (1985): 807–812.
39. H. Wechsler et al., "The Physician's Role in Health Promotion Revisited—A Survey of Primary Care Practioners," *New England Journal of Medicine* 334 (1996): 996–998.
40. E. A. Finkelstein, I. C. Fiebelkorn, and G. Wang, "National Medical Spending Attributable to Overweight and Obesity: How Much and Who's Paying?" *Health Affairs* 12 (2003): 18–24.
41. U.S. Department of Health and Human Services, *Surgeon General's Call to Action to Prevent and Decrease Overweight and Obesity* (Rockville, Maryland: U.S. Government Printing Office, 2001).

CHAPTER 17

Injuries Are Not Accidents

An "Accident" Waiting To Happen

Injuries are the fifth leading cause of death in the United States.[1] (See Table 13–2.) They are even more important than statistics suggest because injuries disproportionately affect young people and thus cause many years of potential life lost (YPLL). Injuries are the number one cause of death among people ages one to forty-four.[2](Table 32) In addition to the people killed by injuries, there are almost as many survivors left with permanent disabilities, a major economic and emotional drain on families and on society in general.

Traditionally, injuries have been thought of as "accidents," unavoidable random occurrences, or the results of antisocial or incautious behavior. It is only recently that public health practitioners have recognized that injuries can and should be treated as a public health problem, analyzable by epidemiologic methods and amenable to preventive interventions. While most injuries are caused to some extent by individual behavior, they are also influenced by the physical and social environment. Public health programs to prevent injury must find ways to change people's behavior by the classic methods of education and regulation, but for many types of injuries, prevention by changing the environment may be more effective.

EPIDEMIOLOGY OF INJURIES

Prevention of injury, like the prevention of most diseases, is based on epidemiology. Data are needed to answer the questions of who, where, when, and how, looking for patterns and connections that suggest where the greatest needs for prevention are as well as ways to intervene to prevent the injury. Fatal injuries are generally categorized as unintentional (sometimes referred to as "accidental") or intentional (homicide or suicide).

Injuries are an especially important cause of death in young people. In 2001, unintentional injuries caused 42 percent of deaths in children aged one to four, 49 percent of deaths in children aged five to fourteen, and 73 percent of deaths in young people aged fifteen to twenty-four.[2(Table 32)]

Race and gender affect injury rates. Males are more likely to sustain injuries than females, with a fatal injury rate more than six times higher than that for females for all age groups combined. African Americans have higher rates of injury mortality than whites. Much of the excess mortality among blacks is due to high rates of homicide among black males age fifteen to thirty-four, which is seven times the rate for white youths.[2(Table 45)]

Injury rates, like other indicators of poor health, are higher in groups of lower socioeconomic status. The death rate from unintentional injury is twice as high in low-income areas as in high-income areas. Housefires, pedestrian fatalities, and homicides are all more common among the poor.[3] The poor are more likely to have high-risk jobs, low-quality housing, older, defective cars, and such hazardous products as space heaters, all of which contribute to higher injury risks.

Figure 17–1 shows the leading categories of injury deaths in the United States. Motor vehicle injuries lead the list, followed by firearms. As a result of the high priority the federal government has placed on prevention of motor vehicle-related injuries, as described in a following section, highway fatalities have declined over most of the past three decades. Firearm injuries, on the contrary, have increased over the same period. The Centers for Disease Control and Prevention (CDC) predicted in 1994 that if trends continued, the number of firearm-related deaths would surpass those related to motor vehicles by the year 2003, as seen in Figure 17–2.[4] The

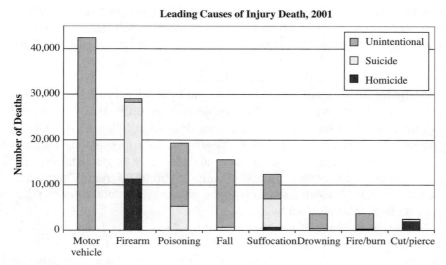

Figure 17–1 Leading Causes of Injury Death, 2001
Source: Data from U.S. Centers for Disease Control and Prevention, *National Vital Statistics Reports* 52(21), June 2, 2004.

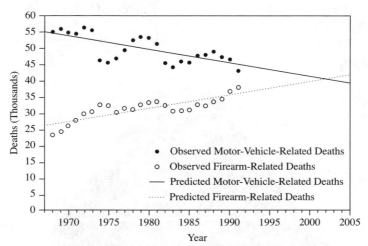

Figure 17–2 Observed and Predicted Firearm- and Motor-Vehicle–Related Injury Deaths, by Year—United States, 1968–2005*
*The lines are predicted numbers of deaths based on linear regression.
Source: U.S. Centers for Disease Control and Prevention, *Morbidity and Mortality Weekly Report* 43 (1994) 38.

trends reversed in 1993 for traffic deaths and in 1994 for firearms deaths, however, and it appears that motor vehicle fatalities will continue to dominate the injury statistics.[5] Other major causes of injury deaths that have drawn significant injury control attention are poisoning, falls and jumps, suffocation, drowning, and fires and burns.

Many injuries are not fatal, of course, but fatal injuries are the ones that are most reliably reported. While there is very little data on nonfatal injuries, they can have serious and even devastating effects. A study in Massachusetts found that for every death due to injury among children nineteen years of age and under, there are forty-five hospitalizations and 1,300 visits to emergency rooms.[6] Using the "injury pyramid" shown in Figure 17–3, it is possible to estimate the impact of nonfatal injuries when data on fatal injuries is known.

Injuries that result in long-term disability, especially head and spinal cord injuries, are particularly costly to society. More than 1.5 million Americans each year sustain a traumatic brain injury. Approximately one quarter million of these are hospitalized and survive, often with lifelong disabling conditions.[7] Many of these victims are young. Caring for these patients costs billions of dollars, much of it paid for with public funds.

Alcohol is a significant factor in a very high percentage of injuries. Forty percent of traffic fatalities in 2003 involved alcohol. High alcohol levels are

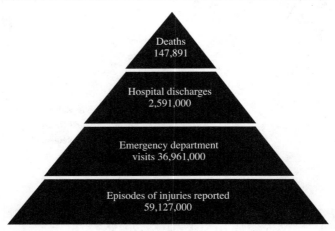

Figure 17–3 Burden of Injury: United States, 1995

Source: U.S. Centers for Disease Control and Prevention, *Health, United States, 1996–1997, and Injury Chartbook,* 18.

found in the blood of more than one-third of adult pedestrians killed by motor vehicles.[8] Many of those fatally injured in falls, drownings, fires, and suicides are under the influence of alcohol, as are many of the perpetrators and victims of homicides. Other drugs may play a role in injury, but because blood alcohol tests are much more commonly done than tests for other drugs, the role of alcohol in injury is better documented.

The importance of alcohol's contribution to injury accounts for its high placement on the list of "actual causes of death" (see Table 13–3). To stress the importance of driving while intoxicated as a cause of death, the authors counted alcohol-related motor vehicle deaths in both the alcohol and the motor-vehicle categories, making alcohol number 3 and motor vehicles number 6.[9]

ANALYZING INJURIES

While injuries are generally brought on by human behavior, injury researchers have increasingly sought to understand the role of the environment in causing an injury-producing event as well as influencing the severity of the resulting injury. The public health approach to injury control analyzes injuries, like infectious diseases, in terms of a chain of causation: the interactions over time between a host, an agent, and the environment. To analyze an injury-causing event requires information about the person who initiates the event and/or suffers the injury, the agent (automobile, firearm, swimming pool), and the environment (road conditions, weather, involvement of other people) before, during, and after the event.

To prevent certain injury-causing events from occurring in the first place—primary prevention—analysts seek to understand the conditions prevailing *before* each such event. For example, characteristics of the host (e.g., alcohol intoxication), the agent (e.g., defective brakes), and the environment (e.g., a dark and rainy night) are all relevant to whether a motor vehicle crash occurs. Conditions prevailing *during* the event affect the outcome of the crash. Thus, wearing a seat belt (host), equipping a car with an airbag (agent), and driving on a divided highway (environment) may allow the driver to avoid serious injury during a crash—secondary prevention. Tertiary prevention depends on conditions *after* the crash that determine whether the victim survives the injury and the extent of any resulting disability. The availability and quality of emergency care are major factors in tertiary prevention.

Because motor vehicle injuries cause so many deaths, they were the first category of injuries to be analyzed and subjected to systematic prevention efforts. Much data are available on conditions surrounding motor vehicle crashes, and methods for preventing motor vehicle injuries are highly developed. National highway safety programs were launched two decades before Congress identified injury as a general public health problem and established the National Center for Injury Prevention and Control at the CDC.

Injury control efforts developed for motor vehicle injuries have served as a model for more embryonic efforts to control other categories of injury. Early prevention strategies focused on changing people's behavior by the classic public health methods of education and regulation. As with many public health issues related to behavior, regulation is usually more effective than education in getting people to change their behavior. In the earliest days of traffic safety efforts, for example, society learned that laws regarding speed limits and traffic lights were necessary to control the chaos on the roadways.

Modern injury control began, however, with the recognition that engineering plays an important role in the causation of injuries and their severity. Sharp objects cause more damage to the human body than blunt ones; an impact distributed over a broad surface results in a less severe injury than that to a smaller surface; if deceleration can be controlled and made less sudden, the body can better withstand the force. In general, automatic protections are more effective than measures that require effort, and the more effort a measure requires, the less likely it is to be employed. Thus the "three E's" of injury prevention are education, enforcement, and engineering.

These insights, first applied in the auto industry, have also been applied to prevention of many other kinds of injury—especially childhood injuries—with considerable success. For example, when the New York City Health Department noted that a large number of children died from falls out of windows, it instituted the "Children Can't Fly" program, requiring landlords to install window guards, and the number of fatal falls was reduced by half.[10] The number of children drowned in swimming pools has been reduced by laws requiring pools to be fenced. Poisonings are prevented by child-proof caps on medicine containers and some household chemicals. The use of smoke detectors has reduced the number of deaths from fires. State and federal regulation of the flammability of fabrics has also saved lives, especially those of children due to laws on children's sleepwear. As a result of these measures and others, fatal injury rates among small children have declined markedly in recent years.[2(Table 32)]

MOTOR VEHICLE INJURIES

Attention was focused on the problem of motor vehicle injuries by Ralph Nader's indictment of the automobile industry in his book, *Unsafe at Any Speed: The Designed-In Dangers of the American Automobile*, published in 1966. Congress responded by passing the National Traffic and Motor Vehicle Safety Act of 1966, which established the National Highway Traffic Safety Administration (NHTSA) and empowered it to set safety standards for new cars, such as installation of seat belts, laminated windshields, collapsible steering assemblies, and dashboard padding. Hundreds of thousands of drivers had died from being impaled on unyielding steering columns. Heads and faces of front-seat passengers had been cut by sharp dashboard edges and glass from broken windshields. The safer designs mandated by the 1966 legislation led to an enormous reduction in both injury and mortality.[10]

NHTSA was also required to collect data on motor vehicle-related deaths and conduct research aimed at prevention of motor vehicle collisions and amelioration of their effects. Among other activities, NHTSA has an ongoing program of crash testing various vehicle models, seeking to understand how further improvements in engineering could protect occupants during a crash. These studies have led to further improvements in automobile design—including headrests that protect their occupants during rear-end collisions, strengthened side bars to protect occupants during side crashes, and airbags—now required by federal law.[11]

While requirements that vehicles more effectively protect their occupants during a crash are an important part of injury control (secondary prevention), preventing crashes from occurring in the first place (primary prevention) is the highest priority. Characteristics of the vehicle such as turn signals and brake lights help prevent crashes. State laws that require annual inspections of these devices, as well as of brakes and tires, are aimed at ensuring that defects in vehicles do not lead to injuries. Environmental features, especially improvements in highway design, have been shown to prevent crashes. Divided highways, raised lane dividers embedded in road surfaces, rumble strips at road edges, and "wrong-way" signs at offramps can help to prevent mistakes by drivers.

Injury control methods that target the driver depend on both education and enforcement, and they exemplify the typical difficulties in getting people to practice healthier behaviors. Because alcohol plays such a major role in fatal crashes, laws against drinking and driving are virtually universal.

Their effectiveness depends on how well they are enforced, however. The activism of volunteer groups such as Mothers Against Drunk Driving (MADD) has helped to raise public consciousness about the extent of the problem, and tolerance for drinking and driving has declined in recent years. In addition to imposing severe penalties for being caught driving drunk, many states have expanded legislation to make establishments that serve alcohol liable for serving minors or persons already obviously intoxicated.

After alcohol, the second most important factor in fatal crashes is youth: 25 percent of drivers in fatal crashes are under twenty-five, even though those under twenty-five make up only 13 percent of all drivers.[12] According to NHTSA, sixteen-year-old drivers have crash rates that are three times more than seventeen-year-olds, five times greater than eighteen-year-olds, and twice those of eighty-five-year-olds.[13] This is believed to be due in part to inexperience: driving is a complex task, and new drivers are more likely to make mistakes. These crashes are also due to risk-taking behavior and poor judgment.

Some states are addressing the issue by implementing graduated driver licensing systems, by which young drivers must pass through two preliminary stages over a period of time before they are allowed a full license. NHTSA has developed a model law that had been adopted by twenty-four states as of the end of 1999. With a learner's permit, a licensed adult must be in the vehicle at all times; the young person must remain crash-free and conviction-free before being allowed to take a road test for a provisional license. Night time driving is restricted for those with a provisional license. Young drivers must remain crash-free and conviction-free for a year before moving to a full license. Graduated licensing has been successful in preventing traffic fatalities among young people: states that have adopted the system have experienced significant reductions in crashes by drivers under twenty years old.[13]

In addition to being inexperienced, young drivers may also be just starting to drink, and learning how to do both together can be fatal. In 2003, 25 percent of drivers fifteen to twenty years old who were killed in crashes had high blood alcohol levels.[12] The federal government and many states have made concerted efforts to reduce drinking and driving among young people. One attempt to deal with the problem was a federal law requiring states to raise the drinking age to twenty-one to receive highway funds (the law became effective in 1988).[10] In 1995, a similar federal law required states to pass zero tolerance laws for drivers under twenty-one.

Since 1998, all states and the District of Columbia have laws setting a limit of .02 percent blood alcohol concentration or below, suspending driver's licenses for those found in violation. The evidence indicates that this is an effective approach to saving lives. Since 1982, a declining percentage of young drivers in fatal crashes have had alcohol in their blood.[14]

Speed limits are an important factor in highway injuries. In 1974 Congress imposed a national speed limit of 55 miles per hour to conserve fuel at the time of the Arab oil embargo. That law, which contributed to a 16 percent decline in traffic fatalities between 1973 and 1974, was revoked in 1995 as part of the deregulation trend.[10] Many states have raised their speed limits as a result, including twenty-eight states that have limits of 70 miles an hour or above.[15] Increased speed is believed to account in part for the rise in highway fatalities in the late 1990s.

The use of seat belts has been shown to reduce fatalities by 40 to 50 percent. Child safety seats can reduce the risk of a child's being killed during a collision or sudden stop by 71 percent.[10] These engineering measures require people to use them correctly, however, and even state laws requiring the use of seat belts and child safety seats are widely ignored. In states that have primary seat belt laws—laws allowing police officers to pull over drivers and ticket them merely for not wearing a seat belt—the rate of seat belt use is higher than it is in states that have secondary laws—laws that permit police to issue tickets for seat belt violations only after stopping a driver for another reason. Currently, twenty states have primary laws, and twenty-nine have secondary laws. New Hampshire has no seat belt law for adults. The federal government is trying to persuade more states to toughen their laws by offering extra highway funds to those that have primary seat belt laws.[16]

In 1968, when implementation of federal traffic safety legislation began, almost 55,000 Americans died each year from motor-vehicle-related injuries. The national effort to reduce this toll has had significant success. By 1993, the number had declined to just over 40,000 fatalities a year despite the fact that many more cars were on the roads and the number of miles driven has more than doubled.[17] Since then, the downward trend has halted, with the number of deaths fluctuating up to 43,000 in 2002.[18] The reversal has a number of causes, including the national move toward deregulation, which has led to a rise in speed limits, repeal of motorcycle helmet laws in many states, and a relaxation of regulations on trucks. The increasing popularity of heavier vehicles such as minivans, pickup trucks, and sport utility vehicles also contributes to increases in traffic fatalities. Crashes between vehicles of widely disparate size and weight cause high risk to the occupants of the smaller vehicle. Sport utility vehicles, mini-vans, and pickup trucks are more likely to roll over in crashes than sedans, however, offsetting the advantage occupants get from their size.[18]

PEDESTRIANS, MOTORCYCLISTS, AND BICYCLISTS

About eleven percent of people killed in motor vehicle crashes are pedestrians, and public health efforts are also directed at preventing these injuries.[19] Elderly people have the highest risk for being killed by a motor vehicle while walking. Sixteen percent of pedestrians killed by motor vehicles are over seventy. Most of these injuries occur in urban areas. A 1985 study investigated reasons for a high fatality rate among older pedestrians along Queens Boulevard in a part of New York City inhabited by large numbers of senior citizens. It was found that elderly persons took an average of 50 seconds to cross the 150-foot wide boulevard, while the "walk" sign allowed only 35 seconds. Moreover, because of the boulevard's width and because vision loss is common among the elderly, many pedestrians could not read the "walk/don't walk" signs, which were located on the far side of the boulevard. The traffic safety unit installed additional signs on the median strips so that they could be more easily seen, and they reset the signs to allow more time for crossing. After implementation of these and other measures, such as stricter enforcement of speed limits, the rate of death and severe injuries among pedestrians fell by 60 percent.[10]

Every year, more than 3,000 motorcyclists and more than 600 bicyclists are killed in crashes.[18] Children aged fourteen and under account for 21 percent of the bicycle-related fatalities, making this one of the leading causes of injury-related death in children.[20] The most important protective measure for bicycle and motorcycle riders is to wear a helmet. Head injuries account for 70 percent of bicycle-related deaths,[20] and are a leading cause of death in motorcycle crashes. Head injuries also cause profound, permanent disability in many survivors.

Public health advocates have devoted considerable efforts to promote the use of bicycle and motorcycle helmets. As discussed in Chapter 3, Congress (as part of the 1966 National Highway Safety Act) mandated that states pass laws requiring motorcyclists to wear helmets, leading to a dramatic decline in motorcycle fatalities.[10] Because of vigorous objections on grounds of personal liberty, the federal law was changed in 1976. In response, twenty-seven states repealed or weakened their laws, and by 1980 motorcycle fatalities increased dramatically.[21] In 2004, nineteen states and the District of Columbia required helmet use for all motorcycle operators and their passengers. In another twenty-eight states, only those under a certain age, usually eighteen, are required to wear helmets. In states where only minors are required to wear helmets, laws are difficult to enforce. Data on crashes in these states show that, despite the law, fewer than 40 percent of fatally-injured minors wore helmets.[22] Only nineteen states and the District of Columbia have laws requiring bicycle helmets, and these laws apply only to children.[20] The bulk of the public health effort regarding bicycle helmets focuses on community education programs.

FIREARMS INJURY—STILL NUMBER TWO

In 1994, firearms injuries had surpassed motor vehicle injuries as the leading cause of injury death in eight states and the District of Columbia. It appeared that firearms would soon become number one nationwide, as projected in Figure 17–3. However, the number of homicides dropped dramatically in 1994 and 1995, and suicides and unintentional gun deaths fell slightly. The number of deaths caused by firearms has continued to decline, falling from almost 40,000 in 1993 to less than 30,000 in 2001. A number of reasons have been proposed for the decline, including tougher gun control laws, community policing, and demographic changes.[23]

Violence is traditionally thought of as a criminal justice issue rather than a public health issue. Certainly no one is arguing that the criminal justice system should abandon its mission. But public health has a different mission: it focuses on prevention as opposed to punishment. The relative success of the public health approach against motor vehicle injuries has inspired calls for it to be applied against violence, especially against firearm violence, the behavior that has the most severe consequences for health.

There are plenty of grim statistics showing that America's permissive attitude toward guns is harmful to people's health. In 1998, firearms killed 30,708 people in the United States. Of these, more than half were suicides, about 40 percent were homicides, and the rest were caused by unintentional shootings, legal intervention, or unknown causes. Teenagers and young adults are especially at risk. About one in four people who die from firearms are between the ages of fifteen and twenty-four. About one-third of these deaths among youths were suicides, and almost two-thirds were homicides. The death rate from firearms is six times higher for males than that for females. Young African American males are especially at risk.[24]

Homicide rates in the United States are far higher than those in other developed countries. Suicide rates are also high, especially among young people.[25] The main reason for these high rates is believed to be the easy availability of guns. Attempts at homicide and suicide are more likely to succeed if guns are used rather than less lethal weapons. In 1999 through 2000, 57 percent of suicides and 64 percent of homicides were committed with guns.[26] Suicide among young people is especially tragic. While rates of suicide among people ten to nineteen years old have declined since 1994, suicide is still the third leading cause of death in this age group. About half of these suicides are by firearms.[27]

About one-third of U.S. households possess firearms, and half of the guns are handguns, the weapon most likely to be used in a fatal injury.[28] While many people own a handgun because they believe it will protect them, a number of studies have shown that the opposite is true. Residents of a household with a gun present in the home are three times more likely to die in a homicide[29] and five times more likely to commit suicide[30] than if no gun is available. Another study found that a gun kept at home was forty-three times more likely to kill its owner, a family member, or a friend than an intruder.[31]

The CDC has been collecting data on patterns of violence for almost two decades, and in the early 1990s the agency stepped up its efforts to identify and evaluate interventions to prevent and reduce the impact of violence. Politically, however, guns have been a much more difficult issue to deal with than motor vehicles. Many conservative politicians, with the support of the National Rifle Association (NRA), regard any attempt to control access to firearms as an attack on the Second Amendment to the Constitution. Limits on the depiction of violence in the media are also vigorously opposed in the name of protecting freedoms, although there is some evidence that viewing violent episodes on television or in the movies increases the cultural acceptance of violence and makes children and youths more likely to behave in aggressive ways.

Opponents of gun control even go so far as to try to prevent the CDC from conducting research on violence as a public health problem. In 1995 and 1996, conservative members of the House of Representatives, backed by the NRA, tried first to eliminate the CDC's National Center for Injury Prevention and Control and then to cut from the center's budget the exact amount—about $2.4 million—that it had proposed for research on firearms injury.[32] President Clinton supported the CDC's work, and attempts to cut the center's budget failed. However, the political opposition has had an impact. Legislation explicitly forbids the CDC from using any of its funding "to advocate or promote gun control."[33(p.190)]

Efforts to reduce firearms injuries are continuing nonetheless. The Harvard Injury Control Research Center, with funding from private foundations, developed a National Violent Injury Statistics System in 1999. Now, the CDC is providing funds to 13 states to implement the system, collecting detailed data on homicides and suicides to better inform policy on violence and suicide, just as data on motor vehicle deaths has informed policy making about traffic safety. Additional states will be added to the system as funds become available.[34]

The successful passage of the Brady Gun Control Act in 1994 showed that there can be political support for limiting access to firearms even in an antiregulatory climate. However, the fact that the Republican Congress did not approve a renewal of the assault weapons ban in 2004 shows that the NRA still has clout in Washington. Some communities have had some success with violence prevention and youth development programs, including education to promote nonviolent resolution of arguments. The economic cost of gun violence in medical care—calculated at about $2.3 billion per year[35]—has helped to persuade some states to pass stricter gun control regulations. About half the medical costs of firearms injuries are borne by taxpayers.

Public health advocates note that guns need not be banned in order to make them safer. The third "E" of injury prevention—engineering—has not been widely applied in the prevention of firearms injuries. Safety catches can be used to make guns childproof, for example, and there are even ways to personalize guns so that they can be used only by the owner. Safety features are required by law for many consumer products that are much less dangerous than guns. When the political climate is ready to support major efforts to prevent firearms-related injuries, the public health approach has much to offer.[36]

OCCUPATIONAL INJURIES

Workplace injuries have been a significant public health problem since the Industrial Revolution, if not further back. In 1907, over 15,000 American workers were reported to have died on the job. Many states implemented occupational safety laws in the late nineteenth and early twentieth centuries. In 1970, the Congress passed a federal law creating the Occupational Safety and Health Administration (OSHA), empowered to set standards, inspect workplaces, and impose penalties for workplace hazards. The law also created the National Institute for Occupational Safety and Health (NIOSH) to conduct research, recommend standards, and conduct hazard evaluations.[10]

The workplace is safer now, with 5,559 fatal injuries reported by the Bureau of Labor Statistics in 2003, despite a large increase in the number of workers.[37] In part, this improvement reflects mandated safety measures and educational programs; in part, it reflects an economy less dependent on heavy industry. However, in addition to the deaths, an estimated 1.4 million Americans suffer an injury each year that lead to lost work days.[37]

As in the pattern of injuries overall, motor vehicles are the leading occupational cause of death, with highway crashes accounting for 25 percent of all worker deaths.[38] Second on the list is "contact with objects and equipment," including events such as "struck by falling objects" and "caught in running equipment or machinery." Violence is third, "assaults and violent acts" having declined significantly between 1992 and 2002. The causes of motor vehicle injuries, in addition to crashes on the highway, include rollovers of agricultural and construction vehicles (tractors, forklifts, bulldozers, and cranes). Construction workers have a high risk of falls. Agricultural workers are at risk for amputations by machinery, electrocutions, and pesticide poisoning.

Over the past decade, a new and rapidly growing category of occupational injury has appeared on the national agenda: repetitive motion injuries, which afflict hundreds of thousands of workers from meatpackers to journalists. While not fatal, these injuries—which most often affect arms, wrists, and hands—can be disabling. Approaches to prevention include such measures as redesign of keyboards and requirements for workers to take regular breaks. OSHA has been working on standards to protect workers from these injuries, but the antiregulatory climate in Washington has been sympathetic to arguments by business that such requirements would be too costly. In the last days of the Clinton administration, the Department of Labor issued standards to protect employees in a wide range of occupations from musculoskeletal injury. However, with the support of the new Bush administration, the Republican Congress overturned the standards in early 2001.[39] OSHA is gradually replacing the standards with voluntary guidelines. According to Labor Department data, repetitive motion injuries cause the longest absences from work of all occupational injuries.[40]

TERTIARY PREVENTION

For any kind of serious injury, the promptness and quality of emergency medical aid play a significant role in whether a victim survives as well as in the extent of permanent disability. Lack of prompt emergency care accounts for the fact that death rates from motor vehicle crashes are higher in rural areas than in more populated ones. The establishment of special trauma centers and the use of helicopters to transport injured patients over long distances have improved the prospects in some locations, but many parts of the country still lack integrated trauma-care programs. Well-trained emergency medical technicians and well-equipped ambulances can make the difference between life and death. There is still a need for research to better understand the biomedical aspects of injury and to devise better treatments.

CONCLUSION

Injuries are a major cause of death and disability in the United States. They are of particular concern to public health because they disproportionately affect young people, and many injuries are preventable. Fatal injuries are categorized as unintentional—commonly called "accidents"—and intentional, a category that includes homicide and suicide. Motor vehicle crashes have been the leading cause of injury deaths for the past several decades, and injuries caused by firearms are second. Alcohol is a significant factor in a very high percentage of injuries. The number of deaths caused by injuries is just the tip of the injury pyramid, which shows that for every death there are many injuries resulting in hospitalizations, many more injuries requiring treatment in emergency rooms and physicians' offices, and even more injuries treated at home.

Analysis of injuries provides guidelines for prevention. The analysis involves considerations of the host, agent, and environment and how they may be altered to prevent an injury from occurring (primary prevention), to minimize the damage (secondary prevention), or to prevent resulting disability by providing prompt treatment (tertiary prevention). This kind of analysis was pioneered in the analysis of motor vehicle injuries, which focused not only on the driver (host) but on making the vehicle (agent) safer and on developing safer highways (environment). Tertiary prevention included the provision of ambulances and trauma centers.

Prevention of motor vehicle injuries also includes campaigns to change people's behavior by persuading them, or requiring them by law, to wear seat belts when riding in motor vehicles and to wear helmets when riding on motorcycles. Bicycle helmets, which are underutilized, are also an important safety measure.

Due to large numbers of firearms injuries, the United States has higher rates of homicides and childhood suicides than other industrialized nations. The easy availability of guns in the United States contributes to the high death rate from firearms injuries. Research has shown that the presence of a gun in the home increases the risk that a resident will be a victim of homicide or suicide. Far from protecting the owner against crime, a gun kept at home is 43 times more likely to kill its owner, a family member, or a friend than it is to kill an intruder.

Public health has made progress in preventing childhood injuries from falls, drowning, poisoning, and fires and burns. Much of this progress comes from laws requiring safety features such as window guards in apartment buildings, fencing around swimming pools, child-proof caps on medicine containers, and fire-proofing of children's sleepwear.

REFERENCES

1. National Center for Health Statistics, "Deaths: Final Data for 2001," *National Vital Statistics Reports* 52, No. 3, 2003.
2. National Center for Health Statistics, *Health, United States, 2003 and Chartbook on Trends in the Health of Americans* (Hyattsville, Maryland: Public Health Service, 2003).
3. S. P. Baker, B. O'Neill, and R. S. Karpf, *The Injury Fact Book* (New York: Oxford University Press, 1992).
4. U.S. Centers for Disease Control and Prevention, "Deaths Resulting from Firearm- and Motor-Vehicle-Related Injuries—United States, 1968–1991," *Morbidity and Mortality Weekly Report* 43 (1994): 37–42.
5. Department of Health and Human Services. *Report on Nation's Health Documents Toll of Injuries in U.S.: Firearm Mortality Down 11%, Traffic Fatality Rates up 2%, 1993–1995*, News Release, July 24, 1997.
6. S. S. Gallagher et al., "The Incidence of Injuries among 87,000 Massachusetts Children and Adolescents: Results of the 1980–81 State-wide Childhood Injury Prevention Surveillance System," *American Journal of Public Health* 74 (1984): 1340–1347.
7. U.S. Centers for Disease Control and Prevention, "Traumatic Brain Injury-Related Hospital Discharges: Results from a 14-State Surveillance System, 1997," *Morbidity and Mortality Weekly Report* 52 (2003): SS-4.

8. National Highway Traffic Safety Administration, "Traffic Safety Facts 2003—Alcohol," *www.nhtsa.dot.gov/people/ncsa*. Accessed October 20, 2004.

9. A. H. Mokdad, J. S. Marks, D. F. Stroup, and J. L. Gerberding, "Actual Causes of Death in the United States, 2000," *Journal of the American Medical Association* 291 (2004): 1238–1245.

10. National Committee for Injury Prevention and Control, "Injury Prevention: Meeting the Challenge," *American Journal of Preventative Medicine* 5, No.3 (Supplement) (1989).

11. National Highway Traffic Safety Administration, "About the National Highway Traffic Safety Administration," *www.nhtsa.dot.gov*. Accessed June 17, 1999.

12. National Highway Traffic Safety Administration, Traffic Safety Facts 2003—Young Drivers, *www.nhtsa.dot.gov/people/ncsa*. Accessed October 20, 2004.

13. National Highway Traffic Safety Administration, State Legislative Fact Sheet, "Graduated Driver Licensing System, 2000," *www.nhtsa.dot.gov/people/outreach/safesobr/21qp/html/fact_sheets*. Accessed October 20, 2004.

14. National Highway Traffic Safety Administration, "Zero Tolerance for Youth: Four States' Experience with Zero Tolerance Laws. 2000," *www.nhtsa.dot.gov/people/injury/traffic_tech/2000/tt229.html*. Accessed October 20, 2004.

15. D. Hakim, "Study Links Higher Speed Limits to Deaths," *New York Times*, November 24, 2003.

16. M. L. Wald, "U.S. Presses States for Strict Seat Belt Laws," *New York Times*, March 5, 2004.

17. U.S. Centers for Disease Control and Prevention, "Deaths Resulting from Firearm- and Motor-Vehicle-Related Injuries—United States," 1968–1991.

18. National Highway Traffic Safety Administration, "Traffic Safety Facts 2003—Overview," *www.nhtsa.dot.gov/people/ncsa*. Accessed October 20, 2004.

19. National Highway Traffic Safety Administration, "Traffic Safety Facts 2003—Pedestrians," *www.nhtsa.dot.gov/people/ncsa*. Accessed October 20, 2004.

20. National Highway Traffic Safety Administration, "Traffic Safety Facts—Laws. Bicycle Helmet Use Laws," *www.nhtsa.dot.gov/people/injury/New-fact-sheet03/BicycleHelmet Use.pdf*. April 2004. Accessed October 25, 2004.

21. G. S. Watson, P. L. Zador, and A. Wilks, "Helmet Use, Helmet Use Laws, and Motorcyclist Fatalities," *American Journal of Public Health* 71 (1981): 297–300.

22. National Highway Traffic Safety Administration, "Traffic Safety Facts—Laws. Motorcycle Helmet Use Laws." *www.nhtsa.dot.gov/people/New-fact-sheet03/Motorcycle Helmet.pdf*. April 2004. Accessed October 25, 2004.

23. Associated Press, "Death Rate Up for Car Crashes, but Down for Shootings in 95," *New York Times* (July 27, 1997), 22.

24. U.S. Centers for Disease Control and Prevention, "Surveillance for Fatal and Nonfatal Firearm-Related Injuries—United States, 1993–1998," *Morbidity and Mortality Weekly Report* 50 (2001): SS-2.

25. World Health Organization. *World Report on Violence and Health*, *www.who.int/violence_injury_prevention/violence/world_report/enfull_en.pdf*. Accessed October 28, 2004.

26. D. Hemenway, "Epidemiology of U.S. Firearm Injuries," *Journal of Public Health Policy* 24 (2004): 380–385.

27. U.S. Centers for Disease Control and Prevention, "Methods of Suicide Among Persons Aged 10–19 Years—United States, 1992–2001," *Morbidity and Mortality Weekly Report* 53 (2004): 471–474.
28. R. M. Johnson, T. Coyne-Beasley, and C. W. Runyan, "Firearm Ownership and Storage Practices, U.S. Households, 1992–2002: A Systematic Review," *American Journal of Preventative Medicine* 27 (2004): 173–182.
29. A. L. Kellermann et al., "Gun Ownership as a Risk Factor for Homicide in the Home," *New England Journal of Medicine* 329 (1993): 1084–1091.
30. A. L. Kellermann et al., "Suicide in the Home in Relation to Gun Ownership," *New England Journal of Medicine* 237 (1992): 467–472.
31. Kellermann and D. T. Reay, "Protection or Peril? An Analysis of Firearm-Related Deaths in the Home," *New England Journal of Medicine* 314 (1986): 1557–1560.
32. N. A. Lewis, "N.R.A. Takes Aim at Study of Guns as Public Health Risk," *New York Times* (August 26, 1995).
33. J. Rovner, "U.S. House Refuses Point-Blank to Restore CDC Gun-Research Funds," *Lancet* 348 (1996): 190.
34. National Violent Injury Statistics System, *www.hsph.harvard.edu/hicrc/nviss/about_main.htm*. Accessed October 28, 2004.
35. P. J. Cook, B. A. Lawrence, J. Ludwig, and T. R. Miller, "Medical Costs of Gunshot Injuries in the United States," *Journal of the American Medical Association* 281 (1999): 447–454.
36. S. B. Sorenson, "Regulating Firearms as a Consumer Product," *Science* 286 (1999): 1481–1482.
37. U.S. Department of Labor, Bureau of Labor Statistics, "Injuries, Illnesses, and Fatalities," *www.bls.gov/iif/home.htm*. Accessed October 29, 2004.
38. U.S. Department of Labor. Bureau of Labor Statistics, "National Census of Fatal Occupational Injuries in 2003," Press Release, September 22, 2004. *www.bls.gov/iif/oshcfoi1.htm*. Accessed October 29, 2004.
39. S. Greenhouse, "Senate Votes to Repeal Rules Clinton Set on Work Injuries," *New York Times* (March 7, 2001), A1.
40. U.S. Department of Labor, Bureau of Labor Statistics, "Repetitive Motion Leads to Longest Work Absences," May 1, 2002, *www.bls.gov/opub/ted/2002/apr/wk5/art03.htm*. Accessed November 2, 2004.

CHAPTER 18

Maternal and Child Health as a Social Problem

The "Back to Sleep" Campaign

The health of pregnant women and children is traditionally one of the highest priorities of public health. In a society concerned with the welfare of its population, everyone should be guaranteed adequate conditions for the best possible start in life. The fetal and infant stages of development provide the foundations of good health throughout life. Moreover, children are the most vulnerable segment of the population and are the first to suffer from any adverse conditions that affect human health in general.

Children's health first became a public concern in the United States at the end of the nineteenth century, prompted by alarm at the high infant and child death rates in the summer from diarrheal diseases.[1] Heat, poor sanitation, and lack of refrigeration contributed to heavy microbial contamination of milk, which was sickening poor children. In 1893, New York City established milk stations that provided safe milk. Similar programs soon followed in other cities. The success of the milk programs in improving children's health inspired the formation of voluntary infant welfare societies with the mission of teaching poor and immigrant mothers about nutrition and hygiene. The federal government got involved in 1912 with the establishment of the Children's Bureau, mandated to "investigate and report on all matters affecting children and child life."[1(p.8)] In 1921 Congress first provided grants to states to develop health services for mothers and children. During the same period, advocates for child health and welfare were fighting to protect children from oppressive and exploitive labor, which was not regulated by the federal government until the 1930s.

Child health programs have, since the beginning, been plagued by a basic philosophical and political conflict: society's responsibility for the well-being of infants and children was sometimes in conflict with the presumed right of parents to provide for, or neglect, their own children.[2] Until the twentieth century, children were regarded as the property of their parents. Passage of the 1912 legislation establishing the Children's Bureau reflected a new view that children were a national resource and that their health and vigor were important for the progress of society. In recent decades, children have increasingly been viewed as having rights on their own, independent of their parents or their prospective role in society. Current controversies concerning the role of government in the protection of children—issues that range from the removal of children from abusive parents to medical treatment for the children of Christian Scientists—are a continuation of a century-long tradition of conflict.

MATERNAL AND INFANT MORTALITY

The infant mortality rate (IMR) is a gauge of a society's attention to children's health and is, in fact, an indicator of the health status of a population as a whole. This rate is a particular concern for U.S. public health professionals because the infant mortality rate in this country is very high compared with that of other industrialized countries. As shown in Table 18–1, the United States ranks twenty-seventh after many Asian and European countries. Japan's infant mortality rate is less than half of that in the United States.

The IMR, defined as the number of infant deaths within the first year of life for every 1,000 live births, has been declining in the United States over the course of the century, as seen in Figure 18–1. The rate fell from 100 in 1915 to 7.0 in 2002. Reasons for the decline include improved socioeconomic status (SES), housing, and nutrition; immunization; clean water and pasteurized milk; antibiotics; and better prenatal care and delivery. The availability of family planning services and legalized abortion in the United States contributed to the lowering of IMR during the 1970s because wanted babies are more likely to thrive than unwanted ones.[3] Progress in recent years is largely credited to technological advances in caring for premature infants and infants with low birth weight.

A very disturbing feature of the trends in infant mortality in the United States is the disparity according to race. The IMR for black Americans

Table 18–1   IMRs (Deaths per 1,000 Live Births), 2000

Singapore	2.1	Israel	5.4
Hong Kong	3.0	Portugal	5.5
Japan	3.2	England and Wales	5.6
Sweden	3.4	Scotland	5.7
Norway	3.8	Greece	6.1
Finland	3.8	Ireland	6.2
Spain	3.9	New Zealand	6.3
Czech Republic	4.1	United States	6.9
Germany	4.4	Cuba	7.2
Italy	4.5	Poland	8.1
France	4.6	Slovakia	8.6
Austria	4.8	Chile	8.9
Belgium	4.8	Hungary	9.2
Switzerland	4.9	Puerto Rico	9.9
Northern Ireland	5.1	Costa Rica	10.2
Netherlands	5.1	Bulgaria	13.3
Australia	5.2	Russian Federation	15.2
Canada	5.3	Romania	18.6
Denmark	5.3		

Source: Data from National Center for Health Statistics, *Health, United States, 2004*. Table 25.

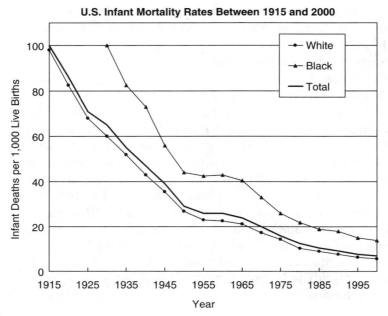

Figure 18–1 U.S. Infant Mortality Rates Between 1915 and 2000
Source: Data from U.S. Bureau of the Census.

is more than double that for white Americans.[4] In fact, the mortality rate for black infants has declined more slowly than that for white infants, so that the racial disparity has increased since 1950.[5] While the high infant mortality among blacks accounts in part for the this country's dismal showing on an international scale, the rate for white Americans is worse than that of twenty-one other countries.

The specific causes of infant mortality have changed over time, and they are different for infants of different races. Prematurity and low birth weight were the leading cause of infant death for all races in 1960[5] and are still the leading cause for blacks.[4] In fact, the mortality rate from low birth weight increased among blacks between 1981 and 1991, while it decreased among whites.[5] Congenital anomalies—birth defects—have become the leading cause of infant death overall, and are also the leading cause for white infants.[4] Sudden infant death syndrome (SIDS) is the third leading cause overall. Earlier in the century, when mortality rates were much higher, infectious diseases were much more significant as a cause of infant deaths.

Maternal mortality rates also declined dramatically in the United States during the twentieth century, so that today the death of a woman in childbirth is a very rare event. Since 1991, an average of twelve women have died each year from causes related to childbirth for every 100,000 live births, as compared with 363.9 in 1940. Like IMRs, maternal mortality rates are significantly higher for black women than for white women—approximately four times higher.[6,7]

INFANT MORTALITY: HEALTH PROBLEM OR SOCIAL PROBLEM?

"Infant mortality is not a health problem; it is a social problem with health consequences." [8(p.473)] In seeking reasons to explain the high IMR in the United States, epidemiologists find that the number one risk factor for infant mortality is poverty. The generally lower SES of African Americans in the United States accounts in large part, but not entirely, for their higher IMR. There are a variety of reasons—environmental, nutritional, behavioral, medical, and social—that poverty leads to high infant mortality. These same factors that raise the risk of infant death also have a more general harmful impact on the health of the children that survive, leading to increased rates of chronic illness and disability, both physical and mental.

An extreme example of an environmental cause of infant mortality is the epidemic of birth defects in Minamata, Japan, caused by mercury contamination of the bay from an industrial source (see Chapter 12). Poor families are more likely to live in such industrial areas, exposing pregnant women and their fetuses to the harmful effects of polluted air and water. Lead, which is highly toxic to the developing nervous system, is a common contaminant in the American inner city, both from deteriorating paint and old plumbing. Other environmental chemicals known to harm the developing fetus are pesticides and organic solvents. More generally, to the extent that air or water pollution or substandard housing harm a mother's health, they harm her ability to give birth to a healthy infant. They may then cause further harm to a sickly infant who is brought home to an unhealthy environment.

Poverty may interfere with a prospective mother's ability to consume an adequate diet for nourishing her fetus. Poor women may lack the knowledge, time, or energy to prepare nutritious meals for themselves and their children. They may live in rural or inner city areas where fresh fruits and vegetables are not readily available or are too expensive. Ignorance or lack of financial resources may carry over to how a baby is fed. Breastfeeding, which provides the best nutrition for an infant [unless the mother is infected with human immunodeficiency virus (HIV)], is less commonly practiced among poorly educated women than it is among those of higher SES.

Maternal behaviors that can harm the health of an infant include smoking, drinking alcohol, and the use of legal and illegal drugs. Women who smoke during pregnancy substantially increase their risk of giving birth to an infant of low birth weight. Moreover, infants are more likely to develop respiratory infections or die of SIDS when family members smoke in the home. Alcohol is a teratogen, and fetal alcohol syndrome is a risk for children of mothers who are problem drinkers. The use by inner city pregnant women of illegal drugs, especially crack cocaine, became a major concern in the late 1980s and early 1990s. So-called "crack babies" were born addicted to the drug, suffered withdrawal symptoms after birth, and some sustained permanent neurological impairment. Unhealthy behaviors are not limited to poor women, of course: affluent women may smoke, drink alcohol, use drugs, and eat unhealthy diets while pregnant. However, these behaviors are more common among poor women, probably for the reasons discussed in Chapter 14.

Social factors that contribute to high-risk pregnancies are those common in poor neighborhoods: young maternal age and low maternal education, out-of-wedlock birth, and violence. Teenage mothers are more likely to deliver premature infants than older women of the same SES, apparently for biological reasons.[9] Poor women are more likely to be single mothers, thus lacking social support. Infants and children of poor families are at greater risk from violence, both the impersonal violence of the neighborhood and child abuse by family members. Poor children are also more likely to die from unintentional injuries, including fires and falls.

The lack of prenatal care has been linked with high risk of infant mortality. Poor women, who are more likely to lack access to medical care for financial and other reasons (see Chapter 26), are less likely to get prenatal care. However, it is not clear to what extent the lack of medical attention in itself contributes to the risk for poor women, since women who do not receive adequate prenatal care are likely to have other risk factors for infant mortality.[10]

Underlying and bound up with these factors that link poverty to infant mortality is the fact that poor women suffer higher levels of stress and lower levels of social support than most women of higher SES. According to one definition, stress is "a state that occurs when persons perceive that demands exceed their ability to cope."[11(p.19)] Poor women may find that even such modest demands as paying the rent and the food bill, getting to work, or finding daycare are too much. Poor housing increases stress when leaky plumbing, malfunctioning appliances, and infestations of vermin must be dealt with. A mother's ability to cope with the needs of a sick child is limited when she has no health insurance, no transportation to a doctor's office, and no one to help her care for other children in the family. A poor, young, single mother may not have the coping skills that might come from experience, education, and the support of the child's father. To make matters worse, this mother is likely to seek stress relief through maladaptive behavior such as smoking, drug use, or entering into abusive relationships.

PREVENTING INFANT MORTALITY

The United States has been successful in substantially reducing IMRs over the past three decades, as seen in Figure 18–1. However, much of this success is due to improved medical treatments for highly vulnerable infants after they are born.[12] The disadvantages of the technological approach are obvious: it disrupts normal bonding between parents and infants; it leaves a significant number of the survivors with long-term developmental disabilities, even severe handicaps; and it is very expensive. The countries that have better IMRs than the United States are generally much less dependent on neonatal intensive care for achieving their successes.

The public health approach to the prevention of infant mortality focuses on two groups: pregnant women in general, most of whom are highly motivated to bear a healthy child and are receptive to information on how to avoid risks; and high-risk women—the poor, young, minority, unmarried women whose infants are most likely to suffer from their socioeconomic disadvantages. Prenatal care provides women with information on how to have a healthy pregnancy and bear a healthy child. Thus prenatal care is the most public-health-oriented kind of care the medical profession provides. Prenatal visits also provide the opportunity to diagnose problems that need medical intervention. For example, studies published in

1995 found that infections of the genital tract are strongly linked to a mother's risk of giving birth prematurely and that treatment with antibiotics could reduce that risk.[13] Beginning prenatal care as early as possible—preferably even before a woman tries to conceive—greatly enhances a woman's prospects of bearing a healthy infant.

Prenatal care is especially important for the women with the lowest SES. Visits to a health care provider may be the only source of the education, services, and social support these women need. Most states recognize the importance of prenatal care and have tried to remove financial barriers by providing insurance or other sources of payment and by establishing prenatal clinics at health departments, hospital outpatient departments, and community health centers. In 2001, more than 83 percent of pregnant women received prenatal care in the first trimester of pregnancy.[14]

However, a number of barriers remain that discourage the women at highest risk from seeking prenatal care, including lack of information about available services, inconvenient hours of service, rudeness and long waits at the clinics, inadequate transportation, and lack of child care for older children. The percentage of black and Hispanic women who receive prenatal care in the first trimester is significantly lower than that for white women (74.5 percent for blacks and 75.7 percent for Hispanics in 2001).[14] Reaching women who do not seek early prenatal care requires active outreach programs including hotlines, community canvassing, and the provision of incentives to the expectant mother.[12] A new barrier arose in the wave of anti-immigrant sentiment and policies included in the 1996 federal welfare reform bill, which resulted in denial of prenatal care for illegal immigrants in some states. From a public health perspective, this is a foolish and expensive policy, since the infants—U.S. citizens—born to these women will be more likely to be premature, unhealthy, and in need of neonatal intensive care.

To be effective in reducing infant mortality, prenatal care for high-risk women should include a broad array of medical, educational, social, and nutritional services. However, political realities too often mean that, although major efforts are made to increase the number of women who receive prenatal care, the clinics that provide it are understaffed, rushed, and not financed adequately to provide the services that could really make a difference in the health of the mother and infant.

Congenital anomalies, the leading cause of infant death overall and the leading cause for the death of white infants, are less linked to SES than are other causes. Many congenital anomalies, such as Tay-Sachs disease, hemophilia, and Down syndrome have a genetic basis and can be prevented by genetic screening and/or prenatal diagnosis, as described in Chapter 12. Newborn screening programs are designed to identify infants born with genetic defects such as phenylketonuria and hypothyroidism that can be remedied by early diagnosis and treatment. Other congenital anomalies may be caused by environmental exposures, such as viruses, heavy metals, or the use of legal or illegal drugs. Public health intervention includes Food and Drug Administration (FDA) regulation of teratogenic drugs such as thalidomide (see Chapter 12) or warnings to pregnant women such as those required on alcoholic beverage containers and on the packaging of legal teratogenic drugs such as the acne drug Accutane or the epilepsy drug dilantin. Infection with the rubella virus—German measles—once a common cause of deafness and mental retardation, is prevented by immunization. As a result of these measures, infant mortality due to congenital anomalies has fallen significantly in both blacks and whites.[15,4]

Nutritional factors may influence the risk of some congenital disorders. Recent evidence indicates that anencephaly (a lethal condition in which all or most of an infant's brain is missing) and spina bifida (protrusion of the spinal cord from the spinal column accompanied by paralysis of the lower body) are caused by a deficiency in folic acid, a B vitamin present in green leafy vegetables, dried beans, liver, orange juice, and grapefruit juice. The damage occurs early in the pregnancy, when the developing spinal column is being formed. Dietary supplementation with folic acid has been shown to reduce the incidence of these neural tube defects by 50 percent or more, but the supplementation must happen during the first month of pregnancy, even before the woman may recognize she is pregnant. Public health campaigns to encourage all women of child-bearing age to take folic acid supplements have had only modest success, and poor, high-risk women are probably the least likely to comply with the recommendation.

Although there was concern that excess folic acid might cause problems in the elderly, the FDA decided to require that foods such as flour, corn meal, pasta, and rice be fortified with folic acid, effective January 1, 1998. Surveys conducted before and after the measure took effect found that fortification reduced the number of affected pregnancies by 26 percent, from about 4,000 pregnancies in 1995 through 1996 to about 3,000 pregnancies in 1999 through 2000. About 40 percent of the affected pregnancies ended in fetal death or elective abortion.[16] The amount of folic acid used for fortification is not sufficient to provide maximum preventive effect, however, and young women are still advised to take supplements. It is especially important for women on low carbohydrate diets to take extra vitamins, because these diets are less likely to include foods that have been supplemented with folic acid.

A great deal of public health attention has been directed toward preventing low birth weight, the leading cause of death among black infants and second leading cause among whites. The primary cause of low birth weight (less than 2500 grams [5.5 pounds]), is prematurity—being born too soon. While the causes of premature labor and delivery are not well understood, many of the environmental, behavioral, nutritional, and social factors previously discussed can contribute to low birth weight. The percentage of infants born with low birth weight has been growing,[17] indicating a public health failure and an increasing reliance on high-technology medical care to maintain the continued decline in IMRs. Black infants are two to three times more likely to be born too small than are white infants. This disparity has decreased slightly in recent years, not because African American mothers are having healthier pregnancies, but because white women are postponing conception until they are older and more likely to have difficult pregnancies or need assisted reproductive technology, leading to multiple births.[17] Improving access to prenatal care, discussed previously, is one approach to reducing rates of low birth weight. Another approach is to reduce rates of adolescent pregnancy, discussed in a following section.

SIDS, the third leading cause of infant death overall, is also not well understood. Almost always the death is unexpected; usually the infant appeared to be healthy before he or she died, and an autopsy fails to establish the cause of death. While SIDS is more common in infants of low birth weight and in infants of smokers or drug users, it is not limited to infants with these risk factors.[18] Until recently, because of the lack of understanding about the causes of SIDS, not much could be done to reduce the incidence.

Then, in the early 1990s, studies done in New Zealand, Australia, and the United Kingdom reported that SIDS occurred more frequently in infants that were sleeping on their stomachs. The American Academy of Pediatrics and the National Institute of Child Health and Human Development began a "Back to Sleep" campaign to educate maternity wards, doctors and nurses, and parents that infants should be put to sleep on their backs. Since the campaign was launched, the number of deaths from SIDS has declined dramatically: by 2001, the SIDS death rate had fallen by over 50 percent.[19, 4] There is still room for improvement: surveys of infant sleeping positions have found that about 20 percent of U.S. infants continue to sleep on their stomachs, and black infants are twice as likely to be placed on their stomachs as white infants.[19]

FAMILY PLANNING AND PREVENTION OF ADOLESCENT PREGNANCY

Because pregnancy is not good for the health of either a teenager or her infant, preventing adolescent pregnancy is a high public health priority. Pregnancy during the teen years has many harmful consequences, including interference with the young mother's education and career prospects, economic hardship, and interference with the formation of a strong family unit. Thus adolescent pregnancy, and all the accompanying socioeconomic consequences, increases the health risks to the child for all the reasons previously described as causes of infant mortality. Teenage mothers are less likely to seek prenatal care than older women and are more likely to have no care at all. They are more likely to smoke and less likely to gain adequate weight during pregnancy. Infants of teenage mothers are at greatly increased risk of low birth weight, serious and long-term disability, and dying during the first year of life.[20]

Rates of adolescent pregnancy in the United States have declined since the 1950s, but in those days, social pressure forced marriage on many girls who became pregnant, producing a more stable economic and family environment for the young child. Today, most teenage mothers are unmarried, and a large increase in adolescent births in the late 1980s alarmed public health advocates and policy makers.[20] However, after peaking in 1991, rates declined steadily through 2002.[21] Birth rates have consistently been higher among African American and Hispanic teenagers than white teenagers, and rates have been lowest among Asian Americans and Pacific Islanders. U.S. adolescent pregnancy rates are the highest in the industrialized world.[20]

Unintended pregnancy in older women is also a matter of concern to public health because it is more likely to lead to poorer health outcomes for mother and child. Some unintended pregnancies are merely mistimed, but many are unwanted, leading to some of the same risks as occur in teenage pregnancies. Surveys have shown that only about half of the pregnancies among American women are planned. A frequent consequence of unintended pregnancy is induced abortion. In the United States, there is approximately one abortion for every four live births.[22] This is a decrease from the ratio of more than one in three live births in the 1980s. From a public health perspective, every pregnancy should be an intended pregnancy.

Adequate access to contraception could go a long way toward reducing rates of unintended pregnancy and abortion. Americans' ambivalent feelings about sex probably contribute to the fact that many women lack access to comprehensive family planning services. Even private health insurance plans often do not provide coverage for contraception. Unmarried women, poor women, adolescents, and African American women are especially likely to encounter difficulty in obtaining and paying for services. A number of federal programs provide financing for family planning services, as do many state programs. However, availability of services varies widely from one state to another and, in many areas, well under half of those in need of subsidized services receive them.[23]

Sterilization is the most common method of contraception in the United States, but it is permanent and is thus inappropriate for young people. Combination oral contraceptives—"the pill"—are highly effective, with a failure rate of only 0.1 percent if used correctly and consistently. Other hormonal contraceptives, such as Depo-Provera and Norplant, which are implanted and act over a longer time, are also very effective, as are intrauterine devices (IUDs). All these methods have drawbacks, although the health risks tend to be overestimated. Barrier methods including the male and female condoms and the female diaphragm and cervical cap can be fairly effective if used correctly (failure rates of 3 to 6 percent) and condoms have the added advantage of reducing the risk of sexually transmitted diseases. However, barrier methods are often used inconsistently and incorrectly. Spermicides used alone (foams, creams, and jellies) have failure rates of 6 percent for perfect use and much worse for typical use.[24]

The "morning after pill," a mixture of estrogen and progestin to be used within seventy-two hours of unprotected intercourse, is an effective backup method, reducing the risk of pregnancy by 75 percent. The hormones prevent the implantation of a fertilized egg in the uterus. This emergency method has not been widely used, apparently because many women and even some medical providers are not aware of its potential.[24] In 2004, pharmaceutical companies requested the FDA to approve the sale of emergency contraceptives without a prescription, which would make the medication more easily available to women who need it. An FDA advisory committee, after reviewing the evidence for safety, recommended that the request be approved. However, in an unusual move widely interpreted as being politically motivated, the FDA did not accept the committee's recommendation.[25] Availability of emergency contraception would be expected to significantly reduce the number of unwanted pregnancies and abortions.

Public health programs specifically aimed at preventing teenage pregnancy include sex education in the schools, which has been found to be effective in delaying young people's initiation of intercourse and increasing their use of contraception when they do have sex.[26] As discussed in Chapter 13, there is considerable controversy about the exact message that should be conveyed in pregnancy prevention programs. The federal welfare reform bill that was implemented in 1998 included funding for programs that teach sexual abstinence only. Many states were reluctant to apply for the money because they believe such programs are much less effective than those that include education on contraception as well. Abstinence-only programs tend to stress the fact that condoms are not perfect and can fail. Studies have shown that teenagers who sign abstinence pledges may delay sex, but when they do initiate intercourse they are less likely to use protection.[27] A study by the Alan Guttmacher Institute found that the decline in teenage pregnancy that occurred between 1988 and 1995 could be accounted for in part by increased abstinence—about 25 percent—but more significantly by increased use of contraception—about 75 percent.[28] Despite the drop in teen birth rates since 1991, rates in the United States are higher than they are in other developed countries.[27]

NUTRITION OF WOMEN AND CHILDREN

Since the establishment of milk stations in the 1890s, nutrition has been an important component of maternal and child health programs. At first, the emphasis was on breastfeeding and the safety of milk and baby foods. As more was learned about vitamins, mothers were given dietary advice on how to feed their children. During the Great Depression of the 1930s, the federal government established several food assistance plans to help the needy. They formed the basis of current federal programs, run by the Department of Agriculture, which originated in the 1960s.[29]

The Special Supplemental Nutrition Program for Women, Infants, and Children (WIC), provides vouchers for milk, fruit juice, eggs, cereals, and other nutritious foods for pregnant women, lactating mothers, infants, and children up to five years old. Nutrition education is also provided, and WIC centers often become a source of many support services for poor, young families. The Department of Agriculture has evaluated the WIC program and found it to be effective in saving medical costs for the women and infants who participated.

The nutritional needs of older children are addressed through the School Meals Program. School lunches, provided at most schools, must meet certain nutritional standards, including offering a meat or meat alternative, fruit and/or vegetables, bread, and milk. Children from households with incomes at or below 185 percent of the poverty level receive the lunches free or at reduced prices. Children from families with higher incomes pay more. A more limited number of children receive free or reduced price school breakfasts, and some schools offer after-school snacks. There is also a Summer Food Service Program, which provides meals during school vacation periods.

A third federal program designed to help low-income families afford adequate food is the Food Stamp Program. Based on the household's size and income, families are issued an electronic benefits transfer card that can be used like a credit card to buy nutritious foods at grocery stores. The Food Stamp Program, which cannot be used for alcohol, tobacco, or non-food items, has come under fire, in part because of some well-publicized abuses. The 1996 federal welfare reform legislation imposed limits on some families' eligibility to receive food stamps, including elimination of benefits for legal immigrants.[30]

Despite food assistance programs, children are at risk of going hungry in the United States. Department of Agriculture surveys have found that 11 percent of households are food insecure, meaning that they have limited or uncertain access to nutritionally adequate foods, and in 3.5 percent of households, someone in the family experiences hunger. Families headed by women with children under eighteen have a 32 percent prevalence of food insecurity.[31]

As discussed in Chapter 16, however, while undernutrition is a real concern for the poorest American families, overeating is a more widespread problem.

CHILDREN'S HEALTH AND SAFETY

Deaths in childhood from infectious diseases have been vastly reduced because of widespread immunization programs, as discussed in Chapter 9. Virtually all children are vaccinated against diphtheria, tetanus, pertussis (whooping cough), polio, measles, rubella (German measles), mumps, and hepatitis B before they enter school, because most of these immunizations are required by law. However, many preschool children are at risk because they do not receive immunizations at the recommended ages. Well-baby care is almost as important as prenatal care for child health, but children of poor families often miss out on these visits to the doctor for the same reasons that their mothers missed prenatal visits, including lack of affordable healthcare.

In 1993, the federal government launched a childhood immunization initiative aimed at increasing vaccination coverage among children ages nineteen months to thirty-five months. The federal government began to provide free vaccines for children who were uninsured or whose insurance did not cover vaccines. Public and private sector organizations and healthcare providers at the national, state, and local levels were enlisted to implement the goals of the initiative, in the hope of virtually eliminating many of the traditional childhood diseases. The initiative was declared a success in 1997 in a statement that 90 percent of American toddlers had received the most critical doses of most of the routinely recommended vaccines by age two.[32] Immunization rates are tracked by the CDC and coverage in 2003 was estimated to be an all-time high.[33] In addition to the eight diseases listed above, four newly developed vaccines are covered by the Vaccines for Children Program: Haemophilus influenzae type b (spinal meningitis), varicella (chicken pox), pneumococcal disease, and hepatitis A.[34] In recent years, there have been shortages of some vaccines. Manufacturers have left the market or produced insufficient supplies because they conclude that profits are not high enough, and they fear lawsuits over possible side effects. How to respond to these shortages is a challenge to the public health system.[33]

Other preventive services of concern to public health because they may be missed by children of low SES who do not get regular well-baby care include screening for tuberculosis, problems with vision and hearing, and scoliosis, or curvature of the spine. Because recognizing these problems as early as possible is important for ensuring a child's future health and ability to learn, these services are usually provided in schools. Diagnosing a problem in a school screening program does not guarantee that the problem will be corrected, however. As Chapter 25 discusses, children who are uninsured or underinsured may be unable to obtain treatment even after the problem is identified repeatedly.

Childhood asthma is a growing public health concern. Asthma prevalence grew dramatically between 1980 and 1995 for reasons that are not well understood. Since then, rates appear to have plateaued. Deaths from asthma are rare, but they also increased over the same period. African American children are at least four times more likely to die of asthma than white children.[35] Environmental factors in the inner city are believed to be responsible, at least in part, for the increase in asthma prevalence. Because asthma can generally be controlled by medication when patients and their parents are educated about self-management techniques, hospitalizations and deaths are thought to be due to lack of access to regular, appropriate medical care.

Although fluoridation of community water supplies and other sources of fluoride have reduced tooth decay among children by more than 50 percent since the 1960s, some children still suffer from painful and debilitating tooth decay.[36] Poor children are especially likely to suffer from dental decay when the water is not fluoridated, and communities vary in the extent to which they provide dental services through clinics or local health departments. In 2000, about two-thirds of the population served by public water systems received fluoridated water.[37]

The fact that most mothers now work outside the home, a major change from the norm in previous decades, means that young children are increasingly being cared for in day care centers. Suddenly, the need for safe and affordable day care has become a public health issue. Infectious diseases spread rapidly among young children, and adequate hygiene when changing diapers is especially important. There are also risks of injury because of an unsafe physical plant or play equipment, inadequate staffing, or unqualified caregivers. These risks can be reduced by state licensing of day care centers, requiring them to meet basic health and safety standards.

Injuries constitute the main risk to the life and health of children once they pass their first year. Public health efforts to prevent childhood injury include education and regulations that encourage use of seat belts, child safety seats, and bicycle helmets. The U.S. Consumer Products Safety Commission monitors toys and children's furniture for safety hazards, issuing warnings and ordering recalls of products that are found to be dangerous to children. Public health efforts directed toward preventing childhood injuries are described in Chapter 17.

While maternal and child health services, like public health in general, focus on prevention of death and disability, there is a long tradition of public concern about the care of children with handicaps. Beginning in 1935, the federal government funded state "crippled children's programs" that provide diagnosis, treatment, and rehabilitative services for children with special needs, many of whom are also eligible for support through Social Security.[1] While in the past many of these children might have been institutionalized, current programs try as much as possible to keep them at home, supporting families and preparing disabled young people to live independent lives.

CONCLUSION

Maternal and child health is one of the highest priorities for public health. In the United States, city, state, and local governments have for over a century conducted programs and enforced legislation aimed at protecting children and promoting their health.

Infant mortality is a gauge of society's attention to children's health and is often used as an indicator of the health status of a population as a whole. The United States compares poorly with other countries on infant mortality, ranking twenty-seventh overall. IMRs, along with other public health improvements, have greatly improved since the beginning of the twentieth century. Like other indicators of health, infant mortality is higher among African Americans than whites and declines with increasing SES.

The three leading causes of infant mortality overall are congenital anomalies, low birthweight, and SIDS. Public health programs to prevent infant mortality because of congenital anomalies, or birth defects, include pre- and postnatal screening and diagnostic programs, as described in Chapter 12. They also include protection of pregnant women from exposure to environmental teratogens. Dietary supplementation with folic acid has been found to prevent some birth defects.

Low birth weight, the leading cause of death among African American infants, is closely linked to SES. Because pregnant adolescents are especially likely to give birth to infants of low birth weight, prevention of pregnancy in teenagers is a high priority for public health.

SIDS deaths declined dramatically during the 1990s after it was found that babies who were put to sleep on their stomach were at increased risk of sudden death. An educational campaign about infant sleeping positions cut SIDS deaths by over 50 percent.

Adequate family planning services are important for public health. Pregnancy in adolescence is risky for both mothers and infants. Comprehensive sex education is effective in preventing teen pregnancy. Political conservatives promote abstinence-only programs, which are less effective than programs that include information on contraception. Unintended pregnancy also increases health risks in older women and their infants. While a variety of effective contraceptive methods are available, many women do not have access to affordable family planning services. Nutrition is an important component of maternal and child health programs. The federal government has, since the 1930s, supported a number of programs that provide supplemental foods for pregnant women, infants, and children. Public sentiment against welfare in the 1990s led to some cuts in nutrition programs, together with cuts in welfare programs.

Other public health initiatives that have a significant impact on children's health include immunization requirements, fluoridation of community water supplies, and injury-prevention measures. Regular access to medical care is important for the health of children, but many poor and minority children do not have this access, as discussed in Chapter 25.

REFERENCES

1. W. M. Schmidt, and H. M. Wallace, "Development of Health Services for Mothers and Children in the United States," in *Maternal and Child Health Practices*, H. M. Wallace, G. M. Ryan Jr., and A. C. Oglesby, eds. (Oakland, California: Third Party Publishing Company, 1988), 3–21.
2. C. A. Miller, "Development of MCH Services and Policy in the United States, in *Maternal and Child Health Practices*, H. M. Wallace, G. M. Ryan Jr., and A. C. Oglesby, eds. (Oakland, California: Third Party Publishing Company, 1988), 39–45.
3. W. S. Nersesian, "Infant Mortality in Socially Vulnerable Populations," *Annual Review of Public Health* 9 (1988): 361–377.
4. National Center for Health Statistics, "Deaths: Leading Causes for 2001," *National Vital Statistics Reports* 52 (2003).
5. G. K. Singh, and S. M. Yu, "Infant Mortality in the United States: Trends, Differentials, and Projections, 1950 through 2010," *American Journal of Public Health* 85 (1995): 957–964.
6. U.S. Centers for Disease Control and Prevention, "Pregnancy-Related Mortality Surveillance—United States, 1991–1999," *Morbidity and Mortality Weekly Report* 52, No. SS02, (2003): 1–8.
7. U.S. Centers for Disease Control and Prevention, "Trends in Infant Mortality Attributable to Birth Defects—United States, 1980–1995," *Morbidity and Mortality Weekly Report* 47 (1998): 773–778.
8. M. G. Wagner, "Infant Mortality in Europe: Implications for the United States," *Journal of Public Health Policy* (Winter 1998): 473–484.

9. A. M. Fraser, J. E. Brockert, and R. H. Ward, "Association of Young Maternal Age with Adverse Reproductive Outcomes," *New England Journal of Medicine* 332 (1995): 1113–1117.

10. J. Huntington, and F. A. Connell, "For Every Dollar Spent—The Cost-Savings Argument for Prenatal Care," *New England Journal of Medicine* 331 (1994): 1303–1307.

11. N. Adler et al., "Socioeconomic Status and Health: The Challenge of the Gradient," *American Psychologist* 49 (1994): 15–24.

12. S. S. Brown, "Preventing Low Birthweight," in *Maternal and Child Health Practices*, H. M. Wallace, G. M. Ryan Jr., and A. C. Oglesby, eds., 307–324.

13. M. Hack, and I. R. Merkatz, "Preterm Delivery and Low Birth Weight—A Dire Legacy," *New England Journal of Medicine* 333 (1995): 1772–1774.

14. U.S. Centers for Disease Control and Prevention, *Health, United States, 2003* (Hyattsville, Maryland: 2003), 30.

15. U.S. Centers for Disease Control and Prevention, "Trends in Infant Mortality Attributable to Birth Defects—United States, 1980–1995," *Morbidity and Mortality Weekly Report* 47 (1998): 773–778.

16. U.S. Centers for Disease Control and Prevention, "Spina Bifida and Anencephaly Before and After Folic Acid Mandate—United States, 1995–1996 and 1999–2000," *Morbidity and Mortality Weekly Report* 53 (2004): 362–365.

17. U.S. Centers for Disease Control and Prevention, "Infant Mortality and Low Birth Weight Among Black and White Infants—United States, 1980–2000," *Morbidity and Mortality Weekly Report* 51 (2002): 589–592.

18. M. Willinger et al., "Factors Associated with the Transition to Nonprone Sleep Positions of Infants in the United States: The National Infant Sleep Position Study," *Journal of the American Medical Association* 280 (1998): 329–335.

19. Task Force on Infant Sleep Position and Sudden Infant Death Syndrome, "Changing Concepts of Sudden Infant Death Syndrome: Implications for Infant Sleeping Environment and Sleep Position," *Pediatrics* 105 (2000): 605–656.

20. S. J. Ventura, S. C. Curtin, and T. J. Mathews, "Teenage Births in the United States: National and State Trends, 1990–96," National Vital Statistics System (Hyattsville, Maryland: National Center for Health Statistics, 1998).

21. Federal Interagency Forum on Child and Family Statistics web site, *http://childstats. gov/ac2004/tables/health9.asp*. Accessed November 3, 2004.

22. Centers for Disease Control and Prevention, "Abortion Surveillance—United States, 2000," *Morbidity and Mortality Weekly Report* 52, No. SS12 (2003): 1–32.

23. J. J. Frost, L. Frohwirth, and A. Purcell, "Availability and Use of Publicly Funded Family Planning Clinics: U.S. Trends, 1994–2001," *Perspectives in Sex and Reproductive Health* 36 (2004): 206–215.

24. U.S. Department of Health Human Services, *Guide to Clinical Preventive Services*, 2nd ed. (Washington, DC: 1996).

25. A. Germain, "Editorial: Playing Politics with Women's Lives," *Science* 305 (2004): 17.

26. A. Gardner, "Female Adolescent Health Care: International Perspective," in *Reproductive Health Care for Women and Babies*, B. P. Sachs et al., eds., (New York: Oxford University Press, 1995), 40–56.

27. J. B. Brody, "Abstinence-Only: Does It Work?" *New York Times* (June 1 2004): F7.

28. J. E. Darroch, and S. Singh, *Why Is Teenage Pregnancy Declining? The Roles of Abstinence, Sexual Activity and Contraceptive Use*. Alan Guttmacher Institute Occasional Report No. 1, December 1999.
29. J. T. Dwyer, and J. Freedland, "Nutrition Services," in *Maternal and Child Health Practices*, H. M. Wallace, G. M. Ryan Jr., and A. C. Oglesby, eds., 261–282.
30. National Anti-Hunger Organizations, *A Blueprint to End Hunger*, June 3, 2004, *www.foodsecurity.org/Blueprint.pdf*. Accessed November 13, 2004.
31. U.S. Department of Agriculture. Economic Research Service. *Briefing Room: Food Security in the United States: Conditions and Trends. www.ers.usda.gov/Briefing/ FoodSecurity/trends/*. Accessed November 13, 2004.
32. U.S. Centers for Disease Control and Prevention, "Status Report on the Childhood Immunization Initiative: National, State, and Urban Area Vaccination Coverage Levels Among Children Aged 19–35 months—United States, 1996," *Morbidity and Mortality Weekly Report* 46 (1997): 657–664.
33. U.S. Centers for Disease Control and Prevention, "National, State, and Urban Area Vaccination Coverage Among Children Aged 19–35 Months—United States, 2003," *Morbidity and Mortality Weekly Report* 53 (2004): 658–661.
34. Centers for Disease Control and Prevention, Vaccines for Children Program, *www.cdc.gov/programs/immun11.htm*. Accessed November 14, 2004.
35. L. J. Akinbami, and K. C. Schoendorf, "Trends in Childhood Asthma: Prevalence, Health Care Utilization, and Mortality," *Pediatrics* 110 (2002): 315–322.
36. U.S. Centers for Disease Control and Prevention, "Achievements in Public Health, 1900–1999: Fluoridation of Drinking Water to Prevent Dental Caries," *Morbidity and Mortality Weekly Report* 48 (1999): 933–940.
37. U.S. Centers for Disease Control and Prevention, "Populations Receiving Optimally Fluoridated Public Drinking Water—United States, 2000," *Morbidity and Mortality Weekly Report* 51 (2002): 144–147.

PART V

Environmental Issues in Public Health

CHAPTER 19

A Clean Environment: The Basis of Public Health

An Environmental Hazard

Humans are designed by eons of evolution to live on the earth: to breathe the earth's air, to drink the earth's water, to eat the plants and animals that grow on the earth's surface. People are adapted to the earth's environment. While there is considerable variation in that environment in different parts of the planet, and humans have found ways to live in many different climates and habitats, people's health depends on the presence of these basic ingredients of life—air, water, and food. There are also natural phenomena in the environment that can harm human health: extremes of heat and cold, ultraviolet rays of the sun, toxic minerals and plants, and other living organisms, from pathogenic bacteria to predatory mammals.

Human beings are social creatures, dependent upon other people to help them navigate the earth's environment. All humans in all parts of the world live in groups, from small bands of hunters and gatherers to the residents of teeming cities. When groups of people settle down to live together in one place, they change their shared environment: the larger the group, the greater the effect on the environment. Some of these changes may be made deliberately, to improve life for everyone; some are the inadvertent results of crowding, with harmful effects on people's well-being.

Archaeological evidence shows that the earliest cities were designed with consideration for the health of their inhabitants. As early as 2000 B.C., cities in India, Egypt, Greece, and South America had devised ways of providing clean water and draining wastes. These ancient systems of water supply, drains, and sewers are the first evidence of public health measures: organized community efforts to provide healthy conditions for the population.

Ensuring a clean water supply and the safe disposal of wastes—functions that fall into the category of environmental health—are still among the most important responsibilities of government. Other environmental health functions necessary in industrial countries are measures to ensure clean air and safe food. All these concerns arise because of the human tendency to live in groups. Most people do not have the means or the desire to grow their own food, draw water from their own well, and dispose of wastes in their own yard. Because people live together in cities and suburbs, they rely on others to provide their food and water and to dispose of their wastes. Because there are so many people, and because of the prodigality of the modern lifestyle, the wastes people produce have unprecedented potential to pollute the air and litter the earth.

ROLE OF GOVERNMENT IN ENVIRONMENTAL HEALTH

Environmental health is clearly the responsibility of government. Many environmental exposures, such as air pollution, are beyond the control of the individual. Others can be avoided only at significant trouble and expense, for example, if people grow their own vegetables, or buy them from farmers whose agricultural methods they have inspected themselves. Governments ensure a healthy environment by various means, sometimes providing services directly, in other cases setting standards and regulating how the services should be provided.

Traditionally in the United States, local governments have provided water for their citizens. They are required by law to meet standards set by state and federal governments. Local governments also traditionally provide sewage systems to dispose of wastes from individual households as well as to handle runoff from the land.

In the 1960s, Americans became increasingly aware that the environment was deteriorating. Lakes and streams were choked with sewage and chemical wastes, which killed fish and other wildlife. Cities were overhung with smog. Citizens were outraged by news stories of neighborhoods poisoned by long-dormant toxic waste dumps. State and federal governments were pressured to assume more responsibility for the environment. In the late 1960s and early 1970s, many new laws set standards for air, water, and waste disposal.

Perhaps the most difficult environmental health issue people face is the threat that human activities worldwide are changing the climate of the earth. The major concerns are depletion of the earth's ozone layer and the accumulation of "greenhouse gases" in the atmosphere. These problems, both of which may significantly affect human health, transcend national boundaries. While the United Nations has sponsored international meetings on these issues and governments have signed treaties designed to bring the problems under control, there is no way of enforcing these agreements.

IDENTIFICATION OF HAZARDS

A major role of the federal government in environmental health is to identify hazards in the environment and to set safety standards that must be met by industry and by state and local governments to protect people from these hazards. Both the identification of a substance as hazardous and the setting of standards are often difficult and controversial. The risks posed by most synthetic chemicals that are discharged into the environment by industrial processes or disposal by consumers are unknown. Testing for potential harmful effects is expensive and time-consuming, and the choice of what chemicals to test may itself be politically controversial. Even in cases where the health risk is obvious—such as the discharge of raw sewage into waterways or the air pollution caused by America's dependence on the private automobile—local governments, industry, and even the average citizen may resist requirements to meet standards because of the expense and inconvenience needed to clean up the environment.

Radiation is an environmental health hazard that people tend to worry about only when it is artificially produced. However, all people are exposed to cosmic radiation, in varying amounts depending on where they live, and natural radioactive materials are found in soils and rocks in many parts of the world. Radon gas, produced by the natural radioactive decay of uranium, is present in many homes, a fact that was recognized only in the mid-1980s. Prolonged exposure to radon is potentially a cause of lung cancer, although the risks from radon in the home are not well understood. Ultraviolet radiation from the sun is a significant cause of skin cancer and melanoma. There is no way these exposures can be regulated by government, except for some testing requirements concerning radon, discussed in Chapter 20.

The discovery in the mid-1890s of x rays, which could pass through flesh and reveal bones, aroused great public excitement and led to extensive human exposures before the danger was recognized. During the early decades of the twentieth century, x-ray treatments were popular as cure-alls for a variety of ailments, and radioactive ingredients were added to patent medicines. The first alarm was raised in the mid-1920s, with the deaths from kidney and bone disease of a number of workers who painted watch dials with radium so they would glow in the dark. They had been touching the paintbrushes to their lips to sharpen the points, thereby ingesting toxic quantities of the chemical. Then in 1932, a rich, socially prominent businessman died agonizingly from the same mysterious ailment, which was diagnosed on autopsy as radium poisoning. He had been dosing himself over a five-year period with hundreds of bottles of Radithor, a radium-containing patent medicine. The publicity surrounding the Radithor scandal led to strengthened Food and Drug Administration (FDA) powers to regulate patent medicines as well as specific limitations on radioactive pharmaceuticals.[1]

Evidence that chronic exposure to low levels of x radiation caused cancer came from epidemiologic studies that began in the 1930s. One study compared death rates of radiologists with those of other medical specialists and found that the average age at death for radiologists was five years younger than that for other specialists.[2] Radiation's damaging health effects were confirmed by long-term follow-up studies of survivors of the atomic bombings of Hiroshima and Nagasaki, Japan, which ended the Second World War. The incidence of leukemia and other cancers was significantly increased among these people. Today, medical and dental x rays constitute the largest source of nonbackground radiation exposure, although equipment has been continuously improved to reduce the hazard. Since about one-third of the medical and dental x rays that Americans receive are estimated to be unnecessary, patients are advised to question whether each exposure is essential.

That some metals have harmful health effects has been common knowledge for decades or longer. This is the case with *mercury*, which was recognized in the nineteenth century to cause neurological damage in workers who made felt hats—the origin of the expression "mad as a hatter" and the inspiration for the character the Mad Hatter in Lewis Carroll's *Alice in Wonderland*. The devastating effects of the mercury discharged by a plastics factory into Japan's Minamata Bay in the 1950s caused some 700 deaths and varying degrees of paralysis and brain damage in 9,000 other people. (See Chapter 12.) The mercury accumulated in fish, which were the staple of the community's diet. Another well-known episode of mercury poisoning occurred in Iraq in 1972, when the substance was used as a fungicide on seed grain. The contaminated wheat was turned into bread, which poisoned more than 6,500 people, 459 of whom died.[3]

In the United States, mercury enters the environment mainly by emissions from coal-burning power plants. The heavy metal falls to earth and becomes a hazard to humans mainly by getting into fish. Because the developing brain is most sensitive to the toxic effects of mercury, pregnant women and women who may become pregnant, as well as nursing mothers and young children are advised to avoid eating fish species that have the highest average amounts of mercury in their flesh: tilefish, swordfish, king mackerel, and shark. Up to twelve ounces per week of other species of fish are considered safe. Mercury is regulated under both the Clean Air Act and the Safe Drinking Water Act. (See Chapters 20 and 21.)

People may be exposed to mercury when the liquid metal is spilled, releasing toxic vapors, for example after a glass thermometer breaks. Mercury may also be found in equipment used in school science labs, and exposure may occur if the equipment breaks or is mishandled. The Environmental Protection Agency (EPA) recommends that mercury-containing products be removed from homes and schools. The sale of mercury-containing fever thermometers is banned in many states; safer alternatives are available. Cleanup of mercury spills requires great caution to prevent droplets of the metal from accumulating in small spaces and releasing vapors into the air. The EPA cautions against trying to clean up mercury with a vacuum cleaner or broom, or pouring it down a drain, because these methods are likely to put more of the toxic vapors into the air.[4]

Lead is another metal known to harm the brain and nervous system, especially those of children. It also damages red blood cells and the kidneys. Lead is believed to be the single most important environmental threat to the health of American children, who may be exposed from a variety of sources. Over the past three decades, evidence has accumulated that even low levels of lead can slow a child's development and cause learning and behavior problems. The federal government recommends that all young children poor enough to be eligible for Medicaid be screened for lead in the blood, and some states have extended the mandate to children of all income levels. Permissible levels of lead have been steadily lowered from 60 micrograms per deciliter of blood in 1970 to 10 micrograms at present.[5]

Lead has been used—and has been causing lead poisoning—since the time of the Roman Empire, when it was a component of wine casks, cooking pots, and water pipes. In fact, the Latin word for lead is "plumbum," the origin of the English word "plumbing." Even today, a major source of lead exposure for millions of Americans is contamination of drinking water from lead pipes or from lead solder used with copper pipes. The use of lead in pipes was phased out in the 1980s, and newer homes use plastic plumbing.

Until the 1980s, lead was a significant air pollutant, emitted from the tailpipes of motor vehicles that burned leaded gasoline. As a result of the phasing out of leaded gas, lead levels in the air have dropped to negligible amounts. Lead was also a component of paint, both interior and exterior, until its use was banned in 1977. Children—especially those who live in old, substandard housing—are still significantly exposed when they chew on chips of old peeling paint or when they put dirty hands in their mouths if the dirt is contaminated with dust from deteriorating paint. Attempts to remove old lead-containing paint can sometimes be even more hazardous if it turns to airborne dust as it is sanded or sandblasted off a surface and is inhaled.

Asbestos is a fibrous mineral valuable for a variety of uses because of its strength and fire resistance. The hazards of asbestos were first recognized in an occupational setting: Inhalation of high concentrations of asbestos dust caused stiffening and scarring of the lungs of miners and other asbestos workers, a condition known as asbestosis, which can be disabling and eventually fatal. Regulations limiting exposure were instituted, but as workers began to live longer many of them developed cancer. They were especially likely to get lung cancer or mesothelioma, a rare cancer of the lining of the chest or abdominal cavity that seems to be caused exclusively by inhalation of asbestos. As a result of a succession of lawsuits brought by injured workers and their families in the 1960s and 1970s, the Manville Corporation—the largest asbestos company in the United States—filed for bankruptcy in 1982.[6] Once the dangers of asbestos were recognized, many uses of the material were banned and standards for occupational exposure were tightened. However, asbestos is still used in some roofing compounds, gaskets, brake linings, and a number of other products.[7]

The general public is most likely to be exposed to asbestos fibers released into the air in the dust from crumbling walls and ceilings of old, deteriorating buildings. This is a special concern in schools, since all schools built or renovated between 1940 and 1973 were required to install asbestos insulation as a fire safety measure. Children's exposure is of special concern because they would live for many years with the fibers lodged in their lungs, and the likelihood of developing cancer would increase with time. In 1986, the Asbestos Hazard Emergency Response Act was passed. It required all primary and secondary schools to be inspected and, if loose asbestos was found, to carry out plans for removing, enclosing or encapsulating material. Unfortunately, the removal was often done improperly, causing more asbestos to be released into the air than if the material had been left intact. Other schools, unable to afford the expense of asbestos removal, ignored the rulings.[3] There is no evidence thus far that exposure to asbestos has been a significant cancer risk to the general population.

However, the population of Libby, Montana, was clearly harmed by decades of exposure to asbestos. The vermiculite ore that had been mined in the Libby area since the 1920s was heavily contaminated with asbestos. A 1999 investigation found that death rates from asbestosis among residents of the area were approximately forty times higher than the rest of Montana and 60 times higher than the rest of the United States.[8] Earlier studies had reported elevated mortality rates from lung cancer, mesothelioma, and other lung diseases among people who had worked in the mines. Follow-up studies found abnormalities in the chest x rays of household contacts of asbestos workers, who presumably were exposed to asbestos dust brought home on the clothes of the workers. Abnormalities were also found in the x rays of children who had played in piles of vermiculite at the processing facilities.[9]

The fallout from the Libby crisis continues. A disease registry has been established to track individuals who were exposed, to learn more about asbestos-related illnesses, and to share information on new therapies and diagnostic tools. A community health center has been established with federal funds to provide medical services. Libby has been declared a Superfund site and is being cleaned up. (See Chapter 22.) W. R. Grace, the company that operated the mines, has been overwhelmed with lawsuits by injured residents and filed for bankruptcy protection in 2001.[10] The EPA is warning that asbestos-containing vermiculite from Libby was used as insulation in millions of homes and businesses across the country and that asbestos fibers could pose a health threat if the insulation is disturbed.

Asbestos exposure is also a concern as a result of the 9/11 attacks on the World Trade Center. Beginning a few days after the collapse of the towers, the EPA and the New York City and New York State Health Departments monitored pollutants in the air, including asbestos. Concentrations near Ground Zero were quite high in the first few days and weeks but decreased to background levels by January or February 2002.[11] These exposures were most likely to affect the thousands of rescue and recovery workers, who are now being monitored for long-term health effects by the Centers for Disease Control and Prevention. One study of these workers found that half of them continued to have respiratory symptoms over a year later.[12]

PESTICIDES AND INDUSTRIAL CHEMICALS

Rachel Carson's best selling book *Silent Spring*, published in 1962, was a wake-up call to the American public, a warning that chemicals in the environment cause harm. The publication of her book, more than any other single event, launched the environmental movement that led to sweeping legislation in the 1970s. *Silent Spring* called attention to the harmful effects of the virtually ubiquitous pesticide DDT. The chemical could be found in lakes and streams, plants and insects. When eaten or drunk by fish and birds, it accumulated in their flesh, to be eaten in turn by predators, which concentrated these chemicals further in their own bodies. A worldwide survey measuring chemicals in the body fat of people on six continents found

DDT in all of them.[13] The use of DDT was banned in the United States in 1972. A number of other insecticides chemically related to DDT were also banned in the 1970s. These chemicals—including chlordane, aldrin, mirex, and Kepone—shared common features of solubility in fatty tissue and persistence in the environment; they break down very slowly, so they continue to cause harm long after their use is halted.

Studies looking for environmental pesticides discovered that a related group of chemicals, polychlorinated biphenyls (PCBs), also turned up often. Unlike pesticides, these chemicals were used mainly in sealed systems— capacitors, transformers, and heat exchangers—but they were still entering the environment in large quantities and getting into the food chain. PCBs frequently entered the environment through discharge of industrial wastes, a route similar to the mercury at Minamata. The contamination of New York's Hudson River with PCBs, discovered by environmentalists in 1975, was traced to two General Electric Company capacitor plants that had been discharging large volumes of PCBs into the river for more than 25 years.[14] Although the discharge was halted, the chemicals will persist in the soil of the riverbed indefinitely. Fish caught in the Hudson River still contain PCBs at concentrations considered unsafe for women of childbearing age and children under fifteen to eat at all, and for others to eat more than once a week. The EPA has developed a plan to clean the river by dredging the contaminated soil, a plan that has generated controversy both because it will stir up the chemicals and cause more contamination of the river water in the short term, and because of vigorous objections by the communities proposed as disposal sites for the contaminated soil. PCBs also entered the environment through release into the atmosphere from contaminated disposal sites or from fires in electrical equipment; they were then deposited on land and water with the help of rainfall. This route is believed responsible for the heavy PCB contamination found in the Great Lakes.[3]

Environmental scientists believe that PCBs are the most widespread chemical contaminant worldwide. The effects on human health of exposure to these chemicals at the levels commonly found in the environment are still uncertain. However, people exposed to large doses of PCBs by a number of industrial accidents were made ill by the chemicals. In western Japan in 1968, a leak at a cooking oil factory contaminated a batch of the rice oil with heat exchanger fluids containing PCBs and related chemicals. Eighteen hundred people were sickened in what became known as the "Yusho" incident ("Yusho" means oil disease in Japanese).[15] Eleven years later, a similar accident occurred in Taiwan, affecting 2,000 people with "Yu-cheng," which means oil disease in Chinese.[16] Two well-known incidents in the United States during the 1970s—a warehouse fire in Puerto Rico that caused PCB contamination of tuna meal used for animal and fish feeds, and a labeling mixup in Michigan that contaminated cattle feed with polybrominated biphenyls, a chemical similar to PCBs— resulted in human exposure to this type of chemicals through the food supply.[17]

Victims of the Yusho, Yu-cheng, and other accidents have been the subjects of epidemiologic studies tracking the victims' health over the years since their exposure. The most conspicuous and consistent symptom is chloracne, a severe skin rash that shows up soon after exposure and may persist for years. Other effects include neurological complaints and immune system defects. An increased risk of some forms of cancer is now becoming apparent. In studies on animals, PCBs and related chemicals disrupt hormonal systems that control reproduction. Infants born to Yusho and Yu-cheng mothers were small at birth and had dark discoloration of the skin, which faded after a few months. There is evidence that prenatal exposure to these chemicals, even at low doses, may have harmful effects on the intellectual development of infants exposed prenatally.[3]

A confounding factor in studying health effects of PCBs is that they are frequently contaminated with dioxins and furans, chemical relatives that are known to be more toxic. This is especially likely if the PCBs were subjected to high temperatures, as would happen in an explosion or fire. When accidental exposure occurs, it is difficult to identify which chemical in a mixture is responsible for the observed health effects. Dioxins have been called the most toxic of all synthetic chemicals: extremely small amounts are fatal to guinea pigs. However, the toxicity is quite different from one species to another, and humans appear to have an average susceptibility to dioxin. Many years of studying the health effects of dioxin and related chemicals suggest that they are carcinogenic in humans but only at high exposure levels. The most significant health effects now being recognized are that these substances act as endocrine disruptors, mimicking sex hormones to alter normal sexual development and adversely affect reproduction.[3]

Production of PCBs was halted in the United States by 1977. However, these chemicals are very stable, and they continue to enter the environment as old equipment is discarded. They tend to remain in the fatty tissues of fish, animals, and humans indefinitely. Although levels of these chemicals are high in the blood and fatty tissues of people who eat fish from contaminated waters, in most Americans the levels appear to be declining.[18]

OCCUPATIONAL EXPOSURES: WORKERS AS GUINEA PIGS

Workers are regularly exposed to larger amounts of toxic substances on the job than most of the population is ever likely to encounter. Consequently, workers tend to be the first and foremost to suffer from any harmful health effects caused by their exposures. Many chemicals that all people encounter in everyday life may have unrecognized effects at low doses, causing unexplained cancer, neurological disorders and reproductive disorders in susceptible individuals. Workers, exposed to larger quantities, may inadvertently serve as the guinea pigs that call attention to the dangers.

That certain occupations carry an increased risk of certain kinds of cancer has long been known, and the information has been helpful in understanding some of the causes of cancer. The first environmentally caused cancer to be recognized was from an occupational exposure: scrotal cancer was common in nineteenth century English chimney sweeps. The soot to which they were exposed contained the same carcinogens found in tobacco smoke—chemicals that are now known to cause lung cancer. Few other cancers can be clearly linked to specific causative agents. Because most exposures are relatively low, and because the time lag between exposure and the development of cancer is long, cause and effect are difficult to establish. Workers are effective though unintentional guinea pigs because exposure on the job is likely to be much higher than that in the general environment. An obvious increase in the rate of a specific cancer in a group of workers who have all been exposed to the same substance clearly throws suspicion on that substance as the cause.

Chemicals identified as carcinogens through occupational exposures include benzidine, which caused bladder cancer in dye factory workers; arsenic, which caused lung and lymphatic cancer in copper smelters; and vinyl chloride, used to make some plastics, which causes angiosarcoma, a rare cancer of the liver.[3] Evidence that radiation exposure causes cancer came from the higher incidence of cancer among radiologists, as discussed earlier.

Neurotoxins, like carcinogens, may be hard to recognize because they act over a long period of time. In fact, nerve poisons may be even more insidious than carcinogens, because the damage they do—deterioration of vision, muscle weakness, failure of memory—may mimic common aspects of aging. Neurological disorders that typically strike workers with specific exposures call attention to those chemicals as neurotoxins. Shoemakers exposed to hexane-containing solvents, dry cleaners exposed to trichloroethylene, pesticide applicators, and many other workers risk nerve damage from neurotoxins.[19]

NEW SOURCE OF POLLUTION: FACTORY FARMS

Over the past two decades, there has been a revolution in farming that threatens to overwhelm the system for regulating environmental pollution. Thousands of hogs, cattle, and poultry are crowded into confined spaces where they can be fed and tended to by automated systems. The environmental problems caused by this approach to farming are the huge volumes of waste produced by these animals, which must be disposed of on a relatively limited amount of land. According to the EPA, the amount of wastes from factory farms is 130 times greater than the total wastes produced by the human population.[20]

The farms deal with the wastes by creating "lagoons" in which the liquids are allowed to evaporate or are sprayed on fields. Lagoons at many of these operations have broken, failed, or overflowed. They emit gases—including ammonia, hydrogen sulfide, and methane—that can be toxic to humans. People living near the farms suffer from symptoms caused by the lagoon gases: headaches, runny noses, sore throats, coughing, respiratory problems, nausea, diarrhea, dizziness, burning eyes, depression, and fatigue. Seepage from the lagoons pollute groundwater that feeds wells used for drinking water. After heavy rains, lagoons may overflow or burst, spilling thousands of gallons of manure into rivers, lakes, streams, and estuaries; such spills have caused massive fish kills in North Carolina, Virginia, Maryland, Minnesota, Missouri, Iowa, and other states.[21]

Most of these farms are owned by a very few major corporations, which have great economic and political power. Some state legislatures have passed laws protecting the industry from regulation. State universities receive funding from the industry and may discourage research that makes the companies look bad.[22] Under the Bush administration, the EPA and the Department of Agriculture have halted enforcement investigations of the farms and suppressed research results unfavorable to the industry.[23] There have been attempts in Congress to protect the corporations against enforcement of existing laws on clean air, clean water, and toxic chemicals. Meanwhile, a number of environmental advocacy organizations, including the Sierra Club, the National Audubon Society, and the Natural Resources Defense Council, have teamed up with organizations that promote family farming and sustainable agriculture to urge the government to force agribusiness to obey environmental laws.[24]

SETTING STANDARDS: HOW SAFE IS SAFE?

Tens of thousands of synthetic chemicals have been manufactured since World War II and, in the United States alone, three to four billion pounds of them are released into the environment each year. Most have not been tested for the capacity to cause cancer, birth defects, neurological damage, or other harmful effects on health. Because of the sheer number of chemicals, it is unrealistic to require testing them all.

The environmental legislation of the 1960s and 1970s tried to establish guidelines for identifying environmental hazards and required standards to be set that protected human health and the environment. Standard setting was required for air quality, water quality, radiation safety, food and drug safety, and the disposal of hazardous wastes. The Occupational Safety and Health Act of 1970 empowered the federal government to set standards for workers' exposure to toxic substances, and the Toxic Substances Control Act of 1976 allowed the government to require testing of potentially hazardous substances before they go on the market and to ban them in certain instances. The Federal Insecticide, Fungicide, and Rodenticide Act, originally passed in 1947 and amended several times since, requires government approval of these substances before they can be used. Congress required a variety of federal agencies to set standards for exposure to toxic substances via various routes: the EPA, the FDA, the Department of Agriculture, the Department of Transportation, the Nuclear Regulatory Commission, the Consumer Products Safety Commission, and the Occupational Safety and Health Administration (OSHA) are among those responsible for various aspects of environmental health.[3]

Standard setting has progressed very slowly, however, since these laws were passed. For example, the Clean Air Act of 1970 required the EPA to develop standards for 320 air pollutants: as of 1993, only eight had been regulated.[3] As of 2004, the National Institute of Occupational Safety and

Health had identified 133 substances as potential occupational carcino-gens; of these, exposure standards for workers had been set for only 26 by OSHA, the agency with the authority to set these standards.[25,26] Under the Superfund Program (discussed in Chapter 22), 1,225 toxic waste sites had been officially listed for cleanup as of 1999, but only 176 had actually been cleaned up.[27]

There are a number of reasons why regulation has progressed so slowly. One factor is the sheer volume of potentially toxic chemicals being manu-factured in the United States, with an estimated 2,000 new chemicals being introduced per year.[28] Another is that each chemical must be regulated separately, with the potential for controversy, legal challenge, and extensive litigation over each proposed regulation. Each standard is likely to have sig-nificant economic impact on some industry, whose members will naturally fight against the potential threat to their businesses and jobs. Emotions on the part of the public often run high, since citizens believe that their health and the health of their children is endangered, and their demands for safety may be perceived as unreasonable. Worst of all, amidst the controversy, scientific data on the potential health effects of most chemicals is lacking: a National Academy of Sciences report in 1984 estimated that information was avail-able to do even a partial health hazard assessment on only about 10 percent of chemicals used commercially other than food additives, drugs, and pesti-cides. For 80 percent of the chemicals, no toxicity information was available at all.[29] The result is often gridlock, with no protections established.

RISK-BENEFIT ANALYSIS

The question "How safe is safe?" has been debated in connection with one potential health threat after another. Increasingly, policy analysts have come to agree that absolute safety is an impossible goal and that attempt-ing to avoid risk of one sort may increase risks of other kinds. Furthermore, in the words of one analyst, "overregulation can cause underregulation"[30] because too much effort is expended setting very strict standards for too few substances. By battling to achieve zero exposure to one carcinogen, for example, public health agencies may be neglecting to investigate other chemicals that are potentially more hazardous. Public health may be better served by aiming for looser, more easily achieved standards. This approach would generate less controversy and opposition, allowing for a stepped-up pace of standard setting.

The argument is also made that prevention of risk must be balanced against other societal goals, including economic well-being. Until recently, the public health approach has been to ignore economic factors in seeking risk reduction. However, an increasing understanding of the fact that economic factors are significant to people's health and well-being (see Chapter 14) has led to greater willingness on the part of public health advocates to consider costs as well as benefits in evaluating risks. Risk assessment and cost-benefit analysis are discussed in Chapter 7.

The Republican Congress elected in 1994 tried to roll back all kinds of regulations under the argument that they were irrational and expensive, examples of government interference that had negative economic impacts on business. The fact that most of these initiatives failed demonstrated that most Americans want the government to protect their health and environment. But the initiatives made people ask how regulations could become more rational, less cumbersome, and more balanced. During the Clinton administration, the political debate focused on how to achieve effective environmental protection while minimizing red tape and government intrusiveness. Today, the Bush administration is even more inclined to favor economic and business interests in policy making on environmental and public health issues.

CONCLUSION

Providing a clean environment, a necessity for human health, is one of the most important functions of government. When people began to live together in cities and towns, they were dependent on the government—traditionally the local government—to provide clean drinking water and safe disposal of wastes. As the American population grew, municipalities and industry discharged their wastes into the air, water, and land, and it became apparent that the environment was deteriorating. Pollution tends to spread beyond local areas, requiring state and federal intervention to be effective. In the late 1960s and early 1970s, a number of significant federal laws were passed that set standards for air, water, and waste disposal aimed at protecting human health and cleaning up the environment.

Identification of hazards is an important first step in creating a safe environment. While environmental health has traditionally focused on microbial pathogens, many other phenomena can also threaten human health. Radiation, both natural and manmade, can be highly dangerous to living organisms, something that was not recognized when x rays were first discovered. Many metals and minerals, including lead, mercury, and asbestos, are toxic to humans. Pesticides and some industrial chemicals have been widely disseminated in the environment, and absorbed into the fatty tissues of animals and humans, where they persist indefinitely, sometimes with harmful effects.

Sometimes hazards of environmental exposures are recognized first in workers who develop occupational illnesses after being exposed on the job. The effects of a number of cancer-causing and neurotoxic substances have been recognized because workers have served as "guinea pigs," the first humans to test the safety of new chemicals.

Federal legislation in the 1960s and 1970s established a number of agencies charged with identifying environmental hazards and setting standards to protect human health. These include OSHA and the EPA. Standard setting was required for air quality, water quality, radiation safety, food and drug safety, the control of toxic substances, and the disposal of hazardous wastes.

Many of these mandates have been politically controversial, in that they have economic impact on various industries. Recent trends have brought greater willingness by public health advocates to weigh costs against benefits in evaluating risks.

Recently, environmentalists have recognized a new hazard—animal wastes from factory farms. These wastes are collected in "lagoons" and may be sprayed on fields, causing air and water pollution. Nearby residents and communities are often powerless to object to the unpleasant odors and, sometimes, toxic fumes. Because of the economic power of agricultural companies, federal and state governments have done little to regulate them.

REFERENCES

1. R. M. Macklis, "The Great Radium Scandal," *Scientific American* (August 1993): 94–99.
2. R. Seltser and P. E. Sartwell, "The Influence of Occupational Exposure to Radiation on the Mortality of American Radiologists and Other Medical Specialists," *American Journal of Epidemiology* 81 (1965): 2–22.
3. A. Nadakavukaren, *Our Global Environment: A Health Perspective*, 4th ed. (Prospect Heights, Illinois: Waveland Press, 1995).
4. U.S. Environmental Protection Agency, "What Should I Do if I Have a Mercury Spill?" *www.epa.gov/epaoswer/hazwaste/mercury/spills.htm*. Accessed May 18, 2005.
5. W. J. Rogan and J. H. Ware, "Exposure to Lead in Children—How Low Is Low Enough?" *New England Journal of Medicine* 348 (2003): 1515–1516.
6. P. Brodeur, *Outrageous Misconduct: The Asbestos Industry on Trial* (New York: Pantheon Books, 1985).

7. Global Environment & Technology Foundation, *Asbestos Strategies: Lessons Learned About Management and Use of Asbestos* (Annandale, Virginia: 2003).

8. U.S. Agency for Toxic Substances and Disease Registry, "Asbestos: Asbestos Exposure in Libby, Montana," *www.atsdr.cdc.gov/asbestos/asbestos_study.html*. Accessed November 16, 2004.

9. L. A. Peipins et al., "Radiographic Abnormalities and Exposure to Asbestos-Contaminated Vermiculite in the Community of Libby, Montana, USA," *Environmental Health Perspectives* 111 (2003): 1753–1759.

10. J. Marbella, "Mine Leaves Lasting Asbestos Scars on Montana Town," *Knight Ridder/Tribune Business News* (July 30, 2003).

11. U.S. Environmental Protection Agency, "Exposure and Human Health Evaluation of Airborne Pollution from the World Trade Center Disaster (External Review Draft)," *http://cfpub.epa.gov/ncea/cfm/recordisplay.cfm?deid_54667/*. Accessed November 16, 2004.

12. U.S. Centers for Disease Control and Prevention, "Physical Health Status of World Trade Center Rescue and Recovery Workers and Volunteers—New York City, July 2002–August 2004," *Morbidity and Mortality Weekly Report* 53 (2004): 807–812.

13. M. Wasserman et al., "World PCBs Map: Storage and Effects in Man and His Biologic Environment in the 1970s," *Annals of the New York Academy of Science* 320 (1979): 69–124.

14. E. G. Horn et al., "The Problem of PCBs in the Hudson River System," *Annals of the New York Academy of Science* 320 (1979): 591–609.

15. Y. Masuda, "The Yusho Rice Oil Poisoning Incident," in Schecter A., *Dioxins and Health* (New York: Plenum Press, 1994), 633–659.

16. C. C. Hsu et al., "The Yu-cheng Rice Oil Poisoning Incident," in Schecter A., *Dioxins and Health*: 661–684.

17. M. J. Schneider, *Persistent Poisons: Chemical Pollutants in the Environment* (New York: New York Academy of Sciences, 1979).

18. U.S. Environmental Protection Agency, *The Foundation for Global Action on Persistent Organic Pollutants: A United States Perspective*. March 2002. *www.epa.gov/nceawww1/pdfs/pops/POPsa.pdf*. Accessed November 20, 2004.

19. P. Spencer and H. H. Schaumburg eds., *Experimental and Clinical Neurotoxicology* (Baltimore, Maryland: Williams & Wilkins, 1980).

20. U.S. Environmental Protection Agency, "EPA Newsroom: Protect Water for Life." *www.epa.gov/epahome/headline_103102.htm*. Accessed November 29, 2004.

21. Sierra Club, "Clean Water & Factory Farms: Reports and Factsheets." *www.sierraclub.org/factoryfarms/factsheets/water.asp*. Accessed November 29, 2004.

22. S. Wing, "Social Responsibility and Research Ethics in Community-Driven Studies of Industrialized Hog Production," *Environmental Health Perspectives* 110 (2002): 437–444.

23. R. F. Kennedy Jr. and E. Schaeffer, "An Ill Wind From Factory Farms," *New York Times* (September 20, 2003).

24. Environmental Integrity Project, "33 Groups: Family Farms, Rural Communities Threatened by Craig Amendment Unleashing Factory Farm Pollution." *www.environmentalintegrity.org/pub252.cfm*. Accessed November 20, 2004.

25. National Institute for Occupational Safety and Health. NIOSH Carcinogen List. *www.cdc.gov/niosh/npotocca.html*. Accessed November 20, 2004.

26. U.S. Department of Labor, Occupational Safety and Health Administration, "10/16/2003—OSHA-Recognized Chemicals as Carcinogens or Potential Carcinogens For Hazard Communication Purposes," *www.osha.gov/pls/oshaweb/owadisp.show_document?p_table-INTERPRETATIONS&p_* . . . Accessed November 20, 2004.

27. OSHA National Toxicology Program, Department of Health and Human Services, "About the NTP," *http:///ntp-server.niehs.nih.gov/index.cfm?objectid=7201637B-BDB7-CEBA-F57E39896A08F1BB*. Accessed November 20, 2004.

28. A. Nadakavukaren, *Our Global Environment: A Health Perspective*, 5th ed. (Prospect Heights, Illinois: Waveland Press, 2000).

29. U.S. National Research Council, "Steering Committee on Identification of Toxic and Potentially Toxic Chemicals for Consideration by the National Toxicology Program," *Toxicity Testing: Strategies to Determine Needs and Priorities* (Washington, DC: National Academy Press, 1984).

30. J. Mendeloff, "Does Overregulation Cause Underregulation?: The Case of Toxic Substances," *Regulation* (September–October 1981).

CHAPTER 20

Clean Air: Is It Safe To Breathe?

Air Pollution

Air pollution caused by coal burning was a problem in London as early as the seventeenth century. With the advent of the Industrial Revolution in the eighteenth and nineteenth centuries, the air of many cities was blackened with smoke from industrial and household furnaces and railroad locomotives. In 1952, an unusual weather pattern caused a particularly severe air pollution crisis in London. A layer of cold, moist air hung motionless over the city for five days, and smoke, fumes, and motor vehicle exhaust accumulated. More than 4,000 deaths from both respiratory and heart disease were attributed to the foul air. Britain's first clean air act was passed soon after.[1]

Earlier, in 1948, the United States had been shocked by a similar deadly air pollution crisis caused by a similar weather pattern. A five-day atmospheric inversion trapped the smoke and fumes of a heavily industrialized Pennsylvania valley. In the small town of Donora, population 14,000, residents suffered eye, nose, and throat irritation and breathing difficulties resulting in twenty deaths.[1]

For most cities, the effects of air pollution were not so dramatic, but air quality was noticeably deteriorating in the United States during the 1950s and 1960s. Increasingly, this was due to automobiles. Los Angeles became known for its photochemical smog, the yellowish-brown haze caused by intense sunlight acting on the complex mix of chemicals emitted in motor vehicle exhaust. The irritating effects of air pollution were obvious to everyone and were especially harmful to the health of children and people with heart and lung diseases.

Efforts by cities and states to regulate pollutant emissions proved unsuccessful, and the federal government began attacking the problem in the mid 1960s. The first emission standards for automobiles were passed in 1965, to take effect with 1968 model year cars. The Clean Air Act of 1970 established strict air quality standards, set limits on several major pollutants, and mandated reduction of automobile and factory emissions. Since then, improving air quality has been an almost constant political battle. Environmental and public health groups have pressed for compliance and even stricter standards, while industries, supported by political conservatives, argue that the cost of pollution control is too high, hurting the national economy. Amendments to the Clean Air Act, strengthening some air quality regulations, were passed in 1977 and 1990. In general, the United States has cleaner air now than it did in 1970, but the battle is far from over.[1]

CRITERIA AIR POLLUTANTS

The Clean Air Act and its amendments require monitoring and regulation of six common air pollutants, called criteria air pollutants, known to be harmful to health and the environment: particulates, sulfur dioxide, carbon monoxide, nitrogen oxides, ozone, and lead.[1] All of these substances enter the air as a result of combustion—for energy in power plants or motor vehicles, or for solid waste disposal or industrial processes.

Particulate matter is the most visible form of air pollution—the smoke, soot, and ash that were so typical of the Industrial Revolution. Aesthetically, particulate matter is objectionable because it reduces visibility, forms layers of grime on buildings and streets, and corrodes metals. Epidemiologic studies have shown that particulates in the air also have harmful health effects. A cohort study conducted by Harvard epidemiologists compared the health of adults and children over the period 1975 to 1988 in six cities with markedly different amounts of particulate pollution in their air.[2] Residents of Steubenville, Ohio, the most polluted city in the study, were more likely to suffer from respiratory symptoms and had poorer lung function than residents of Portage, Wisconsin, the least polluted city. Death rates in Steubenville were 26 percent higher than those in Portage. In a larger study of 151 cities, death rates were increased by 15 percent in the cities with the dirtiest air.

Early air pollution regulation focused on limiting total particulate matter. However a number of studies, including the six cities study, suggest that the smallest particles are the most dangerous because they can evade the body's natural defenses and penetrate deeply into the lungs, becoming a chronic source of irritation. In 1987, the Environmental Protection Agency (EPA) revised the standard so that the smaller particles—those with a diameter less than ten micrometers (PM_{10})—were limited. In 1997, the EPA issued further limits for particles smaller than 2.5 micrometers ($PM_{2.5}$).[1]

Opponents of stricter regulations tried hard to discredit the six cities study and other data, but the evidence was strengthened by a study, published in 2000, that monitored air pollution and death rates from cardiovascular and respiratory illness in twenty of the largest American cities over the period from 1987 to 1994. These researchers concluded that peaks in levels of PM_{10} were significantly associated with a higher number of deaths on the following day.[3] Opponents of the 1997 $PM_{2.5}$ standard sued the EPA, demanding a cost-benefit analysis for implementing the new rules.[4] In 2001, the Supreme Court ruled unanimously that a cost-benefit analysis was not necessary and that the EPA must consider only public health and safety in setting the standards.[5] The importance of $PM_{2.5}$ was affirmed in a large cohort study conducted by the American Cancer Society, published in 2002. The researchers monitored 500,000 residents of metropolitan areas throughout the United States and found that their risk of death from lung cancer, other lung diseases, and heart disease was proportional to the $PM_{2.5}$ levels in the area where they lived.[6] The standard set in 1997 is still in effect, but other actions of the Bush administration throw doubt on the future of clean air regulation, as discussed later in this chapter.

Sulfur dioxide is produced by combustion of sulfur-containing fuels, especially coal. It irritates the respiratory tract, but its most significant impact is as a precursor to acid rain, a major threat to the environment. Sulfur dioxide tends to stick to fine particulates in the air, increasing their potential for causing respiratory damage.[1] Sulfur dioxide levels, which are highest in the vicinity of large industrial facilities, have declined by 52 percent since 1982.[7]

Carbon monoxide is a highly toxic gas, most of which is produced in motor vehicle exhaust. It interferes with the oxygen-carrying capacity of the blood and is therefore especially harmful to patients with cardiovascular disease, who are more likely to suffer heart attacks when exposed to higher concentrations of the pollutant. Carbon monoxide also affects the brain, causing headaches and impairing mental processes. Carbon monoxide levels, which generally are highest in areas of high traffic congestion, have decreased by 62 percent since 1982.[8]

Nitrogen oxides are the chemicals responsible for the yellowish-brown appearance of smog. Like sulfur dioxide, nitrogen oxides are respiratory irritants that contribute to acid rain. They also contribute to the formation of ozone. Nitrogen oxides have proven difficult to control, and emissions have increased by 9 percent since 1982, although concentrations in urban areas have declined. The increase in emissions is believed due to nonroad engines and diesel vehicles.[9]

Ozone, a highly reactive variant of oxygen, is produced by photochemical reactions in which sunlight acts on other air pollutants including nitrogen oxides. It is very irritating to the eyes and respiratory system, and chronic exposure can cause permanent damage to the lungs. Ozone levels in the air are an indicator of various other chemicals produced by motor vehicles and are often used as a general measure of air pollution. As discussed later, ozone is an important protective component of the upper atmosphere, but at low altitudes its effects are harmful.

Ozone levels tend to be highest in suburban areas, downwind from urban centers. They also tend to be high in many national parks, contributing to haze that obscures the views.[10] A study of ninety-five large urban communities in the United States, published in 2004, found that even short-term increases in ozone levels lead to increases in mortality from cardiovascular and respiratory diseases.[11]

When an area does not meet the air quality standard for one of the criteria pollutants, the EPA may designate it a nonattainment area and impose measures designed to force the area to attain the standard. According to the EPA, 124 areas in the nation were classified as nonattainment areas for one or more criteria pollutant in 2002.[12] Poor ozone air quality is especially widespread, affecting broad areas in the Northeast, Mid-Atlantic, Midwest, and California, with smaller areas in the South and south-central United States. In 2003, more than 100 million people lived in the 209 counties with poor ozone air quality.[13]

Lead is a highly toxic metal that can damage the nervous system, blood, and kidneys, posing a special risk to the development of children's intellectual abilities. The main source of lead as an air pollutant was the use of leaded gasoline, which was phased out in the United States during the 1980s. While environmental lead from other sources is still a threat to children, the amount of lead in the air has decreased dramatically, having dropped by 94 percent between 1982 and 2001.[14]

In addition to the criteria air pollutants, which are widespread, a large number of other toxic and carcinogenic chemicals are released into the air by local factories, waste disposal sites, and other sources. The Clean Air Act of 1970 directed the EPA to identify and set emission standards for such hazards, but as of 1993, only eight had been acted on: asbestos, mercury, beryllium, benzene, vinyl chloride, arsenic, radionuclides, and coke oven emissions.[1] As described in Chapter 19, legal battles over each standard have made progress painfully slow.

Clean Air Act amendments passed in 1990 contained a number of provisions designed to speed up the process. Congress identified 188 specific chemicals for the EPA to regulate. Rather than addressing each chemical individually, however, the agency is to identify major sources that emit these pollutants and develop technical standards that will reduce the emissions. Since then, the EPA had issued rules covering over eighty categories of major industrial sources, including chemical plants, oil refineries, aerospace manufacturers, and steel mills, as well as categories of smaller sources such as dry cleaners.[15] It has also identified thirty-three toxic air pollutants that pose the greatest threats to public health in urban areas and developed health risk assessments on them.

STRATEGIES FOR MEETING STANDARDS

Motor vehicles are the number one source of air pollution in urban areas, and the number of motor vehicles is increasing far more rapidly than the population. The standard approach for limiting air pollution from motor vehicles has been limitation of tail pipe emissions by mandating changes both in automobile engineering and in fuel. Significant improvement was achieved by the use of catalytic converters, devices that have been repeatedly improved to meet increasingly strict standards. The newest cars have reduced emissions of carbon monoxide and ozone-producing chemicals by about 90 percent and nitrogen oxides by 70 percent below those of cars without emission controls.[1] The ban on leaded gasoline has almost eliminated lead as an air pollutant.

Because of the continuing increase in the number of cars, however, and because older cars and poorly maintained vehicles continued to emit high levels of pollutants, a number of other requirements were included in the 1990 Clean Air amendments. Special attention was paid to geographic areas that fail to meet standards for one or more criteria pollutants. These requirements include use of less polluting alternative fuels such as ethanol and reformulated gasoline, installation of vapor recovery systems on gasoline pumps, and inspection and maintenance programs that require annual measurement of tailpipe emissions on each car, with mandatory remediation on cars that fail the test. Another mandate that has proved highly controversial is that automakers should develop and market "zero-emission" vehicles—electric cars—a goal that has not as yet been achieved in any practical way. Complicating efforts to reduce tailpipe emissions has been the increase in the number of pickup trucks and SUVs, for which the standards for passenger cars did not apply. The rules were changed in 1999 to require all vehicles to meet the same standards by 2009.[16]

Ideally, the number of cars on the road in highly populated areas should be reduced. Public transportation undoubtedly benefits air quality in New York City and Washington D.C., but too many American cities—including Los Angeles—are not designed for efficient public systems. While Americans support most measures to ensure cleaner air, they consistently resist efforts to move them out of their private automobiles. Many urban areas have developed, with modest success, policies to encourage carpooling by providing high-occupancy vehicle lanes and taxing parking spaces. Substantially higher taxes on gasoline, such as those in most European and Asian countries, would undoubtedly discourage unnecessary driving; but raising gas taxes seems to be considered political suicide by most politicians. Efficient public transport systems require some assistance from public funds—the dreaded increase in taxes.

A variety of strategies have been effective in reducing industrial sources of pollution. Foremost among them have been installation of scrubbers on smokestacks and a move to less polluting fuels, especially away from high-sulfur coal. A new approach included in the 1990 Clean Air Act amendments is the creation of pollution allowances that can be bought and sold. Instead of requiring each factory or power plant to meet defined standards, an overall national or regional emissions goal is set, and that goal is set lower each year. Each potential polluter is assigned a fraction of that amount as an allowance, which can be used or sold. Plants that choose to clean up their technology can recoup some of their investment by selling their allowances to plants that find cleanup too expensive. This market approach was expected to achieve Clean Air Act goals with a maximum of flexibility and a minimum of political pain.[1]

A provision of the 1977 Clean Air Act Amendments that has generated a great deal of controversy is called "New Source Review." When the original Act was passed in 1970, it set standards for newly built power plants, but did not require changes to existing plants. Because this provision led the companies to improve existing facilities without cleaning up their emissions, the 1977 rules required that companies that substantially upgraded their old plants had to bring them into compliance with the standards. Many companies, however, ignored the rules. In the mid-1990s, after years of negotiations with the industry, the Clinton administration sued seven electric utility companies in the Midwest and South to force them to comply with the law and launched investigations of dozens of others.

When the younger President Bush took office in 2001, his administration responded to the complaints of the utilities by setting out to weaken the environmental laws. In 2002, the president proposed the "Clear Skies Initiative," which replaced the New Source Review requirement with a market-based trading system that clearly set lower emissions standards than those required by the Clean Air Act. Congress did not act on the proposal; so the Bush administration began to administratively change the rules. It also dropped the investigations of noncompliant companies. In late 2003, attorneys general of fifteen states, in cooperation with national environmental organizations, filed their own lawsuits against a number of the polluting power plants. Most of the states that are suing are in the Northeast, where air is polluted by emissions blown in from the Midwest. The legal battles are expected to continue for years, and it is not clear that the states will have the legal and financial muscle to prevail against the powerful energy companies. According to a report by the American Lung Association, quoted in the *New York Times*, the Bush administration rule changes are "the most harmful and unlawful air-pollution initiative ever undertaken by the federal government."[17]

In a surprise move toward cleaner air, however, the Bush administration announced, in May 2004, rules that will require vehicles using diesel fuel to meet stricter standards on emissions. Engine makers will need to install emission control systems and refineries will need to produce cleaner-burning diesel fuel. The new regulations will apply to nonroad vehicles such as tractors, bulldozers, locomotives, and barges, as well as to buses and trucks. The change is expected to significantly cut emissions of particulate matter and also, because diesel fuel contains high concentrations of sulfur, to reduce levels of sulfur dioxide in the air, helping to reduce acid rain.[18]

A modest law that took effect in 1988, the Emergency Planning and Community Right-to-Know Act (EPCRA), has had unexpectedly beneficial effects in prodding companies to voluntarily restrict their discharge of air pollutants. The law was passed in response to the infamous Bhopal disaster of 1984, in which a leak of isocyanate gas occurred at a Union Carbide pesticide factory in India, killing over 10,000 people who lived nearby. EPCRA requires businesses to report the locations and quantities of chemicals stored at their sites. This allows communities to prepare for emergencies such as chemical spills. The law also requires that manufacturers disclose information on the kinds and amounts of toxic pollutants they discharge into the local environment each year.[19] Frequently, local communities, alarmed by the information, pressure the industry to cut back on their emissions. The program, known as the Toxics Release Inventory, is credited with reducing industrial releases of toxic chemicals by 49 percent by 2002.[20]

Even before September 11, 2001, some industries were pressuring the EPA to relax requirements of EPCRA, claiming, among other reasons, that publication of such information would increase communities' vulnerability to terrorism.[19] After September 11, the EPA has gone much further in trying to restrict public access to environmental information. Some critics claim that the terrorism argument is being used as a smokescreen to protect industry from lawsuits or bad publicity. As one of these critics is quoted as saying, "What's tricky is finding the right balance between protection from terrorists on one hand and providing information for the neighbors so they can be safe."[21(p.107)]

Urban areas that are having the most difficulty meeting air quality standards by controls on motor vehicles and factories must consider regulating sources of pollution that have thus far been left alone. For example, Los Angeles banned the use of charcoal lighter fluid for barbecues and regulates the exhaust of gas-powered lawn mowers. Dry cleaners, auto body shops, and furniture refinishers are also significant sources of toxic air pollutants that are regulated in the Los Angeles area.[22] In 2004, the region announced a program through which residents could turn in old gasoline lawnmowers in exchange for new, nonpolluting electric mowers. There is also a program in the state of California that offers incentives for people to turn in old cars, trucks, buses, and farm vehicles.[23]

Overall, the United States has made substantial progress in fighting air pollution. As shown in Figure 20–1, emissions of most common pollutants have decreased significantly since 1970 despite significant increases in the nation's population and economic growth. In Los Angeles, concentrations of ozone, historically the most difficult pollutant to control, are now only one half what they were in the mid-1970s; still, ozone levels in Los Angeles air violated federal standards on 120 days in 2003.[24]

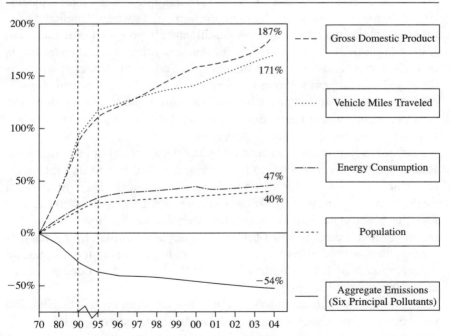

Figure 20–1 Comparison of Growth Areas and Emissions
Source: U.S. Environmental Protection Agency. "Comparison of Growth Areas and Emissions." *www.epa.gov/air/airtrends/econ_emission.html*, Accessed March 3, 2005.

INDOOR AIR QUALITY

While most public concern and political action have focused on outdoor air pollution, the 1980s saw increased attention paid to indoor air quality. In fact, most people spend more time indoors than out, and concentrations of many pollutants trapped inside a building may exceed those outdoors in all but the most polluted cities. The problem is exacerbated by energy conservation measures that minimize the quantity of outdoor air allowed inside. In the extreme, the lack of sufficient ventilation may lead to "sick building syndrome," in which building occupants develop an array of symptoms that disappear when they go outdoors.

The most common indoor air pollutants are tobacco smoke, other products of combustion, radon gas, consumer products that release chemicals into the air, and biological pollutants, including bacteria, mold, dust mites, and animal dander. "Second-hand smoke" has become a political issue in recent years, and many states now ban smoking in various public places. In the homes of smokers—beyond the arm of laws and regulations— tobacco smoke may be the most significant air pollutant and the main source of particulate pollution for children. Smoking also increases levels of carbon monoxide in indoor air and is a source of benzene, which is toxic and carcinogenic. Wood-burning stoves and fireplaces emit significant amounts of particulate matter and gases into the air. Gas ranges and furnaces burn more cleanly than wood stoves, but they produce carbon monoxide and nitrogen oxide.

Radon is a radioactive gas emitted by the decay of radium and uranium. Radon has long been known to be a major health threat to uranium miners, who had a high risk of developing lung cancer. Then in 1984, a nuclear power plant worker set off radiation detection alarms on his way *into* the plant, near Philadelphia.[1] Investigation of his home found that radon gas levels there were 1,000 times higher than normal. Since that discovery, elevated radon levels have been found in homes in most states; an estimated one of fifteen homes in the United States has concentrations above the standard set by EPA.

The health threat from indoor radon pollution is not clear. The EPA and most other public health agencies believe that, extrapolating from the evidence obtained by studying uranium miners, radon in the home must be regarded as a serious cancer threat, causing an estimated 7,000 to 30,000 lung cancer deaths annually.[1] Skeptics believe these estimates are too high, noting that miners' effective exposure is much greater than what is measured, because the radon adheres to dust particles that lodge in the lungs. In miners, smoking acts synergistically with radon in causing lung cancer, meaning that the risk to miners who smoke is many times greater than that of the average smoking non-miner or nonsmoking miner. By analogy, the danger of radon in homes would be greatly enhanced if the residents are smokers.

Radon enters homes by seeping up from the soil and rock through dirt floors, crawl spaces, cracks in cement floors and walls, and through sump holes and floor drains. It may dissolve in well water and be released into the air during showers or baths. Measurement of radon is easily done with inexpensive kits and, in most homes where elevated levels are found, measures to seal cracks and openings are effective in reducing levels.

Other common indoor air pollutants include formaldehyde, a possibly carcinogenic gas that irritates the respiratory system and is contained in insulation, particleboard, plywood, and some floor coverings and textiles. In the past, elevated levels of formaldehyde were common in prefabricated and mobile homes, but since 1985 the Department of Housing and Urban Development has specified that plywood and particleboard must conform to specified formaldehyde emissions limits.[25] Pesticides, dry-cleaning solvents, paints and paint thinners, carpet glues, hair spray, and air fresheners are other chemicals that may pollute indoor air and should be used with caution because of possible adverse health effects. While most biological air pollutants, such as mold, house mites, and animal dander, are a problem only for people who are allergic to them, air-borne microbes can pose serious health hazards: witness Legionnaire's disease, caused by bacteria vaporized from air-conditioning systems; and hantavirus released into the air from rodent urine or feces. (See Chapters 4 and 10.)

GLOBAL EFFECTS OF AIR POLLUTION

Because air pollutants are the most mobile of all forms of pollution, their ill effects may spread far beyond the immediate area where they are released. In fact, evidence is mounting that human activities are actually changing the composition of the atmosphere. The ultimate effects on public health from these changes are still a matter of speculation and controversy, but the effects are unlikely to be beneficial and may be quite harmful.

Acid rain is produced when two common air pollutants—sulfur dioxide and nitrogen dioxide—react with water to form sulfuric acid and nitric acid. In the United States, the industrial areas of the Midwest are a major source of the pollutants that acidify rainfall in the East, since prevailing winds blow from west to east. Acid rain in eastern Canada resulting from U.S. air pollution is a cause of diplomatic tension between the two countries. The environment in Europe, the former Soviet Union, and southern China—everywhere that coal and oil are intensively used—is also seriously affected by acid rain.

Acid rain damages forests, reduces crop yields, and corrodes surfaces of buildings and statuary. It turns the water in lakes and rivers acidic, killing freshwater shrimp, wiping out bacteria on lake bottoms, and interfering with fish reproduction. Some lakes are so acidic that they can no longer support life: all fish species disappear, as do most frogs, salamanders, and aquatic insects. Because many metals, such as aluminum, lead, copper, and mercury are soluble in acid, the increasing acidity of water may lead to toxic levels of metals in drinking water supplies. There is evidence that regulations on industrial pollutants in the United States have helped to bring down levels of sulfur dioxide in the air and have begun to reduce the acidity of rainfall in the Northeast. Improvements in the acidity of lakes and streams is expected to lag behind changes in rain and snow, but a recent EPA publication reported that approximately one-quarter to one-third of formerly acidic surface waters in the Adirondacks, the Upper Midwest, and the Appalachian Plateau were no longer acidic.[26]

Depletion of the ozone layer is another manifestation of the global effects of certain air pollutants. Ozone, which is so harmful to respiratory systems at ground level, is a natural component of the upper atmosphere that provides a layer of protection against ultraviolet radiation. The detection of chlorofluorocarbons (CFCs) in the ozone "hole" which opened over Antarctica in the early 1980s convinced scientists that these chemicals, which were used as refrigerants and spray can propellants, were responsible for the breakdown of ozone. Being very stable, CFCs drift upwards to the ozone layer, where they may cause damage for many decades. The increased ultraviolet radiation that reaches ground level is causing greatly increased rates of cataracts, already a major cause of blindness in the world, and skin cancer. It also has harmful effects on other organisms, including food crops, and could be a major threat to life on the planet.

This global problem clearly required international action. After several years of controversy and denial, diplomats from twenty-nine nations met in Montreal, Canada, in 1987 to sign an agreement aimed at reducing the production and use of CFCs.[1] As evidence of ozone depletion continued to mount, the Montreal Protocol has been strengthened four times, now calling for the elimination of chemicals that deplete ozone.[1] The protocol has been signed by 188 nations, with fewer nations ratifying the revisions.[27] The United States has ended production of CFCs and many other ozone depleting substances. However, millions of pounds of CFCs already in use will continue to be released into the atmosphere for years. The ozone layer appears to have stabilized during the 1990s, and there is hope that it will begin to regenerate during the early twenty-first century.[28]

Carbon dioxide is not strictly an air pollutant—along with nitrogen, oxygen, and argon, it is one of the four major component of the atmosphere—but its increasing proportion in the air has ominous implications for the future of the earth's environment. Carbon dioxide levels have been rising since the beginning of the Industrial Revolution due to the burning of fossil fuel. They are now about 30 percent higher than they were at the beginning of the Industrial Revolution, and they are increasing rapidly.[1]

Atmospheric carbon dioxide acts like the glass of a greenhouse, allowing sunlight to enter but trapping the heat inside. The resulting "greenhouse effect" leads to warmer temperatures at the earth's surface. Evidence is growing that global warming is already under way. It has been hard to definitively prove that the average temperature of the earth's surface is increasing because of the normal fluctuations from year to year and even from one decade to another, but the evidence is now quite strong that the average temperature of the earth has increased by about 1 degree Farenheit since the late 1800s.[1] The causes and effects of global warming are discussed further in Chapter 24.

CONCLUSION

Air pollution, while a conspicuous problem in cities for more than two centuries, was recognized as a severe threat to health in the 1940s and 1950s. Weather-related events together with smoke from the burning of fossil fuels in England and the United States caused local air pollution crises that led to deaths from respiratory and heart disease.

Because air pollution does not respect political boundaries, interventions, to be effective, must be implemented on a national and sometimes global scale. The United States began establishing regulations to control air pollution beginning in the 1960s. Regulations on both automobile and factory emissions have been repeatedly strengthened since the Clean

Air Act of 1970. Each new standard has been highly controversial, opposed by industry, congressional conservatives, and now the Bush administration.

Six criteria air pollutants were identified by the Clean Air Act: particulate matter, sulfur dioxide, carbon monoxide, nitrogen oxides, ozone, and lead. These pollutants must be monitored by the EPA, and levels in the air have fallen since 1970. A larger number of other chemicals have also been identified as pollutants, but standards have been set on only eight of them. The Clean Air Act amendments of 1990 required the EPA to identify major sources of these emissions and to set emission standards for the source categories rather than for individual pollutants.

Strategies for meeting air pollution standards include technological improvements in motor vehicles and factory smokestacks. Congress has encouraged a flexible approach by creating pollution allowances that can be bought and sold, permitting industries to cooperate in meeting the standards. Requirements that industries disclose information on their emissions often result in pressure on companies from local communities to reduce the pollution.

Indoor air may have even more significant effects on health than outdoor air, since most people spend more time indoors than out, and many indoor pollutants are trapped inside buildings at high concentrations. Common indoor air pollutants include tobacco smoke, radon gas, consumer products that release chemicals into the air, and biological pollutants such as bacteria and mold.

Air pollution can create acid rain, which profoundly affects the environment. Depletion of the ozone layer by CFCs increases risk of skin cancer and cataracts and has harmful effects on other organisms. Increases in carbon dioxide concentrations in the air lead to the greenhouse effect, resulting in global warming.

REFERENCES

1. A. Nadakavukaren, *Our Global Environment: A Health Perspective*, 5th ed. (Prospect Heights, Illinois: Waveland Press, 1995).
2. D. W. Dockery et al., "An Association Between Air Pollution and Mortality in Six U.S. Cities," *New England Journal of Medicine* 329 (1993): 1753–1759.
3. J. M. Samet, F. Dominici, F. C. Curriero, I. Coursac, and S. L. Zeger, "Fine Particulate Air Pollution and Mortality in 20 U.S. Cities, 1987–1994," *New England Journal of Medicine* 349 (2000): 1742–1749.
4. J. H. Ware, "Editorial: Particulate Air Pollution and Mortality—Clearing the Air," *New England Journal of Medicine* 343 (2000): 1798–1799.

5. L. Greenhouse, "E.P.A.'s Right to Set Air Rules Wins Supreme Court Backing," *New York Times* (February 28, 2001): A1.

6. C. A. Pope III et al., "Lung Cancer, Cardiopulmonary Mortality, and Long-term Exposure to Fine Particulate Air Pollution," *Journal of the American Medical Association* 287 (2002): 1132–1141.

7. U.S. Environmental Protection Agency, "National Air Quality 2001 Status and Trends: Sulfur Dioxide (SO_2)," *www.epa.gov/air/airtrends/aqtrnd01/sulfur.html*. Accessed November 21, 2004.

8. U.S. Environmental Protection Agency, "National Air Quality 2001 Status and Trends: Carbon Monoxide (CO)," *www.epa.gov/air/airtrends/aqtrnd01/carbon.html*. Accessed November 21, 2004.

9. U.S. Environmental Protection Agency, "National Air Quality 2001 Status and Trends: Nitrogen Dioxide (NO_2)." *www.epa.gov/air/airtrends/aqtrnd01/nitrodox.html*. Accessed November 21, 2004.

10. U.S. Environmental Protection Agency, "National Air Quality 2001 Status and Trends: Ground-Level Ozone (O_3)." *www.epa.gov/air/airtrends/aqtrnd01/gndozone.html*. Accessed November 21, 2004.

11. M. L. Bell et al., "Ozone and Short-term Mortality in 95 U.S. Urban Communities, 1987–2000," *Journal of the American Medical Association* 292 (2004): 2372–2378.

12. U.S. Environmental Protection Agency, "Air Trends: Criteria Pollutants— Nonattainment Areas," *www.epa.gov/airtrends/non.html*. Accessed November 21, 2004.

13. U.S. Environmental Protection Agency, "Air Trends: Introduction," *www.epa.gov/airtrends/2003ozonereport/intro.html*. Accessed November 21, 2004.

14. U.S. Environmental Protection Agency, "National Air Quality 2001 Status and Trends. Lead (Pb)," *www.epa.gov/air/airtrends/aqtrnd01/lead.html*. Accessed November 21, 2004.

15. U.S. Environmental Protection Agency, "Toxic Air Pollutants: About Air Toxics, Health and Ecological Effects," *www.epa.gov/air/toxicair/newtoxics.html*. Accessed November 21, 2004.

16. U.S. Environmental Protection Agency, "National News: Automakers and Gasoline Refiners Join EPA to Celebrate Milestone in Clean Air Program." January 26, 2004. *www.epa.gov/air/oarnew.html*. Accessed November 22, 2004.

17. B. Barcotte, "Up in Smoke: How the Bush Administration Quietly—and Radically— Transformed the Nation's Clean-Air Policy," *New York Times Magazine* (April 1, 2004): 39–44, 66, 73, 76, 78.

18. U.S. Environmental Protection Agency, "New Clean Diesel Rule Major Step in a Decade of Progress" (May 11, 2004). *www.epa.gov/newsroom/*. Accessed November 27, 2004.

19. G. E. R. Hook and G. W. Lucier, "The Right to Know Is for Everyone," *Environmental Health Perspectives* 108 (2000): A160–A162.

20. U.S. Environmental Protection Agency, "National News: EPA Press Advisory: (1) 2002 Toxics Release Inventory Released . . . June 23, 2004." *www.epa.gov/newsroom/*. Accessed November 27, 2004.

21. R. Dahl, "Does Secrecy Equal Security? Limiting Access to Environmental Information," *Environmental Health Perspectives* 112 (2004): A104–A107.

22. W. Boly, "Smog City Wants to Make This Perfectly Clear," *Health* 6, No. 2 (1992): 54.

23. B. Bergman, "To Cut Smog, Los Angeles Places a Bounty on Mowers," *New York Times* (May 5, 2004).
24. South Coast Air Quality Management District, "Historic Ozone Air Quality Trends," *www.aqmd.gov/smog/o3trend.html*. Accessed November 26, 2004.
25. U.S. Environmental Protection Agency, "The Inside Story—A Guide to Indoor Air Quality," EPA Document 402-K-93-007, April 1995. *www.epa.gov/iaq/pubs/insidest. html*. Accessed November 26, 2004.
26. U.S. Environmental Protection Agency, "Response of Surface Water Chemistry to the Clean Air Act Amendments of 1990. January 2003." *www.epa.gov/ord/htm/CAAA-2002-report-2col-rev-4.pdf*. Accessed November 26, 2004.
27. United Nations Environment Programme: Ozone Secretariat. "Table: Status of Ratification." *www.unep.org/ozone/Treaties_and_Ratification/2C_ratificationTable. asp*. Accessed November 27, 2004.
28. U.S. Environmental Protection Agency, "Environmental Indicators: Ozone Depletion." *www.epa.gov/science/indicat/index.html*. Accessed November 27, 2004.

CHAPTER 21

Clean Water: A Limited Resource

Water Pollution

The importance of safe drinking water to public health has been clear since John Snow identified polluted water as the source of London's cholera epidemic in 1855, as described in Chapter 4. Major epidemics of cholera and other waterborne diseases broke out periodically in the United States until the end of the nineteenth century. Ninety thousand people died of cholera in 1885 in Chicago, persuading city officials to stop discharging the city's sewage into Lake Michigan, which was also the source of municipal drinking water.[1] While contaminated water is still a major cause of disease and death in developing countries, Americans expect that their tap water will be safe to drink and, for the most part, it is. Nevertheless,

367

647 outbreaks of waterborne diseases were documented by the Centers for Disease Control and Prevention (CDC) between 1971 and 1994,[2] including the 1993 cryptospiridium outbreak in Milwaukee described in the Prologue. Since 1994, the CDC has recorded an average of twelve outbreaks each year.

Common water pollutants include, in addition to microbial pathogens, a wide range of chemicals that may not only be toxic in drinking water, but have harmful effects on fish and wildlife. Many chemicals have been discharged into waterways as industrial wastes, such as the mercury in Minamata Bay or the polychlorinated biphenyls (PCBs) in the Hudson River. (See Chapter 19.) People may then be poisoned by eating the fish that have accumulated these toxins in their flesh. Other sources of pollution include deposition from the air, as in acid rain, or runoff from the land.

Until the early 1970s, individual states were responsible for the quality of their waterways and the purity of their drinking water. This arrangement was unable to control water pollution for the same reason that it could not control air pollution: the sources of pollution and the communities affected by the pollution may be under different political jurisdiction. For example, New Orleans draws its drinking water from the Mississippi River; it was helpless to stop cities upstream, located in other states, from discharging sewage and industrial wastes into the river.

A number of infamous pollution cases occurred in the United States in the 1960s and 1970s that inspired the passage of federal legislation. The discovery of PCBs in the Hudson River led to a ban on commercial fishing there because the chemicals were so concentrated in the flesh of the fish. Residents of Duluth, Minnesota, were alarmed to learn that the Reserve Mining Company had been dumping asbestos-containing wastewater into Lake Superior, the source of municipal water, for over 20 years.[3] While no one knew whether asbestos was as carcinogenic when drunk as it was when breathed, bottled water was distributed to the population for over a year until a new water filtration plant was completed. The James River was so badly polluted with the insecticide Kepone, discharged from a manufacturing plant in Hopewell, Virginia, between 1966 and 1975, that no practical way has ever been proposed to clean it up. The plant was closed, not because of the environmental damage it caused, but because so many of its employees suffered neurological, liver, and other damage from Kepone poisoning.[4] Perhaps the most dramatic call to action occurred in 1969, when the Cuyahoga River in Ohio caught fire because it had so much oil floating on its surface.[3]

The two goals of cleaning up lakes and rivers and ensuring safe drinking water are distinct but related, and Congress has addressed them in separate legislation: the Clean Water Act of 1972, amended in 1977 and 1987, and the Safe Drinking Water Act of 1974, which was rewritten in 1996.[1] Since half the drinking water in the United States comes from lakes and rivers, success in meeting the goals of the Clean Water Act is obviously a help in achieving the goals of the Safe Drinking Water Act.

CLEAN WATER ACT

The Clean Water Act set national goals that lakes and rivers should be "fishable" and "swimmable" and that all pollutant discharges should be eliminated. First attempts at cleaning up the nation's waterways focused on "point source" pollution—well-defined locations that discharge pollutants into lakes and rivers. Most point source pollution comes from municipal sewage and industrial discharges. The 1972 and 1977 legislation imposed strict controls on these sources; it also provided billions of dollars of funding to assist municipalities in building wastewater treatment facilities. With the success of these efforts, it became apparent that a great deal of pollution washed into waterways from the air and the land. The 1987 reauthorization of the Clean Water Act focused on cleaning up nonpoint source pollution, which has proven to be a much more difficult task.[1]

Laws governing point source pollution set requirements for treating wastewater so that it can be discharged into waterways without causing human health problems or disrupting the aquatic environment. In the case of sewage treatment plants, this requires several steps. The primary step is to remove suspended solids by screening them and then allowing them to settle out by gravity in settling tanks. The secondary stage is to break down the remaining organic material using biological processes: the wastewater is mixed with bacteria and plenty of oxygen, resulting in conversion of the organic wastes into carbon dioxide, water, and minerals. The wastewater is then usually disinfected with chlorine before being discharged into the environment.[1]

While the treatment process produces a liquid discharge that meets standards of environmental safety, it also generates "sludge," the solid waste left behind on screens and at the bottom of settling tanks. Enormous amounts of sludge are generated by municipal sewage plants, creating a major disposal problem. In the past, sludge was often dumped in the ocean or incinerated, but these methods create other pollution problems. Congress prohibited the ocean dumping of sludge in 1992. Some communities bury it in landfills, but landfill space is running low, as discussed in Chapter 22. Since sludge is rich in nutrients, the Environmental Protection Agency (EPA) encouraged the use of treated sludge as a fertilizer and soil conditioner to improve marginal lands and increase forest productivity. Currently, 54 percent of the six million tons of sewage sludge generated every year is used as fertilizer. However, concerns have been raised about the possibility that toxic chemicals and pathogens may be present in the sludge and harm human health. In early 2004, the EPA announced that it would conduct studies to address these concerns.[5]

About 70 percent of the U.S. population is served by sewage treatment plants. Most of the other 30 percent use on-site septic systems, which function as miniature sewage treatment plants including the use of bacteria to break down organic wastes. Like the larger plants, septic systems produce sludge, which must be pumped out periodically. Improperly constructed and poorly maintained septic systems contribute to pollution of waterways and often result in public health problems.[1]

Discharges from industrial sources are the second major category of point source pollution, which is strictly regulated by the Clean Water Act. The EPA is required to develop standards for the release of various categories of pollutants into the environment. Industries that discharge directly into the nation's waterways are required to obtain a permit specifying allowable amounts and constituents of pollutants they may discharge. They must routinely monitor their discharges and report regularly to the EPA.[1]

Industrial wastes may cause special problems if they are discharged into sewer systems and pass through a municipal sewage treatment plant, occasionally with disastrous consequences. In 1977, pesticide wastes illegally dumped into the sewers of Louisville, Kentucky, killed all the microbes responsible for the secondary treatment process, rendering the plant ineffective. For nearly two years while the plant was being cleaned up, 100 million gallons of untreated sewage were discharged into the Ohio River every day. In 1981 in Cincinnati, a paint factory discharged hydrochloric acid into the city sewers, corroding the sewer pipe and causing it to collapse, leaving a hole in the street twenty-four feet in diameter.[1]

To prevent such problems, the Clean Water Act requires pretreatment of industrial wastes that are discharged into sewers. But standards have not been set for many smaller commercial establishments, including car washes and photo processing plants. Hazardous chemicals also enter sewer systems from residences, when people dispose of bleaches, toilet bowl cleaners, paint thinners, and other household substances by flushing them down the drain.

As strict limits have been set on pollution from sewage systems and industry, non-point source pollution has become an increasingly important threat to water quality. These contaminants come from stormwater runoff from farmland, construction sites, and urban streets. Agriculture is the leading source of water pollution in the United States, contributing soil, manure fertilizers, and pesticides that wash into streams and lakes. Agricultural runoff is believed to have been the source of the Milwaukee cryptosporidiosis outbreak. Construction activities also contribute soil to runoff water, together with oil, tar, paint, and cleaning solvents. Contaminants contributed by urban street runoff include sand, dirt, road salt, oil, grease, heavy metal particles, pesticides and fertilizers from lawns, and animal and bird droppings.

A variety of approaches must be used to minimize pollution caused by stormwater runoff. These include preventing soil erosion by planting vegetation on exposed soil, incorporating more green space into urban areas, minimizing the use of chemical fertilizers and pesticides, and controlling litter.

Air pollution is also a source of water pollution. In addition to acid rain, a number of other chemicals are deposited into lakes, rivers, and oceans from the air. These include lead, asbestos, PCBs, and various pesticides. It has been shown that the major portion of PCBs in the Great Lakes comes from the air. Industrial accidents and spills also contribute to pollution of waterways.

SAFE DRINKING WATER

Almost half the drinking water in the United States comes from rivers and lakes. Thus it is likely to be contaminated by the point and non-point source pollutants discussed above. The other half comes from underground aquifers; these are generally of better quality but are increasingly susceptible to contamination by leaching from landfills, leaky storage tanks, and other sources of toxic chemicals. Improvements in surface water quality brought about by the Clean Water Act makes the job easier for community water systems, which must, however, meet much higher standards to produce potable water—water that is safe for human consumption.

All community systems need to treat their water so that, theoretically, all contaminants are removed. The steps needed to produce potable water vary depending on the source of the water and the type of contaminants. The basic steps common to most systems include sedimentation, coagulation, filtration, and disinfection. Incoming water is first allowed to sit quietly while suspended material settles out. Then alum is added, causing small particles to coagulate and settle out. Filtration through beds of sand or similar materials removes the smaller particles that do not settle, and chlorine is added to kill remaining pathogens. In areas of the country where water is "hard"—containing high concentrations of dissolved calcium or magnesium—or where it has objectionable tastes or odors due to dissolved iron or gases, additional treatments may be used. As a last step, fluoride is often added to protect community residents from tooth decay. A typical drinking water purification plant is diagrammed in Figure 21–1.

To ensure that the treatment process is working effectively, regular laboratory tests are generally done on the final product. The traditional measures of water purity are turbidity and coliform levels. Turbidity indicates the presence of suspended particles, a failure of the sedimentation and filtration steps. Suspended particles may interfere with the germicidal action

Figure 21–1 Typical Water Purification Plant
Source: P. A. Vesilind, and J. J. Peirce, *Environmental Pollution and Control* (Boston: Butterworths, 1983), 68.

of the chlorine. After the cryptosporidiosis outbreak, which accompanied an increase in the turbidity of Milwaukee's water, national turbidity standards were tightened. If coliform bacteria are detected, there has probably been a failure of disinfection. These bacteria are common inhabitants of the intestines of humans and other animals and, while they are usually not pathogenic themselves, their presence indicates that other, more harmful microorganisms may have survived the treatment process.[1]

The general approach to water treatment described above is directed primarily against bacterial diseases, the most common and historically devastating type of waterborne disease. It is not very effective, however, against viruses and the parasites cryptosporidia and giardia, which are resistant to chlorine. Furthermore, it does nothing to address the problem of contamination with common chemical pollutants such as pesticides, herbicides, fertilizers, PCBs, lead, and other metals that may be harmful to health. Most community water systems are totally unprepared even to test for these pollutants.

The Safe Drinking Water Act of 1974 required the EPA to set standards for local water systems and mandated that states enforce the standards. Uniform guidelines were set for drinking water treatment, and regular monitoring and testing were required, with the results to be reported to state governments. However, no deadlines were established for the standard setting, and state agencies were lax in enforcing the requirements that were in place. The 1986 reauthorization of the Safe Drinking Water Act specified eighty-three contaminants to be regulated by the EPA and set deadlines for action. In addition, it required water systems to take measures to prevent contamination with giardia and cryptosporidia.[1] The EPA stepped up the pace of regulation. Now, maximum contaminant levels have been set for eighty-seven identified contaminants; some of them are shown in Table 21–1. In addition, secondary standards have been set for fifteen contaminants that do not cause health risks but may affect taste, odor, or color, or cause discoloration of skin or teeth.

In 1996, Congress again strengthened the Safe Drinking Water Act. New measures required that community water systems provide annual reports to their customers on the source of the water, water contaminants, and the health effects of these contaminants.[6] The law also included requirements for source water protection, tightened standards for training and certification of operators, and provided funding to help localities improve their systems. The "right-to-know" measure was expected to evoke public pressure that would result in better compliance with standards.

Table 21–1 EPA National Primary Drinking Water Standards
Selected Contaminants Regulated under Safe Drinking Water Act

Contaminant	MCL (mg/L)	Potential Health Effects from Exposure above MCL	Common Sources of Contaminant in Drinking Water
Arsenic[ioc]	0.010 as of 1/23/06	Skin damage or problems with circulatory systems; may increase risk of cancer	Erosion of natural deposits; runoff from orchards, runoff from glass & electronics production wastes
Asbestos[ioc]	7 million fibers per Liter	Increased risk of benign intestinal polyps	Decay of asbestos cement in water mains; erosion of natural deposits
Benzene[oc]	0.005	Anemia; decrease in blood platelets; increased risk of cancer	Discharge from factories; leaching from gas storage tanks and landfills
Carbon tetrachloride[oc]	0.005	Liver problems; increased risk of cancer	Discharge from chemical plants and other industrial activities
Chlorine[d]	MRDL = 4.0	Eye/nose irritation; stomach discomfort	Water additive used to control microbes
Chlorite[dbp]	1.0	Anemia; infants & young children: nervous system effects	Byproduct of drinking water disinfection
Crypto-sporidium[m]	TT[1]	Gastrointestinal illness (e.g. diarrhea, vomiting, cramps)	Human and animal fecal waste
Cyanide[ioc]	0.2	Nerve damage or thyroid problems	Discharge from steel/metal factories; discharge from plastic, fertilizer factories
2,4-D[oc]	0.07	Kidney, liver, or adrenal gland problems	Runoff from herbicide used on row crops

Dioxin[oc]	0.00000003	Reproductive difficulties; Increased risk or cancer	Emissions from waste incineration and other combustion; discharge from chemical factories
Endrin[oc]	0.002	Liver problems	Residue of banned insecticide
Giardia lambia[m]	TT[1]	Gastrointestinal illness (e.g. Diarrhea, vomiting, cramps)	Human and animal fecal waste
Lead[ioc]	TT[2]	Infants and children: delays in physical or mental development; adults: kidney problems, high blood pressure	Corrosion of household plumbing systems; erosion of natural deposits
Mercury[ioc]	0.002	Kidney damage	Erosion of natural deposits; discharge from refineries and factories; runoff from landfills and croplands
Nitrate[ioc]	10	Infants below the age of 6 months may have shortness of breath, blue baby syndrome	Runoff from fertilizer use; leaching from septic tanks, sewage; erosion of natural deposits
PCBs[oc]	0.0005	Skin changes; thymus gland problems; immune, nervous system, or reproductive difficulties; increased risk of cancer	Runoff from landfills; discharge of waste chemicals
Radium 226, Radium 228[r]	5 pCl/L	Increased risk of cancer	Erosion of natural deposits
Selenium[ioc]	0.05	Hair or fingernail loss; numbness in fingers or toes; circulatory problems	Discharge from petroleum refineries; erosion of natural deposits; discharge from mines

(Continued)

Table 21-1 Continued

Contaminant	MCL (mg/L)	Potential Health Effects from Exposure above MCL	Common Sources of Contaminant in Drinking Water
Total coliforms[m]	5.0%	Not a health threat in itself; used to indicate whether other potentially harmful bacteria may be present	Coliforms are naturally present in the environment as well as feces; fecal coliforms and E. coli only come from Human and animal fecal wastes
Turbidity[m]	TT[1]	Indicator of water quality and filtration effectiveness.*	Soil runoff
Viruses[m]	TT[1]	Gastrointestinal illness (e.g. Diarrhea, vomiting, cramps)	Human and animal fecal waste

Notes: Maximum Contaminant Level (MCL): the highest level of a contaminant that is allowed in drinking water. Treatment technique (TT): a required process intended to reduce the level of a contaminant in drinking water

Contaminant categories:　　d = disinfectant
　　　　　　　　　　　　　　dbp = disinfection byproduct
　　　　　　　　　　　　　　ioc = inorganic chemical
　　　　　　　　　　　　　　m = microorganism
　　　　　　　　　　　　　　oc = organic chemical
　　　　　　　　　　　　　　r = radionuclides

TT[1]　EPA's surface water treatment rules require systems using surface water or ground water under the direct risk of surface water to (1) disinfect the water, and (2) filter their water or meet criteria for avoiding filtration so that microbial contaminants are controlled.

TT[2]　Lead and copper are regulated by a Treatment Technique that requires systems to control the corrosiveness of their water.

* Turbidity is a measure of the cloudiness of water. It is used to indicate water quality and filtration effectiveness (e.g. whether disease-causing organisms are present). Higher turbidity levels are often associated with higher levels of disease-causing micro-organisms such as viruses, parasites, and some bacteria. These organisms can cause symptoms such as nausea, cramps, diarrhea, and associated headaches.

Source: www.epa.gov/safewater/consumer/pdf/mcl.pdf

Ongoing surveillance for waterborne disease by the CDC provides data useful for evaluating the adequacy of existing water treatment technologies and the effectiveness of drinking water regulations. The CDC publishes its findings every two years, analyzing the outbreaks by causative agent, type of water system, type of deficiency in the system, and source of water. The data probably understate the incidence of waterborne diseases, because most cases go unrecognized or unreported.

The most recent available report found thirty-one outbreaks in the two-year period 2001 through 2002, affecting 1,020 people and causing seven deaths.[7] Nineteen of the outbreaks were caused by known infectious agents: five by viruses, five by parasites, and nine by bacteria. Five outbreaks were caused by chemical poisoning, and seven were of unknown origin. According to the CDC, the number of reported outbreaks has been decreasing, beginning with the 1985 through 1986 reporting period. There have been fewer outbreaks affecting community water systems, probably due to better regulations and better enforcement in these systems. Outbreaks that continue to occur are more frequent in small systems, including private wells and other nonpublic systems.

DILEMMAS IN COMPLIANCE

A dilemma currently faced by New York City illustrates why it is so difficult to ensure safe drinking water for many Americans. New York gets most of its tap water from six reservoirs in the Catskill Mountains built in the 1950s and 1960s. For many years, the city was justly proud of the purity and taste of its water. However, population in the watershed region has grown, and the quality of the water has suffered. More than 100 community sewage treatment plants discharge into the watershed area, many in violation of discharge permit standards. Substandard septic tanks also contribute to the problem. Dairy farms contribute tons of manure to the watershed. The amount of coliform bacteria measured in New York's water has frequently violated EPA standards, and the amount of chlorine added to control bacteria has increased to the level that it affects the water's taste. Cryptosporidia have also been found in the city's water. The EPA ordered New York to clean up the pollution or build a filtration plant for the water from upstate reservoirs, setting a deadline of December 1996.[8]

New York City does not now filter its water, and construction of a filtration plant may cost up to $8 billion, a painful price for a city struggling with chronic financial difficulties. As an alternative, the city proposed a plan to protect the watershed by helping communities to upgrade their sewage plants, buying sensitive land near the reservoirs, and making changes in the way farmers dispose of manure. The upstate communities, already angry at the city for taking so much of their land for the reservoirs, are concerned that New York's plan will further harm the region's economy by discouraging development. While most experts believe that all water systems should include filtration, they agree that watershed protection is also important. Milwaukee's cryptosporidiosis outbreak occurred despite the fact that its system filters the water. In early 1997, New York City reached an agreement with the upstate region to implement the watershed protection plan.[9,10] The agreement was for five years; however, three years later the EPA said that the city had fallen behind in fulfilling its side of the agreement and again threatened New York with the need to build the plant. Again, an agreement was reached and the city agreed to increase its efforts at protecting the watershed.[11] Meanwhile, New York is under a court order to build a filtration plant for the more polluted reservoirs in the Croton system, located in suburban areas close to the city, which supply 10 percent of its water.[12]

The cost of ensuring safe drinking water is a major obstacle for many communities, large and small. While the federal government has provided some funds to assist states and localities in regulatory and remediation activities required by the Safe Drinking Water Act, the amount provided is never sufficient. In a report called *The Clean Water and Drinking Water Infrastructure Gap Analysis*, the EPA has shown that spending on water and sewage systems is inadequate to cope with such problems as leaks in aging water pipelines and failures in aging urban sewage systems.[13] In the absence of adequate funding, attempts to upgrade water supplies always involve disputes over who should pay for improvements.

Another dilemma concerning drinking water is that the very chemicals used to kill microbes in water may themselves be harmful to health. Chlorine, the most common disinfectant, reacts with organic matter to form byproducts that, some evidence shows, may be carcinogenic. Other, more expensive disinfection methods include bubbling ozone through the water, but these treatments tend to form other byproducts that may be equally harmful to health. There is no simple solution to this problem— even bottled water is required to meet only the same standards of purity as tap water. General steps to prevent water pollution through eliminating point and non-point sources are helpful, however, since cleaner water sources require less treatment to meet drinking water standards.

A new concern with unknown implications results from a survey of 139 streams across thirty states in 1999 through 2000 by the U.S. Geological Survey. The study found that the water contained trace amounts of a wide variety of hormones, pharmaceuticals, and household chemicals, most of which no one had thought to look for previously. Many of them probably get into wastewater when they are excreted by humans or animals and are not removed by sewage treatment systems. Some of the most frequently detected contaminants were steroids, insect repellants, antibiotics, and non-prescription drugs including caffeine and metabolites of nicotine. The effects on humans, plants, and animals of long-term exposure to low concentrations of these chemicals is not known. One possible concern, for example, is that the persistence of antibiotics could contribute to antibiotic resistance.[14]

IS THE WATER SUPPLY RUNNING OUT?

Although water covers 71 percent of the earth's surface, most of it is in the form of salt water or ice in glaciers or polar ice caps. Less than 1 percent of the total amount consists of fresh water, potentially suitable for drinking, cooking, bathing, farming, and other human needs.[1] In many parts of the world, the supply of fresh water is inadequate for the demands of the local population. Already, political disputes are occurring in the United States over water shortages. Some heavily populated areas, including parts of Texas and New Mexico, are depleting finite underground water sources. In California, large quantities of water are transported to the central part of the state from the mountains to use for irrigation while cities in the south complain of shortages. Water conservation measures of various kinds have been instituted, including legally mandated low-volume toilets and showerheads throughout the United States and limits on car washing and lawn watering in some areas during dry seasons.

As it becomes increasingly clear that pure water is a limited resource, it is also apparent that pure water is essential to public health. The difficulty of ensuring an adequate supply of potable water worldwide is discussed further in Chapter 24.

CONCLUSION

Although Americans take it for granted that their tap water is safe to drink, outbreaks of waterborne illness are not uncommon in the United States; the 1993 cryptospiridiosis outbreak in Milwaukee is the most dramatic. Two federal laws are aimed at keeping the water supply clean and safe.

The Clean Water Act specifies that lakes and rivers should be fishable and swimmable. It imposes controls on point source pollution, mainly discharges from municipal sewage systems and from industry, and non-point source pollution, which is washed into waterways from the air and the land. Laws governing point-source pollution set requirements for treating wastewater before it can be discharged. Non-point source pollution is more difficult to control.

The Safe Drinking Water Act requires the EPA to set standards for local drinking water systems and requires states to enforce the standards. However, the EPA was lax in setting the regulations, and states have been lax in enforcing them. Legislation passed in 1996 requires that community water systems provide annual reports to their customers on water contaminants, in hopes that public pressure will force better compliance with the standards.

Complying with federal drinking water standards is expensive, and many communities do not comply, including New York City, which has been trying to find a way to clean up its reservoirs without building a multibillion dollar filtration plant. Another dilemma concerning drinking water is that chlorine, the most common disinfectant used to kill microbes in the water, may itself cause harmful health effects.

The supply of fresh water on earth is finite, and many areas of the world, including parts of the United States, suffer from shortages.

REFERENCES

1. A. Nadakavukaren, *Our Global Environment: A Health Perspective*, 5th ed. (Prospect Heights, Illinois: Waveland Press, Inc., 2000).
2. U.S. Centers for Disease Control and Prevention, "Surveillance for Waterborne-Disease Outbreaks—United States, 1993–1994," *Morbidity and Mortality Weekly Report* 45, SS-1 (1996).
3. D. Zwick and M. Benstock, *Water Wasteland: Ralph Nader's Study Group Report on Water Pollution* (New York: Grossman Publishers, 1971).
4. W. J. Hayes Jr., *Pesticides Studied in Man* (Baltimore, Maryland: Williams & Wilkins, 1982).
5. J. Lee, "EPA to Study Use of Waste from Sewage as Fertilizer," *New York Times* (January 3, 2004).
6. U.S. Environmental Protection Agency, "Understanding the Safe Drinking Water Act. December 1999." *www.epa.gov/safewater/sdwa/index.html*. Accessed November 28, 2004.

7. U.S. Centers for Disease Control and Prevention, "Surveillance for Waterborne-Disease Outbreaks Associated with Drinking Water—United States, 2001–2002," *Morbidity and Mortality Weekly Report* 53, SS-8 (2004).

8. A. Finder, "Delay Sought on Approving Watershed Plans," *New York Times* (April 7, 1995): B3.

9. A. Revkin, "New York Begins Spending to Save City's Reservoirs," *New York Times* (January 22, 1997): A1.

10. A. Revkin, "Billion-Dollar Plan to Clean New York City Water at Its Source," *New York Times* (August 31, 1997): A1.

11. T. Kelley, "Watershed Deal Calls for City To Act, but Saves It Billions," *New York Times* (November 26, 2002): B2.

12. A. Baker and J. Steinhauer, "Pataki Approves City Water Plant," *New York Times* (July 21, 2003): A1.

13. U.S. Environmental Protection Agency, *The Clean Water and Drinking Water Infrastructure Gap Analysis*. EPA-816-R-02-020. September 2002. *www.epa.gov/safewater/gapreport.pdf*. Accessed November 29, 2004.

14. D. W. Kolpin et al., "Pharmaceuticals, Hormones, and Other Organic Wastewater Contaminants in U.S. Streams, 1999–2000," *Environmental Science and Technology* 36 (2002): 1202–1211.

CHAPTER 22

Solid and Hazardous Wastes: What To Do With the Garbage?

Not in My Backyard

In the spring and summer of 1987, the problem of solid waste disposal was brought to national attention by the plight of the "garbage barge" that could not find a place to unload its cargo. Carrying more than 3,000 tons of commercial trash banned from the local landfill in Islip, New York, the barge's vain search for a disposal site somewhere along the Atlantic or Gulf coasts,

Belize or the Bahamas, made national news over a five-month period. Finally, the barge returned to New York, and the trash was incinerated.[1]

Americans dispose of more than 229 million tons of municipal solid waste each year.[2] In 2001, this amounted to about 4.4 pounds per person per day. Municipal solid waste includes wastes such as durable goods, nondurable goods, containers and packaging, food scraps, yard trimmings, and miscellaneous inorganic wastes from residential, commercial, institutional, and industrial sources. It does not include wastes from other sources such as construction and demolition debris, automobile bodies, municipal sludges, and industrial process wastes, all of which must also be disposed of in some way. Figure 22–1 gives a breakdown of the composition of municipal solid wastes. The greatest portion of it is paper, much of it packaging.

Garbage collection has been an important responsibility of local governments since the late nineteenth century. At that time, it was recognized that rats, flies, and other vermin attracted by garbage carry diseases such as plague and typhus. Even earlier, enlightened cities—including ancient Athens—required that wastes be disposed of outside the city walls.

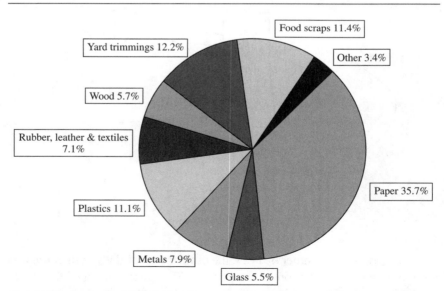

Figure 22–1 Composition of Municipal Solid Waste (MSW), 2001
Source: U.S. Environmental Protection Agency. Municipal Solid Waste in the United States: 2001 Facts and Figures. www.epa.gov/epaoswer/non-hw/muncpl/pubs/msw2001.pdf.

Until the 1970s, little attention was paid to what was done with the garbage after it was taken away from residential neighborhoods. Most often, it was disposed of in open dumps. Sometimes it was burned, either in incinerators or out in the open, at the dump. Another approach was to pour it into nearby rivers, lakes, or oceans. The drawbacks of these methods became obvious as the volume of garbage increased. Garbage washed up on beaches and contaminated drinking water supplies. Incinerators emitted foul odors, noxious fumes, and black smoke. Dumps, in addition to supporting large populations of vermin, produced toxic leachates that seeped through the soil and contaminated groundwater.

Environmental protection laws banned these methods of waste disposal, which merely transferred garbage from one part of the environment to another. The Clean Air Act made most incinerators illegal; the Clean Water Act outlawed dumping into rivers and lakes; and the Marine Protection, Research, and Sanctuaries Act of 1972, with later amendments, prohibited most ocean dumping. Open dumps were outlawed by many states and then by the federal government in 1976 with the Resource Conservation and Recovery Act. RCRA ("rickra"), as it is known, also set standards for sanitary landfills, which have replaced dumps as the most common method of municipal waste disposal.[1]

SANITARY LANDFILLS

Current standards for sanitary landfills require wastes to be confined in a sealed area. A properly designed landfill starts with an appropriate site, which should be dry and consist of impervious clay soil. A large hole is dug and lined with plastic. Refuse is spread in thin layers, compacted by bulldozers, and covered each day with a thin layer of soil. Since decomposing organic matter produces liquids, which may dissolve metals and other toxins, and potentially explosive gases, there must be vents and drains to control these hazards. When the landfill has reached its capacity, it is covered with a two-foot layer of soil. The surface can then be used for a park, golf course, or other recreational facility.

The biggest drawback of sanitary landfills as a method of waste disposal is that they take up a lot of space. In many parts of the country there is no shortage of this commodity, but some urban areas are running out of land. It is expensive to transport garbage from crowded areas to disposal sites with plenty of free space. A measure of the availability of landfill space is the "tipping fee," the cost for disposing of a ton of municipal solid waste. In 2002 the average tipping fee in the United States for burial in a landfill was $33.70. The northeast has the highest tipping fees, at an average of $69.07 per ton.[3] Complicating the problem for cities is the phenomenon known as "NIMBY," meaning not in my backyard. People do not want a landfill in their neighborhood. Even people in areas of the country that have plenty of open space resist the idea of having to accept garbage sent from faraway cities.

The problem is epitomized by the garbage crisis in New York City, brought to a head by residents' complaints about the Fresh Kills landfill on Staten Island, a relatively rural borough located within city limits. Fresh Kills began taking garbage in 1948, and by 1996 it was accepting about 13,000 tons a day. It has never met even minimal environmental standards, and in 1996 the Environmental Protection Agency (EPA) ordered it to cut down on emissions of noxious gases.[4] Meanwhile, the city's Department of Sanitation proposed to conduct regular tours of the site—"the world's largest dump"—a proposal which horrified city authorities and was promptly squelched.[5] Mayor Rudolph Giuliani then proposed to close it down. Fresh Kills was closed, with much fanfare, in March 2001. Except for its use to dispose of World Trade Center debris after September 11 of that year, the site has remained closed. Since then, the city has struggled with the difficulties of sending the wastes to landfills in other states, mostly Pennsylvania and Virginia. City sanitation trucks now take the 11,000 tons per day of wastes to transfer stations in the five boroughs and New Jersey, where it is loaded onto tractor trailers for the trip. The total cost of disposing of a ton of trash in 2002, including transportation costs, had risen to $257—40 percent more than it cost in 1996, and there is concern that the landfills in Pennsylvania are filling up quickly. The city is exploring alternative means of trash disposal, including transporting it in semisubmersible ships to an island in the Caribbean or heating it to 30,000 degrees in a special gasification plant that would break it into elemental components.[6]

ALTERNATIVES TO LANDFILLS

Currently, about 56 percent of municipal solid waste, as well as wastes from other sources, is disposed of in landfills.[7] It is obvious that the garbage crisis could be eased if the volume that goes to landfills could be reduced.

The only way to make landfills last longer is to apply the "three R's": reduce, reuse, and recycle. Prevention of a disposal problem by reducing waste materials at the source is obviously the most efficient approach. Consumer behavior holds the key to successfully reducing waste by this approach. It requires people to buy only the amount of a product that will be used, to choose items without excessive packaging, and to use reusable napkins, towels, diapers, dishes, and cups rather than the disposable variety. The popularity of yard sales is a favorable trend toward achieving reduction of waste through reuse. Although governmental action to encourage the reduction of wastes is still not widespread, there are steps that some communities have taken as incentives. Some residential garbage pickup services charge by the bag, encouraging residents to cut down on volume. Some states impose taxes on hard-to-dispose-of items such as tires, batteries, and motor oil.

Recycling, technically called resource recovery, is rapidly growing as a method of reducing the amount of waste that must be landfilled. In 2001, almost 30 percent of municipal solid waste was recycled nationwide.[7] Providing curbside collection of separated recyclables is a way that communities encourage recycling. Having refundable deposits on bottles and cans is a very effective way to encourage recycling. As of 2004, eleven states require deposits; recycling rates are about 80 percent in these states, about four times the rate in states without bottle bills. Michigan, which raised its deposit to ten cents per bottle, has a recycling rate of 95 percent.[8]

The greatest obstacle to the growth of recycling is a lack of a market for used glass, metal, plastic, and paper. Paper is a special problem; it constitutes such a large proportion of trash, and yet it cannot be recycled indefinitely because the fibers break down. Some states require that newspapers contain a specified minimum percentage of recycled fiber. Since governments use lots of paper, they can make a significant impact on the recycled paper market. The U.S. government mandates that its agencies use paper containing at least 20 percent recycled content, and many states have similar requirements.[1]

Composting is a form of recycling that allows natural decay processes to convert yard and food wastes to mulch, useful in gardening. Composting may be done on an individual or municipal level. Some communities mix their compost with sewage sludge to produce a rich fertilizer for agricultural uses.

Another approach to useful disposal of solid waste is waste-to-energy incineration, which both reduces solid waste and produces heat and energy. Special incinerators for this purpose have been designed to minimize the emission of air pollutants. However, the possibility still exists that they may emit toxic gases, including dioxins and furans from the burning of plastics, lead, cadmium, and mercury vapors from batteries mixed in with municipal wastes. Incinerator ash must be disposed of as a hazardous waste, because it frequently contains dangerous levels of heavy metals. NIMBY opposition tends to make siting of a waste-to-energy incinerator politically difficult, and building and operating one is expensive because of all the safety features required.[1] About 15 percent of municipal solid waste is disposed of by incineration.[7]

HAZARDOUS WASTES

A small but significant percentage of solid waste is hazardous waste. These are materials that are toxic to humans, plants, or animals; are likely to explode; or are corrosive and thus likely to burn through containers or human skin. Two special categories of hazardous wastes that are regulated under separate laws are radioactive wastes and infectious medical wastes.

The problem of hazardous waste disposal first came to public attention in 1978 when Love Canal made the news. Residents of a twenty-year-old housing development in the town of Niagara Falls, New York, had been noticing some alarming phenomena. After a season of heavy rains and snowfalls, noxious chemicals had begun to bubble up in backyards and seep into basements. Chemical odors were prevalent. Children developed rashes and watering eyes after playing outdoors. Heavy rains washed away soil to reveal buried metal drums, which were corroded and leaking. Reports began to circulate of cancer, birth defects, miscarriages, and other health problems among residents of the area. The alarmed citizens demanded that something be done.[1]

The New York State Health Department and the EPA began to investigate. Analyses of soil samples from backyards, air samples in the basements of homes, and water samples in sump pumps and storm sewers revealed contamination by more than 200 different chemicals, including benzene, dioxin, pesticides, and a number of other known carcinogens and teratogens. In August 1978, President Carter declared Love Canal a Federal Disaster Area. Over the next several years, hundreds of Love Canal families were evacuated from their homes.[1]

The source of the problem was an abandoned industrial dump, a trench originally intended to be a canal but never finished, which was used by a chemical company for disposal of its wastes over a ten-year period. In 1952, the trench was declared full and covered with soil. The city took over the property to build a school. By the time home building began in the neighborhood several years later, most people had forgotten about the former activities at the site, and it did not occur to anyone that the area might be hazardous.

Over much of the same period that the Love Canal problems were taking place, another hazardous waste drama was playing out in Missouri. The first act consisted of several episodes in 1971, when waste oil was sprayed on the floors of several horse arenas around the state, a practice used to keep the dust down. After the spraying, a wave of mysterious illnesses began affecting animals and people who came in contact with the dirt. Several children were sickened, some with chloracne, and some had to be hospitalized with severe flulike symptoms. Horses were badly affected, and many died. Hundreds of dead birds were found in the area. The waste oil was suspected, but the hauler claimed there was nothing unusual about the oil. Investigators from the Missouri Department of Health and the Centers for Disease Control and Prevention (CDC) could find nothing unusual in the soil samples or in the blood of the victims. Meanwhile, the same hauler had been hired to spray oil on twenty-three miles of dirt roads in Times Beach, a community of about 2,000 people near St. Louis, during the summer of 1972 and each of the next four summers.[9]

CDC scientists continued to run tests on the soil from the horse arenas, and in 1974 they identified dioxin at concentrations as high as 31,000 parts per billion (ppb). This was plenty high enough to cause human illnesses and the deaths of animals. Further investigation revealed that the oil hauler had been hired by a chemical company to dispose of wastes from the manufacture of Agent Orange, the herbicide used in the Vietnam War. The hauler was mixing this waste oil with used crankcase oil and using it for his spraying operations. The CDC was able to trace the hauler's activities and discovered Times Beach, among other places, where no problems had been suspected. That was in 1982, at just about the time when the community was inundated by a flood which, it was feared, spread the dioxin throughout the town. Tests found dioxin levels of the order of 100 ppb on roads and in yards. Residents were panicked.[10]

In the end, Times Beach, like Love Canal, was evacuated. In retrospect, the decision has been widely criticized as an overreaction. The levels of dioxin in Times Beach were much lower than those in the horse arenas, and more modest remediation would probably have sufficed. However, little was known at that time about the toxicity and carcinogenicity of dioxin in humans. The effects on animals were certainly a cause of concern. Since 1982, extensive studies have been conducted on the residents of both Love Canal and Times Beach. For the most part, although many lives were disrupted and people suffered alarm and anguish, most of the people who lived in these communities appear not to have suffered significant health effects from the chemical exposures.[10]

RCRA, the federal legislation first enacted in 1976 to deal with solid waste disposal, included special regulations on handling of wastes that potentially posed a hazard to health and the environment. These regulations, which were strengthened by amendments to RCRA in 1984, can prevent future Love Canals and Times Beaches. They require that all hazardous wastes be accounted for "from cradle to grave," and there are criminal penalties for those who violate the laws. However, legal disposal of hazardous wastes is expensive, and no one knows how much illegal "midnight dumping" may actually go on today.[1]

RCRA lists many specific wastes that are regulated under the law, including wastes from petroleum refining, pesticide manufacturing, and some pharmaceutical products. Wastes are also considered hazardous if they are ignitable, corrosive, reactive, or toxic. The regulations are stricter for large quantity generators, facilities that generate more than 2,200 pounds per month, than for small quantity generators, facilities that generate between 220 and 2,200 pounds per month. Facilities that generate the smallest amounts of waste are subject to only minimal requirements. The RCRA regulations have two key elements: tracking and permitting. The tracking requirement, illustrated in Figure 22–2, calls for paperwork to document the progress of hazardous waste from its site of generation through treatment, storage, and disposal. Permitting means that any facility that treats, stores, or disposes of hazardous waste must be issued a permit from EPA or the state; the permit prescribes standards for management of the waste. Transportation of hazardous waste, which must be clearly labeled, is regulated by the U.S. Department of Transportation.[11]

In the mid-1990s, the amount of hazardous wastes that was managed annually under the RCRA regulations was 279 million tons. As with municipal solid waste, hazardous waste is managed by practicing the three R's: reduce, reuse, and recycle. One way of reducing the waste is by treating it to make it less hazardous; this can be done, for example, by biological or chemical treatment, by burning the waste at high temperatures, and by separating solids from wastewater to reduce the volume of waste that must be disposed of. A common method of disposing of liquid hazardous waste is by injecting

A manuifest must accompany every waste shipment. The resulting paper trail documents the waste's progress through treatment, storage, and disposal. A missing form alerts the generator to investigate, which may mean calling in the state agency or EPA.

Figure 22–2 Tracking of Hazardous Wastes
Source: U.S. Environmental Protection Agency. *RCRA: Reducing Risk From Waste,* September 1997, 20. www.epaoswer/general/risk/ris-1.pdf.

it under pressure into underground steel and concrete-encased wells. Specially designed landfills are also used for disposing of hazardous waste.[11]

While RCRA was meant to control hazardous wastes as they are generated, it was inadequate to deal with old waste sites that kept turning up in the news after the public consciousness had been raised. In response, in 1980 Congress passed the Comprehensive Environmental Response, Compensation, and Liability Act, known as "Superfund." That law required the EPA to compile a priority list of waste sites that threatened the public health or environmental quality and it authorized $1.6 billion over a five-year period for emergency cleanup of these sites. The cleanup was paid for by a tax on industry, which created the trust fund that gave the program its name. Superfund was reauthorized in 1986 and 1990, allocating additional billions of dollars for cleanup.[1]

The Superfund program has been mired in controversy from the beginning. The pace of the cleanup has been very slow, and the cost has been very high. New sites have been added to the priority list much more rapidly than old sites have been removed: as of 2002, there were 1,223 sites on the list, while only 251 had been cleaned up sufficiently to be removed.[12] Because the legislation calls for polluters to pay, much of the effort has been spent on trying to establish who is liable. One-quarter of all Superfund dollars spent thus far has gone to pay legal fees. Another problem is the shortage of cleanup options: what to do with the toxic materials removed from a site. Creative solutions are urgently needed. There are also disagreements over how clean is clean enough. The EPA's "Brownfields" initiative sets lower standards for sites designated for industrial use, an approach that makes cleanup easier but is less acceptable to some communities.[1]

Congress did not reauthorize the corporate taxes that paid for Superfund cleanup when the taxes expired in 1995, and the trust fund has been exhausted. Although cleanup of many sites is going forward, paid for by the polluters, cleanup of "orphan" sites, for which the responsible company could not be identified or could not pay, is now being paid for with taxpayer dollars. The amount of funds for this purpose in the federal budget has not grown in recent years, and many sites are far short of the funds that are needed.

Americans have been very concerned about hazardous waste disposal and cleanup, especially when it affects their neighborhoods. Some critics believe that the degree of concern is out of proportion to the actual risk to public health. While the release of toxic gases into the air and the leaching of toxic liquids into water supplies are important public health risks because many humans are likely to be exposed to the hazards, risks from toxic substances buried in the ground are much more uncertain. Close to one-quarter of the EPA's entire budget is allocated to the Superfund program, and additional funds are contributed by industry. At present, it is not clear whether this is a rational allocation of spending on the environment. Methods of analyzing risk and understanding the balance between benefits and costs can help make such decisions, as discussed in Chapter 7.

CONCLUSION

As concern about environmental pollution has grown, the problem of disposing of solid wastes has become more difficult to resolve. Traditional solutions, such as dumping garbage into waterways or incinerating it, can no longer be used because they increase water and air pollution. Old-fashioned open dumps cause noxious odors and attract vermin.

Solid waste disposal is now confined to sanitary landfills, which must meet federal standards. But in many parts of the country, there is a shortage of space available for landfills. Communities resist having sanitary landfills sited near them—the NIMBY phenomenon.

The problem of finding space for garbage could be eased if the volume of garbage could be reduced, for example, by eliminating excessive packaging and charging consumers for disposal by volume. Recycling and use of reusable, as opposed to disposable, products also help to reduce the volume of garbage.

Hazardous wastes present an especially difficult disposal problem. Several environmental scandals in the 1970s and early 1980s, including Love Canal in New York state and Times Beach in Missouri, brought national attention to the need for regulation of hazardous waste disposal. Federal legislation known as RCRA requires that all hazardous wastes be accounted for "from cradle to grave." Superfund legislation provides for identification and cleanup of hazardous waste sites dating from before RCRA. Although both programs have shortcomings, they have contributed—along with federal laws on air and water pollution—to a significant improvement in the environment. Congress has not reauthorized the corporate taxes to support cleanup under Superfund, and the future of the program is uncertain.

REFERENCES

1. A. Nadakavukaren, *Our Global Environment: A Health Perspective*, 5th ed. (Prospect Heights, Illinois: Waveland Press, 2000).
2. U.S. Environmental Protection Agency, "Municipal Solid Waste Basic Facts," *www.epa.gov/epaoswer/non-hw/muncpl/facts.htm*. Accessed December 1, 2004.
3. National Solid Waste Management Association, *NSWMA's 2002 Tipping Fee Survey*. NSWMA Research Bulletin 02-03. September 2002.
4. I. Fisher, "EPA Tells Landfills to Curb Gas Emissions," *New York Times* (March 3, 1996).
5. B. Weber, "Broadway, Statue of Liberty and Fresh Kills? World's Biggest Garbage Dump Hopes to Draw Tourists as Well as Gulls," *New York Times* (March 27, 1996): B1.

6. E. Lipton, "City Seeks Ideas as Trash Costs Dwarf Estimate," *New York Times*, (December 2, 2003): A1.

7. U.S. Environmental Protection Agency, *Municipal Solid Waste in the United States: 2001 Facts and Figures*. *www.epa.gov/osw*. Accessed December 2, 2004.

8. Container Recycling Institute, "Bottle Bill Resource Guide," *www.bottlebill.org*. Accessed December 2, 2004.

9. M. J. Schneider, *Persistent Poisons: Chemical Pollutants in the Environment* (New York: The New York Academy of Sciences, 1979).

10. A. Wildavsky, *But Is It True? A Citizen's Guide to Environmental Health and Safety Issues* (Cambridge, Massachusetts: Harvard University Press, 1995).

11. U.S. Environmental Protection Agency, *RCRA: Reducing Risk from Waste*. 1997. *www.epa.gov/epaoswer/general/risk/risk.htm*. Accessed December 3, 2004.

12. T. Zeller, "The Future of Superfund: More Taxing, Less Simple," *New York Times* (March 24, 2002).

CHAPTER 23

Safe Food and Drugs: An Ongoing Regulatory Battle

Meat Inspection

Americans are very concerned about the safety of their food supply. News stories about carcinogenic food additives, pesticide residues on produce, and hormones in milk surface periodically, arousing anxiety in the public mind. Ironically, less attention is focused on the much greater danger of food poisoning caused by microbial contamination, an everyday occurrence. Since only the most serious cases are reported, the frequency of food-borne illness is unclear. The Centers for Disease Control and Prevention (CDC) has estimated that 76 million people contract food-borne diseases each year, with 5,000 deaths.[1]

Nevertheless, the United States is generally thought to have the safest food supply in the world. With some 290 million people eating three meals a day, not counting snacks, the likelihood of getting sick from eating a single meal is extremely small. Many government agencies—local, state, and federal—are involved with regulating food safety. The challenge is enormous: some 6,100 meat and poultry plants, more than 50,000 food processing establishments, about 537,000 commercial restaurants, 172,000 institutional food programs, 190,000 retail food stores, and 1 million food vending locations are subject to government inspection.[2]

The need for government oversight of the food supply, like many other public health measures, arose with the urbanization of the population. City dwellers neither grew their own food nor knew its source and history. Demands for action arose as the public became aware of unhygienic conditions such as those in meatpacking plants—conditions revealed in Upton Sinclair's 1906 novel, *The Jungle*. Other widespread practices that outraged the public included adulteration of supposedly pure food with cheaper materials and the use of sometimes toxic additives to improve color and conceal spoilage. The Federal Food and Drug Act of 1906 established a program to supervise and control the circumstances of manufacture, labeling, and sale of food.[3]

Because similar abuses occurred in the sale of medicines, the 1906 Act included provisions to control manufacturing, labeling, and sale of drugs. The Food and Drug Administration (FDA), created to oversee regulation of food and drugs, was later given authority over cosmetics, medical devices, and feed and drugs for pets and farm animals.

CAUSES OF FOOD-BORNE ILLNESS

Food-borne diseases are generally caused by contamination of foods with bacteria, viruses, or parasites due to breakdowns in sanitation and/or proper food handling practices. Salmonella bacteria, for example, are common contaminants of poultry, meat, and eggs. Infected hens may transfer the pathogens to the eggs as they are being formed in the ovary. Although the bacteria are killed when the food is thoroughly cooked, people who prefer their meat rare or their egg yolks runny are at risk of salmonellosis, especially if the food has been kept at room temperature long enough for the bacteria to flourish. Caesar salad dressing made with raw eggs and homemade eggnog are particularly risky. The symptoms of salmonellosis, like symptoms of most types of food-poisoning, include vomiting, diarrhea, and abdominal pain.

Like salmonella in poultry and eggs, E. coli 0157:H7 is widespread in beef, probably due to the way livestock are raised and processed. To prevent illness and deaths such as those that occurred in 1993 in Seattle (described in Chapter 10), hamburgers must be cooked more thoroughly than the previous standard required. In addition to its occurrence in ground beef, E. coli 0157:H7 has also turned up in other foods, including salami, raw milk, lettuce, alfalfa sprouts, and unpasteurized apple juice. The bacteria are common in the intestinal tracts of cows and are excreted with their feces. The contaminated juice may have been made from apples that fell onto ground where cows had wandered, and the contaminated lettuce was prepared under unsanitary conditions near a cow pen.[4,5] The alfalfa sprouts could have been contaminated by being grown in fields near cattle feed lots and irrigated with water contaminated by manure.[6]

In fact, fresh produce is responsible for an increasing proportion of food-borne illness. In 2000, fruits and vegetables caused almost as many cases of illness as were caused by beef, poultry, fish, and eggs combined.[7] A hepatitis A outbreak among people who had eaten at a Chi-Chi's restaurant in Pennsylvania in fall 2003 was traced to green onions imported from Mexico. More than 600 people were infected, and three people died.[8,9] The microbial parasite cyclospora was the cause of several outbreaks of food poisoning in 1996 and 1997 that included more than 370 cases among people who had attended receptions and banquets in eight states and Canada. Investigators traced the illness to raspberries imported from Guatemala. The source of the contamination was not determined, but suspicions fell on poor sanitary conditions at some of the farms where the fruit was grown.[10]

Fish and shellfish are likely to harbor pathogenic microbes if they are harvested from waters polluted by human sewage. Raw clams and oysters are especially dangerous: because they grow in shallow coastal waters, which are likely to be polluted, these shellfish may carry cholera and related bacteria, hepatitis A virus, and the common Norwalk virus, all capable of causing disease in humans. Fish used uncooked for Japanese dishes such as sushi and sashimi and South American ceviche may also carry parasites harmful to humans.[3]

Some bacterial contaminants cause illness by way of toxins they produce rather than by simple infection. Thus these contaminants are hazardous even after the food is cooked. The best-known—and deadliest—of these are the bacteria that cause botulism. They flourish in the absence of oxygen and are most commonly associated with home-canned vegetables that were inadequately cooked before canning, although a number of botulism outbreaks have been traced to commercially canned foods. Once the toxin is formed, it can be destroyed only by boiling for fifteen to twenty minutes, not a common practice with canned foods. Certain fish and shellfish may also contain toxins—for example, ciguatoxin or scombroid poison—produced by bacteria or algae that the fish feed on or that grow on them, thereby poisoning the flesh for human consumption.[3]

Food may also be contaminated by the actions of food handlers, either if they themselves are infected or if they transfer pathogens from one food to another. For example, a salad might be contaminated with salmonella if the raw vegetables are chopped on a cutting board that had previously been used to cut up uncooked chicken. A number of other bacterial or viral infections tend to be transferred by infected food handlers to raw or cooked foods, such as salads, hot dogs, and delicatessen takeout items. The famous case of Typhoid Mary, described in Chapter 9, illustrates how an infected food handler can spread pathogenic bacteria even when she herself has no symptoms. Hepatitis A virus is also frequently transmitted by food handlers who are careless about hygiene. The disease is most contagious ten to fourteen days before the onset of symptoms.

GOVERNMENT ACTION TO PREVENT FOOD-BORNE DISEASE

A variety of federal, state, and local agencies are responsible for protecting the safety of the food supply. Because of patchwork legislation, division of responsibility, and lack of coordination, there are major inconsistencies among different types of food in the way food safety is regulated. Increasingly, it has become clear that the system depends too heavily on detecting and correcting problems after they occur rather than preventing them. In 1997 the Clinton administration proposed new rules intended to introduce more science-based preventive measures and to increase coordination among the agencies responsible for food safety.[11] However, as nutritionist Marion Nestle states in her book,

Safe Food: Bacteria, Biotechnology, and Bioterrorism, "Today, an inventory of federal food safety activities reveals a system breathtaking in its irrationality."[12(p.55)]

The Food and Drug Administration (FDA) and the Department of Agriculture (USDA) share the primary responsibility for ensuring that foods are safe, wholesome and properly labeled. The laws governing the actions of the two agencies are highly inconsistent. The USDA is responsible for the safety of meat and poultry, including any prepared product that contains more than 3 percent of raw meat or poultry or more than 2 percent of cooked meat or poultry, as well as processed eggs. It is required to inspect all meat and poultry processing plants daily and must have an inspector on site whenever a slaughtering plant is in operation. The USDA has the authority to require food firms to register so that they can be inspected, and it can temporarily detain any suspect foods so that it can seek a court order to seize the food. The plants that the USDA inspects account for about 20 percent of federally regulated foods and 15 percent of food-borne illnesses. Its annual budget for food safety is over $700 million.[13]

The FDA is responsible for all foods other than meat, poultry, and processed eggs, which amounts to about 80 percent of federally regulated foods and 85 percent of reported food-borne illnesses. However, its annual budget for food safety is about $283 million. Because of budgetary constraints, the FDA can inspect food processing facilities under its jurisdiction only once every three to five years, on average. This leads to the paradox that, while the risk of contamination of canned soup comes from the canning process rather than the ingredients, a plant making canned soup with more than 2 percent meat must be inspected every day (by the USDA), while one making meatless soup may be inspected only once every few years (by the FDA). In general, the FDA's authority is limited: it is not mandated to review new foods before they go on the market, and it cannot order recalls of questionable products.[13]

Fish and shellfish are believed to cause 21 percent of all food poisoning cases arising from meat, fish, or poultry. Regulation of the fish industry, which falls mainly under the jurisdiction of the FDA, is especially difficult because most fish are caught in the wild by independent fishermen in relatively small boats. Fish may have been exposed to viruses or bacterial toxins in polluted waters, or they may have been contaminated with scombroid toxin due to inadequate cooling on the boat. Currently no techniques are available that would allow inspectors on the docks to test for these problems. Shellfish should, in theory, be easier to regulate because their source can be determined. However, much of the enforcement is left to the states, and some of them are lax about enforcing standards. There is no requirement for seafood firms to register with the FDA, and so some of them may entirely escape oversight by the agency.

The Clinton Administration chose seafood as the target of its first attempt to apply a new preventive approach to food safety; the new rules took effect in December 1997.[14] Called HACCP ("hassip"), the new system was developed in the 1960s by food processors in cooperation with NASA, to ensure that foods prepared for the astronauts were safe. Rather than relying on inspections, which can never be done frequently or thoroughly enough to ensure complete safety, the HACCP system focuses on procedures, identifying potential problems and devising ways to avoid them. HACCP—which stands for "Hazard Analysis Critical Control Point"—requires an analysis of every step in the process of food production, processing, and preparation, as seen in Figure 23–1. The purpose is to identify each possible hazard and, for each, one or more "control points," which are practices and procedures that will eliminate, prevent or minimize the hazard.[15]

Figure 23–1 The HACCP System
Source: International Association of Milk, Food, and Environmental Sanitarians, Inc.

Many companies are already using HACCP, and the FDA and USDA in the late 1990s moved to encourage more reliance on the system. When fully implemented, HACCP is intended to reduce the need for inspections, relying instead on frequent reviews of procedures to make sure the system is being carried out. Although the meat and poultry industries resisted at first, the USDA reported that by 1999, 96 percent of federally regulated plants were using HACCP, including a requirement that the foods be tested for common pathogens. The FDA implemented HACCP for seafood and then added raw sprouts, eggs, and fresh juice. However, under the FDA, use of the system is voluntary, and in 1999 less than half of federally regulated seafood firms were in compliance.[13]

An increasing proportion of Americans' food is being imported from other countries, especially developing countries, which is a challenge to the food safety system. Although the USDA has the power to bar importing of meat and poultry from countries with inferior food safety systems, the FDA does not have that power for fruits, vegetables, grains, or fish. It must rely on port-of-entry inspections, an expensive and ineffective approach. In 2000, the FDA inspected a mere 1 percent of the imported food under its jurisdiction. Moreover, because the FDA has no authority to detain imports while testing, even if it does identify that a food is adulterated or contaminated, the food might already have been released into the U.S. food supply.[13]

President Clinton requested that Congress tighten import controls on food, but Congress failed to act.[16] According to the Centers for Disease Control and Prevention (CDC), 55 percent of seafood consumed in the United States is imported, as is about 12 percent of vegetables and 33 percent of fruit. Because they are eaten raw, fruits imported from countries with inadequate safety systems are especially risky, causing, for example, the cylosporiasis outbreaks from Guatemalan raspberries and the hepatitis A outbreak from Mexican green onions. As one CDC official is quoted as saying, "We used to believe you had to travel overseas to get travelers' diarrhea. It's a classic example of emerging infections common in Latin America becoming a problem here."[17]

The FDA, in addition to its oversight of food production on a national scale, issues recommendations that state and local governments can use to regulate establishments that deal with food, including retail stores, restaurants, and institutions such as schools and nursing homes. These rules emphasize the importance of hand washing by food service workers and restricting sick workers from direct contact with food. They also include strict guidelines concerning the temperatures at which food may be stored, cooked, and kept in heating trays. To prevent bacterial growth, foods should be refrigerated at 40 degrees Fahrenheit or below, or heated thoroughly so that internal temperatures are above 140 degrees. Special rules apply to large pieces such as roast meats and stuffed poultry because their internal temperatures may lag behind the external changes in temperature, allowing pathogens to grow during roasting or after refrigeration.[3] Local health departments usually enforce these rules by conducting periodic inspections of stores, restaurants, and institutions, and they are usually authorized by local and state laws to close facilities that are significantly in violation.

One potential solution to the problem of foodborne disease is the use of radiation to kill microbial contaminants in food. The idea of irradiating food frightens many people, and the proposal has aroused great opposition among some consumer groups; yet it leaves no radioactive residue, and more than forty years of research have shown it to be safe. It is already used for some foods in the United States and is widely used in some other countries. Radiation treatment kills pests in dried herbs, spices, and tea, controls insects in wheat and flour, and kills the parasites that cause trichinosis when undercooked pork is eaten. It has been shown to greatly reduce the contamination of chicken breasts with salmonella, ground beef with E. coli 0157:H7, and shrimp with cholera bacteria. Because microbial contamination of food is such a common hazard, with potentially deadly consequences, many experts believe that widespread use of irradiation could greatly increase the safety of the food supply. The FDA has approved irradiation of red meat, poultry, pork, fruits and vegetables, seeds, herbs and spices, eggs, and wheat. In 2004, the USDA began to offer irradiated ground beef as part of the National School Lunch Program.[18]

A very important component of any food safety program is epidemiologic surveillance and prompt follow-up of any food-borne outbreak to prevent further spread of disease. With a nationwide food distribution network, local public health authorities may not recognize that a number of seemingly isolated cases of an illness may be caused by contamination at a single source. The CDC has a program called PulseNet, consisting of public health laboratories in all fifty states and Canada that can do DNA "fingerprinting" on food-borne bacteria. The network permits timely comparisons of pathogens that may cause outbreaks in various parts of the country, identifying common sources and enabling public health officials to take action to halt distribution of a contaminated food.[19] The system worked in

1997, when there appeared to be separate outbreaks of E. coli 0157:H7 in Michigan and Virginia. Each state independently investigated its outbreak and found an association with alfalfa sprouts. The PulseNet tests found that the bacteria were identical and traced the infection to a common lot of seeds harvested in Idaho.[6] The seeds were recalled, and the FDA began talks with the sprout industry about methods of seed decontamination.

Another program developed by the CDC is an active surveillance network, called FoodNet, designed to help public health officials better understand the epidemiology of food-borne diseases in the United States.[20] In contrast with the usual epidemiologic surveillance, called passive surveillance, in which the public health agency waits for information to be reported to it by doctors, hospitals, and laboratories, FoodNet investigators conduct active surveillance. They contact laboratories to ask about every case of diarrheal illness they conducted tests on; send surveys to physicians to determine how often and under what conditions they send stool specimens to laboratories; and even call members of the general population to ask if they have had recent diarrheal illnesses, what they think might have caused it, and whether they sought treatment. The data collected by these methods provide information on less severe food-borne illnesses that are often not reported to public health authorities and help officials at the USDA and FDA identify where their regulatory systems should be improved. The FoodNet network includes, in addition to the CDC, investigators at the USDA, the FDA, and nine state health departments. Since FoodNet was implemented in 1996, the incidence of infections caused by E. coli 0157:H7, salmonella, and a number of other pathogens has declined.[21]

Despite some signs of improvement, the patchwork system of federal food safety regulation remains, and there have been repeated calls to establish a single, independent agency that would administer a unified, science-based food safety system. The Institute of Medicine, the President's Council on Food Safety, and the General Accountability Office have each conducted studies on the current system and concluded that laws should be revised to give one federal official responsibility and authority to keep the nation's food supply safe.[12] In fact, the need has become even more urgent since the threat of bioterrorism has become more prominent. In December 2004, when the Secretary of Health and Human Services announced his resignation, he warned of the problem. "For the life of me, I cannot understand why the terrorists have not attacked our food supply because it's so easy to do," Secretary Tommy Thomson said in his final press conference.[22]

ADDITIVES AND CONTAMINANTS

Food safety standards include limits on unwanted substances that accidentally get into food—contaminants—as well as on additives, which are purposely incorporated into food to improve its taste, color, and resistance to deterioration. Contaminants that can be detected by inspection include dirt, hairs, rodent feces, and insect parts. Pesticide residues may be left on food as a result of crop spraying or when livestock eat pesticide-contaminated fodder. The FDA has established tolerance levels—the maximum allowable residues—for all pesticides used on food crops, and it monitors pesticide levels on both domestically produced and imported food. While earlier health concerns focused on cancer, a pesticide law passed by Congress in 1996 requires testing of pesticides for damage to the endocrine system and for effects on developing fetuses, infants, and young children.[23]

However, the monitoring system has been criticized because only a fraction of the food supply is tested, because tests are available for only some of the pesticides, and because when contaminants are detected, it is often too late to prevent the food from being marketed. This is especially a problem with imported foods, which may contain residues of pesticides that are banned in the United States.

Other possible contaminants include hormones and antibiotics. As discussed in Chapter 10, the use of antibiotics in livestock feed is believed to have led to increased antibiotic resistance in many bacteria. The sex hormone diethyl stilbestrol, a form of estrogen, used to be fed to chickens to promote their growth. Because of concerns that hormone residues in the meat might increase breast cancer risk, the practice was banned in 1977. In 1994, the FDA approved the use of bovine growth hormone in dairy cows to increase their milk production. Although hormone residues are generally not found in the milk, many consumers are concerned about the safety of the practice.[3]

Many people choose foods labeled "organic," believing that these foods are safer than foods grown by common commercial methods. Until 2000, however, there was no federal standard that regulated what foods could be labeled organic. A 1990 law required the USDA to set standards, but there was so much controversy and objections from the conventional food industry that it took over a decade for the standards setting process to be completed and the standards to finally become fully effective in 2002. The standards require that organic meat, poultry, eggs, and dairy products must be grown without antibiotics or growth hormones, and organic produce must be grown without pesticides, synthetic fertilizers, or sewage sludge. Genetically engineered products and radiation are also not allowed for organic foods. Then in early 2004, the Bush administration "clarified" the standards, weakening some of the prohibitions on antibiotics and pesticides.[24,25] There was such a clamor of protest that the agriculture secretary reversed the new ruling the next day. Studies have shown that organic produce contains only a third as many pesticide residues as conventionally grown foods and that children fed organic produce and juice had only one-sixth the level of pesticide byproducts in their urine compared with those that ate conventionally farmed foods.[26,27]

Additives are put into food for a variety of reasons. One purpose is to prevent deficiency diseases that used to cause serious public health problems in the United States. For example, the addition of iodine to table salt has virtually eliminated goiter; vitamin D added to milk has done away with rickets; and niacin, a B vitamin, is added to bread to prevent pellagra. As discussed in Chapter 18, the FDA mandates that folic acid be added to flour and rice products to prevent some birth defects. Another purpose of food additives is as a preservative, to retard spoilage or prevent fats from turning rancid. Other additives are used to improve color or to enhance flavor or texture.[3]

Because of public concern about the safety of many food additives, Congress passed legislation in 1958 that required FDA approval for any proposed food additive. Additives already in use were exempted and placed on the GRAS list—"generally regarded as safe." Since then, several additives on the list have been removed because they turned out not to be safe, among them several food colors that were shown to be carcinogenic.

DRUGS AND COSMETICS

As its name makes clear, the FDA is also responsible for the safety of drugs. This responsibility includes both prescription drugs and over-the-counter drugs—those available without a prescription. Both types of drugs must be proven safe and effective before they can be approved by the FDA.

The FDA does not test drugs itself. Companies seeking to market new drugs are required by law to conduct the tests and submit the evidence to the agency. FDA staff than review the data and determine whether the evidence supports the new drugs' safety and efficacy.

There is an orderly procedure for collecting the evidence on new prescription drugs. Several stages of exchange of information between the pharmaceutical company and the FDA are required. The company files a new drug application (NDA) for an investigational new drug, providing evidence that the drug has the desired effect in animals and satisfies some basic safety criteria. If the FDA approves the NDA, the company is allowed to test the drug in humans in clinical trials. The trials go through three phases: In phase I, the new drug is given to a small number of people who are extensively tested to measure absorption, distribution, metabolism, and excretion, and to look for side effects and toxicities. Phase II tests a larger number of patients for signs that the new drug is effective. Phase III is a full-scale controlled trial, as described in Chapter 5, in which patients are assigned randomly to two groups. People in the experimental group receive the new drug. Members of the control group receive either a placebo or standard treatment.[28]

The FDA also has a system of postmarketing surveillance, in which doctors and patients can report adverse reactions to an approved drug. On occasion, evidence arises after a drug is on the market that it has risks that were not recognized in preapproval studies. The FDA has revoked its approval of a number of drugs based on such evidence. The FDA's drug approval process has for years involved great political controversy, as described later in this chapter.

Cosmetics are more loosely regulated by the FDA. They do not need preapproval. In fact, there is no requirement for safety testing of cosmetics, but a warning label must be attached to any product that has not been tested. A number of ingredients that were used in the past have been shown to be harmful to health, and their use is prohibited by law. These include several chlorinated compounds as well as some color additives and most compounds containing mercury.

FOOD AND DRUG LABELING AND ADVERTISING

The scandals that inspired passage of the original Pure Food and Drugs Act of 1906 were cases of economic fraud as much as they were threats to public health. Expensive imports such as tea, coffee, and spices were frequently adulterated with dried leaves of native trees or ground native nuts and berries.[29] Thus, accurate labeling was one of the important provisions of the 1906 act. Labeling requirements have become increasingly elaborate over the years. Recently, as it has become clear that overall dietary behavior has far more impact on health than food contamination does (see Chapter 16), the FDA has placed more emphasis on empowering consumers to eat a healthy diet. Regulations established in 1994 require labels to contain information on fats, fiber, vitamins, and other nutrients, along with recommended daily intakes for these nutrients. Because the kinds of fats in the diet have an important effect on health, especially heart disease, labels are required to list the amount of artery clogging saturated fat. A new labeling requirement was announced in 2003. Effective on January 1, 2006, foods will be required to add to their labels the amount of trans fats in a serving of the product. Trans fats, which have been used since the 1980s as substitutes for saturated fats, have been found to be almost as harmful to arteries as saturated fats.[30]

Accurate labels on drugs are also required by the FDA. Here the emphasis is on ensuring that claims of safety and efficacy are accurate and communicate information about hazards directly to the consumer. This is especially important for over-the-counter drugs, for which the label may be the sole basis on which consumers choose to buy and consume the product. Oddly, advertising of over-the-counter drugs is regulated by the Federal Trade Commission rather than the FDA.

Unfounded claims for health benefits from certain foods, drugs, and vitamins have had popular appeal in the United States since the nation's birth, despite governmental efforts to enforce accuracy in labeling and advertising. In the late nineteenth and early twentieth centuries, patent medicines contained alcohol and sometimes opium, which helped patients feel better but did little to cure the underlying problems. Still today, desperate patients suffering from incurable diseases turn to quack therapies, at best just wasting their money, but in some cases turning their backs on therapies that might do some good. The FDA can act when labels on a food or drug contain false or misleading claims; accompanying leaflets are considered labels. However, nothing can be done to suppress articles and books containing unsubstantiated health claims about foods and "nutritional supplements" if the writings cannot be classified as labels.[31]

Among the most persistent nutritional misconceptions has been the belief that if it is "natural," it must be safe. Accordingly, Congress in 1994 succumbed to intense lobbying by the health food industry and passed the Dietary Supplement Health and Education Act, which was signed by President Clinton. The Act forbids the FDA from requiring safety testing of herbs and food supplements. Consequently, a number of products known to have quite potent physiological effects are sold freely in health food stores, although they may turn out to be harmful once they are better understood. For example melatonin, promoted as a sleep aid and treatment for jet lag, is sold as a nutritional supplement despite the fact that it is a hormone with unknown and potentially powerful effects on the brain and the reproductive and immune systems.

In 1996, people were shocked by news stories that a college student on spring break had died after taking an herbal product called "Ultimate Xphoria" (also called "Herbal Ecstacy"), which contained ephedra, a potent natural stimulant similar to amphetamines. Ephedra-containing compounds were marketed as energy boosters, aids to weight loss, sexual stimulants, and a way to get high.[31] Soon after the CDC reported that eight deaths and 500 adverse health affects including heart attacks, seizures, and psychoses, had occurred nationwide among people who had consumed ephedra-containing products.[32] While some state and local governments banned these products, the FDA could not stop their sale and use. Finally, after the highly publicized death in early 2003 of a twenty three-year-old Baltimore Orioles pitcher who used ephedra to lose weight at the beginning of spring training, the FDA banned the substance. It was the first time that the FDA had removed a dietary supplement from the market since 1994, and the action succeeded only after the agency had reviewed some 16,000 reports of adverse reactions, commissioned a study by a nonprofit research agency, and received tens of thousands of comments from the public.[33]

POLITICS OF THE FDA

The FDA regulates products amounting to over 20 percent of consumer dollars spent in the United States.[34] Not surprisingly, it has made itself unpopular with some of the industries financially impacted by its decisions. These industries can place intense political pressures on Congress and the White House to rein in the agency's actions, as illustrated by the success of the dietary supplement industry in getting itself exempted from FDA oversight.

One of the most frequent criticisms of the FDA has been that it is too slow in approving new drugs. This complaint comes from the pharmaceutical industry, which argues that companies must wait too long to recoup their investments in research and development, as well as from patients with intractable diseases, who feel they are being denied promising new treatments. AIDS activists were especially critical of the FDA's caution, arguing that they would inevitably die if the process of new drug approval was not accelerated. Citing the thalidomide disaster that was averted in the United States by a cautious FDA official (see Chapter 12) was no longer enough to deter calls for "reform." In 1992, Congress acted constructively to speed up the approval process by requiring drug companies to pay a fee for the processing of NDAs, which allowed the agency to hire more reviewers.[35]

However, after the 1994 election, the pro-business Republican Congress stepped up its calls for FDA reform, including proposals to privatize the process of reviewing new drugs and medical devices. Consumer groups are strongly opposed to the reform proposals, arguing that they will lead to conflicts of interest that may jeopardize the system that has done a good job of protecting Americans from food, drugs, and medical devices that have harmed people in other countries.

The FDA's political troubles were exacerbated by Commissioner David Kessler's declaration that nicotine is an addictive drug and his proposals to regulate the sale of tobacco to children, an issue that enraged conservatives and became a factor in the 1996 presidential campaign (see Chapter 15). After prolonged debate, a moderate FDA reform bill was passed in 1997; the bill did not privatize the review of new drugs, but did permit review of some medical devices by private contractors. Other controversial provisions included allowing manufacturers to advertise drugs for "off-label" uses, applications of a drug or medical device in a way that was not specifically approved by the FDA.[36] Consumer advocates claim that the FDA is now too ready to approve new drugs, a claim supported by the necessity in recent years to recall several drugs because of adverse effects that became evident only after they were on the market. For example, the diet drug known as "fen-phen" had to be recalled a year after it was approved because it caused serious heart valve problems.[37]

Further doubts about the drug approval and monitoring process surfaced in 2004 when the Merck pharmaceutical company withdrew from the market Vioxx, a pain killer that was one of the most widely advertised drugs in the world and had earned $2.5 billion for the company since it was approved by the FDA in 1999. Merck had found in a new study that people taking the drug doubled their risk of heart attacks and strokes. Questions were raised about why the FDA had not recognized the problems with Vioxx and recalled it earlier. In a hearing by the Senate Finance Committee, FDA employees disagreed with one another on whether the agency was too likely to surrender to the demands of the industry. As described in a *New York Times* news report on the hearing, "the clash was a rare public airing of tensions that have simmered in the agency for decades." The conflict is clearly one that also reflects the opposing views Congress has held on the agency. After years of congressional pressure on the FDA to protect the interests of the pharmaceutical industry, the FDA is now accused of neglecting the safety of consumers.[38]

Critics complain that since the 1992 law permitting pharmaceutical companies to pay "user fees" to speed up drug approval, the agency has become too cozy with the companies. They note that the number of recalls of new drugs has increased dramatically, amounting to over 5 percent in the period 1997 to 2001, implying that the drugs are being approved too easily.[39] Moreover, the law has forced the FDA to spend almost 80 percent of its budget, supplemented by the user fees, for drug approvals, with too little allocated for safety monitoring after the drugs have been approved. Postmarketing surveillance relies on the drug companies to report adverse effects, a system that is inadequate at best and rife with conflicts of interest on the part of the companies. There are now calls for an independent drug safety board to oversee postmarketing surveillance.[39,40]

Another problem with the drug approval process gained attention in 2004 and has led to calls for change in the way clinical trials are reported. For years there have been concerns that the pharmaceutical companies selectively publish trials that show a drug to be effective while remaining silent about negative results. In June 2004, New York State attorney general Eliot Spitzer sued the British drug maker GlaxoSmithKline for fraud, claiming that the company had heavily promoted its antidepressant Paxil for children and adolescents with depression, basing its claims on one clinical trial, while it suppressed results of other trials that failed to show a benefit or showed that Paxil actually increased the risk of suicide.[41] British drug regulators had already banned the use of all antidepressants except Prozac for children and teens based on a thorough analysis of published and unpublished data. The extensive publicity about the issue prompted by Spitzer's lawsuit and by a public hearing of an FDA advisory committee called attention to the problem of selective publication. There were calls for all clinical trials to be publicly registered when they began, so that reviewers could put positive results in perspective. In September 2004, a group of editors of eleven prestigious medical journals, including the *New England Journal of Medicine* and the *Journal of the American Medical Association*, announced that they would not publish the results of clinical trials unless they had been registered at the start.[42] The editors' statement urges all biomedical journals to adopt the same policy.

The American Medical Association and the Association of American Medical Colleges have urged the federal government to create a database and require companies to register their clinical trials at the outset and to report the results in the database. A voluntary database already exists, developed by the FDA and the NIH, and Congress is considering legislation that would make such a database mandatory. Prospects are uncertain that such a law will be enacted by a federal government controlled by industry-friendly Republicans.[43]

CONCLUSION

Although the U.S. food supply is thought by many to be the safest in the world, food-borne illness occurs more often than generally believed. Common sources of illness include salmonella bacteria in poultry, meat, and eggs, as well as a variety of viruses and parasites in fish and shellfish. Over the past decade, E. coli 0157:H7 has emerged as a serious threat in ground beef and other foods as well as in unpasteurized fruit juice.

Governmental responsibility for food safety is distributed among a variety of federal, state, and local agencies. The laws are inconsistent and, in many cases, paradoxical. The USDA has significant authority over meat and poultry safety. The FDA is responsible for most other foods, including fish and seafood, but its financial resources for inspection and monitoring are limited, and it has little power to act.

In the wake of several highly publicized food poisoning incidents, the Clinton administration took steps to improve the U.S. food safety system. The focus now is on preventing problems before they occur rather than depending on inspections to detect food that is already contaminated. The system, called HACCP, analyzes every step in the process of food production, processing, and preparation, with the objective of identifying possible hazards and instituting practices that will eliminate or minimize them.

Another feature of the food safety initiative is a strengthened surveillance system for rapid detection of food-borne disease outbreaks so that their sources can be identified and they can be halted early.

In addition to its role in the prevention of microbial contamination of food, the FDA regulates food additives and chemical contaminants, as well as food labeling and advertising. It sets standards for foods to be labeled "organic." The agency also has oversight over the safety of drugs and medical devices. This responsibility has led to considerable controversy, as the pharmaceutical industry and patient groups complain about the slow pace of new drug approval. The conservative Congress has made repeated efforts to weaken the FDA's authority and force it to act more quickly on drug approvals. One resulting law is the Dietary Supplement Health and Education Act of 1994, which prohibits the FDA from regulating herbs and food supplements. Another is a reform bill that passed in 1997 and allows private contractors to conduct the reviews of some medical devices. Consumer groups are concerned that these laws, together with the climate of pressure to speed up drug approvals, endanger public health by allowing unsafe products on the market.

Several scandals occurred in the early 2000s that confirmed fears that drugs are approved too easily and that the system for detecting safety problems after approval is inadequate. Evidence that pharmaceutical companies selectively publicize clinical trials that show benefits of their drugs while suppressing negative results has led to calls for mandatory registration of clinical trials at the outset, so that all the evidence will be available publicly. Whether Congress will support this remedy is uncertain.

REFERENCES

1. P. S. Mead et al., "Food-Related Illness and Death in the United States," *Emerging Infectious Diseases Journal* 5 (1999): 607–625.
2. W. M. Laydon, "Food Safety: A Patchwork System," *GAO Journal* (Spring-Summer 1992): 48–59.
3. A. Nadakavukaren, *Our Global Environment: A Health Perspective*, 5th ed. (Prospect Heights, Illinois: Waveland Press, 2000).
4. C. Drew and P. Belluck, "Deadly Bacteria—a New Threat to Fruit and Produce in U.S.," *New York Times* (January 4, 1998): A1.
5. P. Belluck and C. Drew, "Tracing Bout of Illness to Small Lettuce Farm," *New York Times* (January 5, 1998): A1.
6. T. Breuer et al., "A Multistate Outbreak of Escherichia coli O157:H7 Infections Linked to Alfalfa Sprouts Grown from Contaminated Seeds," *Emerging Infectious Diseases Journal* 7 (2001): 977–982.
7. M. Burros, "Produce Becoming Increasing Source for Food Illnesses," *New York Times* (November 23, 2003): 1.
8. L. Polgreen, "Hepatitis Inquiry Moves Deliberately from Farm to Plate," *New York Times* (November 18, 2003): A20.
9. D. W. K. Acheson and A. E. Fiore, "Preventing Foodborne Disease—What Clinicians Can Do," *New England Journal of Medicine* 350 (2004): 437–440.
10. U.S. Centers for Disease Control and Prevention, "Update: Outbreaks of Cyclosporiasis—United States and Canada, 1997," *Morbidity and Mortality Weekly Report* 46 (1997): 521–522.

11. U.S. Food and Drug Administration, *Food Safety from Farm to Table: A New Strategy for the 21st Century*, February 1997. *http://vm.cfsan.fda.gov/~dms/fs-draft.html*. Accessed July 2005.

12. M. Nestle, *Safe Food: Bacteria, Biotechnology, and Bioterrorism* (Berkeley, California: University of California Press, 2003).

13. R. A. Robinson, *Food Safety and Security: Fundamental Changes Needed to Ensure Safe Food*, General Accounting Office. Testimony Before the Subcommittee on Oversight of Government Management, Restructuring and the District of Columbia, Committee on Governmental Affairs, U.S. Senate. October 10, 2001. *www.gao.gov/new.items/d0247t.pdf*. Accessed December 14, 2004.

14. Food and Drug Administration, FDA/Seafood Industry Food Safety Initiative Goes Into Full Effect, December 18, 1997. *www.cfsan.fda.gov/~lrd/haccp.html*. Accessed July 2005.

15. Committee on Communicable Diseases Affecting Man, *Procedures to Implement the Hazard Analysis Critical Control Point System* (Ames, Iowa: International Association of Milk, Food, and Environmental Sanitarians, Inc., 1991).

16. T. Weiner, "Proposal Would Bar Food Exported by Some Nations," *New York Times* (May 11, 1998): A10.

17. M. Burros, "President to Push for Food Safety," *New York Times* (July 4, 1998): A1.

18. M. T. Osterholm and A. P. Norgan, "Role of Irradiation in Food Safety," *New England Journal of Medicine* 350 (2004): 1898–1901.

19. U.S. Centers for Disease Control and Prevention, "What Is PulseNet?" *www.cdc.gov/pulsenet/what_is.htm*. Accessed December 14, 2004.

20. U.S. Centers for Disease Control and Prevention, "What is FoodNet?" *www.cdc.gov/foodnet/what_is.htm*. Accessed December 9, 2004.

21. U.S. Centers for Disease Control and Prevention, "Preliminary FoodNet Data on the Incidence of Infection with Pathogens transmitted Commonly Through Food—Selected Sites, United States, 2003," *Morbidity and Mortality Weekly Report* 53 (2004): 343.

22. R. Pear, "Departing Health Secretary Warns of Flu Risk and Attacks on Food," *New York Times* (December 3, 2004).

23. U.S. Environmental Protection Agency, "EPA Announces Comprehensive Plans for Protecting Food Safety, Regulating Pesticides Under the 1996 Food Quality Protection Act," EPA Headquarters Press Release, March 18, 1997.

24. M. Burros, "Last Word on Organic Standards, Again," *New York Times* (May 26, 2004): F4.

25. M. Burros, "Agriculture Dept. Rescinds Changes to Organic Food Standards," *New York Times* (May 27, 2004): A17.

26. M. Burros, "Study Finds Far Less Pesticide Residue on Organic Produce," *New York Times* (May 8, 2002): A29.

27. C. K. Yoon, "Exposure to Pesticides is Lowered When Young Children Go Organic," *New York Times* (March 25, 2003): F2.

28. K. Flieger, "Testing Drugs in People," *FDA Consumer, Special Issue: From Test Tube to Patient: New Drug Development in the United State*s (January 1995).

29. R. M. Deutsch, *The New Nuts Among the Berries: How Nutritional Nonsense Captured America* (Palo Alto, California: Bull Publishing Company, 1977).

30. M. Burros, "F.D.A. Announces Label Requirement for Artery Clogger," *New York Times* (July 10, 2003): A1.
31. M. Burros and S. Jay, "Concern Grows Over Herb That Promises a Legal High," *New York Times* (April 10, 1996): C1.
32. U.S. Centers for Disease Control and Prevention, "Adverse Events Associated with Ephedrine-Containing Products—Texas, December 1993–September 1995," *Morbidity and Mortality Weekly Report* 45 (1996): 689–692.
33. S. G. Stolberg, "U.S. To Prohibit Supplement Tied to Health Risks," *New York Times* (December 31, 2003): A1.
34. U.S. Food and Drug Administration, "FDA: The Nation's Premier Consumer Protection and Health Agency," January 2002. *http://www.fda.gov/opacom/brochure/fdahealthbro/.html.* Accessed December 14, 2004.
35. R. Stone, "Kessler's Legacy: Unfinished Reform," *Science* 274 (1996): 1603–1604.
36. U.S. Food and Drug Administration, "FDA Modernization Act of 1997," FDA Backgrounder, November 21, 1997.
37. L. Johannes and S. Steckgow, "Dieting Dilemma: Withdrawal of Redux Spotlights Predicament FDA Faces on Obesity," *Wall Street Journal* (September 16, 1997): A1.
38. G. Harris, "FDA Failing in Drug Safety, Official Asserts," *New York Times* (November 19, 2004): A1.
39. P. B. Fontanarosa, D. Rennie, and C. D. DeAngelis, "Postmarketing Surveillance—Lack of Vigilance, Lack of Trust," *Journal of the Medical Association of America* 292 (2004): 2647–2650.
40. "Editorial: Industry Distortion of the FDA," *New York Times* (December 8, 2004).
41. G. Harris, "New York State Official Sues Drug Maker Over Test Data," *New York Times* (June 3, 2004): A1.
42. C. De Angelis et al., "Clinical Trial Registration: A Statement from the International Committee of Medical Journal Editors," *New England Journal of Medicine* 351 (2004): 1250–1251.
43. D. Kennedy, "Clinical Trials and Public Trust," *Science* 306 (2004): 1649.

CHAPTER 24

Population: The Ultimate Environmental Health Issue

The Population Bomb

Population biology is a science in itself. Studies of animal, plant, and microorganism populations have yielded some concepts and insights that can be applied to human populations. However, application of these studies' findings to human populations is an inexact science, and predictions are always highly controversial. Interest in the dynamics of the human population arises from concern about its continuing growth and its increasing impact on the environment.

All organisms tend to produce more offspring than would be needed to maintain a stable population. Pressures from the environment, such as availability of food and prevalence of predators, tend to limit the survival of those offspring. The difference between the birth rate and the death rate is the population's rate of growth.

Studies of organisms newly introduced into a closed environment have shown two general patterns of population growth: the S curve and the J curve, illustrated in Figure 24–1. Both patterns start out with a rapidly expanding population, but they differ in their response to environmental limitations. In the more common S pattern, environmental pressures increase gradually as the population approaches the number known as the

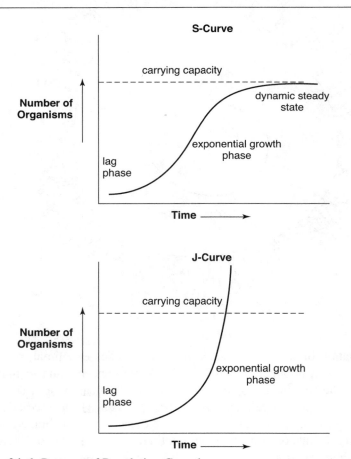

Figure 24–1 Patterns of Population Growth

Source: Reprinted from: *Our Global Environment: A Health Perspective*, 4th ed. (p. 51) by A. Nadakavukaren with permission of Waveland Press, 1995.

carrying capacity—the number of organisms that can be supported in a given environment without degrading that environment. In the J pattern, the population expands rapidly past the carrying capacity and then crashes, because once the carrying capacity is exceeded, the environment is degraded, and the carrying capacity is reduced. For example, the J pattern is seen in lemmings and locusts, species famous for huge population explosions followed by massive numbers of deaths when the food supply is exhausted.[1]

It is not yet clear whether the human population is growing in an S or a J pattern. The world population has grown steadily, with minor irregularities, for the past million years, with a major surge beginning about 200 years ago. About that time, when the population of the earth was about one billion, the British clergyman and economist Thomas Malthus raised an alarm that population growth was outpacing the food supply; he predicted that the resulting crowding would lead to famine, war, and disease. However, Malthus's dismal predictions did not come about, and his warnings were discredited. Progress in agricultural technology and migrations from highly populated areas in Europe to the open spaces of the Americas and southern Africa relieved pressures on populations, allowing the expansion to continue.[1]

In 1968, when the world's population was 3.5 billion, Paul Ehrlich, an American ecologist, published *The Population Bomb*, a best seller that repeated and expanded upon Malthus's warning.[2] Perhaps in part due to the attention paid to Ehrlich's book, the rate of the world's population growth has slowed since then, from an all-time high of 2.1 percent per year between 1965 and 1970 to about 1.2 percent in 2002.[3] There is a tremendous momentum to population growth, however, and the numbers continue to increase dramatically. In 1990, when the population had reached 5.3 billion, Ehrlich and his wife, Anne, published another book, *The Population Explosion*, arguing that many of his dire predictions have already begun to be realized.[4] And in 2004, with the world's population at 6.4 billion, they published *One with Nineveh*, which further examines the consequences of overpopulation and the linked problems of overconsumption and political and economic inequity—consequences that include the prospect of increasing terrorism.[5]

Most environmentalists and public health experts agree with Ehrlich. However, like Malthus, he has his detractors. There are pro-growth advocates—mostly economists—who argue that human ingenuity will always find ways of overcoming any problems created by crowding. In response, the Ehrlichs quote Kenneth Boulding: "Anyone who believes exponential growth can go on forever in a finite world is either a madman or an economist."[4(p.159)] Some of the world's major religions oppose population control measures, making it easier for politicians to listen to growth advocates and simply ignore the problems created by overpopulation.

It is very difficult to predict what the future population of the world will be. There are indications, as the Ehrlichs point out, that environmental pressures opposing population growth are increasing, especially in developing regions of the world. There are also indications that international family planning efforts are paying off in slowing growth rates in many parts of the world. The United Nations predicted in that, if current trends continue, the population will reach 9.3 billion in 2050 and stabilize just after the year 2200 at somewhat under 11 billion.[6] It is not clear, however, if the earth's carrying capacity is large enough to support that many people. If not, irreversible forces may be building for a sudden J-type population crash. By the time the Ehrlichs would be proved right, it would be too late to do anything to prevent the disaster.

PUBLIC HEALTH AND POPULATION GROWTH

Public health has had a major role in bringing about the dramatic growth in the world's population over the past several decades. Public health improvements—clean water, immunization, pest control measures, inexpensive oral rehydration treatment of diarrheal diseases—in developing countries have led to major declines in death rates, especially among children. According to the United Nations Children's Fund (UNICEF) the number of children who die before reaching their fifth birthday declined by almost 60 percent since 1960.[7] Because birth rates remained constant, populations grew rapidly in the developing countries.

In developed countries, which instituted public health measures over a period of many decades in the nineteenth and twentieth centuries, birth rates tended to fall in response to falling death rates, a process known as the "demographic transition." The fall in birth rates is a rational response to parents' knowledge that their children are likely to survive to adulthood. In an industrialized, urban society, children are an economic liability—expensive to feed, clothe, and educate.

In the developing world, however, many public health measures were introduced by international agencies over a short period of time after

World War II. International aid for population control efforts has not been as generous. This is, in part, because of cultural resistance to contraception within some societies; and, in part, because of the religious and political controversy surrounding family planning, especially in the United States, which has limited the amount of aid this nation provides.

Because of continued high birth rates, the public health in many developing countries is now, ironically, threatened by the crowding that has resulted from public health improvements. In all parts of the world, there has been a trend toward urbanization, because rural areas whose main industries are agricultural do not need the increasing numbers of workers. This trend has been most marked in developing countries, where migrants from rural areas flock to the cities. From 1950 to 2004, the percentage of people living in cities increased from 29 percent to 48 percent.[1,8] According to the World Bank, Africa is becoming urbanized at the rate of 5 percent a year; the annual rate of urbanization in Asia is almost 4 percent.[9] Governments struggling to provide adequate drinking water and sewage services to their citizens cannot keep up with the influx. Many of the migrants settle on the outskirts of the cities in shantytowns totally lacking in water and sanitation. Others are completely homeless, simply living on the streets.

These conditions threaten to reverse all the progress in public health made through earlier efforts. Cholera and other diarrheal diseases are rampant in these third-world slums. Malaria, measles, whooping cough, and diphtheria are also common. Polio is still a threat in Africa, as discussed in Chapter 9. Cases of tuberculosis and AIDS are surging. In sub-Saharan Africa, 7.5 percent of the adult population is HIV positive, and in some of these countries, prevalence is shockingly high: 38.8 percent in Swaziland and 37.3 percent in Botswana. The number of children orphaned by AIDS was estimated at fifteen million in 2003.[7] In fact, AIDS has dwarfed all other public health problems in Africa. Life expectancy in several countries in southern Africa has fallen by twenty years, and the rate of population growth has dropped to almost zero, not because of low birth rates as in developed countries, but because death rates are almost equal to birth rates. The United Nations predicts that the population of Botswana will fall by 43 percent between 2004 and 2050.[8]

The desperate conditions in third-world urban slums lead to the disruption of traditional lifestyles and the breakdown of normal social constraints, including sexual and parental restraints. Prostitution is common; children are abandoned to fend for themselves. These were the conditions that are believed to have led to the origin of AIDS as an epidemic threat (see Chapter 10), and they contribute to the continuing disaster of the epidemic. Such conditions may be the breeding ground for other emerging infections in the future. These conditions also encourage crime and violence. Even if, as predicted, population growth rates continue to decline, 95 percent of the two or three billion people added to the world in the next twenty-five to fifty years will be in the poorest countries, and most of that growth will occur in cities.[1]

Even the United States and other developed countries are affected by some of the pressures described above, although the rate of population growth in this country is under 1 percent, and in Japan and most European countries, it is close to zero. The American population is becoming increasingly urban, with over 75 percent living in communities with more than 2,500 residents.[1] Sixteen percent of children live in families with incomes below the poverty line; a high percentage of these children live with both housing and food insecurity.[10]

The United States is also affected by the social consequences of population growth in developing countries. Highly publicized problems with illegal immigrants from Mexico and Central America are linked with poverty and social problems caused by population growth in those countries. As conditions in those areas become more crowded and desperate in the future, the pressures on people to seek less crowded, more prosperous surroundings will increase, making it more difficult for the United States to remain isolated. As discussed in Chapter 10, infectious diseases have no respect for political boundaries. With international travel and commerce so rapid and widespread, Americans are at risk from diseases imported from anywhere in the world. Furthermore, as discussed in the following section, human population growth threatens to change the environment of the entire globe, posing health threats that no one could escape, even if the nation's borders were sealed.

GLOBAL IMPACT OF POPULATION GROWTH—
DEPLETION OF RESOURCES

The carrying capacity of the earth—the population size that the earth can support without being degraded—is determined by a number of factors, some of which can be altered by technological intervention and human behavior. These factors, which are related, include the availability of fresh water, the availability of fuel, the amount and productivity of arable land, and the amount and disposition of wastes, both biological and technological. There are signs that the carrying capacity is already exceeded in some parts of the world: as the environment is degraded, the size of the population that can be supported shrinks, leading to further environmental degradation and a vicious circle of hunger, disease, and death.

The supply of fresh water, which is basic to human life, is one of the factors that limits the earth's carrying capacity. Water is essential for drinking, cooking, and washing. It is also used for agriculture, irrigating dry fields to grow the increasing amounts of food required by expanding populations. Water is a renewable resource, due to cycles of evaporation and precipitation, but the rate at which water supplies are renewed is fixed. Only a small percentage of the water on earth is suitable for human use: while there are methods of removing the salt from sea water, the technology is expensive and uses large amounts of energy. Pollution resulting from the use of fresh water supplies for disposal of wastes also renders potential sources of water unsuitable for human use.

Availability of fresh water is highly variable according to geographic area and precipitation patterns. In drier parts of the world, especially the Middle East, water rights become volatile international issues because some countries depend on water sources that originate beyond their borders. For example, the Nile flows into Egypt from Ethiopia and Sudan, and the flow of the Tigris-Euphrates into Syria and Iraq may be altered by dam construction in Turkey.

In the United States, water supplies have been sufficiently plentiful so that Americans are accustomed to lavish consumption, watering lawns, washing cars, and filling private swimming pools, even in relatively dry areas of the Southwest. The annual per capita use of water in the United States, including industrial usage, is more than seventy times higher than it is in Ghana.[11] An example of wasteful practices is the draining of the Ogallala Aquifer, the world's largest underground water reserve, which underlies portions of six southwestern states. The water accumulated during the last ice age and cannot be replenished. Yet it is being used, among other things, for industry and irrigation, attracting people to the area who will be left literally high and dry when the water runs out.

The amount of fresh water on earth is theoretically sufficient to support a population of twenty billion people if evenly distributed.[11] Many countries have taken steps to conserve fresh water supplies and clean up the pollution. In poorer, drier countries, however, the available water is insufficient to support the growth in population that is occurring. The lack of water for cooking and washing, and the pollution of drinking water with human and industrial wastes, is already harming the public health. According to a 1997 United Nations report, one-third of the world's population, mostly in Africa and south Asia, lives in regions with water shortages, and that number will grow to two-thirds by 2025.[1]

Predictions about the earth's carrying capacity have most often centered on food, attempting to estimate the limits of agricultural productivity. Malthus's warnings were built on concerns about limited growth in food supplies, which nevertheless continued to grow rapidly for almost two centuries. Now, unhappily, it is beginning to look as if Malthus may finally be proven right.

With increasing populations needing greater amounts of food, the amount of land used for agriculture grew quickly during the period between 1850 and 1950. Then, despite continued population growth, the expansion of arable land slowed down and ceased altogether in the late 1980s.[12] Food production continued to keep pace with population growth during the 1960s and 1970s, however, because of the "green revolution," the development of genetic strains of wheat and rice that yielded harvests two to three times greater than conventional strains. Crop yields also grew because of increasing use of fertilizers, irrigation, and chemical pesticides.

Such increases in yields are unlikely to continue, however, because of water shortages, depletion of soil, and the development of resistance by pests to chemical pesticides. The amount of land under cultivation worldwide has declined in the past decade, in part because of spreading urban centers, in part because the soil is depleted of nutrients or has become salty from irrigation. Erosion of topsoil due to overgrazing and poor agricultural practices has contributed to the loss of arable land.[12] The demand for agricultural land for farming has led to widespread clearing of forests, although forested land may be only marginally suitable for cultivation. Deforestation also occurs as a result of people gathering wood for fuel. The need by growing populations for firewood for cooking and, in colder climates and mountainous regions, heating as well, has resulted in vast treeless areas around towns and villages throughout Africa, Asia, and Latin America. The loss of forests increases soil erosion and contributes to catastrophic flooding in areas subject to monsoons.

Population growth has also caught up with the seemingly limitless supply of food from the sea. Fish catches increased dramatically between 1950 and 1989 but have declined since then. The United Nations Food and

Agriculture Organization has concluded that 70 percent of the major fish species are either fully exploited or overexploited. Pollution of coastal waters has also contributed to the decline of harvests, especially those of shellfish. On the bright side, the practice of aquaculture is growing rapidly, and in 2000 one out of every four fish eaten worldwide was raised on a fish farm.[1]

GLOBAL IMPACT OF POPULATION GROWTH— CLIMATE CHANGE

Perhaps the most threatening effect of population growth is that it is beginning to change the composition of the earth's atmosphere, with potentially drastic consequences. As discussed in Chapter 20, the depletion of the ozone layer, which protects the earth's surface from ultraviolet radiation, is known to increase risks of skin cancer, melanoma, and cataracts. It may also have a harmful impact on plant and animal life.

Although international agreements have led to policies effective in slowing and possibly even reversing damage to the ozone layer, there is less hope of preventing climate change caused by other human activities. Alteration in the relative concentrations of the four major constituents of air—nitrogen, oxygen, argon, and carbon dioxide—is causing global warming due to the "greenhouse effect," in which the energy of sunlight is absorbed by carbon dioxide in the air and turned into heat rather than radiating back into outer space.

The balance of atmospheric gases has been maintained over the millenia by the photosynthetic activities of green plants, which take up carbon dioxide and release oxygen. The reverse process occurs during combustion of wood, coal, oil, and gas: oxygen is consumed and carbon dioxide is released. Since the beginning of the Industrial Revolution, with the ever-increasing use of fossil fuels, the levels of carbon dioxide in the atmosphere have been rising. The trend is made worse by the loss of photosynthetic action that accompanies widespread destruction of forests through logging and, worse, by the burning of vegetation, including tropical rain forests, to clear land for agriculture and human settlement. Green plants are being lost from the ocean also, through poisoning of phytoplankton by pollution of the seas. The concentration of atmospheric carbon dioxide has grown by nearly 30 percent since the beginning of the Industrial Revolution and is expected to double by about 2100.[1,13] Other gases also contribute to the greenhouse effect, especially methane, which is released by microbial activity in the intestines of cattle and in paddy fields where rice is grown.

Although the evidence was strongly disputed for many years, it is becoming increasingly clear that global climate change has begun: the earth's average temperature has risen by almost a full degree Fahrenheit over the past century, as seen in Figure 24–2. Predictions for the year 2100 range from three to eight degrees Fahrenheit higher than today.[13] The implications for human health are complex and far-reaching and entail a certain amount of speculation. Oceans will rise, inundating coastal towns and cities, displacing as many as 20 percent of the world's people.[14] Precipitation patterns will change, and the intensity of storms and hurricanes will increase. Food supplies will be affected, as optimal temperature and rainfall conditions for agriculture shift northward and marginally dry lands turn to desert. Insect pests will become more active, adversely affecting crops even further. Already, glaciers are melting, coral reefs are dying, the Antarctic ice sheets are disintegrating, species extinction is accelerating, and sea levels are rising.

As temperate zones become hotter, vector-borne diseases that now plague tropical regions will enlarge their territory, spreading even to industrialized countries. Mosquitoes that carry the dengue and yellow fever viruses and malaria parasites threaten to move northward into the

Figure 24–2 Global Temperature Changes (1880–2000)
Source: U.S. National Climatic Data Center, 2001.

United States from Central America. A warmer climate may be responsible for the emergence of hantavirus infections, described in Chapter 10, in the United States, and the 1991 outbreak in South America of epidemic cholera, the first seen in the Western hemisphere in more than a century.[1] Extreme heat waves, such as the ones that occurred in Chicago in 1995 and in Europe in 2003, greatly increase the risk of death, especially among elderly city dwellers.

Prospects for slowing the process of global warming appear dim, in part because population pressures in developing countries contribute to continuing deforestation but, more importantly, because the United States and other industrialized countries contribute disproportionately to the production of greenhouse gases, as seen in Figure 24–3. The United States, with less than 5 percent of the world's population, contributes over 20 percent of the world's greenhouse emissions. By contrast, India has 17 percent of the people in the world while contributing only 5.5 percent of the world's greenhouse emissions.[7,15] The high per capita production of carbon dioxide is part of the affluent life style, one that poorer countries strive to emulate and may begin to achieve if they can control the growth of their populations.

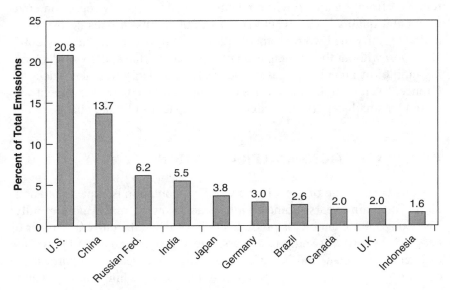

Figure 24–3 Top 10 Greenhouse Gas Emitters
Source: Data from World Resources Inst.

However, that hope is countered by the probability that environmental damage caused by the continued rise in the earth's temperature will cause increases in human suffering, especially in the poorest countries.

Recognizing the dangers of global climate change, delegates to the United Nations' Earth Summit in 1992 negotiated an agreement that called for voluntary reductions in greenhouse gas emissions. It soon became obvious, however, that the nations were failing miserably at achieving any reduction in emissions, and negotiations were resumed in 1997 in Kyoto, Japan. At that conference, representatives from 171 nations agreed on mandatory reductions, with individualized goals for each country. The United States was assigned the goal of reducing its emissions to 7 percent below 1990 levels by 2012. The Kyoto Protocol was to become legally binding after being ratified by fifty-five countries representing 55 percent of the 1990 emissions.[1]

Prospects for ratification by the U.S. Congress looked bleak even when Bill Clinton was president, but upon the election of George W. Bush, it was clear that the United States would not participate. President Bush withdrew the nation from the Kyoto Protocol soon after he was inaugurated. He has rejected evidence that global warming is occurring, to the extent that political pressures forced all reference to climate change to be removed from a major Environmental Protection Agency report on environmental quality.[16] (See Chapter 2.) In 2004, Russia became the 121st nation to ratify the Kyoto Protocol, allowing it to take effect in early 2005. However, without the participation of the United States, the world's leading emitter of greenhouse gases, the treaty is unlikely to make much difference. Even if all the signatories meet their targets, the achievement will be only a small step toward reducing the impact of climate change.[17]

DIRE PREDICTIONS AND FRAGILE HOPE

At its current rate of growth, the world's population is expected to double in forty-nine years. Some countries are growing much more rapidly: The Congo, for example, is predicted to have twice the current number of people in as little as twenty-two years; Nicaragua also has a doubling time of twenty-two years and Nigeria's is twenty-three years. In contrast, the doubling time of the U.S. population is 116 years, while that in Japan is 318 years. As discussed in the Prologue, in Russia, as well as in several European countries, the population is shrinking.[1]

Many third world countries are already suffering from shortages of natural and economic resources, including limited agricultural land and a lack of nonagricultural employment. Such regions may have already passed a threshold of irreversibility. The speed and magnitude with which populations are outstripping the available resources are unprecedented in history. The result is expected to be an increase in migrations and violent conflicts. Already, wars and civil violence are being fought over scarce resources such as water, farmland, forests, and fish. Some analysts predict a total breakdown in the social fabric of the planet.[18]

If there is any hope for saving the earth from the direst of these predicted fates, it must come from control of population growth. Unfortunately, international agreement on this issue is exceedingly difficult. Three United Nations conferences on population have been held at ten-year intervals, most recently in 1994; all were fraught with ethical, religious, and political controversy. Rich countries blame poor countries for the destruction of natural resources, while poor countries blame the rich for profligate consumption. Poor countries demand help from the rich, which attach unwelcome conditions to the aid they provide. Opposition to contraception by Roman Catholic and Muslim authorities, as well as the incendiary politics of abortion in the United States, obstruct rational attempts at limiting population growth.

Although the 1994 conference held in Cairo was as contentious as the two previous meetings, a consensus emerged on a new approach to population policy, one that focused on individual rights, especially women's rights, including their right to make reproductive decisions. The conference produced a twenty-year "Programme of Action" that included, among other goals, education for women.[19] Educated women prefer fewer children, and they have more bargaining power in the family and in society, studies have shown. Thus the optimum path to a world population that is within the earth's carrying capacity and to the development of resources in a sustainable way may be achievable by the relatively uncontroversial measure of providing girls in the developing world with a basic education.[20]

The United States is sheltered from some of the realities of the population problem because of the nation's relative isolation from the most crowded regions of the planet. However, Americans cannot afford to be complacent about the dangers posed by world crowding. Global warming, air and ocean pollution, and loss of biodiversity are environmental effects of overpopulation that are certain to affect public health in the United States, even if the nation could close its borders to all international travelers. Without global population control, other public health efforts would ultimately be a losing battle.

Population control cannot be imposed by force, however. As Paul and Anne Ehrlich point out in their most recent book, *One with Nineveh*, stabilization of the world's population is closely tied to modernization and economic viability of the poorest countries.[5] This agrees with the conclusions of the 1994 Cairo conference, and it is the goal that the United States and other developed nations should be striving toward. The Ehrlichs quote Lester Pearson, former prime minister of Canada and president of the United Nations General Assembly, "A planet cannot, any more than a country, survive half slave, half free, half engulfed in misery, half careening along toward the supposed joys of almost unlimited consumption. Neither our ecology nor our morality could survive such contrasts."[5(p.234)]

CONCLUSION

The earth's human population has been growing rapidly and continuously for centuries. While the rate of growth appears to be slowing, the science of population biology suggests that a disastrous population crash is possible, a result of environmental pressures.

Paradoxically, public health measures such as clean water, immunization, and pest control have contributed to population growth by saving lives. While improved life expectancy has led to a fall in birth rates in industrialized countries, in the developing world population control efforts have not kept up with other public health efforts. The resulting crowding threatens to reverse the advances that have been made in public health. Migrants from rural areas, in search of jobs, settle in urban shantytowns that lack adequate drinking water and sewage services. These conditions lead to frequent epidemics of infectious diseases, and the accompanying social breakdown contributed to the rise of the AIDS epidemic. The AIDS epidemic in turn is so severe in parts of Africa that it has put a stop to population growth in those countries.

Many analysts believe that the carrying capacity of the earth—the population size that the earth can support without being degraded—is being reached. Factors that limit carrying capacity include the availability of fresh water, the availability of fuel, the amount and productivity of arable land, and the amount and disposition of wastes. Fresh water is already in short supply in some parts of the world, and many sources of fresh water are being degraded by pollution with human and industrial wastes. Arable land is being depleted through overcultivation and erosion. Deforestation is occurring on all continents, and even the sea is being depleted of fish.

In addition to the impact of resource shortages on human populations, overpopulation is bringing about global climate change. Increased atmospheric concentrations of greenhouse gases brought about by human activities are causing warming of the earth's surface. This in turn causes melting of the polar ice caps and a rise in ocean levels. Weather patterns may already be changing. Warming of temperate zones may account for the recent emergence in the United States of a number of infectious diseases formerly confined to more tropical regions. At an international conference in Kyoto, Japan in 1997, an agreement was reached for countries to reduce their greenhouse gas emissions. However, President Bush has tried to cast doubt on the evidence for global warming, and he has withdrawn U.S. support for the Kyoto Protocol.

The United Nations has held three conferences on population, all fraught with ethical, religious, and political controversy. Rich countries and poor countries blame each other for the problems that result from overpopulation and overconsumption. At the third United Nations conference, held in Cairo in 1994, a new approach to population control was agreed upon. This consensus builds on evidence that education and empowerment of women lead them to choose smaller families and brings a fragile hope that stabilization of the population may be achieved by helping the poorest nations to modernize and become economically stronger.

REFERENCES

1. A. Nadakavukaren, *Our Global Environment: A Health Perspective*, 5th ed. (Prospect Heights, Illinois: Waveland Press, 2000).
2. P. R. Ehrlich, *The Population Bomb* (New York: Ballantine Books, 1975).
3. J. E. Cohen, "Human Population: The Next Half Century," *Science* 302 (2000): 1172–1175.
4. P. R. Ehrlich and A. Ehrlich, *The Population Explosion* (New York: Simon and Schuster, 1990).
5. P. Ehrlich and A. Ehrich, *One with Nineveh: Politics, Consumption, and the Human Future* (Washington, DC: Island Press, 2004).
6. D. Peck, "The World in Numbers: Population 2050," *Atlantic Monthly* (October 2002): 40–41.

7. United Nations Children's Fund, *State of the World's Children 2004* (New York: 2004).
8. Population Reference Bureau, "2004 World Population Data Sheet," *www.prb.org/pdf04/04WorldDataSheet_Eng.pdf.* Accessed December 17, 2004.
9. World Bank. Urbanization and Cities—Facts & Figures. *www.web.worldbank.org.* Accessed December 17, 2004.
10. "Federal Interagency Forum on Child and Family Statistics: America's Children," *www.childstats.gov/ac2004/pressrel.asp.* Accessed December 19, 2004.
11. J. W. Maurits la Riviere, "Threats to the World's Water," *Scientific American* (September 1989): 80–94.
12. J. Bongaarts, "Can the Growing Human Population Feed Itself," *Scientific American* (March 1994): 36–42.
13. R. E. Kerr, "Three Degrees of Consensus," *Science* 305 (2004): 932–934.
14. J. D. Mahlman, "Uncertainties in Projections of Human-Caused Climate Warming," *Science* 278 (1997): 1416–1417.
15. World Resources Institute. Climate Change and Energy. *http://poclimate.wri.org/pubs_content_text.cfm?ContentID-2639.* Accessed December 19, 2004.
16. E. Stokstad, "EPA Report Takes Heat for Climate Change Edits," *Science* 300 (2003): 201.
17. S. Mydans and A. C. Revkin, "With Russia's Nod, Treaty on Emissions Clears Last Hurdle," *New York Times* (October 1, 2004): A1.
18. R. D. Kaplan, "The Coming Anarchy," *Atlantic Monthly* (February 1994): 44–76.
19. J. DeJong, "Role and Limitations of the Cairo International Conference on Population and Development," *Social Science and Medicine* 51 (2000): 941–953.
20. B. Herz, "Importance of Educating Girls," *Science* 305 (2004): 1909–1910.

PART VI

Medical Care
and Public Health

CHAPTER 25

Is the Medical Care System a Public Health Issue?

Public Health Issues?

Even in an ideal world, where public health functioned perfectly, there would be a need for medicine. The medical system provides preventive care: immunizations against infectious diseases, monitoring of pregnancies and provision of "well-baby care" to ensure that children develop normally, testing of adults for risk factors (such as high cholesterol and blood pressure) that lead to cardiovascular disease, and secondary prevention measures—screening for early detection of diabetes and cancer, for example, and early interventions to correct problems. Even people with the healthiest lifestyle get sick or injured. Medical care saves lives and prevents suffering and disability and, therefore, must be considered necessary for public health.

Medical care is even more necessary when public health is not functioning perfectly. There are many gaps in the public health system because of a lack of resources, lack of political will, and the emergence of new health threats. Also, competing values in society lead people to behave in unhealthy ways. The medical system is called on to deal with the consequences of failures in public health. Doctors are asked to repair the damage when an unvaccinated child contracts an infectious disease, when a community is sickened by water or food contaminated because of deficiencies in sanitary practices, when someone is injured in a motor vehicle accident caused by a drunk driver, or when a smoker develops cancer after years of exposure to tobacco smoke.

The fact that medical care can and does make a difference in people's health raises a number of fundamental social questions. Who is responsible for providing medical care when it is needed? Medical care is expensive, and the costs have been rising dramatically over the past several decades. Who should pay for that care? Vastly greater sums of public money are spent each year on medical care than on public health measures aimed at preventing disease and disability. Is that a rational allocation of resources? Should U.S. citizens have the same right to medical care as they have to education in childhood? And, if there are limits on the community's responsibility for providing medical care, how should those limits be determined?

The medical profession has fought governmental involvement in addressing these questions, regarding itself as the ultimate authority over all matters of health.[1] However, public health concerns have repeatedly forced government action on a piecemeal basis to challenge medicine's sovereignty. Public health has always seen a role for itself as the provider of last resort, offering needed medical care to people who cannot afford to pay for it. This is part of the assurance function that the Institute of Medicine identified as one of public health's core functions (see Chapter 1). Government regulation has also been found necessary to set standards for the practice of various health care services, to discipline medical professionals when they are thought to be acting unethically or incompetently, and to set policy when ethical dilemmas have arisen that transcend the individual sickroom.

WHEN MEDICAL CARE IS A PUBLIC HEALTH RESPONSIBILITY

Some forms of medical care are more important to the health of the community than others. Medical treatment of communicable diseases is particularly important because of the possibility that one sick individual could infect many others. Consequently, public health has taken a major interest in all aspects of infectious disease control, from the early days when quarantines were the only effective way of controlling epidemics, to immunization programs, to the provision of free medical treatment for those who do not have health insurance and cannot afford to pay for care. City and county health departments have traditionally operated clinics for diagnosis and treatment of infectious diseases. Today, the threat of re-emerging tuberculosis is taken seriously enough that, for example, the New York City Department of Health provides a program of directly observed therapy (see Chapter 10) in which public health nurses are sent to track down patients and make sure they take their medicine. The fact that AIDS is a communicable disease accounts, at least in part, for the major investment that the federal and some state governments have made not only in research, but also in providing treatment for patients.

A second area in which communities have an undisputed interest in the universal availability of medical care is the provision of emergency services. Emergencies are by definition unpredictable and can strike individuals at any time and in any place. In an increasingly mobile society, heart attacks and motor vehicle crashes may occur when people are far from home, with no family or friends present to provide first aid or call the doctor. It is in the interest of everyone to save lives first and ask questions later. Beginning with the Highway Safety Act of 1966, the federal government began to pressure states and localities to develop procedures for providing quick access to emergency care. Since then, in accordance with federal standards, communities have developed 911 phone response networks, trained emergency medical technicians, dispatched ambulances using a centralized system, regulated the availability of hospital emergency rooms, identified trauma centers, and provided evacuation helicopters in rural areas. Still, the quality and effectiveness of emergency response systems vary considerably in different parts of the country.[2]

A number of federal and state laws require that emergency rooms provide treatment to any patient that arrives with a life-threatening condition until he or she is stabilized, regardless of ability to pay. When the emergency situation has passed, however, many hospitals transfer poor and uninsured patients to public or charity hospitals. Some states have laws that prohibit hospitals from denying admission based solely on inability to pay, but in many parts of the country hospitals can and do turn away patients for financial reasons. Once medical treatment is under way, however, a patient's rights are greatly enhanced. There are laws against "abandonment," and hospitals cannot simply discharge patients because they are poor and uninsured.

Although most U.S. citizens do not have a general right to medical care, there are several exceptions, including veterans and prisoners. The hospitals and clinics of the Department of Veterans Affairs (VA) were designed to treat war-related injuries, but they also serve as a safety net for low-income veterans who do not have other sources of medical care. Seventy percent of veterans seeking care through the VA system earn less than $20,000 a year; many of them suffer from psychiatric disabilities or have substance abuse problems.[3] Prisoners are entitled to medical care because, as wards of the state, they are unable to seek care on their own. The courts have ruled that to deny them care would be the cruel and unusual punishment forbidden by the Constitution.[4] The medical care provided in prisons, however, is often substandard.

THE CONFLICT BETWEEN PUBLIC HEALTH
AND THE MEDICAL PROFESSION

Most Americans get health insurance as part of an employee benefit package. The insurance covers the worker and his or her family. This approach to paying medical bills became dominant after World War II, when unions bargained actively to obtain health benefits for workers. The arrangement satisfied most groups over the next three or four decades. Workers and their families could receive necessary medical care without worrying about cost; doctors and hospitals were happy because they could provide care as they saw fit and not worry about getting paid; unions took credit for forcing employers to provide the benefits; employers did not object because the cost at first was modest and the benefits inspired loyalty in their workers.

Traditional health insurance, the kind of insurance provided by most employers until quite recently, is like car insurance. Regular premiums are paid to the insurance company to cover the worker and his or her family. When covered individuals get sick, they go to the doctor or other medical provider of their choice, and that provider then sends them bills for services rendered. The patients pay the bills and are reimbursed by the insurance company. Sometimes the policy, like many car insurance policies, calls for a deductible that the patient must pay first before the insurance kicks in. Sometimes the patients must also pay a flat fee or a fixed percentage of the remainder of the bill, called a copayment. This way of paying for medical care is called "fee-for-service." The fee-for-service approach permits doctors to make decisions about a patient's care with no consideration of cost. As discussed in Chapter 26, this freedom has led to escalating medical costs and increasing numbers of uninsured citizens whose access to care is limited.

The medical profession has strongly resisted efforts to be included in the domain of public services. Since the end of the nineteenth century, with the discovery of bacterial causes of diseases, public health has claimed the prevention and treatment of infectious disease as its responsibility, and doctors have resisted that claim. While tolerant of public health's efforts at cleaning up the environment, private practitioners regarded diagnosing and curing sick people as their domain. Early in the twentieth century, they fought reporting requirements for cases of tuberculosis and venereal disease, and they opposed the creation of public health clinics and centers, which they perceived as an attack on their economic interests. This struggle continued throughout the century, and although public health has had some victories, the medical establishment has been able to prevent the United States from providing for its citizens the public assurance of needed medical care.[1]

Still, there is a long history of providing charity care for the nation's poor. Often, treatment was provided by part-time volunteer physicians who combined their services with research and the teaching of medical students. This practice began in the late eighteenth century, with the establishment of free dispensaries in eastern cities, many of them connected with medical schools. These services were controversial. Private practitioners were suspicious that free care was being provided to those who could afford to pay for it, and there was great concern about "dispensary abuse." The poor, on the other hand, were distrustful of the dispensaries, where they were forced to wait hours for hasty and superficial attention.[1]

In the early twentieth century, city health departments began setting up clinics for the control of infectious diseases and the prevention of infant mortality. Baby clinics emphasized the teaching of hygienic practices and promotion of improvements in child care, diet, and living patterns. Clinics for tuberculosis and venereal disease provided diagnosis and advice about hygiene and diet but left treatment to private physicians, who objected strongly when they felt that the clinics were trespassing on their territory. The New York City Department of Health ran into trouble when its diagnostic bacteriologic laboratory began producing diphtheria antitoxin, selling it to drugstores, and making it available to poor patients for free, prompting complaints of socialism and unfair competition that forced it to cease all sale of the antitoxin. Despite the early opposition of the medical profession, however, an uneasy truce has evolved that allows city and county health departments to provide treatment for the poor, often under the uncomfortable conditions that prevailed in the old dispensaries.[1]

Community health centers provide another source of basic medical care for the poor. These centers are supported by federal grants as well as by payments by public and private health insurance for services provided. There are about 900 community health centers in the United States. They are located in inner cities and isolated rural areas where there are shortages of medical and social services. Community health centers provide primary and preventive care to people who might otherwise not be able to afford it. Services may be paid for by government programs (see below), or patients may pay a fee based on a sliding scale according to income. Community health centers serve as an important safety net for low-income families; however, they serve only about 10 percent of uninsured persons.[5]

The health of schoolchildren has been a public health concern since the late nineteenth century. To control the spread of communicable diseases, cities began to employ medical inspectors to examine children who were thought to be sick and exclude them from school if they had a communicable disease. School doctors and nurses also began testing children for eye problems and other physical impairments that might interfere with learning. Because of the opposition of the medical establishment, they were not allowed to provide medical treatments. With the development of effective vaccines, the law began requiring that children be immunized— by their private physicians or in public clinics—before they started school, and the threat of epidemics in the schools has receded. In some cities, school health programs treat minor problems; sometimes they merely send notes home to parents recommending treatment. It is a source of frustration to public health practitioners that there is no integration of school health programs with medical services, leaving many children with health problems that are repeatedly diagnosed but untreated.[1]

Throughout the twentieth century, there have been repeated attempts in the United States to provide some kind of national health insurance plan to ensure that everyone would have access to needed medical care. During this period, most industrialized countries were setting up such programs, some of them run by the national government, others more loosely organized. Germany established the first national system of compulsory sickness insurance in 1883. Over the next thirty years, Austria, Hungary, Norway, Serbia, Britain, Russia, and the Netherlands followed Germany's example. Canada implemented a national health insurance plan in the 1970s.[1]

In the United States, efforts to establish a national health program were made before World War I but were derailed by the war. Another attempt was made during the 1930s as part of President Franklin D. Roosevelt's New Deal, but health insurance was not included in the Social Security Act. After World War II, President Harry S. Truman proposed a single health insurance system that would apply to everyone; again the attempt failed. Each time, the medical profession opposed governmental involvement in medical care as "socialized medicine," and various other political interests joined to defeat the proposals.[1]

In 1965, a significant victory over the medical establishment's opposition was achieved under President Lyndon Johnson: legislation for Medicare, which provides insurance for the elderly, and Medicaid, a welfare-type program for the poor, were passed. These programs were designed to remedy what people considered the main problems with employer-based insurance: it stopped when a worker retired, and it left the poor and unemployed out of the system.[1]

Medicare, created in 1965 as a mandatory insurance program for people over the age of 65, is part of the Social Security system. (Younger people who are entitled to Social Security because of disability are also eligible for Medicare.) Workers pay into the system through deductions from their paychecks; employers pay a tax on their payroll; and workers are entitled to benefits when they reach retirement age. The Medicare program has two parts: Part A, which covers hospital insurance, and Part B, which pays doctor bills and other outpatient costs. Virtually all people are automatically enrolled in Medicare Part A when they reach age 65. Part B is voluntary and requires participants to pay a monthly premium. Medicare is much like traditional health insurance, in that most doctors and other providers are paid on a fee-for-service basis. Like private insurance, the patient is required to pay deductibles and copayments. In 2003, legislation was passed that created a new Medicare prescription drug plan. The new benefit, which will become effective in 2006, is optional and will require an additional monthly premium.

Medicaid was created, also in 1965, as a welfare program for the poor, with costs shared by the federal government and the states. Eligibility is determined by income and varies from one state to another. Medical bills are paid directly by the government to the provider, usually at a low, fixed rate for each service.

In the early 1970s, President Richard Nixon tried to expand these programs, proposing a national plan to cover everyone, but his efforts were derailed by the Watergate scandal. No further efforts were made until President Bill Clinton was elected in 1992, promising to provide health insurance for all; his proposal was also defeated. However, because of increasing concern about the problem of children without access to medical care, President Clinton and Congress negotiated a program called the State Children's Health Insurance Program (SCHIP). This is a joint federal-state program, similar to Medicaid, which expands coverage to children in families that earn too much to qualify for Medicaid, usually up to 200 percent of the federal poverty level.[6]

The United States remains the only industrialized nation, except South Africa, that does not have a national plan ensuring medical care for all its citizens. In early 2003, almost 19 percent of the American population under 65 had no health insurance.[7] For many of these people, there is no guaranteed access to health care except for emergency care. While most public health advocates believe that the government should ensure access to basic medical care for anyone who needs it, the American political system has not supported that view. Clinical medicine, always more prestigious and better financed than public health, has been able to fend off public health's attempts to integrate medical treatment into a rational system that would maximize the health of all Americans. In response to increasing evidence that the U.S. health care system is dysfunctional, as discussed in Chapter 26, there has been a move by some physicians in recent years to profoundly change the system.[8]

LICENSING AND REGULATION

While the medical profession has resisted government efforts to ensure and fund medical care for all Americans, it has been willing to submit to some forms of government regulation. Licensure of qualified medical practitioners, including physicians, nurses, and other health professionals, protects the prerogatives of the professionals from encroachment by non-licensed practitioners and also ensures quality of care for patients. Physicians, nurses, and dentists must be licensed to practice in every state. Licensing requirements for other health care professionals vary from state to state. States may establish requirements, such as continuing medical education, for physicians and nurses to maintain or update their skills to retain their licenses. States also have the power to discipline medical professionals for incompetence or misconduct with the ultimate threat of revoking their licenses.

States also license and regulate medical facilities such as hospitals and nursing homes. To confirm that they provide high-quality care, health care institutions also may seek accreditation by a private organization, generally the Joint Commission on Accreditation of Healthcare Organizations (JCAHO). Since Medicare, Medicaid, and many private health insurers usually require institutions to be accredited in order to pay them for patient services, maintaining accreditation is important. Schools of medicine, nursing, and public health as well as training programs for advanced medical specialties also seek accreditation as a measure of their quality. As medical care is increasingly being provided by managed care organizations (see Chapter 26) and as methods are developed to evaluate the quality of care provided by these organizations (see Chapter 27), accreditation of managed care organizations is becoming more widespread.

As discussed in Chapter 26, governments have attempted to use regulatory approaches to restrain the growth of medical costs by requiring certificates of need before new facilities can be built or expensive new equipment purchased. These efforts have generally been ineffective and most have been abandoned.

ETHICAL AND LEGAL ISSUES IN MEDICAL CARE

Although the United States has chosen not to establish a broad right to medical care, it has been forced repeatedly to deal with individual cases that attract public attention and demand community response. Consequently, there are many legal requirements and restrictions on medical care that have arisen from specific cases. Usually, such cases have come to the attention of the courts when medical professionals disagreed with each other or with patients' families. Decisions in these cases have set legal precedents for how medicine can be practiced in certain situations. Many of these situations involve the beginning and end of life, and many of the precedents have profound implications for public health.

Abortion is one of the most controversial medicolegal issues, pitting the "right to life" of the fetus against the right of the pregnant woman to control her own body. Abortion was illegal in most states until 1973, when the Supreme Court decided in *Roe v. Wade* that women have a constitutional right to an abortion, at least in the first trimester of pregnancy. The controversy continues, however, with right-to-life activists trying, with some success in some state legislatures, to place limits on the circumstances under which women can exercise their rights.

Similar controversy raged in the late 1990s over whether mentally competent, terminally ill patients have the right to physician-assisted suicide. Dr. Jack Kevorkian was making a career of helping to end the lives of people who were suffering or were afraid that they would suffer painful or degrading deaths. While laws were passed outlawing Dr. Kevorkian's activities, juries sympathized with the patients and refused to convict him. However, in 1999, he was convicted of second degree murder because he went beyond assisting suicide and administered a lethal drug himself to a patient who wished to die. The death of a fifty-two-year-old man with Lou Gehrig's disease was aired on the CBS program *60 Minutes*. Dr. Kevorkian is still serving his sentence of ten to twenty-five years in prison.[9]

Ironically, while there is no legal requirement to provide medical care to people who want and could benefit from it, many of the most contentious legal cases have concerned the system's insistence on providing expensive, intrusive, and unwanted treatment to patients whose conditions are judged medically hopeless. In the 1976 case of Karen Ann Quinlan, a young woman left permanently unconscious from an overdose of drugs and alcohol, the New Jersey Supreme Court eventually ruled that she could be removed from a ventilator at the request of her parents over the objections of hospital personnel. However, in the fourteen months of the court battle, the young woman had been weaned from the ventilator and was able to breathe on her own, although she remained unconscious. She was transferred to a nursing home where she survived for ten years in a persistent vegetative state.[10]

In the similar case of Nancy Cruzan, a young Missouri woman in a persistent vegetative state resulting from an automobile crash, the Supreme Court decided in 1990 that states could set the standards for when life support could be removed. Cruzan's father had to move her to another state in order to remove the feeding tube and let her die.[11] Now, after a number of other cases have been tried in the courts, the precedent is well established that competent patients can refuse medical treatment and that life-support measures are not required for an incompetent patient who has specified in advance the conditions under which he or she would not want them. The most reliable way for an individual to ensure that his or her wishes would be followed is to sign a durable power of attorney over to a trusted friend or family member who can make medical decisions if he or she becomes incompetent.

The lack of such an advance directive led to the politically charged battle in early 2005 over removing a feeding tube from Terri Schiavo, a young Florida woman who had been in a persistent vegetative state for 15 years. Florida law provided that Ms. Schiavo's husband was entitled to decide that the feeding tube should be removed; he contended that she would not have wanted to be kept alive in this condition. However, Ms. Schiavo's parents objected, maintaining that she recognized them and might improve with treatment. Inspired by "right to life" political pressures, the Florida governor and legislature, the U.S. Congress, and President Bush attempted to block removal of the feeding tube, but the Florida courts, the federal appeals court, and the Supreme Court upheld the husband's right to decide. Ms. Schiavo died 13 days after the tube was removed. Such family disputes over withdrawing life support, while common, would be easily resolved if the individual had prepared a "living will" that specifies her wishes.[12]

But what happens if a patient indicates that he or she wants all possible measures taken to preserve his or her life, even if there is no hope of regaining consciousness? This is what happened in 1991 in the case of Helga Wanglie, an 87-year-old woman in a persistent vegetative state who was being kept on a ventilator and feeding tube in a Minneapolis hospital. Her husband and children refused to allow life support to be removed, stating that they were praying for a miracle. The hospital went to court, claiming that the treatment was futile and merely prolonged death. The court refused to intervene, and the patient remained on life support until she died six months later.[13] However in some states, including California and Texas, the law allows health care institutions to withdraw life support when further treatment is judged futile, even against the wishes of the patient as expressed in an advance directive.[12] Not often mentioned in the legal arguments is the cost of the care. Most often, the costs of caring for brain-damaged patients are borne by the taxpayer, since few families have the resources to pay for the necessary care.

Similar quandaries occur at the beginning of life, when decisions must be made about treating infants whose prospects are limited. Several notable cases occurred in the 1980s involving babies born with Down syndrome, characterized by mental retardation and often accompanied by physical defects that are lethal but correctable by surgery. The difficult question with which parents are confronted, while still reeling from the news that their infant is not normal, is whether to authorize the surgery, allowing the infant a chance to live although his or her quality of life will be uncertain. In 1982, the Infant Doe case drew public attention to the problem. Infant Doe was a Down syndrome baby born in Bloomington, Indiana, with tracheoesophogeal fistula, a hole between the respiratory and digestive tracts. The parents chose not to operate, but hospital administrators and pediatricians went to court to force the surgery. The judge ruled that the parents had the right to make the decision; each level of appeal supported the parents, and the baby died before the case reached the Supreme Court.[10]

However, the publicity over Infant Doe attracted the attention of the Reagan Administration, which firmly supported the right-to-life viewpoint. On the grounds that nontreatment of newborns constituted discrimination against people with disabilities, the Justice Department implemented the so-called Baby Doe rules, which mandated treatment of all newborns with birth defects. Large posters were to be displayed outside all neonatal intensive care units stating that "Discriminatory failure to feed and care for handicapped infants in this facility is prohibited by federal law." A toll-free 800 number, the "Baby Doe hotline," was posted to report abuses, and "Baby Doe squads," composed of lawyers, government administrators, and physicians, investigated complaints. Later court action struck down the Baby Doe rules; but in 1984, Congress passed a law declaring that nontreatment in Baby Doe cases is child abuse except when the child is chronically and irreversibly comatose.[10]

It is not only Down syndrome infants that must be given aggressive medical treatment. The 27,000 infants born every year with low birth weight are also provided with advanced, high-technology care. Many of these infants survive to lead normal lives, but many others—especially those with very low birth weight (less than 3.3 pounds) die or are left with permanent impairments. Infants with low birth weight that survive are at increased risk of such long-term disabilities as cerebral palsy, autism, mental retardation, vision and hearing impairments, and other developmental problems.

The costs of medical treatment for these infants, like the costs of providing life support for nearly dead adults, are not generally considered when decisions are made about whether aggressive treatment should be given. Frequently, the cost is very high; in one case of an infant "rescued" by a Baby Doe squad the medical bills added up to $400,000, although doctors said the infant had "zero chance for a normal life expectancy."[10] An estimate of the total national hospital bill for prematurity in 2000 was $11.9 billion.[14] If these babies survive with major handicaps, medical and care-taking costs will continue throughout their lives.

From a public health perspective, the American health care system is unfair and unethical. Vast resources are spent on a relatively few desperately ill patients, many of whom have no prospect of a reasonable quality of life, while millions of Americans have no access to the most basic medical services that could relieve pain and prevent long-term disability. Richard Lamm, a former governor of Colorado who has been an outspoken critic of the inequities of the system, laments that medical ethicists debate agonizingly over the treatment of a few individuals while little attention is paid to social ethics, a neglected and much needed examination of the allocation of resources for the entire system. Lamm argues that "it is axiomatic that public funds should buy the most health for the most people,"[15(p.14)] a view consistent with that of public health. Chapter 26 discusses further the financing of U.S. medical care and the flaws in the system.

ETHICAL ISSUES IN MEDICAL RESOURCE ALLOCATION

While public health advocates believe that the inequities in access to care are the most important ethical dilemmas concerning the medical system, numerous other situations call for public participation in medical decisions. Sometimes the issue is access to scarce resources other than money. For example, when hemodialysis (blood-cleansing) was first developed in 1970 to help failing kidneys, there was a shortage of dialysis machines. To choose which patients should be dialyzed, "God Committees" were formed. The committees consisted of laypeople who would select the most worthy candidates for the life-saving treatment. The committees tended to favor those who had jobs, family responsibilities, youth, good general health, and strong motivation. The judgment process made many people uncomfortable.[10] After dramatic publicity about the plight of patients with kidney failure who were denied the dialysis treatment, Congress passed the 1972 End-Stage Renal Disease (ESRD) Act, which funded dialysis treatment for all Americans without selection criteria. Subsequently, the program's funding was extended to include kidney transplants.

The ESRD Act created a new group of citizens with a right to medical care based on their diagnosis. Advocates for patients with other conditions, such as hemophilia and heart and lung disease, tried to persuade Congress to fund their diseases as well; however, the cost of kidney dialysis and transplants skyrocketed due in part to the open-ended funding, and Congress declined to extend the benefit to people other than kidney patients.[10]

As organ transplantation has became increasingly successful due to improved antirejection drugs, the problem of how to distribute scarce resources has resurfaced, since the number of donor organs is never adequate to fill the need. Livers are in especially short supply, and there is no substitute treatment, like kidney dialysis, for failing livers. More than 4,000 patients receive liver transplants each year, but in 2004, there were over 17,000 people on regional waiting lists. Hundreds of people die waiting.[16]

The policy on distributing organs has been controversial. The task of matching available organs with waiting patients is handled by a non-profit organization under contract with the Department of Health and Human Services (HHS). The organization, the United Network of Organ Sharing (UNOS), maintains a computerized network of sixty-eight organ recovery centers in eleven geographic regions of the nation. When an organ becomes available, a suitable recipient is first sought within the same region. If a suitable match is not made within the region, the computer looks at waiting lists in other regions.[17]

In 1998, because organs were allocated first within local areas, the times patients had to wait for an organ varied greatly from one geographic locality to another. Donna Shalala, Secretary of HHS, proposed that local priority lists should be eliminated and a national list be established, based on the urgency of patients' needs. The proposal provoked objections from Congress, with members trying to protect patients and transplant centers in their districts. After months of controversy, a compromise was reached that led to the current system of regional distribution. The allocation process is a life or death matter because each year about 6,000 patients die while waiting for an organ.[18]

The acrimony over rationing of organs, which is unavoidable because of obvious shortages, demonstrates how difficult it is politically to make rational decisions in the allocation of medical care. Chapter 26 argues that rationing currently exists throughout the medical system and should be addressed openly, although very few politicians or medical professionals are willing to face this fact.

CONCLUSION

While public health's focus on prevention of disease aims to minimize the need for medical care, access to medical care is an important part of the assurance function of public health. Medicine has always resisted attempts to include it as part of the public health system, with considerable success. Most Americans have private health insurance provided through their employers. However, public health concerns have overcome the opposition of the medical profession on some issues.

The urgent need to control the spread of communicable diseases has led to significant government involvement at the local level in providing medical care. Governments also coordinate, and often provide, emergency services to ensure prompt response when lives are at stake. Public health clinics that provide care for the poor have been grudgingly accepted by organized medicine, but there is no general right to medical care for Americans, as there is in most other industrialized countries.

There have been repeated attempts throughout the twentieth century to enact a universal health insurance system in the United States. All have been defeated. However, in the 1960s, Congress created the Medicare program, which guarantees medical care for the elderly, and the Medicaid program, which provides health care for the poor.

Public health has a role in monitoring and ensuring the quality of medical care through licensing of physicians, nurses, and other health professionals. Health care institutions such as hospitals and nursing homes also must be licensed by states. By requiring institutions to be accredited in order to receive Medicare and Medicaid payment for services, the government can help to ensure that the services provided meet a standard of quality. In the 1990s, a joint federal-state program called SCHIP was created to provide medical care for poor children.

Government involvement in medical issues also occurs in connection with ethical and legal debates about life and death—issues that impact both medicine and public health. Such questions are especially painful when they concern removal of life support from permanently unconscious patients or nontreatment of severely handicapped newborns, situations that involve the provision of costly and probably futile care, usually at the public's expense.

Public participation in medical decisions is also necessary when scarce resources other than money are distributed. When hemodialysis for kidney failure was developed, there was a shortage of dialysis machines, and committees were formed to decide which patients could have the life-saving treatments. This was such a difficult political issue that Congress decided on the expensive solution of funding treatment for all Americans with kidney failure. Currently, patients with failing livers are in a similar life-and-death situation, with a liver transplant being their only hope of survival. However, there is a shortage of livers available for transplant, and the federal government has been embroiled in controversy over how these organs should be distributed.

REFERENCES

1. P. Starr, *The Social Transformation of American Medicine* (New York: Basic Books, 1982).
2. M. Peisert, *The Hospital's Role in Emergency Medical Services Systems* (Chicago: American Hospital Publishing, 1984).
3. N. J. Wilson and K. W. Kizer, "The VA Health Care System: An Unrecognized National Safety Net," *Health Affairs* 16 (1997): 200–204.
4. L. I. Palmer, *Law, Medicine, and Social Justice* (Louisville, Kentucky: Westminster/ John Knox Press, 1989).
5. National Association of Community Health Centers, "About Health Centers," *www.nachc.com/about/aboutcenters.asp*. Accessed December 23, 2004.
6. Centers for Medicare and Medicaid Services, "Welcome to the State Children's Health Insurance Program," *www.cms.hhs.gov/schip/about-SCHIP.asp*. Accessed April 25, 2004.
7. Agency for Health Care Research and Quality. "Health Insurance Coverage in America—1996 to 2003: Estimates for the U.S. Population Under Age 65. Medical Expenditure Panel Survey Statistical Brief #45." *www.meps.ahrq.gov/papers/st45/ stat45.pdf*. Accessed December 23, 2004.
8. Physicians' Working Group for Single-Payer National Health Insurance, "Proposal of the Physicians' Working Group for Single-Payer National Health Insurance," *Journal of the American Medical Association* 290 (2003): 798–805.
9. Kevorkian News, *www.fansoffieger.com/kevonews.htm*. Accessed December 24, 2004.
10. G. E. Pence, *Classic Cases in Medical Ethics: Accounts of the Cases That Have Shaped Medical Ethics, with Philosophical, Legal, and Historical Backgrounds* (New York: McGraw-Hill Publishing, 1990).
11. G. J. Annas, "Nancy Cruzan and the Right To Die," *New England Journal of Medicine* 323 (1990): 670–672.
12. L. O. Gostin, "Ethics, the Constitution, and the Dying Process: The Case of Theresa Marie Schiavo," *Journal of the American Medical Association* 293 (2005): 2402–2407.
13. L. Belkin, "As Family Protests, Hospital Seeks an End to Woman's Life Support," *New York Times* (January 10, 1991): A1.
14. W. A. Silverman, "Commentary: Compassion or Opportunism?" *Pediatrics* 113 (2004): 402–403.

15. R. D. Lamm, "Ethics of Excess," *Hastings Center Report* 24 (1994): 14.
16. OPTN/SRTR Annual Report, *www.optn.org/AR2003/default.htm*. Accessed December 24, 2004.
17. UNOS: United Network of Organ Sharing, "The Organ Donation Process," *www.livertransplant.org/patientguide/unos.html*. Accessed December 24, 2004.
18. S. G. Stolberg, "U.S. Renews Organ-Donor Contract," *New York Times* (September 29, 2000).

CHAPTER 26

Why the U.S. Medical System Needs Reform

Inequalities in Access

It was obvious almost as soon as Medicare and Medicaid were enacted that the U.S. health care system still had problems. Medical costs in the United States, which had been rising more rapidly than general inflation, rose even more rapidly, putting a strain on all forms of health insurance. Figure 26–1 shows the growth in medical care expenditures in the United States since 1960. In that year, approximately $27 billion was spent on medical care. In 1970, the figure had grown to $74 billion. By 2002, national health expenditures were $1.6 trillion dollars a year.[1] The rate of

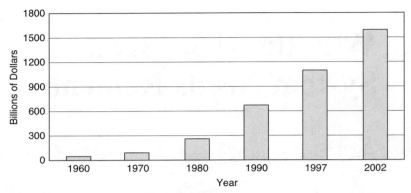

Figure 26–1 U.S. Health Care Expenditures Between 1960 and 2002
Source: Data from *Health Affairs* 1994; 13 (5), 14–31, and 2004; 23 (1), 147–159.

increase averaged about 4.8 percent above the general rate of inflation. Because medical costs grew faster than the economy as a whole, they have constituted a larger and larger percentage of the nation's gross domestic product (GDP). In 1960, medical expenditures were about 5 percent of the GDP; in 2002, they were 14.9 percent.[1]

Although expenditures on health have risen all over the world, the United States spends far more on medical care per person than any other country in the world. In 2001, an average of $4887 was spent on health costs for each American, more than twice the average of a group of 30 industrialized countries that are members of the Organization for Economic Cooperation and Development (OECD). (See Figure 26–2.) Spending as a percentage of GDP is also highest in the United States, amounting to 13.9 percent in 2001; Switzerland follows at 11.1 percent and the average for the 30 countries was 8.1 percent.[2]

There is no evidence that Americans are healthier as a result of the greater expenditures. As measured by the common indicators of health status used for international comparisons, the United States does poorly. Of thirty-seven countries compared in 1999 and 2000, the United States ranked twenty-seventh in infant mortality and twenty-third in life expectancy at birth for both males and females. This country did better in life expectancy at age sixty-five, ranking thirteenth for males and seventeenth for females.[3]

Despite the large expenditures, many Americans have difficulty getting access to medical care when they need it. Nearly forty-five million people,

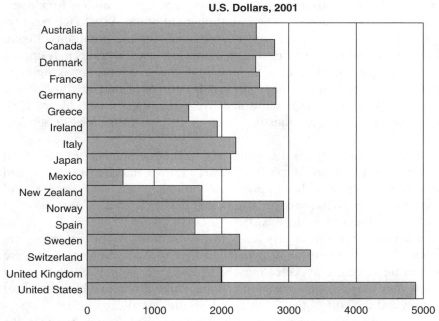

U.S. Dollars, 2001

Figure 26–2 Per Capita Health Spending in Selected OECD Countries
Source: Data from *Health Affairs* 2004; 23 (3), 10–25.

or 15.6 percent of the population, lacked health insurance at any given time during 2003; as many as fifty to sixty million people are without it at some time during a calendar year.[4] The numbers have been increasing and are predicted to continue to rise. Most of the uninsured are poor but not poor enough to qualify for Medicaid. About one in five are children. Members of racial and ethnic minority groups are more likely to be uninsured than white Americans: almost 20 percent of African Americans and more than 32 percent of Hispanics were uninsured in 2002 through 2003, compared with 14.4 percent of whites.[5] Many of the uninsured are patients with chronic diseases who are closed out of the market because of policies that deny coverage for pre-existing conditions or charge exorbitant premiums for people whose health is poor.

The problem of access to medical care is closely related to the problem of its cost. As monthly premiums have risen in proportion to wages, it has become increasingly expensive for employers, especially small businesses, to provide health insurance for employees and their families. Employers have cut back on their coverage, shifting more of the costs to the employees by requiring them to pay a larger share of the premiums, higher deductibles, and higher copayments. Some low-wage workers may choose to remain uninsured because their share of the premiums is too high; yet these workers earn too much to qualify for Medicaid in most states. Nearly 83 percent of the uninsured live in families headed by workers. Uninsured workers are mostly employed in blue-collar jobs or service-sector jobs.[6]

No other industrialized country has such large numbers of uninsured citizens as the United States. The Western European countries, Japan, and Canada have national health plans that virtually guarantee coverage to all citizens. They spend less per capita and devote a smaller percentage of their economies to medical costs.

Lack of insurance clearly leads to poorer outcomes when people are sick. People who are uninsured tend to postpone seeking medical care when they need it, and they may be denied care. If they are sufficiently sick, they may go to an emergency room, which is required by law to treat them, and the cost of their care may be borne by shifting it to other payers, increasing the charges for insured patients. This is not, however, the most effective form of medical care. The uninsured are more likely to be hospitalized for preventable illnesses than insured patients, and they are less likely to survive a serious illness.[6]

Although Medicare has ensured that most of the elderly have access to medical care when they need it, escalating costs have had an impact here too. Each year the program pays out more than it collects in premiums, and Congress has repeatedly tried to make adjustments to save the system from bankruptcy. This is a delicate political issue because the elderly are fiercely protective of their entitlements. Deductibles and copayment requirements have risen so that—with the overall increase in costs—the elderly now pay a higher percentage of their income out-of-pocket for medical care than they did before the Medicare program was created.

Medicaid has never worked as well as it was expected to. Although federal law requires coverage for all children under six and pregnant women whose family income is below 133 percent of the federal poverty level, eligibility for families is set by the states, and the national average is less than 50 percent of the poverty level.[7] In some states, the fixed fees that the program pays to providers are so low that doctors are unwilling to participate in the program, making it difficult for families that have coverage to find someone to treat them other than poor quality "Medicaid mills." Even so, the growing costs of Medicaid are placing a strain on many state budgets. The states are constantly trying to find ways to extract more Medicaid funding from the federal government, while the federal government tries to limit the amount that goes to the states. In most states, the proportion of the budget spent on Medicaid is higher than the amount spent on education.[8]

Overall, although the American medical system is the most expensive in the world, it is highly inefficient. The United States spends a higher proportion of its resources on health care than other countries; at the same time a significant proportion of the population is denied services, a situation almost unheard of in other countries. Moreover, the health status of the American population is poor in international comparisons—evidence that all the spending on medical care cannot compensate for failures in the public health system, as discussed in Chapter 27.

WHY DO COSTS KEEP RISING?

A number of factors are responsible for the high and rising cost of medical care in the United States, some of them common to all industrialized countries, some unique to the American system. The aging of the population, for example, is a problem common to most countries. Because older people generally have more need for medical care, aging populations are driving up medical expenditures everywhere. In fact, several other countries have older populations than the United States. The problem of medical costs and aging is discussed in Chapter 28.

Another factor that increases costs everywhere is the continual development of new medical technology and high-tech procedures. New instruments such as computed tomography (CT) scanners and magnetic resonance imaging (MRI) devices and new procedures such as arthroscopic and laparoscopic surgery and cardiac catheterization are expensive. They can be very effective in diagnosing and treating illness and so are used widely—perhaps too widely. Although such new technologies are available in all advanced countries, their use is more widespread in the United States than many other countries.[9] As in the case of kidney dialysis described in Chapter 25, the United States has been unable to make choices that limit access to high-tech procedures. For example, almost four times the number of coronary bypass operations are done in the United States per capita than the average for OECD countries. This nation also has a higher rate of bone marrow transplants and patients undergoing dialysis than most other industrialized nations.[9] Other countries establish criteria for the use of such technologies that enable them to control costs more successfully.

When inflationary factors that are unique to the American system are considered, administrative costs are one of the favorite targets of blame. According to one recent estimate, 31 percent of the American medical budget is spent on administration. Twenty-seven percent of medical workers in the United States spend most of their time on paperwork, up from 18 percent in 1968.[10] Because many different insurers pay for medical care, each with its own forms and documentation requirements, the process of billing and paying for care in the United States is much more time consuming and expensive than in countries where the government pays for everything. Moreover, some insurance companies, in trying to control costs, institute additional administrative procedures, for example requiring doctors to justify the need for certain treatments; this has the paradoxical effect of increasing paperwork and the percentage of effort and expense that goes to administration. As one eminent health economist lamented: "I look at the U.S. health care system and see an administrative monstrosity, a truly bizarre mélange of thousands of payers with payment systems that differ for no socially beneficial reason."[11]

Another peculiarly American characteristic that adds to medical costs is our tendency to sue for malpractice when something goes wrong. Doctors complain about the exorbitant price of malpractice insurance, and occasional news stories tell of a multimillion dollar jury award to an unfortunate patient who was harmed by some medical procedure. Although these costs do not in themselves have a significant overall impact, the fear of malpractice suits may affect a physician's decisions. Doctors may practice "defensive medicine," ordering more diagnostic tests and medical procedures than necessary, to document in court that they did "everything possible" for the patient.

In fact, studies have shown that the whole system of malpractice compensation is inefficient and unjust. Most patients who are harmed by poor medical treatment are not compensated, and many patients who have suffered a bad outcome sue and win, even when the medical provider was not negligent.[12] However, because the United States does not have a national health plan, winning a malpractice suit may be the only way an injured patient will be able to pay for treatment of his injury.

Among the most significant factors driving up medical costs are financial incentives for medical providers. In the "fee-for-service" system of payment, doctors and hospitals are motivated to provide more services in order to increase their income. Moreover, the performance of surgical procedures and the use of high-tech diagnostic equipment are more profitable than the more time-consuming practices of talking, listening, observing, and touching. Along with the growth of new medical technologies has come the growth of specialization among physicians. Fewer than 50 percent of doctors in the United States work in primary care, which includes family practice, general internal medicine, pediatrics, and obstetrics/gynecology. The majority of American physicians practice the more lucrative, technological specialties such as radiology, anesthesiology, surgery, cardiology, gastroenterology, and urology.[13]

Conspiring with providers in forcing up costs are the expectations of the medical care "consumer"—the patient. Patients with traditional insurance do not have to consider the costs of their care in making decisions on how they should be treated, because the bills will be paid by their insurance company. Thus they demand "the best" in technology, treatment by specialists, and prompt service. Economists point out that the medical marketplace is different from classical markets, which are sensitive to the price of goods and services. In the medical marketplace, the seller (the doctor) rather than the buyer (the patient) determines what the buyer needs. Sellers also set the price, and because the bill is paid by a third party (the insurance company), there is no incentive for the buyer to select less expensive options.

By the end of the twentieth century, the fastest growing segment of health care costs was prescription drugs.[1] Contributing to the growth of drug costs is the practice of direct-to-consumer advertising, which encourages people to ask their doctors for specific medications that are often more expensive than other, equally effective drugs. Although the amount spent on drugs is only about 10 percent of total health care costs, the burden was especially heavy for the poor elderly, because Medicare did not pay for drugs. News stories about old folks having to choose between paying for drugs or food led to the passage by Congress of a Medicare prescription drug benefit, which will become fully effective in 2006. Unfortunately, lobbying by the pharmaceutical industry persuaded the politicians to resist measures, such as bulk purchase of popular drugs by Medicare, that might have helped control the cost of this benefit.

APPROACHES TO CONTROLLING MEDICAL COSTS

Of the total amount spent on medical care in the United States, 45.2 percent is paid by federal, state, and local governments. About 37 percent is paid by private health insurance sponsored by employers.[1] Thus, both governments and employers have reason to try to control costs, and they have tried a variety of approaches to achieve that goal. The first cost control effort by the federal government was the imposition of price controls by President Nixon from 1971 to 1974. Although the policy moderated cost increases temporarily, providers adapted to the lower fees paid for each service by increasing the quantity of services. Total spending continued to rise.

Another regulatory approach to cost control focused on limiting spending on new facilities and technology. This is a major strategy used by other OECD countries to control their costs. In the 1970s the federal and some state governments tried to constrain the supply of hospital beds and high-tech equipment by establishing regional planning agencies that would assess the need for capital expenditures and issue certificates-of-need for new investments. Without limits on budgets, however, there were few incentives for state or local governments to control these expenditures. Considerable political pressure also served to force approval of new projects. In the 1980s, certificate-of-need programs were gradually abandoned as ineffective.

In the 1980s, the Medicare program tried a different approach to cost control. Because the greatest expenditures were payments to hospitals, the program devised a payment system designed to provide incentives for hospitals to limit the length of hospital stays. Medicare paid a flat fee for each hospital stay, an amount based on the illness category of the patient, or diagnosis related group (DRG), and the average cost of treating similar patients throughout the country. If a hospital could cure the patient in a shorter time than average, it could keep the extra cash. If a longer stay was necessary, the hospital had to swallow the additional cost. Hospitals, in response, began charging private insurance companies more to make up for their losses from the government; so several states adopted DRG-type rate-setting systems for all payers, forcing hospitals to accept the same rates for everyone. One result of policies limiting payments to hospitals was to move more treatment out of the hospital. Hospital stays are on average much shorter now than they were two decades ago, and outpatient surgery and diagnostic testing have become the rule. The DRG system was effective in reducing expenditures for hospital care, but overall costs continued to rise because there was no DRG system for outpatient care.

MANAGED CARE—NOT A PANACEA

Employer-based private insurance plans have tried a number of approaches to limiting costs by bargaining with providers—doctors and hospitals—for discounts on services. The result is a variety of plans that fall under the category of managed care. For example, in preferred provider organizations (PPOs), patients are required to seek care from participating providers who have agreed to provide services at lower rates. In some of these plans, patients are not allowed to see a specialist without a referral from a primary care physician, a strategy for limiting access to expensive high-tech care as well as for ensuring coordination of the care received by the patient from various providers. A variation on the PPO arrangement allows patients to go to nonparticipating providers but requires them to pay a higher percentage of those costs out of their own pockets.

The most stringent form of managed care is the health maintenance organization (HMO), so called because—in theory at least—the organization "has a financial incentive to maintain the health of its members. An HMO acts as both insurer and provider. In return for a fixed monthly or annual payment, the HMO agrees to provide all the medical care the individual needs. Conventional HMOs hire a staff of physicians, nurses, and other health care workers who earn a salary and thus have no incentive to provide expensive treatments when not necessary. Moreover, HMOs have incentives to provide preventive care and health promotion programs, adopting some of the goals and objectives of public health.

Managed care flourished in the 1990s. With the continued rise of medical costs and the failure to enact President Clinton's plan for health care reform, employers moved to restrict the choices of their employees to plans that incorporated cost control measures. In 1995, almost three-quarters of workers covered by employer-sponsored insurance were in managed care plans.[14] States began to move Medicaid recipients into managed care plans in the hope of providing them with higher quality of care and more continuity of care, as well as controlling Medicaid costs. The Medicare program also tried to encourage more of the elderly to enroll in managed care plans. The result was a dramatic slowing of medical inflation in the 1990s.[1] However, the slowdown did not last.

With the success of managed care came some major criticism and what was called "the HMO backlash."[15] Patients understood that the financial incentives encouraged denial of treatment, and they were outraged, even when some of the treatments denied were of unproven efficacy. Some for-profit HMOs had especially objectionable practices of giving bonuses to physicians who were most successful in denying care. Patients also objected to limits on their choice of doctors to consult. News stories told of HMO "gag rules" that forbade physicians from recommending treatments for which the HMO would not approve payment. Many state legislatures passed laws prohibiting gag rules. Similarly, states passed laws regarding "drive-through deliveries" and "drive-through mastectomies" in response to managed care plans that limited hospital stays for women giving birth or having cancer surgery. In 1996 alone, fifty-six laws were passed in thirty-five states aimed at regulating or weakening HMOs.[15] The result of such laws, together with some important decisions in federal courts that favored consumers' right to sue HMOs for denial of care, meant that managed care organizations lost much of their ability to manage medical care in a cost-conscious way.[16]

Despite the complaints about managed care, including well-publicized instances of patients' being denied expensive procedures that might have saved their lives, there is no evidence that patients are harmed by the cost-control measures. In many ways, managed care has an advantage over fee-for-service in providing high-quality care. The emphasis on prevention and health education may indeed help to keep members healthy. Coordination of care and use of interdisciplinary teams for disease management can help to prevent patients with chronic diseases from developing severe and costly complications. The use of primary care physicians as gatekeepers for controlling patient access to specialists may help to prevent unnecessary procedures that could put patients at risk. Managed care organizations, because of centralized recordkeeping, have the ability to monitor patients' health and evaluate the quality of care they receive, as discussed in Chapter 27.

The result of the weakening of managed care organizations' cost control methods was that medical spending began to grow again in the late 1990s and early 2000s. Plans became less restrictive and PPOs became more popular because they allow more choices. Health insurance became less affordable. More of the costs are shifted to the patients. The problems of the uninsured have grown worse. When fee-for-service was the norm, hospitals could charge higher rates to insured patients to cover the costs of treating the uninsured, as they are often required to do by law. (See Chapter 25.) Now, however, managed care organizations, even the weaker ones, negotiate reduced payments for treatment of their members, and hospitals are less able to cost-shift, causing financial pain for the hospitals. While some states provide special payments to hospitals to cover bad debt and charity care, anti-tax sentiment discourages such public funding for the poor. Private hospitals select the most profitable patients and stories of patient "dumping" have become common. Public hospitals in inner cities bear the brunt of caring for the sickest uninsured patients, and many are at risk of closing because of lack of funding.[17]

RATIONING

In the late 1980s, the state of Oregon tried an experiment. Realizing that its Medicaid budget was not large enough to provide comprehensive coverage for all its poor citizens, the state legislature undertook a plan to spread its resources over a larger number of people by limiting the services for which it would pay. Its first move was highly controversial. It decided to no longer pay for organ transplants, with the justification that the funds required for thirty-four transplants could provide for prenatal care and delivery for 1,500 pregnant women.[18] When a young boy with acute leukemia was denied a bone marrow transplant and died as a result, there was a national uproar.

The legislature, led by John Kitzhaber, a physician who was then president of the state senate and later became governor, decided to develop a more acceptable policy for broadening Medicaid eligibility. The new approach focused on life-saving treatments for serious conditions and tried to eliminate less effective therapies for less serious conditions. The state decided to develop a prioritized list of health services and draw a line below which treatments would not be covered. The goal was to cover all citizens whose incomes were below the poverty level, and to use managed care plans to provide medical care.

A commission was formed to develop the list by consulting as much as possible with the citizens of the state. Public hearings and town meetings were held to determine the relative value placed on various medical services by the public. The commission established seventeen categories of health problems according to thirteen criteria, including life expectancy, quality of life, the cost-effectiveness of a treatment, and the likely number of people who would benefit. The highest priority was placed on acute problems that could be fatal and for which treatment would provide full recovery. Surgery for appendicitis is an example of a high priority procedure. Other highly ranked services included maternity care and preventive care for children. At the bottom of the list were treatments known not to be effective, or those that did not improve quality of life or extend life, such as some treatments for cancer and AIDS.[19]

The Oregon plan provoked opposition on legal, social, and ethical grounds. In 1991 the Department of Health and Human Services denied permission for Oregon to implement the plan on the basis that it violated the Americans with Disabilities Act, because the list undervalued the quality of life of people with disabilities. After some revisions, the plan was finally approved by the Clinton administration in 1993. More than 100,000 Oregonians were added to the Medicaid program as a result.[19]

Many critics have pointed out that the policy would be more fair, and the decisions would be much less difficult, if everyone—not just the poor—were included in the rationing proposal. The medical system as a whole is rich enough to provide necessary care for everyone; the need to ration care for the poor is a consequence of failures of the system to provide adequate and affordable care for everyone. However, the plan is politically popular in Oregon, and complaints about the list are unusual.[19] Health policy experts have praised its focus on medical necessity so that all appropriate care and no inappropriate care is covered. It calls attention to the need for more research on outcomes of various treatments to permit better informed decisions on medical necessity (see Chapter 27).

The Oregon experiment makes many people uncomfortable. People don't like to confront the idea that rationing of medical care might be necessary or desirable. In fact, however, rationing of medical care has been going on all along: care has been rationed on the basis of ability to pay, but the rationing is not explicitly admitted. When a story hits the news about an uninsured child denied treatment for leukemia, for example, the public and politicians purport to be shocked that such a thing could happen in our society. Yet it is politically impossible to raise taxes so that such children could be provided with medical insurance or public hospitals could afford to provide effective care.

Our society has never been willing to discuss tradeoffs between costs and quality of medical care.[20] Because third parties—usually the government or insurance companies—pay for care, people have come to believe that cost should not be considered when decisions are made about medical treatments. When asked about a particular patient or situation, people will say that no effort should be spared in trying to achieve the best possible outcome. It is an easy thing to say when they are not paying the bills. At the same time, people naturally seek out insurance plans with the lowest premiums. It is a catch-22 situation: society demands that the health care system maximize quality while minimizing costs, but has placed a taboo on consideration of cost.[20]

Rationing is a dirty word when it applies to medical care. But rationing is inevitable. In economics, "rationing is simply the process of allocating goods in the face of scarcity."[21] Since most people are unwilling to pay an unlimited amount of money to receive a small benefit, decisions are continually being made on allocation of medical services. What is needed is an open discussion on how those decisions should be made. Should kidney dialysis be denied to the elderly or to people with diabetes so advanced that they have lost their vision? Should we tolerate long waiting lists for hip replacements? Should the rich receive care and the poor be denied it? Should we allow for-profit health care systems that make large profits for their stock holders while refusing to care for patients with expensive chronic diseases?[22] These are difficult questions for medicine and for public health, but we need to openly discuss them and decide on a societal basis.

CONCLUSION

The U.S. medical care system is the most expensive in the world. At the same time, it has many faults, including lack of access for the uninsured, about 16 percent of the American population. Medical care costs have risen continuously, and the rising costs contribute to the inability of many to afford health insurance.

There are a number of reasons for the high and rising costs. An aging population needs more medical care; expensive new medical technologies are regularly developed; administrative costs are high in the United States; malpractice suits lead to defensive medicine; and financial incentives often favor overtreatment.

A number of attempts to impose cost-containment measures on medical care have been relatively unsuccessful in controlling costs. Managed care slowed the growth in health care costs in the 1990s and has consequently become the dominant form of employer-sponsored health insurance. Managed care organizations negotiate reduced payments to health care providers and employ various strategies to limit patients' access to treatments considered non-essential or too expensive for the expected benefit. Despite its successes, managed care has been unpopular with the public, and it has not improved access for the uninsured. Because of its unpopularity, managed care has suffered legislative and legal setbacks that have weakened its ability to control costs. Medical care expenditures have resumed their escalation, and it is not clear how the nation can pay for medical care in the future.

Many health policy makers believe that some form of rationing will ultimately be necessary to ensure access to high-quality medical care for the whole population. They point out that care is already rationed by cost. In Oregon, the Medicaid program, using an explicit method of ranking various treatments and cutting off access to lower priority procedures, has significantly expanded the number of people covered by the plan. Discussion of rationing is largely taboo in the current political climate, but if the problems of the system continue to grow, Americans may be forced to consider cost and fairness when making decisions about medical care.

REFERENCES

1. K. Levit et al., "Health Accounts Team. Health Spending Rebound Continues in 2002," *Health Affairs* 23 (January–February 2004), 147–158.
2. U. E. Reinhardt, P. S. Hussey, and G. F. Anderson, "U.S. Health Care Spending in an International Context," *Health Affairs* (May–June 2003): 10–25.
3. National Center for Health Statistics, *Health, United States, 2004 with Chartbook on Trends in the Health of Americans* (Hyattsville, Maryland: Author), 140–142.
4. K. E. Thorpe, "Perspective: Protecting the Uninsured," *New England Journal of Medicine* 351 (2004): 1479–1481.
5. C. DeNavas-Walt, B. D. Proctor, and R. J. Mills, U.S. Census Bureau, "Current Population Reports," P60–226, *Income, Poverty, and Health Insurance Coverage in the United States: 2003* (Washington, DC: U.S. Government Printing Office, 2004), *www.census.gov/prod/2004pubs/p60-226.pdf*. Accessed December 27, 2004.
6. P. Fronstin, "Sources of Health Insurance and Characteristics of the Uninsured: Analysis of the March 2004 Current Population Survey," *Employee Benefit Research Institute Issue*, Brief No. 276. December 2004, *www.ebri.org*. Accessed December 27, 2004.
7. U.S. Institute of Medicine, *Insuring America's Health: Principles and Recommendations* (Washington, DC: National Academy Press, 2004).
8. P. Belluck, "Governors Unite in Fight against Medicaid Cuts," *New York Times* (December 26, 2004).
9. U. E. Reinhardt, P. S. Hussey, and G. F. Anderson, "Cross-National Comparisons of Health Systems Using OECD Data, 1999," *Health Affairs* (May/June 2002): 169–181.

10. S. Woolhandler, M. H. A. Campbell, and D. U. Himmelstein, "Costs of Health Care Administration in the United States and Canada," *New England Journal of Medicine* 349 (2003): 768–775.
11. H. J. Aaron, "Costs of Health Care Administration in the United States and Canada—Questionable Answers to a Questionable Question," *New England Journal of Medicine* 349 (2003): 801–803.
12. T. A. Brennan, C. M. Sox, and H. R. Burstin, "Relation Between Negligent Adverse Events and the Outcomes of Medical-Malpractice Litigation," *New England Journal of Medicine* 335 (1996): 1963–1967.
13. D. A. Kindig, "Counting Generalist Physicians," *Journal of the American Medical Association* 271 (1994): 1505–1507.
14. G. A. Jensen, M. A. Morrissey, S. Gaffney, and D. K. Liston, "The New Dominance of Managed Care: Insurance Trends in the 1990s," *Health Affairs* (January/February 1997): 125–136.
15. T. Bodenheimer, "The HMO Backlash—Righteous or Reactionary?" *New England Journal of Medicine* 335 (1996): 1601–1604.
16. M. G. Bloche and K. M. Studdert, "A Quiet Revolution: Law as an Agent of Health System Change," *Health Affairs* (March/April 2004): 29–42.
17. K. Sack, "Public Hospitals Around Country Cut Basic Services," *New York Times* (August 20, 1995): A1.
18. R. M. Kaplan, *The Hippocratic Predicament: Affordability, Access, and Accountability in American Medicine* (San Diego, California: Academic Press, 1993).
19. T. Bodenheimer, "The Oregon Health Plan—Lessons for the Nation," *New England Journal of Medicine* 337 (1997): 651–655.
20. D. M. Eddy, "Balancing Cost and Quality in Fee-For-Service Versus Managed Care," *Health Affairs* 16 (May/June 1997): 162–173.
21. D. A. Asch and P. A. Ubel, "Rationing by Any Other Name," *New England Journal of Medicine* 336 (1997): 1668–1671.
22. J. P. Kassirer, "Our Endangered Integrity—It Can Only Get Worse," *New England Journal of Medicine* 336 (1997): 1666–1667.

CHAPTER 27

Health Services Research: Finding What Works

Will Back Surgery Help?

In the late 1960s and early 1970s, the medical establishment was shaken by a number of reports that documented wide variations in the way physicians treated their patients for common health problems. One study found that in Morrisville, Vermont, nearly 70 percent of the children had their tonsils removed by the time they were fifteen years old, whereas in nearby Middlebury, only 8 percent of children underwent the operation. Another study in Iowa reported that more than 60 percent of the male population of one community had their prostate glands removed by age eighty-five, whereas the rate was only 15 percent in another area. And the rates at which women underwent hysterectomy varied from 20 percent in one part of Maine to 70 percent in a city less than twenty miles away.[1]

The reasons for these differences were unclear. The populations of the comparison communities were not substantially different from one another. There was no reason to believe that the residents of one community were sicker than those of another or that their insurance coverage was more comprehensive. It seemed obvious that these procedures were being overused in some geographical areas or underused in others. However, the studies could not determine which was true or decide what the appropriate use rates should be.

This method of examining medical practice, known as small area analysis, has been applied over the past two decades to a broad range of medical practices and procedures. Repeatedly, wide variations have been found, with no apparent reason for the differences in practice. In 1996, Dr. John Wennberg, a professor at Dartmouth Medical School and a pioneer in the field who had conducted the studies in Vermont, Maine, and Iowa, published the *Dartmouth Atlas of Health Care*, an analysis of 1993 Medicare data.[2] (Since the Medicare program maintains files on everything it pays for, including services to virtually all Americans sixty-five and older, it provides valuable data for this kind of research.) All over the country, variations occur in treatments for prostate cancer, breast cancer, heart disease, and many other common conditions. Rates of surgery for low back pain were seven times higher in Provo, Utah, than in Kingsport, Tennessee. Breast sparing surgery for women with breast cancer ranged from just over one percent in Rapid City, South Dakota, to 49 percent in Elyria, Ohio.

Small area analysis called attention to the lack of scientific evidence on which doctors and patients base decisions about how various medical conditions should be treated. The surprising results of the early studies have led to a new field of research—health services research. This research attempts to understand the reasons for the observed variations in medical practice and to determine, from observations of the everyday practice of medicine, what treatments lead to the most desirable outcomes. Health services research studies the effectiveness, efficiency, and equity of the health care system. It is a way of trying to assess the quality of medical care. This research also may lead to insights on how to control costs and improve access.

REASONS FOR PRACTICE VARIATIONS

A number of explanations have been suggested for variations in medical practice, most of which can be tested, and most of which can be shown to play a role in the observed differences. It is clear that the variability in the use of different treatments reflects the degree of uncertainty facing physicians regarding their relative efficacy. Variations in practice are far greater for some medical conditions than for others. For example, most physicians agree that surgery is the appropriate treatment for appendicitis and broken hips. Correspondingly, the geographic variability in the treatment of those conditions is much smaller than the variability in rates for tonsillitis and disorders of the uterus, on which there is much less evidence about when surgery is needed.

In many cases, doctors are unaware that their way of treating a condition is unusual, and they will change their patterns of practice when presented with evidence that they are deviating from the norm. In the early 1970s, Wennberg confronted the physicians of Morrisville, Vermont, with data showing that they were doing tonsillectomies far more frequently than other doctors in the state. The Morrisville physicians reconsidered the indications for the procedure, instituted a policy of obtaining second opinions before deciding on surgery, and ended by reducing the tonsillectomy rate to less than 10 percent of what it had been.[1]

It is easy to suspect that inappropriate use of invasive procedures is responsible for the observed variations in the frequency with which they are done. While this suspicion is supported by the Vermont experience in reducing tonsillectomy rates, other studies have found that inappropriate use explains only a small part of the wide variability observed for many procedures.

In one small area study of three procedures commonly done on Medicare patients, panels of expert physicians examined the files of a random sample of patients who had undergone each procedure. The experts

Table 27–1   Appropriate and Inappropriate Use of Three Procedures

Procedure	Site No.	Rate per 10,000 Elderly	Appropriateness Category, %			Sample Size
			Appropriate	Equi- vocal	Inappropriate	
Coronary	1	50	72	10	18	628
angiography	2	23	77	7	17	514
	3	22	81	4	15	535
Carotid	1	23	37	34	30	600
endarterectomy	2	6	42	29	29	210
	4	16	30	30	40	492
Upper GI tract	1	102	72	14	15	614
endoscopy	2	144	73	8	19	462
	5	149	71	11	18	509

Source: Adapted from M. R. Chassin et al., *Journal of the American Medical Association* 258 (1987): 2534.

compared the indications for the test in high-use areas with those in low-use areas. They were asked to determine, for each patient, whether the decision to do the procedure was appropriate, equivocal, or inappropriate. Results are shown in Table 27–1. Coronary angiography—used to identify blockages in the blood vessels of the heart—was performed more than twice as frequently in the high-use area as in the low-use area. Yet even in the high-use area the experts considered it inappropriate in only one sixth of the cases. Carotid endarterectomy, which had an almost four-fold variation in frequency, was the procedure most often judged inappropriate. A risky procedure intended to remove blockages in the arteries that carry blood to the brain, carotid endarterectomy was deemed inappropriate in about one third of the cases done in the high-use area. However, the procedure was considered by the experts to be inappropriate almost as frequently in the low-use area.[3]

This evidence suggests that for many medical conditions, more than one response may be appropriate. When faced with a patient suffering from a specific illness, one physician may prefer conservative treatment using drugs and "watchful waiting," while another physician may believe that immediate surgery is indicated. These opinions tend to be shared by the physicians within a community. Wennberg has called these differences, the "practice style" factor. For most of the conditions in question, there is not enough scientific evidence to determine which treatment yields a better outcome for the patient. In many cases, the choice of treatment involves weighing benefits against risks, a trade-off that different patients might evaluate differently if they were given the opportunity to choose.

THE FIELD OF DREAMS EFFECT

One factor that has consistently been shown to influence practice styles is the availability of services in a community. The presence of a greater number of surgeons is accompanied by the performance of a larger number of surgeries; higher numbers of hospital beds lead to higher rates of hospitalization. This effect was dramatically illustrated in Maine during the early 1980s, when two neurosurgeons moved to a community and devoted themselves to performing laminectomies—disc surgery for low back pain. The number of laminectomies for the whole state nearly doubled as a result of the work of these two surgeons, although only 20 percent of the population of Maine lived in that community and the adjacent referral area.[4] This high rate of surgery, like the tonsillectomies in Vermont, came down after the surgeons were confronted with data on practice patterns in other communities.

Research has consistently demonstrated an influence of supply on usage when hospital beds are concerned. A study done in the 1980s comparing Boston, Massachusetts, with New Haven, Connecticut, found that Boston had 4.5 hospital beds per thousand people, whereas New Haven had only 2.9 beds per thousand. Approximately the same percentage of beds was filled in the two cities, meaning that the population of Boston was hospitalized at a higher rate than that of New Haven. When Wennberg and his colleagues interviewed physicians in the two cities, they found that New Haven doctors were not purposely trying to ration care and that neither group of doctors was aware that they hospitalized patients more or less frequently than average.[4] Mortality rates and other measures of quality of care were almost the same in the two cities. In the 1990s, when managed care came to both cities, hospitalization rates fell, but by about the same percentages, so that Boston doctors still hospitalized their patients much more frequently than New Haven doctors.[5]

The Dartmouth researchers' analysis of Medicare data found that the number of hospital beds in a community significantly influences the kind of care received by dying old people.[6] Medicare patients in New York City, Newark, New Jersey, and Memphis, Tennessee, are much more likely to spend their final days in a hospital, often in an intensive-care unit, than elderly patients in Portland, Oregon, or Salt Lake City, Utah, who are more likely to die at home. Based on 1994 and 1995 data, the rates at which Medicare patients die in the hospital correlate closely with the number of hospital beds per thousand residents in their community. Researchers call this correlation the "Field of Dreams Effect," after the line in the 1989 movie about a baseball field: "If you build it, they will come."

While there is little evidence to show that patients are helped or harmed by the more intensive care they receive in Boston, Miami, and other high-use areas of the country, the differences in use have a major impact on medical care costs. For example, the average hospital bill for each Medicare enrollee's final six months of life is $16,571 in the New York City borough of Manhattan, as opposed to an average of only $6,793 in Portland, Oregon.[6] In the Boston-New Haven comparative study, Boston's per capita hospital expenditures are about double those of New Haven.[7] Wennberg calculated that overall hospital expenditures for the 685,000 residents of Boston were $300 million higher in 1982 than they would have been if the usage rates of New Haven applied.

Wennberg does not specifically argue that conflict of interest or pecuniary motives enter into decisions that determine use rates of medical serves. However, many studies suggest that financial considerations may enter into some physicians' medical decision making. For example, there is evidence that when physicians stand to profit from the performance of diagnostic tests, they are much more likely to order such tests. Until the practice was outlawed by Congress, physicians who owned an interest in clinical laboratories were more likely to refer patients for laboratory tests than similar physicians who referred patients to labs in which they had no financial interest.[8] Similarly, physicians who own diagnostic imaging equipment are more likely to use it than comparable physicians who must refer patients elsewhere for such examinations.[9] A recent surge in complex spinal fusion operations has been linked to the high rates Medicare will pay to surgeons and hospitals, although there is no evidence that the procedure is more effective at curing back pain than laminectomies or even less invasive approaches.[10]

OUTCOMES RESEARCH

As we have seen, variations in medical care are greatest for medical conditions about which the least is known concerning the effectiveness and appropriateness of various diagnostic and treatment approaches. The solution to the uncertainties raised by small area analysis, therefore, is to study outcomes of these various diagnostic and treatment approaches in order to determine what works. Many policy makers believe that such research will allow the development of guidelines for medical practice, leading not only to more effective medical care but also to cost savings through the elimination of unnecessary care.

Outcomes research is the epidemiologic study of medical care. Whereas epidemiology usually examines the disease-causing effects of exposure to agents such as viruses and toxic chemicals, medical care epidemiology examines the health effects of exposure to medical interventions. Controlled clinical trials are one form of medical care epidemiology, but there are practical, financial, and ethical barriers that prevent conducting controlled trials aimed at answering many important questions about medical care. Outcomes research collects and analyzes data generated by the everyday practice of medicine in order to reach conclusions on benefits and risks of various interventions for various types of patients.

Prostatectomy is the most common major operation performed on males over sixty-five; some 354,000 prostatectomies were performed in the United States in 1984, and the rate at which the operation is done has increased many-fold since then.[4,11] It is a high-variation procedure, with prostatectomy rates varying from 20.4 per 100,000 patients in Rhode Island to 428.5 per 100,000 in Alaska.[11]

Prostatectomy, the surgical removal of the prostate gland, is used as a treatment for cancer of the prostate and for benign hypertrophy of the prostate (BHP), a common condition in older men that causes difficulties with urination. Other treatments are available for both conditions, including watchful waiting, since many cases of prostate cancer never progress to become life threatening. Proponents of the surgical procedure argue that it can reduce symptoms and improve the quality of men's lives. Skeptics point out that surgery often has unwelcome side effects.

Wennberg and his colleagues, in trying to identify the reasons for variations in prostatectomy rates, conducted a major analysis of Medicare records to determine outcomes of surgery for BHP. They found that published reports significantly overstated the benefits of prostatectomy and understated the complications. Although only about one percent of men died in the hospital, 2 to 5 percent of the patients died in the weeks following the surgery. Moreover, within four years of the surgery, almost half of the patients had required further treatment for urinary tract problems. After eight years, about one in five had needed a second prostatectomy.[4] When researchers interviewed a series of 300 patients three, six, and twelve months after surgery, they found additional complications. Five percent of men who were sexually active before surgery reported impotence for the full year afterwards. Three percent had problems with incontinence throughout the year.[12] Some of these patients wished they had not had the surgery.

The results of these studies indicate a need for better informing patients of their choices and the likely outcomes of each choice. Men's feelings about their symptoms, their willingness to accept risks of the surgery, and their assessment of the possible outcomes vary substantially among individuals. Outcomes research should enable them to make informed decisions based on their own values. As Wennberg has pointed out, "current rates of use of invasive high-technology medicine could well be higher than patients want . . . particularly when risks must be taken to reduce symptoms or improve the quality of life, patients tend to be more averse to risks than physicians. Given an option, patients will on average select less invasive strategies than physicians."[7(p.1203)] Effective drug therapies have been developed for BHP, and the number of surgeries performed for this condition declined in the 1990s, perhaps due to evidence contributed by outcomes research.[13]

The number of prostatectomies for cancer has increased, however, due in part to the development of a new screening method that became widely used in the 1990s. The test measures prostate specific antigen (PSA) in the blood, levels of which have been correlated with the presence of cancer. However, low-grade prostate cancer is very common in older men, and many cases never progress to cause a problem. The follow-up testing and treatment of men whose PSA levels are elevated is invasive and may have undesirable side effects. The problem with the use of PSA screening is that there is no evidence that it reduces mortality from prostate cancer. In a study conducted by the Dartmouth researchers, Medicare data was used to compare two cohorts of men who lived in areas with different practice patterns for screening and treatment. In the Seattle-Puget Sound area, men were tested at a rate 5.39 times the rate in Connecticut. The researchers found that more than twice as many men in the Seattle area, compared with Connecticut men, were subjected to biopsies of the prostate to confirm the presence of cancer. The Seattle area men were over five times more likely to have a prostatectomy as the Connecticut men. However, after eleven years of follow up, there was no significant difference in the mortality rates from prostate cancer between the two groups of men.[14]

In 1989, Congress established the federal Agency for Health Care Policy and Research (AHCPR), hoping that studies such as those on BHP would encourage a reduction in high-technology medicine and save money on medical costs, especially for Medicare and Medicaid. The Agency was mandated to examine the reasons for the wide variations in health care practices around the country, develop guidelines for treatment, and find effective ways to disseminate its research findings and guidelines.[15] However, the Agency—and Congress—discovered to their surprise that the research results were not always welcome.

One of the health conditions that the AHCPR tackled early was low back pain. It is a widespread problem, ranking second only to the common cold as a reason that people go to the doctor. Treatment of low back problems costs over $20 billion a year in the United States. Surgery for low back pain is a high-variability procedure, ranging from a low in the Northeast to a rate in the Northwest that is more than three times higher. The guidelines developed by AHCPR's panel of experts and released in December 1994 recommended treating most acute, painful low back problems with nonprescription pain killers and mild exercise, followed in about two weeks by conditioning exercises. Surgery benefits only about 1 in 100 people with acute low back problems, according to the chairman of the panel, a professor of orthopedic surgery at the University of Washington School of Medicine.[16]

Back surgeons responded with rage and political action. With the Republican Congress intent on budget cutting in 1995, legislators were sympathetic to claims by the back surgeons' lobbying group that AHCPR was a waste of money, that the government should not be telling doctors how to practice medicine, and that the Agency should be eliminated.[17] Defenders of the Agency pointed out that the guidelines could save billions of dollars and accused back surgeons of merely trying to protect their incomes. When the federal budget was finally approved that year, AHCPR had survived, although its budget was cut substantially. Its leaders decided that developing clinical guidelines was too dangerous politically, but the agency continued collecting evidence that allowed other organizations to do so, and it maintains a national guideline clearinghouse of evidence-based clinical guidelines developed by other organizations.

There was a new emphasis on quality of care and patient safety, and the agency's name was changed to the Agency for Healthcare Research and Quality (AHRQ). Four years after its "near-death experience," AHRQ had regained all the funding it lost, and by 2002 the budget had grown to more than double its pre-1995 level.[18]

QUALITY

The AHCPR drama came at a time when there had been a series of dramatic, highly publicized medical errors. A thirty-nine-year old health reporter for the *Boston Globe* died after receiving an overdose of a chemo-therapy drug while being treated for breast cancer at one of the most presti-gious hospitals in the country. A fifty-one-year old diabetic man had the wrong leg amputated in a Florida hospital. And an eight-year old boy in another Florida hospital died due to a drug mix-up during "minor" surgery.

A number of studies were published in the 1990s documenting that pre-ventable medical errors occurred in 1.5 to 2 percent of hospitalizations, and that many of these errors caused the patient's death. The Institute of Medicine (IOM) was asked to investigate the issue and recommend a strategy that would lead to improvements in quality of care. The study led to the publication in 1999 of a report, *To Err Is Human: Building a Safer Health System.*[19] The report estimated that 44,000 to 98,000 deaths a year in the United States were caused by medical errors, more than motor vehi-cle accidents, breast cancer, or AIDS, placing medical errors among the top ten causes of death.

Before the IOM report was published, medical errors were blamed on failures by individual doctors and nurses; practitioners who made mis-takes were sued for malpractice, and some had even been prosecuted as criminals. The report shifted the blame to the medical care system—or "non-system," according to some critics—characterizing it as decentral-ized and fragmented, rife with confusion, miscommunication, and lack of incentives for improvements in safety. The IOM committee compared the medical care industry unfavorably with other high-risk industries that had been much more successful at improving safety and preventing injury, especially the commercial airline industry. The report made a number of recommendations, beginning with the creation of a Center for Patient Safety within the AHRQ, which would set national goals, track progress, develop a research agenda, evaluate methods for identifying and preventing errors, and disseminate information. Another recommendation was that, as in the airline industry, accidents and near-misses should be reported so that errors could be investigated, leading to an understanding of the underlying factors that contribute to them. A mandatory, non-punitive system should be developed that encourages providers to learn from their mistakes.[19]

Recognizing that many adverse events involve medication errors, the report recommended that the Food and Drug Administration should require that drug naming, packaging, and labeling be designed to minimize confusion. Because of doctors' notoriously poor handwriting, procedures should be developed to ensure accurate communication of prescriptions and other orders.

In 2004, a paper published by the prestigious health policy journal, *Health Affairs*, evaluated progress in implementing the IOM report's recommendations five years later.[20] Stating that "we appear to be 'at the end of the beginning'," the author, R. M. Wachter, describes progress on some of the measures and failures on others. He praises policies by the hospital accrediting agency that mandate standardized procedures for many aspects of patient care. He noted that although the AHRQ is investing in valuable research, it is seriously underfunded. Error-reporting systems have been only partially implemented, and there is no evidence that the reports are being used to improve the system. Overall, "I would give our efforts an overall grade of C+, with striking areas of progress tempered by clear opportunities for improvement."[20]

MEDICAL CARE REPORT CARDS

The rise of managed care (see Chapter 26) contributed to an increasing interest in the measurement of quality and efficiency, or cost-effectiveness, of medical care. Managed care's focus on cutting costs ran up against the common assumption that, when it comes to medical care, more is better—an assumption that is challenged by outcomes research that suggests that sometimes less may be better and be less expensive as well.[21] However, many people are suspicious that managed care companies, which have a financial incentive to do less for their patients, may have an inherent conflict of interest. The suspicion is especially strong in the case of for-profit managed care plans, which have an obligation to maximize profits for their investors, perhaps at the expense of the patients.

In the medical care marketplace, where economic factors are becoming increasingly significant, outcomes research has an important role to play in evaluating the quality and efficiency of different medical plans. In theory, when given enough information, customers—both the employers who choose which plans to offer and the employees who must choose among the plans that are offered—can make informed decisions, weighing quality and cost.[22] Moreover, patients are increasingly becoming more active participants in their own care. In part because of growing distrust of the medical system, patients want information on risks and benefits of available treatments and, if possible, on the competence of their physicians and other medical providers. Outcomes research provides some of this information.

Although managed care is often regarded with skepticism, it is more easily evaluated than the traditional fee-for-service form of medical practice. The organization of services that allows care to be "managed" also makes it possible for those services to be assessed in a formal way, something that is not realistic to do when each medical provider acts independently. Through an accreditation process conducted by the non-profit National Committee for Quality Assurance (NCQA), it is possible to rate managed care plans on their performance with respect to a number of standards. Information on the accreditation status of a plan can influence a business's decision on whether to offer the plan to its employees, and the information can be used by employees to choose among plans offered. In its 2004 State of Health Care Quality report, 563 health plans covering about one out of four Americans provided data to NCQA on sixty different measures of health care quality. NCQA reported that the plans were improving their performance on most of the measures.[23]

Many of the most easily measured standards used by NCQA focus on preventive care: for example, whether children receive a full set of immunizations and whether women get mammograms and Pap tests. Other standards evaluate how a plan manages care for patients with common diseases. The findings of outcomes research can be used, for example, to measure performance of an HMO in treating elderly heart attack victims. Research supported by AHCPR found that patients sixty-five years of age and older were 43 percent less likely to die after a heart attack if they were treated with beta blockers than if they did not receive these drugs.[24] Using that information, NCQA established, as one of its standards for evaluating a plan, the use of beta blockers for treatment of heart attacks. In 1996, when reporting of this measure was instituted, only an estimated 40 percent of patients in the United States who should have received the drugs were given them. In 2003, the average reported by the health plans was almost 95 percent, and many plans reported 100 percent.[23]

Outcome research can also be used in some circumstances to evaluate the performance of individual medical providers. The findings offer a basis not only for patients to choose where to go for treatment, but also for providers to compare their performance with that of their peers. Since 1989, New York State has measured the outcomes of coronary artery bypass surgery for treatment of blocked arteries in the heart, monitoring each of the thirty-one hospitals where the operations are performed. Mortality rates in 1989, adjusted for patients' risk factors such as age, diabetes, and hypertension, ranged between 0.88 percent and 10.02 percent.[25] Data has also been collected on outcomes achieved by individual surgeons.

One of the study's findings was that hospitals that perform large volumes of coronary surgery have better outcomes than those that perform few of the operations, a result that has also been found true of other types of surgery. The New York study also found that surgeons who perform more than 150 bypass operations per year have only half the mortality rate of surgeons who perform fewer than fifty. The publicity that followed release of the 1989 data on individual hospitals led to a dramatic decline (41 percent) statewide in mortality rates associated with the surgery over the next three years.[26] Data collection and analysis continues, and mortality rates have continued to fall. By 1992, New York had the lowest risk-adjusted mortality rates of any state in the nation, and New York's rates continued to be lower than other states', at least through 1999. Thus, the information provided by outcomes research led to improved quality of surgical care statewide. An analysis of how the improvements were accomplished show that hospitals identified as performing poorly reacted strongly, for example, by restricting the surgical privileges of some low-volume surgeons whose patients were more likely to die from the operation.[27]

Despite the successes, health services research has a long way to go before it can be widely used to help people make decisions about health care based on quality. Most of the indicators of managed care quality measured by accrediting agencies focus on preventive care for the healthy. Although this approach is important from a public health perspective, what matters most to patients is the quality of care they receive when they are ill.[21] Detailed analyses of providers' performance are available for only a limited number of procedures in New York, and most states would probably not be willing or able to carry out such ambitious programs. Surprisingly, although New York's annual reports on cardiac surgery are made public, it appears that neither managed care companies nor patients use the information to choose hospitals and surgeons.[27]

INEQUITIES IN MEDICAL CARE

Health services research has thrown light on an unpleasant reality that pervades the American medical care system. Not only is care rationed by ability to pay, as discussed in Chapter 26, but there are racial inequities in how care is delivered even when individuals are able to pay for it. As documented in a 2002 Institute of Medicine report, *Unequal Treatment: What Healthcare Providers Need to Know about Racial and Ethnic Disparities in Healthcare*,[28] African Americans and Hispanics are less likely than whites to receive the most effective treatments for heart disease, human immunodeficiency virus (HIV) infection, asthma, breast cancer, and many other conditions, even when their income and insurance status are equal to whites.

Regarding heart disease, for example, the work of the New York State researchers described above has also found racial differences in access to coronary artery bypass surgery. It seems that physicians are less likely to recommend surgery to patients from ethnic minority groups than to comparable white patients. Studying files of patients who had undergone diagnostic testing in eight New York hospitals, and using guidelines developed by the RAND Corporation for "appropriateness" and "necessity" of the operation, the researchers selected 1,261 patients who would benefit from a coronary artery bypass. Returning to the files three months later, the researchers found that African American and Hispanic patients were significantly less likely to have had the surgery than comparable white patients. It was not that the blacks and Hispanics had decided against the surgery; for the overwhelming majority, their physicians had not recommended it.[29]

Childhood asthma is a chronic disease that can usually be kept under control by providing patients and their families with prescriptions for inhaled medications and education on how to use them. A study that examined records of young children hospitalized for asthma found that racial minorities were less likely than whites to have taken the most effective medications before they were hospitalized and were less likely to be given prescriptions for such medications when they were discharged. Thus African American and Hispanic patients received poorer quality care than whites, an observation that was especially disturbing because the prevalence of asthma in minority children is higher than in whites—25 percent higher.[30]

Other studies have found that African American women with breast cancer are less likely than white women to receive appropriate care as recommended by an expert panel of the National Cancer Institute, a factor that may help to explain the fact that survival rates are lower for black patients.[31] Doctors are also less likely to recommend mammograms to black women than white women.[32] Blacks and Hispanics who are infected with HIV are less likely to receive antiretroviral therapy than non-minorities with HIV. Even after adjusting for insurance status, CD4 cell count, and other factors, minorities were 24 percent less likely than whites to receive protease inhibitors or other advanced drugs.[28]

These studies provide evidence that inequities in medical care extend significantly beyond disparities in health insurance status and the corresponding financial barriers to care common in members of minority groups. The IOM report concluded that "although myriad sources contribute to these disparities, some evidence suggests that bias, prejudice, and stereotyping on the part of healthcare providers may contribute to differences in care."[28]

THE RELATIVE IMPORTANCE OF MEDICAL CARE FOR PUBLIC HEALTH

Health services research, in addition to studying medical care epidemiology, has tried to answer questions on the proper place for medical care in the public health system. To what extent does medical care contribute to improving the health of the population as a whole? Some skeptics have argued that medicine's effectiveness is limited and its impact on health marginal at best. As discussed in Chapter 1, much of the improvement in life expectancy over the past century resulted more from public health measures and improvements in the population's economic status than from improvements in medical interventions.

In focusing on the population perspective, analysts weigh the contribution of medical care in comparison with other factors that contribute to people's health (Figure 27–1). There is little agreement on the relative importance of the various factors, which include genetics, lifestyle, and the environment, in addition to medical care. However, any consideration of these factors calls attention to the fact that, in the United States, resources

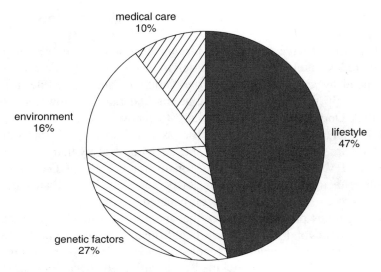

Figure 27–1 Contribution of Medical Care to Health
Source: Data from P. R. Lee, C. L. Estes, editors. *The Nation's Health.* (Sudbury Mass.: Jones & Bartlett Pub., 2001), p. 50.

devoted to medical care are far out of proportion to its contribution to health. In fact, the enormous American investment in medical care uses up resources that would otherwise be available to address other factors that affect health, such as education, housing, and the environment. In that sense, it may be that the greater the expansion of the medical care system, the more negative the impact on the population's health.[33]

Evidence from small area comparisons in the United States, as well as comparative studies of industrialized nations, has clearly indicated that health is not correlated with resources devoted to medical care. This was true, for example, in Wennberg's comparison of health care costs and the population's health status in Boston and New Haven. Similarly, an international study of mortality rates in 18 developed nations found no consistent relationship with levels of medical care resources.[34] In fact, health was found to depend primarily on wealth: mortality rates declined with increasing gross domestic product (GDP) per person. Paradoxically, countries with a higher number of physicians per population tend to have higher mortality rates, supporting the view that investment in medicine may be at the expense of other health-promoting factors. This conclusion is supported by a 2003 study by Wennberg's group that looked at patients with heart attacks, hip fractures, or colorectal cancer who lived in geographical areas with high Medicare spending compared with similar patients in areas with lower spending. The researchers found that patients in the high spending areas had more physicians visits, more tests and procedures, and spent more time in the hospital than those in the low spending areas, but the outcomes were not better and, in fact, included a small increase in the risk of death. Apparently, the higher intensity practice patterns caused harm to the patients.[35]

As discussed in Chapter 26, the United States does not get its money's worth for the resources allocated to medical care. Health services research that focuses on the efficiency of the health care system can offer evidence on how the nation could keep costs under control while achieving better health. A number of studies have investigated the effects of different methods of paying for care on the use of care and on health outcomes. One influential study was the RAND Health Insurance Experiment.[34] This study compared use of services, expenditures, and health outcomes among several groups of consumers who were assigned randomly to receive free care or to pay copayments of varying amounts. The evidence showed, not surprisingly, that higher copayments discouraged patients from seeking care. The more consumers had to pay, the less medical care they consumed, and the free care group used services costing 50 percent more than those who had to pay the most. The extra services were not found to have any impact on the typical participant's health status. Thus, many health care services provided to Americans with generous insurance policies may be wasted in that they do not contribute to better health.

However, for those who were poor and chronically ill, free care did provide significant benefits in health status. These are the people most likely to lack access to medical care because of financial barriers. They are the ones who may need care the most, but may be least likely to get it. This is the tragedy of the American health system which, despite the highest rate of health care spending in the world—much of it probably unnecessary—leaves 16 percent of the population uninsured.

Unfortunately, although political interest in the health care system remains high, little of the attention at present is focused on improving access. Despite evidence that the poor and sick are the ones who could most benefit from access to medical care, their prospects for receiving it are not likely to improve any time soon. Research on the efficiency of the health care system demonstrates that a significant proportion of the resources spent on medical care in the United States does not contribute to better health in the population. If the nation were to muster the political will to really reform how medical care is paid for in this country, the system could be made much more efficient and equitable than it is today, and the health of the American population could be significantly improved.

CONCLUSION

One hope for reducing costs of medical care and improving its quality is health services research, which studies the effectiveness, efficiency, and equity of the health care system. Small area analysis, a form of health services research, has found that physicians in different geographical areas vary widely in how they treat common health problems. This observation suggests that for some conditions, decisions on treatment are somewhat arbitrary, and that different treatments may be equally valid—or invalid.

The observed differences may be due in part to the varying availability of services in a community. Larger amounts of surgery are done in communities with higher numbers of surgeons. More people are hospitalized in communities with higher per capita numbers of hospital beds. Other variations seem to be merely variations in practice style, which tends to be shared by all physicians in a community. Comparisons of high-usage areas with low-usage areas have not found significant differences in health status, indicating that the variations are not caused by greater severity of illness in some areas, and there is no evidence that high usage helps or harms people's health. However, medical costs are proportionately high in the high-usage areas, suggesting that adopting the practices of low-usage areas could save substantial sums.

Outcomes research, the epidemiologic study of the everyday practice of medicine, holds hope for reaching conclusions on the benefits and risks of various treatments for high-variation conditions. For example, prostatectomy for benign prostate disease is a common surgery performed on older men. However, it is not always effective in relieving symptoms, and it can have undesirable complications such as impotence and incontinence. Results of outcomes research have made it clear that people should be informed of the risks of surgery and the possible outcomes before they make choices about their treatment. PSA screening for prostate cancer is also of questionable value since it leads to many biopsies and prostatectomies but does not appear to lower mortality rates.

Outcomes research can be used to evaluate the quality of managed care plans, assessing whether plans provide services that have been demonstrated to be effective. The research can also be used to compare the performance of hospitals and surgeons. New York State has done this research, an exercise that has resulted in improved quality of coronary surgery in that state.

Health services research has documented extensive evidence that the delivery of medical care is inequitable and that ethnic and racial minorities receive poorer quality care than do white Americans. This is true even after differences in health insurance status have been taken into consideration.

Although health services research has been proven capable of improving the quality of medical care, it also shows that medical care is a less important influence on people's health than some other factors, including education, housing, and the environment. In fact, health services research suggests that if the United States spent less on medical care, and instead invested the savings in these other areas, the population's health might be improved.

REFERENCES

1. J. E. Wennberg, "Dealing with Medical Practice Variations: A Proposal for Action," *Health Affairs* 3 (1984): 6–32.
2. J. E. Wennberg and M. M. Cooper, eds. *Dartmouth Atlas of Health Care* (Chicago: American Hospital Publishing, 1996).
3. M. R. Chassin et al., "Does Inappropriate Use Explain Geographic Variations in the Use of Health Care Services? A Study of Three Procedures," *Journal of the American Medical Association* 258 (1987): 2533–2537.
4. J. E. Wennberg, "Small Area Analysis and the Medical Care Outcome Problem," in L. Sechrest, E. Perrin, and J. Bunker, *Conference Proceedings: Research Methodology: Strengthening Causal Interpretations of Nonexperimental Data*, AHCPR. May 1990, 177–201.
5. G. Kolata, "In the U.S., All Medicine is Local," *New York Times* (February 4, 1996): 5.
6. J. E. Wennberg and M. M. Cooper, eds. *Dartmouth Atlas of Health Care 1998* (Chicago: American Hospital Publishing, 1998).
7. J. E. Wennberg, "Outcomes Research, Cost Containment, and the Fear of Health Care Rationing," *New England Journal of Medicine* 323 (1990): 1202–1204.
8. M. Waldholtz and W. Bogdanich, "Warm Bodies: Doctor-Owned Labs Earn Lavish Profits in a Captive Market," *Wall Street Journal* (March 1, 1989): A1.

9. B. J. Hillman, et al., "Frequency and Costs of Diagnostic Imaging in Office Practice—A comparison of Self-Referring and Radiologist-Referring Physicians," *New England Journal of Medicine* 323 (1990): 1604–1608.

10. R. Abelson and M. Petersen, "An Operation to Ease Back Pain Bolsters the Bottom Line, Too," *New York Times* (December 31, 2003): A1.

11. G. L. Lu-Yao, D. McLerran, J. Wasson, and J. E. Wennberg, "Assessment of Radical Prostatectomy. Time Trends, Geographic Variation, and Outcomes. The Prostate Patient Outcomes Research Team," *Journal of the American Medical Association* 269 (1993): 2633–2636.

12. F. J. Fowler et al., "Symptom Status and Quality of Life Following Prostatectomy," *Journal of the American Medical Association* 259 (1988): 3018–3022.

13. J. H. Wasson et al., "Transurethral Resection of the Prostate Among Medicare Beneficiaries: 1984–1997. For the Patient Outcomes Research Team for Prostatic Diseases," *Journal of Urology* 164 (2000): 1212–1215.

14. G. Lu-Yao et al., "Natural Experiment Examining Impact of Aggressive Screening and Treatment on Prostate Cancer Mortality in Two Fixed Cohorts from Seattle Area and Connecticut," *British Medical Journal* 325 (2002): 740–746.

15. J. Kosterlitz, "Cookbook Medicine," *National Journal* (March 9, 1991): 574–577.

16. Agency for Health Care Policy and Research, "AHCPR Releases Low Back Pain Guideline" *Research Activities* (January 1995): 15–16.

17. N. A. Lewis, "Agency Facing Revolt After Report: Enraged Back Surgeons Recruiting Republicans for a Battle," *New York Times* (September 14, 1995).

18. B. H. Gray, M. K. Gusmano, and S. R. Collins, "AHCPR and the Changing Politics of Health Services Research," *Health Affairs* (June 25, 2003); web exclusive.

19. Institute of Medicine, *To Err Is Human: Building a Safer Health System*, (Washington, D.C.: National Academy Press, 1999).

20. R. M. Wachter, "The End of the Beginning: Patient Safety Five Years After 'To Err Is Human,'" *Health Affairs Web Exclusive*, November 30, 2004. *http://content. healthaffairs.org/cgi/reprint/hlthaff.w4.534v1.*

21. C. R. Gaus, and L. Simpson, "Reinventing Health Services Research," *Inquiry* 32 (1995): 130–133.

22. M. Angell and J. P. Kassirer, "Quality and the Medical Marketplace—Following Elephants," *New England Journal of Medicine* 335 (1996): 883–885.

23. National Committee for Quality Assurance, *State of Health Care Quality 2004. www.ncqa.org/communications/SOMC/SOHC2004.pdf.*

24. S. B. Soumerai et al., "Adverse Outcomes of Underuse of Beta-Blockers in Elderly Survivors of Acute Myocardial Infarction," *Journal of the the American Medical Association* 277 (1997): 115–121.

25. E. L. Hannan et al., "Improving the Outcomes of Coronary Bypass Surgery in New York State," *Journal of the American Medical Association* 271 (1994): 761–766.

26. E. L. Hannan et al., "Decline in Coronary Artery Bypass Graft Surgery Mortality in New York State: The Role of Surgeon Volume," *Journal of the American Medical Association* 273 (1995): 209–213.

27. M. R. Chassin, "Achieving and Sustaining Improved Quality: Lessons from New York State and Cardiac Surgery," *Health Affairs* (July/August 2002): 40–51.

28. Institute of Medicine, *Unequal Treatment: What Healthcare Providers Need to Know about Racial and Ethnic Disparities in Healthcare* (Washington, DC: National Academy Press, 2002).

29. E. L. Hannan et al., "Access to Coronary Artery Bypass Surgery by Race/Ethnicity and Gender Among Patients Who Are Appropriate for Surgery," *Medical Care* 37 (1999): 68–77.

30. J. A. Finkelstein et al., "Quality of Care for Preschool Children With Asthma: The Role of Social Factors and Practice Setting," *Pediatrics* 95 (1995): 389–394.

31. P. Diehr et al., "Treatment Modality and Quality Differences for Black and White Breast-Cancer Patients Treated in Community Hospitals," *Medical Care* 27 (1989): 942–954.

32. M. S. O'Malley, J. A. Earp, and R. P. Harris, "Race and Mammography Use in Two North Carolina Counties," *American Journal of Public Health* 87 (1997): 782–786.

33. R. G. Evans and G. L. Stoddart, "Producing Health, Consuming Health Care," *Social Science and Medicine* 31 (1990): 1347–1363.

34. L. A. Aday, *Evaluating the Medical Care System: Effectiveness, Efficiency, and Equity* (Ann Arbor, Michigan: Health Administration Press, 1993).

35. E. S. Fisher et al., "The Implications of Regional Variations in Medicare Spending. Part 2: Health Outcomes and Satisfaction with Care," *Annals of Internal Medicine* 138 (2003): 288–298.

CHAPTER 28

Public Health and the Aging Population

Getting Older

The U.S. population is getting older. The "baby boom" generation, which is approaching sixty, will begin to retire in a few years. The prospect is causing great alarm among health planners because of the increasing pressure it will place on medical costs. Medicare spending has grown dramatically since the program began, both because of growing medical care costs and because of the aging population. Politicians know

489

that they must do something to remedy the situation, but there is no agreement on how or on what should be done. Present trends are unsustainable: if growth in Medicare and Social Security continued at the present rate, together they would consume the entire federal budget by 2070.[1]

Older people tend to be in poorer health than younger ones. They tend to have more chronic illness and are more likely to suffer limitations on their ability to participate fully in the activities of their community. These truths have two unhappy consequences: the quality of life of the elderly is on average poorer than that for younger people and their medical costs are higher. Both issues are of great concern for public health.

Quality of life in later years depends significantly on lifestyle in youth and middle age. Therefore, to the extent that public health succeeds in promoting healthy behavior throughout life, there is a payoff in improved health and quality of life for older people. Public health must also address the inevitability that there will be limits to society's willingness to pay the medical costs of the aged. Although the Medicare program was created in the hope of enabling all older people to receive adequate care, financial barriers are increasing and, like the system as a whole, medical care for the elderly is being rationed. The challenge for public health is twofold: first, to improve the health of older people by prevention of disease and disability; and second, to confront the issue of how costs can be controlled in an equitable and humane way. Although these public health goals for older people are no different from those for other age groups, there is special urgency in the case of the elderly because society has made a unique commitment to this group through the Social Security and Medicare programs, a commitment that is now in jeopardy.

THE AGING OF THE POPULATION—TRENDS

The population is getting older by a number of measures. The median age of the American population—the age at which half the population is younger and half older—increased from 20 in 1860 to 35.3 in 2000.[2] The U.S. Census Bureau predicts that the median age will peak at 39.1 in 2035. The number of older Americans has increased much more rapidly than the overall population: from 1900 to 2000, the population sixty-five and older increased more than eleven-fold, while the number of those under sixty-five grew only 3.4-fold.[2,3] The increased number of older people was accompanied by an increase in life expectancy at birth, from 47.3 in 1900 through 1902 to 76.9 in 2000.[4]

As people are living longer, most people aged sixty-five—the traditional retirement age—are still relatively vigorous. To reflect this reality, the elderly are categorized into three component groups, which have quite different characteristics and needs: the "young old," ages sixty-five to seventy-four; the "aged," who are seventy-five to eighty-four; and the "oldest old," those eighty-five and older. In 2000 there were 4.2 million oldest-old people in the United States, and this is the fastest growing age group in the population. The Census Bureau predicts that there will be about 21 million people age eighty-five and older by the year 2005.[5] Obviously these projections have important implications for the Social Security and Medicare systems, because the numbers of working-age people—who will be expected to pay to support the elderly—are growing at much slower rates.

Figure 28–1 shows the age distribution of the population in 2000. The baby boom generation—those born between 1946 and 1964—is making its way through the age groups like the proverbial pig through a python and will account for an explosive increase in the numbers of elderly beginning in 2011. Predictions of future population size depend both on the birth rate—which is currently fairly stable—and immigration rates, which are somewhat unpredictable and depend on federal policies.

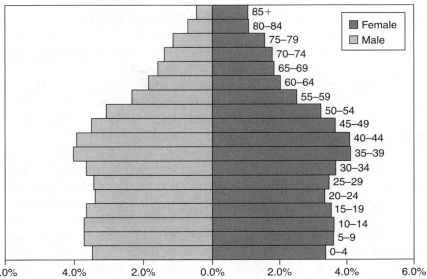

Figure 28–1 Age Distribution of U.S. Population, 2000
Source: U.S. Census Bureau.

Females increasingly outnumber males in older age groups. Among the oldest old, there are more than twice as many women as men. This is a consequence of the fact that women have a longer life expectancy than men. After the age of seventy-five, most women are widowed and live alone, while most men are married and live with their wives. Racial and ethnic diversity among the elderly is expected to increase: non-Hispanic whites constituted 83 percent of the older population in 2003, but that proportion is projected to shrink to 61 percent in 2050. As in younger age groups, older whites are in better health than older people of racial and ethnic minorities. Life expectancy for both men and women at age sixty-five is 1.7 years longer for whites than for blacks. However, racial differences in health grow smaller in the oldest populations, and there is even some evidence that African Americans who survive to join the oldest-old category are healthier than whites of the same age.[5]

Social Security and Medicare have helped most of the sixty-five-and-over age group to stay out of poverty. The percentage of people sixty-five and older living in poverty declined from 35 percent in 1959 to about 10 percent in 2002. Elderly women (12 percent) were more likely to be poor than elderly men (8 percent). Poverty rates were higher for older blacks (24 percent) and Hispanics (21 percent) than for whites (8 percent).[5]

HEALTH STATUS OF THE OLDER POPULATION

The greatest public health concern for Americans over sixty-five is long-term chronic illness, disability, and dependency. The majority of the older population, especially those in the younger groups, are in good health. In national surveys of noninstitutionalized persons, about 80 percent of the young old who are white consider their health to be good, very good, or excellent, as do about 71 percent of those over 75. Blacks and Hispanics report poorer health than whites. With more advanced age, many older people have chronic conditions that cause them to require assistance with the activities of daily living. Overall, less than 5 percent of people aged sixty-five and over live in nursing homes, but that proportion increases to about 18 percent of the oldest old. About 15 percent of the eighty-five-and-over group who are not institutionalized require assistance with everyday activities.[5]

The causes of death of older people are pretty much the same as the causes of death in the overall population, with cardiovascular disease and cancer leading the list. (Figure 28–2.) Death rates from motor vehicle crashes and suicide are also significant causes of death, among older men far more than for older women. Men are likely to die at a younger age, whereas older women are more likely to suffer from chronic, disabling diseases. Heart disease, cancer, and stroke, in addition to killing people, can contribute to chronic health problems and dependency. Many of the elderly, especially women, suffer from arthritis, diabetes, osteoporosis, and Alzheimer's disease, conditions that limit their independence and may force them into nursing homes.

A still unanswered question with very important implications for public health is whether longer life expectancy means more healthy years for most people or, alternatively, if it leads to longer periods of chronic illness and disability. The financial solvency of the Medicare system will be highly dependent on the answer. Experts on aging agree that the trend of the twentieth century has been a "compression of mortality," shown in Figure 28–3, meaning that deaths are increasingly concentrated in a relatively short age range at about the biological limit of life span. What is less certain is whether the compression of mortality will be accompanied by a compression of morbidity—the rates of chronic disease and disability.

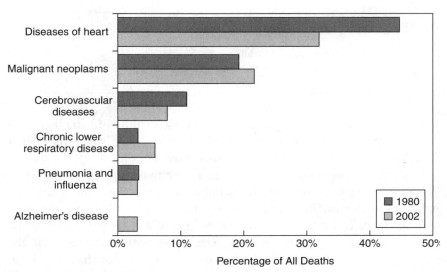

Figure 28–2 Leading Causes of Death, Individuals Sixty-Five Years and Over
Source: Data from National Center for Health Statistics, *Health, United States, 2004.*

Figure 28–3 Compression of Mortality
Source: U.S. Census Bureau. *65+ in the United States*, 1996, p. 3-2.

Ideally most people would prefer to live a long, healthy life and then suddenly drop dead, like the "wonderful one-hoss shay," a scenario that would also save massive amounts of Medicare money.

Evidence is beginning to emerge that a compression of morbidity is indeed taking place.[6] An ongoing national survey of Medicare recipients indicates that disability rates among those over sixty-five declined steadily, from 26.2 percent in 1982 to 19.7 percent in 1999. Other national surveys have had similar findings. The 2000 census showed that the percentage of older people living in nursing homes has declined. The Framingham Heart Study, which tracked the health of a cohort of original participants and their offspring (see Chapter 4), found that the younger generation had less disability than their parents at the same ages.[7] This trend is a measure of success for public health and an indication that more investment in health promotion could be cost-effective for the future.

GENERAL APPROACHES TO MAXIMIZING HEALTH IN OLD AGE

There is still a great deal to learn about how public health can continue to achieve a compression of morbidity, improving quality of life for those who benefit from the compression of mortality that has already occurred. Although a variety of factors might influence the risk of disability in old age, health-related behavior is one important variable that would be expected to make a difference. A study that tracked 1,741 older alumni of the University of Pennsylvania found that, indeed, a healthy lifestyle reduced not only their risk of dying but also their disability in later years. The study subjects, who had attended the University in 1939 and 1940, were surveyed on their smoking habits, body-mass index (BMI), and exercise patterns and, beginning in 1986, chronic conditions, use of medical services, and extent of disability. The alumni were classified into three risk groups, the highest risk belonging to obese, inactive smokers. Those in the highest risk group had twice the cumulative disability of those with low risks, and the onset of disability was postponed by almost eight years in the low risk group.[6,8]

This evidence indicates that, as in younger age groups, the behaviors that most significantly affect health in older people are smoking, obesity, and physical inactivity.[6] However, the recently observed compression of morbidity cannot entirely be explained by improvements in these factors. The reduced prevalence of smoking over the past several decades, discussed in Chapter 15, is no doubt responsible in part for the fact that the elderly are healthier than they used to be. But the increased prevalence of overweight, obesity, and physical inactivity would be expected to have the opposite effect, leading to increased disability in older people.

Smoking is always a major risk factor for cardiovascular disease and cancer, still the leading causes of death in those over sixty-five. Chronic obstructive pulmonary disease is caused almost entirely by smoking. Osteoporosis and disorders of the mouth are also made worse by smoking.

It is significant that prevalence of smoking drops off with increasing age, in part because many older people have succeeded in quitting and in part because many smokers die before they reach old age. In 2002, only about 10.1 percent of American men aged sixty-five and over smoked. The rate among older women was only 8.6 percent.[4]

Nutrition and physical activity are the other most important determinants of health in old age. As seen in Chapter 16, diet and exercise affect the risk of cardiovascular disease and cancer. Overweight and obesity, the result of overnutrition and lack of exercise, increase the risk not only of the leading killers, but also of diabetes and arthritis of the weight-bearing joints. Interestingly, the percentage of the population that is overweight and obese decreases after age sixty-five, as seen in Figure 28–4. The reason for this is not known, but one theory is that, like cigarette smokers, obese people die at an earlier age. This may explain in part the apparent paradox between the obesity epidemic and the trend toward better health in the older population. Because obese people are more likely to report poor health than people of normal weight, it is likely that the compression

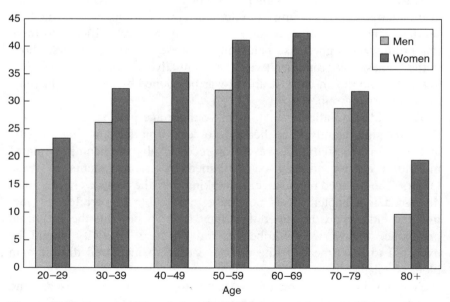

Figure 28–4 Percent of Population Obese by Age and Sex, 1999–2000
Source: Data from K. M. Flegal et al., Prevalence and trends in obesity among adults, 1999–2000, *Journal of the American Medical Association* 288 (2002): 1725.

of morbidity seen in recent years will be reversed unless the obesity epidemic can be halted.[9]

Obesity is not the only outcome of poor diet and lack of exercise. Elderly individuals need physical activity to maintain muscle strength, balance, and cardiovascular fitness, which protect them against osteoporosis and falls. The special nutritional needs of the elderly are not well understood, but adequate calcium is clearly important for the strength of bones and teeth. Despite fragmentary evidence about special effects of individual nutrients such as vitamins C and E in protecting against the diseases of the elderly, the best advice is, as for younger people, to eat a varied diet low in fat and rich in fruits and vegetables.

Through the 1990s more and more evidence appeared suggesting that hormone replacement therapy (HRT) might have broad health advantages for older women in addition to its well-known efficacy in fending off the symptoms of menopause. A number of epidemiologic studies, including the 60,000-woman cohort in the Nurses' Health Study, showed that estrogen therapy was associated with lower rates of heart disease and osteoporosis and perhaps Alzheimer's as well. On the other hand, the hormone increases the risk of breast and uterine cancer. In a 1997 publication, the investigators concluded that HRT reduced women's overall risk of dying as long as they took the hormones.[10] The hopes for estrogen's anti-aging effects were crushed, however, with the publication of the clinical trial conducted as part of the Women's Health Initiative, as discussed in Chapter 6. The trial found that although HRT helped to prevent osteoporosis and the symptoms of menopause, it actually increased the risk of heart disease, strokes, and even Alzheimer's disease. It seems that the apparent benefits of estrogen were caused by the confounding factor that women who chose HRT were healthier and more likely to have a healthy lifestyle than those who chose not to use the hormone.[11]

Other aspects of medical care have probably contributed to reductions in disability among the elderly. For example, secondary prevention such as the use of drugs to treat diabetes, high blood pressure, and high cholesterol have undoubtedly reduced morbidity and mortality in many older people. The number of total joint replacements for arthritis and cataract surgeries has doubled over the past two decades, greatly reducing disabilities and improving quality of life. Still, access to medical care has not improved, and access to prescription drugs is limited for many poor elderly.[12] It remains to be seen whether the new Medicare prescription drug benefit will actually improve the health of people sixty-five and over.

PREVENTING DISEASE AND DISABILITY IN OLD AGE

Much of the disease and disability common in later life is linked to unhealthy behavior in earlier years. However, there are preventive measures that the elderly and their caregivers can take to improve their quality of life and prospects for independence even after health has begun to fail. Some of these measures are well known and easily available, such as vaccination against pneumonia and influenza. Some are beneficial and appropriate for people of any age, such as smoking cessation and blood pressure control. Others are not widely recognized or well understood. Research is needed on how to prevent many of the debilitating conditions and how to minimize their impact on quality of life for the elderly. In a 1990 report, the Institute of Medicine identified a number of the most common problems of the elderly and made recommendations for combating them.[13] These problems commonly and uniquely afflict the elderly and have severe impact on their quality of life but are not among the leading causes of death.

Medications

Although chronic conditions that afflict many of the elderly can be helped by prescription drugs, some of these treatments have unwanted side effects that may seriously impair health and quality of life. Little is known about how the body's ability to metabolize drugs changes with age. Kidney and liver function are often impaired in older people, leading to increased sensitivity to drugs. In older bodies, a higher percentage of body weight is fat, which metabolizes drugs less actively, causing an increased risk of overdoses. Moreover older people often take a number of medications for various chronic conditions. This could lead to unexpected interactions between drugs, including over-the-counter drugs, because patients tend not to inform their doctors about these medications.

Reducing the risks from adverse drug reactions requires education and vigilance by everyone involved. Elderly patients' needs for medications should be reassessed regularly. In some cases, the potential benefit provided by a drug—for example, improved heart function—may not be worth the damage it could cause to other aging organs, for example, the brain. According to the Institute of Medicine, there is an urgent need for more research on risk versus benefit of various types of drugs in the elderly. There is also a need for better coordination and monitoring of medical care, a need that might be better filled by managed care than by fee-for-service care, which currently dominates in serving the Medicare population.

Osteoporosis

Bone loss is common with age, especially in women. This loss leads to osteoporosis—"porous bones," which tend to break easily. Bone loss among women is greatest in the years following menopause. Smoking and alcohol consumption increase the risk of osteoporosis; obesity reduces the risk (one of the few health benefits of being overweight). White women have the greatest risk for the condition; black men have the lowest, and Asians have intermediate risk. A number of medications commonly used by older people cause bone loss. Some diseases also cause bone loss. The degree of osteoporosis depends on bone density earlier in life, which is determined by a number of factors including genetics, diet, and physical activity. Thus, drinking milk and exercising during youth can protect women against osteoporosis in old age. Unfortunately, girls tend to not take the threat seriously when these habits could do them the most good. Surveys have found that the average amount of calcium women obtain in their diet is significantly below the recommended amount.[14]

Osteoporosis itself has no symptoms, and most older people are unaware that they have the problem until they suffer a broken bone. Hip fractures are the most serious consequence of osteoporosis; there is a significant risk that a hip fracture might lead to substantial disability and death. Of those aged sixty-five or older who suffer a hip fracture, about 20 percent die within a year.[14] About 20 percent of the survivors end up in nursing homes because they are unable to walk or care for themselves. Wrist fractures are also a frequent result of osteoporosis, but there is little data on their frequency. Fractures of the vertebrae, even more common, might go unrecognized but often lead to progressive loss of height and the curvature of the upper spine called "dowager's hump." Some osteoporotic fractures are untreatable and cause chronic, debilitating pain. A Surgeon General's report on bone health, published in 2004, estimated that about 1.5 million people a year suffer a bone fracture related to osteoporosis, and the cost of caring for these patients is up to $18 billion a year.[14]

Considerable research has been done on how to prevent osteoporosis. The Framingham Study, among others, found that taking estrogen after menopause can protect women from bone loss and reduce the risk of hip fracture.[15] However, HRT is no longer recommended for older women, as previously discussed. The Surgeon General's report makes a number of recommendations for preventing osteoporosis. These include getting adequate amounts of calcium (1,000 milligrams (mg) per day for adults under fifty years and 1,200 for those over fifty) and vitamin D (200 mg per day for everyone up to fifty years, 400 for those fifty-one to seventy, and 600 for those over seventy). Good source of calcium are milk, leafy green vegetables, soybeans, yogurt, and cheese. Vitamin D is produced in the skin by exposure to the sun and is found in fortified milk and other foods. Other recommendations include being physically active at least thirty minutes a day for adults and sixty minutes a day for children, including weight-bearing activities, which have been shown to increase bone strength.[14]

Bone scan tests can screen for risk of osteoporosis, and the Surgeon General's report recommends that the test be used to screen all women over sixty-five and younger men and women who have risk factors, including previous fractures. When the test shows bone thinning, drugs are available that help to prevent further loss of bone mass. The drugs have been found to reduce the fracture rate by about 50 percent.

Falls

Most osteoporotic fractures occur when elderly people fall. Thus, in addition to osteoporosis prevention, public health efforts focus on preventing falls. More than one third of people sixty-five and older fall each year; many of them fall repeatedly. About one in ten falls results in a serious injury, such as a fracture or head injury. Many older people have a high risk of falls because of medical conditions that affect their mobility, such as arthritis, stroke, and Parkinson's disease. Other risk factors include vision impairment, muscular weakness, problems with balance, and the side effects of medications. The use of four or more prescription drugs is considered a risk factor for falls. Psychoactive drugs such as antidepressants, tranquilizers, and sleeping pills are especially dangerous.[16]

The easiest and most common approach to protecting against falls is to educate the elderly and their families to fall-proof their environment by such means as covering floors with tacked-down carpets, keeping walkways clear of obstacles, equipping bathrooms with grab bars around toilets and tubs, keeping stairways well lit, and using night lights. The elderly can also protect themselves against falls by having physical therapy and doing regular muscle strengthening exercises, which can significantly increase their mobility, strength, and balance. Clinical trials have shown that vitamin D supplements can reduce the risk of falls independently of its value in osteoporosis prevention. The vitamin appears to directly improve muscle strength.[17]

For people with osteoporosis who have an especially high risk of falling, hip protectors are available, which cushion the hips if a fall does occur.

Impairment of Vision and Hearing

Loss of vision and hearing are among the most prevalent conditions among elderly Americans. Either condition may be disabling, limiting the individual's ability to interact with the environment and communicate with others. Loss of vision increases the risk of falls and other injuries. It may restrict the individual's ability to drive, a significant handicap in many parts of the country. Impairment of either vision or hearing is likely to lead to social isolation, a risk factor for poor health at any age (see Chapter 14) and an even greater risk factor in the elderly. Sensory loss also is associated with depression and cognitive impairment in the elderly.

The leading causes of visual impairment among the elderly are cataracts, glaucoma, macular degeneration, and diabetic retinopathy. Cataracts—clouding of the lens—are the most prevalent cause of eye disease; by age eighty, more than half of Americans either have a cataract or have had cataract surgery. Exposure to sunlight contributes to the lens damage, so wearing sunglasses and hats with brims can help protect the eyes. Smoking increases the risk of cataracts. Most cataracts can be effectively corrected by surgery in which the clouded lens is removed and replaced with a synthetic lens.[18]

Glaucoma is a gradual increase in pressure within the eye that causes damage to the optic nerve. It is not known why this occurs or how it can be prevented. It is a common cause of blindness, especially in African Americans and Hispanics. People with a family history of the disease have an increased risk. Secondary prevention is the best approach to controlling glaucoma: regular eye checkups can catch the increase in pressure before it causes harm, and the pressure can be reduced with medication in the form of eye drops.

Macular degeneration involves the breakdown of the light-sensing cells in the macula, the central part of the retina. The risk of macular degeneration increases with age. Whites are at greater risk than blacks, and women have a higher risk than men. Smoking may increase the risk. The cause of macular degeneration is not well understood, and there is no known way to prevent the disease. There is also no known treatment for the most common form of macular degeneration. Researchers are studying whether certain vitamins and minerals might help to slow the progress of the disease.

Diabetic retinopathy is a common complication of diabetes that poses a major risk to vision. The condition occurs when high blood sugar damages the tiny blood vessels in the retina. Strict blood sugar control helps to reduce the extent of this damage, and the condition can be treated with laser surgery.

The most common form of hearing loss among the elderly is characterized by reduced sensitivity to higher frequency tones and, therefore, difficulty in comprehending speech. This pattern is similar to that associated with exposure to excessive noise. In fact, populations living in relatively noise-free environments are less likely to suffer age-related hearing loss. The proportion of Americans affected by hearing impairment ranges from about 23 percent of individuals sixty-five to seventy-four to almost half of people aged eighty-five and older, and that proportion is expected to increase with the aging of generations that thrive on rock concerts and boomboxes. Many products can help people to hear better, including hearing aids, telephone amplifying devices, and assistive listening devices in public places such as movie theaters, churches and synagogues, and auditoriums.

One barrier that limits the access of many older individuals to services and devices that correct the effects of sensory loss, such as glasses and hearing aids, is that Medicare does not cover them.[13]

Oral Health

As people age, they suffer increasingly from diseases and impairments of the mouth, including tooth loss, dental caries, periodontal disease, salivary dysfunction, cancer and precancerous conditions, and chronic pain. Such problems can have a severe impact on quality of life. They may impair the individual's ability to chew, taste, and swallow, thereby posing a threat to physical health and nutrition far beyond the anatomical parts that are primarily affected. Like sensory impairments, disorders of the mouth may diminish social functioning by affecting speech, facial esthetics, and self esteem. Oral health in old age, like overall health, depends on healthy behaviors throughout life, but older people can improve their health status by instituting healthier habits at any time. They can quit smoking, use better oral hygiene self-care practices, and use professional dental services. Unfortunately, many of the elderly do not have access to dental services for financial reasons, and Medicare does not cover them.[13]

Alzheimer's and Other Dementias

Alzheimer's disease is one of the most dreaded afflictions of old age. It robs the individual of memory and individuality, and eventually reduces him or her to the helplessness of an infant. Caring for someone with Alzheimer's imposes a crushing emotional, physical, and financial burden on a family. Dementia among the elderly is a major public health problem, currently affecting about four million people in the United States at a cost of up to $100 billion per year; much of this cost is for long-term care in nursing homes.[19]

Alzheimer's is the most common cause of dementia in the elderly, although there is no definitive diagnostic test for the disease, which can be identified for certain only on autopsy. The risk of dementia increases with age, becoming especially high in the oldest age group. In one survey conducted in East Boston, nearly half of the people over eighty-five were found to have major impairments in thinking and memory. With the rapid increase in the oldest-old population, it is estimated that by the middle of the twenty-first century, up to fourteen million Americans could be suffering from Alzheimer's disease.[19]

While a few types of dementia are treatable, there is no cure for Alzheimer's. Until recently, virtually nothing was known about its cause or how the disease could be prevented. However, the magnitude of the problem has stimulated a great deal of research. The hope is that a better understanding of Alzheimer's could lead to methods of postponing its onset. Some experts predict that merely delaying the onset of Alzheimer's by five years could reduce the number of cases by half, because many potential victims are nearing the end of their lives for other reasons.

Biomedical scientists have learned a great deal about the changes in the brain that are typical of Alzheimer's disease. These changes include characteristic tangles of fibers within brain cells, deposits of the protein beta-amyloid, called plaques, in extracellular spaces, and the death of brain cells. Several genes have been identified that influence the risk that an individual will develop Alzheimer's disease. In fact, a mouse model of Alzheimer's has been developed by genetically engineering a mouse with a mutant human gene. The mice develop memory loss as they age, and their brains have the protein plaques characteristic of Alzheimer's, though not the tangles.[20] The scientists hope that studies of these mice will help them understand the relationship between the abnormal protein, the death of brain cells, and the cognitive losses of Alzheimer's disease.

Much of what is known about Alzheimer's disease has come from studies of an early onset form of the disease, which is largely determined by genetics.[21] Recent evidence suggests however, that the more common form of Alzheimer's that occurs in older people may have a component that is caused by vascular disease and unrecognized strokes. Risk factors for cardiovascular disease increase the risk of Alzheimer's as well. This suggests that preventive measures against heart disease, such as weight control, physical activity, avoidance of smoking, treatment of high blood pressure and cholesterol, and aspirin, might help against dementia as well.[22]

An increasing body of evidence indicates that non-genetic factors play a significant role in the development of Alzheimer's. A study of elderly Japanese American men living in Hawaii found that they had a higher rate of Alzheimer's than men of the same age living in Japan, suggesting that lifestyle and environment might affect risk.[23] Other studies have found that people with more education are less likely to develop the disease and that participation in cognitively demanding leisure activities in late life, such as reading, playing board games, and playing a musical instrument, may protect against dementia.[21]

A number of approaches are being tested to treat or prevent Alzheimer's disease. Vaccines against beta-amyloid have been tested in humans with mixed results. Some encouraging results have come from preliminary trials of statins, which lower cholesterol levels. Drugs that act on the neurotransmitters—chemicals that carry signals between nerve cells—have been shown to delay progression of some symptoms, and these drugs have been approved by the FDA. Trials are also under way, testing the effect of vitamin E. There was great hope that HRT would protect against

Alzheimer's, as discussed earlier in this chapter, but the Women's Health Initiative has found evidence to the contrary.[19]

There is some evidence that taking non-steroidal anti-inflammatory drugs (NSAIDs) could reduce the risk or Alzheimer's disease. Arthritis patients who take regular doses of these drugs—such as aspirin, ibuprofen, naproxen—to control their pain have been observed to have an unusually low risk of dementia.[24] Inflammation is found in the brains of Alzheimer's patients, further supporting the approach of treating them with NSAIDs. However, in December 2004, the National Institutes of Health halted a major clinical trial testing whether Celebrex—one of a new type of NSAIDs called COX-2 inhibitors—could prevent Alzheimer's. When Vioxx, another COX-2 inhibitor, was pulled from the market for increasing the risk of heart disease, as discussed in Chapter 23, questions were raised about other drugs of the same type. A number of studies testing this group of NSAIDs for cancer prevention were also halted as a result of the new data on risk to the heart. COX-2 inhibitors had been thought safer than the older NSAIDs because they were less likely to cause bleeding in the digestive tract. Now, there is uncertainty about the safety even of some of the older NSAIDs.[25] Since the older people who have the greatest risk for Alzheimer's are also likely to have a greater risk for heart disease, the wisdom of treating them long-term with anti-inflammatory drugs now seems questionable.

MEDICAL COSTS OF THE ELDERLY

Medicare, the federal program that pays medical bills for elderly Americans, is already feeling the strain of the aging population. The number of people enrolled for Medicare coverage has more than doubled since 1967, from 19.5 million then to 41.7 million in 2004, and the numbers will swell much more rapidly as the baby boomers retire.[26] The number of workers whose earnings contribute to the system is growing at a much slower pace. The same problem applies to Social Security, the retirement system for the elderly. In 2002, there were 3.2 workers supporting every retiree; by the year 2030, only two workers will be expected to support each retiree.[27] The government projects that, at the current rate, the system will go into the red in 2012, but the Social Security trust fund will keep the program solvent until 2042.[28] Medicare's problems are worse than

Social Security's, however, because its costs are less predictable. Not only is the number of people enrolled growing, but the cost per enrollee is also rising, even faster than health care cost inflation overall. The average annual expenditure for each Medicare enrollee rose from about $1,200 in 1980 to over $6,800 in 2004.[26] The new prescription drug benefit, passed by Congress in 2003, to be fully implemented in 2006, will add to the growth in costs.

Despite the large expenditures that threaten Medicare's solvency, the program pays only 53 percent of the health care costs of its enrollees. About 12 percent of overall costs are paid by private "Medigap" insurance policies that help pay for expenses not covered by Medicare. Medicaid, with funding provided jointly by federal and state government, pays about 12 percent of costs and acts as a Medigap policy for the poor elderly. The Medicaid program, which was intended to serve the poor and poor children in particular, has increasingly been called on to pay for services for the elderly that Medicare does not provide, especially nursing home care and home health care. Because of the high costs, most nursing home patients rapidly deplete their savings and become poor enough to qualify for Medicaid, which does cover such care. Almost half of all nursing home costs are paid by Medicaid, which like Medicare, has seen its budget mushroom, from $24 billion in 1980 to almost $170 billion in 2004. While the elderly constitute only 10 percent of the persons enrolled in Medicaid, they consume 28 percent of the Medicaid budget.[26] This aspect of the crisis in health care costs for the elderly has received less attention than the problems of Medicare.

Past efforts to rein in the growth of government expenditures for the elderly's medical bills have meant that these patients bear a higher percentage of the costs through higher premiums and copayments. By 1999, 19 percent of the medical costs of the elderly were paid by the elderly themselves and that does not include premiums for Medicare and private Medigap policies. Most elderly households have annual incomes below $40,000, and the poorest households spend an average of 29 percent of their household income on medical expenses.[26] This trend threatens the Medicare population with rationing by ability to pay, a matter of great concern to them.

Another approach to controlling growth of costs has been to reduce reimbursement to medical providers, a strategy that, it is feared, could induce some providers to refuse treatment to Medicare patients. In 1997, Congress tried to control Medicare costs by providing incentives for the elderly to enroll in managed care plans, an approach that had been successful in younger groups. However, over the next few years, there were many problems with the plans, in part because of Congress's efforts to control costs. The plans raised premiums and reduced benefits; providers withdrew from the plans; and a large number of plans withdrew from the Medicare program. In 2003, only 12 percent of Medicare enrollees chose managed care despite incentives to encourage them to do so.[29] Moreover, costs to Medicare were higher for beneficiaries enrolled in the private plans than for those who chose fee-for-service. The 2003 legislation that established prescription drug benefits also contained provisions meant to encourage the use of private managed care plans like those established by the 1997 law. There are many questions about how the new policies will work and predictions that the high costs will force the Medicare program into crisis sooner than ever.[29,1]

On the Medicaid side, costs for the program have increased faster than those of Medicare, putting immense strain on state budgets. Twenty-nine percent of Medicaid spending is for long-term care, not only for the elderly, but also for the disabled.[26] Many states set low reimbursement rates for long-term care providers in order to save money. Some states try to control costs through regulations limiting the number of available nursing home beds. In response, nursing homes tend to preferentially admit patients who can pay their own bills, usually at higher rates than allowed by Medicaid. Consequently, there is a large and growing unmet need among the less affluent elderly for nursing home care.

Unless the baby boom generation turns out to be significantly healthier and more independent than the aged and oldest old of today, their need for nursing homes and other forms of long-term care is likely to reach critical proportions. In the past, and even today, most elderly Americans who need help with the activities of daily living have been cared for by their families, with primary responsibility borne by a daughter or daughter-in-law. A number of trends make these arrangements less feasible in the future. Baby boomers have fewer children to share the burden of caring for them in old age than did previous generations. The increased divorce rate has led to more complicated family arrangements, which may make it more difficult for the younger generation to take their parents into their homes. A more mobile society means that many children live far away from their parents. Moreover, most women work outside the home. Thus, just as the government is reducing social services for the elderly, old people may be less able to depend on their families for the help they need.

PROPOSALS FOR RATIONING

As it has become obvious that the growth in health care costs for the elderly has become unsustainable, various proposals have been made for controlling the costs through a systematic process that would be fair and equitable, such as rationing. Richard Lamm, a former governor of Colorado, was one of the first to draw attention to the idea by suggesting in 1984 that older persons have a duty to die and get out of the way.[30] His concern was that as the elderly consume increasing amounts of medical care, society is cutting back on care for children and working people, jeopardizing their future and the productivity of society as a whole. Moreover, as medical costs—largely for the elderly—consume an increasing proportion of the national budget, the government is making cutbacks in other social programs, such as education or food programs targeted for the young, which are important for the future health and prosperity of the country.

Most of the proposals for rationing involve denying expensive life-prolonging technology to people over a set age, to people seen as causing their own medical problems through unhealthy behavior, or to people who are not expected to achieve a substantial improvement in quality of life from the treatment. However, careful analyses have shown that most expenditures for old people are not for high-technology interventions and that age-based rationing would not achieve much in cost saving.[31] Many people believe that any attempt to ration health care should include people of all ages, not just the elderly or the poor, a model that would only be possible through a coherent national system.

Considering how the nation should care for its increasing numbers of elderly citizens requires examination of our ethics and values as a society. The questions raised are difficult to answer, and most people would prefer not to think about them. However, refusal to take responsibility for solving the problems that will inevitably face us will lead to desperation among the elderly and those who must care for them, especially people who do not have the resources to pay for needed care.

The current interest in assisted suicide is one consequence of ill and elderly patients' fear that they will not receive humane care as they lose control and independence. Euthanasia is only a step further, and its widespread use would certainly cut the costs of caring for the dying, an incentive feared by its opponents. Desperate families might increasingly resort to "granny dumping"—abandoning in a public place an unidentified elderly person, most often someone with Alzheimer's disease—when they feel they can no longer cope with caring for a difficult dependent.

Perhaps the greatest hope for reducing costs in an aging population is the possibility of improved health for the elderly, the compression of morbidity that most people would wish for as they look forward to longer lives. This is a realistic hope in that the baby-boom generation is relatively well educated as compared to preceding generations, and more education correlates with better health in the elderly as in other age groups. A consortium of opinion leaders has proposed that this goal could be more readily achieved through a conscious policy of integrating public health and medical services with the aim of reducing the need and demand for medical care.[32] The advocates include James F. Fries, author of the University of Pennsylvania alumni study described earlier in this chapter,[8] who has long argued that compression of morbidity is already occurring, and former Surgeon General C. Everett Koop. Fries and Koop propose that the goal of an integrated health care system should be to postpone the onset of chronic infirmity—which accounts for the bulk of illness in the population—by reducing risk factors such as smoking, dietary fat intake, lack of exercise, and failure to wear seat belts, measures that would reduce the need for medical care. In addition, they suggest that demand for medical care could be reduced by educating individuals to assume more responsibility for their own health, including self-management of chronic disease. The Fries-Koop consortium's proposal is in effect an integration of the missions of public health and medicine, a "doubly positive policy goal," they write; "it promises better health for the individual and lowering of the medical costs that now consume a dangerously high share of our nation's productivity."[32]

CONCLUSION

The American population is aging. Because older people tend to use medical services more than younger people, there are fears that the reliance of an increasing percentage of the population on Medicare to pay for their medical costs will overwhelm the system.

Factors that increase the risk of chronic disability in the elderly—and thus drive up medical costs—are similar to those that cause premature mortality in younger people. These include smoking, poor diet, physical inactivity, and unsafe driving practices. Public health aims to prevent the major killers, such as cardiovascular disease, cancer, and injuries, but it also has a role in secondary and tertiary prevention of a number of problems common in elderly patients that can adversely affect their independence and quality of life. These include overmedication, osteoporosis, falls, impairment of vision and hearing, impairments of the mouth, and Alzheimer's and other dementias.

A key question in planning for the future is whether the compression of mortality—the increasing probability that people will survive until the biological limit of life span—will be accompanied by a compression of morbidity, permitting people to remain healthy until shortly before they die. As medical costs of the elderly have grown, and as the baby boom generation approaches retirement, it has become clear that current trends would cause the system to be overwhelmed. Various proposals for rationing medical care have been put forward. The best hope for avoiding the need for rationing, and at the same time for improving quality of life for the elderly, would be to devise a way of integrating public health measures with the medical system to prevent chronic disease in the elderly, thereby reducing the need and demand for medical care.

REFERENCES

1. M. W. Serafini, "The Real Medicare Crisis Ahead," *National Journal* (June 5, 2004).
2. U.S. Bureau of the Census. Press Release: Nation's Median Age Highest Ever, but 65-and-over Population's Growth Lags, Census 2000." Press Release (May 15, 2001).
3. U.S. Bureau of the Census. Current Population Reports, Special Studies, P23-190. *65+ in the United States* (Washington, DC: U.S. Government Printing Office, 1996).
4. National Center for Health Statistics. *Health, United States, 2004, with Chartbook on Trends in the Health of Americans. Older Population Age 65 Years and Over, 2004, www.cdc.gov/nchs/products/pubs/pubd/hus/older.htm.* Accessed January 4, 2005.
5. Federal Interagency Forum on Aging-Related Statistics. *Older Americans 2004: Key Indicators of Well-Being, www.agingstats.gov/* Accessed January 4, 2005.
6. J. F. Fries, "Measuring and Monitoring Success in Compressing Morbidity," *Annals of Internal Medicine* 139 (2003): 456–459.
7. S. H. Allaire et al., "Evidence for Decline in Disability and Improved Health among Persons Aged 55 to 70 Years: The Framingham Heart Study," *American Journal of Public Health* 89 (1997): 1678–1683.
8. A. J. Vita, R. B. Terry, H. B. Hubert, and J. F. Fries, "Aging, Health Risks, and Cumulative Disability," *New England Journal of Medicine* 338 (1998): 1035–1066.

9. R. Sturm, J. S. Ringel, and T. Andreyeva, "Increasing Obesity Rates and Disability Trends," *Health Affairs* 23 (March/April 2004): 199–205.
10. F. Grodstein et al., "Postmenopausal Hormone Therapy and Mortality," *New England Journal of Medicine* 336 (1997): 1769–1775.
11. National Institutes of Health, "Menopausal Hormone Therapy Information," *www.nih.gov/PHTindex.htm.* Accessed January 8, 2005.
12. J. F. Fries, "Reducing Disability in Older Age," *Journal of the American Medical Association* 288 (2002): 3164–3166.
13. U.S. Institute of Medicine, *The Second 50 Years: Promoting Health and Preventing Disability* (Washington, DC: National Academy Press, 1990).
14. U.S. Department of Health and Human Services, *Bone Health and Osteoporosis: A Report of the Surgeon General* (Washington, DC: Government Printing Office, 2004).
15. D. T. Felson, "Effect of Postmenopausal Estrogen Therapy on Bone Density in Elderly Women," *New England Journal of Medicine* 329 (1993): 1141–1146.
16. M. E. Tinetti, "Preventing Falls in Elderly Persons," *New England Journal of Medicine* 348 (2003): 42–49.
17. H. A. Bischoff-Ferrari et al., "Effect of Vitamin D on Falls: A Meta-analysis," *Journal of the American Medical Association* 291 (2004): 1999–2006.
18. National Eye Institute. Health Information, *www.nei.nih.gov/health.* Accessed January 6, 2005.
19. Alzheimer's Disease Education and Referral Center, "Alzheimer's Disease: Unraveling the Mystery," *www.alzheimers.org/unraveling/02.htm.* Accessed January 6, 2005.
20. J. Marx "New 'Alzheimer's Mouse' Produced," *Science* 274 (1996): 177–178.
21. J. T. Coyle, "Use It or Lose It—Do Effortful Mental Activities Protect against Dementia?" *New England Journal of Medicine* 348 (2003): 2489–2490.
22. J. P. Blass, and R. R. Ratan, "Silent Strokes and Dementia," *New England Journal of Medicine* 348 (2003): 1277–1278.
23. L. White et al., "Prevalence of Dementia in Older Japanese-American Men in Hawaii," *Journal of the American Medical Association* 276 (1996): 955–960.
24. L. Helmuth, "Protecting the Brain While Killing Pain?" *Science* 297 (2002): 1262–1263.
25. J. Couzin, "FDA Panel Urges Caution on Many Anti-Inflammatory Drugs," *Science* 307 (2005): 1183–1184.
26. Centers for Medicare and Medicaid Services, "The CMS Chart Series," *www.cms.hhs.gov/charts/default.asp.* Accessed January 7, 2005.
27. W. Ritchie, "Ask an Actuary—Part IV: Social Security's Long-Range Financial Outlook," February 1995, updated December 9, 2002 by H. C. Ballantyne *http://www.ssa.gov/OACT/ASKACT/part4.html.* Accessed January 7, 2005.
28. Social Security Administration, "Status of the Social Security and Medicare Programs: Summary of the 2004 Annual Reports," *www.ssa.gov/OACT/TRS>UM/trsummary.html.* Accessed January 7, 2005.
29. B. Biles, G. Dallek, and L. H. Nicholas, "Medicare Advantage: Déjà vu All Over Again?" *Health Affairs Web Exclusive http://content.healthaffairsorg/egi/reprint/hlthaff.w4.586v1.* December 15, 2004.
30. "Old Age and the Rationing of Health Care," in R. H. Binstock and S. G. Post, eds. *Too Old for Health Care? Controversies in Medicine Law, Economics, and Ethics* (Baltimore, Maryland: The Johns Hopkins University Press, 1991), 1–12.

31. D. W. Jahnigen, and R. H. Binstock, "Economic and Clinical Realities: Health Care for Elderly People," in R. H. Binstock and S. G. Post, eds. *Too Old for Health Care?* 13–43.

32. J. F. Fries et al., "Beyond Health Promotion: Reducing Need and Demand for Medical Care," *Health Affairs* (March/April 1998): 70–84.

PART VII

The Future of Public Health

CHAPTER 29

Emergency Preparedness, Post-9/11

Emergency Response

The events of September 2001, discussed in the prologue, confronted the United States with a new awareness of vulnerability. The attacks on the World Trade Center and the Pentagon made clear that the nation was threatened by enemies who wished to terrorize it using nonconventional weapons and that military and intelligence agencies were unprepared to

515

defend against them. The anthrax-containing letters sent through the mail, while causing only minimal loss of life, exposed a threat from another non-conventional weapon, suggesting the equally terrifying possibility of epidemics for which health agencies were unprepared. The successes and, mostly, the failures of the nation's response to these events forced national soul-searching and mobilization of resources to ensure that the United States would not again be caught unprepared.

The plane crashes and the intentional spread of pathogenic bacteria required law-enforcement responses with the purpose of identifying responsibility, punishing the perpetrators, and preventing further harmful actions. These events also prompted public health responses to deal with the consequences of the incidents and prevent further injury and illness. The public health role in responding to these emergencies was not unprecedented. It was similar to the response seen in many other natural and manmade disasters. Actions taken since 9/11 by governmental and nongovernmental agencies to improve America's preparedness for terrorist attacks will, it is hoped, better prepare the nation to deal with future emergencies of all kinds.

TYPES OF DISASTERS AND PUBLIC HEALTH RESPONSES

Disasters cause death, injury, disease, and property damage on a scale beyond the routine emergencies to which the health system is accustomed. However, many natural disasters are predictable—for example, hurricanes, blizzards, and forest fires—and vulnerable areas generally have plans to deal with them. These plans usually include prior evacuation of the population in affected areas to minimize negative health effects and loss of life. Other natural disasters may be unpredictable, like earthquakes, but even these unpredictable disasters tend to occur in specific geographic areas—California, for example—and therefore allow communities to be prepared through strict building codes, requirements that appliances be secured, easy turn-off of gas and electricity, and so on.

Manmade or technological disasters are generally unpredictable, although the potential can sometimes be identified and the possibility minimized through government regulation and community planning. Typical technological disasters include industrial explosions, hazardous material releases, building or bridge collapses, and transportation crashes that may also cause a chemical or radioactive release. The presence of an industrial facility or a nuclear power plant should prompt a community to conduct emergency planning appropriate to the facility and the likely exposures. Plane crashes and crashes of trains or trucks carrying hazardous materials are more complicated to plan ahead for in detail. Most terrorist events fall into the category of technological disasters. An act of bioterrorism could cause a disaster, but it would be expected to mimic a natural disease outbreak and demand the same public health response that a natural epidemic would require.

Most disasters, natural or manmade, cause immediate injury to many residents of the affected area. Sometimes specially trained and equipped rescue personnel are needed to locate and extricate people buried in the rubble of collapsed buildings or to move people out of harm's way in fires or floods. Police and firefighters are often on the front line in combating a disaster. The injured require emergency medical care and transportation to hospitals. If hazardous materials are involved, measures must be taken to protect the rescuers and medical personnel. The situation can get even more complex when volunteers join the rescue efforts. In some cases, family members might be wandering around anxiously searching for loved ones. These individuals may also need protection from hazards in the affected environment. When there are many deaths, procedures must be established to identify victims and communicate with their families. In situations such as this, there is a critical need for coordination of activities.

Disasters create conditions that cause health risks for the survivors. These tend to be amplifications of the general environmental hazards that public health deals with routinely: contamination of air, water, and food; exposure to toxic chemicals or radioactivity; and injury hazards such as fallen power lines and unstable buildings. The survivors need food and potable water; some people with chronic diseases may urgently need medications such as insulin or cardiac drugs. People may be left homeless by the disaster, or they may be displaced and need temporary shelter.

What is the role of public health in all these activities? One of its most important functions is planning in advance of the emergency, working with other agencies to ensure coordination of all the activities of the responders. Local public health authorities should be knowledgeable about the community and its resources because they have the responsibility to protect the health of the survivors. One of the outcomes of the September 11 attacks was a recognition of the weaknesses in coordination and communication of the emergency responders. This has led to a concerted effort, organized by the federal government, to ensure that all communities have disaster response plans in place so that any future attack may be met by an effective response. This planning process has the added benefit of preparing the nation to deal with other natural or manmade disasters. In fact, many private and public organizations actively promote the need for "all-hazard planning."

NEW YORK'S RESPONSE TO THE WORLD TRADE CENTER ATTACKS

When two jet planes hit the World Trade Center towers at 8:46 and 9:02 A.M., New York City police, firefighters, and emergency medical workers rushed to the site. The firefighters and police launched rescue and evacuation efforts, and emergency medical workers set up temporary medical posts to treat injured survivors. The city's Office of Emergency Management (OEM) began directing activities from its headquarters nearby at 7 World Trade Center. Ambulances came from all over the city, and hospitals in all five boroughs prepared to receive large numbers of patients.

Between 13,000 and 15,000 people were successfully evacuated from the towers before the south tower collapsed at 9:59 A.M. and the north tower at 10:28 A.M.[1] Two thousand eight hundred and one people died, including 149 passengers on the planes.[2] The fact that so many people survived the disaster showed that in many ways the emergency response efforts were successful. Subsequent to the 1993 bombing at the World Trade Center, improvements in fire safety measures had been established, including better lighting in the stairways and evacuation drills. However, many things went wrong on September 11. The building housing OEM headquarters was severely damaged by the collapse of the north tower soon after the attack and had to be evacuated, significantly undermining OEM's ability to coordinate the rescue efforts. Moreover, OEM's communication depended on an antenna located on the roof of the north tower.[3] The Police Department and the Fire Department each had its own radio communications system, but they used different frequencies and could not communicate with each other. Poor communication led to confusion for some evacuees when some stairways were blocked, and they were not informed of alternative routes down. Doors to the roof were locked, trapping people who worked above the impact sites who tried to escape by climbing upwards. Tragically, the Fire Department radios worked only sporadically in the high-rise buildings, so, despite attempts to warn them, at least 121 of the 343 firefighters who died were in the north tower when it collapsed. They had not realized that the south tower had fallen.[4]

After the buildings collapsed, the air was filled with dust, soot, and smoke, posing a threat to the thousands of rescue workers, cleanup workers, and later residents and people who worked in downtown Manhattan who were allowed to return to their offices. An estimated 5,000 tons of asbestos had been released into the air due to the destruction of the buildings.[5] Lead, other metals, dioxin, and PCBs were also detected in the soot, as fires continued to burn for months after the disaster. Although workers at the site should have been wearing respirators to protect their lungs, few of them did in the early days, and many of them developed the notorious "World Trade Center cough." It was not clear which agencies were responsible for determining when the area was safe. A priority at the highest levels of government was to get the downtown area back in business, especially Wall Street, which was opened only six days after the collapse. Politicians rushed to reassure New Yorkers that the environment was safe, but there was no scientific basis for these reassurances, and their statements were received with appropriate skepticism.[6] The Environmental Protection Agency was accused of covering up the risk.

The Departments of Health of New York City and New York State had the responsibility to carry out routine public health functions, under not-so-routine conditions, during the period after the disaster. They issued death certificates and burial permits. They monitored food and drinking water served to emergency workers to ensure that it was safe. They cleaned up food in abandoned restaurants at the site to prevent outbreaks of rodents. Because there was concern that the attack might have included biological agents, the Centers for Disease Control and Prevention (CDC) sent officers to monitor hospital emergency rooms for patients with unusual symptoms. Later ongoing surveillance activities included sampling of dust and debris near the site to assess risk and monitoring of symptoms of cleanup workers and area residents. In addition to respiratory symptoms, insomnia, headaches, and dizziness, millions of survivors and workers suffered from psychological distress suggestive of post-traumatic stress disorder. Mental health agencies arranged for counseling. Victim location services were established for families with missing relatives, and shelters for displaced residents were set up. At least nineteen city, state, and federal government agencies, as well as several academic, medical, and other organizations, were involved in the public health and medical response to the disaster.[2]

PRINCIPLES OF EMERGENCY PLANNING AND PREPAREDNESS

The evident weaknesses in the response to the 9/11 attacks called attention to the need for advance planning for possible future disasters. Two essential ingredients of an emergency plan missing in New York City were coordination and communication. In part, the lack of these functions resulted from the fact that the emergency management headquarters and communication antenna were disabled in the event. This situation highlights the importance of emergency system redundancy. A backup plan for managing the crisis in the absence of these resources should have been in place. Redundancy in the communication system would have ensured that critical information about evacuation routes could have been shared with everyone in the buildings. The situation was aggravated by a history of competition between police and fire departments and the OEM.

Because any disaster will require a coordinated response from a number of different agencies, the basic principle used in the immediate response to an emergency is the Incident Command System (ICS).[7] This approach puts a single person, who has responsibility for managing and coordinating the response, in charge at the scene. Disaster response is generally managed by authorities from local government agencies, because the response must be immediate and local authorities are closest to the scene and know the territory. The lead agency is often the fire department or the police department. The state and federal government provide technical assistance and back-up resources.

Agencies involved in the ICS might include an emergency operations center, the fire department, the police department, the emergency medical system, the public health agency, the American Red Cross, the electric company and gas company, and, sometimes, the highway department or, as in the case of the World Trade Center, the Port Authority, and the manager of the buildings. Most of these agencies would know their responsibilities in an emergency and would have practiced them as part of their planning and preparedness process. Different agencies might have different communications networks, but it is critically important that all communication is integrated. The public health agency, in coordination with emergency medical services and hospitals is responsible for directing patients to the appropriate level of care and for dispatching ambulances according to the availability of appropriate resources such as operating rooms and intensive care units. On September 11, one nearby hospital was swamped with "walking wounded" and critical patients, while a trauma center only three miles away sat idle.[3] The Federal Emergency Management Agency is now working on a system called the National Incident Management System, which standardizes the organizational structures, processes, and procedures that communities should employ in planning for an emergency.

In a guide to *Public Health Management of Disasters* published by the American Public Health Association, the author lists twelve tasks or problems likely to occur in most disasters.[7] All the following must be sorted out and practiced ahead of time.

- Sharing information: Two-way radios are often the most reliable way to communicate, but it is important to choose a common frequency.
- Resource management: personnel should identify themselves at a check-in area and be given an assignment and a radio; arrival of equipment and supplies should be logged in and distributed where they are needed most.
- Warnings should be issued and evacuations ordered by the appropriate agencies. The warnings should be delivered, usually by the mass media, in a manner that will prompt appropriate action by the population.
- Warnings must be unambiguous and consistent and include specific information on who is at risk and what actions should be taken.
- Search and rescue operations should be coordinated so that casualties are entered into the emergency medical services system and the health care system.
- Using the mass media to warn the public about health risks after the disaster is an effective public health measure.
- Triage: A method for sorting survivors by severity of their injury and need for treatment should be established at the scene by trained medical personnel.
- Casualty distribution: Protocols should be established to ensure that patients are distributed among available hospitals or other facilities.
- Tracking of patients and other survivors is difficult but, to the extent it is possible, will avert difficulties later.
- Establishing methods to care for patients with all levels of need should be part of the advance planning. Many survivors seek care for

minor injuries or may need prescription medications for chronic medical conditions.

- Management of volunteers and donations should be planned for; resources should be collected, organized, and distributed at a site outside the disaster area to not disrupt ongoing emergency operations.
- Expect the unexpected. Be ready to respond to unanticipated problems.

The plan should be practiced at least once, and preferably once a year. The exercises can be desktop simulations, field exercises, or drills. The time for partners to meet each other is before, not after, the disaster strikes.

Since September 11, the federal government has provided substantial resources to states and major metropolitan areas for public health preparedness, including preparedness for natural disasters, bioterrorism, and chemical and radiological disasters. In June 2004, the Department of Health and Human Services announced that since 9/11, it had invested more than $3.7 billion in strengthening the nation's public health infrastructure.[8] The money is being used for planning, training, improving communication and coordination, strengthening hospitals and laboratories, and improving epidemiology and disease surveillance in state and local areas. A Strategic National Stockpile (SNS) includes medical supplies, antibiotics, vaccines, and antidotes for chemical agents. In the event of an emergency, SNS personnel can deliver these supplies to the people who need them anywhere in the United States within twelve hours.

An evaluation of the progress made by twelve metropolitan areas between September 11 and May 2003 found that emergency preparedness had improved but gaps still remained. The researchers highlighted three communities of different sizes that they found to be especially strong in their level of preparedness: Syracuse, New York, Indianapolis, Indiana, and Orange County, California.[9] The success of these three communities is credited in part to previous experience with public health threats. Syracuse, for example, has a nuclear power plant nearby, which had stimulated the population's concern about a nuclear accident or a terrorist attack. Indianapolis has done extensive planning over the years for the annual Indianapolis 500 auto races and other large sporting events. Orange County had experience in disaster planning because of the ongoing threat of earthquakes and fires; a nuclear power plant is also located nearby. Other factors that contributed to readiness, the researchers concluded, are strong leadership, successful collaboration, and adequate funding.[9]

BIOTERRORISM PREPAREDNESS

The anthrax letters attack of fall 2001, discussed in the Prologue and Chapter 10, constituted a terrorist attack just as surely as the hijacking and plane crashes, and similarly spread terror in the American population, although it caused few deaths. The anthrax letters were recognized to be a terrorist attack in part because of the heightened alertness created by the events of 9/11, and in part because anthrax is such a rare pathogen in humans. Anthrax had been identified as a possible agent of bio-warfare in the planning that the federal government had been carrying out during the late 1990s. If a less conspicuous pathogen had been used, the attack might not have been recognized as quickly. For example, the 1984 salmonella outbreak in Oregon, described in Chapter 10, was not recognized as a deliberate attack until much later, when the cult members quarreled publicly about the attack, and a criminal investigation was launched.[10]

Bioterrorism requires a very different kind of preparedness strategy than the response needed for dramatic disasters such as an earthquake or the attack on and collapse of the World Trade Center towers. The greatest challenge in bioterrorism preparedness might be the ability to recognize that an attack is underway. Accordingly, the CDC has been coordinating extensive efforts throughout the nation to improve the public health infrastructure, understanding that the response to a biological attack must be the same as that for a natural disease outbreak. As Dr. Julie Gerberding, the director of the CDC said, "We are building . . . capacity [to handle biological terrorism] on the foundation of public health, but we are also using the new investments in [combating] terrorism to strengthen the public health foundation" because "these two programs are inextricably linked."[11]

The CDC has listed pathogens most likely to be used in a terrorist attack. Category A agents, shown in Table 29–1, include smallpox, anthrax, Ebola, and other hemorrhagic fever viruses discussed in Chapter 10. These agents can be easily disseminated or transmitted person-to-person and cause high mortality, with potential for major public health impact. Recommendations for preparing for biological attacks are shown in Table 29–2.

The public health capacities that are being strengthened to improve recognition of a disease outbreak include (1) educating physicians and other medical workers to recognize unusual diseases, (2) monitoring emergency rooms for certain patterns of symptoms, (3) opening new laboratories with the capability of identifying unusual viruses and bacteria, and (4) improving

Table 29–1 Category A Bioterrorism Agents

Category A

The U.S. public health system and primary health care providers must be prepared to address varied biological agents, including pathogens that are rarely seen in the United States. High-priority agents include organisms that pose a risk to national security because they

- can be easily disseminated or transmitted person-to-person;
- cause high mortality, with potential for major public health impact;
- might cause public panic and social disruption; and
- require special action for public health preparedness.

Category A agents include

- variola major (smallpox);
- *Bacillus anthracis* (anthrax);
- *Yersinia pestis* (plague);
- *Clostridium botulinum* toxin (botulism);
- *Francisella tularensis* (tularaemia);
- filoviruses,
    - — Ebola hemorrhagic fever,
    - — Marburg hemorrhagic fever, and
- arenaviruses,
    - — Lassa (Lassa fever),
    - — Junin (Argentine hemorrhagic fever) and related viruses.

Source: U.S. Centers for Disease Control and Prevention, *Morbidity and Mortality Weekly Report* 49 (2000), RR-4:5.

communication between public health agencies at the local, state, and federal level and the professionals and facilities most likely to first encounter affected patients. Surveillance activities include emergency room visits, calls to 911 and poison control centers, and pharmacy records to detect increased use of antibiotics and/or over-the-counter drugs. (One early indication of the 1993 cryptosporidiosis outbreak in Milwaukee discussed in the Prologue was that pharmacies were selling out of medications for diarrhea.) Similar measures are important for recognizing chemical attacks as well, and the CDC now has a laboratory that can test for 150 chemicals that could be used by terrorists to attack humans.[11] The Department of Agriculture is similarly conducting surveillance for animal diseases and other agricultural threats.

Table 29–2   Steps in Preparing for Biological Attacks

- Enhance epidemiologic capacity to detect and respond to biological attacks.
- Supply diagnostic reagents to state and local public health agencies.
- Establish communication programs to ensure delivery of accurate information.
- Enhance bioterrorism-related education and training for health-care professionals.
- Prepare educational materials that will inform and reassure the public during and after a biological attack.
- Stockpile appropriate vaccines and drugs.
- Establish molecular surveillance for microbial strains, including unusual or drug-resistant strains.
- Support the development of diagnostic tests.
- Encourage research on antiviral drugs and vaccines.

Source: U.S. Centers for Disease Control and Prevention, *Morbidity and Mortality Weekly Report* 49 (2000), RR-4:5.

Animal health is an important component of homeland security, both because of the need to protect the food supply and because many animal diseases are also a threat to humans. Seventy-five percent of emerging infections that have recently been identified in humans originate in animals—for example, bird flu, SARS, hantavirus, mad cow disease, and E. coli O157:H7.[12] Computer networks serve to alert public health officials about significant or unusual findings from surveillance data. In addition to public health efforts to improve the ability to recognize a bioterrorist attack and identify the agent, the CDC has taken steps to improve response to the event, including the SNS, as previously described.

The spread of West Nile encephalitis across the country has provided an opportunity and a challenge for the public health and medical care systems to develop and practice response to a new infectious disease. When West Nile virus first appeared in 1999 in New York City (see Chapter 10), bioterrorism was considered as one possible explanation for its origin. That hypothesis was soon discarded, but the disease has been closely monitored as it spreads to areas where it is unfamiliar. The mechanisms used to deal with the spread of West Nile virus are the same as those that would be used in a bioterrorist event.

The prospect of bioterrorism has raised other issues that affect the nation's ability to respond effectively. Among the most important of these is that public health officials need to have the legal power to take action to protect the public and contain an outbreak of an infectious disease. For example, the officials have to be able to isolate and quarantine people. Public health activities are, for the most part, controlled by state law, and the public health laws in many states predate modern scientific understanding of disease. The laws may be outdated, inadequate, and inconsistent. For example, some states have laws that prevented sharing of surveillance information with other states; private property laws might prevent destruction of contaminated property or the imposed distribution of drugs and medical supplies to where they are needed; privacy laws might interfere with public health agencies' ability to obtain information from hospitals or pharmacies; quarantine laws might be challenged by affected individuals and thus prevent prompt action.[13]

After the anthrax attacks of 2001, the CDC requested a group of legal and public health scholars to develop a Model State Emergency Health Powers Act that state legislatures could follow to update their laws. The suggested provisions include measures to encourage planning for emergencies; surveillance; managing property to ensure availability of vaccines, pharmaceuticals, and hospitals; powers to compel vaccination, testing, treatment, isolation, and quarantine when necessary; and provision of information to the public. These measures would be activated when a public health emergency is declared and would include legal safeguards to protect personal rights while promoting the common good.[13] The model act was released in December 2001 and, as of July 1, 2004, forty-four states have introduced legislation based on the model act, and thirty-three have passed at least some of the measures.[14]

Another issue that has been raised but not so readily addressed is the problem of the forty-four million Americans who lack health insurance. If the first individuals to be exposed to an infectious agent are uninsured, they may choose not to seek medical care or may delay visiting an emergency room, thus spreading the pathogen and delaying the recognition that an outbreak is under way. "Their lack of insurance is a known risk to their own health, but it must now also be recognized as a risk to the nation's health," noted two public health experts.[15] The problem is compounded by the federal law, passed in 1996, that prohibits federally funded medical clinics from treating illegal immigrants. Unless it is made clear to the whole population that everyone with symptoms of a contagious illness should seek treatment and that they will not suffer legal or financial consequences from presenting themselves for a medical evaluation, the United States will be vulnerable to bioterrorism in a way different from any other developed country.

A terrorist event, in addition to being a public health challenge, is a crime. The response, therefore, involves not only medical and public health professionals, but also law enforcement officials. This may result in turf battles and duplication of effort. The two disciplines use different methods and are held to different standards of evidence. Criminal investigations require that a chain of evidence be maintained for microbiologic specimens in anticipation of criminal prosecution. Public health workers are familiar to medically underserved communities, which distrust law enforcement officials and might be unwilling to share information with them. In the investigation of the anthrax attack, the CDC and the Federal Bureau of Investigation (FBI) had already developed a relationship in planning for bioterrorism, and the two agencies worked well together. Interviews with exposed persons were conducted by teams including an epidemiologist and an investigator from the FBI or local police, which reduced the number of times people had to be interviewed. It also maximized the possibility that important clues might be recognized by interviewers with different expertise and experience. It is important in all bioterrorism preparedness planning that both public health and law enforcement personnel be included.[16] Despite this cooperation, some public health workers had the sense that the FBI did not share important information with the CDC about the nature of the anthrax attacks, which could possibly have led to some unnecessary exposures and inadequate prevention measures.

While the CDC is taking a major role in planning for bioterrorism, the Department of Homeland Security has been developing technological methods of detecting biological and chemical attacks, in the hope of recognizing an attack faster, even before people begin developing symptoms, and identifying the biological or chemical agent. Monitoring devices with sensors that detect bacteria, viruses, and toxins were used at the Salt Lake City Olympics in 2002, and these devices have been installed in more than thirty major American cities. The devices suck air through filters, which are periodically changed, and the filter paper taken to a laboratory for testing. It is not clear how effective these detectors would be in an attack, and many scientists are skeptical about the value of the monitoring systems. The Department of Homeland Security is supporting research to develop more sophisticated systems for environmental monitoring.[17]

SMALLPOX

Smallpox is the most dreaded of the possible bioterrorism agents, and after the initial shock of the anthrax events in 2001, a great deal of government planning efforts were devoted to the possibility of a bioterrorist attack using smallpox. As discussed in Chapter 9, there are concerns that, although smallpox was officially eradicated in the 1970s, rogue nations might have obtained stocks of the virus from the former Soviet Union. A smallpox attack would be devastating. The disease is highly contagious; there is no effective treatment; about 30 percent of those infected die. Virtually everyone in the world is susceptible to some extent, because immunizations have not been given in twenty-five years. As described in a CDC planning document, a covert release of the virus that causes smallpox would not have any impact until a week or two later, when patients would appear in doctors' offices and emergency rooms, complaining of various nonspecific symptoms. By the time characteristic rashes appeared, "the terrorists would be far away and the disease disseminated through the population by person-to-person contact."[18, p.3]

After the events of fall 2001, the urgency about smallpox was heightened. The nation's lack of preparedness had been made clear by a war game, called "Dark Winter," that had been conducted less than three months before 9/11 by policy scholars and former senior government officials. The participants played the roles of decision-makers such as the President, Secretary of State, Secretary of Defense, Secretary of Health and Human Services, Attorney General, Director of the Central Intelligence Agency, Director of the FBI, governors, and media executives, who acted as they believed the actual officials would behave in such circumstances.

The exercise started with the assumption that anonymous terrorists covertly sprayed smallpox virus in three shopping malls, one each in Oklahoma City, Atlanta, and Philadelphia. About two weeks later, according to the game scenario, the CDC informed the National Security Council that twenty cases of smallpox had been confirmed in Oklahoma, and there were reports of suspect cases in Georgia and Pennsylvania. Six days into the epidemic, a total of 2,000 smallpox cases had been reported in fifteen states, with 300 deaths. The epidemic had spread to Canada, Mexico, and the United Kingdom. The media were covering the situation around the clock. After another week, a total of 16,000 smallpox cases had been reported in twenty-five states, 1,000 people had died, and the vaccine supply was exhausted. Predictions were that the epidemic would expand to as many as 3 million cases, with 1 million deaths.[19]

On July 23, 2001, former senator Frank Nunn, who played the President of the United States in the exercise, testified before a congressional committee about the war game and the lessons learned from it. Among the conclusions were:

- Public health is now a major national security issue.
- An attack on the United States with biological weapons could cause massive civilian casualties, breakdowns in essential institutions, disruption of democratic processes, civil disorder, loss of confidence in government, and reduced U.S. strategic flexibility.
- Government currently lacks adequate strategies, plans, and information systems to manage a crisis of this type or magnitude.
- Constructive media relationships become critical for all levels of government.
- Containing the spread of a contagious disease delivered as a bioweapon will present significant ethical, political, cultural, operational, and legal challenges.[20]

The most effective way to prevent a smallpox attack from becoming a disaster would be to vaccinate the whole population. However, there are a number of significant reasons why the federal government has not recommended vaccinating everyone. First, when the government began to address the issue, there were insufficient supplies of vaccine, which had been stored for decades, and there were questions about its continued efficacy. Moreover, the vaccine, which contains live virus related to smallpox, has side effects that people might not be willing to accept, considering that the risk of exposure would be so remote. The Bush administration developed a plan to vaccinate 500,000 public health and health care workers so that, in case of a biological attack, they would be prepared to care for smallpox patients and to interview them for purposes of contact tracing. About 500,000 members of the military were also to be vaccinated, in preparation for the invasion of Iraq, which was believed to have biological weapons. The vaccinations in the military occurred relatively uneventfully, but fewer than 38,000 civilian health workers had volunteered to be vaccinated by the time the program was discontinued in June 2003.[21] If smallpox was known to be at large and the risk was real, more people might recognize the importance of being vaccinated.

The government has now stockpiled enough smallpox vaccine to vaccinate everyone who might need it in an emergency. The vaccine has the advantage of being effective in preventing the disease if used within about four days after a person has been exposed to the virus. If there were an attack, the preferred public health response would be "ring vaccination," which includes isolation of confirmed and suspected cases, and vaccination of people who have had contact with these cases.[22,23] Vaccinating and monitoring a "ring" of people around each case would be the most efficient way of protecting people at risk, while minimizing adverse effects of the vaccine. However, it is controversial whether this approach is adequate. Some experts argue that it would be safer to provide vaccinations to everyone on a voluntary basis. Release of an aerosolized virus amidst a population that has no immunity, especially if it occurs in many places at once, could overwhelm the public health system. Moreover, it is possible that the vaccine might be ineffective against a genetically engineered virus.[24] Widespread immunity to smallpox would eliminate smallpox as a possible bioterrorist weapon.

CONCLUSION

Public health has an important role in responding to all kinds of emergencies and disasters, natural or manmade. The immediate response to a disaster must include emergency medical care for the injured and evacuation of survivors. Later there is the need to ensure that air, water, and food are not contaminated and that injury hazards such as fallen power lines and unstable buildings are eliminated. Generally the disaster response is carried out by a number of agencies, and coordination among them is very important. After 9/11, the federal government provided funding for all communities to develop disaster plans, in which all the relevant agencies should participate.

The response in New York to the World Trade Center attacks demonstrated a number of weaknesses, offering lessons that should be incorporated in planning for any future emergencies. The most serious problem was poor communication between response agencies. The city's emergency management center was damaged by the attack, as well as the antenna it used for communication, and the Fire Department and Police Department could not communicate with each other. Although more than 13,000 people escaped from the towers, some of the 2,801 deaths could have been prevented by better communication and coordination. The air in lower Manhattan was contaminated for months after the attacks, and many of the cleanup workers at the site did not use respiratory protection devices. Critics complained that government agencies were more intent on reassuring the population than on telling them the truth about health risks.

There are well-established principles for management of disasters that should be understood by all medical and safety responders. All agencies involved should participate in planning; all responders should be familiar with the plans, and the response should be practiced at least once a year. Since 9/11, the federal government has invested more than $3.7 billion in strengthening the public health infrastructure. The preparations improve the nation's ability to respond not only to disasters, but also to naturally occurring disease outbreaks and other public health emergencies.

Preparedness for bioterrorism requires that the public health system would carry out its normal surveillance functions. A biological attack might be recognized only after patients start showing up in hospitals and doctors' offices; even their symptoms may not be unusual—most of the pathogens that might be used as bioweapons first cause flu-like symptoms. The CDC has provided funding for states and major cities to develop surveillance of hospital emergency rooms, 911 calls, calls to poison control centers, and pharmacies. The CDC has opened new laboratories capable of testing for biological and chemical agents, and it maintains a Strategic National Stockpile (SNS) of medical and emergency supplies. The Department of Agriculture conducts surveillance for animal diseases.

Other issues that might affect the nation's readiness for a biological attack are state public health laws that might need updating, the widespread lack of health insurance that could prevent infected people from seeking medical care, and lack of coordination between public health and law enforcement agencies.

The threat of an attack by a rogue nation or terrorist using smallpox virus is particularly terrifying. The disease is highly contagious; almost everyone is susceptible; there are no effective treatments; the fatality rate is about 30 percent. A 2001 war game, called "Dark Winter," concluded that, in the case of a smallpox attack, public health could be a major national security issue. In the exercise, which started with terrorists covertly spreading smallpox virus in three shopping malls, the resulting epidemic expanded to as many as 3 million cases with 1 million deaths.

As a result of concerns raised by the events of fall 2001, the "Dark Winter" exercise, and the planned war in Iraq, which was suspected of having bioweapons, the Bush administration developed a controversial plan to vaccinate health professionals and members of the military. This plan was only partially carried out.

REFERENCES

1. U.S. Centers for Disease Control and Prevention, "Preliminary Results from the World Trade Center Evacuation Study—New York City, 2003," *Morbidity and Mortality Weekly Report* 53 (2004): 815–817.
2. S. Klitzman, and F. Freudenberg, "Implications of the World Trade Center Attack for the Public Health and Health Care Infrastructures," *American Journal of Public Health* 93 (2003): 400–406.
3. R. Simon, and S. Teperman, "World Trade Center Attack: Lessons for Disaster Management," *Critical Care* 5 (2001): 317–319.
4. J. Dwyer, K. Flynn, and F. Fessenden, "9/11 Exposed Deadly Flaws in Rescue Plan," *New York Times* (July 7, 2002): A1.
5. J. Shufro, "Perspective on the Tragedy at the World Trade Center," *American Journal of Medicine* 42 (2002): 557–559.
6. G. D. Thurston, and L. C. Chen, "Risk Communication in the Aftermath of the World Trade Center Disaster," *American Journal of Industrial Medicine* 42 (2002): 543–544.
7. L. Y. Landesman, *Public Health Management of Disaster: The Practice Guide* (Washington, DC: American Public Health Association, 2001).
8. U.S. Department of Health and Human Services, "News Release: HHS Awards $849 Million to Improve Public Health Preparedness," (June 17, 2004). *www.hhs.gov/news/press/2004pres/20040617.html*. Accessed August 15, 2005.
9. M. McHugh, A. B. Staiti, and L. E. Felland, "How Prepared Are Americans for Public Health Emergencies? Twelve Communities Weigh In," *Health Affairs* (May/June 2004): 201–209.
10. T. J. Torok et al., "A Large Community Outbreak of Salmonellosis Caused by Intentional Contamination of Restaurant Salad Bars," *Journal of the American Medical Association* 278 (1997): 389–395.
11. L. K. Altman, "Disease Control Center Bolsters Terror Response," *New York Times* (August 28, 2002): A14.
12. N. Marano, and M. Pappiaoanou, "Historical, New, and Reemerging Links between Human and Animal Health," *Emerging Infectious Diseases* 10 (2004): 2065–2066.
13. L. O. Gostin et al., "Model State Emergency Health Powers Act: Planning for and Response to Bioterrorism and Naturally Occurring Infectious Diseases," *Journal of the American Medical Association* 288 (2002): 622–628.
14. Center for Law and the Public's Health at Georgetown and Johns Hopkins Universities, "Model State Public Health Laws," (July 1, 2004). *www.publichealthlaw.net/Resources/Modellaws.htm*. Accessed January 15, 2005.
15. M. K. Wynis, and L. Gostin, "Bioterrorist Threat and Access to Health Care," *Science* 296 (2002): 1613.
16. J. C. Butler et al., "Collaboration between Public Health and Law Enforcement: New Paradigms and Partnerships for Bioterrorism Planning and Response," *Emerging Infectious Diseases* 8 (2002): 1152–1156.

17. K. Brown, "Up in the Air," *Science* 305 (2004): 1228–1229.
18. U.S. Centers for Disease Control and Prevention, "Biological and Chemical Terrorism: Strategic Plan for Preparedness and Response," *Morbidity and Mortality Weekly Report* 49 (2000): RR-4, 3.
19. T. O'Toole, M. Mair, and T. V. Inglesby, "TV. Shining Light on 'Dark Winter,'" *Clinical Infectious Diseases* 34 (2002): 972–983.
20. Center for Strategic and International Studies, "Dark Winter: Bioterrorism Exercise: Nunn, Hamre to Testify on Lessons Learned," (July 19, 2001): *www.csis.org/press/ma_2001_0723. htm* (July 19, 2001). Accessed January 16, 2005.
21. D. G. McNeil, Jr., "2 Programs to Vaccinate for Smallpox Come to a Halt," *New York Times* A13.
22. U.S. Centers for Disease Control and Prevention, "Vaccinia (Smallpox) Vaccine: Recommendations of the Advisory Committee on Immunization Practices (ACIP), 2001," *Morbidity and Mortality Weekly Report* 50 (2001): RR 10.
23. U.S. Centers for Disease Control and Prevention, "Recommendations for Using Smallpox Vaccine in a Pre-Event Vaccination Program," *Morbidity and Mortality Weekly Report* 52 (2003): RR 7.
24. M. M. Weiss, P. D. Weiss, G. Mathise, and P. Guze, "Confronting Biological Weapons: Rethinking Smallpox," *Clinical Infectious Diseases* 39 (2004): 1668–1673.

CHAPTER 30

Public Health in the Twenty-First Century: Achievements and Challenges

The Future of Public Health

The United States in the twentieth century saw great progress in public health. As a field of practice, public health has advanced in knowledge and methodology. Biomedical scientists have identified many of the organisms that cause infectious diseases and have developed methods to control them. Epidemiologists have recognized risk factors that lead to many chronic diseases, information that can be used to reduce people's risk of illness. Efforts to clean up the environment have resulted in air and water that are much safer than they were a half-century ago. Intensive health

535

education efforts have even persuaded Americans to improve some health-related behaviors, leading to reductions in tobacco use and drunk driving. The ability to assess the state of the public's health and to evaluate the impact of medical and public health interventions has also advanced dramatically because of vast stores of health-related data and computer software capable of analyzing them. These achievements have greatly improved the health of Americans. The average lifespan has increased by thirty years since 1900 (when it was forty-seven), and twenty-five of those years are attributed to improvements in public health.[1]

In 1999, the Centers for Disease Control and Prevention (CDC) published a "top ten" list of great public health achievements of the twentieth century.[1] These accomplishments were chosen for the positive impact they have had and will continue to have in reducing deaths, illnesses, and disabilities in the United States. Following is the CDC's list (not in order of importance).

- Routine use of *vaccination* has resulted in a dramatic reduction in infectious diseases, including the eradication of smallpox; the elimination of polio in the Americas; and control of measles, rubella, tetanus, diphtheria, and a number of other infectious diseases in the United States and other parts of the world (see Chapter 9).
- Improvements in *motor vehicle safety* have contributed to large reductions in motor vehicle-related deaths. This has been achieved through engineering efforts to make vehicles and highways safer and through success in persuading people to adopt healthier behaviors, such as using seat belts, child safety seats, and motorcycle helmets, and to not drink and drive (see Chapter 17).
- *Safer workplaces* have resulted in a dramatic reduction in fatal occupational injuries—down 90 percent since 1933—and illness. This achievement results from improvements in safety in mines and in the manufacturing, construction, and transportation industries (see Chapter 17).
- *Control of infectious diseases* has been achieved by (in addition to vaccination) improved sanitation, cleaner water, safer food, the discovery of antibiotic drugs, and methods of epidemiologic surveillance and follow-up (see Chapters 4, 9, 21, and 23).
- A *decline in deaths from heart disease and stroke* has resulted from the identification of risk factors (see Chapters 4 and 11) and people's

significant success in changing their behavior to reduce cholesterol levels and to stop smoking (see Chapters 15 and 16). Secondary prevention methods, such as early detection and treatment of high blood pressure, also contribute to the lower number of deaths.

- *Safer and healthier foods* have almost eliminated major nutritional deficiency diseases such as rickets, goiter, and pellagra in the United States. Microbial contamination of food has been reduced, and nutritional supplementation and labeling have made possible a healthier diet (see Chapter 23).

- *Healthier mothers and babies* are the result of better hygiene and nutrition; availability of antibiotics; greater access to health care, including prenatal care; and technologic advances in medicine. Since 1900, there has been a 90 percent reduction in the infant mortality rate and a 99 percent reduction in the maternal mortality rate (see Chapter 18).

- *Access to family planning and contraceptive services* has contributed to healthier mothers and babies through smaller family size and longer intervals between the birth of children; increased opportunities for preconception counseling and screening; and improved control of sexually transmitted diseases (see Chapter 18).

- *Fluoridation of drinking water* has reduced tooth decay in children by 40 percent to 70 percent, and tooth loss in adults by 40 percent to 50 percent (see Chapter 5).

- *Recognition of tobacco use as a health hazard* and subsequent public health anti-smoking campaigns have helped to prevent people from beginning to smoke, to promote quitting, and to reduce exposure to environmental (second hand) tobacco smoke. The resulting decrease in the prevalence of smoking among adults has prevented millions of smoking-related deaths (see Chapter 15).

CHALLENGES FOR THE TWENTY-FIRST CENTURY

As the twenty-first century begins, public health faces many challenges, both old and new. There are renewed threats from infectious diseases, such as AIDS, antibiotic resistance, and foodborne pathogens. The global economy has increased Americans' vulnerability to many of the health threats faced by residents of less developed nations brought about by international travel and importing of agricultural products. Paradoxically, past successes have led to new threats, such as climate change caused by overpopulation and rising costs of medical care for the aging population. The challenge of understanding and altering human behavior—the factor that now contributes most substantially to premature mortality—remains to be confronted by the public health practitioners of the twenty-first century. The decline in cigarette smoking has slowed; rates of alcohol and illicit drug use among adolescents are largely unchanged over the past decade; physical inactivity and unhealthy diets contribute to the increasing prevalence of obesity among Americans; and violence is still a major cause of injury and death.[2]

Ironically, the successes of public health in the twentieth century led to cutbacks in resources and support for preventive activities. During the second half of the century, the medical approach—curing health problems rather than preventing them—gained acceptance. Public health's many achievements, including those described above, were taken for granted while rapidly increasing resources were devoted to medical care. This problem was recognized in the 1988 Institute of Medicine's report, *The Future of Public Health*.[3] This report prompted public health agencies, policy makers, and academic institutions to initiate a national discussion on the role of public health and the steps necessary to strengthen its capacity to fulfill its role. Attempts were made to coordinate public health efforts at various levels of government, to develop public-private partnerships in communities, and to undertake strategic planning aimed at achieving defined goals and objectives. The Institute of Medicine undertook a new analysis to follow up on the 1988 report and made recommendations for enhancing understanding of public health and developing a framework for assuring the public's health in the new century.[4]

The events of fall 2001, particularly the bioterrorist attacks using anthrax, brought new attention to the American public health system and revealed the weaknesses in the public health infrastructure—workforce, information systems, laboratories, and other organizational capacity—which was suffering from neglect. It became clear to policy makers and the public that the public health system is the front line of defense in protecting the population from bioterrorism and other threats. Concerns about preparedness led to a flow of federal funds into public health agencies and activities. These funds have helped state and local agencies to begin strengthening their capacity to respond to public health challenges; however public health officials are concerned whether the efforts can be sustained.

Budget deficits at the federal and state levels threaten to derail the upgrades just when their importance is being recognized. The Institute of Medicine's report, *The Future of the Public's Health in the 21st Century*, was published in 2003 and includes lessons learned from the 2001 attacks.[4]

The 2003 Institute of Medicine report states that, "the public health system that was in disarray in 1988 remains in disarray today." It notes that the United States is not meeting its potential in the area of population health, in part because of the nation's emphasis on (1) medical care rather than preventive services and (2) biomedical research rather than prevention research. It also notes the serious and persistent disparities in health status among various population groups, according to race and ethnicity, gender, and socioeconomic status. The report recommends that the public health workforce needs better education and training, that changes are needed in public health laws to bring them up-to-date and to ensure better coordination among states and territories, and that advances in information technology should be used more effectively to provide adequate surveillance and communication. Although the resources to rectify some of the deficiencies have been provided in the wake of 9/11, the Institute of Medicine report stresses the need for these efforts to be sustained for the long term.

STRATEGIC PLANNING FOR PUBLIC HEALTH

With so many different agencies at so many different political and organizational levels involved in implementing public health's mission, it became apparent some time ago that there was a need for planning and coordination. Beginning in 1979, the Public Health Service adopted "management by objectives," a process that was becoming increasingly widespread in the private sector. This technique requires that managers jointly define a set of measurable goals, use these goals as a guide to their actions, and regularly measure progress toward achieving them. The management-by-objectives approach is especially useful in decentralized organizations, where many different actors must coordinate their efforts, and thus is well suited to the needs of the public health system.[5]

To develop goals for the year 1990, the Public Health Service enlisted a broad range of participants from both within and outside of government to specify a set of health status objectives. The national goals, published as *Healthy People: The Surgeon General's Report on Health Promotion and Disease Prevention*,[6] set targets for reducing mortality rates in different age groups, with specific objectives designed to meet each target. For example, to achieve the goal of a 25 percent death rate reduction for ages twenty-five through sixty-four, progress had to be made in reducing the prevalence of cigarette smoking, high blood cholesterol, and high blood pressure among adults. Any state, community, or research group that applied for federal funds for a public health program had to justify its request by showing how its project would contribute to achieving one or more of the *Healthy People* goals. When the results of the first planning cycle were tallied in 1990, the numerical mortality goals were met for three of the four age groups: infants, children, and adults aged 25 through 64. Only targets for adolescents and young adults were not met, because of continued high rates of fatal motor vehicle injuries, homicides, and suicides.[5]

The *Healthy People* planning process encourages states and local communities to use the national objectives as a basis for developing objectives of their own. One problem that became obvious during the first decade of the program was a lack of data systems that could track progress, especially at the local level.

In 1987 the Public Health Service began the process of setting objectives for the following decade. *Healthy People 2000*, a 692-page book sets three overall goals, with over 300 measurable objectives divided into twenty-two priority areas, as shown in Figure 30–1.[7] As in the previous *Healthy People* publication, these objectives set targets for individual behavioral change, environmental and regulatory protections, and access to preventive health services. *Healthy People 2000* also addressed the problem of inadequate data, which had hindered evaluation of progress toward the 1990 objectives. Implementing, tracking, and reporting on the goals and objectives involved many agencies of the federal government, as well as hundreds of state agencies, national organizations, academic institutions, and business groups. Most states developed their own year 2000 objectives. The individual states' objectives either paralleled or modified the national objectives to suit the states' own needs and priorities.

In 2001, a final review was published that evaluated the nation's progress in meeting the *Healthy People* objectives.[8] Progress was achieved on over 60 percent of the objectives. Targets were met in reducing deaths from coronary heart disease and cancer, reducing AIDS incidence, and reducing homicide, suicide, and firearm-related deaths. Tobacco-related

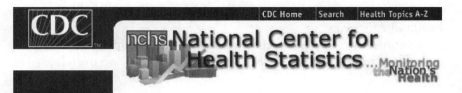

Healthy People 2000

Priority Areas at a Glance (22)

1. Physical Activity and Fitness
2. Nutrition
3. Tobacco
4. Substance Abuse: Alcohol an Other Drugs
5. Family Planning
6. Mental Health and Mental Disorders
7. Violent and Abusive Behavior
8. Educational and Community-Based Programs
9. Unintentional Injuries
10. Occupational Safety and Health
11. Environmental Health
12. Food and Drug Safety
13. Oral Health
14. Maternal and Infant Health
15. Heart Disease and Stroke
16. Cancer
17. Diabetes and Chronic Disabling Conditions
18. HIV Infection
19. Sexually Transmitted Diseases
20. Immunization and Infectious Diseases
21. Clinical Preventive Services
22. Surveillance and Data Systems

Figure 30–1 Healthy People 2000
Source: U.S. Centers for Disease Control and Prevention. www.cdc.gov/nchs/about/
otheract/hp2000/2000pa22.htm.

mortality targets were met. Goals for infant mortality and the number of children with elevated blood lead levels were nearly met. There was progress toward reducing health disparities. However, for 15 percent of the *Healthy People 2000* objectives, the nation moved away from the report's targets. Notably, these included the prevalence of overweight and obesity, especially among adolescents, an ominous sign for the future health of Americans.

Healthy People 2010, launched in January 2000, set public health goals and objectives even higher.[2] *Healthy People 2010* has two overall goals:

1. Increase quality and years of healthy life, and
2. eliminate health disparities.

These are similar to the goals of *Healthy People 2000*, except that Goal 1 places a new focus on quality of life, and Goal 2 no longer sets different targets for racial and ethnic minorities, aiming to ensure that all groups in the United States will be equally healthy.

Healthy People 2010 is organized into twenty-eight focus areas, many of which are the same as the priority areas in *Healthy People 2000*. In addition, a set of ten leading health indicators have been chosen for special attention. These indicators, shown in Figure 30–2, were chosen based on their ability to motivate action, the availability of data to measure their progress, and their relevance as broad public health issues.

Inspired by the Institute of Medicine reports and the success of the Public Health Service's planning initiative, and recognizing that most public health activities take place at a local level, a group of public health associations have been working on ways to help local public health agencies apply the management-by-objective approach. The participating organizations—the CDC, the Public Health Foundation, the American Public Health Association, the Association of State and Territorial Health Officials, the National Association of Local Boards of Health—have developed guidelines for local public health agencies to conduct their own strategic planning process, involving all sectors of the community in both planning and implementation.[9] With funding from the Robert Wood Johnson Foundation, the participating organizations have developed a program called *Turning Point: Collaborating for a New Century in Public Health*.[10] Turning Point has created partnerships with twenty-one state and local public health and community-based organizations to serve as models for a more effective and responsive public health system. Public health advocates hope that the increased capacity and involvement of local communities in public health planning and implementation will make the first decade of the twenty-first century even more successful in achieving its goals than the efforts of the 1990s.

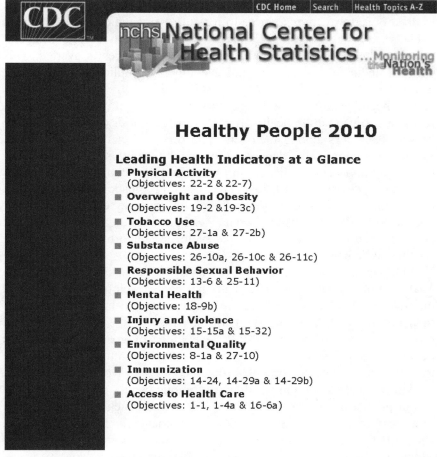

Figure 30–2 Healthy People 2010
Source: U.S. Centers for Disease Control and Prevention. www.cdc.gov/nchs/about/
otheract/hpdata2010/abouthp.htm.

HOPE FOR THE INTEGRATION OF PUBLIC HEALTH AND MEDICAL PRACTICE

Because of the high and continuously rising cost of medical care, managed care became more prevalent in the 1990s, as discussed in Chapter 26. Managed care moves the incentives of medicine closer to the mission of public health—keeping people healthy. While traditional fee-for-service medicine focuses on people who seek care, offering financial rewards to doctors for providing services to patients, managed care organizations (MCOs) are responsible for all their members, yielding financial rewards when the need for expensive medical services is averted. This shift in medicine's perspective has a number of implications for public health.

The incentives for MCOs to keep their patients healthy encourage medical plans to use public health strategies to prevent disease and promote healthy behaviors among members. The financial incentives also make medicine economically dependent on public health's effectiveness in preventing unnecessary disease in the community. Public health failures can be expensive for MCOs. The 1993 cryptosporidiosis outbreak in Milwaukee described in the Prologue, for example, caused $15.5 million in medical costs.[11] Thus, the changes in how medical care is financed and delivered encourage the medical sector to support adequate funding for the public health sector.

With managed care, medicine is driven by the same kind of measurable goals and objectives that public health has been developing. As discussed in Chapter 27, MCOs are forced to collect data on the effectiveness of their services and the health status of their members. They are evaluated on their success in achieving the same kinds of goals and objectives detailed in the *Healthy People* process. These common goals provide medicine and public health with strong incentives to work together.

Unfortunately, from the standpoint of public health, managed care has lost its popularity since the late 1990s. There was a backlash against many of its cost-control measures, and the benefits that come from incentives to keep MCO members healthy were not obvious to the public. State Medicaid programs continue to rely heavily on managed care, however.

For the majority of Americans, whose health insurance is provided by their employers or through Medicare, the future is uncertain. The cost of medical care is again rising rapidly, and the trend is economically unsustainable. Employers are shifting the costs to their employees, who are paying an increasing share through higher premiums and co-payments. Congress will soon be forced to make another attempt to reform Medicare to control its costs. It is likely that the number of Americans who lack health insurance will continue to rise. As the 2003 Institute of Medicine report comments, "the loss of trust in the idea of managed care is also the loss of a great opportunity to improve quality and restrain costs."[4(p.241)]

INFORMATION TECHNOLOGY

Advances in information technology offer extraordinary opportunities for collaboration between public health and medical care. For example, epidemiologic surveillance using the Internet would allow a system linking state and local health departments, public health laboratories, hospitals, and doctors' offices to collect data in real time and rapidly analyze it to detect unusual disease patterns. Such a system could simultaneously disseminate the information among all participants. However, at this time, there is no single system. Instead, there are multiple systems that do not necessarily communicate with each other.

Even before 9/11, the Department of Health and Human Services recognized the desirability of linking information networks to form a national health information infrastructure.[12] A departmental advisory committee has developed recommendations for a strategy to implement a network that would include consumers, healthcare providers, and public health agencies. The committee released its recommendations in 2001, with a plan that would include safeguards for privacy, confidentiality, and security and that would be implemented in ten years.[13]

Meanwhile, the CDC is developing its Public Health Information Network (PHIN), which provides a framework for a health and disease tracking information system shared by public health agencies. PHIN has five key components: detection and monitoring, data analysis, knowledge management, alerting, and response.[14] A major component of PHIN is the National Electronic Disease Surveillance System, which can rapidly integrate data from public health agencies, laboratories, and clinical settings. The system is designed to identify and track emerging infectious diseases and potential bioterrorism attacks, investigate outbreaks, and monitor disease trends. The CDC provides the software for the system to state health departments and requires the software to be used for the states' surveillance systems.[15] Another component of PHIN is the Health Alert Network, which provides emergency information through high-speed Internet connectivity.[16]

As the 2003 Institute of Medicine report notes, the anthrax attacks of fall 2001 demonstrated the weaknesses of public health communication and information systems being used at the time. Only half of the nation's state, local, and territorial health departments had Internet capability. Another 20 percent of these health agencies lacked email. Federal funding for bioterrorism preparedness has helped to bring many of the local health departments up to modern standards of information technology, but continued funding will be necessary to overcome their extensive deficiencies.[4]

In addition to being used in epidemiologic surveillance, information technology is already transforming the assessment and evaluation activities so important to the practice of public health and that promise also to improve outcomes in the practice of medicine. States and some counties maintain electronic databases on vital statistics, notifiable diseases, chronic diseases, hospital discharges, and immunizations. Billing records on patients covered by the Medicare program have proven useful in assessing outcomes of medical care, as seen in Chapter 27. Some states are developing similar records on Medicaid patients, hoping to improve the efficiency and effectiveness of medical care for the poor.[17]

Information networks are also being developed by MCOs and other nongovernmental providers of health services. Giant health care companies have streamlined procedures for storing and exchanging data on medical tests, procedures, costs, and outcomes. However, as noted by Paul Starr, historian of the relationship between medicine and public health (see Chapter 25), "National policy has yet to resolve two of the most fundamental questions about computerized health information: how to keep private what ought to be private, and how to make public what ought to be public."[18(p.103)]

A federal law passed by Congress in 1996, which became effective in 2003, was designed to protect the privacy of medical records. The Health Insurance Portability and Accountability Act (HIPAA) forbids "wrongful disclosure of individually identifiable health information." While this provision helps to eliminate some abuses, it has raised concerns that the privacy measures obstruct the use of medical data for many useful purposes. For example, researchers have complained that they cannot conduct outcomes studies, such as comparisons of different treatments for cancer.[19] The privacy rules also have discouraged the creation of public databases that consumers could use to make optimal decisions concerning their health and health care.[18]

The rise of the Internet presents major new opportunities and challenges for individuals who wish to understand and make choices concerning their personal health. People have access to vast quantities of health information—and misinformation—on the Internet. As discussed in Chapter 8, many state and federal public health agencies provide the latest and most accurate information about health issues on their Web pages.

Many nongovernmental sites also offer good advice and information, which can raise people's awareness of health risks, provide them with motivation and skills to reduce these risks, offer a helpful sense of connection to others who are in similar situations, and furnish information about difficult choices. However, caution is necessary in using the information presented on Web sites that lack authoritative sponsors. This information may be biased because of the Web site creators' commercial interests, distrust of science, or ignorance.

The Internet poses challenges to government agencies charged with regulating medical care because of the lack of accountability on the part of those who create Web sites. For example, doctors set up Web sites to diagnose and prescribe for patients' ills without examining the patients. Prescription drugs are sometimes sold over the Internet to people without valid prescriptions. Drugs that are not approved in the United States can be ordered from foreign markets. Even prescription drugs that are available in the United States may cost more here than in other countries, including Canada, and many people choose to buy them over the Internet to save money. The traditional role of the Food and Drug Administration (FDA) and other governmental agencies—to protect consumers from fraudulent and irresponsible medical practice—is made much more difficult by the free-wheeling culture of Internet commerce. At the same time, the FDA's opposition to importing cheaper drugs from Canada has begun to seem like a ploy to protect the American drug industry's profits, generating skepticism about the integrity of the agency's mission.

THE CHALLENGE OF BIOTECHNOLOGY

Biotechnology promises to solve many medical problems with new drugs and procedures that will contribute to the spiraling costs of medical care. It also offers unprecedented possibilities, such as that of choosing the characteristics of future children through genetic engineering and cloning or of slowing the aging process. These developments will raise many legal and ethical issues, which will have to be faced through public debate and difficult policy choices. Developments in biotechnology also raise what is perhaps the ultimate challenge to public health in the twenty-first century: How many of these "miracles" can our society afford, and how should priorities be set when resources are limited?

THE ULTIMATE CHALLENGE TO PUBLIC HEALTH IN THE TWENTY-FIRST CENTURY

"If public health's mission is to fulfill society's interest in assuring conditions in which people can be healthy [*The Future of Public Health* definition], public health has yet to succeed in fostering a national debate on the relative return on investment to improve population health."[20(p.xxiii)] Public health agencies are chronically starved for funding to carry out essential public health services that are clearly cost-effective in raising the health status of communities. As Jonathan E. Fielding noted in a review of public health in the twentieth century, the enormous expansion of the medical care system—a system that is largely inaccessible to much of the population that needs it most—occurred without consideration of whether this investment could have yielded more benefits to health if invested elsewhere.[20]

Health is determined by the social, physical, and economic environments; health behaviors; and genetics. Health is affected only marginally by medical interventions. The challenge for public health continues to be to educate the public and policy makers about the role of these nonmedical factors in determining people's health and to convince people of the importance of the core public health functions in protecting and promoting the health of the entire population. As it becomes increasingly apparent that advances in high-technology medical care have become economically unsustainable, the nation must focus on assuring conditions in which people can be healthy—the mission of public health—in the twenty-first century.

CONCLUSION

The United States has made great progress in public health during the twentieth century. The threat of infectious diseases has been greatly reduced, risk factors for some chronic diseases are well understood, the environment has been substantially cleaned up, and a great deal has been learned about how health is affected by behavior. The ability to assess the state of the public's health and to evaluate the impact of medical and public health interventions has advanced dramatically because of the existence of vast stores of health-related data and computer software capable of analyzing it.

During the twentieth century, the life expectancy of Americans has been extended by thirty years. Much of this improvement came from ten great public health achievements identified by the CDC: vaccination, motor vehicle safety, safer workplaces, control of infectious diseases, decline in deaths from coronary heart disease and stroke, safer and healthier foods, healthier mothers and babies, family planning, fluoridation of drinking water, and recognition of tobacco use as a health hazard.

Still, public health faces many challenges in the twenty-first century. Some of these challenges come from new forms of familiar public health problems such as infectious diseases and environmental pollution. Others are posed by efforts to change people's unhealthy behavior, the factor that now contributes the most to premature mortality.

A trend toward decentralizing governmental responsibilities and authority has prompted public health to adopt a planning process called "management by objectives." This process involves setting measurable goals and objectives and periodically assessing progress. The federal government has led this planning process over the past two and a half decades, and involvement has expanded to include state, county, and local communities. The result has been substantial progress toward achieving public health goals.

The trend toward managed care as a strategy for controlling medical care costs moved the incentives of medical practice closer to the mission of public health. However, the unpopularity of managed care and the failure to communicate the health benefits it offers has led to a backlash. Consequently medical costs have resumed their upward spiral, raising concerns that medical care will become even less affordable in the twenty-first century, and the number of uninsured will continue to rise.

Advances in information technology have led to great improvements in public health surveillance capabilities. The bioterrorism attacks of fall 2001 stimulated a flow of federal funds to state and county health departments for preparedness, allowing improvements in information systems at all levels of government. Information technology also makes possible much of the assessment and evaluation activity that is becoming important to the practice of public health and medicine. However the vast quantities of data available on individual and community health pose the challenge of how to keep private what ought to be private and how to make public what ought to be public. The rise of the Internet as a source of information and commerce also poses challenges to individual consumers on how to evaluate the information and to government regulators on how to protect consumers from fraudulent and irresponsible medical practice.

Perhaps the most important challenge faced by public health in the twenty-first century will be to encourage a society-wide debate on how public resources should be allocated to most effectively improve the health of the population as a whole.

REFERENCES

1. U.S. Centers for Disease Control and Prevention, "Ten Great Public Health Achievements—United States, 1900–1999," *Morbidity and Mortality Weekly Report* 48 (1999): 241–243.
2. U.S. Department of Health and Human Services, *Healthy People 2010: Understanding and Improving Health*, 2nd ed. (Washington, DC: U.S. Government Printing Office, November 2000).
3. U.S. Institute of Medicine, *The Future of Public Health* (Washington, DC: National Academy Press, 1988).
4. U.S. Institute of Medicine, *The Future of the Public's Health in the 21st Century* (Washington, DC: National Academy Press, 2003).
5. J. M. McGinnis, and D. R. Maiese, "Defining Missions, Goals, and Objectives," in F. D. Scutchfield, and C. W. Keck, eds., *Principles of Public Health Practice* (Albany, New York: Delmar Publishers, 1997), 131–146.
6. U.S. Department of Health, Education, and Welfare, *Healthy People: Surgeon General's Report on Health Promotion and Disease Prevention* (Washington, DC: PHS Publication 79–55071, 1979).
7. U.S. Department of Health and Human Services *Healthy People 2000: National Health Promotion and Disease Prevention Objectives* (Washington, DC: PHS publication 91–50212, 1990).
8. National Center for Health Statistics, *Healthy People 2000 Final Review* (Hyattsville, Maryland: Public Health Service, 2001).
9. M. F. Katz, and M. W. Kreuter, "Community Assessment and Empowerment," in F. D. Scutchfield, and C. W. Keck, eds., *Principles of Public Health Practice* (Albany, New York: Delmar Publishers, 1997), 147–157.
10. Robert Wood Johnson Foundation, *Turning Point: Collaborating for a New Century in Public Health, http://turningpointprogram.org*. Accessed January 23, 2005.
11. R. Lasker, *Medicine and Public Health: The Power of Collaboration* (New York: New York Academy of Medicine, 1997), 37.
12. U.S. Department of Health and Human Services, "National Committee on Vital and Health Statistics. Work Group on National Health Information Infrastructure," *http://ncvhs.hhs.gov/nhichrg.htm*. Accessed January 24, 2005.
13. U.S. Department of Health and Human Services, *Information for Health: A Strategy for Building the National Health Information Infrastructure* (November 15, 2001). *http://aspe.hhs.gov/sp/nhii/Documents/NHIIReport2001*. Accessed January 29, 2005.
14. U.S. Centers for Disease Control and Prevention, *Public Health Information Network (PHIN). Overview of PHIN, www.cdc.gov/phin*. Accessed January 24, 2005.
15. U.S. Centers for Disease Control and Prevention, *National Electronic Disease Surveillance System, www.cdc.gov/nedss*. Accessed January 24, 2005.

16. U.S. Centers for Disease Control and Prevention, *Health Alert Network*, *www.phppo. cdc.gov/han/*. Accessed January 29, 2005.

17. D. N. Mendelson, and E. M. Salinsky, "Health Information Systems and the Role of State Government," *Health Affairs* 16 (3) (1997): 106–119.

18. P. Starr, "Smart Technology, Stunted Policy: Developing Health Information Networks," *Health Affairs* 16 (3) (1997): 103.

19. J. Kaiser, "Privacy Rule Creates Bottleneck for U.S. Biomedical Researchers," *Science* 305 (2004): 168–169.

20. J. E. Fielding, "Public Health in the Twentieth Century: Advances and Challenges," *Annual Review of Public Health* 20 (1999): xiii–xxx.

Index